THE GLOBAL ECONOMY

Resource Use, Locational Choice, and International Trade

BRIAN J. L. BERRY

EDGAR C. CONKLING

D. MICHAEL RAY

Prentice Hall
Englewood Cliffs, New Jersey 07632

Library of Congress Cataloging-in-Publication Data

BERRY, BRIAN JOE LOBLEY, (date)
  The global economy : resource use, locational choice, and
international trade / Brian J.L. Berry, Edgar C. Conkling, D.
Michael Ray.
      p.   cm.
  Rev. ed. of: Economic geography. c1987.
  Includes bibliographical references and index.
  ISBN 0-13-357997-2
  1. Economic geography. 2. Natural resources. 3. Industry—
Location. 4. International trade. I. Conkling, Edgar C.
II. Ray, D. Michael (David Michael), (date). III. Berry, Brian
Joe Lobley, (date) Economic geography. IV. Title.
HC59.B52 1992   92-8346
330.9--dc20   CIP

Acquisition Editor: Ray Henderson
Editorial/production supervision and
       interior design: Judi Wisotsky
Copy Editor: Linda Thompson
Cover design: Wanda Lubelska
Prepress buyer: Paula Massenaro
Manufacturing buyer: Lori Bulwin
Editorial assistant: Joan Dello Stritto
Cartography: Maps and diagrams were prepared under the
   direction of Greg Theisen, Cartography Laboratory,
   Department of Geography, State University of New York
   at Buffalo; Christine Earl, Department of Geography,
   Carleton University, Ottawa, Canada; and at the Bruton
   Center for Development Studies, University of Texas
   at Dallas.

Portions of this volume previously appeared in
*Economic Geography: Resource Use, Locational Choices,
and Regional Specialization in the Global Economy.*

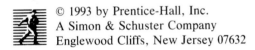 © 1993 by Prentice-Hall, Inc.
A Simon & Schuster Company
Englewood Cliffs, New Jersey 07632

Printed in the United States of America
10 9 8 7 6 5 4 3 2 1

ISBN 0-13-357997-2

Prentice-Hall International (UK) Limited, *London*
Prentice-Hall of Australia Pty. Limited, *Sidney*
Prentice-Hall Canada Inc., *Toronto*
Prentice-Hall Hispanoamericana, S.A., *Mexico*
Prentice-Hall of India Private Limited, *New Delhi*
Prentice-Hall of Japan, Inc., *Tokyo*
Simon & Schuster Asia Pte. Ltd., *Singapore*
Editora Prentice-Hall do Brasil, Ltda., *Rio de Janeiro*.

Contents

PART TWO
Fundamentals of Economic Geography: People and Resources

PART THREE
Fundamentals of Spatial Economics

PART FOUR
Principles of Locational Choice

Preface

The global economy and world trade are experiencing changes that are unprecedented both in their magnitude and their speed. The world is now a global marketplace, not only for goods but for services, capital, and technology as well. Nation after nation is shifting toward market-driven rather than government-directed solutions to national economic problems. The differences in the productive capabilities of many less-developed countries are narrowing, compared to developed countries. The changes confirm the argument of classical theorists that open markets remain the best route to broad-based improvements in economic growth and prosperity. World trade achieves these improvements by linking the forces of specialization, competition, and adjustment to change. Specialization allows countries to produce those goods and services they produce best and to buy what others produce best. Competition spurs innovation, efficiency, and excellence. Rapid adjustments to change, even though they bring problems to some, improve overall economic growth and prosperity. Trade impels countries to adapt more quickly and efficiently to the changing world economy.

So rapid have been the adjustments that we, too, have had to change. This book is a substantial reconstruction of our earlier text on economic geography, introducing many new ideas and perspectives, reinforcing those that were introduced tentatively in the previous book and have stood the test of time, and discarding others that appear to be less useful as the global economy evolves. Yet not all is change. There are ideas of lasting value that we have preserved, seeking only to clarify them with contemporary illustrations, maps, graphs, and tables based on the latest statistical information.

What is new? Chapter 1 now focuses on the forces that are reshaping the global economy and the new sequence of stages of economic development that is emerging, as well as upon the cultural differences among nation-states that seem to be reinforcing themselves as countervailing pressures to globalization. Critically important to any understanding of differences in economic growth and performance are differences in type of political economy, yet these differences have not yet been incorporated into relevant geographic theory. In this book we focus on the forces behind globalization, yet we point to the crafting of culturally conditioned theories of specialization and economic development as a future path for research in economic geography.

The most significant actors in global specialization and trade are multinational enterprises (MNEs), many of which are bigger than the economies of most member-nations of the United Nations. MNEs are given new and expanded treatment in Chapters 10 and 14. Yet alongside the expanding role of MNEs, small enterprise is increasingly important as a source of innovative new growth (Chapter 10). This reflects the phase of the economic long wave through which the world economy is now passing (Chapter 11), as well as the changing balance of economies and diseconomies of scale and scope and the renewed importance of externalities (Chapter 7). What is emerging are information-age "thoughtware" economies (Chapter 11). There are implications for resource use (Chapter 5), for the relative importance of size of enterprise and type of specialization (Chapter 10), and for the dynamics and patterns of world trade and investment (Chapters 13 and 14).

What is enduring? We retain and update our discussion of the intellectual heritage of economic geography as it moves from one interpretive paradigm to another, redefining the relevant facts and the accepted modes of explanation (Chapter 2). We continue to discuss the continuing realities of population growth, resource use, and environmental impact—whether we are heading towards Malthusian disaster or a brave new world of unparalleled prosperity (Chapters 3–5).

And we believe that there are bodies of theory that are of continuing utility: spatial microeconomics (Chapters 6 and 7), behavioral decision theory (Chapter 8), theories of land use and location (Chapters 9 and 10), and the theory of international trade (Chapter 12). Each of these bodies of theory is evolving; thus, at the appropriate places we also discuss imperfect competition, bounded rationality, economies of scope, and what happens to location and trade as information age factors come to prevail.

We hope that this mix of the new and the enduring will provide students and faculty alike with a rich array of insights into the changing global environment in which we all live. Students who intend to move to more advanced studies will find that the book provides a platform for that work, combined with suggestions as to where further research might be undertaken. Economic geography is a rapidly changing field. Its continuing vitality depends upon the research that these students will undertake. We look forward to learning from their exploration and discovery.

Brian J. L. Berry
Edgar C. Conkling
D. Michael Ray

About the Authors

Brian J. L. Berry

Edgar C. Conkling

D. Michael Ray

Brian J. L. Berry is the Lloyd Viel Berkner University Professor, Professor of Political Economy, and Chair of the Bruton Center for Development Studies at The University of Texas at Dallas. He received his B.Sc. (Economics) degree at University College, London in 1955, and then traveled to the U.S. for graduate work at the University of Washington, Seattle, receiving his M.A. in Geography, in 1956, and the Ph.D. degree in 1958. In 1958 he joined the University of Chicago, rising to Irving B. Harris Professor of Urban Geography, Chairman of the Department of Geography, and Director of the Center for Urban Studies. In 1976 he became the Williams Professor of City and Regional Planning, Chairman of the Ph.D. Program in Urban Planning, Director of the Laboratory for Computer Graphics and Spatial Analysis, Professor in the Department of Sociology, and Faculty Fellow of the Institute for International Development at Harvard University. Leaving Harvard in 1981, he became Dean of the School of Urban and Public Affairs and University Professor of Urban Studies and Public Policy at Carnegie-Mellon University, positions that he held until moving to Texas in 1986. In 1975 he was elected a member of the National Academy of Sciences, and in 1976 a Fellow of the American Academy of Arts and Sciences. In 1978-79 he was President of the Association of American Geographers, and in 1987 was awarded the James R. Anderson Medal by the A.A.G. In 1988 he received the Victoria Medal from the Royal Geographical Society, and in 1989 was elected a Corresponding Fellow of the British Academy. He is the author of several hundred books, articles and other professional publications. Throughout his career he has been concerned with bridging theory and practice, and has been heavily involved in urban and regional development planning and policymaking in both advanced and developing countries.

Edgar Conkling is Professor Emeritus at the State University of New York at Buffalo, where he was on the faculty of the International Trade Concentration, a graduate program that prepares students for careers in international business. In the ITC program he taught international trade theory, as well as courses dealing with the problems of conducting business in foreign cultural realms. He also served as chairman of the Geography Department at SUNY/Buffalo and as editor of *The Professional Geographer* and co-editor of *The Annals of the Association of American Geographers*. Educated at the University of Chicago and Northwestern University, he was for several years manager of the home office of a multinational corporation headquartered in Chicago. In addition to his works on international trade, he has published on the subjects of rural land use theory and regional development. Since retiring from active teaching in 1989, he has continued writing on the changing spatial patterns of world trade and on the regional variations in cultures that are encountered by businesses operating abroad.

Michael Ray was born in Cornwall, England in 1935. His keen interest in economic geography emerged during his B.A. studies at Manchester University with a thesis on industrial location in part of the London area. It further developed with an M.A. at Ottawa, a Ph.D. at Chicago, and a series of National Science Foundation fellowships in quantitative methods, computer techniques, and regional science. The computer and quantitative training made possible the detailed analysis of regional policy and opened a career of alternating university and government posts involving the development of methodology and the evaluation of regional policy alternatives. He is currently Professor of Geography at Carleton University and has also lectured at Ottawa, Waterloo, and the State University of New York at Buffalo. Policy issues addressed have included the regional impact of foreign investment by multinational corporations for the government of Canada and for the International Labor Office, employment generation by small firms and statistical techniques for defining homogeneous regions for Statistics Canada, as well as urban growth and regional policy issues for various federal and provincial Canadian government agencies. This work, together with membership of a number of commissions of the International Geographical Union focused the need for a new textbook on economic geography which encapsulated the changing nature of economic geography, the changing regional economic concerns that face decision makers and the consequent changing demands placed on geography graduates. His previous books include *Market Potential and Economic Shadow*, *Dimensions of Canadian Regionalism*, and *Canadian Urban Trends*.

1

The Forces Reshaping Global Economic Geography

OVERVIEW

Global economic geography is being transformed by the extraordinary events that began in 1989, including the collapse of socialism and the end of the Cold War. The working concepts that we use must change along with this transformation. A new paradigm is needed to explain the competitive advantage of nations in global markets as well as why, under the pressures of globalization, nations assert deep-rooted cultural traditions to maintain their distinctiveness.

The competitive advantage paradigm provides new insights into the stages of economic growth. Nations pass from an early factor-driven stage of development to one that is investment-driven, from that to an innovation-driven stage, and finally to a stage that is wealth-driven. At each of these stages, different factors determine competitiveness.

The reassertion of cultural traditions, exemplified by the breakup of the Soviet Union and Yugoslavia into ethnically-based states, reemphasizes that politics and economics are closely intertwined, and that their interrelationships must be appreciated if current shifts in global economic geography are to be thoroughly understood.

OBJECTIVES

- to place the subject of economic geography within the framework of world events
- to outline the factors that determine the competitive advantage of nations
- to offer a new concept of stages of economic development
- to identify the cultural factors that differentiate the world's nation-states
- to classify the principal types of political economies that determine the ground rules for growth and development

THE TRIUMPH OF MARKETS

With the opening of the Berlin Wall in November 1989, an extraordinary sequence of events began to unfold that seems destined to transform global economic geography.

Communist governments were ousted throughout Eastern Europe, and then in the former Soviet Union itself. The two Germanies became one and the Cold War ended, promising reductions in the trillions of dollars going to support the military-industrial complex. In 1990 former Soviet President Gorbachev's drive to restructure the Soviet economy took on a new urgency as the Soviet empire vanished, the Soviet republics asserted their right to self-determination, and the old guard fought back to preserve communist dictatorship. By the end of 1991, Gorbachev, the old guard, and the Soviet Union were all gone, replaced by independent states seeking to eliminate the consequences of Communism.

Underlying the shifts was a simple truth. Centrally directed socialist systems do not work and cannot compete. They produce only sporadic growth (see Box 1.1), assure only a low-level equality that is violated by party-member privilege, and quite demonstrably have been far more destructive of the environment than political and economic systems of any other kind. The nuclear disaster at Chernobyl rendered vast areas of Belarus uninhabitable. Former East Germany's nuclear plants are equally dangerous and must be closed, as must that territory's chemical factories. The Aral Sea is vanishing. Even once-pristine Lake Baikal is being polluted by pulp mill effluent.

What Mikhail Gorbachev realized when he called for *perestroika* was that the rules determining the economic geography of a major section of the globe were going to have to change if growth is to produce rising levels of welfare. The socialist system of central direction and party control would have to be replaced by individual initiative and the discipline of markets in the economic arena, and by individual freedoms and democratic institutions in the sphere of politics. Private

---

BOX 1.1   The Benefits of Democratic Market Institutions to the Developing Nations

In his 1991 doctoral dissertation at The University of Texas at Dallas entitled "The Impact of Government Size on Economic Growth," James S. Guseh discovered not only that greater governmental size takes a toll on economic growth, but also that the type of economic and political freedoms present in a country affects the magnitude of this toll. Using the annual growth rates of real per capita gross national product of 59 middle-income developing countries for the period 1960–1985 as his measure of economic growth, and controlling for other variables that affect the growth rate, he discovered that if the share of gross national product consumed by government increases by 10 percent, different types of economic and political freedoms take the following tolls of growth relative to democratic market economies:

		Political freedoms		
		Democratic Institutions	Partially Democratic	Nondemocratic
Economic freedoms	Market Economy	Base Case	0.07% slower	1.2% slower
	Mixed Economy	No Difference	0.03% slower	0.8% slower
	Socialist Economy	1% slower	1.7% slower	2.2% slower

For the 59 middle-income developing countries he studied, the price of a 10 percent increase in government size in a socialist economy was a 1 percent reduction in the annual growth rate, compared with the base case of a market economy. The price of nondemocratic political institutions was a 1.2 percent per year comparative reduction in the growth rate. Combining the two, nondemocratic socialist systems had annual growth rates that were 2.2 percent slower than democratic market systems. Little wonder, then, that democratic market systems are triumphing across the globe!

enterprise would have to replace state monopoly; competition would have to replace the dictatorship of the proletariat. It took only his first tentative initiatives for the world order crafted by Lenin and Stalin to start to disintegrate. It took only the first pains of disintegration for Russian conservatives to demand a return to that country's deeply embedded authoritarian traditions, setting in motion a continuing political debate about that country's future.

As transformation of the former Communist world runs its course, the working concepts we use to help us understand global economic geography will have to change. The rest of the world is not remaining static as Communism retreats. No longer can we think of the differences between the First (Western), Second (socialist), Third (developing), and Fourth ("basketcase") Worlds of economic development. All are becoming parts of a global system of markets. There is need for a new paradigm to explain the competitive advantage of nations: why some nations grow and others do not; why countries differ in the industries in which they specialize; why particular countries become the home of many of the world's leaders in particular industries—Germany in chemicals; Switzerland in pharmaceuticals; Japan in electronics, cameras, robotics, and facsimile machines; the United States in computers, software, movies, and commercial aircraft. Part of the explanation resides in the growth factors that are of global significance. A countervailing part resides in the cultural traditions that both enable and force nations to remain distinctive.

GLOBAL COMPETITIVE ADVANTAGE

After a 4-year study of 10 important trading nations in which he paid particular attention to the competitive advantage of firms in global industries, Michael Porter of Harvard University's Business School concluded that there are, today, four broad attributes of nations that shape the environment in which local firms compete, and that thus promote or impede the creation of competitive advantage: (1) factor conditions, (2) demand conditions, (3) the nature of related and supporting industries, and (4) firm strategy, structure, and rivalry. Together, these attributes suggest a new typology and sequence of national economic development.

Factor conditions are what economists have conventionally termed the "factors of production"—land and other resources, labor, and capital. Much of the conventional theory of international trade rests on these factors. Porter believes that a new grouping of these factor endowments is necessary to understand

the ways in which they now impinge on the competitive advantage of nations. He distinguishes among the following:

1. *Physical resources.* The abundance, quality, accessibility and cost of land, water, mineral, and timber deposits, together with other physical traits such as location, time zone, and climate.
2. *Human resources.* The quantity, skills, and cost of personnel, including cultural factors that bear on the work ethic.
3. *Infrastructure.* The type, quality, and user cost of the transportation and communications systems, health care, cultural institutions, and so on.
4. *Knowledge resources.* The nation's supply of scientific and technical knowledge and know-how.
5. *Capital resources.* The amount, type, and cost of capital available to finance industry. Important variables include national savings rates, the structure of capital markets, and governmental policies that affect the money supply and interest rates.

This list includes what Porter terms *basic factors,* such as resources, climate, location, and numbers of people, and *advanced factors,* such as educated personnel, research and development capabilities, and advanced digital communications infrastructure. Figure 1.1, a map of the country-to-country variations in the percentage of gross domestic product derived from agriculture, gives some indication of the dependence upon basic factors today. Figure 1.2, which maps the distribution of scientists and technicians per 1000 people, focuses attention on the regions where advanced factors have assumed priority.

Basic factors are of diminishing necessity and widened global availability because of changes in product design, together with improved transportation and communications facilities. Advanced factors are now the most significant for competitive advantage, and in contrast to basic factors they can be improved and created through education and investment in research. The difference is important. Many basic factors such as natural resources are fixed in availability and may place upper limits to growth. Advanced factors impose no such limits.

Demand conditions are, Porter says, those that obtain in domestic markets: the composition of buyer needs; the size and pattern of growth of domestic demand; and the ways in which domestic preferences are

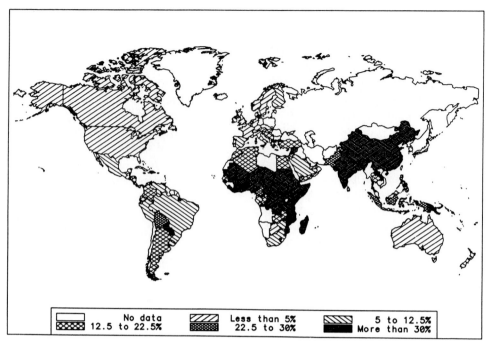

FIGURE 1.1   Percent of GDP in agriculture, 1988. GDP (gross domestic product) is the total output for final use of the goods and services produced by an economy by both residents and nonresidents. It differs from GNP (gross national product), which is composed of GDP plus or minus net factor income from abroad—the income residents receive from abroad for factor services minus payments made to nonresidents who contribute to the domestic economy. [*Source:* Data from The World Bank, *Poverty, The World Development Report, 1990.* (New York: Oxford University Press, 1990), p. 182.]

transmitted to foreign markets. They influence the ability to achieve economies of scale in production, and the rate and character of improvement and innovation. Sophisticated and demanding domestic buyers force local firms to meet high standards in terms of product features, quality, and service, and thus pressure them to be more innovative, upgrading competitive advantage as they do it. Japanese home market conditions, for example, have led to pressure to innovate and produce products that are *Kei-haku-tan-sho* (light, thin, short, small), and the result is a stream of products that are exceedingly successful internationally.

Related and supporting industries are part of the environment that fosters success. Especially important are supplier industries: Sweden's innovative ball bearing and cutting tool producers could not flourish without the country's strength in specialty steels. It was the Swiss dye industry that created conditions leading to a successful move into pharmaceuticals, which in turn has led to world dominance in production of food flavorings. The relationships with home-based suppliers are particularly important in the pro-

cess of innovation and upgrading. Italy's leather manufacturers work closely with shoe producers, monitoring fashion trends and planning new products. The advantages are those of external economies, helping create new products and finding ways to reduce costs.

Firm strategy, structure, and rivalry involve corporate goals and management systems. It is important for competitiveness whether firms are small and production is fragmented, or whether there are relatively few firms producing standardized products on large-scale production lines. It is important whether firms seek to maximize profits each quarter, or are willing to accept a lower return to ensure long-run market advantages. Where companies are owned by investors who seek rapid growth of share prices, pressure is upon the company to produce the best quarterly earnings statements, and thus to maximize profits in the short run. Elsewhere, as in Germany and Switzerland, long-term capital gains have been exempt from taxation, and corporate strategy is directed to corporate performance over much longer periods of time. In Sweden, there is great suspicion of wealth, and taxa-

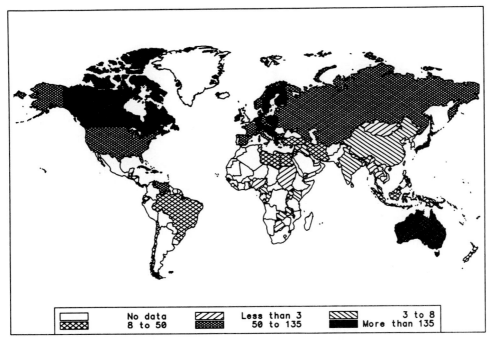

FIGURE 1.2   Scientists and Technicians per 1000 people, 1987. [*Source:* Data from United Nations Development Programme (UNDP), *Human Development Report, 1990* (New York, Oxford University Press, 1990), p. 136.]

tion prevents its accumulation, a powerful disincentive to business initiative—the very contrast to the United States, where the rate of new business formulation is, accordingly, much higher. Vigorous domestic rivalries result from new business formation, encouraging competitiveness.

Four Stages of Economic Development

Putting the factors together, Porter says that he now sees four stages to national competitive development: (1) factor-driven, (2) investment-driven, (3) innovation-driven, and (4) wealth-driven. Economies progress by upgrading their positions in global markets through achieving higher-order competitive advantages in existing industries and developing the capability to compete successfully in new higher-productivity industries. Part of this upgrading process involves the simultaneous loss of position in industries that are more price sensitive or that require less sophisticated skills and technology. These become the domain of nations further down the skills ladder. Thus, as economic growth occurs, all nations are linked on the ladder of success as they compete to supply global markets.

The first, or *factor-driven,* stage is one in which competitive advantage is based almost exclusively on the basic factors of production: natural resources and abundant, cheap semiskilled labor. Firms compete on the basis of price in industries that use simple, widely available technologies imported from other nations, frequently financed by foreign capital. For the resource-dependent, there is extreme sensitivity to world economic cycles and to exchange rates, because these affect demand and prices. As Figure 1.3 reveals, most nations in the world remain at the stage of merchandise exports dominated by primary commodities. Some of these nations, painfully poor, are pressed to the threshold of subsistence. Others, like Saudi Arabia and the Gulf States, have flourished because of the earnings of their staple exports. Some have progressed beyond physical resource dependence by applying their abundant supplies of inexpensive labor to produce, for example, textiles and clothing; see Figure 1.4.

The second, or *investment-driven,* stage is based upon the willingness and ability to invest in modern, efficient facilities representing the best technology available in global markets. It not only involves investment in new technology, but the upgrading of factors of production from the basic to the advanced, development of modern infrastructure and domestic rivalry that pushes down costs, improves quality, introduces new products, and modernizes processes. Firms still compete in relatively standardized, price-sensitive markets, especially those where domestic demand is

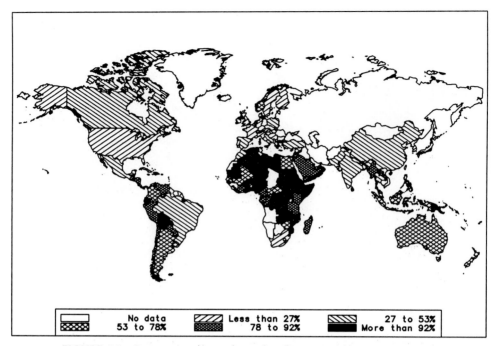

FIGURE 1.3   Percentage share of merchandise exports in primary commodities, including fuels, minerals, and metals, 1988. [*Source:* Data from The World Bank: *Poverty, The World Development Report, 1990,* p. 208.]

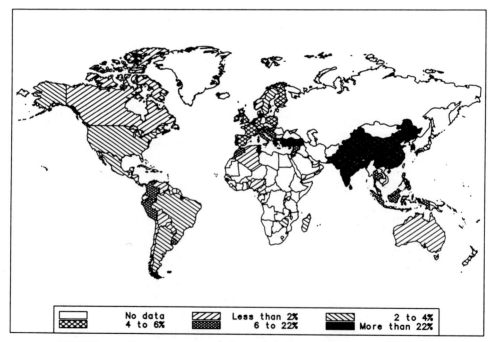

FIGURE 1.4   Percentage share of merchandise exports in textiles and clothing, 1988. [*Source:* Data from The World Bank, *Poverty, The World Development Report, 1990,* p. 208.]

large. The focus, however, is upon industries with significant scale economies and capital requirements, a large labor cost component, producing standardized products with a readily transferable technology. A typical example is the manufacture of machinery and transport equipment; see Figure 1.5. The significant competitive advantages are low labor costs and modern facilities. During this stage, industrial employment increases rapidly, as do wage and other factor costs, but over time this erodes competitive advantage.

Sensitivity to world economic cycles and exchange rates remains. Prime examples of successful investment-driven economies are Japan after World War II, and Korea and Taiwan in the last quarter-century. The results have been startlingly different: South Korea's economy is dominated by very large-scale firms and that of Taiwan by large numbers of highly competitive small-scale enterprises.

The third, or *innovation-driven,* stage is different because at this stage firms actively create new technologies, new products, and new markets. The capacity to innovate opens up new industries that compete internationally in narrower market segments. Competitive advantage is no longer based upon factor costs, but on productivity derived from high skill levels and advanced technology. Firms became multinational, competing globally with self-contained strategies and their own international marketing organizations, ser-

vice networks, and brand reputations. They also begin to produce in many nations, fabricating components and subassemblies in some, and finished products in others. Two trends are unfolding simultaneously. Industry clusters *deepen* as supplier industries expand, compete, and specialize, and *widen* as the range of products expands and new industrial clusters emerge. Within the industry clusters, innovation leads to spinoffs and to a rapid rate of new firm formation. Critically important are highly skilled human resources, high-quality service industries and infrastructure, and the most advanced transportation and communications facilities. The service industries, in particular, rise to account for more than 75 percent of the labor force; see Figure 1.6. At this stage, rising skills, education, and incomes breed growing domestic demand for new products and sophisticated services that can become the basis of new international competitiveness. And once again, as nations move to more sophisticated competitive advantage, their less-advanced industries are lost to countries further down the technology ladder. An accompanying problem may be sharpening regional differences within countries between those areas receiving innovation-led growth and those areas losing factor-driven and investment-driven economic activity.

The final *wealth-driven* stage is reached if a nation achieves levels of affluence that induce erosion of

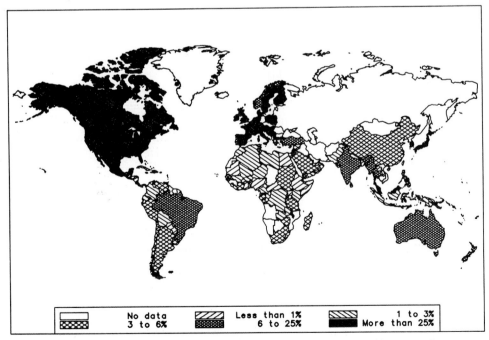

FIGURE 1.5 Percentage share of merchandise exports in machinery and transport equipment, 1988. [*Source:* Data from The World Bank, *Poverty, The World Development Report, 1990,* p. 208.]

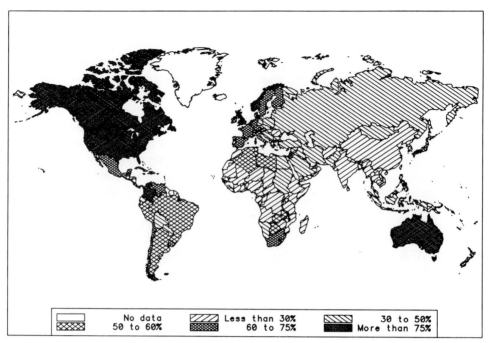

FIGURE 1.6   Percentage of labor force employed in the service industries. [*Source:* Data from UNDP, *Human Development Report, 1990,* p. 156.]

the drive to succeed, undermining innovativeness and investment. As Figure 1.7 reveals, it has not been the former world leaders in the North Atlantic region that have grown most rapidly in the past quarter-century. The problem is that people, business leaders, and politicians can become complacent and self-indulgent. Priorities are based upon use of already-accumulated wealth and come to be dominated by risk-reducing stewardship rather than by risk-taking leadership. Preservation and stability come to dominate over creativity and change. Competitive rivalry is lost, there are declining motivations to invest, and powerful firms collude with each other and with government to insulate their positions by fixing prices and protecting markets. There may be less interest in technical education and a switch of priorities to social goals. A wealth-driven nation with apparently successful large-scale companies will come to be affected by sagging growth, rising long-term unemployment, and burdensome taxation. The United Kingdom has been a classic case in point, losing its competitive edge in the final decades of imperial power and experiencing the consequences when domination of imperial markets was ended by the independence of former colonies after World War II. The new ''mini-Britain'' suddenly had to compete in world markets, but was saddled with old industries and infrastructure, corporate leaders who had forgotten how to be innovative, and labor organizations seeking redistribution of old wealth rather than cre-

ation of new enterprise. In three decades, the former world leader sagged as other European nations forged ahead. It took the period of conservative government under Margaret Thatcher, with all its disruptive (and for some regions disastrous) social consequences to privatize state-run enterprises and to reintroduce incentives for innovation-led growth. The side effect of such growth is that some benefit far more than others, and some may lose. Social tensions increase, and along with them calls for greater fairness. Unfortunately, efficiency and equity are tradeoffs, and achieving balance is an art, not a science—a task for the world of politics, not of economics.

This is why the nation-state remains important. Michael Porter places great emphasis upon economics—global markets, multinational competition, and competitive advantage. But many of the important changes that are unfolding lie at the interface of politics and economics, in the world of political economy. Former Soviet President Gorbachev's decisions were political; so were those of former British Prime Minister Thatcher. Government not only influences the factors shaping competitive advantage; politics also determines the kind of social and economic system that will prevail. Hence the importance of the nation-state, the entity that encloses a group of people sharing common laws, government, citizenship, and coming to share common values, myths, and symbols (See Box 1.2).

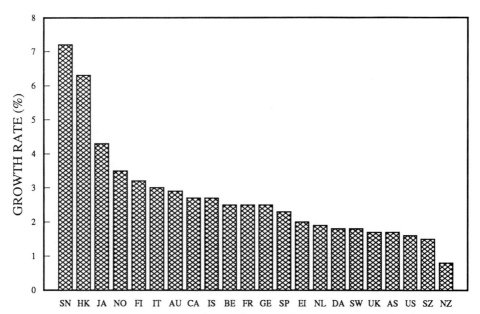

FIGURE 1.7 Average annual growth rates of per capita GNP for the world's high-income non-OPEC economies, 1965–1988. The countries are, in ranked order from highest to lowest growth rates: Singapore, Hong Kong, Japan, Norway, Finland, Italy, Austria, Canada, Israel, Belgium, France, West Germany, Spain, Eire (Ireland), Netherlands, Denmark, Sweden, United Kingdom, Australia, United States, Switzerland, and New Zealand. [*Source:* Data from The World Bank, *Poverty, op. cit.,* p. 178.]

BOX 1.2   *The Nation-State: Core Identities and Cultural Differences*

The globe is covered by a mosaic of nation-states of different sizes and histories. Each state's central government has a legitimate monopoly over the authorized use and regulation of force within its boundaries; has defined responsibilities for maintaining the system of which it is part; and can impose sanctions and use the police power to implement the society's main collective goals, maintain its internal order, and regulate its foreign relations.

The basic activities of the nation-state are *legislative,* in which the society's primary goals are determined and the general rules are formulated for maintaining (or changing) the existing social order; *administrative,* which deals with the execution of these basic rules and with the organization of the technical activities needed for their efficient execution; *party-political,* which mobilizes support for different mea-

sures and rules and for the holders of different political positions; and *juridical,* concerned with testing the validity of the rules and laws by applying them to concrete cases in society. The body of law serves to define the range of acceptable behavior and imposes sanctions on those who transgress.

Within the nation-state men and women are socialized to a uniform and shared way of life, to a common belief system that defines the essential traits of national character. Where this has not occurred, the state is in jeopardy. As the world's successful territorial states emerged, diverse groups were merged through centralization, unification of the economy, provision of common legal systems, and the growth of mass public educational systems. The result was a set of *core identities* that imposed themselves as the mainstream paradigms of economic, politi-

cal, and social life. Each core identity defines a self-sufficient system of action that is capable of existing longer than the lifespan of the individuals who belong to that society. It persists as an organized body of custom, consisting of traditional ideas and values that are both the products of action and the conditioning elements of further action. Part consists of the norms for and the standards of behavior. Another part consists of ideologies justifying and rationalizing selected ways of behaving. If society is an organized set of individuals with a given way of life, the core identity is that way of life. If society is an aggregate of social relations, then the core identity is the content of those relations. It is this core identity that we call *culture.* Differences in culture are at the basis of differences in political-economic life.

THE CULTURAL FOUNDATIONS
OF DISTINCTIVENESS

Porter pointed to cultural factors that bear on the work ethic, on the nature of domestic demand, on preferences for one type of organizational structure over another, and on attitudes to risk-taking and experimentation, as particularly important elements of the factor conditions helping determine national competitiveness. Berry (1989) says:

> In an increasingly tightly knit global economy, multinational corporations play their locational games interactively with nation-states on the checkerboard of culture . . . (but) . . . as the activities of these multinationals bring the world's inhabitants closer than ever before, differences in beliefs, goals, planning, and action have come into sharper focus. . . . (These) differences are rooted in *culture*—the philosophical ideals, values, ideologies, religious beliefs, and passions that give meaning to people's lives. Culture is the differentiator that is sharpened by increasing interdependence.

To Dutch anthropologist Geert Hofstede (1980) culture is the "collective programming of the mind" that differentiates the motivation and behavior of members of one society from those of other societies. It is through culture that societies give meaning to their environments, organizing their life around particular symbols and myths. Culture shapes perceptions and behavior by directing that selective attention be paid to some details of reality, permitting some actions and forbidding others.

Central to this programming of the mind is the transmission of *values,* broad preferences for one state of affairs over others. People face moral dilemmas, ambiguous circumstances where several choices of proper behavior are possible. Values are priorities for sorting out and implementing one code of behavior rather than others. The act of prioritizing involves emotional commitment. The commitment arises because values are learned during the process of childhood socialization, when individuals come to accept that a particular form of life is meaningful.

What people are socialized to is a particular paradigm, a dominant set of beliefs that organizes the way they and other members of their group perceive and interpret the world around them: A social paradigm contains the survival information needed for the maintenance of a culture. It results from generations of learning whereby dysfunctional beliefs and values are discarded in favor of those most suited to collective survival. An individual element of a social paradigm is difficult to dislodge once it becomes firmly entrenched because shared definitions of reality are anchored in it. The values, norms, beliefs, and institutions of paradigms are not only beliefs about what the world is like. They are guides to action and they serve the function of legitimating and justifying courses of action, i.e., they function as ideologies, and ideologies drive politics.

Is each culture idiosyncratic, or are there systematic variations? This was the question asked by Geert Hofstede as he worked for a large multinational corporation that was seeking to understand why the same facts and instructions sent from headquarters to corporate officers based in different cultures produced different results. After completing attitudinal surveys in 40 different countries and analyzing the results, Hofstede concluded that differences among cultures were far greater than differences within them, lending strong support to the idea that most countries were characterized by a dominant cultural mainstream (social paradigm). He also concluded that the different mainstream cultures varied along four separate dimensions. He called the first three *individualism-collectivism, power-distance,* and *uncertainty avoidance,* and the fourth, *masculinity.* A better term for the latter would be sex-role differentiation. Let us look at each of these, and then see how they combine to differentiate the world's cultures.

Individualism versus Collectivism

The first important dimension of variation was between cultures in which the individual is the locus of responsibility and action and cultures in which it is the collectivity that matters. In individualist cultures Hofstede's respondents said that individuals should look after their own interests and the interests of their immediate family (husband, wife, and children). On the other hand, in collectivist cultures it was said that any person through birth and later events belongs to one or more cohesive collectives ("in-groups"), from which he or she cannot detach himself or herself. The in-group (for example, the extended family with grandparents and either paternal or maternal uncles, aunts, and cousins—or on a larger scale, the nation and its governmental institutions) should protect the interests of its members but in exchange can expect their permanent loyalty. Study Table 1.1.

Individualist cultures tend to share the following traits:

- Market economies
- Balanced-power political systems

TABLE 1.1

Contrasts between individualist and collectivist cultures

Traits of Highly Individualist Cultures	Traits of Collectivist Cultures
(i) Emphasis on individual initiative, decisions, and achievement	(i) Emphasis on belonging to groups and organizations that make decisions and protect people in exchange for their loyalty
(ii) The belief that in society, everyone is supposed to take care of himself or herself and his or her immediate family	(ii) "We" consciousness and collectivity orientation: identity rooted in the social system
(iii) "I" consciousness and self-orientation: identity based in the individual	(iii) Emotional dependence of the individual on organizations and institutions
(iv) Emotional independence of the individual from organizations or institutions	(iv) The invasion of private life by organizations and clans to which the individual belongs: opinions predetermined
(v) Belief that everyone has a right to a private life and opinion	(v) Expertise, order, duty, security provided by the organization or clan
(vi) The idea that the same value standards should apply to all: universalism	(vi) Value standards that differ for in-groups and out-groups: particularism

- Greater occupational mobility
- More press freedom
- Protest potential
- Atomized labor movements
- Worship of the independent actor
- Protestant (modernist) ethic
- Involvement of individuals with organizations primarily calculative
- Organizations not expected to look after employees from the cradle to the grave
- Policies and practices that allow for initiative and apply to all (universalism)
- Promotion from inside and outside, based on market value (cosmopolitanism)

Collectivist cultures, on the other hand, are most typically characterized by:

- Nonmarket economies
- Unbalanced-power political systems
- Less occupational mobility
- Less press freedom
- Repression potential
- United labor movements
- Stress on identity and roots
- Traditionalist ethic
- Involvement of individuals with organizations primarily moral
- Organizations that have great influence on member's well-being (Employees expect organizations to look after them like a family.)

- Policies and practices that are based on loyalty and individual sense of duty and vary according to specific social relations (particularism)
- Promotion from inside, based on family and friendship networks (localism)

Hofstede showed that the degree of individualism correlates highly with contemporary levels of economic development across the globe, as measured by per capita gross national product ($R = 0.82$; see Figure 1.8). His "individualism" scores are charted in Figure 1.9.

Power-Distance

Power-distance is the characteristic of a culture that defines the extent to which the less-powerful persons in society accept inequality in power and consider large social distances to be normal. Inequality exists within all cultures, but its extent and the degree of it that is accepted vary from one culture to another. The belief patterns of "high P-D" and "low P-D" cultures are contrasted in Table 1.2. High-inequality cultures have the following typical traits:

- Autocratic or oligarchic governments
- Sudden changes in form of government (revolution and/or instability)
- Polarization between left and right with a weak center if political parties exist
- Tax system protects the wealthy
- Success of religions stressing stratification
- Ideologies of power polarization
- Elitist theories about society

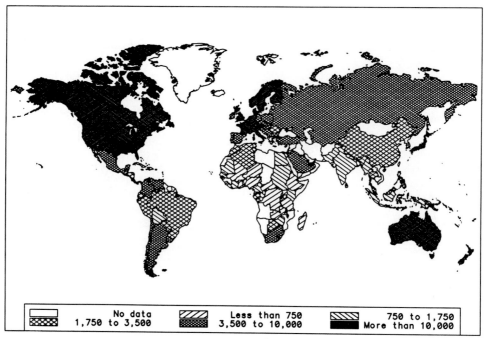

FIGURE 1.8 Real gross domestic product (GDP) per capita, 1987 in PPP$. Real GDP is GDP that has been adjusted to account for the fact that official exchange rates to U.S. dollars frequently do not reflect the relative purchasing power of currencies. The United Nations International Comparison Project developed models of real GDP on an internationally comparable scale using purchasing power parities (PPP) instead of exchange rates as conversion factors. It is the resulting "international dollars" that are reflected here. However, we now know that the information for the USSR and Eastern Europe was overstated for propaganda purposes. New 1990 estimates place Soviet GNP per capita (for the difference between GNP and GDP see Figure 1.1) at barely one-fifth that of the United States, a ratio exceeded slightly by Czechoslovakia and Hungary, but greater than that for Poland, Romania, Bulgaria, and poverty-stricken Albania. [*Source:* Data from the United Nations Development Programme (UNDP) *Human Development Report, 1990* (New York: Oxford University Press, 1990), p. 158.]

TABLE 1.2

Contrasts between high P-D and low P-D cultures

Belief Patterns in High P-D Cultures	Belief Patterns in Low P-D Cultures
(i) There is and should be an order of inequality in which everyone has his or her rightful place: high and low are of different kinds and are protected by this hierarchical order.	(i) Inequality and hierarchy in society should be minimized: All should be interdependent and should have equal rights.
(ii) A few should be independent: most should be dependent.	(ii) Any power that is used should be legitimate and is subject to the judgment between good and evil.
(iii) Power is a basic fact of society that antedates good or evil: Its legitimacy is irrelevant.	(iii) The way to change a social system is by redistributing power.
(iv) The way to change a social system is by dethroning those in power.	(iv) There is an underlying harmony between the powerful and the powerless.
(v) There will always be conflict between the powerful and the powerless.	(v) Cooperation among the powerless can be brought about based on solidarity.
(vi) Cooperation among the powerless is difficult to bring about because of the low faith that people have in each other.	

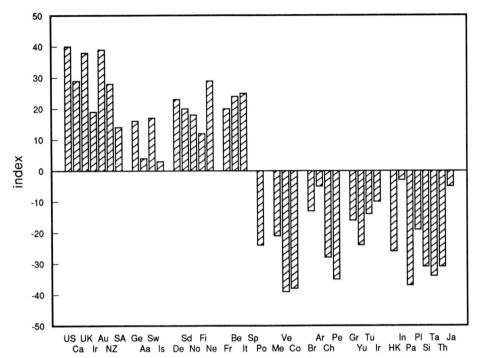

FIGURE 1.9 Hofstede's individualism index scores plotted for groups of countries as deviations from the mean.

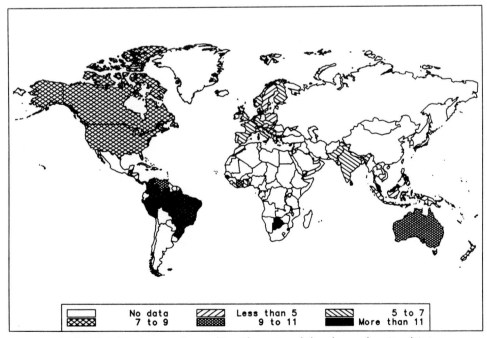

FIGURE 1.10 Income inequality. The ratio of the share of national income of the wealthiest 20 percent to that of the poorest 20 percent. Adequate information on the distribution of incomes is simply unavailable for much of the globe, but such data as are available reveal the greater inequalities in Latin America. [*Source:* Data from UNDP, *Human Development Report, 1990,* p. 158.]

- Greater centralization and tall organization pyramids with a large proportion of supervisory personnel
- Large wage differentials

An analogous list of traits for low-inequality cultures is as follows:

- Pluralist governments based on outcome of majority votes
- No sudden changes in form of government (evolution and stability)
- Political parties that exist tend to be in the center, with relatively weak left and right wings
- Tax system aimed at redistributing wealth

- Success of religions stressing equality
- Ideologies of power equalization
- Pluralist theories about society
- Less centralization and flatter organization pyramids with small proportion of supervisory personnel
- Smaller wage differentials

A useful indicator of power-distance is the degree of income inequality within countries. For a map showing the global variations see Figure 1.10. Hofstede's P-D scores are charted in Figure 1.11. If countries are cross-classified using their individualism and P-D scores, insights are provided about the principal types of political economies to be found in the world today. Refer to Box 1.3.

BOX 1.3   A Typology of Political Economies

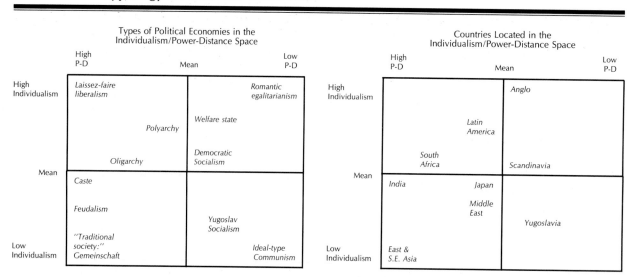

The two diagrams above show where different types of political economies lie in the two-dimensional individualism/collectivism versus power-distance space, and where individual nation-states are located in this same space.

The top left-hand corner (high individualism, high power-distance) is occupied by *ideal-type laissez-faire liberalism,* the main features of which are the following:

- *View of human nature.* Humans are highly individualistic and competitive, motivated by rational calculation of self-interest.

- *Nature of social system.* Free markets and private property are the foundation of economic and political freedom. The "invisible hand" of the market is the allocator. Society is the sum of the individuals who make it up: If individuals maximize their welfare,

this will produce the greatest social good.

- *Central values.* Values include individual liberty and private property (laissez-faire) as well as freedom from restraint.

- *Orientation to social change.* Change occurs in an incremental way as a result of individual actions.

- *The ideal system.* Free-market capitalism exists. Production is

Uncertainty Avoidance

The third of Hofstede's axes of cultural variation is that of "uncertainty avoidance"—that characteristic of a culture that defines the extent to which people within the culture are made nervous by situations they consider to be unstructured, unclear, or unpredictable, and the extent to which they try to avoid such situations by adopting strict codes of behavior and a belief in absolute truths. Table 1.3 contrasts the belief patterns of "high U-A" and "low U-A" cultures.

The traits of high uncertainty-avoidance cultures are

- Greater dependence of citizens on authorities and less tolerance for citizen protest

- More elaborate legal system
- More intolerant activist state religions
- Popularity of ideological thinking
- More structuring of activities
- More written rules
- More ritual behavior

On the other hand, the traits of more tolerant cultures are

- "Looser" societies
- Stronger feelings of citizen competence and more tolerance for citizen protest
- More casuistic approach to legal issues
- De facto religious tolerance

---

increased through individual decisions. Least government is the best government.
- *Concept of community.* The concept is "Community of Limited Liability"—the marketplace as community.

The bottom right-hand corner (low individualism, low power-distance) is occupied by *ideal-type communism,* the main features of which are these:

- *View of human nature.* Humans have no meaning that is not provided by the community of which they are part; the individual's interest is subjugated to that of the collectivity.
- *Nature of the social order.* Social order is based on equality, to eliminate the class conflict that destabilizes capitalism.
- *Central values.* Equality and community solidarity are important.
- *Orientation to social change.* Change is produced by inherent conflicts and contradictions within the system; it is dialectical.
- *Ideal system.* Worker/community ownership and control of the means of production through democratic decision-making processes exists.
- *Conception of community.* Community is the solidarity of equal

power based on the abolition of social classes.

The main diagonal, running from top left to bottom right, is readily recognizable as the axis along which capitalism and socialism are opposed.
Off the diagonal, in the lower-left quadrant, the central values are those of *authoritarian conservatism,* including feudal and other aristocratic systems, as well as caste-stratified and fascist societies. Its main features are these:

- *View of human nature.* Cynical view of humans as inherently aggressive, selfish, competitive and hierarchical, motivated by biological urges.
- *Nature of the social order.* Humans need society to protect themselves from each other. Inequality and hierarchy are natural and necessary.
- *Central values.* These values involve authority, order, and tradition as well as freedom within prescribed bounds.
- *Orientation to social change.* Change is disruptive and should be minimized.
- *Ideal system.* Paternalistic capitalism exists, where there is stability through elite-controlled growth.
- *Conception of community.* "Ge-

meinschaft," as illustrated in the feudal estate, is ideal.

The top-right quadrant is best typified by the twentieth-century philosophy of the *welfare state:*

- *View of human nature.* This view is the same as liberalism, but not as cynical. Individuals can be motivated by altruism under certain circumstances.
- *Nature of social system.* Social system has tendencies toward instability, concentration of power, and injustice; it requires government fine-tuning to keep it running smoothly. Capitalism with a meritocratic structure is the best form of society.
- *Central values.* Individual civil rights and equal opportunity are important.
- *Orientation to social change.* Humans, through the vehicle of the state, must intervene to make appropriate modifications in the system. Social change is evolutionary.
- *The ideal system.* Welfare-state capitalism exists. Expand and adjust the pie through state-guided development.
- *Concept of community.* "Community without Propinquity:" Social networks and associations are not bound by territoriality.

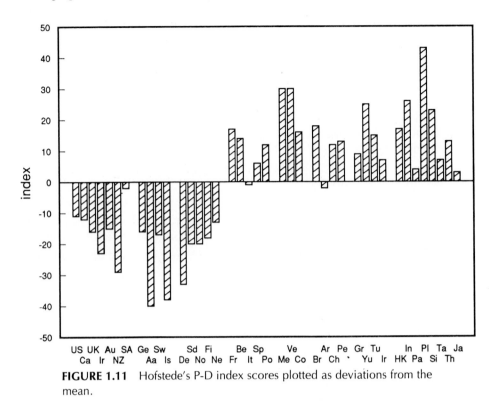

FIGURE 1.11   Hofstede's P-D index scores plotted as deviations from the mean.

- Popularity of pragmatic thinking
- Less structuring of activities
- Fewer written rules
- Less ritual behavior

Hofstede's "U-A" scores are charted in Figure 1.12. One indicator of the extent to which economic uncertainty prevails and/or has been avoided is the inflation rate mapped in Figure 1.13. If countries are cross-classified on the basis of their P-D and U-A scores, fascinating contrasts in social organization are revealed. Refer to Box 1.4.

Sex-Role Differentiation

The final dimension identified by Hofstede arises because cultures use the biological difference between men and women to define vastly different social roles

TABLE 1.3

Contrasts between high U-A and low U-A cultures

Belief Patterns in High U-A Cultures	*Belief Patterns in Low U-A Cultures*
(i) High anxiety and stress: There is an inherent uncertainty in life that is a continuous threat.	(i) Ease, lower stress: The uncertainty inherent in life is more easily accepted and each day is taken as it comes.
(ii) Strong superegos and more showing of emotions: Assertive nature of self and others is accepted.	(ii) Weaker superegos and less showing of emotions: Assertive behavior is frowned upon.
(iii) Strong need for consensus: Conflict and competition can unleash aggression and should therefore be avoided.	(iii) More acceptance of dissent: Conflict and competition can be contained on the level of fair play and used constructively.
(iv) Intolerance: Deviant persons and ideas are dangerous.	(iv) Deviance is not felt as threatening; there is greater tolerance.
(v) Concerns with security in life: Conservatism, law, and order are essential.	(v) There is more willingness to take risks in life and less conservatism.
(vi) Achievement is defined in terms of security.	(vi) Achievement is determined in terms of recognition.
(vii) Search for ultimate, absolute truths and values is ongoing.	(vii) Relativism and empiricism exist.
(viii) Written rules and regulations are needed.	(viii) The belief exists that there should be as few rules as possible.
(ix) Belief in experts and their knowledge exists: Ordinary citizens are incompetent versus the authorities.	(ix) There is a belief in generalists and common sense and that the authorities are there to serve the citizens.

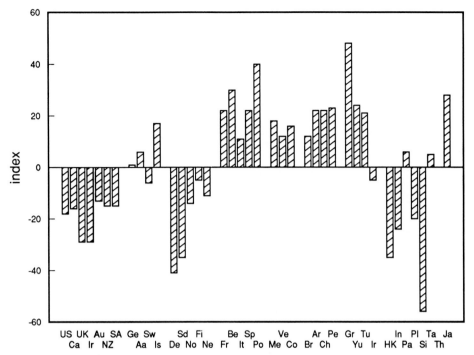

FIGURE 1.12   Hofstede's U-A index scores, plotted as deviations from the mean.

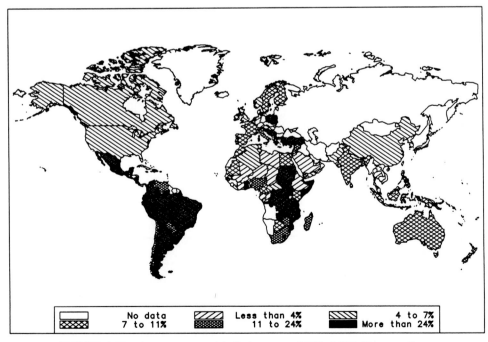

FIGURE 1.13   Average annual inflation rate, 1980–1988 [*Source:* Data from The World Bank, *Poverty, The World Development Report, 1990,* p. 202.]

BOX 1.4   Types of Social Organization

	Small Power-Distance	Large Power-Distance
Weak uncertainty avoidance	Countries: Anglo, Scandinavian, Netherlands Organization type: implicitly structured Implicit model of organization: market	Countries: Less-developed Southeast Asian Organization type: personnel bureaucracy Implicit model of organization: family
Strong uncertainty avoidance	Countries: German-speaking, Finland, Israel Organization type: workflow bureaucracy Implicit model of organization: well-oiled machine	Countries: Latin, Japan, Near Eastern, Socialist Organization type: full bureaucracy Implicit model of organization: pyramid

If power-distance is cross-classified with uncertainty avoidance, contrasts in social organization are revealed. One sees, for example, the Germanic well-oiled machine (lower-left quadrant) contrasting with Southeast Asia's family-type personnel bureaucracies (upper-right quadrant). The principal diagonal contrasts Anglo-Saxon and Latin Europe.

---

for the sexes. Highly masculine cultures expect men to be assertive, ambitious, and competitive, to strive for material success, and to respect whatever is big, strong, and fast. They expect women to nurture, to care for the quality of life, for children, and for the weak. Less-masculine cultures define overlapping social roles for the sexes, in which men need not be ambitious or competitive but may put the quality of life over material success and may respect whatever is small, weak, and slow. In both masculine and nonmasculine cultures, the dominant values within political and work organizations are those of men. In masculine cultures these organizational values stress material success and assertiveness; in nonmasculine cultures they stress quality of life and welfare for the weak.

The belief patterns of more- and less-masculine cultures are contrasted in Table 1.4. Highly masculine cultures share the following traits:

- The emphasis is on aggressive pursuit of success.
- Men and women follow different types of higher-level education.
- Men are breadwinners, and women are cakewinners.
- Some occupations are considered typically male, others, female.
- There are fewer women in more-qualified and better-paid jobs.
- Fertility is based on male income.

TABLE 1.4

Contrasts between more- and less-masculine cultures

Belief Patterns in Highly Masculine Cultures	Belief Patterns in Less-Masculine Cultures
(i) Men should behave assertively and women should care.	(i) Men need not be assertive but can also take caring roles.
(ii) Sex roles in society should be clearly differentiated: father used as a model by boys; mother by girls.	(ii) Sex roles in society should be fluid: both father and mother used as models by boys and girls.
(iii) Men should dominate in all settings: there is a machismo (ostentative manliness) ideal; women can be kept ignorant.	(iii) Differences in sex roles should not mean differences in power; unisex and androgyny ideal; more equal partnership of men and women.
(iv) Weaker position of the mother in the family: male-dominated fertility decisions.	(iv) Stronger position of the female: female leadership in fertility decision.

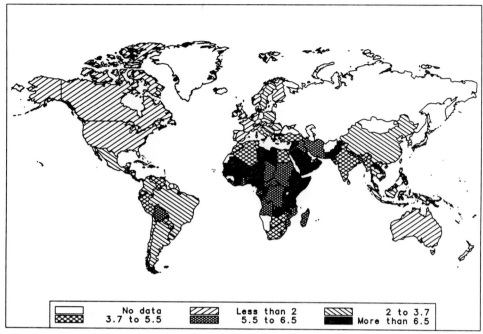

FIGURE 1.14   Total fertility rate, 1988. [*Source:* Data from The World bank, *Poverty, The World Development Report, 1990,* p. 230.]

In cultures with less sex-role differentiation, the dominant traits are as follows:

- Emphasis is on caring and sharing.
- Men and women follow the same types of higher education.
- Men and women can both be breadwinners.
- There is less occupational segregation.
- There are more women in more-qualified and better-paid jobs
- Fertility is controlled by female labor force opportunity

Among the indicators of sex-role differentiation and therefore of degree of masculinity are the total fertility rate, the extent of female labor force participation, and the extent to which women participate in the political process. These are mapped in Figures 1.14, 1.15, and 1.16. Hofstede's "masculinity" scores are charted in Figure 1.17. For the results of cross-classifying countries on their U-A and masculinity scores see Box 1.5.

From Family to Nation-State, An Explanation of Cultural Traditions

Another anthropologist, Emmanuel Todd, has offered a bold hypothesis to explain why distinct cultural traditions persist and reproduce contrasting political ide-

ologies. *Family relations,* he says, *serve as the model for political systems by defining the relationship between the individual and authority.* The family shapes the worldview of its children, reproducing people who share the same beliefs and values. Each generation absorbs parental values and bases its own child-rearing upon those values; the system is self-perpetuating. In turn, the values shape the individual's expectations about larger social, economic, and political relationships beyond the family at the level of region and nation-state. The resulting political ideologies are no more than family relations writ large.

There are across the globe, he argues, only eight basic family types. These are mapped in Figure 1.18. The first four types are derived by cross-classifying the opposing forces of liberty-authority and equality-inequality (Hofstede's individualism/collectivism versus power-distance) to define the essential features of the four fundamental family types found in Europe:

	Inequality	Equality
Liberty	1. Absolute nuclear family	2. Egalitarian nuclear family
Authority	3. Authoritarian family	4. Community family

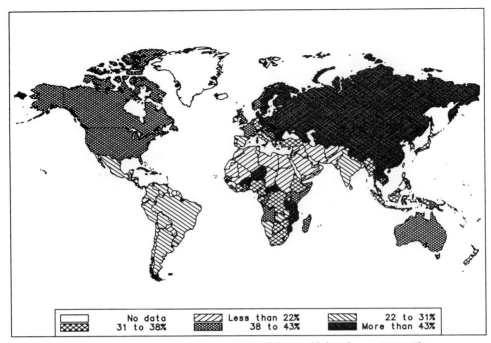

FIGURE 1.15   Women as a percentage of the total labor force, 1988. That the lowest rates are in Islamic countries, followed by many Catholic nations, India, and Japan reveals that religious values are among the strongest factors in establishing and maintaining sex-role differentiation. [*Source:* Data from UNDP, *Human Development Report, 1990,* p. 156.]

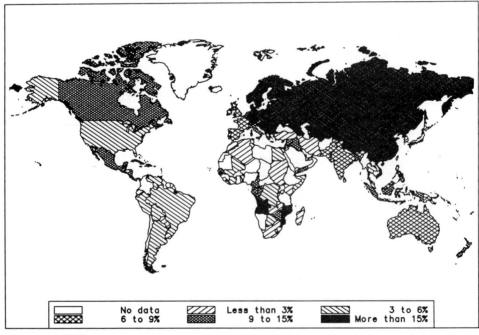

FIGURE 1.16   Females as a percentage of male legislators in the national parliament, 1988. [*Source:* Data from UNDP, *Human Development Report, 1990,* p. 144.]

BOX 1.5   *Types of Motivation Driving Behavior*

	Low Sex-Role Differences	*High Sex-Role Differences*
Weak uncertainty avoidance	Countries: Northern Europe and Netherlands Motivation by success and belonging Success measured partly collectively and partly by the quality of human relationships and the living environment.	Countries: U.S., Great Britain and former Dominions Motivation by individual achievement Success measured by wealth, recognition, and self-actualization
Strong uncertainty avoidance	Countries: Socialist Motivation by security and belonging Success measured by group solidarity and performance rather than by individual wealth	Countries: Japan, German-Latin, Greece Motivation by personal security Success measured by wealth, and by hard work within the organization

Cross-classification of countries on the uncertainty-avoidance and masculinity axes provides insights into four different types of motivation that drive behavior. In the diagram above, "Anglo" achievement orientation contrasts with the collective-security orientation of the socialist state; likewise, Northern European concepts of individual success combined with belonging contrast with German-Japanese notions of personal security secured by hard work within the organization.

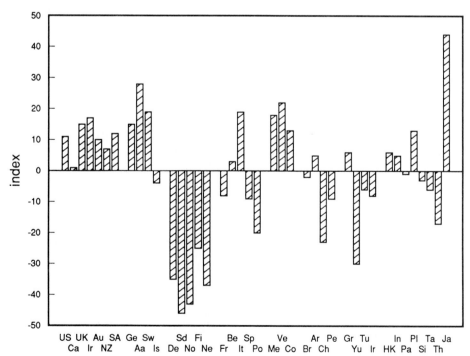

FIGURE 1.17   Hofstede's masculinity scores, plotted as deviations from the mean.

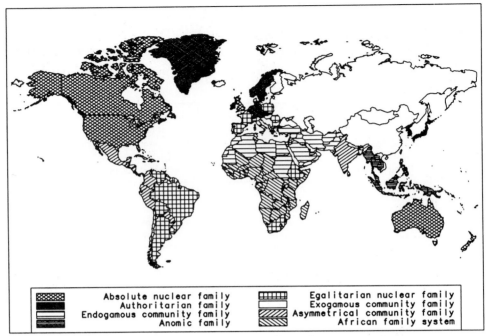

FIGURE 1.18   Global distribution of principal family types. This map is generalized from Todd's illustrations, which show detailed regional variations within nation-states, particularly in western and southern Europe. [*Source:* Data from Emmanuel Todd, *The Explanation of Ideology* (Oxford: Basil Blackwell, 1985), p. vi.]

The first of the family types, the *absolute nuclear family* of the Anglo-Saxon world, socializes children to individualized values: They must strive to succeed to be able to support their own independent nuclear family units. One result has been a preference for utilitarian concepts of individual rights and liberties: Individuals must be the ones to act to maximize their own welfare; the best society is one in which each individual has maximized his or her own happiness. The kind of philosophy that comes to characterize such a society is laissez-faire liberalism.

Opposed to the individualist nuclear family is the *exogamous community family,* characterized by equality between brothers and cohabitation of married sons and their parents. The principal regions in which this family form has dominated historically are: Russia, Albania, central Italy, China, and Vietnam. In these regions, in Todd's view, modern revolutionary movements have transferred the egalitarian values of the family to the level of the state. Individual rights are crushed by the political system in the same way they were destroyed in the past by the extended family.

The *authoritarian family* involves inequality of brothers laid down by inheritance rules, with transfer of an unbroken patrimony to one of the sons. The traditional regions dominated by this family form were Germany, Austria, Bohemia, peripheral regions of

France, northern Spain and Portugal, Japan, and Korea. Primogeniture implies inequality, and with inequality there is a presumption of the dominance of the powerful and the deference of the weak. The result at the societal level is the use of authority to guarantee stability, frequently manifested in the development of elaborate bureaucratic hierarchies and of large-scale organization. Thus, feudal aristocratic systems, fascism, bureaucratic socialism, and Catholicism can and often have coexisted. There is also strong tendency to demand conformity and to persecute that which is alien or different: The notion of cultural "purity" is strong. What results are the mainstream values of authoritarian conservatism.

Dialectically opposed to the authoritarian family type is the *egalitarian nuclear family* of northern France and Italy, central and southern Spain, central Portugal, Greece, Romania, Poland, and Latin America. The defining features are equality of brothers laid down by inheritance rules. The outcome of socialization by his family type is a continual tension between the individualism demanded by the nuclear family and the equality built into the rules of inheritance. The first demands individual effort that can only result in inequality; the second requires rules and regulations to ensure that the goal of equality is met. As a result of this fundamental contradiction, Todd says, one sees a continuing tension at the societal level between liberal democracy on the one hand and bureaucratized central controls on the other, and at its worst, between anarchy and militarism.

These four family types lie at the basis of Europe's political economies and those parts of the world colonized by Europeans. But to complete his world map, Todd found it necessary to identify four additional types. The fifth family type socializes children in the Arab world, Turkey, Afghanistan, Azerbaijan, Turkmenistan, Uzbekistan, and Tadzhikistan. The *endogamous community family* is characterized by equality between brothers established by inheritance rules, cohabitation of married sons with their parents, and frequent marriages among cousins. This is the anthropological reality, says Todd, that lies beneath the theological appearance of Islam, built of close-knit groups and clans. The extended household remains all-important, but the authoritarian role of the father is replaced as a regulatory mechanism by custom. Relationships tend to be horizontal rather than hierarchical and vertical, and the power of the fraternal bond surpasses the others, a bond that is strengthened by the presumption of equality. Islamic tradition recognizes two fundamental institutions, religion and the family. Accordingly, central administration and the state remain relatively weak, and this weakness of the state results in political fragmentation. Islam rejects both the Western notion of the freely acting individual who escapes both the family and the state and the communist notion of the individual escaping from his family into the body of the state; instead it recognizes only two levels of social integration, the family and the community of believers (the *Ummah*).

A sixth family type is the *asymmetrical community family* of central and southern India and Sri

---

BOX 1.6   The "Indian Problem"

Source: Paraphrased from the *Economist's* Survey of the Indian Economy, May 4, 1991.

India's future looks more threatened than for many years. This is not the fault of wicked colonial masters or wicked western capitalists or the cruel hand of fate. It is largely India's own doing. Nowhere else, not even in communist China or the Soviet Union, is the gap between what might have been achieved and what has been achieved as great. The country is rich in the resources that matter most for economic advance—not physical resources (which it also has) but human resources. Indians are capable of punishingly hard work; remarkably for people so poor, they are thrifty; they are entrepreneurial; they are ambitious and materialistic. When Indians have ignored the Hindu injunction never to cross the "black sea" and travel abroad, they have prospered within a generation. Only at home are so many imprisoned, in their hundreds of millions, in a sink of despair and degradation. The country is divided by violence over caste and religion. Economic growth is slowing, and poverty on a scale that defies the imagination seems beyond all remedy.

The problem is twofold. Since independence in 1947 India has pursued a policy of self-sufficiency, managed by a proliferating bureaucracy that has combined the worst of central-planning ideas borrowed from the Soviet Union with the traditional rigidities of caste. Major industries were nationalized. Licenses and direct controls regulated much of the rest of the economy. Firms were told where to locate and what to charge. Small, labor-intensive firms were favored over bigger, capital-intensive ones; hand-loom weavers were favored over power looms, and so on.

After a fashion, the policy succeeded. A civil servant can show you the view from his window and tell you with pride that almost everything you see in his country—cars, buses, scooters, radios, televisions, you name it—was made in India. True, he will admit, our quality is not all it might be. Agreed, our designs are not bang up-to-date. (Only in India is it possible for a car buyer to choose between a brand-new 1950s Austin and a factory-fresh 1950s Hillman.) "But then ours is a poor country, what can you expect?"

In excuses for failure, too, India can supply all it needs. India has two great excuses. The first is sheer weight of people. It is undoubtedly true that India is already overpopulated, and the continuing growth of numbers is a heavy burden on the economy. The second excuse is that poverty tends to be self-reinforcing. India started from behind; it is a struggle merely to prevent the gap from growing. The country's educated elite talks complacently of the "Hindu rate of growth": "Never forget that India was crippled by its colonial past, that the rich First World will refuse to let it catch up, that democracy costs India one or two percentage points of growth a year."

The real problem is that of culture and religion. Hinduism promotes acceptance and resignation by those of lower caste. The centrally directed state created by the post-independence intellectuals used the moral imperative of Hindu philosophy to blunt the spur of competition, and reproduced in the bureaucracy administrative hierarchies as rigid as those of caste. The ambition and materialism unlocked when Indians move elsewhere is constrained at home by rigidities inherited at birth, reinforced both by childhood socialization and by the directed management of the state.

Lanka, dominated by systems of *caste*. The essential family features are equality between brothers defined by inheritance rules and cohabitation of married sons with their parents. Such families socialize children to a society in which groups within society are separated from each other, obsessed by fear that physical contact is polluting. Endogamous marriage is enforced within the subcaste, the small localized groups corresponding to particular occupations and regions. An overarching ideology is that of racism, of the superiority of certain castes and the inferiority of others, with people born into positions in which they must remain throughout their lives. The only way out is through reincarnation, provided that people behave in ways exemplary of their given status in the present life. The orientation, then, is antithetical to change, demanding obedience, guaranteeing the stability of the caste hierarchies, and promoting structured inequality. See Box 1.6.

An *anomic family* form is characteristic of Burma, Cambodia, Laos, Thailand, Malaysia, Indonesia, the Philippines, Madagascar, and the South American Indian cultures, Todd says. It is defined by uncertainty about equality between brothers, inheritance rules that are egalitarian in theory but flexible in prac-

tice, cohabitation of married children with their parents rejected in theory but accepted in practice, and consanguineous marriage possible, often frequent. A particular type of social and political system characterizes states with this family form, not centralized and hierarchical (which is associated with vertical family systems) but "centrified." The anomic family works in a particular way, unregulated, permissive, not accustoming its members to the principle of discipline, and only weakly integrated by communitarian ideas of neighborhood cooperation. So the centrified state, equally weakly integrated, with the family and the communitarian idea the only basis of cohesion, is likewise equally weakly structured. There are advantages: relative equality of men and women; absence of constraint that permits rapid inroads to be made by new ideas and technologies, and their ready absorption into the structure of the family and society. The disadvantages reside in the absence of traditional power bases for organizing and running a modern state, a task that therefore frequently falls into the lap of the only hierarchically organized, goal-oriented bureaucracy available, the military.

A final category is reserved by Todd for *African family systems*, characterized by absence of stable in-

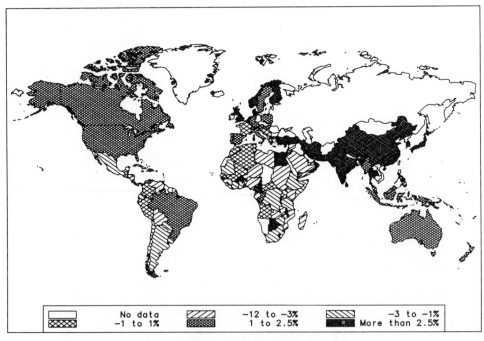

FIGURE 1.19   Annual growth rates of per capita GNP, 1980–1987. This map reveals the major beneficiaries of the period of accelerated growth following the global "stagflation" crisis of 1980–1981, when inflation skyrocketed and much of the world plunged into recession. Note also that there were many countries, especially those in Africa, that experienced declining national product per capita. [*Source:* Data from UNDP, *Human Development Report, 1990,* p. 170.]

terpersonal relationships, except between mother and children, and by polygyny. Vertical (patrimonial) power relationships are limited, weakening socialization to the concept of authority, and undermining the idea of discipline. The instability of relationships doomed to failure the experiments in democracy that the colonial powers left in place. With weak bases for state formation, the army has become preeminent, the only organized game in town, often acting in support of the charismatic leader. But lack of stability has meant frequent power shifts that drive a vicious circle: Because there is instability, there is poor economic performance; because economic performance is weak, there is more instability. See Figure 1.19.

Todd's hypotheses are provocative, providing an explanation for the persistence of deep-seated cultural differences that serve as a counterweight to the globalizing force of multinational enterprise. As a management consultant, Hofstede realized the importance of these differences. There are, he said, no universal solutions to organization and management problems, only culturally relative ones. Thus, the Confucian work ethic has provided a particular way of achieving growth in East Asia (Box 1.7). The ways in which the multinational firm structures its operations must be relative to the values and expectations of the host culture if it is to succeed. Different nations have different cultural heritages that are largely invisible but have

---

BOX 1.7   Cash Value of the Confucian Work Ethic

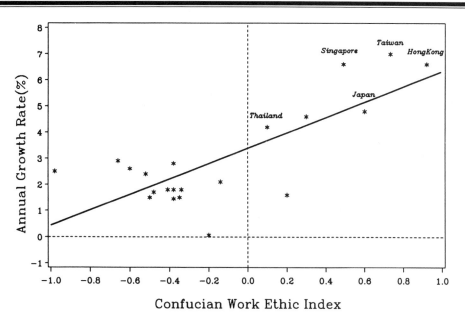

The Confucian work ethic involves a number of ideas: that the government must assume full responsibility for the well-being of its people; that leadership is obligated to provide, to enrich, and to educate the people; and that bureaucrats are not merely functionaries, but leaders, intellectuals, and teachers. Driven by this ethic, Japan and the "Four Dragons" of East Asia have transformed themselves into "development states" with single-minded attention to wealth and economic power that has centered on the ability of the central government to forge

bonds of trust with the business community, the intelligentsia, and the working class. To measure the consequences Michael H. Bond and Geert Hofstede developed a "Confucian Work Ethic" index. This index was estimated for a group of 21 countries. Values were compared with the average annual growth rates of per capita GDP from 1965 to 1984, as in the accompanying graph, and it was found that there was a strong relationship between the two ($R = 0.77$). Bond and Hofstede concluded that the Confu-

cian work ethic had a real "cash value"; i.e., that it was the driving force behind "Confucian capitalism," predicated upon harmony and consensus rather than competitive conflict in the market, leading to coordination of actions between government, business, and labor. See Michael H. Bond and Geert Hofstede, "The Cash Value of Confucian Values," in Stewart R. Clegg and S. Gordon Redding, eds., *Capitalism in Contrasting Cultures* (Berlin & New York: Walter de Gruyter, 1990), pp. 383–389.

powerful consequences, not only for multinational operations but for economic growth and political life viewed more broadly. The invisible part—the *collective unconscious*—consists of the values that are held by a majority of the population and are transferred from generation to generation through early life experience in family and schools and through socialization in organizations and institutions. The stability of national cultures over long periods of history is achieved through a system of constant reinforcement, because societal norms lead to particular political, organizational, and intellectual structures and processes, and these in turn lead to self-fulfilling prophecies in peoples' perceptions of reality that reinforce the societal norms. National culture, in its turn, defines the preferred type of political economy, and therefore the ways in which growth and development are achieved.

TOPICS FOR DISCUSSION

1. To what extent do countries formerly classified as members of the "Fourth World" fit into Michael Porter's factor-driven stage of economic development? In what ways are their development potentials limited by their factor dependence?

2. It is said that the former Second World's socialist economies will be unable to enable the transition to market systems without first reintroducing private property. Why should this be so?

3. The world's top 500 major multinational corporations are headquartered in only 19 urban regions (North America: New York, Chicago, Los Angeles, San Francisco, Philadelphia-Wilmington, Dallas–Fort Worth, Houston, St. Louis, Detroit, Pittsburgh; Asia: Tokyo, Osaka-Kobe, Seoul; Europe: London, Paris, Ruhrgebiet, Frankfurt, Randstadt, Rome). Does this mean that the current world economy is organized around these 19 regions in a multicentered fashion, or is it possible that modern communications are linking the regions into a single dispersed "polycenter"?

4. Michael A. Goldberg and John Mercer offer the following contrasts between the United States and Canadian cultures in their book *The Myth of the North American City* (Vancouver: University of British Columbia Press, 1986):

CANADA	UNITED STATES
Deferential behavior	Assertive behavior
Collective	"Frontier" individualism
Respect for authority	Distrust for authority
Elitist/oligarchic	Egalitarian/democratic
Self-restraint	Self-indulgence
Social liberalism	Economic conservatism
Cautious/evolutionary	Dynamic/experimental
Peace/order/good government	Pursuit of happiness

What differences in the structure of the Canadian and U.S. economies might be a consequence of these cultural variations?

5. What steps should a wealth-driven economy take to reestablish innovation-driven growth? What problems are likely to arise if a country makes such a transition? Think of examples from Margaret Thatcher's Britain and Ronald Reagan's United States.

FURTHER READINGS

BERRY, BRIAN J. L. "The Howard G. Roepke Lecture in Economic Geography. Comparative Geography of the Global Economy: Cultures, Corporations, and the Nation-State," *Economic Geography*, 65, No. 1 (January 1989), 1–18.

Provides an overview of the principal cultural dimensions that shape the worldview, goals, and decision criteria of actors in the global economy.

DOTI, JAMES L. and DWIGHT R. LEE. *The Market Economy: A Reader.* Los Angeles: Roxbury Publishing Co., 1991.

A collection of important essays on the political, economic, and philosophical underpinnings of a market system.

HOFSTEDE, GEERT. *Culture's Consequences: International Differences in Work-Related Values.* Beverly Hills, Calif.: Sage Publications, 1980.

Presents an empirically based framework for understanding cross-national variations in culture.

PORTER, MICHAEL E. *The Competitive Advantage of Nations.* New York: The Free Press, 1990.

Provides a new look at the factors responsible for economic growth, and a new classification of the stages of economic development.

SIMON, JULIAN L. *The Ultimate Resource.* Princeton, N.J.: Princeton University Press, 1981.

The "ultimate resource" is humankind. This book presents the possibility of evolution in social organizations.

2

The Changing Nature of Economic Geography as a Field of Study

OVERVIEW

*Economic geography is primarily concerned with the location of economic activity, the spatial organization and growth of economic systems, and people's use and abuse of the earth's resources. Economic geography traces its roots to the emergence of the highly practical field of **commercial geography**. This new subject provided prospective merchants and governments with information on products and exports of the principal regions of the world.*

*From 1900 until the early 1930s, an analytic, explanatory approach based on a philosophy of **environmentalism** dominated the discipline. In this approach, the dependence of people's activities upon the natural environment was emphasized.*

*The following 25 years saw a variety of regional and topical approaches to the study of the **areal differentiation** of economic activities, accompanied by a growing concern for conservation and the wise management of the earth's resources.*

*From the mid-1950s, interest grew in **locational analysis, spatial organization, and the dynamics of spatial systems,** and then in the 1970s economic geographers began to explore **behavioral approaches to individual decision making,** as well as to reintroduce **ecological concerns** for the relationships of people and nature, and to respond to the alternative ideological perspectives of Marxism and of postmodern philosophies.*

*As a result of this evolution, economic geography now is characterized by a **complex mosaic** of ideas and approaches.*

OBJECTIVES

- to help you understand contemporary thinking by following the steps by which ideas have been developed
- to describe the work of geographers who have played a leading role in shaping the subject
- to illustrate the difficulties of developing new theory, and the resulting succession of probes into theory and retreats into fact
- to indicate the concerns about the images of humanity that underlie macrotheories about the interrelationships between population and resources as well as microtheories of how the decisions are made that determine the spatial organization and growth of economic systems

DISTINCT PERIODS IN THE HISTORY OF ECONOMIC GEOGRAPHY

The rapid changes in global economic geography discussed in Chapter 1 have led to calls for new bodies of theory to help explain the evolving realities. Before we throw out the old, however, it is important that we place these challenges and the call for new theory in perspective. Throughout its history, economic geography has been concerned with an enduring set of issues: the relationships between population, economy, and resources; the similarities and differences from place to place in the ways people make a living; the factors that determine locational choice; the reasons for regional specialization and the trade flows that they generate; the explanations of economic development and the associated disparities in living standards. Over the years, the approaches to studying these issues and the theories used to explain them have changed, resulting in several distinct periods in the history of the field.

The emphasis at first was on the facts of *commerce,* in an effort to form some reasonable forecasts of future commercial development that might serve as a guide to business interests and to governments. The search for better explanations led next to a more theoretical economic geography that focused on the study of the relationships between economic activity and the physical environment. However, *environmental determinism,* the theory that economic differences were caused by environmental factors, failed to explain the diversity of economies in similar physical environments, and ignored the freedom of individuals to make their own choices, within limits, of what they produced. A retreat from theory back to fact followed. A third economic geography emerged that concerned itself with *areal variation* in production, and the economic regions that resulted.

Beginning in the 1950s, economic geographers made new attempts at creating a theoretical approach, building on the work of economists, and relying heavily on quantitative methods to understand the *spatial organization* of economic systems. Some economic geographers subsequently retreated from this approach because they rejected the underlying image of the "economic maximizer," seeking instead a new *behavioral* economic geography and a more comprehensive understanding of the motivations that divide decision-makers. Others, Marxists in particular, rejected capitalist assumptions and offered *structuralist* interpretations of locational differences. They, in turn, have given way to the "New Age" philosophies of the *radical humanists* who, once again, reject the search for general theory.

The history of these shifts in economic geography is a fascinating subject worthy of study in its own right. Thomas Aquinas is reputed to have said that "no-one believes anything he first does not believe to be believable." In other words, the preferred explanation depends upon the observer's belief system—usually, the prevailing image of humanity, but also the dissident's alternative to it. As the image changes, so does the explanation of a given set of facts. We thus need to learn why images change. The difficulties in establishing a theoretical approach to the subject and the traps into which economic geography has fallen need to be relearned by each new generation of students.

Kenneth Boulding once observed that "nothing fails like success." It is perhaps also true that nothing succeeds like failure. Out of the constant questioning and frequent rejection of approaches to economic geography there may yet emerge new and more powerful approaches. In tracing the history of the subject, we therefore attempt to draw out the progression of ideas that have contributed to current thinking in the field. We pinpoint some of the geographers who dominated the subject and describe their work. We underline the insights that have propelled the subject forward, and the excesses that have sidetracked it. We also direct attention to the components that we believe must be integrated into any new synthesis. We begin at the beginning with the emergence of commercial geography.

COMMERCIAL GEOGRAPHY

Modern economic geography traces its roots to commercial geography. Commercial geography had grown up as the Western European nations expanded their trading relationships and empires across the globe, creating a demand for commercial information about world regions that previously had been unknown to the Europeans. One of the first textbooks in the field was written in the middle of the seventeenth century by the geographer Bernardus Varenius to provide practical commercial information for Amsterdam merchants. Later, other volumes were published: Patrick Gordon's *Geography Anatomized,* which had 20 editions in England between 1693 and 1728; William Guthrie's *New System of Modern Geography,* published in 1770 and revised through 1843; and Jedidiah Morse's *Geography Made Easy.* These books were the world's first financially rewarding educational publications.

George G. Chisholm

Commercial geography reached its zenith in the work of a Scottish scholar, G. G. Chisholm, who founded the school of geography at the University of Edinburgh in 1908. Chisholm's *Handbook of Commercial Geography* was first published in 1889 and reached its tenth edition in 1925 when he was 77 years old. This distinguished book, subsequently rewritten by L. Dudley Stamp and others, still occupies an important place in the literature and may well have had a more profound and lasting influence on economic geography than any other single book.

The *Handbook,* which provided a precise account of world production and trade, was organized first by commodity, using as a basis such factors as climate and geology, which Chisholm thought helped explain the world distribution of commodity production, and second by country, to describe the detailed locality of production. Chisholm was a stickler for accuracy and detail, but he argued that the most important contribution of commercial geography was not the facts themselves, but the clues they provided to the likely future course of commercial development.

Production and Trade.

Chisholm introduced the first edition of his book with this essential truth: "The great geographic fact on which commerce depends is that different parts of the world yield different products, or furnish the same product under unequally favorable conditions." The view that particular geographic conditions offer absolute advantages to the production of specific commodities, whose production will therefore tend to become concentrated in those regions, became more firmly entrenched in geographic thinking with each new edition of the *Handbook.*

Chisholm also elaborated the interdependence of production and trade. Regional concentration in production is not possible without the transportation facilities to distribute the goods to their markets. Trade is thus the great equalizer, increasing the variety of goods available in any location and reducing differences in price for a good between any two regions to the costs of transportation and any tariffs involved. Improvements in transportation technology, he found, reduced regional price differences and increased the range of commodities traded. Chisholm noted that early Egyptian, Assyrian, and Phoenician trade was in only the most expensive and transportable luxuries— gold, silver, precious stones, ebony and fine woods, ivory and inlaid work, incense, perfumes, balsams and gums, apes, peacocks, panther skins, and slaves. By the time he wrote the first edition of the *Handbook,*

these commodities had been displaced by bulk items. In Chisholm's day, one drug, opium, shipped mainly to China, held a leading place by value in world exports, but trade was otherwise dominated by raw materials and manufactured items in common use, such as wheat, wool, iron, and ironware.

Concentration and Deconcentration.

Improvements in transportation technology, Chisholm observed, had led to more concentrated patterns of production and to increases in regional specialization. Distant centers, previously unable to compete in local markets because of shipping costs, found that they could undersell local producers as transportation costs fell. More particularly, established centers with highly skilled labor and more advanced equipment benefited most from improvements in transportation technology. Along with this, these improvements tied the world's distant raw-material-producing regions into a single system, revolving around a Western European industrial "heartland." Chisholm cited the example of the refrigeration technology that was just developing as his first edition went to press in 1889 and that played such an essential role in the establishment of the commercial dairy and livestock industries in countries such as New Zealand, Australia, and Argentina. Shipment of these low-cost agricultural goods to Europe stimulated the further concentration of manufacturing activity in Europe at the same time that the animal industries concentrated in the Southern Hemisphere. Improvements in transportation and trade encouraged increasing concentration of production.

Chisholm also identified countervailing forces of decentralization, and he believed these forces would in the end outweigh the forces of concentration and would lead to a more equal worldwide distribution of industrial activity. One of the primary forces of decentralization was what he called the "Law of Diminishing Returns" (more correctly, the "Law of Vanishing Assets"). Given a choice, industrialists will mine raw materials such as coal and iron ore where they are most favorably located. Thus, the thickest, richest coal seams, those closest to existing manufacturing activity, will usually be mined first. Once these best, most conveniently located reserves are used up, the costs of production can be expected to rise, imposing an increasing cost burden on older industrial centers and forcing both raw materials and industrial production into new locations.

Chisholm did not address questions of limits to growth, however. In the years that he was working on the various editions of his *Handbook,* 1889 to 1925, he was interested in the effects that *local* depletion of resources (not shortages at the global scale) would have on the distribution of industry. Improved transportation technology, he thought, could be expected to alleviate the effects of any local resource depletion. If there were to be any problems of shortages, they would be shortages of workers, not resources. Thus, he wrote in the introduction to his fourth edition:

> Demands are constantly made for more men for our mercantile navy, for agriculture, and for various industries, while it is notoriously the case that more men are finding employment in the service of the rich and well-to-do, and in connection with amusement and education, including under one or other of these last two heads all the varied forms of literature. When such demands are made the population returns raise the question, Do the men exist to meet them?[1]

Chisholm worked on his *Handbook* in an age of rapid technological change. The last few decades of the nineteenth century saw the coming into general use of hydroelectric power, refrigerated steamships, subways, the telephone, electric light, steel skyscrapers, and the elevator. Industrial technology was changing rapidly, with the Gilchrist-Thomas process of steelmaking in Germany in 1879. The manufacture of calcium nitrate by the fixation of atmospheric nitrogen began in Norway in 1905, providing artificial fertilizers for world agricultural output. New agricultural lands were opening up, and the Canadian prairies enjoyed a wheat boom made possible by new strains of fast-maturing wheats. A subdued optimism thus characterized Chisholm's writing.

ENVIRONMENTAL DETERMINISM

Economic geography developed as a separately named field of study in the United States at the time when Chisholm was writing successive editions of his *Handbook,* but it followed a different path. The first article to use the term *economic geography* in the United States was published in 1888. Some years later, World War I proved a great stimulus to this field of study; economic geographers were called upon to provide knowledge about sources of food and raw materials in the world, and for understanding of the economic problems of different countries. By the early 1920s the field was well established, and a special journal, *Economic Geography,* appeared in 1925. Despite the calls

of some early advocates, this new economic geography was not closely related to economics, but instead was a discipline whose ideas were consistent with the philosophies of *environmentalism* that dominated the social sciences as they emerged out of natural philosophy in the latter part of the nineteenth century.

The Environmental Idea

The basic environmentalist idea was clearly expressed by the first president of the Association of American Geographers, William Morris Davis, in his 1906 presidential address: "Any statement is of geographic quality if it contains . . . some relation between an element of inorganic control and one of organic response." To Davis, human society was an organism that survived by adjustment to the physical environment; the nature of its growth was environmentally prescribed.

Davis was a tireless scholar who sought for many years to impose the environmentalist concept on American geographic education. This viewpoint is best illustrated in the following quotation from one of his contemporaries.

> Man is a product of the earth's surface. This means not merely that he is a child of the earth, dust of her dust; but that the earth has mothered him, fed him, set him tasks, directed his thoughts, confronted him with difficulties that have strengthened his body and sharpened his wits, given him his problems of navigation or irrigation, and at the same time whispered hints of their solution.[2]

The Geographical Theory

The environmentalist idea was so strong that when sociologist Pitirim A. Sorokin published his masterful review and critique, *Contemporary Sociological Theories Through the First Quarter of the Twentieth Century,* he devoted one-sixth of his study to what he termed *The Geographical Theory:* "Almost since the beginning of man's history," he wrote, "it has been known that the characteristics, behavior, social organization, social processes and historical destiny of a society depend upon the geographical environment."[3]

Among the phenomena Sorokin noted that the environmentalists tried to explain by environmental

---

[1] G. G. Chisholm, *Handbook of Commercial Geography,* 4th ed. (London: Longmans, Green and Co., 1903), p. xxv.

[2] Ellen Semple, *The Influences of Geographic Environment* (New York: Henry Holt & Co., 1911), p. 1.

[3] P. A. Sorokin, *Contemporary Sociological Theories Through the First Quarter of the Twentieth Century* (New York: Harper & Row, 1928), p. 99.

causes were: population distribution and density, housing types, road location, clothing, and the amount of wealth produced and owned by a society. A dominating belief was that all brilliant and wealthy civilizations of early times occurred in "favorable" natural environments, whereas "unfavorable" climates and inaccessible or isolated areas bred backwardness and savagery. The location and nature of industry, business cycles, and the rhythms of economic life, race, and physiological, social, and historical differences among societies all were explained on the basis of environmental determinants. So were health, energy and efficiency, suicide, insanity, crime, birth, death, and marriage rates, religion, art, and literature, and the social and political organization of society!

Ellsworth Huntington

The strongest hypotheses about civilization and climate were those of a geographer named Ellsworth Huntington, who argued that climate was the decisive factor in health and physical and mental efficiency; and that since a civilization is the result of the energy, efficiency, intelligence, and genius of the population, ergo, climate is the "mainspring" factor in the progress or regress of civilizations.

How does one establish a link between civilization and climate? Ellsworth Huntington began by writing to 214 well-traveled and well-read geographers, historians, diplomats, business people, and others in 27 countries to help him. They were asked to rate the level of civilization in each of a given list of regions on a scale of 1 to 10.

Huntington provided them with a definition of civilization:

> Qualities (of civilization) find expression in high ideals, respect for law, inventiveness, ability to develop philosophical systems, stability and honesty of government, a highly developed system of education, the capacity to dominate the less civilized parts of the world, and the ability to carry out far-reaching enterprises covering long periods of time and great areas of the earth's surface.[4]

How objective are the replies likely to be when individuals are asked to rate the level of civilization in all regions across the world, including their own? In one respect, Huntington considered himself lucky. He undertook the enterprise in 1913 before the hopes for international objectivity and cooperation were dashed by World War I. Nevertheless, his expert eye detected some bias in the replies he received. Thus, he noted that Americans put America, particularly its more backward parts, higher than what one would expect. To reduce this bias he grouped the replies (54 in all) by the region in which the respondent lived and produced regional averages. In this way the American replies (numbering 25) carried no more weight than that of the Teutonic Europeans (6) or Asiatics (also 6).

The disparities in the averaged ratings revealed systematic spatial patterns. The North America map, for example, showed that, in general, the lower the rating for a region, the greater the disparity in the rating suggested by different contributors (Figure 2.1). The highest rating given was for the manufacturing belt stretching from New York to Chicago (rating 95 to 100). The Canadian Prairies rated 64 points (out of 100), and Greenland a mere 50. But the range in average maximum and minimum values ranged from 1 for New York, to 30 for Manitoba, to 51 for Greenland.

An ethnocentric bias is even more obvious. Contributors tended to rate their own immediate regions higher than more distant contributors. The Austrian Alps are rated 90 by "Teutons," but 74 by Americans. Southern China is rated 84 by all Asiatics, but only 44 by the British. One exception to the tendency of ratings to drop with the distance of the contributor is Quebec Province. The lowest rating for Quebec was by the North American contributors (85), which compares with 89 by British contributors.

The major objective of the maps of civilization was to determine "much more fully than has yet been the case, how far various moral and mental qualities are influenced by physical environment, race, historical development, biological variations and other causes."[5] The method of rating civilization and the disparities in the results obtained dispel any respect for the work among those not repelled by the very idea of ranking civilization itself.

Huntington's writing on civilization has caused subsequent geographers acute embarrassment. Taken for what it pretends to be, the work is blatantly ethnocentric and ludicrously pompous. Thus, when British geographer T. W. Freeman included a chapter on Huntington in his book *The Geographer's Craft* (1967), an American reviewer was in a gloomily humorous vein and was "led to wonder if some, perhaps unconscious, anti-American bias had not motivated the writer to

---

[4] Ellsworth Huntington, *Civilization and Climate* (New Haven: Yale University Press, 1915), p. 150.

[5] Ibid., p. 151.

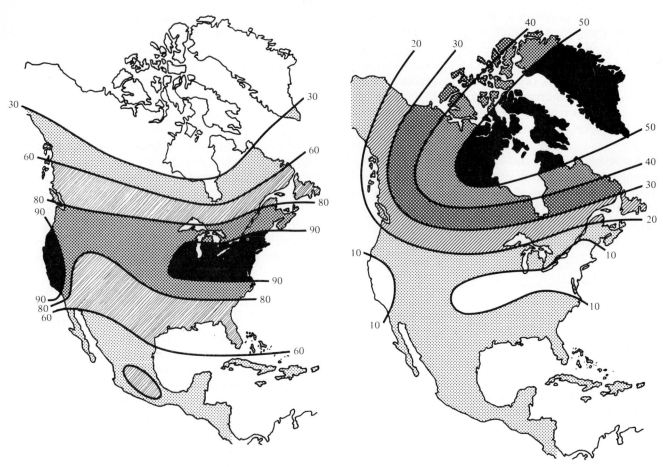

FIGURE 2.1   The level of civilization (left) and range of civilization scores (right) in North America: Huntington, 1915. The strongest hypotheses about civilization and climate were those of Ellsworth Huntington. The map of civilization in North America appears in *Civilization and Climate* (New Haven: Yale University Press, 1915), p. 173, and was used to bolster the preposterous argument that the northeastern United States had the ideal climate to stimulate the highest levels of "civilization."

choose the figure whom most contemporary American geographers might most avidly choose to forget."[6]

Whereas geographers are trying to forget about the work of Huntington and the conclusions he made between climate and civilization, some contemporary economists are beginning to ponder whether in fact such a relationship might not exist. Thus, economist Michael Todaro, writing on the differences between initial conditions of the developed world before its economic takeoff and those of the developing world today, notes climate as one of eight major differences:

Almost all Third World countries are situated in tropical or subtropical climatic zones. *It is a his-*

[6] Andrew H. Clarke, quoted in Geoffrey J. Martin, *Ellsworth Huntington: His Life and Thought* (Hamden, Conn.: Archon Books, 1973), p. 251.

torical fact that all successful examples of modern economic growth have occurred in temperate zone countries. Such a dichotomy cannot simply be attributed to coincidence: it must bear some relation to the special difficulties caused directly or indirectly by differing climatic conditions.

One obvious climatic factor directly affecting conditions of production is that in general the extremes of heat and humidity in most poor countries contribute to deteriorating soil qualities and the rapid depreciation of many natural goods. It also contributes to the low productivity of certain crops, the weakened regenerative growth of forests, and the poor health of animals. Finally, and perhaps most important, these extremes of heat and humidity not only cause discomfort to workers but also weaken their health, reduce their desire to engage in strenuous physical work and generally lower their levels of productivity and efficiency.[7]

In his own day, Huntington's work had a much weaker impact in the United Kingdom than in North America. Chisholm was among the wide circle of academics with whom Huntington corresponded regularly. Chisholm thought highly of Huntington's work in general, but wrote in one review that "the tendency to lack due care in generalizing cannot be denied, and there are . . . too many evil consequences thereof."[8] Chisholm is not among the list of those British geographers who agreed to contribute to the map of civilization. Nor did Huntington's work have any visible impact on Chisholm's *Handbook of Commercial Geography*.

J. Russell Smith

One geographer who did agree to contribute to the map of civilization was the American J. Russell Smith. Smith, asked in 1916 to evaluate Huntington's work, could say categorically, "Huntington is doing what I regard as the most important geographical work now being carried out." Smith's view is important because he wrote the first and one of the most influential textbooks in economic geography in the United States, and because his approach to the subject was strongly influenced by Huntington's work.

J. Russell Smith began his university studies in economics at the Wharton School of Finance and Economy at the University of Pennsylvania, and he began his teaching career there in 1903 as an instructor in commerce. He later became Professor of Geography and Industry and then became Professor of Economic Geography at Columbia University in 1919. Smith claimed he was dissatisfied with Chisholm's textbook because he found it too descriptive. Notwithstanding his own early training as an economist, he felt the need for a book that would analyze the underlying relationships among the physical environment and people's economic activities and resource utilization.[9] The result was Smith's *Industrial and Commercial Geography,* published in 1913, with various editions (with M. O. Phillips and his son T. R. Smith) ending in 1961.

The first edition of Smith's *Industrial and Commercial Geography* predates Huntington's *Civilization*

and Climate, but the first chapter bears the imprint of Huntington's work and refers at length to one of Huntington's earlier papers. Thus, Smith begins his book with a chapter titled "Our Changing Environment" and the words, "A group of people can only prosper, increase and grow powerful when their environment furnishes them an abundance of food and of other materials for making appliances to supply the other necessities of existence."[10] But like Huntington, he believed in a challenge-response element in development. Smith viewed civilization as a product of adversity, advancing most where nature restricted production to certain seasons, requiring people to work and to save to keep themselves during the other season. Where things were too good, "the native may sit and doze most of the time, as for untold generations, his ancestors have done before him—enervated by plenty."[11] Civilization, he thought, had gained by moving north into the cold regions.

Cold is a great stimulus to activity. Men and animals alike want to move more rapidly on a brisk, cold day of winter than on a sultry summer afternoon. This is as true of nations as of persons. The most energetic and powerful nations, therefore, are those living in a climate where frost forces them to activity and where the warm summer enables them to produce vast supplies of food.[12]

Like G. G. Chisholm, J. Russell Smith viewed commerce as the key to the distribution of commodities in all regions, few of which could produce the complete range needed. But the term *civilization* constantly reappears in the opening chapter of his book even when discussing commerce and transportation. Nevertheless, Smith's discussion of trade and commerce makes the same basic points as did Chisholm. Improvements in transportation were recognized to have changed the staples of trade to the cheap, bulky items, and to have evened out in time and space the supply of foods.

The very strong environmentalism evident in the opening chapter of the first edition of Smith's book was modified in later editions. Nevertheless, a reference to Huntington's *Civilization and Climate* appeared in virtually identical form after its publication in 1915 in all later editions of Smith's book.

Three world maps were presented; the first two

[7] Michael Todaro, *Economic Development in the Third World* (New York: Longman, 1981), pp. 100–101.

[8] Quoted in Martin, *Ellsworth Huntington*, p. 133.

[9] See Virginia M. Rowley, *J. Russell Smith* (Philadelphia: University of Pennsylvania Press, 1964), p. 50.

[10] J. Russell Smith, *Industrial and Commercial Geography* (New York: Henry Holt & Co., 1913), p. 1.

[11] Ibid., p. 7.

[12] Ibid., pp. 9–10.

were from Huntington: distribution of human energy on the basis of climate, and the level of civilization. The civilization map has been discussed. The climate-energy map was equally ethnocentric, with "best" physical health and energy placed at an averge temperature of 64°F at night to 70°F by day, and "best" mental health at somewhat lower temperatures. Smith then added a third map that showed the percentage of the labor force in manufacturing activity. The connection among the three maps was inescapable. Smith concluded:

> By a strange coincidence these areas of high civilization in Europe and North America happen to have the best and most accessible coal in the world. Suppose that coal had been in the Amazon, Congo, and lower Mackenzie valleys![13]

It is unlikely that Huntington would have approved of such extreme statements. In one letter in 1932, Huntington wrote, "I used the words *control* and *determine*. Now my tendency is very strongly to say *permit* and *favor* [Huntington's italics]. I think that what the environment does is mainly first to offer a choice of different conditions which man may utilize, and then favor one type of activity rather than another." An article written by Huntington in 1931, which reflected his thinking on "The Content of Modern Geography," was, however, rejected by the editors of the *Annals of the Association of American Geographers,* who felt that their journal should concentrate on the results of original field investigations.[14]

T. Griffith Taylor

The environmental relationships between energy resources and economic development, voiced in such a simplistic way by Smith, were stated much more astutely by the Australian T. Griffith Taylor, a determinist who also maintained an active correspondence with Ellsworth Huntington. Griffith Taylor probably was the most controversial geographer ever, and his biography makes interesting reading. He had become a world celebrity because of his participation in Robert Scott's last expedition to the Antarctic, his work in both surveying and naming Australia's new capital, Canberra, and his fierce disagreement with government officials on the settlement possibilities of Australia.

Taylor established the first university depart-

ments of geography in both Australia (at Sydney in 1920) and Canada (at Toronto in 1935). He wrote major books on both countries, with titles that left no doubt about his deterministic leanings. His *Australia* text (first published in 1941) was subtitled, "A Study of Warm Environments and Their Effect on British Settlement." His *Canada* book (first published in 1947) was subtitled, "A Study of Cool Continental Environments and Their Effects on British and French Settlement." Australia's description certainly sounds cozier than Canada's, but Taylor was very pessimistic about its settlement future, at least by the standards of the day. He castigated as irresponsible claims that Australia could support 100 million population or more. His own assessment was based on a careful appraisal of the distribution, reliability, and total amount of rainfall across the country, for he believed that rainfall would prove to be the single most important factor limiting settlement. He therefore summarized his thinking in a set of maps emphasizing environmental control (Fig. 2.2). The government of Australia banned some of his books, and Griffith Taylor left his post for a professorship at the University of Chicago and later at the University of Toronto.

Taylor was more optimistic about settlement possibilities in Canada. His inaugural address at Convocation Hall, Toronto, Ontario, given in 1935 and attended by the lieutenant-governor and other dignitaries of the province, as well as the president of the university, seems as prescient today as it must have appeared far-fetched at the time.

Griffith Taylor predicted in that address that Alberta would probably become the most powerful province in Canada. Calgary, he said, might one day be larger than Montreal or Toronto, although at the time Calgary's population was about one-tenth that of Montreal and Toronto. He based these predictions on Alberta's oil and coalfields, and he then accused the Canadian government of neglecting their development. The day would come, he predicted, when the capital of Canada would be moved from Ottawa to Calgary and Canada itself would become the center of the British Empire. He also had encouraging words about the Mackenzie River Valley. It might, as Smith emphasized, lack coal, but it has a warmer summer climate than the Gaspe Peninsula. Northern Canada could duplicate the Russian experience and establish a string of cities with populations of more than 20,000 each.

Taylor also made careful estimates of the total population that the world could support. The figures depended on the standard of living expected; thus, Australia's population could climb to 60 million, given European living standards, or 30 million at Australian living standards. Taylor believed in "carrying capac-

[13] J. Russell Smith and M. O. Phillips, *Industrial and Commercial Geography*, 3d ed. (Henry Holt & Co., 1946), p. 15.

[14] Martin, *Ellsworth Huntington*, pp. 242–244.

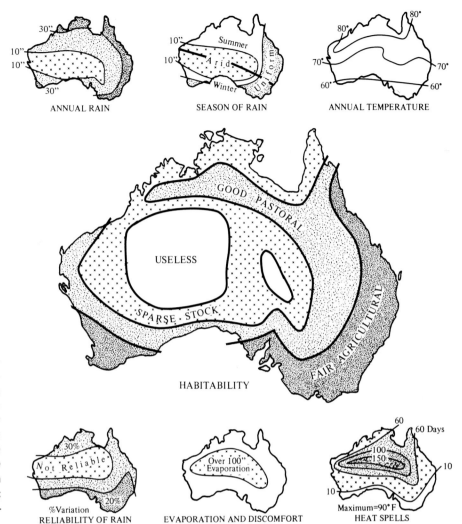

FIGURE 2.2 Environmental determinants of Australian settlement: Griffith Taylor, 1940. Journalists and politicians anticipated that Australia's population would grow to 100 million or more. Taylor suggested that environmental limits, as described in these maps, set a reasonable limit at 20 to 30 million. He was called unpatriotic, and some of his books were banned. His views were later vindicated, and in 1952 he returned to Australia to retire in Sydney. The university there named its geography building after him. [*Source:* Griffith Taylor, *Australia: A Study of Warm Environments and Their Effect on British Settlement* (London: Methuen and Co. Ltd., first published 1940; seventh edition reprinted 1966), frontispiece.]

ity'' and limits to growth. Had he lived to see the publication of the Club of Rome's studies he would have been quick to point out that, whereas Meadows and colleagues based population limits on an undifferentiated world, and Mesarovic and Pestel on a world of only 10 regions, he had used 74 economic regions for his estimates as far back as 1922. All that without the help of any computer!

Taylor summarized his thinking about the relationship between population and physical environment, and the role of the geographer, in a paragraph that reappeared in many of his books. He wrote:

> The writer is a determinist. He believes that the best economic program for a country to follow has in large part been determined by Nature, and it is the geographer's duty to interpret this program. Man is able to accelerate, slow or stop the progress of a country's development. But he should not, if he is wise, depart from the directions as indicated by the natural environment— What the Possibilists fail to recognize is that Nature has laid down a ''Master Plan'' for the World—This pattern will never be greatly altered; though man may modify one or two percent of the desert areas, and extend the margins of settlement. It is the duty of geographers to study Nature's plan, and to see how best their national area may be developed in accord with temperature, rainfall, soil, etc., whose bounds are quite beyond our control in any general sense.[15]

---

[15] Quoted in John K. Rose, ''Griffith Taylor, 1880–1963,'' *Annals of the Association of American Geographers,* 54, No. 4 (December 1964), 622–629.

The Waning of Environmentalism

Even as environmentalism reached its height, geography was developing new ideas that were to supersede it, however. Frederic Le Play, a French geographer, developed the first scientific method for the study and analysis of social phenomena, and he correlated the character of places with the type of work, forms of property, types of family organization, and other institutions and social processes, emphasizing the *mutual interdependence* of place, economy, and culture, rather than single-factor causation by environment.

The idea of the interdependence of culture and nature was developed more fully by another French geographer, Vidal de la Blache, in his *Principles of Human Geography* (1926). According to de la Blache:

> The dominant idea in all geographical progress is that of terrestrial unity. The conception of the earth as a whole, whose parts are coordinated, where phenomena follow a definite sequence and obey general laws to which particular cases are related, had early entered the field of science by way of astronomy.[16]

What was emerging out of environmentalism was an early concern in geography for *ecology*. Vidal de la Blache thought that "every region is a domain where many dissimilar things, artificially brought together, have subsequently adapted themselves to a common existence" and in which "the influences of environment are seen only through masses of historical events which enshroud them." He also believed that the physical environment sets limits or margins within which humans are free to work, rather than controlling people directly.

The gradual change in thinking can be traced in the following series of quotations from successive editions of Nels August Bengtson and William Van Royen's textbook *Economic Geography*. In 1935, the authors indicated that "differences in the natural environment not only affect the physical activities of man, but generally they also lead to fundamental differences in thoughts and ideals. . . . The Norwegians of today—strong, agile, alert, and serious—are in large measure the product of the environment which has fostered them." The next edition of the text (1942) made certain adjustments. The first edition's "differences in environment lead to differences in activities" became "differences in productive activities are often results of differences in environment." Again, "the

Norwegians of today—virile, agile, alert, and sincere—in large measure have been shaped as a regional group by the environment which has fostered them." The subtle change is noteworthy. Finally, in 1956 the authors indicated that "the physical environment does not determine the economic activity and the mode of life of man." Evidently some old dogs were willing to learn new tricks!

AREAL DIFFERENTIATION: 1930s TO THE 1960s

Retreat from Theory

"The simple faith in the determining influence of natural environment has almost disappeared," wrote Jan Broek in "Discourses on Economic Geography," which appeared in *The Geographical Review* for 1941. In the face of increased questioning, environmental determinism was abandoned by economic geographers, who began to look for new explanations based on the principles of economics. W. H. Carter and R. E. Dodge, for example, argued that economic geography "should analyze . . . universally applicable economic principles that underlie our whole industrial life."[17] There was some experimentation with industrial location analysis. O. E. Baker made use of David Ricardo's rent theories in his studies of land use. Other American geographers became concerned with resources and the conservation of the environment during the Great Depression and the New Deal of the 1930s. Some geographers moved into problem-solving roles in President Franklin Roosevelt's National Resources Planning Board and in the Tennessee Valley Authority.

This initial flirtation with economic theory was short-lived, however. Rejecting not only environmentalism but also most attempts to theorize, the majority of economic geographers from the 1930s to the 1960s returned once again to a very descriptive approach. The tentative generalizations about commodity production and trade in George G. Chisholm's introduction to his *Handbook of Commercial Geography* and sweeping assertions about economy and environment in J. Russell Smith's *Industrial and Commercial Geography* were dropped. In their place came a variety of organizations of subject matter, each simply a "container" for facts.

Economic geography, according to two textbook authors, once again became

---

[16] Vidal de la Blache, *Principles of Human Geography* (London: Constable, 1926), 6–7.

[17] W. H. Carter and R. E. Dodge, *Economic Geography* (New York: Doubleday, Doran and Co., 1939), p. vi.

an inquiry into similarities, differences and linkages within and between areas in the production, exchange, transfer, and consumption of goods and services.[18]

The study of the areal variation of the earth's surface in mans' activities related to producing, exchanging and consuming wealth.[19]

Some economic geographers organized their books by regions or countries and described their principal products and exports. Some authors described world-scale maps of the spatial patterns of production and trade of particular commodities. Still others organized their works around "activity systems," such as primitive subsistence economies, commercial grain-livestock farming systems, and industrial-urban complexes.

There were, to be sure, some changes over the years. The regionally oriented approaches dominated the 1940s, although there was a gradual shift toward topical organization. But the described variety of phenomena and the increasing abundance of facts led the describers to despair of ever again having a unified field of economic geography. In 1954, a review of the field appeared in *American Geography: Inventory and Prospect,* and it noted:

> General economic geography [has] ceased to exist as a research specialty. . . . More and more the scholar who claims penetration in his research thinks of himself as a specialist in land utilization, in resources, in manufacturing geography, in the geography of transportation, or some other special aspect, and he makes no pretense to competence in research in economic geography as a whole.[20]

On the other hand, it was admitted that

> There is a central theme, however, common to all the topic specialities within the general limits of economic geography. Economic geography has to do with the similarities and differences from place to place in the ways people make a

living. The economic geographer is concerned with economic processes especially as manifested in particular places modified by the phenomena with which they are associated.[21]

The tone of the subject of economic geography in this third phase is illustrated by one popular text that went through many editions, namely, Clarence Fielden Jones's *Economic Geography,* first published in 1935. The descriptive approach in the book was set by the opening sentences, which are in sharp contrast to those of the Chisholm and Smith texts quoted earlier. Jones began a chapter titled "The Distribution of People" quite simply: "Everyone likes to travel. Most of us wish to visit distant lands." What followed was a description of the work people do in various lands, organized on an activity basis. Eight main activities were identified: hunting and fishing, grazing, farming, forestry, mining and manufacturing, and commerce. These then become the main sections of the book. Each chapter typically included a map of a representative farm and farming region. The farm maps were at a scale of 1 inch equals $\frac{1}{4}$ mile, and were accompanied by a detailed description of the farm itself and the annual rhythm of activity. Discussion of physical factors affecting production led into a map depicting the limits of the agricultural region represented by the farm. Where necessary, further maps at intermediate scales were included. Thus, a map of a farm village in hilly land in Kiangsu Province, China, showed how farm plots were allocated among village farmers. The descriptions went far beyond the detail offered in the early commercial geographies and stressed economic geography as a field of study that should be directly involved in travel, observation, mapping, and original data collection, rather than one depending on governmental statistics, as Chisholm had suggested.

Ultimately, the areal differentiation approach in economic geography became bound up with the definition and mapping of *economic regions.* Regions had always been important in economic geography, but they had received less attention in earlier approaches. Commercial geographers had employed countries as convenient units to present data on world commodity production and trade. Environmental determinists employed physical regions based largely on climate. In both cases, regions were a means to an end. In areal differentiation, definition of regions became an end in itself, the ultimate in descriptive generalization.

To younger geographers in the late 1930s, this was problematic, and they began to complain about

[18] Richard S. Thoman, "Economic Geography," *International Encyclopedia of the Social Sciences,* Vol. 6 (New York: Macmillan, 1968), pp. 124–128.

[19] J. W. Alexander, *Economic Geography* (Englewood Cliffs, N.J.: Prentice Hall, 1963), p. 9.

[20] Raymond E. Murphy, "The Field of Economic Geography." In *American Geography: Inventory and Prospect,* ed. P. E. James and C. F. Jones (Syracuse, N.Y.: Syracuse University Press, 1954), pp. 242–243.

[21] Ibid., pp. 242–243.

the sterility of the regional focus. Change was halted by World War II, however, and after the war economic geography took new and different directions.

THE "QUANTITATIVE REVOLUTION"

Adoption of Location Theory

Wartime military intelligence and economic planning required applied geographic studies in which inferences had to be drawn from limited data with the help of sound theory. Younger geographers recognized they had been poorly trained for this work, and after World War II they expressed their dissatisfaction with areal differentiation, and voiced the need for sound theory and reliable methods of inference.

The search for theory intensified in the 1950s and 1960s, a time when the social sciences were becoming increasingly interdisciplinary, when computer technology was beginning to revolutionize quantitative analysis, and when governments were subsidizing research, particularly for planning and policy-oriented studies. There were many suggestions and calls to action. Geographers rediscovered the classical economic theories of location of J. H. von Thünen, Alfred Weber, Walter Christaller, and the newly translated (in 1954) work of August Lösch (these theories are discussed in Chapters 9, 10, and 11). At the same time, an economist, Walter Isard, was sparking a renewed interest in the economics of location. Because he felt that both economics and geography had let the development and application of location theory fall into the gaps between them, he called for creation of a new discipline, *regional science,* to take a leadership role. Partly as a result of Isard's challenge, economic geographers' work became more highly analytic and quickly embraced location theory as an intellectual core.

So pervasive and swift were the results that geographers dubbed the change the "Quantitative Revolution." By 1968 Richard Thoman could write:

> . . . the past decade has marked the emergence of a new school of thought. . . . This school has chosen an explicitly theoretical approach, emphasizing nomothetic (law-seeking) research and depending . . . upon mathematic abstracting.[22]

An assessment of the changes was made by the U.S. National Academy of Sciences' National Re-

search Council in a 1965 report titled *The Science of Geography:*

> Several traditional subfields of geography, including economic, urban and transportation geography, are not discussed . . . as they once might have been. . . . It would appear that the three . . . subfields have been joined in a problem area which we entitle . . . location theory studies. . . . The development, testing and refinement of location theory, related studies of the geographic organization of economic life, and of urban and transportation systems, have been fundamental. . . . The applicable body of theory includes . . . abstract concepts concerning spatial distributions and space relations. . . . Very recently a new synthesis has begun to emerge based upon: (1) the identity of spatial concepts and principles developed in (several) subfields of geography; and (2) emphasis upon the interaction of economic, urban and transportation phenomena in interdependent regional systems that are the material consequences of man's resource-converting and space-adjusting techniques. *This emerging synthesis thus results from a concerted application of systems theory within geography* [italics added].[23]

What is systems theory? It deals, in Arthur Koestler's words, with economies

> as an organization of parts-within-parts, because all living matter and all stable systems have a parts-within-parts architecture, which lends them articulation, coherence, and stability.[24]

A system is simply an entity consisting of a set of interdependent and interactive parts: land uses, business firms, trade flows, regions, or, more abstractly,

> *movements,* that (produce) the channels along which the movements occur, the *network,* structured around *nodes,* organized as a *hierarchy,* with the interstitial zones viewed as *surfaces.*[25]

---

[22] Thoman, "Economic Geography," p. 124.

[23] Edward A. Ackerman, Brian J. L. Berry, Reid A. Bryson, Saul B. Cohen, Edward J. Taaffe, William L. Thomas, Jr., and M. Gordon Wolman, *The Science of Geography* (Washington, D.C.: National Academy of Sciences-National Research Council, 1965), p. 44.

[24] Arthur Koestler, *The Ghost in the Machine* (New York: Macmillan, 1967), pp. 82–83.

[25] Peter Haggett, *Location Analysis in Human Geography* (London: Edward Arnold, 1965), p. 18.

Some emphasized not only systems theory but *normative* considerations involving control of these systems to reach specific goals. Many geographers, both East and West, began to think of their discipline as

> a science concerned with the laws of development of dynamic spatial systems formed on the earth's surface in the process of interaction of nature and society, and with control of these systems . . . the science dealing with the laws of development of geosystems and their control.[26]
>
> . . . economic geography emphasizes the need of *control* in the spatial allocation of our resources. It . . . (involves) . . . *geocybernetics,* the study of spatial organization.[27]

[26] Y. G. Saushkin and A. M. Smirnov, "The Role of Lenin's Ideas in the Development of Theoretical Geography," *Vestnik Moskovskogo Universiteta, Geografiya,* No. 1 (1970), pp. 3–12.

[27] Commission on College Geography, *A Systems Analytic Approach to Economic Geography* (Washington, D.C.: Association of American Geographers, 1968).

Behavioral Assumption: The Economic Maximizer

This new theoretical economic geography involved not only a focus on location theory and on the spatial structures that resulted (Figure 2.3), but it implied a particular image of humanity, and it led to a concern with a quite different set of geographic concepts. Of all of these components, none has caused more subsequent concern or dissatisfaction than the underlying behavioral assumption that each individual is an "economic maximizer."

An economic maximizer, quite simply, has perfect knowledge of present circumstances and future events so that he or she has powers of perfect prediction. This individual is also entirely rational and driven by a single goal—to maximize profits. In some cases this goal may be achieved by locating economic activity so as to minimize transportation costs. In other cases, profits are maximized by seeking the "highest and best" land use. But most location decisions with which this economic person must grapple involve tradeoffs. Higher land rents are charged for the most

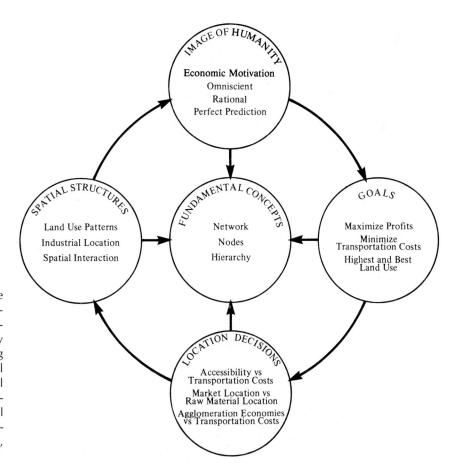

FIGURE 2.3 Building a normative economic geography. This conceptual framework was built upon an image of humanity as motivated solely by economic considerations, having particular goals, making locational decisions, and resulting in spatial structures of land use, industrial location, and settlement. Fundamental concepts in understanding these spatial structures include networks, nodes, and hierarchies.

accessible locations where transportation costs are lower, whereas less-accessible locations may involve higher transportation costs and lower rents. One set of tradeoffs may therefore involve accessibility—rents versus higher transportation costs. To cite a different example, an industrialist can minimize costs of obtaining raw materials by locating close to them, and can minimize marketing costs by locating close to markets. How should this person weigh a market location versus a raw material location? And how should he or she weigh tradeoffs relating to the scale of production? Unit costs of production tend to fall with increasing scale of output; larger industrial plants have lower unit costs than smaller plants, everything else being equal. But larger plants must serve a larger market area, which in turn involves higher transportation costs. Thus, economies of large-scale operation must be weighed against increased transportation costs.

Location theories that deal with these issues describe rational economic landscapes based on optimal decisions of economic maximizers. These landscapes are not a product of differences in climate and soils, as the environmental determinist would have argued. Instead, they are constructed in an abstract space devoid of environmental differences. In this respect, the new economic geography of the 1960s represented a complete break with the past. George Chisholm stressed in his commercial geography the intrinsic physical advantages that each part of the world offered for the production of particular products. J. Russell Smith related production to climate. Clarence Jones described regional patterns. None of them would have predicted that complete economic landscapes could emerge out of rational decisions by profit maximizers, regardless of environmental considerations.

The completeness of the break with the past may be demonstrated by comparing four books, those of Chisholm, Smith, and Jones, already discussed, and a book titled *Readings in Economic Geography,* by Robert Smith, Edward Taaffe, and Leslie King. In this last book, regional studies are used to illustrate theory, and no attempt is made to provide systematic coverage of either all commodities or world regions. This work was a response to the growing interest of geographers in locational analysis and the increasing proportion of economic geography students completing courses in economics and quantitative analysis. The book was a substantial break from economic geographies based upon the idea of areal differentiation, and the editors noted that they were "quite aware that there are other approaches to the large and diverse subject of economic geography." Its closest affinity is with texts in regional economics, although the main thrust is a natu-ral extension of ideas suggested as early as Chisholm's *Handbook.*

Coping with Uncertainty

Every theory in science implies a particular image of humanity. Changes in scientific theories involve changes in our image of ourselves. The new theoretical geography of the 1960s thus involved a new model of how decisions are made about the location of economic activity. This model replaced the stimulus-response theory of people as robots dancing to the rhythm of their physical environment, which was developed by the environmental determinists, with the concept of rational scientific human beings in control, able to achieve goals and to maximize welfare.

One test of a theory is the acceptability of its particular image of humankind. All theory entails some simplification of reality. The image of humanity similarly entails some truncation of the complexity of human nature. The concept of the economic maximizer simplified reality by removing uncertainty from life and by making us single-goal directed. The image was accepted in the 1960s, even though it is a gross simplification of reality, for two reasons. First, the results of profit maximization provided a norm, or yardstick, with which to examine reality. Indeed, the great German location theorist August Lösch turned the argument around. The time had come, he said, to test reality against theory, not theory against reality. That is, we can judge people by the extent to which they are rational maximizers, rather than whether economic rationality captures the reality of human behavior. This argument does have a certain appeal. Economic geographers can see some merit in knowing what the world would look like under the idealistic circumstances of omniscient, rational, profit maximizers, if only to know how far reality departs from this version of what is the optimal. But they also know that individuals are not all-knowing—that they have to cope with uncertainty, even if a "law of large numbers" takes care of uncertainty for the population as a whole.

The collective ability of economic systems to deal with uncertainty was first explained by Armen Alchian in an allegory.[28] Imagine that thousands of

---

[28] See Armen Alchian, "Uncertainty, Evolution, and Economic Theory," *Journal of Political Economy,* 58 (June 1950), 211–221; Charles Tiebout, "Location Theory, Empirical Evidence and Economic Evolution," *Papers and Proceedings of the Regional Science Association,* Vol. 3 (1957), 74–86.

TABLE 2.1

People against the environment

| | | Fishing strategies[a] | |
		In-shore	*Off-shore*
Environmental conditions	Current	Win	Lose
	No current	Lose	Win

[a] Jamaicans who earn their living fishing have two possible strategies, in-shore and off-shore fishing. Conditions of the physical environment can be either with an off-shore current, or with no current. Knowing the chances of an off-shore current and the premium in price for off-shore fish, the individuals can develop an optimal mix of the two strategies, which maximizes their "wins."

motorists set out on a long journey picking their routes entirely at random. They are unaware that all the service stations are closed except along one route. The travelers who follow this route and so reach their destinations may appear to have acted rationally, and even with considerable foresight. In fact, the route of the survivors is just the same whether they act rationally or not. Similarly, the argument goes, the locational pattern of surviving firms will look much the same whether the surviving firms selected only the locations where they could survive (that is, economic *adaption* occurs) or whether they locate randomly and the economy *adopts* the lucky ones.[29]

The manner in which adoption and adaption occur in real situations has been illustrated using game theory, a mathematics for optimizing under conditions of uncertainty.[30] The technique is discussed in Chapter 8, so here we need note only the nature of the problem, as illustrated by a Jamaican fishing village. Those who make their living from catching fish have two strategies: in-shore or off-shore fishing. Off-shore fish fetch a better price, but unpredictable currents can cause high losses. The trick is to go for a mixed strategy in which the proportions of in-shore and off-shore fishing are determined jointly by the risk of off-shore currents, and the premium that off-shore fish can earn (Table 2.1). Game theory demonstrates that the mixed strategy developed in this Jamaican village over years of trial and error is indeed the optimal one.

BEHAVIORAL APPROACHES

Many geographers were critical of the new theoretical economic geography. Some said that land-use patterns are not dictated by geometry and the cash register. The relevance of the new theory to understanding the real world was questioned. The validity of the statistical procedures employed was considered doubtful by some. And it was noted by others that even some economists were replacing the image of an economically motivated person with a new model in which the decision-maker was a "satisficer."[31]

The Satisficer Concept

People do not necessarily achieve, or even wish to achieve, maximum profits. They seek a variety of goals and are prepared to trade off some income to achieve these other goals. Thus, they select, from among a set of satisfactory alternatives, that alternative which is most compatible with their aggregate goals.

The shift in the image of humanity accompanying this idea of "satisficing" has produced new kinds of studies in economic geography. Rather than assuming self-interested maximization and building a theoretical geography, increasing emphasis has been placed on how risks and opportunities are perceived and how these perceptions influence decision making. This new emphasis is particularly evident in studies of resource management.[32]

This research demonstrates that experience is a good teacher only when it is repetitive and consistent. Where risks are low, and perils infrequent, decision-makers become prisoners of their own fragmentary experience and often underestimate the chances of disaster. Hence the paradox that increased expenditure on flood control in the United States has been associated with increased, not decreased, flood damage.

This new emphasis on the importance of how the perception of an uncertain environment influences the decisions we make is being reinforced by philosophical shifts in geographic thinking. Locational analysis of the 1960s was in tune with a prevailing philosophy termed *logical positivism*. Logical positivism involved empirical analysis within a normative (theory-building)

[29] Alchian, "Uncertainty, Evolution, and Economic Theory," pp. 214–215.

[30] William Davenport, "Jamaican Fishing: A Game Theory Analysis," *Yale University Publications in Anthropology*, 59 (1960), 3–11; Peter Gould, "Man Against His Environment: A Game Theoretic Framework," *Annals of the Association of American Geographers*, 53 (September 1963), 290–297.

[31] Julian Wolpert, "The Decision Process in Spatial Context," *Annals of the Association of American Geographers*, 54 (December 1964), 537–558.

[32] T. F. Saarinen, *Perception of Environment* (Washington, D.C.: Association of American Geographers, Resource Paper 5, 1969).

framework. Data could be collected to test location theory, and the theory developed on the basis of many test results. However, in the 1970s, a number of influential articles appeared in geography that put forward the contrasting philosophy of phenomenology.

Phenomenology

Phenomenology stresses the importance of an individual's "lived-world" experience. It rejects individual maximizing behavior and the notion that there exists some "objective" world. Instead, there is the belief that life takes on meaning only through one's experience and needs. Research must be guided, therefore, not by the preconceived notions of the researcher, but by a more humanistic empathy between the observer and the observed, in which the researcher views the problem from the respondent's viewpoint. Because viewpoints are individual, there is little room for general theory.

Phenomenology thus argues for a step back from the location theory of the 1960s toward a more humanistic orientation within the discipline. Anne Buttimer warns that this approach offers no clear-cut operational procedures to guide the researcher. Rather, she said, it offers perspectives that point to exploration of new facets of geographic inquiry. It is thus a preamble to theory.[33] Others, "postmodern" or "New Age" thinkers, the descendants of nineteenth-century Romantics, denying the validity of the notion of objectivity, reject all theoretical aspirations.

A simple illustration of the phenomenological approach is work on "mental maps."[34] When people are asked to rank places in terms of their personal preferences as to where they would like to live, some fairly clear patterns emerge. First, they tend to rank where they live highest. Places farthest from them rank lowest. This is similar to the results of Huntington's survey of civilization. Second, they are very discriminating in ranking areas around their home region, which they know best, but tend not to differentiate more distant places. But there is also a relationship between population density and rank. Perhaps people like to be at the center of things. Perhaps the density of population is high because these are desirable places to be. Whatever the reason, London ranks high among its residents, and New York high among American residents. The amenity factor is evident too, with high

rankings for the southern coast of England, and in the United States, California and Colorado.

Such mental maps can be prepared at all scales, from local to global. Mental maps, drawn at the local scale by children, illustrate a fundamental distinction between the vertical world of children living in high-rise apartments and the horizontal world of children living in houses. William Bunge has made effective use of such maps in diagnosing problems in urban planning.

It is too early to judge the contributions that will flow from behavioral geography. It is obvious that the shift has brought economic geography back to earth, and this return to reality was needed. One reason for uncertainty is that the new humanism has become "radical humanism" as it has adopted Marxist concepts, even as Marxism is falling into global disrepute.

THE MARXIST CHALLENGE

The Vietnam War sparked an antiwar movement that soon created a counterculture. Rejecting the individualist tenets of American society, members of this counterculture embarked upon a radical critique of the society's institutions and images of humanity. The alternative image that was advanced was Marxist. Economic geography was not seen as the outcome of either the behavior of rational maximizers or of satisficers; rather it was assumed to be the product of exploitation by capital of labor. According to the Marxist interpretation of world history, feudalism was succeeded by capitalism, and within countries capitalists structured economic life to benefit their own class at the expense of exploited workers. Similarly, in the world economy, it was capitalist imperialists who structured the unequal relations of an urban-industrial core and the poverty-stricken, resource-dependent periphery. Thus, in the Marxist worldview, class interest, class conflict, and the use of political and economic power to structure geography are central. Among others, radical feminists have taken these ideas and applied them to the relations between the sexes: Men have structured the world in their own interest and suppressed the legitimate rights and aspirations of women.

Yet what has been structured can also be destructured and restructured. If the self-interested activities of the capitalist class had structured the world economy to their advantage, it also was possible for the resulting social and spatial inequities to be removed and social justice guaranteed by restructuring in the interest of the working class. This restructuring was most likely, Marxists thought, when capitalism

---

[33] Anne Buttimer, "The Dynamism of Lifeworld," *Annals of the Association of American Geographers,* 66 (1976), 277–292.

[34] Peter Gould and Rodney White, *Mental Maps* (Harmondsworth, U.K.: Penguin Books, 1974).

entered a final crisis precipitated by internal contradictions produced by the inequality that it had created. The working class would rise, a revolution would occur, political power would be seized and used, justice would be achieved by creating a society in which private property was replaced by common ownership of the means of production, individual self-interest by collective welfare, competition by cooperation, and competitive markets by state monopolies under the "dictatorship of the proletariat." To advance these ideas, a Marxist special-interest group was formed in the Association of American Geographers as the Vietnam War ran its course. A Marxist economic geography began to be written by such geographers as David Harvey.

One of the most recent restatements of the Marxists' argument is in a paper by Eric Sheppard, published in 1990 in *Economic Geography*. Sheppard sets in stark contrast what he calls the neoclassical and Marxist paradigms. The neoclassical paradigm takes as axiomatic that an industrial capitalist economy results from the behavior of large numbers of economic actors who interact in freely operating, competitive commodity markets. The self-serving behavior of these individuals produces an optimal allocation of resources and maximizes aggregate social welfare. The Marxists criticize this view, saying that the key actors are social classes, not individuals, and that economies are structured by the class that controls the process of production and determines how economic surplus is allocated. Capitalism, the Marxists say, systematically favors the capitalist class at the expense of workers, produces and maintains inequality between the classes, and as a result is inherently unstable and crisis-prone. Resolution of inequality, they say, is a political rather than an economic issue, demanding collective action by the state. If capitalists have structured the economic system in their own self-interest, it is possible for workers to restructure the system by capturing political power. The controlling force of central government can be used to eliminate inequality and therefore to guarantee stability, because the source of capitalist crises is removed.

Radical Humanism

Except for a few, however, counterculture radicals are backing away from such classical Marxism, especially since the collapse of the Soviet Union, because centrally directed socialist strategies have not worked. Some radicals, influenced by phenomenology, have been *deconstructionist*. Since all experience is personal, they say, no theory is valid. Such postmodern or New Age thinkers deny the very idea of objectivity.

Others have become increasingly *humanistic*. Because they hold that all values are personal, the role of the scholar is to observe them by trying to experience them through the eyes and the feelings of those who are being studied. The drive to a new humanism has been particularly strong among alienated intellectuals who resent the obscurity of scientific vocabulary and mathematics that prevent otherwise educated people from participating in the advance of knowledge. The strongest movement is that of the *radical humanists*. Members of this group advocate a new orthodoxy, what they term "politically correct" thinking about race, ecology, feminism, culture, and foreign policy. Reminiscent of Marxist structuralism, they argue that Western society has been dominated for centuries by a white male power structure, a "patriarchal hegemony" that is inherently unfair to minorities, women, and members of deviant subcultures, exploitive of the environment and of the Third World. "Politically correct" scholarship takes as axiomatic the notions of domination and exploitation and seeks to expose the consequences.

In economic geography today, the greatest tension is between the neoclassical theories and analyses that became ascendent during the Quantitative Revolution, and this new brand of radical scholarship. The neoclassical approaches provide the insight into global markets and growth. Radical scholarship provides insights into the political debate about negative side effects of that growth.

CONTINUITY AND CHANGE

The history of economic geography, like that of all academic disciplines, is punctuated by major shifts in thinking. Distinct economic geographies have emerged: commercial geography, environmental determinism, areal differentiation, location theory, and now radical humanism.

The cycle of advance into theory and retreat into fact, with each stage involving changes in the content and organization of the subject matter, should be noted. Commercial geography was a practical geography serving the day-to-day needs of business and government for factual information on production and trade. Environmental determinism emphasized physical, particularly climatic, causal factors and painted people as "robots" stimulated and challenged by their environment. Areal differentiation required detailed field work and the preparation of maps delimiting regions of agricultural production such as the U.S. "cotton belt." Location theory sought to describe economic landscapes created by economic maximizers in which areal differentiation results not from intrinsic differences in climate, soils, or physiography, but instead from accessibility, transportation costs, and economies of scale. Now, Marxists look to class conflict for explanations, and new humanists seek to understand each individual's "lifeworld."

This restless search for new economic geographies may have involved too quick a rejection of what is good in the old. Marvin Mikesell has been led to ponder whether such changes in approach reflect the fickleness of geographers seeking the latest fashion rather than the refinement of science (see Topic 7 at end of the chapter). Others have suggested that a progressive development is evident in the succession of approaches. What is probably the case is that the quest of economic geography is directed by both internal and external forces. The discipline must not only deal with the changing realities of the world but also must satisfy the intellectual demands of its practitioners. The external forces are harder to document than the internal forces that have shaped the discipline, but it seems likely that these forces have been as much geographic, technological, and social as they have been political. Not all locations are of equal productivity: They differ in resource endowment and accessibility. Technology is not constant: It becomes more sophisticated through time and diffuses out from centers of innovation, changing the relative value of resource endowment and geographic location. And society changes: The Vietnam War bred the radical counterculture; concern for individual values drifts into New Age mysticism.

Environmental factors may provide a satisfactory explanation of economic activity and use of resources where geography and technology combine to restrict choice in small-scale and highly localized societies. As the range of options increases, nonenvironmental considerations can be expected to influence decisions as to resource use and economic activity. Determinism yields to possibilism. Given a range of satisfactory alternatives, optimization may yield to satisficer behavior. With increasing affluence, goals may shift from material success to a more inward-looking search for "self-actualization." But the problems facing the world in this age of crisis make it evident that both satisficing and self-actualization are luxuries not available to all the people of the world. And even if all the basic human needs and wants could be fulfilled, we would still face social limits to growth. Not all of us can have the best jobs, highest incomes, and most attractive locations. And what is true for individuals is also true for countries. Countries compete for industry and none wants to be relegated to the position of "hewers of wood and drawers of water."

Whatever the correct interpretation of the changing nature of economic geography and the dual role of internal and external forces, we should not ignore the lessons and contributions of each of the economic geographies described in this chapter. Hence, in organizing this book we have attempted to integrate the mosaic of ideas into their geographic and economic fundamentals, to elaborate the theories of location and interaction that result, and then to return to the problems identified by the critics of capitalism.

TOPICS FOR DISCUSSION

1. How similar in approach are the discussions of particular commodities or regions in current bank reports and business news to the accounts given in the old commercial geographies such as Chisholm's *Handbook?* Why have such accounts failed to satisfy the goals of economic geography as an academic discipline?

2. How essential are environmental differences to a geography of commodity production? How important are environmental influences to the existence of geography as a science? (You may want to reconsider your answer after reading Chapters 9 to 11.)

3. H. A. Innis argued the need for a "geography of geographers" [*Geographical Review,* 35 (1945), 301–311]. How far are the views of geographers influenced by where they live and when they live? Discuss this question in relation to a specific geographer or geographers.

4. Describe the dominant characteristics in approach and content during each of the main periods in the history of economic geography.

5. Each school of thought in economic geography has favored a particular concept of region. Commercial geography used political regions; environmental determinism, climatic; areal differentiation, regions based on cropping patterns or analogous characteristics of areas; and location theory, regions based upon flows and interdependencies. How true is this generalization? Give examples and exceptions. Does the argument extend to Marxist theory and to "politically correct" radical humanist theory?

6. What is the image of humanity implied by each of the schools of economic geography? Why is this image important?

7. "One is always tempted to ask whether the changing fashions of geography reflect the refinement of a science or simply the fickleness of human nature."[35] Examine this assertion by reviewing representative economic geography textbooks of each of the periods.

8. How were questions of world population and world food supplies assessed by each school of economic geography?

9. Give examples of economic "adaption" and "adoption" as observed at the local urban scale.

10. The contribution of individual economic maximization is as a norm against which to compare decision making in the real world. Discuss.

11. The potential links between economic geography and economics were weakened by the advent of environmental determinism. Determinism involved "taking each phenomenon in turn and relating it to the physical environment, whereby the mutual relationships between the phenomena have been underemphasized."[36] Discuss.

12. Exploitation, not markets, structures global economic geography. Discuss.

[35] Marvin Mikesell, in B. J. L. Berry, ed., *The Nature of Change in Geographic Ideas* (Dekalb, Ill.: Northern Illinois University Press, 1980), p. 19.

[36] Michael Chisholm, *Geography and Economics* (London: G. Bell & Sons, 1966), p. 24.

FURTHER READINGS

ALCHIAN, ARMEN A. "Uncertainty, Evolution, and Economic Theory," *Journal of Political Economy,* LVIII (June 1950), 211–221.

Economic systems cope with uncertainty through a process of adoption and adaption. The process is explained by an allegory.

CHISHOLM, GEORGE C. *Handbook of Commercial Geography.* London: Longmans, Green and Co. First edition, 1889; tenth edition, 1925; subsequent editions revised and rewritten by L. Dudley Stamp and others. Last revision, the twentieth, revised edition, 1980.

The main development in the first 10 editions was a progressive development of the introduction. It is well worth reading the introduction to one of these early editions to gain a feeling of the shift in thinking that occurred with environmental determinism.

CHISHOLM, MICHAEL. *Geography and Economics.* London: G. Bell & Sons, 1966.

Chapter 2, "Relations Between Geography and Economics," pp. 4–28, traces the history of development in and relationships between both geography and economics. This is an important and readable summary.

DAVENPORT, WILLIAM. "Jamaican Fishing: A Game Theory Analysis," *Yale University Publications in Anthropology,* 59 (1960), 3–11.

Brought to the attention of geographers by Peter Gould, this paper concluded that fishermen, as a group, maximize their income in the face of uncertainty, perhaps through trial and error over a long period of adaption and adoption.

FREEMAN, T. W. *The Geographer's Craft.* Manchester, U.K.: Manchester University Press, 1967.

Contains seven biographies, including Ellsworth Huntington (pp. 101–123), a geographer, it was said, many Americans would sooner forget.

HUDSON, JOHN C. (Ed). *Annals of the Association of American Geographers Special Issue: Seventy-Five Years of American Geography,* Vol. 69 (March 1979).

A series of personal observations by 27 of those who were participants in events leading up to the present. It provides fascinating insights on differences in the approaches between leading centers of geography as well as changes over time.

JOHNSTON, R. J. *Geography and Geographers: Anglo-American Human Geography since 1945.* London: Edward Arnold, 1979.

The key for a more detailed overview of the changing nature of economic geography.

JONES, CLARENCE FIELDEN. *Economic Geography.* New York: Henry Holt & Co., 1935.

An example of areal differentiation in economic geography using the activity systems approach. This popular textbook was later published by the Macmillan Co. in three editions, 1951, 1954, and 1965, coauthored with G. G. Darkenwald.

MARTIN, GEOFFREY J. *Ellsworth Huntington: His Life and Thought.* Hamden, Conn.: Archon Books, 1973.

Huntington was a prolific and controversial writer. For a balanced view of his thinking and contribution read Chapter XIV, "The Geography of Ellsworth Huntington: Some Thoughts and Reflections," pp. 232–253.

POWELL, J. M. "T. G. Taylor: 1880–1963." In *Geographers, Bibliographic Studies,* Vol. 3, pp. 141–154. Edited by T. W. Freeman and Philippe Pirichemel. London: Mansell, 1979.

One of an excellent series of biographies. Contains a particularly useful chronology of events.

ROSE, JOHN K. "Griffith Taylor, 1880–1963," *Annals of the Association of American Geographers,* 54, No. 4 (December 1964), 622–629.

A concise summary of the highlights of Taylor's career.

ROWLEY, VIRGINIA M. *J. Russell Smith: Geographer, Educator and Conservationist*. Philadelphia: University of Pennsylvania Press, 1964.

Smith's *Industrial and Commercial Geography* is reviewed on pp. 49–60.

SHEPPARD, ERIC. "The Howard G. Roepke Lecture in Economic Geography. Modeling the Capitalist Space Economy: Bringing Society and Space Back," *Economic Geography,* 66 (1990), 201–228.

A review and restatement of the central tenets of a Marxist economic geography.

SMITH, JOSEPH RUSSELL. *Industrial and Commercial Geography*. New York: Henry Holt & Co. First edition, 1913; fourth edition (coauthored with M. Ogden Phillips and Thomas R. Smith), 1955; reprinted, 1961.

The first major textbook in economic geography in the United States, it presented in its early editions the environmental determinist viewpoint. Its aim was to interpret the earth in terms of its usefulness to humanity, but the first chapter, "Our Changing Environment," described civilization as the product of adversity. The environmental stand was much reduced by the fourth edition.

SMITH, ROBERT H. T., EDWARD J. TAAFFE, and LESLIE J. KING. *Readings in Economic Geography: The Location of Economic Activity*. Chicago: Rand McNally, 1968.

A most useful collection of classical statements, empirical studies, and theoretical restatements. It illustrates the fourth period of economic geography and reveals a sharp break with past economic geographies.

TIEBOUT, CHARLES M. "Location Theory, Empirical Evidence and Economic Evolution," *Papers and Proceedings of the Regional Science Association,* 3 (1957), 74–86.

Elaborates the argument of Alchian that the economic system adopts those industrial entrepreneurs who choose the correct locations, regardless of how those decisions come to be made.

3

The Challenges of Population Growth and Change

OVERVIEW

Modern technological developments in the production and distribution of food and other human needs have made it possible to support large numbers of people even as medical advances have increased the survival rate and longevity of human populations. The result has been a remarkable acceleration in the rate of population growth in recent times.

A number of theories have arisen to help find meaning in the phenomenon of population growth and to aid in predicting its future course. One line of study has pursued the relationship between population growth and economic development. This work aims to help in coping with present and anticipated problems of population growth in factor-driven economies and to provide an understanding of the problems of adjustment that population decline is beginning to raise in some industrialized countries.

Added to the strains of differential rates of population growth is the migration of peoples from one country or region to another. Great numbers of people still migrate from one region to another within countries, and the developing countries are experiencing a growing rural-urban movement that is creating new metropolises that dwarf those existing in the older industrialized countries.

OBJECTIVES

- to describe the processes by which populations grow or decline and to examine the theories that have been advanced to explain them
- to outline demographic transition theory, relating population growth and economic development
- to examine the causes and nature of human migrations and to note their social and economic effects upon supplying and receiving regions
- to explain the changing character and the consequences of international and interregional migration

POPULATION AND RESOURCES:
THE BASIC VARIABLES

Whatever approach economic geographers may take to their subject matter, the most basic variables remain *population* and *resources*. Recall from Chapter 1 how Porter called these the basic factors in factor-driven economic systems. In Chapters 3 and 4 we shall deal with the population factor and then, in Chapter 5, we shall turn to key resource issues: food supply, energy, industrial materials, and environmental quality.

People are the most fundamental factor of all. They are the consumers of what is produced; the workers who do the production; the investors and managers who organize the transformation of raw materials into finished products and the distribution of these products to their consumers. The circuits of interdependency may be local, as in the world's few remaining relatively isolated self-sustaining communities, but they are more likely today to be regional, national, and increasingly global.

People living in an isolated community, with limited technologies at their disposal, are closely tied to their immediate resource base. Their resources have a finite ''carrying capacity,'' and if population approaches that limit, social, economic, and political strains are likely to reduce efficiency and even endanger existence. If population overshoots the carrying capacity, the consequences may be calamitous: famine, sickness, and premature death.

Carrying capacity depends on technology. What at one time may be a problem of population pressure may subsequently become one of relative abundance, even in an isolated self-sustaining community, if new technologies become available, such as improved agricultural practices or new crops.

The narrow insecurity that stems from localized dependence on immediate resources may be offset in other ways, though—by increasing specialization and trade, and by widening radii of interdependence that provide everyone with access to a broader resource base and the security of more alternatives. Emerging global interdependence and rapid technological change make the question of the earth's ultimate carrying capacity a matter of continuing concern and debate, however.

To be sure, numbers of people *are* important even in the global equation. Canada's labor-short economy produces and exports goods very different from those of India's labor-surplus economy, and the two countries have followed contrasting paths of economic development. An adequate labor supply is a recognized precondition for locating a new productive enterprise: Managers cannot safely assume that a large establishment will inevitably attract the necessary work force from distant areas. Likewise, regional and national economies may fail to attain their full growth potential if too few people are available to permit adequate exploitation of opportunities. In many parts of the world, however, the opposite problem is more common today; such countries as Bangladesh, Egypt, and El Salvador find their economic development hindered and their political stability threatened by overpopulation and by the very rate at which their populations grow.

Yet the question is not limited to mere numbers of people. The particular qualities of human populations—education levels, age structure, the availability of crucial skills, health and longevity, social attitudes—are at the core of the advanced factors so central to contemporary economic growth. A major consideration is the unevenness with which human populations and their cultural characteristics are distributed in space, not only among countries but also within countries.

This chapter deals with the processes of population change. What are the principal components of such change? What influences produce a rise (or fall) in numbers of people and cause them to move from one part of the earth to another? How does population change affect the material welfare of societies?

Based on this discussion of population dynamics, Chapter 4 will analyze the spatial distribution of populations. We shall be asking such questions as these: Where are particular kinds of people concentrated? Why is the spatial pattern so uneven? How do we expect future maps of world population to look? Is the earth capable of supporting a human population of the ultimate size now being projected?

NATURAL INCREASE

Two dynamic processes are responsible for the growth of populations and for regional variations in numbers of people: These processes are *natural increase* and *migration*. Natural increase results from an excess of births over deaths within a given area. Populations are growing throughout most of the world today, even though the rate of increase has slackened in the industrial countries and zero growth has been attained by a few maturer societies. The unprecedented rate of world population growth in the latter half of this century has aroused general concern, and widening regional disparities in rates of natural increase pose new dangers to world security and human welfare.

2.6 Million Years of Population Growth

Anthropologists believe that human existence on earth extends back at least 600,000 years and possibly more than 2 million years prior to that. Quantitative information before A.D. 1650 must be estimated from circumstantial evidence based on our knowledge of how early human beings gained their livelihood and of the capacity of the land to support primitive economies. We know, for example, that subsistence gathering and hunting and fishing, as practiced by primitive peoples today, require as much as two square miles per person. Even the most rudimentary agriculture, on the other hand, can normally support much denser populations. Supplementing such estimates as these are the scattered records of early communities, particularly those of the Roman Empire, together with other archaeological and historical evidence.

Accelerating Growth.   These estimates of early populations, together with data accumulated from modern censuses and projections of current growth trends, provide enough information for us to construct curves of world population growth like that shown in Figure 3.1. The main impressions given by this curve are its persistent upward trend and its accelerating rise in recent times. Note that until the modern era, world population increased slowly, with periods of actual decline. Only within the past 300 years—a tiny fraction

of human tenure on earth—has world population grown at consistently high rates.

During the preagricultural era, before 8000 B.C., when only rudimentary tools and weapons were in use, not more than 5 million people inhabited the earth. Numbers increased to between 200 million and 250 million by the beginning of the Christian era and possibly as many as 257 million by the end of the first millennium. Within the next 300 years the population of Europe began to rise, and the world total may have reached as much as 384 million by A.D. 1300.

The following century brought a series of plagues that reduced Europe's population so drastically that the population of the world as a whole declined. From 1400 to 1650, however, European civilization enjoyed a rebirth, and European peoples began an energetic conquest of new lands. Although Europe's population likely rose at more than twice the world rate during this period, the indigenous population of the Americas probably declined sharply as a result of the impact of European invasion. Population estimates undertaken in 1650 indicated a world total of about 500 million. Within the next two centuries the total rose even more rapidly, doubling to approximately 1 billion people by 1850. By 1930 the population had reached 2 billion, and by 1970, 3.6 billion. This was a significant event considering that the world contains about 3.6 billion acres of arable land. Thus in that year (1970) there was one acre of cropland for every person in the world. The amount of land per person has since diminished even further as world population has continued its climb, reaching 5 billion in 1986.

The Growth Curve.   Accelerating growth has thus caused a continual steepening of the population curve. In A.D. 1300, the annual rate of growth for the world was perhaps 0.11 or 0.12 percent, but between 1650 and 1750 it was probably nearer −0.3 percent. By the 1930s the annual rate had reached 1.0 percent, and by the 1960s it had risen to 2.1 percent. Another way of looking at this is to note the number of years it takes for the world's population to double. Between 8000 B.C. and A.D. 1650 this doubling required 1500 years; but the next doubling, between 1650 and 1850, took only 200 years. Eighty years later, by 1930, population had doubled again, and it had once again doubled by 1975, a mere 45 years.

If instead of plotting world population on an arithmetic scale as in Figure 3.1 we use a double-logarithmic scale (Figure 3.2), which emphasizes rates of change, we discover a number of details obscured in the previous diagram. We now find that three main surges of population have likely occurred during hu-

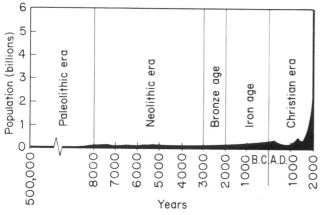

FIGURE 3.1 Growth of world population. Note that, after having gained but little during the thousands of years of early human life, population began a slow rise during Roman times, slipped backward during the Dark Ages, and began to rise again by the fourteenth century, when the bubonic plague brought a sharp but temporary decline. Since then, population growth has accelerated rapidly. [*Source: After Population Bulletin,* 18, No. 1.]

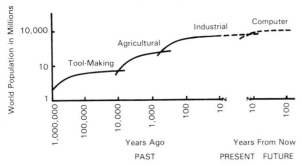

FIGURE 3.2 Technological revolutions and world population growth. Population growth for the past million years plotted on a log-log scale shows a series of surges, each associated with a technological revolution that has increased the earth's capacity to support human life. Some technological optimists have also suggested that widespread adoption of computers may lift productivity sufficiently to support a new surge of population growth in coming decades. [*Source:* Adapted with modifications from Deevey, "The Human Population." Copyright © 1960 by Scientific American, Inc. All rights reserved.]

man history rather than only one, and that each surge was apparently associated with a technological breakthrough that increased the capacity of the world economy to support more people. The developments that fostered these bursts of population were the tool-making, agricultural, and industrial revolutions. Figure 3.2 also suggests a fourth technological revolution in the making, a possible result of advances in the use of computers and robotics and in knowledge use in an "information society," which promise quantum increases in productivity in the near future.

As we shall note shortly, population growth rates are not likely to continue indefinitely at recent high levels, despite increases in human efficiency that a computer revolution may bring. The threat to finite world supplies of food and nonrenewable natural resources and the growing effects of environmental pollution would seem to dictate upper limits to the number of people this planet can support. Indeed, for the first time in modern history, the rate of global population growth has lately begun to slip, falling from 2.1 percent in the early 1960s to 1.8 percent by the end of the 1980s. In its report, *The State of World Population 1990,* therefore, the United Nations Population Fund forecasts that world population could stabilize at something under 11 billion during the coming century, depending upon current national and international campaigns to limit growth.

Thus, the ordinary exponential curve may prove in the end to be less appropriate for describing the

current phase of world population development than a logistic curve, one that eventually levels off and perhaps even declines. Precedent for this is seen in the experience of such mature populations as those of Western Europe. More recently, the curve of population growth in the United States has begun to assume such a shape, as Figure 3.3 shows.

The Growth Mechanism

What are the components of natural increase (or decrease)? The basic ingredients of this process are numbers of births and deaths within a specified time. Whether a population increases or decreases (assuming no migration) depends upon which of these components is greater. A variety of events may influence the relationship between the two.

Birth Rates, Death Rates, and Rates of Natural Increase. Birth rates are commonly expressed in terms of yearly births per thousand people. For example, at the beginning of 1980, the population of the United States was 222,100,000 people, and the number of births in that year was 3,598,000. Dividing the number of births by the population and multiplying by 1000 gives a birth rate of 16.2 for the year. Similarly, we obtain the 1980 death rate for the United States by dividing the number of deaths, 1,986,000 by the population and multiplying by 1000, which gives a rate of 8.9. The rate of natural increase is the difference between the birth and death rates, or 7.3 per 1000. It is customary, however, to express the rate of natural increase as a percentage, that is, so many people per 100 per year, which in this case would be 0.73 percent. This rate for the United States is typical of industrialized countries, but it is well below the rate of 1.8 per-

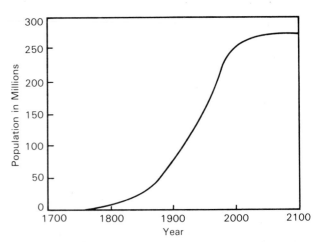

FIGURE 3.3 Logistic growth of the United States population from A.D. 1700 projected to A.D. 2100.

cent for the world as a whole. Note that the rate of natural increase can be affected by a rise or fall in either the birth rate or death rate.

Although these are the most commonly used forms of birth and death rates, meaningful population analyses and predictions require more refined measures. The *crude birth rate* described above is not as revealing as the *fertility rate,* which is the number of births in a given year per thousand women of child-bearing age (15 to 49). Thus, fertility rates are more useful for comparing anticipated changes in a young population having a large number of females with those of a more mature population. Fertility rates are also generally higher in rural areas than urban ones, among lower classes than upper classes, and among blue-collar workers than professionals, although these differentials have diminished in more advanced countries as educational levels and the quality of mass communications have risen.

Likewise, the *crude death rate* does not give as much information as the *age-specific death rate,* defined as the number of deaths per thousand in a particular age group. One widely used age-specific death rate is the *infant mortality rate,* or the number of deaths in the first year of life per thousand live births. This is one of the more valuable indices of socioeconomic well-being. Another measure that performs a similar function is *life expectancy,* that is, the average age at death of the inhabitants of a given area.

Events Affecting Population Increase.   Although primitive peoples ordinarily have birth rates approaching 50 per thousand, these are generally balanced by similarly high death rates. Consequently, the rates of natural increase remain low in such societies unless some event alters the birth or death rates and tips the balance.

Until modern times the death rate was the more volatile of the two measures. The most dramatic effects on death rates have been those resulting from disease, famine, and war. The bubonic plague (A.D. 1348 to 1350), for example, quickly reduced Europe's population by at least one-fourth, and the London plague of 1665 eliminated one-third to one-half of that city's population. Endemic diseases, such as malaria, have been almost as destructive to certain populations, even in more recent years.

Many of the deaths attributed to disease in some parts of the world, however, are merely the indirect effects of hunger and malnutrition; indeed, the correlation between disease, hunger, and death rates is very high. Periodic famine, caused by floods, droughts, insect plagues, and war, was one of the earliest population controls. Between A.D. 10 and 1846, for example,

Britain recorded approximately 200 famines. China had an estimated 1828 famines between 108 B.C. and A.D. 1911, an average of about one per year. Nine to 13 million Chinese died between 1869 and 1876 alone. Nor are famines unknown to this present century. In all, the USSR suffered 5 million to 10 million deaths attributable to famine between 1918 and 1922 and between 1932 and 1934. India lost from 2 million to 4 million in 1943, and similarly large numbers of famine deaths occurred during Bangladesh's struggle for independence from Pakistan and Biafra's attempt to secede from Nigeria.

Receiving more public attention, though, are the wartime deaths resulting directly from the fighting. The two world wars in this century reduced populations throughout Europe. Among some primitive peoples, as in the Indonesian province of West Irian, intertribal wars have been a major and customary cause of death.

Famines, epidemics, and war also affect birth rates, by reducing the ability to conceive and by disrupting normal family life; however, the voluntary means of reducing births have had the most pervasive and prolonged effects upon population growth. Although birth control has been the most effective means of population control in modern times, even early societies limited population growth by such means as infanticide, sexual taboos, killing the sick and aged, and marriage restrictions. Abortion has been of growing significance in many industrialized countries as they have liberalized and paid more attention to women's rights, although there is also a conservative religious backlash. Contraception, an ancient practice mentioned in the Bible, is the most common way of preventing births. The extent to which birth control is practiced, as well as the choice of methods, is influenced by cost and the availability of information, within a framework of religions, customs, attitudes, technological development, and degree of urbanization.

Population Theory

The steeply rising curve of world population shows clearly that the balance between births and deaths has been seriously disturbed in recent times. This increasingly urgent problem has given rise to a body of population theory, the most familiar being that of Thomas Malthus. The eighteenth century had been a period of optimism concerning the perfectibility of humankind, combined with the view that a large population is a source of national strength. By the end of that century, however, a reaction had taken place. The Industrial Revolution in Britain had revealed the evils of the factory system, economic growth had brought with it a rapid increase in population, and the appearance of bad times soon caused these numbers to seem excessive. A period of poor harvests, high food prices, and much human misery provided the setting for Malthus's pessimistic statement of 1798.

Malthus.   Thomas R. Malthus was an English clergyman, historian, and economist, born in 1766 to the English landed gentry and educated at Cambridge. In his famous *Essay on the Principle of Population,* intended originally as an answer to the Utopians, he strongly expressed the view that it is not desirable for a population to expand indefinitely without the assurance that the means for supporting that population can keep pace. Malthus concluded that population has a natural tendency to increase rapidly as long as food, or "subsistence," is available. If unchecked, population will go on doubling itself every 25 years, that is, it will increase at a "geometric ratio" (2, 4, 8, 16, 32, etc.). At the same time, however, even under the most favorable circumstances, the food supply cannot increase faster than at an "arithmetic ratio" (3, 6, 9, 12, 15, etc.). The number of people to be fed will thus quickly overtake and exceed the food supply.

Malthus believed that the *ultimate* check to population growth, as in the case of the lower animals, is exhaustion of the food supply at the point when the two growth curves cross. This ultimate check to population growth would, of course, cause death from starvation, but more usually either of two kinds of *immediate* checks intervenes. One is the *preventative* check, resulting from the ability of human beings to recognize the consequences of their behavior. This preventative check Malthus termed "moral restraint," by which he, being a good churchman, did not mean birth control. To Malthus, moral restraint meant postponement of marriage, "accompanied by strictly moral behaviour"—the purpose being to avoid having children before the parents are able to support them. The second intervening influence is the *positive* check, "all of those causes which tend in any way prematurely to shorten the duration of human life." These include "vice"—those misfortunes we bring upon ourselves, such as war and the various consequences of immoral behavior—and "misery"—unavoidable products of the laws of nature, especially plagues and famines. Note that the positive checks act to limit population growth by raising death rates, whereas the preventative checks accomplish this same result by reducing birth rates.

According to Malthus, the lowest stratum of society is most affected by positive checks. In mature societies these forces cause the population to rise and fall in a cyclical fashion. In times of prosperity young people can support a family at an earlier age, there are thus more children, and the population increases, but this in turn causes the price of labor to fall and the cost of living to rise. The ensuing hard times bring the Malthusian checks into play, the age at which young people marry increases, and the population decreases until once again the labor force is in balance with job opportunities. Prosperity then returns, bringing with it new opportunities for earlier marriage and a repetition of the population growth cycle. Malthus indicated that this cycle is not confined to advanced lands but is seen even in tribal societies, where populations are subjected to a whole range of positive checks upon reaching the limits of subsistence.

Malthus saw no lasting way out of this dilemma through charity or emigration, which can bring only temporary relief from population pressure. His proposed solution was the general adoption of "moral restraint," that is, postponement of marriage, together with mass education (including the teaching of population principles) and increased respect and personal liberty for single women.

Malthus was enormously influential. His basic ideas had a pervasive effect not only on philosophical, economic, social, and political thought but also on the physical sciences, legislation, and popular education. Out of his work grew a school of population study that, with modifications, persists today.

Later in the nineteenth century Malthus's population theory fell into disfavor as the populations of Western European countries and their colonies experienced accelerated growth while enjoying unprecedented improvements in their standards of living. This appeared to refute Malthus, who had failed to anticipate the important effects of the social, economic, and technological changes then taking place. Yet it has since become apparent that Malthus's perspective held some validity for the long run: Today, human populations do indeed threaten to increase to that point beyond which the world's resources can no longer support them.

Other Population Theories.   As Malthus's predictions failed to be realized in Western Europe, other theorists attempted to correct the deficiences in the Malthusian thesis. Like Malthus, many early theorists sought "natural laws" of population growth, but they tended to look more to the newly emerging social sciences for these laws. Michael Sadler, for example, maintained that as population densities increase, fertility rates will drop. Herbert Spencer suggested that the increasing complexity of modern life would divert human energies from procreation and cause a reduction in the capacity to produce children. And, as recently as 1929, Corrado Gini claimed that population growth is directly related to the rise and fall of nations.

Some nineteenth-century writers proposed population theories to substantiate their political and social ideas. For example, Karl Marx, who misinterpreted Malthus's writings, insisted that it was not overpopulation that produced poverty and hardship, but rather the failure of the economic system. Henry George maintained that his "single tax" would provide land for everyone who needed food and that this would increase agricultural productivity and expand the food supply indefinitely.

A more modern theorist, Alexander Carr-Saunders, suggested that the rate of population growth was determined by human perception of the densities that are economically desirable for a particular way of life. Although he agreed with Malthus's assessment of the growth trends of population and food supply, he believed that other checks operate to limit population. Contemporary theorists disclaim any "natural law" of population growth but attribute differences in birth and death rates to social, cultural, economic, and physical conditions. And directly countering Malthus, modern theorists such as Julian Simon claim that it is people who are the "ultimate resource," capable of using their brainpower to overcome any temporary restrictions by inventing new activities and improved lifestyles.

Demographic Transition

As we observed earlier, the rapid growth of Europe's population confirmed Malthus's predictions, but the remarkable increase in European prosperity did not. Moreover, he did not anticipate the effects that development might have on those forces determining population size. Today we have come to recognize the close interrelationship between the processes of development or "modernization" on the one hand and those of population growth on the other, lending growing support to the views of the anti-Malthusians.

The European Experience. The demographic history of modern Europe illustrates some of these relationships. Prior to the Industrial Revolution, when death rates and birth rates were very high, Europe's population was fairly stable. Urban death rates were especially high, and city growth was made possible only by heavy in-migration. The unwholesome urban conditions responsible for such mortality rates resemble those of many cities in less-developed countries today: uncertain food supply, contaminated water, in-

adequate housing, lack of sewage disposal, and poor medical service.

The Industrial Revolution that began in Britain during the second half of the eighteenth century had profound effects on both death and birth rates in Western Europe. The application of inanimate energy to mining and manufacturing greatly increased total and per capita output of goods. The rising incomes that resulted from greater production made possible the purchase of food in larger quantities and of higher quality. Incomes also provided financial support for better sanitary practices and for medical research. Although these improvements in food supply and public health evolved gradually, their cumulative effect was to reduce death rates substantially and to make cities capable of sustaining their populations. Much of the total rise in population during the succeeding two centuries since the Industrial Revolution can be attributed to improved conditions in the cities.

Related to these urban and industrial developments, and essential to them, was the accompanying revolution in agriculture. Previously, British agriculture had consisted mainly of subsistence farms producing very little surplus for cash sale. Even the richest agricultural regions were unable to grow sufficient food to support more than 15 percent to 20 percent of their populations in urban activities, such as manufacturing, commerce, and government. Near the end of the eighteenth century, however, in response to growing urban demands, farmers began to breed higher-quality livestock, introduce new high-yielding crops, and develop farm techniques that increased the output of traditional commodities. Through the "enclosure movement," medieval open fields and common lands were reallocated into compact and individually owned farmsteads, and the many landless laborers who were displaced made their way to the growing cities. Thus, as the Industrial Revolution made larger urban concentrations necessary, new developments in agriculture supplied the additional food required to support a growing nonfarm population, and reorganization of the agricultural landscape (which took the form of waves radiating from the new cities) forced surplus farm workers into the growing urban labor force.

Important innovations in transportation took place at the same time as these industrial and agricultural developments. The construction of roads, canals, and railways, and the invention of new types of vehicles, greatly expanded the range of distribution and collection. No longer was it necessary for communities, or even countries, to be self-sufficient in raw materials and foodstuffs. Local crop failures thus became far less likely to cause hunger and famine among European peoples. Not only goods but also people and ideas circulated freely over greater distances, thereby accelerating the rate of scientific discoveries, including those related to health.

As these events combined to bring about a steady decline in death rates, birth rates were also dropping, although at a slower rate. The Industrial Revolution influenced birth rates in ways not anticipated by Malthus. It did this first of all by concentrating people into towns and cities, where they no longer had the need for large families that they once had on the farm. At the same time, the decline in infant mortality removed an important incentive for large numbers of births. And as ideas of the French Enlightenment spread over Europe, more time was devoted to women's education, and age at marriage rose. With effective changes in attitude toward family size, the practice of contraception spread. Beginning among upper-income groups in urbanized areas, contraception diffused to lower levels of society and into rural areas. Malthus could not have foreseen this, and he would not have approved of it if he had.

The development of contraception did not exert its full force until this present century, however. Most of the nineteenth-century reductions in birth rates came from increased age of marriage. Europe was only able to escape what might have been excessive population pressures because its surplus peoples migrated in large numbers to newly discovered lands in both the Western and Southern Hemispheres. These migrants in turn brought rich virgin lands into cultivation and shipped an ever-increasing supply of grain and other commodities back to the markets of their former homelands. In this century, the population of Western Europe has stabilized, as new low death rates and birth rates have come into balance. As the same demographic trends have diffused throughout the lands settled by Europeans, the advanced countries seem to have eluded the Malthusian trap. The immediate worry today is for the less-developed countries, where rapidly growing populations threaten to fulfill Malthus's gloomy prophesy.

Population Growth in the Less-Developed World. Some of the densely settled lands of eastern and southern Asia, especially China and India, likely reached their optimum population densities as agriculturally based peasant societies centuries ago. The Chinese population apparently fluctuated at a high level over an extended period, despite war, plague, and famine. Evidently it followed a cyclical pattern like that described by Malthus, rising in good times and falling in bad times. This pattern was disturbed by the coming of European colonial control, which brought a new burst of population growth in such lands as Indonesia and India. Colonial administrations reduced internecine fighting among native populations and introduced economic improvements, causing death rates to fall below persistently high birth rates.

Since World War II, much of the less-developed world has experienced a population crisis as improved public health delivery and better food distribution brought a rapid drop in mortality rates. Unlike the gradual reduction of death rates in today's developed countries, which had to await a whole series of medical advances over a period of two centuries, today's less-developed countries were able to import low-cost, highly effective death-control measures that were ready-made. Many primitive villages otherwise untouched by modernization have benefited from sophisticated medical technology. So successful have these programs been that crude death rates in the less-developed world as a whole had fallen from 24.3 in 1950 to only 9.9 per thousand by the 1990, hardly different from the rate of 9.8 for developed countries. Death rates for several Third World countries have actually dropped below those of the developed world. Thus, left with an unusually young population after years of runaway population growth, Costa Rica had a death rate of only 3.8 by 1987.

Meanwhile, birth rates remain high throughout most of the Third World. As Figure 3.4 shows, crude birth rates exceeding 40 per thousand are typical of countries at the lower levels of development. Some African countries—Kenya and Zambia, for example—have crude birth rates of 50 per thousand or more. In 1990 Eastern Africa as a whole had a rate of natural increase of more than 3.0 per annum, and Western Africa was increasing at a rate of 3.26. In both regions, growth rates have risen substantially in recent decades. Another area of concern is the Middle East, where rates of natural increase are high and still rising, especially around the Persian Gulf. For instance, by 1990 Iraq's population was increasing by 3.48 percent per annum, Saudi Arabia's by 3.96 percent, and Qatar's by 4.15 percent. This explosion of population in the Third World will have added another billion people to the world total by the final decade of the present century.

Unlike the European colonial powers of the previous century, the less-developed countries of today cannot ship their surplus populations to new lands in other continents, although some, such as Indonesia and Brazil, are attempting to send people from their overcrowded "heartlands" into lightly populated outlying regions. Consequently, rates of natural increase for Third World countries remain exceedingly high—2.1 percent for less-developed countries as a whole in 1990.

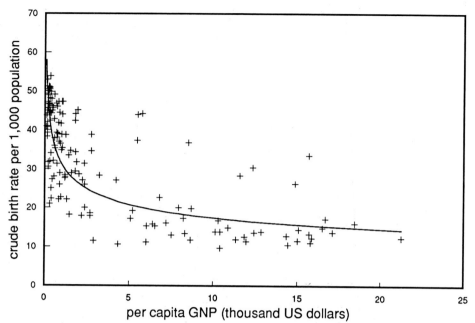

FIGURE 3.4 Relationship between birth rates and per capita GNP, 1987. Countries at the lowest levels of development tend to have the highest birth rates. Tightly clustered at the upper left of the diagram are nearly 50 low-income African and Middle Eastern nations. At higher levels of per capita GNP, the extreme positive anomalies (those countries lying above the regression line in this diagram) are Middle Eastern oil exporters. This suggests that, although the relationship between income and birth rates is strong ($R^2 = 0.615$), cultural factors play an important part, too. The role of culture is likewise apparent in the clustering of low-income East Asian countries at the lower left of the diagram. European countries, plus Japan, constitute most of the cases below the line at higher income levels. The United States lies very close to the line, suggesting a birth rate corresponding closely to what might be expected of a country with its per capita GNP. [*Source:* Based upon data from the *1990 Britannica Book of the Year* (Chicago: Encyclopaedia Britannica, 1990).]

At the same time, rates of population growth continue to diminish among advanced countries, falling to only 0.53 percent for the group in 1990. This represents a decline of about one third within one decade. Population growth has essentially halted in Western Europe, where several countries—notably Hungary, Denmark, Austria, and Germany—are actually seeing their populations shrink. Even in their periods of most rapid growth, during the nineteenth century, the more-developed countries of today never attained rates of population increase approaching present rates in the Third World.

The already-crowded lands of Asia and Africa have felt the most immediate and obvious impacts of this growth, but the less densely populated Latin American countries are also seriously affected. Having achieved their independence from European powers a century or more earlier, they were free to begin the process of reducing death rates sooner than those lands emerging from colonial control in more recent times.

One important consequence of high growth rates is a youthful age distribution. Figure 3.5 compares the age structure of a rapidly growing population, Ethiopia, with that of a mature population, Switzerland. In Ethiopia 47 percent of the population is below the age of 15, as opposed to only 17 percent in Switzerland. Africa as a whole has more than 45 percent of its population in this dependent age group, the highest African country being Kenya, with 52.1 percent under 15. The Islamic lands of Southwest Asia have similarly high percentages of the young, as do some Central American countries.

Transition Theory. This international comparison of demographic characteristics suggests that countries undergo a *demographic transition* as they ascend the ladder of development. The study of this process

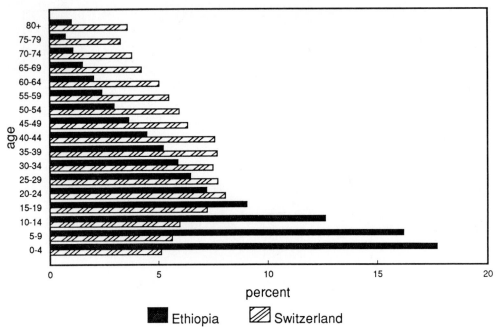

FIGURE 3.5   Comparison of age structures of Ethiopia and Switzerland. With 46.5 percent of its population under the age of 15, Ethiopia is typical of less-developed countries having high birth rates and low death rates. Only 16.7 percent of Switzerland's population is in the under-15 group, which is common for more-developed countries with birth rates and death rates that are both low. Note also that in the Swiss example the 5-year age groups below 20 years become progressively smaller, indicating that the birth rate is still falling. In the higher ages the circumstances of the two countries are reversed. More than 1 out of every 10 Swiss are 65 years or older; fewer than 3 percent of Ethiopians attain that age. [*Source:* Based upon data from *United Nations Demographic Yearbook* (New York: United Nations; 1989).]

has given birth to a *transition theory*, which serves as a tool for predicting future population changes of developing countries and offers a means for anticipating the problems that accompany these changes. According to this theory, a country passes through three demographic phases as it develops (see Figure 3.6).

In the first phase the population remains fairly stable. It is kept in equilibrium by the combination of a high birth rate and a similarly high, but fluctuating, death rate. This describes the demography of societies as diverse as preindustrial Europe, premodern China, and contemporary primitive peoples in the rain forests of the Amazon and Congo basins.

When the development process commences, the country enters the second phase. As diets and health improve, the death rate drops; but the birth rate remains high throughout the earlier stages of the development process before it too begins to decline. During Phase II, therefore, the two curves diverge, producing

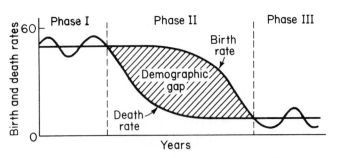

FIGURE 3.6   Transition theory. At the beginning of a country's development the death rate tends to drop quickly, whereas the birth rate remains high for an extended period before it too begins to decline. The divergence of these two rates creates a demographic gap, or "population explosion," which continues until equilibrium is finally reestablished during the later stages of development.

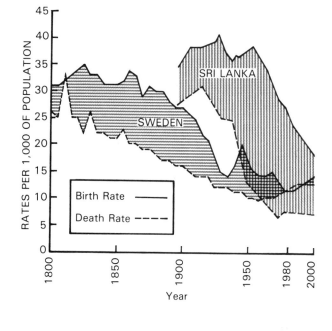

FIGURE 3.7 Contrast between demographic transitions in Sri Lanka and Sweden. Sweden's transition extended over nearly two centuries and has now concluded with birth and death rates at a low equilibrium. Sri Lanka's transition began a century later and is proceeding rapidly. Note that Sri Lanka's death rate has declined steeply and is now actually lower than Sweden's because of Sri Lanka's much younger population. Sri Lanka's birth rate is still far higher than its death rate, resulting in continued rapid population growth. [*Source:* From Halfdan Mahler, "People," *Scientific American,* 243, No. 3 (September 1980), 66–77. Copyright © 1980 by Scientific American, Inc. All rights reserved.]

a *demographic gap*. This is the period of rapid population growth, or "population explosion." Much of Latin America and the Middle East and parts of Africa and southern and eastern Asia are at this point. Subsequent maturing of the economy brings urbanization, higher per capita incomes, and various social changes, especially better-educated women, all of which favor smaller families. The accompanying changes in social attitudes therefore act to reduce the birth rate during the latter part of Phase II.

When at last the birth rate has fallen to a level approximating that of the already-low death rate, Phase III has been reached. Note that in this final phase it is the birth rate that fluctuates about some mean, a response mainly to rises and falls in the business cycle. When times are good, more women enter the labor force, and child-rearing is deferred. It is when times are bad, ironically, that women are more likely to stay home and choose instead to raise a child. The countries of Western Europe, Anglo-America, and Oceania, as well as Japan, have attained this new low-level equilibrium.

Transition theory actually represents a generalization of the Western European experience. Recent events, however, have shown that the history of today's industrialized nations offers a less-than-perfect model for predicting demographic change in today's less-developed countries. For one thing, current fertility rates in less-developed countries are much higher than they were in premodern Europe. This is a result of religious beliefs, marriage customs, land tenure ar-

rangements, and other cultural factors. People will eagerly accept innovations that improve their health and increase their longevity, but they do not easily relinquish traditional attitudes toward marriage and the home.

Illustrating this problem, Figure 3.7 contrasts the demographic changes now taking place in Sri Lanka (formerly Ceylon) with those experienced previously by Sweden. After a century and a half of declining birth and death rates, Sweden has now reached the point of "zero population growth," where it will likely remain for the foreseeable future. Although Sri Lanka's demographic transition began only a few decades ago, it is progressing far more rapidly than Sweden's. Note that at the start of this process Sri Lanka's birth and death rates were both much higher than Sweden's had been and that the death rate has dropped more steeply, actually falling below that of Sweden because of Sri Lanka's very young population. The resulting population bulge will continue well into the next century.

Adding to the difficulties of applying transition theory to contemporary conditions is the fact that the largest of the less-developed lands, especially India and China, are more densely populated than was preindustrial Europe. A further complication is the differing demographic histories of some developed countries; Germany, for example, reached population equilibrium much later than did France.

Despite these problems, the central features of the transition theory remain valid. First, the death rate

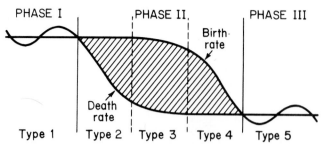

FIGURE 3.8 United Nations' classification of countries according to population growth types. Phases I, II, and III correspond to the major stages of demographic transition, whereas Types 1 through 5 refer to classes of countries according to their demographic characteristics.

always begins its decline before that of the birth rate, except perhaps in totalitarian countries where individual choice is restricted. Second, changes in the death rate are the main determinant of population size in less-developed lands, but fluctuations of the birth rate are the principal determinant in advanced societies.

A Demographic Classification of Countries. Most population forecasts and regional analyses now make use of transition theory in some manner. The Population Division of the United Nations has devised a classification system that subdivides the second phase of demographic transition into three parts. It is important to know whether a country is just entering this critical period of rapid population expansion and thus has the major part of its population growth ahead of it, whether it is in the middle or most explosive part of the phase, or if it is about to emerge from this part of the cycle.

The diagram in Figure 3.8 illustrates this application of transition theory, and Figure 3.9 shows how the countries of the world fit into the scheme. The shaded portion of the diagram (Figure 3.8), which indicates

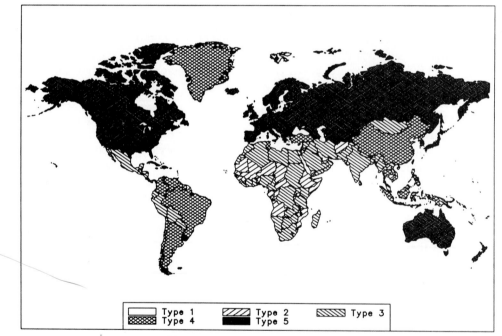

FIGURE 3.9 World map of population growth types. The 1980s have seen important demographic changes throughout the world. During that period most of Africa has shifted from the ominous Type 2 category into the explosive Type 3 stage of the demographic transition. In this it has been joined by the Middle East and densely populated South Asia, together with Mexico, Central America, and parts of Andean South America. On the other hand, East Asia has made encouraging progress toward population stability. This is especially true of China, with its billion people (now Type 4), and Japan and Korea (Type 5 countries). The older industrialized lands have long ago completed their demographic transitions, and some European populations are now beginning to shrink. [*Source:* Based upon data from the *1990 Britannica Book of the Year* (Chicago: Encyclopaedia Britannica, 1990).]

the dimensions of the demographic gap, has been subdivided into three subcategories designated with arabic numerals. Five population growth types result. Type 1 countries have high birth rates and high, fluctuating death rates, producing stable populations with growth rates generally under 1 percent. Although several densely populated underdeveloped countries had these characteristics at an earlier time, the combination is now rare. Most former Type 1 countries have now at least begun their demographic transitions.

The transition process commences with the Type 2 countries, which have high birth rates and high but declining death rates. The two curves are beginning to diverge (Figure 3.8), indicating the start of the expansionary Phase II of the demographic transition. Population growth is well over 1 percent and climbing. A few African lands remain at this stage, with its looming threat of accelerated growth, as well as a handful of southern and southeastern Asian nations. Most Type 2 countries of a decade ago, however, have now proceeded to the next level of growth.

By the end of the 1980s the majority of African nations could be classified as Type 3 countries, having entered the most explosive part of Phase II. This combination of high birth rates and low death rates results in very rapid population growth. Sharing this critical stage are most of the already-crowded lands of the Middle East and South Asia, notably India with its 836 million people. Mexico, Central America, and a few South America countries are also in this part of the demographic transition.

The distinguishing features of Type 4 countries are a declining birth rate and low death rates. The effect of this is shrinking growth rates as these nations move closer to low-level equilibrium. A major part of Latin America has progressed to this point, as well as Turkey, Sri Lanka, and Indonesia—populous countries that are gaining in the struggle to bring birth rates under control.

With their low but fluctuating birth rates and low death rates, Type 5 countries have attained the final phase of the demographic transition. Growth rates rarely exceed 1 percent, and in many cases they are much less. All the world's older industrialized nations are at this state, and several European countries are at or below zero population growth.

Consequences of Population Growth and Decline

The relationship between population growth and food supply was Malthus's chief concern, and this subject continues to preoccupy most writers on population today. Vital as the question of feeding an expanding world population may be, however, this is by no means the only problem resulting from population increase. As most Third World countries have discovered, rapid population growth creates many other economic, social, political, and environmental problems that complicate the developmental process. Meanwhile, some mature industrial societies are having to adjust to another kind of demographic change—zero population growth, or even decline.

Problems of a Growing Population. All too frequently a less-developed country finds its developmental gains wiped out by overly rapid population growth. Arriving at the end of the year with increased output, it discovers that these additional goods must be divided among a still larger number of people. The problem of diminishing per capita food supplies is one of the most worrisome effects of excessive population growth, not only because of humanitarian concerns but also because of its political and economic consequences.

Figure 3.10 shows that many of the less-developed countries are finding it difficult to supply the daily nutritional needs of their people. The diagram suggests a fairly close relationship between daily per capita food energy (calories) and level of development (measured by per capita *gross national product,* GNP). Even so, the average developing-world family spends a larger proportion of its income on food than does the typical family in advanced societies. Referred to as *Engel's law,* this relationship is illustrated by the case of Ghana, where half of family income goes for food, or Honduras, where a family spends more than two-fifths of its income in this manner. By contrast, a Danish family spends less than one-fourth of its income on food, and a Canadian family spends about one-fifth.

Not only do most people in the developing world consume less food per day but they are also more likely to suffer from dietary deficiencies. The poorer the population, the more dependent the people are upon starchy foods, such as grains and root crops. The essential "protective" foods, which are most costly, are generally lacking in the diets of the poorest peoples, as shown by the relationship between GNP and consumption of proteins (Figure 3.11), and especially animal proteins (Figure 3.12). These associations between diet and development imply that a rise in per capita income should bring a drop in the percentage of income spent on food, an increase in the total amount consumed (until some optimal level is reached), and a shift from cheaper starches to more expensive and nutritious foods, especially animal products ("indirect calories").

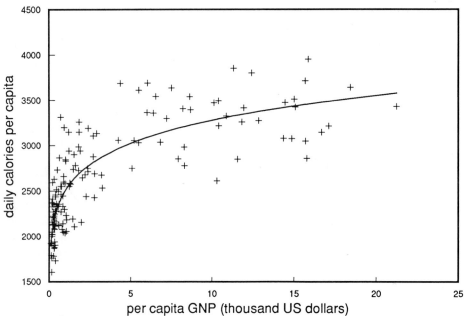

FIGURE 3.10 Relationship between per capita calorie consumption and level of development ($R^2 = 0.704$). This diagram lends support to Engel's Law, which says that poor families allocate larger proportions of their incomes to food than do richer ones. Note that the regression line climbs steeply at first but quickly tapers off at higher levels of per capita GNP. Clustered in the lower-left corner of the diagram are 43 impoverished countries with daily calorie consumptions averaging below the 2240 considered essential to support normal human health and activity. Twenty-five of these countries are in sub-Saharan Africa, 11 are in Asia, and most of the remainder in Latin America. The more affluent nations vary considerably in the amounts of food they consume, mainly as a result of cultural differences in dietary patterns. Thus, Japan and the newly industrialized countries of East Asia are well below the regression line, as is most of Scandinavia. The lands of central and southern Europe are generally well above the line. What these country averages do not disclose, however, are the large numbers of poorly fed people within some of the wealthiest nations. [*Source:* Based upon data from the *1990 Britannica Book of the Year* (Chicago: Encyclopaedia Britannica, 1990).]

Despite the difficulties of feeding their growing populations, most underdeveloped countries employ a majority of their labor forces in agriculture (Figure 3.13). Much of this agriculture is of an unproductive sort. Consider the plight of Asian or African peasants on their plots of exhausted land, which are so tiny that they must be devoted almost entirely to grains and other foods for direct human consumption. In their poverty these peasant farmers are caught up in a vicious circle. Unable to afford machinery, fertilizer, or improved seeds, they can only apply increased quantities of human labor in their efforts to raise levels of output. This provides a motivation to have large families, which in turn means more mouths to feed. High rates of population growth in less-developed countries therefore tend both to reduce the quantity and quality

of per capita food consumption and to affect adversely the conditions for producing that food.

In addition to its impact on food supply, rapid population growth causes economic stress. Inflation, once a localized problem affecting only individual countries, has now become a global phenomenon. Business cycles in the industrial world have become increasingly synchronized, creating a simultaneous growth in demand for finite supplies of resources and pushing up world prices. As the most accessible and highest-quality resources are used up, it becomes necessary to turn to less-productive farmlands, grazing lands, fisheries, and forests, and to mineral deposits that are more remote and of poorer quality. The resulting decline in output for each additional new unit of input—referred to as the *law of diminishing returns* (to

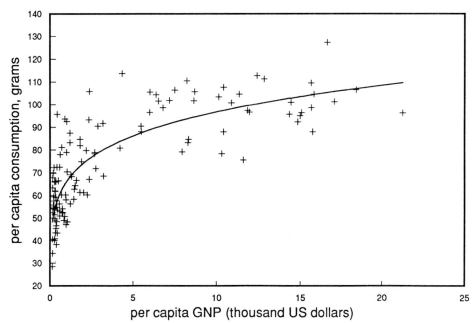

FIGURE 3.11 Relationship between per capita protein consumption and level of development ($R^2 = 0.654$). In addition to the issue of providing a sufficient quantity of food for the world's people (see Figure 3.10) is the question of ensuring its nutritional quality, measured here by the amount of protein in the average daily diet. At the lower end of this scale are 63 countries whose populations consume less than 75 grams per person; none of the 63 has an annual per capita GNP exceeding $1800. The majority of these are African or Asian, including such populous nations as India and Pakistan, but a few are Latin American. Among the higher-income nations are a number that consume unusually large quantities of protein. These are mainly economies with large animal industries (Argentina and New Zealand) or fisheries (Iceland). Several Mediterranean lands, especially Greece, are big consumers of protein and thus appear well above the regression line in the diagram. Prominent among those better-off countries consuming less-than-expected quantities of protein are Japan and the newly industrialized nations of East Asia, all with ancient traditions of rice culture. [*Source:* Data from *FAO Production Yearbook 1987* (Rome: Food and Agriculture Organization of the United Nations, 1988); and the *1990 Britannica Book of the Year* (Chicago: Encyclopaedia Britannica, 1990).]

be discussed in Chapter 9)—adds further upward pressure on global commodity prices. Growing scarcity provides opportunities for the creation of cartels, such as the Organization of Petroleum Exporting Countries (OPEC), which are able to set artificially high prices for the commodities over which they share effective oligopolistic control. Meanwhile, overexploitation of physical resources brings environmental deterioration.

Population growth underlies the worsening global problem of unemployment. In the industrialized lands, when young people born during the "baby-boom" era of the 1950s and 1960s reached an employable age, they entered the labor force more rapidly than jobs could be created for them; consequently, those age groups have since experienced abnormally high unemployment rates. The problem is far worse, however, in the less-developed countries, where high birth rates are flooding labor markets with millions of new workers. In these mainly agricultural nations, available farmland quickly becomes overcrowded, and fledgling industries cannot generate manufacturing employment rapidly enough to absorb the overspill from the countryside. The result is high unemployment rates, which would be even greater if they included all the *underemployed*. These are the surplus workers who remain on the family farms even though their labor is not really needed there. Thus India, already burdened with massive unemployment and underemployment, has little hope of finding sufficient work for the more than 5 million young people entering the la-

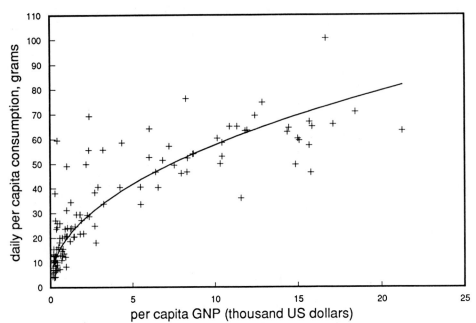

FIGURE 3.12 Relationship between per capita animal protein consumption and level of development. Consumption of animal proteins offers a better measure of nutritional quality than does the total amount of protein in the diet (see Figure 3.11), and it is highly correlated with per capita GNP ($R^2 = 0.768$). Looking at the availability of the higher-quality proteins found in meat, fish, and milk products gives a different view of nutrition in several major world areas than does access to total protein alone. Some of the world's poorest populations derive most of their protein from vegetable sources of inadequate nutritional value. This is true of the impoverished countries of Africa and South Asia shown tightly clustered in the lower left-hand corner of the above diagram. Many Latin Americans also rely upon vegetable sources for much of their protein (beef-producing Argentina and Uruguay are exceptions). Most Western Europeans consume ample quantities of animal proteins, especially in those countries with large animal industries, such as Ireland. Australia and New Zealand also rank high for this same reason. The world's leading consumer of animal proteins, however, is Iceland, where fishing is the leading industry and supplies a principal item of diet. [*Source:* Data from *FAO Production Yearbook 1987* (Rome: Food and Agriculture Organization of the United Nations, 1988); and the *1990 Britannica Book of the Year* (Chicago: Encyclopaedia Britannica, 1990).]

bor force each year. In neighboring Bangladesh at least one-third of the work force is unemployed.

Other related economic and social ills result from overly rapid population growth. With millions of job-seekers pouring into their cities each year, many developing countries are wrestling with a host of severe urban problems: overcrowding, inadequate housing, and lack of sanitation and health services, in addition to severe unemployment.

A further burden for developing countries with high birth rates is the large number of people in the dependent ages. With one-third to one-half of their people under the age of 15, these countries find it ex-

ceedingly difficult to provide the necessary extra services, especially education. So many children are reaching school age each year that schools cannot be built or staffed fast enough to accommodate them. Compulsory education laws are thus of little practical significance, and literacy rates are in some cases actually falling. This, of course, diminishes the quality of labor forces.

Thus, plagued by excessive population growth, many less-developed countries are trapped in a vicious circle of poverty, malnutrition, and disease. Despite the relative improvements in public health delivery that have reduced death rates and therefore fueled the

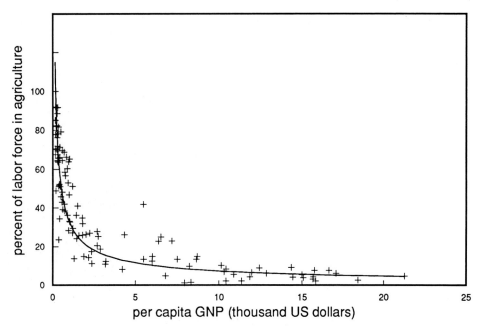

FIGURE 3.13   Relationship between level of development and percent of labor force in agriculture. This association is very strong ($R^2 = 0.805$). In the poorest countries of sub-Saharan Africa and southern Asia, agriculture engages virtually all the working population. Among the extreme cases are Nepal (92.1), Burundi (91.7), and Rwanda (91.8). This percentage drops steeply with increasing levels of per capita GNP, however, tapering off gradually thereafter. Among the higher-income countries, the primary occupations employ relatively small numbers of workers, even in such major exporters of agricultural commodities as Canada, the United States, Australia, and Argentina. Most of Western Europe is below the regression line. Prominent among those middle- and upper-income countries rising above the line are several oil-rich states in the Middle East, together with the USSR and East European countries, whose agricultural sectors use labor inefficiently. [*Source:* data from *FAO Production Yearbook 1987* (Rome: Food and Agriculture Organization of the United Nations, 1988); and the *1990 Britannica Book of the Year* (Chicago: Encyclopaedia Britannica. 1990).]

very population expansion that retards their development efforts, the countries of the Third World still lag behind the industrialized nations in quality of health care. Indeed, such indicators of health as life expectancy are strongly correlated with level of development, which is measured by per capita GNP (see Figure 3.14). A direct link exists between birth rates and the health of women and children: After repeated pregnancies, mothers become increasingly debilitated and vulnerable to death in childbirth, and the mortality rates of their infants rise.

Finally, rapid population growth may have adverse political consequences. The many economic and social problems of rapidly growing populations are ma-

jor sources of internal political instability in many developing countries. Declining domestic farm output, for instance, can undermine the stability of governments, as shortages and rising prices bring popular unrest. Food riots in Egypt during the 1970s and later in Poland underscored the political dangers of an inadequate food supply. Many countries are forced to divert ever-larger amounts of scarce foreign exchange from development needs to pay for food imports. At the same time, differential rates of population growth among countries often produce international political strains. If, for example, the population of one country is increasing faster than the populations of its neighbors, this may arouse fears that the overcrowded

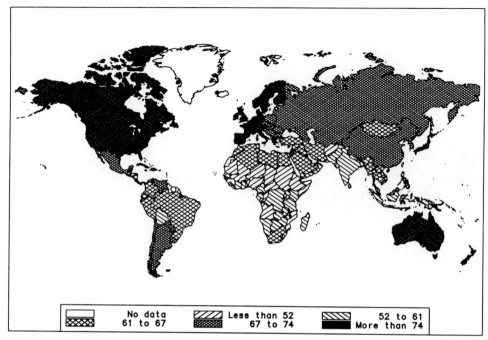

FIGURE 3.14   Life expectancy at birth. A measure of the general level of health in a population, life expectancy ranges from less than 45 years in some poorer countries to more than 80 years in the richer ones. The lowest life expectancies are concentrated in sub-Saharan Africa and parts of South Asia, which are also areas of poor nutrition (see Figures 3.12 and 3.13). Life expectancy continues to rise in the industrialized countries. Japan and Iceland are the current leaders, but life expectancies exceeding 75 years are common throughout Western Europe. Longevity is rising steadily in the newly industrializing countries of East Asia and in such South Asian countries as Sri Lanka and India, complicating the problem of containing population growth in those crowded lands. [*Source:* Data from the *1990 Britannica Book of the Year* (Chicago: Encyclopaedia Britannica, 1990).]

country may attempt to seize adjacent lands to relieve internal population pressures. The suspicious attitude toward Iran held by other Persian Gulf countries, whose populations are much smaller, stems partly from this source; Indochina has endured centuries of warfare between overpopulated neighbors contending for the rice-basket areas of the Mekong delta. History offers innumerable examples of wars of conquest prompted by the desire on the part of one country for relief from overcrowding.

Problems of Declining Populations.   In the industrialized countries of Western Europe and North America, uneasiness is arising over an opposite demographic trend—population decrease. Despite some disagreement about the precise consequences of population decline, it is generally conceded that these consequences are pervasive. The demographic effects are the most obvious. Population growth depends not only upon birth rates but also upon the number of women reaching childbearing age. Hence, until recently, the

arrival of postwar babies into this age group has ensured a substantial growth in population, despite a continuing decline in birth rates. Even though family size in the United States has now dropped to a two-child average, which is below the replacement level, births will exceed deaths for the rest of the century. Meanwhile, the age structure of the United States population has begun to change, affecting the mix of goods and services demanded. Smaller and smaller numbers of children are entering the schools, whereas the proportion of the population aged 65 and above is growing. In these trends the United States is following on the heels of the European countries. Most of these have arrived at the point of zero population growth, and some are beginning to see their populations shrink.

A declining population is an aging population. As life expectancy increases and people live to more-advanced ages at a time when birth rates are declining, the proportion of a country's citizens in the retirement ages rises accordingly. A nation in which this process

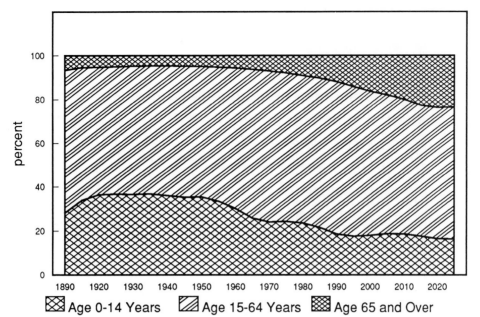

FIGURE 3.15 Japan's aging population. Although Japan's industrialization began in the latter part of the nineteenth century, its population structure resembled that of a Third World country until after World War II. The birth rate was high and life expectancy was low, forcing those Japanese in their economically active years to support large numbers of dependent children, but relatively few elderly persons. This diagram illustrates the extraordinary speed with which postwar Japan brought its birth rate under control and extended the life span of its citizens. Today, the Japanese have the world's highest life-expectancy rate (along with the Icelanders), posing a wholly new set of dependency problems. [*Source:* For 1890–1985, Japan, Bureau of Statistics, *Population Censuses;* for 1990–2025, Institute of Population Problems, Ministry of Health and Welfare, *Population Projections for Japan, 1985–2085* (Tokyo, 1987).]

is occurring with remarkable rapidity is Japan (Figure 3.15). With what is now the world's highest life expectancy, the Japanese population is being transformed from one that has been relatively young into one that is quickly aging.

The changing nature of the dependency problem is evident from Figure 3.16, which illustrates the diverse conditions that exist today in major world regions, together with the situation that the United Nations expects to prevail in A.D. 2025. The developed regions, with their mature, stable populations contrast sharply with the less-developed regions, whose populations are still very young. If we compare the child-dependency ratios (the child population under 15 expressed as a relationship to the number in the productive years from 15 through 64) with the elderly-dependency ratios (the number 65 or older as a proportion of those in the intermediate years), it is apparent that a comparatively small number of Africans and Latin Americans in the economically active age group must support very large numbers of children but few

elderly persons. In Canada and the United States, and in Europe, a mainly middle-aged work force must provide for a great many retirees. The U.N. projections for A.D. 2025 suggest that the heavy burden of child dependency will diminish somewhat for the Third World as population growth begins to come under control, especially in East Asia. For the developed regions, however, caring for a growing elderly population will become increasingly onerous.

The aging of its population confronts a society with new kinds of problems. Prominent among these is the heavy cost of providing adequate national pension programs, as shown by the strains that have emerged in the U.S. social security system. A response to the longer-term problem of declining numbers of active workers has been to reverse a trend toward earlier retirement; in the United States, the customary age of retirement has shifted from 65, and in most cases mandatory retirement rules are being eliminated altogether.

A second cost burden imposed by an aging popu-

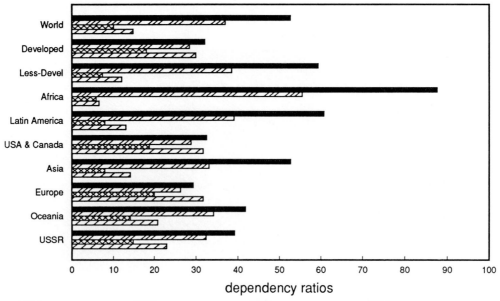

FIGURE 3.16 Age-dependency ratios for the world and major regions, 1990 and 2025 (U.N. medium-variant projections). The child-dependency ratio represents the ratio of the population 0–14 years of age, to the economically active group aged 15–64, per 100. The elderly-dependency ratio is the ratio of the population aged 65 years and older, to the population of intermediate age, per 100. This measure indicates the relative number of persons in each dependency category that must be supported by the economically active population. In the least-developed areas, the working-age population must support relatively large numbers of dependent children; in the more-developed areas, workers must provide for large numbers of retirees. By the year 2025 the more-developed regions can anticipate having to support more elderly people than children. For the less-developed areas, the huge burden of child dependency will likely diminish somewhat. [*Source:* Data from *World Population Prospects 1988* (New York: United Nations, 1989.]

lation stems from rising medical bills for treating diseases of the elderly. Indeed, in the United States there is a continuing crisis over the soaring expenditures for health care, exacerbated by a rapidly developing medical technology that prolongs life at an ever-rising cost.

Helping to compensate for higher outlays for pensions and health care in a mature population, a falling birth rate may serve to hold education expenditures in check. But the educational level of the labor force is a major determinant of economic growth, especially in an era when new knowledge-intensive industries, such as computers and robotics, have begun to replace older industries that employ unskilled workers in assembly-line production. The need for adult education and retraining for older employees displaced from declining industries such as steel and automobiles is growing as fewer young workers, many of whom have above-average education levels, enter the

labor force, and as a surplus work force of displaced workers in their fifties grows.

The product mix of consumer demand changes as the population shifts from the "Pepsi generation" to the "Geritol generation" and as needs shift from high chairs to wheelchairs. Adjusting production levels to changes in the demand mix is more difficult if the labor force is aging and the proportion of new, more mobile, workers is falling, although this may hasten the adoption of new computerized technologies: robots on the assembly line and computer terminals that enable information rather than people to be moved. Certainly, most current innovations in industry are substituting capital for labor in the production process, calling on smaller numbers of better-trained higher-quality workers.

Finally, a decline in population can have an impact on public opinion and policymaking. An older population generally holds more conservative views on public questions. Furthermore, as we discovered during the 1930s, when birth rates dropped steeply in North America and Europe in response to the Great Depression, many people react to zero population growth with feelings of extreme anxiety, fearing an adverse effect on national prosperity and security. Although population decline does indeed pose problems of adjustment, these merely signal the need for a creative public policy rather than call for a program to encourage higher birth rates. Students of such problems generally believe that the average person will be substantially better off economically if population growth follows a two-child family pattern rather than a three-child family, or more.

MIGRATION

The second dynamic population process is *migration,* the permanent movement of human beings from one place to another. Migration is a complex phenomenon, and the study of it is all the more difficult because official data are so variable in quality.

The Migration Process

Viewed broadly, migration is similar to trade, with flows of people substituting for flows of merchandise. As in the case of commodity movements, one area supplies a surplus population, or at least provides some "push" that causes people to want to leave. At the other end of the journey, an area of demand exerts a "pull" because of a population deficiency or the presence of some other positive attraction. Between the regions of supply and demand, a variety of barriers interpose obstacles to the movement of people.

Here the analogy to trade ends. Goods are passive, whereas people are active agents ordinarily free to decide for themselves whether or not to migrate. Exceptions are numerous, however, and involuntary movements of people are not unusual. Many of history's large population transfers have taken place as a result of actions by government or other official agencies, which offered little or no choice to the migrants. Then, too, children and other dependents usually have decisions about migration made for them.

Why People Migrate. Perhaps the most familiar explanation for migration is that offered by the classical economic model of *factor mobility.* Underlying this model are the assumptions that migrants are motivated by the desire to maximize their incomes and that they are fully aware of the opportunities for employment in other locations, as well as the wages prevailing in each place. A further assumption is that the workers are numerous and are identical in skills, values, and needs. Finally, the model assumes the absence of barriers to migration. Under these conditions labor will migrate from Region *A* to Region *B* as long as *real wages* (wages expressed in terms of how much they will buy) are higher in *B* than in *A*. The expected outcome is a labor market that is everywhere in equilibrium, with a job for every worker and all vacancies filled.

This focus upon economic reasons for migration finds some justification in both less-developed and advanced countries. In India, for example, one study found that the decisions of individuals to move hinge largely upon their expectations of job opportunities in the new area. In another case, it was shown that 85 percent of the labor movements between regions of the United States are associated with changes in unemployment levels. In other words, people tend to migrate to those places where new jobs are opening up most rapidly in relation to the number of persons entering the labor force.

Even so, the assumptions of the classical model have limited applicability. People have other than economic motives for moving, and few are able to decide with complete objectivity. Much rationalization is connected with most decisions to move, knowledge about conditions at the other end of the journey is usually imperfect, and there are many barriers in the way of the prospective mover. Prospective migrants must weigh their perceptions of their present locations against those concerning the proposed locations. In this evaluative process, economic reasons do not tell the whole story, and sometimes they do not even give the most important part.

Often the most compelling reasons for moving are of a cultural nature. Religion has been an important migration factor: Throughout history many individuals and groups have moved to new places where they could practice their beliefs unhindered. Kinship, friendship, and linguistic and ethnic ties have also played important parts in decisions to migrate.

Cultural groups have tended to produce "streams" of migrations into particular places. During the American colonial period large numbers of German migrants settled in Pennsylvania, where they came to be called "Pennsylvania Dutch." The Mormons, in their organized westward movement, followed distinct paths and settled in certain selected areas. In Canada, Finns chose to congregate at the head of Lake Superior and Mennonites in southern Manitoba. In the Italian migrations to the Western Hemisphere, those from southern Italy went mainly to the

United States and those from the north of Italy tended to go to the Rio de la Plata region of South America. Meanwhile, some migrants changed their minds, or perhaps decided to return home to marry or to retire, thereby creating "counterstreams."

Political considerations have been prominent in decisions to migrate. Persons seeking relief from political persecution, expelled from their homelands because of unpopular beliefs, or fleeing because of war have figured importantly in migrations to new lands. In addition, governments have forcibly resettled large numbers of people and have sent sizable groups to colonize new areas.

Some demographers have attempted to classify the many possible explanations for migrating. Sociologist William Petersen devised a fivefold classification, further subdividing each category as to whether it is "innovating" or "conservative." Migrants whose moves are innovating are undertaking a new way of life; those whose moves are conservative are preserving their accustomed way of life in new surroundings. Petersen's five classes of migrants are as follows:

1. *Primitive migration* describes movements of peoples at very low levels of development in response to conditions of the physical environment over which they have little control. In its *conservative* form, primitive migration is exemplified by the wanderings of the herders of Central Asia, the subsistence farmers of Amazonia, or food gatherers in the Congo. The *innovative* form is indicated by the settling of Middle Eastern nomads into an urban way of life in Egypt or Syria.

2. *Forced migration* is the compulsory transfer of a people, usually by a political agency. The resettling of populations as a result of the westward shift of Poland's borders following World War II was a conservative type of forced migration, whereas the African slave trade was an innovative type.

3. *Impelled migration* is similar to forced migration in that migrants are under some form of duress, but it differs in that they retain some ability to decide whether or not to move. The flight of ancient Britons before the Saxon invaders was a conservative form of impelled migration; those who chose not to escape to the security of the Welsh mountains had the option of remaining behind to be enslaved. Jewish victims of the Russian pogroms, who could have stayed at home under subjection, elected instead to leave their rural homeland to pursue urban trades in American cities.

4. Individual movements for economic betterment or mere adventure are referred to as *free migration*. The westward migrations of pioneer farmers in the United States and Canada were a conservative type of free migration, whereas migrations of modern

Americans or Canadians leaving their cities for the farms, logging camps, or mines of Alaska or the Northwest Territories are innovating.

5. As the name suggests, a *mass migration* involves large numbers of participants. In such movements the migrants tend to submerge their individual motives and may not even be fully informed of what to expect in their new settlements. Entire rural communities from the Westlandit region of southwestern Norway migrated to North America in this way. Some found opportunities to establish farms in their new environments, but others did not.

Migrations differ in the degree of governmental control to which they are subjected. Before World War I the United States accepted virtually all immigrants; following the war, however, it admitted immigrants according to a rigid quota system that excluded some nationalities altogether. Thus, a policy of *selective* immigration replaced one of *unrestricted* immigration.

Typologies of migration have more than academic uses: They aid policymakers and other agencies in dealing with the numerous problems created by emigration or immigration. In general, the analytical approach to this subject offers a better understanding of the pressures and motivations underlying the present global urbanization trend, the movement of people from the U.S. Northeast to the Sunbelt, and other contemporary migrations.

Barriers to Migration. The question of *why* people move must be distinguished from that of *how many* actually do so. Often many persons would, or should, move but are prevented from doing so because of certain barriers to migration. These are of three types: distance, political restrictions, and those characteristics of would-be migrants that reduce their mobility.

One of the most imposing barriers to migration is distance, which therefore figures prominently in most analyses. Such studies invariably show that most people move short distances and that the frequency of moves declines with an increase in distance from the migrants' original homes. Migrants may find that long-distance moves simply entail too much transport cost or that such moves exact too high an "opportunity cost"—that is, the income that would have to be foregone at the old locations.

A variety of noneconomic considerations further reduce the number of long-distance moves. For one thing, people's knowledge about other areas, and the opportunities that may exist there, grows dimmer with increasing distance from home. Moves to remoter places, especially to foreign lands, also cause many personal disruptions owing to the unfamiliar customs and languages and the lack of family and community ties in the new locations. These pose "psychic costs" for migrants.

Because distance has such an effect upon human migration, "gravity" models are often used for the study of this subject, following in the footsteps of Newton's laws in physics. The basic hypotheses underlying this approach are, first, that the propensity to migrate from region i to region j is inversely related to the distance separating them (or, more commonly, the square of the distance) and, second, that the number of persons moving to a particulate point is directly proportional to the population living at each end of the journey. In its simplest form, the following expression describes the relationship:

$$M_{ij} = \frac{P_i P_j}{d_{ij}^x} \times k$$

where

M_{ij} = number of migrants moving from region i to region j

P_i, P_j = size of population in regions i and j, respectively

d = distance separating regions i and j

x = a factor that describes that rate of decline of migration with distance

k = a measure of proportionality

Certain adjustments in this model are usually required. It is necessary to make some kind of allowance in the formula for the nature of employment opportunities in the new place. This provides a better measure than does population alone. Account must also be taken of any intervening opportunities that may appear along the routes of travel from the place of origin. Studies of labor migration in Sweden, for example, have shown that proximity to other employment centers tends to siphon off sizable numbers of migrants from more distant places. Another useful variable indicates the number of friends and relatives who may already have moved to the new location, persons who can be depended upon to give information about opportunities in that place, and perhaps even to provide food and shelter at the outset. Finally, the model should allow for other attractive qualities of the destination, such as a benign climate. Studies of interregional migration in the United States have confirmed that this can be an important variable.

Because of the influence of distance, therefore, the areas nearest the prime source of migrants tend to fill up first. Migration thus usually takes the form of a diffusion outward from the center. This has been apparent in studies of local, regional, and international migration.

Political barriers may be especially difficult for migrants to penetrate. As in the case of trade, international movements encounter more obstacles of this type than do interregional ones. This has become increasingly true in recent years: Only in this century have national governments closely controlled immigration and emigration, but the trend has now proceeded to the point where free international migration has nearly ceased. During periods of high unemployment, the industrialized countries have become increasingly reluctant to issue work permits to foreigners.

Despite generally rising bars to immigration, Western countries do not ordinarily restrict emigration. By contrast, the Communist countries permitted few of their citizens to leave. The most visible evidence of this policy was the Berlin Wall, built to prevent the East German economy from being weakened by the outflow of its best-trained young adults. When Hungary and Czechoslovakia provided an alternative exit, the pent-up pressures were irresistible, however: The dam burst, sweeping not only the wall but also communist East Germany away with it.

Where people are free to move at will, as in most interregional migration, some are prevented from doing so by still other, more subtle, barriers. Among the strongest are the family and cultural ties that bind would-be migrants to their home areas. Such links have prevented many unemployed people in depressed areas of Appalachia, the Ozarks, and the old manufacturing districts of the Northeastern United States from going to more dynamic areas where jobs are available. Home ties have likewise been strong deterrents to interregional migration in Britain and China.

Certain members of a society are less bound by such links than others. The most mobile persons are young adult males between the ages of 15 and 30. The more prosperous among the elderly, however, may retire to areas with warmer climates. Studies have shown that fewer women than men leave their home areas. Migrants also tend to be better educated and more skilled and to have better health than those remaining behind.

Not only are some people more likely to migrate than others, but they are also more inclined to move at certain times. Migration is much greater when the business cycle is ebbing in the source region and rising in the receiving region. The life cycle of the individual also affects migration decisions: People are more inclined to move upon completing their education and entering the labor market, when they are retiring, or when they are undergoing changes in marital status. During the long intervals between such landmark events in an individual's life, most people are reluctant to undergo the financial and emotional strains of leaving friends and accustomed surroundings for a new way of life in a strange place.

Effects of Migration.

Because it is a selective process, migration can have important effects on both the supplying and receiving regions. Immigration and emigration alter the age composition, sex ratios, literacy rates, and demography of the affected areas; they can also create social and economic problems.

For a region of heavy out-migration, the departure of predominantly young adults in their most productive years leaves behind a population consisting mostly of the very young and the elderly. Conversely, an area of in-migration usually has a preponderance of young and middle-aged adults. Exceptions are regions with warm, sunny climates, such as Florida and Arizona, which attract large numbers of retirees.

Migration also affects the sex ratio: the proportion of males to females in a population. This ratio is obtained by dividing the number of males by the number of females and multiplying by 100. High sex ratios, indicating proportionately larger numbers of males than females, are characteristic of newly settled areas. This is because men tend to be the most mobile members of the population. The relatively larger numbers of women remaining behind give low sex ratios to areas of heavy out-migration. The greater life expectancy of women further reduces the sex ratios of older, more stable, areas. The low ratio of the United Kingdom (94.9) is typical of Western Europe, which has experienced continued emigration over a long period. By contrast, Singapore's higher ratio (103.8) is representative of countries still receiving immigrants.

As time passes, the sex ratios of newer countries and regions gradually decrease. Throughout its earlier years the United States had proportionately large numbers of males owing to heavy immigration. In 1910 the sex ratio was 106.2, by 1940 it had fallen to 100.8, and by 1969 it was only 95.2. The lowest ratios in the country are those of New England, whereas the highest are in the West. In Alaska, for instance, the ratio is 132.3.

The loss of young adults results in lower birth rates in regions of much out-migration and correspondingly higher birth rates in the receiving areas. In this way the selectivity of migration accentuates the population losses and gains of the two areas. Ultimately, however, the influx of immigrants to a new region accelerates the growth of urbanization, which is normally attended by falling birth rates.

The effects of migration upon death rates are complex. Paradoxically, the influx of retirees to Arizona, many of whom are attracted by the reputed healthfulness of the desert climate, has given that state a higher-than-average death rate, simply because in-migration has raised the age level.

The social effects of migration are likewise mixed. Although emigrants tend to be the more physically healthy members of a source population, their mental health and emotional stability often range from the very best to the worst. The problems of adjusting to a new environment may contribute to increased incidence of crime, lawlessness, and disintegration of families among in-migrants. Such stresses apparently underly many of our most difficult urban problems. In addition, cultural conflicts between newcomers and an indigenous population can produce antagonisms, social unrest, and even violence.

Economically, a region that receives large numbers of immigrants may benefit in many ways, at least in the earlier stages. This seems to have been true of the United States prior to World War I. The influx of immigrants during that era has been credited with increasing the growth rate of the country's total gross national product, and possibly even raising it in per capita terms. This apparently resulted from the addition of large numbers of persons mainly of working age who were healthy, skilled, conditioned to hard work, and possibly of better-than-average intelligence: In other words, the United States benefited from the added *human capital*. As they prospered, these persons offered a rapidly expanding market for goods of all kinds and especially those of the newly developed manufacturing industries. These conditions in turn created an attractive investment market for the European capital required for further expansion.

The economic effects upon those regions supplying migrants have varied. For the Western European countries of the nineteenth century, emigration of their surplus peoples to the New World gave temporary relief during downward swings of the business cycle. The large numbers of farmers moving to agriculturally rich lands in the Americas also supplied Europe with abundant new supplies of foodstuffs at low prices. At the same time, the industrial nations gained rapidly expanding markets for their manufactured goods in these overseas areas.

For today's less-developed countries and regions, emigration is often detrimental, for the emigrants are the most enterprising, skilled, and educated members of the population. Many potential business leaders and professionals receive educations abroad, then elect to pursue their careers in advanced countries, where the financial rewards and opportunities are greater than at home. Because the developing nations often desperately need such skills, this type of migration has perverse effects.

The recent migration of people from the United States Snowbelt to the Sunbelt of the South and Southwest offers many examples of the problems that such population movements can create. The out-migration of people and industries is not only costing the northern states some of their more enterprising people, but it is increasing the burden on local governments, which must try to maintain public services with diminished tax revenues from industry, property, and personal income, as well as retail sales. Meanwhile, the Sunbelt states, though benefiting from the influx of new business and industry, are hard-pressed to install new roads, streets, sewers, and other forms of infrastructure required by economic growth and the flood of new people. Local governments encounter new and unaccustomed problems of law enforcement and provision of social services.

Patterns of Migration

Let us now examine briefly some of the main patterns of migration that have contributed to the current distribution of populations. Migration patterns are apparent at three scales of observation: worldwide, within continents, and within countries.

International. The earliest human migrations were group movements of clans and tribes; individual movements and migration streams appeared much later. The first primitive migrations were impelled mostly by climatic changes or by calamities, such as hostile invasions. Considering the comparatively small number of inhabitants on earth during the period of prehistory, it is paradoxical that one of the probable reasons for early migrations was population pressure. We must remember, however, that primitive means of livelihood were (and still are) highly extensive in their use of land. Because the support of every individual required so much land, primitive folk constantly had to adjust their activities to an uncertain food supply. When their numbers increased to the point that their traditional lands became inadequate, migration to new areas became necessary. Physical features of the landscape, such as mountain passes, ice bridges, and wide plains and valleys, dictated their routes of travel.

Modern migrations, however, have dwarfed all such primitive movements. Whereas earlier migrations often involved the encroachment of primitive peoples upon the lands of more advanced cultures, as with the Mongol invasions of China, most modern migrations have reversed this process. An estimated 60 million Europeans and Africans took part in the great migrations since A.D. 1500. These migrations began slowly. Although from 10 million to 20 million African slaves were transported to the new lands, relatively few Europeans moved permanently prior to 1800, probably no more than 2.5 million in all.

The European exodus accelerated during the nineteenth century, particularly after 1830, and reached a peak on the eve of World War I with an annual flow of 1.5 million. These persons were mainly escaping rural overpopulation in Scandinavia, Ireland, Scotland, Germany, and Italy, as well as political upheavals, religious persecution (such as the Russian pogroms), and economic depressions, although many came in a spirit of adventure. Most of the movements formed streams to particular locations. Of the total, almost two-thirds went to the United States, but large numbers moved to Canada and other British Commonwealth countries as well. South America attracted immigrants mainly from the Mediterranean lands.

Intracontinental. Changes in national policy following World War I quickly altered these familiar flow patterns. The Great Depression reversed migration flows during the early 1930s, when some Western European countries actually experienced net gains, mostly from returnees. For a time the United States, Australia, New Zealand, Argentina, and Uruguay had net losses of migrants. Since that period the most significant population movements have taken place within continental areas.

Intra-European migrations have been particularly large since the beginning of World War II, the war itself being responsible for wholesale displacement of populations. Just prior to the war about 400,000 persons (mostly Jews) had escaped from Nazi Germany, and during the war the Germans imported 8 million foreigners as forced labor. In all, the Nazis uprooted an estimated 30 million or more persons. The postwar boundary changes produced large population shifts, especially the westward expansion of the Slavic area at German expense. This resulted in the displacement of 11 million Germans and a very large exchange of populations between the USSR and Poland along their new border. Another million Germans subsequently escaped from East Germany into West Germany. In all, 25 million or more people moved during the time of postwar resettlement.

Among the prospering nations of postwar Western Europe a new pattern of population movement emerged. Surplus labor from the southern Mediterranean region, North Africa, and Asia Minor streamed into labor-short Germany, France, Switzerland, and the Low Countries. When economic recession appeared in the late 1970s, it brought with it an alarming rise in unemployment in those countries. Losing their jobs, many of these "guest workers" from the south returned to their homelands, although some remained in their new locations, creating social and economic problems for host governments. Also during this period a great many unwanted immigrants from Commonwealth countries in the Caribbean, Africa, and Asia poured into already-overcrowded Britain, resulting in urban unrest and racial strife. Several countries of Africa and Asia, newly freed from colonial control, have had very large migrations, mainly unrecorded, of peoples uprooted by famine, intertribal conflict, and war.

As the final decade of the twentieth century arrived, the number of people displaced from their homelands by military conflict and political repression continued to swell, posing humanitarian problems of immense proportions. One of the most gripping events of 1989 was the spectacle of hundreds of thousands of people escaping to the West from the crumbling Communist regimes of Eastern Europe and the USSR. The majority of these were ethnic Germans seizing the opportunity to find freedom in West Germany, but they also included a great many Soviet Jews taking advantage of the relaxation of Soviet exit restrictions to escape to Israel and the West.

During this same period the ruthless suppression of the pro-democracy movement by the Chinese government led to an accelerated migration from the British crown colony of Hong Kong. Apprenhensive about their futures after the colony reverts to Chinese rule in 1997, ethnic Chinese have been leaving in ever-greater numbers. By some estimates, as many as 600,000 will have migrated by 1997, principally to Canada, the United States, Australia, and Britain.

More dramatic still was the massive exodus of refugees following the Iraqi seizure of Kuwait late in the summer of 1990. Hundreds of thousands of Kuwaitis and resident foreigners hurriedly made their escape from the harsh military occupation of that Persian Gulf emirate. Of the many nationalities represented in this flight the largest contingent consisted of Pakistanis, Indians, and other South Asian oil-field workers. The forced return of these masses only confounded the population problems of their already-crowded homelands.

Prior to these additions, the combined total of refugees around the world had already reached an esti-

mated 13 million. Africa saw the greatest accumulation of refugees—Sudanese, Ethiopians, Somali, Mozambicans, and others escaping from revolutions, wars, and famines in their home countries. A similar problem area was Southeast Asia, where camps in neighboring lands sheltered escapees from continuing turmoil in Cambodia. Added to these refugee populations were an estimated five million Afghans, a hundred thousand or so Iraqi Kurds, and many thousands of exiled Salvadorians and Nicaraguans in Central America. Thus the human toll of regional armed conflicts has steadily mounted in recent years.

Internal.   Although migrations between countries and within countries stem from the same basic causes, internal movements are of much greater relative magnitude today because of rising international barriers to migration. The two main types of internal migration, *interregional* and *rural-urban,* are both still evident in the United States, although these are now taking some new turns. As the historically important westward movement continues, it has been joined by a southward flow from the Northeast and North Central states. One result of this is the wide variation in growth rates among the nation's metropolitan areas.

The U.S. population as a whole grew by nearly 11 percent between the 1980 and 1990 censuses, but the increase was shared unequally among the various states and regions (Figure 3.17). Continuing a trend of the 1970s, the new decade saw a further "hollowing out" of the country's midsection as more and more people moved to the coasts.

This out-migration resulted largely from the long-term decline of the region's mature industries—especially basic metals and motor vehicles—victims of a restructuring of domestic and world economies. Increasingly, the stress is placed on the manufacture of high-technology goods, which are less materials- and energy-intensive than the traditional products of the old manufacturing belt. Except for New Hampshire, which benefited from spillovers of high-technology growth from eastern Massachusetts, none of the states of the Northeast gained population at the national rate, and the four industrial states of Ohio, West Virginia, Illinois, and Michigan formed a pocket of population decline.

The agricultural economies of the nation's midsection lagged throughout this period as the family farm continued to wither, leading to a steady departure of young people from the Great Plains region. Three farm states—Iowa, North Dakota, and Wyoming—suffered absolute losses of population, and the interior Farm-Belt region as a whole grew at rates well below the national pace. In the deep South, Louisiana also

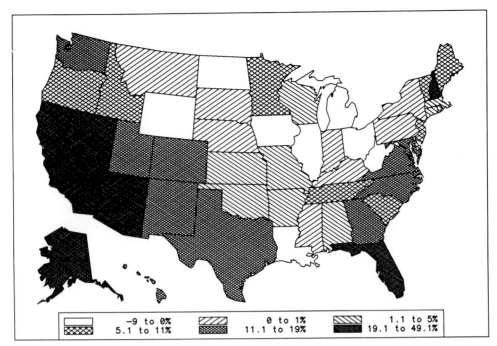

FIGURE 3.17 Population shifts in the United States during the 1980s. The "hollowing out" of the continental interior that had begun in the previous decade continued through the 1980s. This persistent movement of people away from the center toward each of the seacoasts occurred in response to (1) the push of declining manufacturing industries and a prolonged recession in the farm economy of the nation's midsection, and (2) the pull of growing high-technology production in Sunbelt areas of the Southwest and Southeast, which offered the additional enticement of benign climates. [*Source:* U.S. Bureau of the Census, *1990 Decennial Census, Housing and Population Counts* (Washington, D.C.: U.S. Government Printing Office, 1990).]

lost population, owing to a decline in its mining industries.

The great majority of the out-migrants headed for the states of the Southwest and Southeast, commonly termed the Sunbelt. An unbroken expanse of high growth extends along the Atlantic coast southward from Delaware and Maryland, to culminate in the flourishing states of Georgia and Florida. A continuous phalanx of seven rapidly growing states likewise stretches from Texas to California, with outliers in Alaska, Hawaii, and Washington state. In the southeast, Florida and Georgia enjoyed similar expansions. As in the previous decade, the largest absolute gains during the 1980s were made by California, which added 5.6 million people, Florida (3.0 million), and Texas (2.6 million). These three states together accounted for nearly half the entire U.S. population increase between the 1980 and 1990 censuses.

The 1990 census also revealed that the rate of population growth in metropolitan areas had accelerated since the 1970s. Furthermore, it showed that the metropolitan population had expanded much more rapidly during the decade than the nonmetropolitan population—11.6 percent as against only 3.9 percent. By 1990 the metropolitan centers held 77.5 percent of the entire U.S. population.

This renewed growth of metropolitan areas apparently reversed what for a time had seemed to be a trend away from metropolitan living. During the 1970s and early 1980s the United States had appeared to experience the beginnings of a dispersal of populations away from the largest metropolises, rather like that occurring in Western Europe. Smaller towns and cities and nonmetropolitan areas were gaining people at a rate higher than that of the country as a whole. Smaller centers had become increasingly attractive to new manufacturing industries and other activities because of lower operating costs and taxes. As places to live, too, they were favored not only because of lower living costs but also because of better job opportunities as well as the perception that they were safer places and offered better environments. The interstate highway network and other changes in transportation and communications had increased the accessibility of these smaller centers to national markets. A sharp decline in U.S. manufacturing during the 1980s, however, reduced job opportunities in the small industrial centers at a time when employment in the services was climbing steeply. Much of this service growth took place in metropolitan centers, whose populations expanded accordingly.

Growth rates among metropolitan areas varied widely, however, between the 1980 and 1990 censuses (Figure 3.18). The resulting pattern of change closely resembles that of the states. As might be expected, the main metropolitan centers of the high-growth Sunbelt

areas registered the largest increases. During the decade the country's second-largest city, Los Angeles, grew at an annual rate of 2.2 percent, further narrowing the gap between it and first-place New York City and widening its lead over Chicago. San Francisco passed Philadelphia to capture fourth place, and Dallas overtook both Washington, D.C. and Houston. Other Sunbelt cities achieved similar gains in national ranking at the expense of older "Rust Belt" metropolises, as they absorbed large numbers of migrants from other parts of the country.

Canada, too, has had important internal migrations, both interregional and rural-urban. Canada's interregional migrations have had two spatial compo-

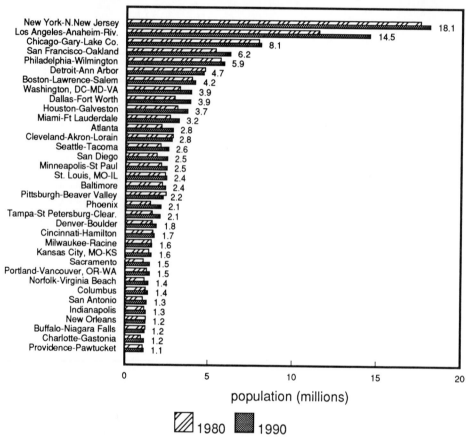

1980 1990

FIGURE 3.18 Twenty-five largest metropolitan areas in the United States, 1980 and 1990. Ninety percent of the nation's growth in the 1980s occurred in the metropolitan areas. By 1990, 77.5 percent of all Americans lived in such areas, and 43 percent of these were in the 25 top regions shown here. Population growth of the Sunbelt cities continued to outstrip that of the older metropolises of the Northeast during the 1980s. Los Angeles further narrowed New York City's lead, and several other Sunbelt metropolises—San Francisco, Dallas, Miami, Atlanta, Seattle, San Diego, Phoenix, Tampa, and Denver—rose still higher in national ranking. Most northern cities grew but little during the period, and several lost population, notably Detroit, Cleveland, and Pittsburgh. [*Source:* U.S. Bureau of the Census, *Press Release CB91-66* (Washington, D.C.: U.S. Department of Commerce, February 21, 1991).]

nents: east to west and hinterland to heartland. The east-west trend was prevalent until World War II, with the result that each province, with few exceptions, had a net gain of people from every province to its east and lost population to every province to its west. At the same time, streams of migrants converged on the Ontario Industrial Belt from resource-oriented hinterland regions. Increasingly since the war, both immigration from abroad and internal migration have tended to follow these trends.

Other advanced countries have had similar internal migrations, both rural-urban and interregional. Italy, for example, has experienced a substantial flow of Calabrians, Sicilians, and others from the overpopulated and economically depressed rural south to the prosperous industrial cities of the north. Large-scale internal migrations have likewise occurred in many less-developed nations, particularly rural-urban movements. As we shall see in the next chapter, the most rapidly growing cities in our present era are in the Third World.

AN ASSESSMENT: POPULATION GROWTH AND MIGRATION IN THE CONTEMPORARY WORLD

Though large-scale movements of people within countries continue in many parts of the world, permanent migrations between countries, as we have noted here, have become relatively less significant in the latter part of the twentieth century. Despite growing population pressures throughout the Third World, migrants from less-developed countries are finding borders closed to them nearly everywhere. This declining role of international migration highlights the growing importance of differential rates of natural increase among countries as an agent of global population change.

The basic questions posed by Malthus and his successors are therefore being asked once again. Lending credence to the claim of early theorists that population growth is linked to the earth's carrying capacity, the evidence suggests that past surges of population increase occurred in response to technological breakthroughs that enhanced the productivity of earth resources. Some observers believe that the computer revolution now under way has the potential to power yet another such surge of population growth. Nevertheless, an eventual end to the long process of human multiplication seems likely, when at last the earth's finite supplies of resources approach exhaustion and environmental deterioration grows more threatening. Current indications are that the rate of natural population increase has already begun to decline. U.N. projections of this decline have lately proved overly optimistic, however; the rate of population growth has diminished more slowly than earlier anticipated. Experts now doubt that their previous prediction that global population would stabilize at about 10.5 billion before the end of another century will be realized. Their present best hope seems to be that the world total will ultimately taper off at slightly under 11 billion.

As we saw, Malthus did not anticipate the effects of development upon the basic factors of population growth, namely, birth rates and death rates. Demographic transition theory holds that as development commences, death rates fall more rapidly than birth rates, causing a demographic gap, or "population explosion," which continues until equilibrium is finally reestablished in the later stages of development. Recent events, however, show that transition theory, which is based upon Europe's experience, has not accurately predicted demographic change in today's less-developed countries, whose fertility rates are generally much higher than in premodern Europe and whose death rates have fallen much more rapidly. Current population densities also are far greater. Nevertheless, transition theory retains some validity because it predicts the sequence of demographic events, if not their precise magnitude and timing. It thus provides a useful basis for attacking the problems of population change.

Our examination of this subject has shown that the problems of growing populations are different from those of declining ones. Rapid population growth can wipe out the gains from development, reduce food supply, produce dietary deficiencies and disease, and cause poverty, inflation, unemployment, urban problems, and high levels of dependency, all of which contribute to political instability. The aging of a population, on the other hand, creates the need to restructure the economy in response to the changing nature of demand. It substitutes one kind of dependency for another and introduces new kinds of social, psychological, and political problems. In the long run, population stability appears to be the optimal state.

At present the disparities between countries in their rates of population growth are still widening. With most of the industrialized world approaching zero population growth, Third World nations are doubling their numbers every 20 to 35 years. Undoubtedly, therefore, the world population map of A.D. 2025 will look very different from today's, and international migration will have much less to do with the pattern than will differential rates of natural increase. The existing pattern of world population, which evolved in response to past events, and the new patterns expected to result from trends now in motion, will be the topic of the next chapter.

TOPICS FOR DISCUSSION

1. Why did world population grow so slowly prior to the seventeenth century, and why has its growth accelerated since? What gave rise to the three surges of population growth that occurred in the past? Describe the new developments that promise a quantum change in the world's productive capacity and explain why these developments are less likely to produce a renewed surge in world population growth.

2. Define the following: crude birth rate, crude death rate, rate of natural increase, fertility rate, age-specific death rate. Which of these measures are the most useful for assessing population change? What do they tell us about a society?

3. What did Malthus perceive as the "ultimate" check to population growth? Describe his "preventative" and "positive" checks. What solution to the problem of excessive population growth did he advocate? Why might we regard Malthus as a pioneer in the movement for women's liberation? Explain why Malthus's predictions for Western Europe failed to materialize. Where in the world today are his predictions apparently being borne out to some degree? Why?

4. Explain "demographic transition" and discuss the historical basis for transition theory. What is a "demographic gap"? Why is transition theory a less-than-perfect model for today's developing nations?

5. Show how transition theory serves as the basis for the United Nations' classification of countries according to their demographic characteristics. Discuss the five U.N. demographic types, illustrating each with country examples. Which types of countries give the greatest cause for concern?

6. Explain Engel's law and show how it applies to less-developed countries. Discuss the economic, social, health, and political problems that these countries encounter because of rapid population growth.

7. Contrast the problems of dependent populations that face Mexico with those confronting Germany. What are some of the other kinds of new problems that countries with declining populations must solve?

8. Explain the changing relative importance of natural increase and migration as determinants of national and global population patterns in recent times. Why do people migrate? Describe the various types of migration, giving examples.

9. How do the social, economic, political, and demographic effects of migration differ for supplying and receiving regions? Give some examples of migration streams.

FURTHER READINGS

BROWN, L. R., et al. *The State of the World, 1989*. New York: Norton, 1989.

In this recent annual assessment, the president of Worldwatch Institute warns of a number of converging trends that threaten the habitability of the planet for future generations and proposes a program of stabilizing population, developing new energy strategies, and reducing the degradation of the environment. Based upon careful interdisciplinary analyses by the institute's scientific research staff.

DEMKO, GEORGE J., HAROLD M. ROSE, and GEORGE A. SCHNELL. *Population Geography: A Reader*. New York: McGraw-Hill, 1970.

A durable collection of geographical writings on the spatial distribution of populations and the nature and problems of population growth and human migration.

EHRLICH, PAUL R., and ANNE H. *The Population Explosion*. New York: Simon and Schuster, 1990.

A sequel to Ehrlich's best-selling 1968 book, *The Population Bomb,* which warned of impending disaster if humankind failed to rein in its rampant population growth. In this new work the authors declare that now "the population bomb has exploded." They make a convincing case for their contention that overpopulation is responsible for the deteriorating physical environment. A well-documented introduction to the hazards of unrestrained human proliferation.

HAUB, CARL, and MARY KENT. "1990s a Crucial Decade for World Population Stabilization." News Release, Population Reference Bureau. Washington, D.C.: Population Reference Bureau, May 24, 1989.

The authors indicate that this decade brings us to a crossroads in the effort to stabilize world population at a sustainable level. Stubborn political, social, and cultural obstacles remain to be overcome before this goal can be achieved, and the timing will be close.

JONES, HUW R. *Population Geography*. New York: Harper & Row, 1981.

In this geographical treatise on population, Jones emphasizes the spatial-temporal processes shaping current patterns of fertility, mortality, and migration at global, national, and subnational scales. He also discusses the social and economic consequences of contemporary trends and their policy implications, especially for developing countries.

MAHLER, HALFDAN. "People." *Scientific American*, 243 (September 1980), 66–77.

Comparing demographic trends in developed and less-developed countries, the Director General of the World Health Organization describes the adverse effects that rapid population growth has on the general level of health in a society and examines the implications for development.

SADIK, NAFIS. *The State of World Population 1990: Choices for the New Century.* UNFPA United Nations Population Fund. New York: United Nations, 1990.

The executive director of UNFPA declares in this report that the "choices of the next ten years will decide the speed of population growth for much of the next century; they will decide whether world population trebles or merely doubles before it finally stops growing; they will decide whether the pace of damage to the environment speeds up or slows down. . . . They may decide the future of the earth as a habitation for humans." Stresses the vital role of education for women in reducing high fertility rates in the Third World.

SMITH, ROBERT S., FRANK T. DEVYVER, and WILLIAM R. ALLEN. *Population Economics: Selected Essays of Joseph J. Spengler.* Durham, N.C.: Duke University Press, 1972.

Reproduced in this volume are some of the more enduring works on population economics by a noted authority.

4

Changing Patterns
of World Population

OVERVIEW

Human populations are spread very unevenly over the world: Great numbers of people concentrate within a relatively few regions, leaving vast land areas virtually empty. Today's population pattern is the cumulative result of countless human actions over a very long period of time. This pattern has been shaped by the physical needs of human beings for food, comfort, and opportunities for a livelihood, as well as their desires, perceptions, and social and cultural relationships. The world map shows four great population concentrations and several lesser ones. The spatial irregularity of population distributions extends also to subnational levels.

As rates of population growth diverge among regions, a very different population map of the future takes shape. Most developed areas are already at or near zero population growth, ensuring that their share of global population will continue to shrink. Though 95 percent of future population growth will occur in less-developed countries, some will grow faster than others. Within a century Africa will likely hold a quarter of all humanity, and most of the world's largest cities will be in less-developed countries.

Population projections are not at all certain for the world's poorest areas, however, and for some of these they are mere guesses. Such uncertainties raise crucial questions: Can the world support nearly 11 billion people before the end of the next century? Can human populations reach such concentrations without irretrievable damage to their living space?

OBJECTIVES

- to examine both the existing spatial pattern of human populations and the factors that have caused that pattern to assume such an irregular shape
- to observe present demographic trends and show how these vary among countries at different levels of development
- to predict the changes in the population pattern that the twenty-first century will bring if current trends persist
- to consider the implications of these evolving patterns, noting the problems they will likely pose for future generations

PRESENT DISTRIBUTION
OF HUMAN POPULATIONS

The spatial pattern of world population is exceedingly uneven, as Figure 4.1 shows. This has led some people to question the growing concern with overpopulation. They note that large numbers of human beings are concentrated in a few relatively small areas whereas vast expanses of the earth's surface remain only lightly occupied or entirely vacant. Why, they ask, should we not settle our surplus populations in these little-used areas? In this chapter we shall look at some of the reasons why the problem is not so simply solved. The existing pattern of world population is a product of the dynamic processes of natural increase and migration described in the previous chapter. Let us now see how these processes, working together through the many ages of human existence, have favored certain areas over others. What are the characteristics of those regions that have attracted large numbers of people and of those that have been avoided?

The second main task in this chapter is to learn where current population trends are likely to lead us. With the increasing restrictions on international migration, the future map of world populations will be shaped largely by differences among countries in their rates of natural increase. How will that map differ from today's, and what problems are present population trends likely to bring in future years?

The circumstances that have produced the present spatial distribution of population reflect the whole range of human requirements, desires, perceptions, and social and cultural interrelationships. At the most basic level, the physical environment has tended to limit the range of habitation, based upon the biological needs of human beings as organisms, as well as the physical opportunities for them to gain a livelihood—the needs of people as economic beings. Within this material framework many other influences have helped shape the pattern we see today. In Chapter 3 we noted the ways in which political organization and control, the policing and regulatory powers exercised

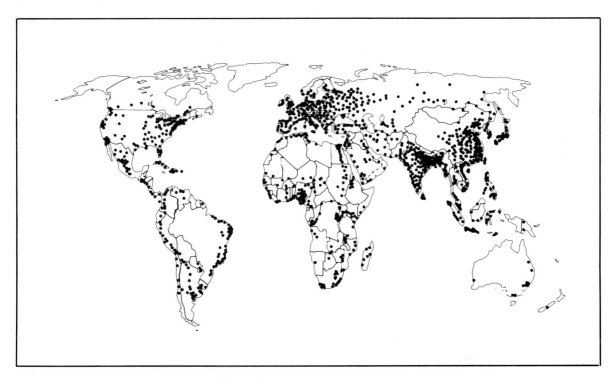

FIGURE 4.1 World population (1 dot = approximately 3 million people). Although this scale of representation can give only a general impression of the world pattern, the four major population nodes stand out clearly. The two largest concentrations are in East Asia, especially Eastern China and the southeastern coast of Japan, and in South Asia, where the main focus is upon the deltas of the Ganges and Brahmaputra rivers. Somewhat smaller, the European node reaches its peak in the lower courses of the Rhine and Thames. The smallest of the four nodes is in the northeastern United States and adjacent border areas of Canada. For more precise information on world population, see Figure 4.2 and Tables 4.1, 4.2, and 4.3.

by governments over their territories, may directly or indirectly affect migration and demography. Also influencing population patterns are the divisive or cohesive forces resulting from racial, linguistic, and religious affiliation, the traditions associated with marriage and the family, and other forms of group behavior.

The population patterns we see today, therefore, represent the cumulative effects of innumerable human actions in the long past, including those dictated by a technology and social organization different from that of today. Despite the many new developments of recent times, however, past patterns persist because of the limited mobility of human populations, especially at the global scale. As is true of most geographical phenomena, the scale of observation affects the kinds of comparisons that are possible—whether between continents, countries, or regions and localities within countries. The quality of population data also varies with scale, as well as from place to place.

Numbers of People: International Comparisons

The chief sources of population data are official records, especially those compiled by national governments and the United Nations. Some of this information is of doubtful reliability, however, particularly that relating to less-developed countries; for some states in Africa, Asia, and Latin America no dependable statistics exist at all. Interpreting data of such uncertain quality requires caution, all the more so when one is making temporal comparisons. Studies by

the United Nations have disclosed, for instance, that official censuses in parts of Africa have suffered from underenumeration and that the populations of some of these countries are much larger than had been suspected. Only in 1982 did the People's Republic of China, which contains nearly a quarter of all humanity, undertake its first real census; only rough estimates had hitherto been possible. Complicating comparisons of data over time are the many boundary changes of recent decades, such as that resulting from the separation of Bangladesh from Pakistan. Furthermore, measures of population characteristics and definitions of urbanization are not standardized internationally.

Comparative analyses thus require judgment and careful qualification. The problem is less acute for developed countries, which have fairly reliable data. To minimize data problems among Third World countries it is often desirable to aggregate information by continental groupings.

Population Size.   From Table 4.1 and Figure 4.2 it is apparent that the continents differ greatly in population size. Asia contains nearly three-fifths of the world's people, even when we exclude the former USSR, which in 1990 was the third most populous country. The most rapidly growing population, however, is that of Africa, which overtook Europe during the 1980s to become the second largest among the continents. With only 0.5 percent of the world's people, Oceania (Australia, New Zealand, and the islands of the South Pacific) has the smallest population of all the

TABLE 4.1

World distribution of population by region, 1990

Region	Population[a] (thousands)	Percent of World Population	Density (population per square kilometer)	Cropland[b]	
				Hectares per Person	Total Hectares (thousands)
World	5,292,178	100.0	39.5	0.278	1,473,590
Africa	647,518	12.2	21.4	0.286	185,033
Asia (excluding USSR)	3,108,476	58.7	112.7	0.145	451,219
Europe (excluding USSR)	497,741	9.4	102.2	0.280	139,535
Northern America[c]	275,880	5.2	14.3	0.855	235,925
Latin America[d]	448,096	8.5	21.8	0.400	179,341
Oceania	26,476	0.5	3.3	1.853	50,293
Former USSR[e]	287,991	5.4	12.9	0.806	232,244

Sources: United Nations: *World Population Prospects 1988.* Department of International Economic and Social Affairs, Population Studies No. 106 (New York: United Nations, 1989); Food and Agriculture Organization of the United Nations, *Production Yearbook 1987* (Rome, 1988).

[a] Projected.

[b] Cropland includes arable land and land in permanent crops.

[c] Northern America consists of Canada and the United States.

[d] Latin America includes all the lands south of the U.S. border: Mexico, Central America, the Caribbean, and South America.

[e] The USSR of 1990 broke into 15 independent states in 1991.

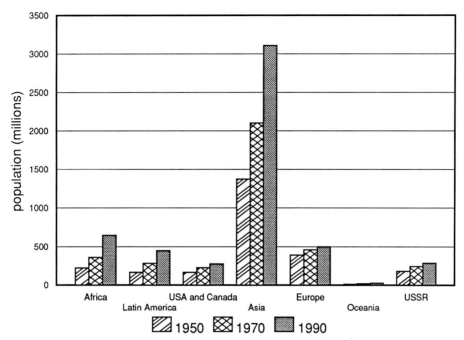

FIGURE 4.2   Regional shifts in world population 1950–1990. The major continental areas differ greatly in the numbers of people they contain, and the disparities among them have widened still further during the past four decades. Asia, which holds two of the world's largest population concentrations, has continued to increase its numbers. Also on the ascendancy is Africa, which in the 1980s passed Europe to take second place among the continents. Latin America, another growth area for Third World populations, is steadily gaining on Europe. Northern America (the United States and Canada) lags slightly behind fifth-place USSR. Oceania (Australia and New Zealand, plus the islands of the South Pacific) accounts for only 0.5 percent of the world's people. [*Source:* Data from *World Population Prospects 1988* (New York: United Nations, 1989).]

continental groupings. The former USSR appears separately in Table 4.1 because of its large land area, nearly 15 percent of the world total, because it is partly in Europe and partly in Asia, and because it did not break apart into 15 separate states until 1991.

In Table 4.2 the individual countries with the largest populations are listed in rank order. Altogether, 78.3 percent of the world's people live in these 25 nations. One in every five lives in China, and one in six lives in India. Note that 13 of the countries are Asian, not counting the former USSR. It is clear from Tables 4.1 and 4.2, however, that continental and country totals do not give an accurate impression of crowding. One reason for this is that the world's populous countries differ so greatly in areal extent (Table 4.2, column 3).

Population Density.   Differences among countries become still more obvious if we relate numbers of people to land area, to derive a measure of population density (Table 4.2, column 5). Thus, the former USSR

and the United States rank third and fourth, respectively, in population size, but the people in those two countries are spread over immense territories, resulting in low density figures. The simplest measure of density is that used in Table 4.2, namely, *arithmetic density,* which is the total number of people divided by the total land area. Some of the greatest densities occur in tiny city-states such as Monaco, with 15,316 persons per square kilometer. This is similarly true of those city-states occupying small islands, as, for example, Hong Kong (5,506 people per square kilometer) and Singapore (4,229 per square kilometer). Excluding such cases, as well as all island nations smaller than 10,000 km², we find that the 25 countries listed in Table 4.3 are the most densely populated in the world. Of these, Europe contributes seven, a number that has steadily dwindled in recent years as swelling Third World populations have crowded industrialized nations off the list. Less-developed countries that have risen in this ranking during the period are Bangladesh, Taiwan, South Korea, India, Sri Lanka, the Philip-

TABLE 4.2

Twenty-five countries with largest populations in 1989

Country (ranked according to size)	Population (thousands)	Area Square Kilometers (thousands)	Percent of World	Density (population per square kilometer)	Percent of World Population
1 China	1,104,275	9,573	6.4	115.4	21.1
2 India	835,812	3,166	2.1	264.0	16.0
3 Former USSR	287,800	22,403	14.9	12.8	5.5
4 United States	248,777	9,529	6.3	26.1	4.8
5 Indonesia	177,046	1,919	1.3	92.2	3.4
6 Brazil	147,404	8,512	5.7	17.3	2.8
7 Japan	123,120	378	0.3	325.7	2.4
8 Pakistan	118,820	880	0.6	135.0	2.3
9 Nigeria	115,973	924	0.6	125.5	2.2
10 Bangladesh	110,290	144	0.1	765.9	2.1
11 Mexico	84,275	1,958	1.3	43.0	1.6
12 Vietnam	64,747	332	0.2	195.0	1.2
13 West Germany	61,131	249	0.2	245.5	1.2
14 Philippines	59,906	300	0.2	199.7	1.1
15 Italy	57,436	301	0.2	190.8	1.1
16 United Kingdom	57,218	244	0.2	234.5	1.1
17 France	56,107	544	0.4	103.1	1.1
18 Turkey	55,541	779	0.5	71.3	1.1
19 Thailand	55,258	513	0.3	107.7	1.1
20 Iran	54,333	1,648	1.1	33.0	1.0
21 Egypt	51,748	998	0.7	51.9	1.0
22 Ethiopia	48,898	1,224	0.8	39.9	0.9
23 South Korea	42,380	99	0.1	428.1	0.8
24 Myanmar (Burma)	40,810	677	0.5	60.3	0.8
25 Spain	39,159	505	0.3	77.5	0.7
Total	4,098,264	67,799	45.2	60.4	78.3
World Total	5,234,000	150,157	100.0	34.9	100.0

Source: 1990 Britannica Book of the Year (Chicago: Encyclopaedia Britannica, 1990).

pines, Vietnam, North Korea, and Pakistan—all in East or South Asia—Rwanda and Burundi in East Africa, and El Salvador, Jamaica, Haiti, and the Dominican Republic in Latin America. Also appearing in Table 4.3 are two small neighbors at the eastern end of the Mediterranean, Lebanon and Israel. Note that 8 of the 25 densest populations belong to island nations: Taiwan, Japan, Sri Lanka, the United Kingdom, Jamaica, Haiti, the Philippines, and the Dominican Republic.

The Food and Agriculture Organization (FAO) of the United Nations has estimated the proportion of land available for crops, that is, *arable* land, in each of the major regions. From this information it is possible to derive a measure of *physiological density,* which relates the size of a population to amount of cropland (arable land and permanent crops) available for its support. Table 4.1 lists this information for each of the continental areas and for the world as a whole. Note that in 1987 the average person in the world could draw upon only one-quarter of a hectare (two-thirds of

an acre) of cropland (column 5 in Table 4.1); 15 years earlier the amount available per person had been 0.4 hectares (one acre). A majority of the world's people live in areas having less than the world average of one-quarter hectare. The number of hectares per person has declined throughout the Third World; in Asia it is now only 0.145 ha. Although Europe as a whole has a larger ratio of cropland to total land area than any other continent, its population densities are so great that the average European can draw upon only 0.28 ha.

Physiological density is only a rough measure, however, for it does not take into account the variable quality of cropland. Although the per capita supply of cropland in Africa is slightly above the world average, the productivity of the land is generally much below that of North America or Europe. A large part of Latin America's cropland is of poor quality also. Similarly misleading is the large amount of cropland per person shown for Oceania, a sparsely populated region with only 1.4 percent of the world's total cropland.

TABLE 4.3

Most densely populated countries, 1989.

Country (ranked according to density)	Density (population per square kilometer)	Area (thousands square kilometers)
1 Bangladesh[a]	765.9	144
2 Taiwan	556.2	36
3 South Korea[a]	428.1	99
4 The Netherlands	354.6	42
5 Japan[a]	325.7	378
6 Belgium	323.7	31
7 Lebanon	283.2	10
8 Rwanda	265.4	26
9 India[a]	264.0	3166
10 Sri Lanka	256.7	66
11 West Germany[a]	245.8	249
12 El Salvador	244.2	21
13 United Kingdom[a]	234.4	244
14 Israel	220.4	21
15 Jamaica	216.2	11
16 Haiti	201.5	27
17 Philippines[a]	199.7	300
18 Vietnam[a]	195.2	332
19 Italy[a]	190.6	301
20 Burundi	189.9	28
21 North Korea	183.2	122
22 Switzerland	162.0	41
23 East Germany	153.4	108
24 Dominican Republic	144.7	48
25 Pakistan[a]	135.1	880

Source: 1990 Britannica Book of the Year (Chicago: Encyclopaedia Britannica, 1990).

Note: Includes only those countries with areas of more than 10,000 sq km.

[a] Also appears on list of countries with largest populations, Table 4.2.

Limits of Habitation.   Population density figures for entire continents, or even countries, can convey only limited information, however. As the population map (Figure 4.1) demonstrates, densities are rarely consistent throughout national territories, and many major population concentrations cross national boundaries. Let us explore the reasons why certain areas are more heavily occupied than others.

For the most part, the pattern of world population we see today took form at a time when human beings gained their livelihood directly from the land. It is not surprising, therefore, that those parts of the earth's land surface with little or no human habitation—about three-fifths of the total—are physically unsuited to agriculture. Figure 4.3 provides a generalized view of those regions that are too dry, too wet, too cold, or too mountainous for the ordinary forms of cultivation. In some cases two or more of these negative conditions coincide in a particular area. Note, however, that few of the major world regions are entirely devoid of human beings. Within some broad nonarable areas are localities that have special conditions permitting the practice of agriculture—desert oases, for example. Some areas that lack farmland contain nonagricultural settlements, located near valuable mineral deposits, biotic resources (such as forest products), recreational facilities, or other special assets.

Excessive aridity virtually excludes farming from large portions of the world. The amount of moisture available to crops varies according to the evaporation rate in an area. At least 10 inches of annual rainfall are usually required in the middle latitudes, but 30 inches or more may be needed in the tropics to replace evaporation losses. Much of the earth's surface is either desert (less than 10 inches of rain per year) or steppe land (between 10 and 20 or 30 inches) and thus mostly unsuited to agriculture. Within such dry lands, however, exceptional circumstances may permit irrigated agriculture in certain favored localities. For example, "exotic" rivers such as the Nile or the Colorado, with sources in regions of high rainfall, pass through arid lands where their waters may support large agricultural populations. In some desert areas, oases grow up around local springs or wells drawing upon deep underground veins of water. Vast expanses of the Sahara and other major deserts, however, are either remote from water supplies or lack true soils to permit agriculture on their barren sandy or rocky surfaces. Arid regions with deposits of valuable minerals such as petroleum, nitrates, or metallic ores may attract some human habitation, but such activities normally require only small numbers of workers and rarely affect the general population pattern to an important degree.

On the other hand, some large regions support only small populations because they receive too much rainfall. The great equatorial basins of the Amazon and Congo rivers support a dense rain forest vegetation, leading some people to believe that these lightly populated areas could become productive agricultural lands suitable for resettlement of the world's surplus millions. Scientific evidence, however, does not support this idea, and the catastrophic results of Brazil's recent large-scale attempts to develop Amazonia cast further doubt on it. The basic problem is the inherently low quality of tropical rain forest soils. Heavy rains throughout the year leach the soluble mineral plant food elements out of the soil and carry these to depths beyond the reach of ordinary shallow-rooted food plants. The deceptively lush growth of native trees results from the ability of these forest giants to send their taproots deep into underground deposits of nutrients. Most areas with tropical rain forest climates are thus lightly settled; Amazonia, for instance, supports

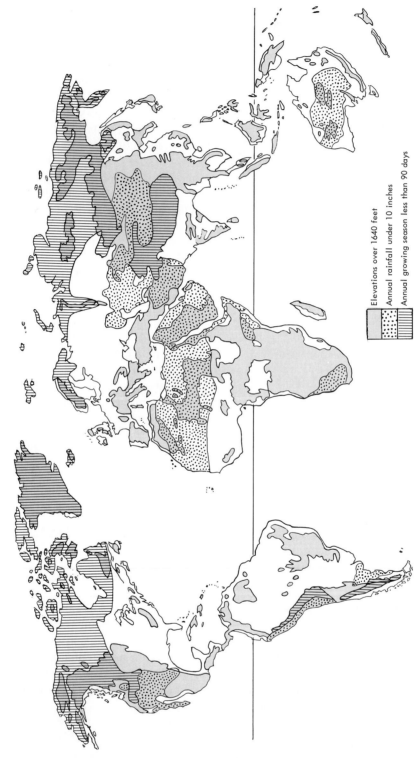

FIGURE 4.3 Limits of agricultural production. Much of the earth's land surface is too mountainous or too dry or has too short a growing season to support the usual forms of agriculture.

Elevations over 1640 feet

Annual rainfall under 10 inches

Annual growing season less than 90 days

only one person per square kilometer. Important exceptions are to be found in certain areas where local soil conditions permit successful farming despite heavy rainfall and rapid leaching. Thus, the Indonesian island of Java is able to support some of the world's highest rural population densities on its rich soils, which are periodically renewed by volcanic deposition. In some other places, sizable numbers of people obtain a livelihood from the cultivation of tropical tree crops such as rubber, bananas, and cacao.

Possibly the most forbidding of all climatic features is excessive cold. Ice and snow permanently cover great areas near the poles and on the higher mountains. Adjacent to the polar sheets are even greater expanses where low temperatures and short growing seasons prevent ordinary agriculture. Because most food plants require at least three months without frost to reach maturity, the limit of the 90-day growing season usually represents the poleward boundary of agricultural production (Figure 4.3). The colder climates, however, do support some human habitation: Exploitation of minerals employs limited numbers in certain favored localities, fishing provides a livelihood along the coasts of the northern continents, and forest products support scattered populations along the southern margins where temperatures are high enough for tree growth.

Farming is impossible in those mountainous areas with slopes too steep for soil to cling. The higher mountains are also too cold for ordinary crops because of the tendency for temperatures to drop with increasing elevation. In the middle and upper latitudes, forestry is confined to the lower slopes because temperatures at higher elevations are too low for trees to grow. Nearer the equator, however, the moderate temperatures and gentler slopes of highland basins provide ideal farming conditions; in tropical America these are the preferred places for human habitation (compare Figure 4.1 with Figure 4.3).

Grazing is often possible in areas that are too dry or cold for agriculture. With their sparse natural covering of grasses and herbaceous plants, the steppe lands are much used for this purpose, as are the basins and upper slopes of some mountainous regions. Reindeer herding takes place even in the far north of Eurasia and Alaska. Such lands have a meager carrying capacity for grazing animals, however, and they therefore support only scattered human populations.

Although such extreme climatic conditions tend to limit the spread of human beings into the more hostile areas, physical capabilities of the land do not bear a perfect relationship to the patterns of population density elsewhere. One important influence is length of settlement. In those parts of Asia and the Middle East where people have lived continuously since the emergence of human life on earth, rural overcrowding has become severe despite the submarginal quality of much of the land and poor agricultural conditions generally. In these places the steady growth of population over a very long time has diminished the capacity of the land to support human life. By contrast, farmlands of superior quality in the more recently settled Americas have far smaller population densities.

A further reason why maps of population density do not correspond perfectly with those of physical conditions is the governmental limits placed on immigration. Thus, sparsely settled Australia long excluded peoples seeking to migrate from the populous lands of nearby southern Asia.

Modern technology has further modified the influence of physical factors on settlement patterns. Today, if human beings have a compelling reason to live in an inhospitable area, they manage to create their own artificial environments. Heating, air conditioning, desalinization of water, and drainage are some of the costly measures that technology offers for residents of otherwise inhospitable surroundings. Perhaps the ultimate artificial environments are those found in great cities. These places develop an economic momentum of their own, attracting and providing for their populations regardless of the inherent physical characteristics of the land on which they are built.

The Empty Areas. Having noted the factors that limit human habitation, we may now examine some of those regions that have few people (Figures 4.1 and 4.3). One almost empty area is the enormous arctic region of North America, which includes northern Alaska, Canada, and Greenland. Also sparsely settled are the dry lands of western North America. Two virtually unpopulated regions in South America are the tropical rain forests of Amazonia and the great deserts of the south: the Atacama of Chile and Peru and the Patagonian region of Argentina. Africa has three prominent empty areas: the vast Sahara Desert in the north, the tropical rain forests of equatorial Africa, and the Kalahari and Namib deserts of the south. Even Eurasia, the most populous of continents, has two extensive negative areas, the great polar fringes of Russia and Scandinavia, and the deserts of central Asia and the adjacent highlands. Of all the inhabited continents, Australia, with its "dead heart," has the largest proportion of unoccupied land. Antarctica, which is covered by a huge ice sheet up to 2 miles thick, has no permanent human habitation at all.

The Major Population Nodes.   Contrasting with these empty areas are four great population nodes, which dominate the world population map. The three largest, all in Eurasia, have at least half a billion people each; together they comprise more than three-fifths of humanity. Leading them all, the *East Asian* node includes Japan, Korea, and eastern China. Each of these areas has a middle-latitude location with generally favorable climatic conditions for agriculture. The inhabitants of this node are particularly concentrated within the large river floodplains and deltas on the Chinese mainland and the densely packed coastal plains and river valleys of mountainous Japan and Korea. As the birthplace of one of the principal human races, this region has an ancient history of habitation. Further contributing to the high population densities here are religious and cultural traditions that favor large families. Although intensive agriculture supports high rural densities, a large and efficient industrial economy enables Japan to sustain a population more than half that of the United States and to do so on a group of mountainous islands having a combined area less than that of Montana.

Second in size is the *South Asian* node, which includes most of India, Pakistan, and Bangladesh, in addition to the island of Sri Lanka (formerly Ceylon) and parts of Burma. Here the greatest population densities are in areas with a heavy monsoon rainfall. The only limit on the growing season is the availability of water, as warm temperatures prevail 12 months of the year. The largest cities and highest rural densities are found in the river deltas and floodplains and along the coastal plains, but even the drier interior of the Indian peninsula bears large numbers of people. Despite the generally poor quality of the soil—exhausted after several millennia of continuous use—agriculture remains the chief life support. High birth rates, however, continually strain food supplies.

Europe and the western Soviet Union constitute the third great population node. This region enjoys one of the most reliable of all agricultural climates, especially in its western portions. With moderate temperatures, a dependable supply of rainfall well distributed throughout the year (except along the Mediterranean), and a long growing season, Europe produces some of the world's best crop yields. Of all the continents, Europe also has the largest proportion of its land area devoted to agriculture. Despite their productivity, however, Western Europe's farms employ only a small proportion of the labor force. Relatively few people are engaged in exploiting Europe's ample mineral and biotic resources; most are employed in manufacturing and service activities; hence, the high degree of urbanization. Like the other population nodes of Eurasia, this is a region of long settlement, dating at least to the end of the last Ice Age.

The population node of *Eastern North America,* large as it is, has only a fraction of the people contained in each of the three major Eurasian concentrations. This region includes the "megalopolis" of the Middle Atlantic seaboard of the United States with its westward extension in the Great Lakes region of the Middle West and southern Ontario and Quebec, together with the associated rural populations of this important farming area. Despite a temperate climate, the growing seasons are decidedly shorter here than in most parts of the other three population nodes. Eastern North America also has important natural resources, including coal, iron ore, natural gas and oil, and a variety of other raw materials. Unlike the other three population nodes, this region was settled fairly recently and experienced rapid growth mainly through immigration and natural increase during its formative period. As in Western Europe, agriculture in Eastern North America is efficient and productive but occupies only a small percentage of the labor force.

Lesser Population Clusters.   In addition to these major concentrations, at least 14 smaller population clusters appear on the world map. One is the *Los Angeles–Central Valley–San Francisco* area of California, until recently the fastest-growing concentration in the United States. The magnificent scenery and benign climate of this area have been prime attractions, but shortages of water and other environmental and economic problems threaten its continued growth. Another small cluster includes the *Vancouver* and *Puget Sound–Fraser River* areas of the Pacific Northwest, likewise a region of pleasant physical surroundings.

Mexico City and adjacent parts of the central plateau offer some of the most attractive climatic conditions in Mexico. Although agriculture is limited, this area contains a large part of the country's population and has become the center of a growing industrial district. The valleys of the *Central American highlands* contain most of the population of the isthmian region. Although widely separated from each other, the *islands of the Caribbean* are among the most densely populated areas of the Western Hemisphere.

The rapidly increasing population of South America is mainly concentrated at various points along the continental margins. Largest of these clusters is the *Central Plateau and Northeast Coast of Brazil,* the leading industrial area of Latin America and one of its principal agricultural districts as well, despite the difficult problems of supporting a swelling population. The *Rio de la Plata* district is the heart of Argentina's and Uruguay's populations; it contains most of the industry and is the focus of commercial agriculture. *Middle Chile,* another area of pleasant climatic conditions and productive agriculture, contains the majority of that country's people. The *Highland Basins of the Northern Andes,* extending from La Paz, Bolivia, northward through Peru, Ecuador, Colombia, and Venezuela, provide an attractive environment similar to that of the Central American highlands.

One of the most unusual population concentrations occupies the *Valley of the Lower Nile River* in North Africa. Here some of the highest rural densities in the world are compressed within the narrow confines of the irrigated floodplain and delta of an exotic stream that flows from the humid East African highlands through one of the driest of deserts (less than 1 inch of rainfall per year). The *Gulf of Guinea* coast of West Africa supports large numbers of people, especially in Ghana and Nigeria, where subsistence agriculture is the main occupation. In *East Central Africa,* some of the world's highest fertility rates are producing high levels of population growth despite widespread disease and frequent intertribal conflicts. Another concentration of people in that continent is the *Republic of South Africa.* The coastal belt of this country has a pleasant Mediterranean-type climate and its interior is rich in valuable minerals, including gold, diamonds, coal, and iron. The final population node includes *Eastern Australia and New Zealand.* Australia's people live mainly along the southeast coastal lowland, which, by contrast with the arid center and west, receives adequate rainfall, has moderate temperatures, and offers most of the country's agricultural potential.

Intracountry Variations

Regional Concentrations. As we have seen, the national population figures for most countries obscure large internal variations in density. Even a country as small as Belgium, with an overall density of 324 persons per square kilometer, has its lightly populated Ardennes uplands. Though the United Kingdom as a whole has a high density, several regions, such as central Wales, the Pennine uplands, and the Scottish Highlands, have few people. Even greater differences occur in Brazil, where the large and economically active population of the São Paulo–Rio de Janeiro region and the crowded rural northeast contrast markedly with the virtually empty Amazonian north. Likewise, the densely peopled Toronto–Golden Horseshoe district of Canada is entirely different from the nearly vacant Arctic lands of the Canadian north.

Some of the greatest regional variations are in China. Despite a huge population of 1104 million, Chi-

na's overall density is only 115 persons per square kilometer. This is lower than the densities of most of its neighbors in eastern and southern Asia and much less than those of Western Europe. China's population is concentrated mainly in the coastal and central provinces, where most of the cultivated land is found. The Chengtu Plain in Szechwan Province supports exceedingly high rural population densities, whereas great areas in the arid west remain nearly unpeopled.

Why does the Chinese population remain so unevenly distributed after more than 40 centuries? One reason is the extreme variation in the physical capabilities of the land. Wide differences in soils, temperatures, and rainfall have profoundly influenced the locational choices of this predominantly agricultural people. Even where underused agricultural opportunities seem to exist, however, the Chinese have been unusually reluctant to move, owing to the influence of ancestor worship, of traditionally strong ties to family and village, and of regional language differences that hamper communication. Furthermore, extreme poverty has been endemic in China for centuries. Lacking savings, being vulnerable to a variety of natural calamities, and having little assurance of bettering themselves elsewhere, the Chinese have preserved a remarkably stable population pattern. Communist control appears to have had little overall effect in redistributing population among provinces, although important shifts have occurred locally.

Urbanization. The ultimate population concentration, of course, is in cities. One of the notable events of recent decades has been the rush of people from farms to cities and from smaller urban places to larger ones. By 1989, 77 percent of the people in the world's most industrialized countries lived in urban places, as opposed to 71 percent in 1965.

Gregariousness among human beings appears to be instinctive: The survival of early peoples depended upon their living close to others of their kind. Throughout history, people have established cities for defense as well as for the various social and economic advantages of cooperative efforts. Both commerce and industry enjoy numerous savings by locating within urban areas, as later chapters will show. Among their other important roles, cities also serve as centers for administrative control, education, and culture, and as points of convergence for transportation routes.

Nevertheless, the very large city is a phenomenon of modern times; indeed, the word "civilization" is derived from the Latin term for city. Primitive human activities provided an insufficient surplus of food to support a large non-food-producing population. Subsistence gathering, hunting and fishing, herding, and agriculture supply barely enough food for tribal members and are very extensive in their use of land; migratory peoples may require five square kilometers or more to feed each individual. Although the well-organized Romans were able to mobilize production to support sizable urban populations, this capacity was lost in Europe when the Roman legions vanished. As Marco Polo discovered, however, the Chinese were able to maintain large cities throughout the period when medieval Europe's urban centers remained small.

Modern urban growth resulted from three essential developments. The first was the agricultural revolution of the late eighteenth century, which, for the first time, allowed European farms to feed a large non-agricultural population. Farm yields increased because of improved cultivation methods, new crops, scientific breeding of both plants and animals, consolidation of

land holdings, and better communications and transportation. Transmitted across the Atlantic, the agricultural revolution brought similar results to the United States, where agricultural employment steadily declined as a percentage of the total labor force. In 1820, farm labor represented 72 percent of the gainfully employed, but by 1900 this figure had dropped to 37 percent; in 1980, only 2.6 percent of the labor force worked on farms, where they grew enough food not only to support the other 97.4 percent of the population but also great quantities for export overseas.

Beginning about the same time, the Industrial Revolution brought the factory system, which displaced the earlier cottage industry and hastened the growth of large concentrations of people. Simultaneously, the transportation revolution permitted cheap, fast, and dependable distribution of food, industrial raw materials, and other goods required by an

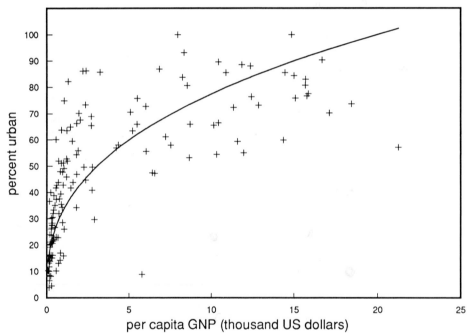

FIGURE 4.4   Relationship between urbanization and per capita gross national product ($R^2 = 0.614$). Although the correlation is fairly close for nations at the lower end of the developmental scale, it is less strong for the more-advanced economies, which differ considerably in their degree of urbanization. A number of European states are not as urbanized as their per capita GNPs would suggest, notably the Alpine lands of Switzerland and Austria and the southern countries of Italy, Portugal, and Greece. Also falling below the regression line are the former USSR and most of Eastern Europe. By contrast, the United Kingdom and The Netherlands are well above the line. Unusually high levels of urbanization are likewise found in Australia, New Zealand, and the southern-cone countries of South America. Predictably, the city-states of Singapore and Hong Kong appear at the very top of the diagram. [*Source:* Data from *1990 Britannica Book of the Year* (Chicago: Encyclopaedia Britannica, 1990).]

expanding urban population. Meanwhile, these three developments helped expand the commercial hinterlands that acted as markets for the goods and services of the growing urban centers.

The ultimate result of the agricultural, industrial, and transportation revolutions has been the creation of great metropolises. The population of metropolitan London increased eightfold during the most recent century and a half, reaching 10.6 million people in 1990. During that same period, New York's metropolitan area attained a population of 15.7 million. Eclipsing New York's population today are Tokyo (20.5 million) and two Third World cities: Mexico City (19.4 million) and São Paulo (18.4 million).

The degree of urbanization in a country usually corresponds to its level of economic development: In general, the most urbanized countries also have the highest per capita gross national products (see Figures 4.4 and 4.5). Studies have shown that those countries ranking highest in urbanization also tend to rank highest on indices of transportation, communications, energy production and consumption, national and per capita incomes, and foreign trade. In developed countries, urban pursuits—manufacturing and the services—employ most workers, including a majority of those actually residing in rural areas.

As Figure 4.4 shows, however, several developed countries are exceptions to this general relationship. Thus, among the richer industrialized countries, a few are less urbanized than their per capita GNPs would suggest. Switzerland, for example, is only 57 percent urbanized and Finland is only 60 percent urban. On the other hand, not counting such city-states as Singapore and Hong Kong, one of the most urbanized of all is Australia, with an urban population of 86 percent—hardly the picture of a nation of sheep growers and wheat farmers.

Within countries the degree of urbanization varies from one region to another. Urban development in the United States has produced dense concentrations of cities along each coast and on the shores of the Great Lakes. Elsewhere in the country, urban centers tend to be smaller and more scattered. In the lightly settled, largely rural plains and Rocky Mountain states, most cities exist in semi-isolation, although several urban centers in the intermontane west are growing very rapidly at present.

The typically lower levels of urbanization in less-developed countries stem mainly from their greater dependence upon agricultural employment. Even many of those persons living in cities and towns go daily into the countryside to work in the fields. Some

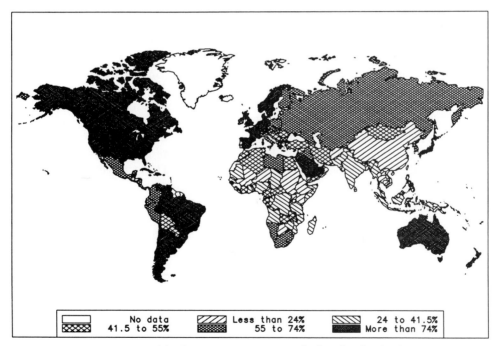

FIGURE 4.5 World urbanization. Exceptionally low levels of urbanization are seen in Southeast Asia and in the Himalayan kingdoms. A second region that is little urbanized is sub-Saharan Africa. In much of the Third World, however, the movement to the cities is accelerating, especially in Latin America and the Middle East. [*Source:* See Figure 4.4.]

of the lowest percentages of urbanization are in Asia, especially such remote, mountainous countries as Bhutan and Nepal, which have only 4 percent and 6 percent urbanization, respectively. Even in a country as large as Bangladesh, only 16 percent of the people live in cities. More striking yet is China, where 21 percent of a total population of 1.1 billion live in urban places. In India, 24 percent of the nation's 836 million people are urban. Levels of urbanization are likewise exceedingly low in sub-Saharan Africa; for example, Burundi (8 percent), Rwanda (5 percent), Mozambique (13 percent), and Tanzania (14 percent). On the other hand, in the semi-industrialized Republic of South Africa 56 percent of the population is urban.

Urbanization has proceeded much further in Latin America than in Africa or in South and East Asia. Several of the more prosperous countries of South America have now attained higher levels of urbanization than found in North America or most of Europe. Venezuela, Uruguay, Argentina, and Chile all have well over 80 percent of their people in urban places, and Mexico and Brazil are two-thirds urban. Much lower levels prevail, however, in some Andean countries, in most of the Caribbean, and in parts of Central America.

Another Third World area that is substantially urbanized is the Middle East (Figure 4.5). Contrary to the usual image of the Islamic world, the Middle East is a region of large cities. Moreover, the exceptionally high rates of natural increase prevalent among urban-dwelling Middle Easterners are further swelling the populations of those centers.

Indeed, despite the mainly rural character of most lower-income countries, some of the world's great cities are in less-developed lands. Only the most backward societies lack cities altogether. Typically, a less-developed country has only one truly large city and this dwarfs all other urban places in the land. For instance, Ethiopia's capital, Addis Ababa, is 5 times as large as second-place Asmara; Guatemala City, capital of Guatemala, is 12 times the size of Quetzaltenango; Costa Rica's capital, San José, is 20 times Limón; and the capital of Thailand, Bangkok, is 27 times Nakhon Ratchasima.

In addition to the usual commercial functions of a large urban place, the primate city of a less-developed land dominates the economically active parts of the country and is the focus of national political, social, and cultural life. In those countries at the lower end of the developmental scale, however, the functions of their principal cities tend to be limited in scope. Manufacturing, transportation, and communications are usually poorly developed, except insofar as

they link demands of the developed world to the resources of the primate cities' hinterlands.

FUTURE POPULATIONS

Predictions

The spatial patterns of human population we have been describing are even now undergoing changes that will make tomorrow's world population map look very different from today's. Working to effect these changes are the dynamic forces discussed in the previous chapter: migration and differential population growth. With international migration now largely curtailed, however, the evolving population map increasingly reflects spatial variations in fertility and mortality rates. The kinds of demographic change now occurring create innumerable problems for the present and threaten even graver ones for the future.

If we are to devise strategies to cope with such problems, we must have forecasts of future population growth that are sufficiently reliable to pinpoint the trouble spots and to suggest the amount of potential danger. In the past, population forecasting was notoriously poor; most earlier projections greatly underestimated the rates at which growth was to occur. Thus, in 1949 Colin Clark forecast a world population of 3.5 billion by 1990, a figure that was exceeded before 1970. The main reason for such errors was the failure of demographers to anticipate the important declines in mortality and increases in life expectancy that advances in medical technology and the provision of public health care would bring. Today's forecasts have become more reliable, as demographers sharpen their analytical tools and receive better information. The 1980–81 series of censuses around the world tended to confirm the improved quality of United Nations projections. These projections benefited from much improved data on fertility and mortality, especially from larger countries, such as China, India, Bangladesh, and Indonesia. Furthermore, the growth rate of world population seemed to be easing, thereby making demographic trends somewhat more predictable and reducing the range of forecasting error.

By the end of the 1980s, however, the euphoria that some population experts had begun to feel concerning future growth trends was shaken by indications that the latest projections had been overly optimistic. Furthermore, no forecast can allow for the unexpected: catastrophes such as global wars, massive famines, or the spread of AIDS, or unanticipated developments in technology or social organization that

reduce birth rates, or medical breakthroughs that increase longevity.

The World in the Twenty-first Century

Based upon existing evidence, the United Nations
Population Division has concluded that the decade of
the 1990s will be a crucial period for the future of
world population. We appear to be at a turning point.
The directions that trends take in this decade will determine the shape of things in the first century of the
new millennium.

The U.N. assessment of information at hand suggests that population growth rates will follow the paths
shown in Figure 4.6. The steep rise in growth rates for
the world as a whole during the 1950s resulted from a
sharp drop in mortality, accompanied by only a slight

retreat in the birth rate. World population reached a
peak growth rate of 2.06 percent at the end of 1960s
then receded during the 1980s to a plateau of about
1.73 percent in the 1980s. The United Nations predicts
that the world rate will resume its decline in the 1990s
and will continue to slide in the new century.

The effects that these growth-rate changes have
had on the numbers of people in the world are apparent from Figure 4.7. Having risen from only 2.3 billion
people in 1940, global population had reached 5.3 billion by 1990 and, according the United Nations, will
arrive at the 6 billion mark in 1997. In that same year,
the United Nations predicts, annual additions to world
numbers will peak at 97 million people. This means
that during each year of this decade, the world will be
adding the equivalent of Mexico to its total population.

Note that this peak year for increases to total

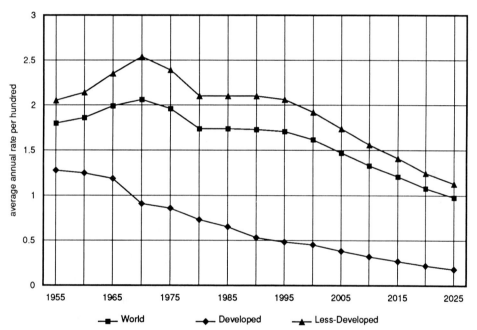

FIGURE 4.6   Population growth rates, 1950–1985 projected to A.D. 2025,
for the world and developed and less-developed regions (5-year averages).
The growth rate for the world as a whole rose steeply during the 1950s and
early 1960s, owing mainly to declining death rates. At the end of the 1960s
the world rate peaked at an annual rate of 2.06 percent then fell sharply for
a time, misleading population forecasters concerning true underlying
trends. The United Nations expects the world rate to resume its decline in
the 1990s. The most significant influences on these world trends come
from the Third World, where growth rates have yielded only reluctantly
to downward pressures. Population growth rates for the more-developed
regions, already low by the 1950s, have maintained a consistent downward trend. U.N. experts expect a rate of only 0.18 percent for this group
by A.D. 2025, a level consistent with a shrinking population. [*Source:* Data
from United Nations, *World Population Prospects 1988* (New York: United
Nations, 1989).]

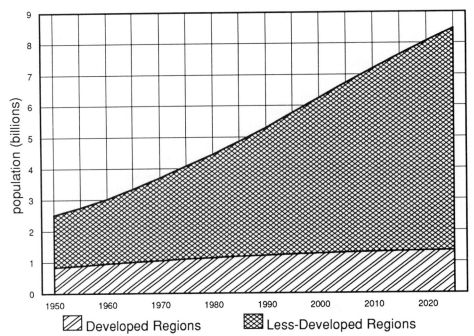

FIGURE 4.7   Population of the world and developed and less-developed regions, 1950–1985, projected to A.D. 2025. The slope of the curve for total world population continued to rise more steeply until the 1990s. Thereafter, based upon the growth rate trends shown in Figure 4.6, it is expected to slow its ascent. According to optimistic U.N. projections, total world population should level off during the latter part of the twenty-first century. Note that by far the greater share of the additions to total world population come from the less-developed regions. Populations in the more-developed regions are scarcely growing at this time and will likely begin to shrink in the coming century. [*Source:* Data from United Nations, *World Population Prospects 1988* (New York: United Nations, 1989).]

world population, 1997, follows by almost exactly three decades the period during which the world growth *rate* had peaked. This illustrates the principle of *population momentum*, which refers to the propensity of a previously increasing population to continue expanding for a generation or more after growth rates have fallen. This is a natural consequence of the youthfulness of a rapidly growing population.

The numbers now anticipated for the year A.D. 2025 (Figure 4.7) are higher than those previously projected by the United Nations during the mid-1980s. The excessive optimism underlying those earlier projections was based upon an apparent easing of population growth rates everywhere except Africa and parts of South Asia. Most of all, forecasters were lulled by a decline occurring in China's growth rate at that time owing to a government policy that severely restricted family size. Obviously, any event affecting China's population—more than one-fifth of the world's people—is of great importance to demographers.

The population division offers several explana-

tions for the overshooting of its earlier population forecasts. One source of the increased numbers has been an unforeseen rise in the Chinese birth rate since 1985. An even larger portion of the unexpected increase, however, comes from South Asia. Fertility rates, which had earlier shown promise of lessening in that heavily populated region, have declined but little during the past decade. Death rates, on the other hand, have dropped even faster than anticipated. Together, China and India account for 37 percent of total world population; hence, any demographic events in those lands have exaggerated impacts on global trends.

These developments have forced the United Nations to reassess its projections (see Figure 4.7). The expectation now is for world population to reach 6251 million by the end of this century, an extra 129 million above earlier forecasts—equivalent to adding another Japan to the total. Likewise, the newly projected total for A.D. 2025 is 8467 million, 260 million above the previous figure.

The steeply rising curves in Figures 4.6 and 4.7

during the first decades following World War II thus appear to confirm Malthus's ominous prediction of exponential population growth. The tendency in subsequent years for growth to subside, however, suggests that ultimately the growth curve will assume the characteristic S-shape of logistic growth, something Malthus did not foresee.

Projecting these trends still further, United Nations demographers expect the world as a whole to attain zero population growth (ZPG) toward the end of the twenty-first century. In 1984 the United Nations confidently projected an eventual total of 10.2 billion by that time; in 1988 it revised that estimate to 11.3 billion. This is the U.N. ''medium,'' or ''most likely,'' figure. Note, however, that the United Nations still bases its projections on optimistic assumptions, in particular the notion that fertility rates in Africa, Asia, and Latin America will drop by one-third within the next 30 to 40 years. This must be considered more a hope than a firmly grounded expectation.

According to the latest U.N. scenario, the world as a whole would reach ZPG by the end of the twenty-first century, but the various world regions would attain that level at different times (Figure 4.6). Since 1950 the rate of population growth in the more-developed regions has fallen from 1.3 percent to only 0.5 percent and is expected to reach zero soon after A.D. 2025. By contrast, the growth rate of less-developed populations, after achieving a high of 2.5 percent at the end of the 1960s, is still 2.1 percent and giving ground only grudgingly. Whether the latter will attain ZPG by the year 2100 is problematical. A select group of more prosperous less-developed countries, however, will likely have stationary populations much sooner than the rest.

As a result of these diverging trends, the share of world population accounted for by each of the two major categories of countries is changing (Figure 4.7). The more-developed regions contained one-third of the total in 1950 but only a quarter by 1990, and this proportion is expected to fall to one-fifth by A.D. 2025. The magnitude of these predicted population shifts is unprecedented and holds important implications for the future of the human race.

The United Nations bases its projections on a number of demographic trends, reflected in the contrasting age-sex structures of populations in more-developed and less-developed countries. Sweden and Kenya exemplify these two groups. With only 17 percent of its people below the age of 15 and more than 18 percent 65 years and older, Sweden has the typical old-age distribution of a mature population (Figure 4.8a). Kenya, on the other hand, has much higher levels of fertility and mortality and hence a very young

population (Figure 4.8b). More than 51 percent of its inhabitants are under 15 and only 2 percent are 65 or older.

Reinforcing the growth effects of a youthful population, the inhabitants of less-developed countries are living much longer than they did a few years ago (Figure 4.9). In 1950 the life expectancy at birth of people in less-developed regions was only 41 years; by 1985 it had risen to 57.6 years, and by A.D. 2025 it is expected to reach 70.4 years. The corresponding figures for people in developed regions are 65.7 years in 1950, 72.3 in 1985, and 78.7 in 2025. Thus the gap between the two regions is quickly closing, from a difference of 24.7 years in 1950 to a mere 8.3 years in 2025.

It is apparent, therefore, that most of the population growth of the next 100 years will be in less-developed areas. Growth has already diminished in Europe, North America, and Russia, and it has begun to slow in East Asia (Figure 4.10). Latin American growth is easing somewhat also. Elsewhere, the expansion continues little abated. The region that is contributing the largest absolute numbers to world population is Southern and Southwestern Asia, but Africa is the area with the most rapidly climbing population.

Another way of viewing the effects of different growth rates on future population distributions is to compare doubling times—the number of years it will take for populations to grow to twice their present sizes. Note from the map (Figure 4.11) that if current growth rates continue, many countries in Africa and the Muslim Middle East will have doubled their populations within 22 years or less. Most of the other lands in these two regions, along with nearly all of South Asia, will have accomplished this within 22 to 35 years. Contrast these with Western Europe, where most populations will require as much as 700 years to double; indeed, some have already begun to shrink. Next, let us examine more closely the growth trends and their effects in major world areas.

The More-Developed Regions

With low birth rates closely balanced by low death rates, the more-developed regions are classified as Type 5 countries according to the U.N. system (see Figure 3.8, Chapter 3). Fertility rates (*total fertility* is the average number of children born by a group of women in the childbearing ages if they experienced no mortality) in these regions have declined steadily since 1950 and are now below replacement levels. This trend is a consequence of circumstances that discourage having children: high incomes, urbanization, high levels of female education, large numbers of women in the work force, postponement of marriage, wide-

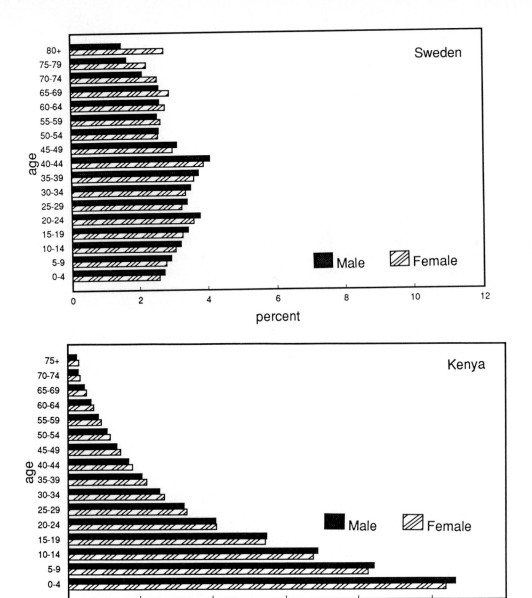

FIGURE 4.8 Contrasting age-sex structures of a more-developed and a less-developed country, Sweden and Kenya. Sweden's mature population, with a fairly even distribution of people in all age groups, forms the tubular-shaped structure typical of older industrialized countries. The diagram for Kenya forms the broad-based triangle of a rapidly growing population common among countries at lower levels of development. More than half of Kenya's population is under 15 years of age, and each new cohort of children is larger than the one preceding it. Because few Kenyans live to old age, the cohorts at higher age levels are severely diminished in size. Note also the differences between the two populations in their sex ratios (the proportion of males to females) at increasing age levels. As is usual for all human beings, males in both countries outnumber females during the early years, but the higher mortality of males causes the ratio to fall in later years. In Sweden's case, however, the excess of males over females continues until their late fifties, owing to superior medical care. After that, the proportion of females steadily increases until, beyond age 80, it constitutes half of the population. The decline in Kenya's sex ratio begins at age 20 but the shift is gradual thereafter. [*Source:* Data from *United Nations Demographic Yearbook* (New York: United Nations, 1989).]

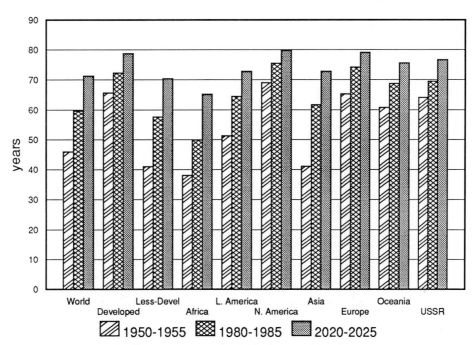

FIGURE 4.9 Life expectancy at birth, both sexes, for the world and for developed and less-developed regions, 1950 to A.D. 2025. The life expectancy of populations in less-developed countries was only 41 years in 1950, but it has continued to rise in the years since and is anticipated to reach 70 years by A.D. 2025. Life expectancy has likewise risen in the more-developed populations, but the rate of increase has been slower, partly because it was higher to begin with (65.7 in 1950) and partly because mortality rates are harder to reduce at the ages now attained by most people in those countries. Life expectancy in the latter group is projected to rise to 78.7 by A.D. 2025. The United Nations therefore predicts that the gap between the life expectancies of developed and less-developed populations will have shrunk from 24.7 years in 1950 to only 8.3 years in 2025. If this trend continues, the difference between the two populations would be eliminated before the end of the twenty-first century. The implications of this for the growth of future populations are profound. [*Source:* Data from United Nations, *Population Prospects 1988* (New York: United Nations, 1989).]

spread use of contraception, delayed age of giving birth to the first child, and rising divorce rates. Life expectancy is rising at a reduced rate because most illnesses are largely under control except for those related to old age, which tend to be more intractable.

Population stability has thus become general throughout the industrialized regions, and the projected size of future populations in those areas is likely to increase only slowly and at a diminishing rate. Indeed, this modest increase is occurring despite essentially zero growth in the number of births, simply because of a steady decline in deaths. The more-developed peoples now total a little more than 1.2 billion, and they will probably rise to no more than 1.4 billion before leveling off during the first half of the next century. They will therefore become an ever-smaller proportion of global population (Figure 4.12). Neverthe-

less, population growth rates vary somewhat among developed countries because of differences in their circumstances and in the timing of their demographic change.

Europe, the first region to experience a demographic transition, has the most mature population of all. Fertility is so low that some European countries have already begun to decline in numbers (see Figure 4.11). As recently as 1950 Europe had 15.6 percent of the world's people; today it has only 9 percent, and by A.D. 2025 it is expected to have only 6 percent. Though growth rates are diminishing fastest in Northern and Western Europe, they are declining in all parts of the continent. Italy, for example, recorded the world's lowest fertility rate in 1989.

In Northern America (Canada and the United States) societal changes have brought fertility levels to

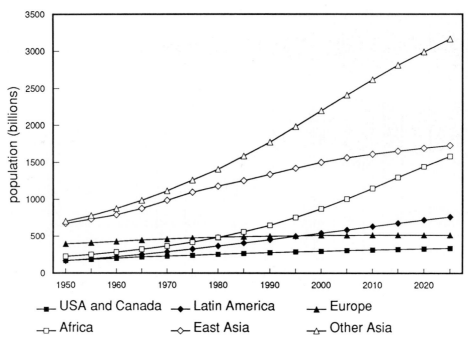

FIGURE 4.10 Estimates and projections of world population by major world regions, 1950 to A.D. 2025. As the populations of the more-developed regions mature, they will begin to level off and decline early in the next century, according to U.N. projections. The rate of population growth in East Asia (Japan, North and South Korea, China, Taiwan, Hong Kong, and Mongolia) is also easing somewhat, as is that of Latin America. Elsewhere in the Third World the rate of growth continues little abated. Other Asia (the remainder of the continent after East Asia is subtracted) will be contributing the greatest absolute numbers to future populations, but the region whose population is climbing at the most alarming rate is Africa. Thus, future additions to world population are to come predominantly from two major problem areas in the less-developed world. (The former USSR is not shown here because its growth curve would have been obscured by that of the USA and Canada, to which it closely corresponds). [*Source:* Data from United Nations, *Population Prospects 1988* (New York: United Nations, 1989).]

historic lows. Despite the large number of women from the postwar baby boom generation who reached childbearing age during the 1970s and 1980s, birth rates did not rise proportionally. Northern America's population is therefore projected to increase at an annual rate of only 0.6 percent in the 1990s. Having fallen from 6.6 percent of world population in 1950 to its current 5.2 percent, Northern America is expected to comprise only 3.9 percent of the total by A.D. 2025 (Figure 4.12).

An interesting case is that of Japan, which had an exceedingly high birth rate until the end of World War II (refer to Figure 3.15). At that time official policy changed abruptly, as the Japanese saw the difficulties of accommodating a rapidly expanding population within a small island nation no larger than California. Thus, they quickly brought population growth under

control by using such means as contraception, abortion, and other measures. Small families are now the rule in Japan, and the growth rate and age structure are similar to those of the United States.

The former USSR has also entered the ranks of U.N. Type 5 countries. Now growing at only 0.68 percent annually, the population of that area about equals that of Northern America (Figure 4.12) and is following a very similar growth path. There is, however, unusual variability among its newly-independent republics (which are generally drawn up along ethnic lines). Births have fallen below replacement levels among the ethnic Russians. In the Central Asian Republics, however, fertility remains surprisingly high—nearly double that of Russia and comparable to rates found in less-developed lands. This puzzles demographers because the high-growth areas have literate fe-

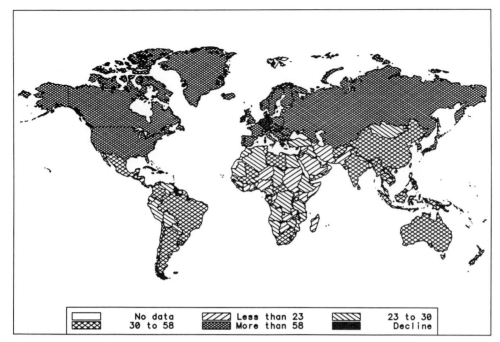

	No data		Less than 23		23 to 30
	30 to 58		More than 58		Decline

FIGURE 4.11 Number of years to double population, based upon 1984–89 growth rates. If current trends were to continue unchanged, much of Africa, the Middle East, and the tropical Americas would have twice as many people within another generation as they do now. Little future growth is expected, however, in Northern America, Europe, most of the former USSR, or Japan and the newly industrializing lands of East Asia. Indeed, several countries of central and northern Europe are already seeing their populations begin to shrink. [*Source:* Based upon data from *1990 Britannica Book of the Year* (Chicago: Encyclopaedia Britannica, 1990).]

male populations and low death rates. A likely cause is a firmly embedded cultural bias among these Muslim minorities favoring very large families. Another unique demographic feature of the Russian population is its unusual age distribution. The 65 to 69 age group has a disproportionately small number of males, a result of heavy casualties during World War II. At the same time, the 40 to 44 age group is relatively small because these are the children of those who fought the war.

The Less-Developed Countries (LDCs)

As the populations of the more-developed regions stabilize, those of the less-developed areas continue to soar. The United Nations expects the poorer countries to account for 95 percent of world population growth between now and the middle of the next century. Although birth rates are beginning to decline in some important areas, they generally remain very high elsewhere. Meanwhile, throughout much of the less-developed world, mortality rates are falling and people are living longer.

Although continued population growth is the dominant trend among less-developed countries, each region seems to be taking its own path. Moreover, some of these paths are easier to predict than others, mainly because fertility rates vary greatly from region to region. Several less-developed countries have achieved surprisingly low levels of fertility, whereas others have fertility rates as high as ever. Fertility is a complex matter: Although high fertility is closely linked to poverty, it has deep cultural roots as well (see Chapter 3). Thus, we cannot be certain when it will start to fall in those areas where it is currently high, nor can we be sure how fast its decline will be.

Figure 4.13 shows the widely differing expectations for future total fertility rates. Demographers at the United Nations predict that fertility will continue to decline rapidly in eastern Asia, that it will decrease more rapidly in southern Asia than in Latin America, and that it will lag far behind the others in Africa.

For the remainder of this century Asia will remain a serious problem area, not just because of its high rate of growth but because of the enormous population to which those rates apply. The situation differs

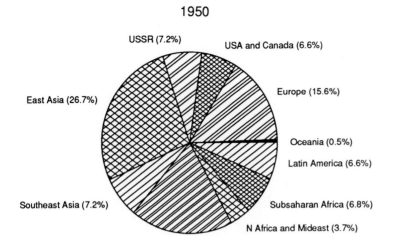

1950

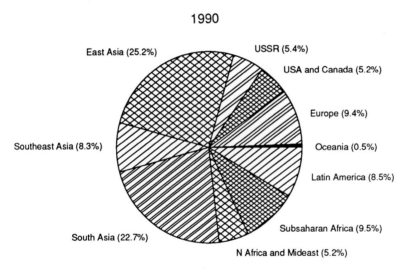

1990

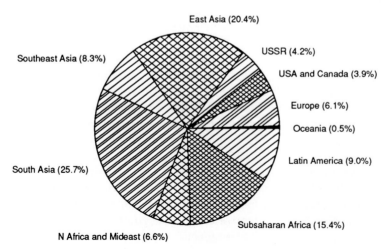

AD 2025

FIGURE 4.12 Regional shares of world population, 1950, and projected for 1990 and A.D. 2025. The population growth trends indicated previously in Figure 4.10 would produce major changes in regional shares, as revealed sequentially in these diagrams. Here we see each of the more-developed regions gradually shrinking in relative size, especially Europe. During this same period most of the less-developed regions experience explosive growth, notably South Asia, Subsaharan Africa, Latin America, and the Islamic lands of North Africa and the Middle East. According to this United Nations scenario, however, East Asia's share of world population declines as China and other populous lands in that crucial area reach the final stages of the demographic transition. [*Source:* See Figure 4.10.]

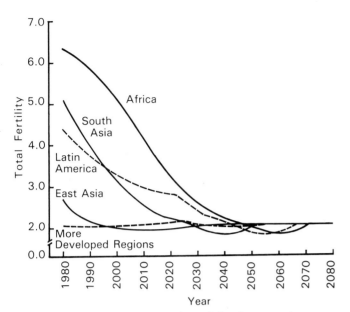

FIGURE 4.13 Projected total fertility rates by world regions—U.N. medium variant, 1980 to 2080 as assessed in 1980. The United Nations anticipates wide variation among regions in the timing of the decline in their total fertility (average number of births per couple during their lifetime). Rates will likely remain very high in Africa well into the twenty-first century. [*Source:* After U.N. Population Division, *Population Bul.* No. 14, 1983.]

from one country to another, however. Some countries have begun to make substantial progress and may attain zero population growth early in the next century; others are disappointingly slow. Both types are present in southern Asia. Fertility rates are dropping rapidly in the industrialized city-state of Singapore, where total fertility is now well below the replacement level of two children per family. Despite low incomes, the island nation of Sri Lanka is also progressing. On the other hand, several other low-income countries— Kampuchea, Bangladesh, Nepal, Afghanistan, and Pakistan—still have very high fertility and mortality rates. The same is true of the Muslim countries of Southwest Asia—both those that are rich in oil and those that are not. A notable exception among Islamic nations is semi-industrialized Turkey, which maintains a strict separation between religion and the state and is beginning to get its population under control. The other countries of southern Asia, nearly a billion people in all, are making only slow progress.

Perhaps the brightest spot in the developing world is eastern Asia. Even though China's recent census has forced an upward revision in the estimated total population of the region, a dramatic reduction in

population growth is taking place throughout the area. This is occurring not only in the middle-income industrialized countries—Taiwan, South Korea, and the city-state of Hong Kong—but most notably in China, a low-income nation that has made startling progress in population control. Prior to the 1949 revolution, China was truly a U.N. Type 1 country: a very high birth rate balanced by a similarly high death rate. The new government effected a remarkable reduction in the death rate by improving food distribution, raising literacy levels, and introducing health-care facilities in virtually every rural community. The result was explosive population growth, adding 400 million people—almost as many as in all of Europe—to an already-overpopulated agricultural country.

Influenced by Mao Tse-tung's utopian philosophy, China's rulers at first did nothing to stem this growth, believing that the more people the better. Subsequently, a more pragmatic leadership awoke to the fact that 30 percent of national income was being drained off to support the additions to China's population. The government therefore established a new policy, setting a target of zero population growth by A.D. 2000, with a standard of one child per family, backed by a combination of rewards and penalties. This policy quickly reduced fertility, cutting the former birth rate of 40 per thousand to only 18 per thousand in 1984 and 1985.

Enforcement of such a radical change in traditional practices, however, has been exceedingly difficult in a country as large and diverse as China and especially in the countryside. During the second half of the 1980s, therefore, birth rates began creeping up, forcing the government to raise its estimates for the period to 23.3 per thousand. The rise came as a result of the arrival to childbearing ages of the baby-boom generation of the 1960s, as well as a relaxation of the official one-child-per-couple policy. Small as the increase in birth rate may appear, when applied to a population of more than a billion people it translates into a truly significant addition to the world total. Nevertheless, China's progress in population control has been impressive: The country is compressing its demographic transition into an uncommonly short time span.

This dramatic reversal of China's tradition of large families compares with similar changes achieved earlier by ethnic Chinese populations living in Taiwan, Hong Kong, Singapore, and elsewhere in Asia. This has prompted demographers to speculate that the Chinese culture is particularly receptive to the idea of lower fertility. The abruptness of this shift in mainland China is clear from the current age structure of that country, as shown in Figure 4.14. Note that, although

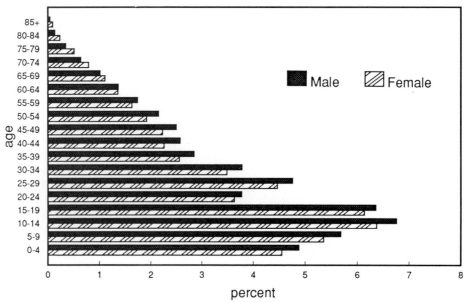

FIGURE 4.14 Age-sex structure of China's population, 1982. The shape of this diagram is typical of less-developed countries except for the unusual constriction in the sizes of the youngest age groups, evidence of the effectiveness of the Chinese government's strict population policy. When new data become available, they will show a slight increase for the under-5-year-olds caused by the coming of China's baby-boom generation to childbearing age and also by difficulties in enforcing the country's one-child-per-couple policy. Another unique feature of China's population structure is the substantial excess of males over females, a result of traditional cultural practices limiting the number of girl babies. Note also the reduced size of those groups born during the social upheavals of the "Great Leap Forward" and the "Cultural Revolution." [*Source:* Data from *United Nations Demographic Yearbook* (New York: United Nations, 1989).]

the diagram assumes the broad-based form typical of less-developed countries with young populations, it contracts sharply in the lowest age groups owing to the recent decline in birth rate. Trends such as these underscore U.N. predictions that East Asia's population, now 25 percent of the world total, will drop to only 20 percent by A.D. 2025, yielding its first-place position in Figure 4.12 to South Asia.

Africa is the only continent where population growth rates have actually risen during the past two decades. All of Africa is a demographic problem area, but the most serious threat comes from sub-Saharan Africa. Two-thirds of the world's poorest nations are in this region, confirming the much-noted poverty-population link. Recent data indicate that fertility rates are still rising, forcing the United Nations to revise upward its estimates of the future size of the region. In 1950, Africa south of the Sahara held only 6.8 percent of the world's people, roughly equivalent to Northern America's population at the time; today this proportion has risen to 9.5 percent, and by A.D. 2025 it is projected to reach 15.4 percent (Figure 4.12).

The nature of the worsening population crisis in this impoverished region is illustrated by the widening demographic gap in one troubled area, East Africa (Figure 4.15). Note that the overall birth rate is little diminished since 1950 (the suggested decline after the 1990s is no more than a hope) but that the death rate is steadily dropping. Throughout tropical Africa are some of the highest total fertility rates ever recorded—for example, 7.2 children per woman in Zambia, 8.12 in Kenya, and 8.49 in Rwanda. Only in war-afflicted Ethiopia has fertility eased somewhat; in most of these countries it has increased. Many demographers have concluded that the populations of this region have a greater cultural propensity to high fertility than other peoples at similar levels of development. Populations are exceedingly young, as Kenya's age structure illustrates (see Figure 4.8b above). Thus, sub-Saharan Africa is only now entering the most explosive phase of the demographic transition. Although Africa's demographic future is clouded at this point, one thing is sure: The twenty-first century will see continued population growth, posing grave problems in a region where

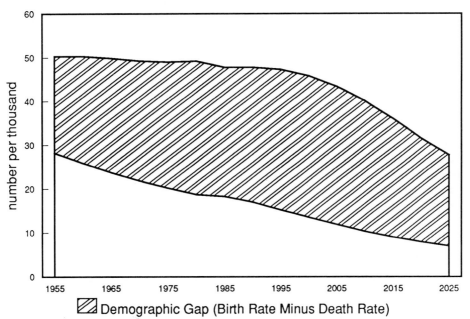

Demographic Gap (Birth Rate Minus Death Rate)

FIGURE 4.15 Birth and death rates in East Africa, 1955–1990 and projected to A.D. 2025. The widening demographic gap in East Africa is typical of all sub-Saharan Africa, where a population explosion is now in progress. Death rates are steadily declining but birth rates remain stubbornly high. The decline in birth rates projected by the United Nations to begin around the turn of the century is no more than a hope; no evidence for it now exists. Indeed, current fertility rates for these countries are the highest ever recorded anywhere. [*Source:* Data from United Nations, *World Population Prospects 1988* (New York: United Nations, 1989).]

many people are already pressing the resources of the land. If Malthus is to be vindicated, it will be here.

A strong cultural bias toward large populations also characterizes the male-dominated Islamic lands of North Africa and the Middle East. Fertility rates are high, especially in those countries with the most-conservative religious traditions, such as Libya (7.12 children per woman) and Saudi Arabia (7.28). Yet, as urbanization and development proceed in parts of the area, some signs of diminishing growth rates have appeared. Turkey and Egypt, two of the more advanced countries in the group, are leading the way with moderate decreases in fertility, especially in the larger cities. Tunisia is following closely behind, suggesting that some other countries of the region will eventually take the same path. Yet the ultimate outcome in this region is not at all certain, given the recent upsurge of Muslim fundamentalism.

Latin America's population began to soar in the early post–World War II period, the result of successful programs to reduce death rates. Birth rates remained high, however, and most Latin American nations have exceedingly young populations. Latin America in general has all the conditions conducive to high fertility: widespread poverty, female illiteracy,

and a cultural bias toward large families, reinforced by religious strictures against birth control. As life expectancy continues to rise, this region comprises an expanding share of total world population (Figure 4.12).

Latin America is very diverse, however, and some parts fit this description better than others. A number of low-income countries—notably Honduras, Haiti, and several smaller island nations of the Caribbean—have persistently high levels of fertility and galloping population growth. Certain other high-fertility countries, somewhat less impoverished, have very low death rates and exploding populations. Prominent in this group are Bolivia, Ecuador, Paraguay, and parts of Central America. On the other hand, a number of countries have achieved some reduction in fertility and thus moderated their rates of population growth. Among these are Brazil, Venezuela, Colombia, Peru, Mexico, Costa Rica, Panama, and Cuba. Finally, in southern-most Latin America, semi-industrialized Argentina, Uruguay, and Chile have already attained low levels of fertility and mortality and should be reaching zero population growth early in the next century.

Despite this evidence of demographic change, Latin America's population is destined to rise from 8.5

percent of the world total now to 9 percent by A.D. 2025 (Figure 4.12). At the end of World War II, Latin America had fewer people than Northern America; in another hundred years it will have more than three times as many. As yet only a few countries in Latin America are actually overcrowded, notably El Salvador and several Caribbean islands. Although densities are otherwise well below those common in Asia and West Africa, present trends will doubtless change this. Furthermore, even those growing Latin American populations that have not experienced physical crowding are finding it increasingly difficult to feed, educate, and employ the new additions to their numbers. One troublesome result is the mounting spillover of Latin Americans into Northern America.

With 95 percent of the world's future population growth taking place in the less-developed regions, it is to be expected that several Third World countries will assume top rank among the most populous nations, leapfrogging a number of industrialized countries along the way. In Figure 4.16 the 16 million-plus countries of A.D. 2025, as projected by the United Nations, are arrayed in order of their anticipated population

sizes in that year. Note that only three industrialized countries remain in this top group—the former USSR, the United States, and Japan. With their static populations, all European countries have been crowded off the list. This would seem to suggest that less-developed nations will necessarily exert an increasing influence in global affairs, if only because of their overwhelming size.

Changes in Structure and Spatial Distribution

In addition to their changing demography, the developing countries are experiencing profound changes in the structure and spatial distribution of their labor forces. As development proceeds, it substantially alters the occupational makeup of a population, which in turn reinforces the flood of people to the cities, as described previously. In this section we look at the expectations for structural change in developing economies and examine projections of future urban growth as it affects the major cities in those areas.

As we compare work-force structures of countries at different stages of economic development, a

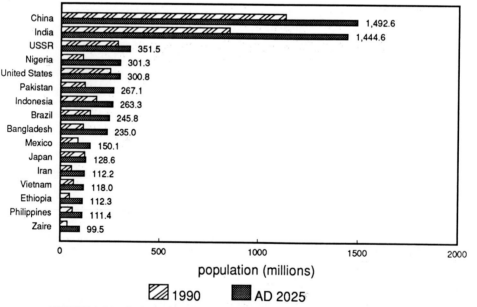

FIGURE 4.16 Projected largest countries in A.D. 2025, U.N. medium variant. As an outcome of the divergent growth trends of developed and less-developed regions, the most populous countries of the future will be mainly in the Third World. China, already by far the largest, is projected to have a population of nearly 1.5 billion by the end of the first quarter of the new century. Even more striking is the projected population of India, which is expected ultimately to exceed that of China. Note that by the year 2025 Nigeria will have replaced the United States as the fourth largest nation, and Bangladesh and Mexico will have passed Japan. [*Source:* Data from United Nations, *World Population Prospects 1988* [New York: United Nations, 1989).]

fairly consistent pattern of change takes place, as illustrated in Figure 4.17. Before industrialization, the primary sector—agriculture, forestry, and fishing—employs a major part of the work force. Secondary forms of production, mainly handicrafts, occupy relatively few workers. The non-goods-producing activities, likewise poorly developed, consist of two parts. The tertiary sector, including retailing and wholesaling, is often inflated in numbers by the inefficient nature of marketing and by the prominence of personal and domestic service in less-developed economies. The quaternary sector—administration, higher education, research and development, medicine, and other more specialized activities—is severely limited and rudimentary. Typical of such economies is Honduras, where 57 percent of the work force is in primary activities, only 18 percent is in industry, and the remaining 25 percent in the services. In some of the poorest countries of Africa and southern Asia, the primary sector accounts for nine-tenths or more of all employment.

When industrialization commences, demand for workers in secondary occupations grows at an accelerating pace until eventually manufacturing becomes a major employer. Meanwhile, increased efficiency in the use of farm labor leads to a steady drop in primary employment. The tertiary and quaternary activities develop less slowly because services and administration still come mainly from outside the country. One such newly industrializing country is South Korea, which

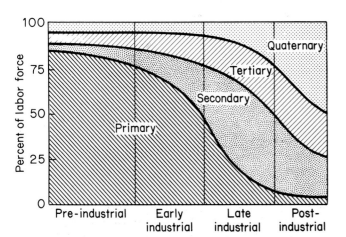

FIGURE 4.17 Effects of economic development upon the structure of the labor force. As a region rises in the scale of development, the proportion of its labor force engaged in primary activities diminishes. The percentage employed in secondary activities increases until industrialization is essentially completed, at which time it begins a relative decline. The proportion in the services, both tertiary and quaternary, consistently rises.

now employs 34 percent of the labor force in agriculture, 29 percent in industry, and 37 percent in the services.

The late-industrial stage, which arrived in the United States during the 1920s, sees an accelerating decline in agricultural employment. Manufacturing employment continues to grow, although at a declining rate as labor productivity rises and finally reaches a maximum by the end of the period. Meanwhile, tertiary activities expand steadily to satisfy the proliferating demands of supporting services for manufacturing and to supply the growing requirements of an ever-more-prosperous population. Though initially slow to develop, the quaternary sector eventually expands and becomes increasingly sophisticated as the economy and society grow more and more complex.

The postindustrial stage, which began soon after World War II in the United States and arrived in Western Europe and Japan in the 1960s, is marked by a declining emphasis upon material goods and a growing interest in the quality of life. Agriculture becomes so capital-intensive and efficient that only a small number of farm workers provide the food and industrial raw materials needed by the rest of the population. Meanwhile, automation reduces labor requirements in industry. Tertiary activities, now more specialized than ever, begin to reach saturation; but the quaternary sector steadily expands, developing an elaborate division of labor and supplying a whole new set of societal needs. Thus, in the United States less than 3 percent of the work force runs the farms that feed 249 million people and that produce a major share of the country's export earnings. Industrial employment has fallen to 27 percent, but the services now require 70 percent of the work force.

As newly developing nations follow along this path, presumably their labor forces will undergo the same kinds of structural changes as those that have taken place in the developed countries. The shift of workers out of primary employment, however, accelerates the flow of people into those large cities where jobs in industry and the services are concentrated. Hence, the pace of urbanization now under way in developing countries will likely continue well into the next century.

The effects of this trend are apparent from Figure 4.18, which lists in rank order the 25 largest cities in A.D. 2000, according to United Nations projections. For comparison, Figure 4.18 also shows the populations of those same cities in 1990. Note that 19 of the 25 are in less-developed countries and that only 2 of the top 10 are in more-developed lands. In 1950, seven of the 10 largest cities were in developed countries. As we have noted previously, the flight of people from the

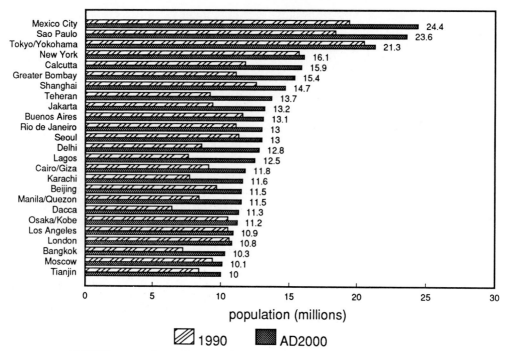

population (millions)

⊘ 1990   ▓ AD2000

FIGURE 4.18 The 25 largest urban agglomerations in A.D. 2000. Populations for 1990 are also shown for comparison. Accelerating urban growth in the Third World is rapidly changing the lineup of megacities. The turn of the new century will find only six metropolises from industrialized countries remaining on this list of the world's largest. The current world leader, Tokyo, will have slipped to third place. Some of these newly prominent cities may come as a surprise—Lagos, Nigeria, and Dacca, Bangladesh, for example. [*Source:* Data from United Nations, *The Prospects of World Urbanization: Revised as of 1984–1985* (New York: United Nations Department for International Economic and Social Affairs, 1989).]

countryside in less-developed countries is proceeding more rapidly than jobs or services can be provided for them, posing enormous urban problems. Can these already-burgeoning cities really absorb the numbers predicted for them?

ASSESSMENT: WHAT TO DO WITH 11 BILLION PEOPLE

This is a crucial period for the issue of world population; much depends upon what happens between now and the end of the present century. By the 1980s the number of human beings inhabiting the earth had reached levels previously considered unthinkable, and most of this increase had occurred within the modern era. As we have seen in this chapter, today's population of more than 5 billion people is crowded into a comparatively small portion of earth space, mainly regions that in earlier times held special attractions to

migrants and offered optimal conditions for the multiplication of human populations. Chief among these conditions was the presence of favorable agricultural environments for a people who obtained their livelihood directly from the soil. Today the largest population concentrations are in those regions with the earliest histories of habitation, but the areas most densely packed with humanity are the great urban metropolises that have evolved in modern times—end products of the agricultural, industrial, and transportation revolutions.

Evidence presented in this chapter suggests that the world has entered an important era of demographic change. The slope of the global growth-rate curve is no longer steepening, an indication that world population growth may have peaked. Indeed, U.N. experts anticipate a further slackening in the rate of growth and predict that the global population will have stabilized before the end of the twenty-first century. But these long-range projections are based upon unsure assumptions about a remote future. Forecasting techniques have improved sufficiently for us to be fairly sure about what will happen in the developed world, where detailed information is available and trends are well established. For the less-developed regions, however, the future is less clear because circumstances are so varied and cultural influences so important.

Demographers are already breathing easier about East Asia, where fertility rates are dropping much sooner and far more rapidly than any had dared to hope. Japan's success in reversing its high fertility at the close of World War II is being emulated today, three decades later, throughout the Orient, most notably in China. This is an important development, considering that East Asia's present population is so huge and densities are so great. The situation is less sure in Latin America and southern Asia, where some countries have made progress but several very large ones have done less well.

The greatest uncertainty focuses upon sub-Saharan Africa and the Islamic lands of the Middle East and North Africa. The social pressures for large families among Muslim peoples threaten to offset the moderating effects of urbanization upon fertility rates. When directed toward African countries south of the Sahara, however, predictions become mere guesses. Extreme poverty, illiteracy, and cultural propensities combine in those areas to create conditions for explosive population growth. U.N. projections for the entire region are hardly more than hopes; no one knows when the present high rates of fertility will begin to drop, or even whether this will happen at all.

We have also noted that the populations of developing countries are being transformed in other, related ways, especially the structural changes in their labor forces that take place as workers are shifted progressively out of primary occupations into manufacturing and service activities. A visible manifestation of this is the accelerating rate of urbanization within the Third World, which by A.D. 2000 will contain the majority of the world's largest metropolises, together with all the economic, social, environmental, and political strains these bring.

At every scale—global, regional, or urban—population predictions are horrendous, even if they prove correct. This chapter has shown that rapid population growth intensifies nearly every serious problem of humanity: unemployment, illiteracy, poor housing, ill health, political instability, and, most basic of all, inadequate food supply and environmental degradation. The adverse impact of population growth afflicts most severely the poorest areas and most impoverished people. And, when these problems become sufficiently severe in one area, they spill over into others: Even the richest, most stable populations cannot escape their consequences in an ever-shrinking world. Thus, the question for us all is whether or not the world is able to support 11 billion people. The next chapter looks for answers to this.

TOPICS FOR DISCUSSION

1. What are the relative merits of each of the following measures for comparing populations: population size, population density, physiological density?

2. Discuss the various physical limits to human habitation, and explain how these have contributed to the shaping of contemporary population patterns. Why is the correlation between population density and physical conditions an imperfect one?

3. Describe the principal population nodes that appear in Figure 4.1, and discuss their relative importance. Why do lightly populated areas exist within the territories of some of the most densely populated countries? Give examples.

4. What causes human beings to congregate in cities, and why have truly large cities appeared only in modern times? In what countries does urbanization reach its highest levels today and why? Account for the current rush of people to the cities of Third World countries, and identify those cities most likely to be the world's largest by the end of this century.

5. Analyze the main demographic forces at work to change the world population map. Why has population forecasting failed so badly in the past, and why are demographers more confident of today's forecasts?

6. Describe and explain the differences in age composition of populations in advanced countries and those in less-developed ones. How do the occupational structures of these two categories of countries differ and why? What economic and social problems do these population characteristics create in each case?

7. How is a world population map for the year 2080 likely to differ from a map of today's population? Explain the wide variations in population growth projected for different Third World areas. Which world regions are of greatest concern to students of population? Explain.

FURTHER READINGS

BOGUE, DONALD J., and AMY ONG TSUI. "Zero World Population Growth?" *The Public Interest,* Spring 1979, pp. 99–113.

Explores the reasons for recent declines in birth rates and the implications of these for bringing world population growth under control.

BOUVIER, LEON F., with HENRY S. SHRYOCK and HARRY W. HENDERSON. "International Migration: Yesterday, Today, and Tomorrow," *Population Bulletin* 32, No. 4. Washington: Population Reference Bureau, Inc.

Looks at modern trends of international migration and envisions massive migrations of African workers to Western Europe similar to the legal and illegal migrations of Latin Americans to the United States.

COALE, ANSLEY J. "A Reassessment of World Population Trends." *Population Bulletin of the United Nations,* No. 14-1982. New York: United Nations, 1983.

Reassesses trends in mortality and fertility and their long-term implications for population growth, with special reference to earlier projections, one of which has proved very accurate. Using this latter method, the author examines trends in a large number of countries. He finds a great diversity of levels and trends of fertility among developing countries, and he concludes that future rates of increase in Third World areas depend upon the unpredictable timing and pace of the reduction of childbearing in those populations where fertility continues to be high.

COALE, ANSLEY J. "Recent Trends in Fertility in Less-Developed Countries." *Science,* 221 (August 26, 1983), 828–823.

Coale notes that in the 1960s the world birth rate began to decline more rapidly than the death rate, but that the rate of decline varied greatly among Third World countries. He predicts that the momentum of growth will bring continued population increase for several decades even in countries where fertility has fallen the most and that these increases will be very large in those populations whose fertility has not yet begun to decline.

DAVIS, CARY. "The Future Racial Composition of the United States." *Intercom* 10, No. 9/10 (1982), 8–10.

Projects annual migrations, legal and illegal, to the United States and predicts a Hispanic-Black-Asian majority for the country by the middle of the twenty-first century.

KATES, ROBERT W. *The Human Environment: Penultimate Problems of Survival.* Natural Hazards Research and Applications Center, Special Publication No. 6. Worcester, Mass.: The Center for Technology, Environment, and Development, Clark University, 1983.

Considers three related sets of issues: population growth and resource use, income disparities and their potential for widespread unrest and conflict, and environmental problems resulting from technological change.

TSUI, AMY ONG, and DONALD J. BOGUE. "Declining World Fertility: Trends, Causes, Implications," *Population Bulletin* 33, No. 4. Washington: Population Reference Bureau, Inc., 1978.

Projects population growth rates for A.D. 2000. African populations are expected to continue growing very rapidly, but rates will be declining in Latin America and most of Asia.

UNITED NATIONS. *World Population Prospects 1988.* Population Studies No. 106, Population Division of the Department of International Economic and Social Affairs. New York: United Nations, 1989.

The first revision by the Population Division of its estimates and projections of population and other demographic variables since its 1984 report, which has since proved overly optimistic. Summarizes the assessments by United Nations demographers of current trends relating to population size and growth, fertility and mortality, and population structure. Also analyzes the demographic events that caused world population growth to overshoot previous U.N. projections. Contains tables of demographic data for all countries, areas, and regions of the world from 1950 through 1985, with projections to A.D. 2025 using a medium (most likely) variant, high (worst-case) variant, and low (best-case) variant.

VAN DE WALLE, ETIENNE, and JOHN KNODEL. "Europe's Fertility Transition: New Evidence and Lessons for Today's Developing World." *Population Bulletin* 34, No. 6. Washington: Population Reference Bureau, Inc., 1980.

Analyzes changes in marital fertility among European populations since the eighteenth century. The wide differences among countries in the timing of fertility decline suggests the influence of cultural factors.

5

Resources: Food, Energy, Materials, and Environment

OVERVIEW

Continuing population growth brings into question the earth's capacity to provide the necessary food, energy, and industrial raw materials during the coming century. The Third World, being the last to achieve population equilibrium, will exert most of the new pressures upon resources. Thanks to new technology, the global food supply will probably be adequate for the near term; beyond A.D. 2000, however, the outlook is not yet assured. Already the Third World is a net importer of food.

Population growth and industrialization likewise exert pressures upon nonrenewable resources. Recurring oil crises since the early 1970s have focused attention upon energy supplies. Like other minerals, the fossil fuels are concentrated in a few countries and regions, some politically unstable. Oil and gas output

will peak early in the new century; coal should last much longer, although hampered by problems of pollution and shipping cost. In the longer run, new technologies will take over. The outlook for other minerals is less promising. Although a few are plentiful, many have limited life spans, and all draw upon other scarce resources in their production and use. It appears unlikely that the world as a whole can ever consume many of these at current U.S. levels.

The intensifying use of the earth's resources also threatens the quality of the environment. Pollution wastes valuable resources even as it poisons the atmosphere and water. Although costs of remedial measures are high, the future habitability of a crowded planet requires that these measures be taken.

OBJECTIVES

- to understand the nature and availability of the earth's resources
- to appreciate the difficulties of ensuring an adequate supply and equitable distribution of food for future populations
- to distinguish between short- and long-run political, economic, technical, and environmental problems of global energy supply
- to evaluate future prospects for mineral raw materials and possibilities for extending their life spans
- to describe the impacts of population increase and industrialization upon environmental quality

CAN THE WORLD SUPPORT ITS FUTURE POPULATIONS?

Growing Pressures

Does the earth have enough material resources to provide for the 11 billion people expected eventually to live here? This is the much-debated question that closed the previous chapter. The answer depends upon what happens to the two parts of the resources/population ratio. In Chapter 4 we examined those elements influencing the denominator of this fraction—numbers of people. Here we consider the many complex issues affecting the numerator: the problems of how much food, energy, and raw materials the earth can be made to yield and whether the physical environment can remain habitable with intensifying human use.

The shape of future world populations is now beginning to emerge. Drawing upon better data and improved predictive techniques, demographers generally feel that we are approaching that turning point when the population growth curve, which has risen exponentially for so long, will start to moderate its rate of climb and will eventually assume the characteristic S-shape of the logistic curve. Although the world's population as a whole is expected to reach a steady state some time in the latter part of the next century, however, the timing of this will vary greatly from one part of the world to another. Population equilibrium will arrive last in the poorest countries, where growth still remains high. Hence, it is safe to predict that the future drain on resources will come increasingly from parts of the Third World.

While population is assuming a new global pattern, the other side of the Malthusian ratio is likewise changing. Two things are happening to the resource part of the fraction: Per capita resource use is growing, and new kinds of resource needs are arising. The main reason for increased consumption of food, energy, and raw materials per person is the general rise in level of development. If the global economy were to continue growing at its 1980–1987 rate through the remainder of this century, the gross product of the world as a whole would have expanded by more than one-third by the year 2000 (see Figure 1.19). Economic growth is not occurring equally in all regions, however, As Box 1.7 shows, certain newly industrializing countries are increasing their output at rates well above those of the world. This group includes not only the "Five Little Tigers" of Asia—South Korea, Taiwan, Hong Kong, Singapore, and Malaysia—but, more significant for

the drain on global resources, also such populous lands as Brazil, Turkey, China, and India.

Furthermore, as Robert Kates has noted in his book *The Human Environment: Penultimate Problems of Survival* (1983), the numerator of the Malthusian ratio is changing in composition and in the relative importance of its constituent parts. When Malthus first posed the problem in 1798, food supply was the all-important factor limiting population growth. By the middle of the next century, however, the supply of mechanical energy had joined food as a necessary requirement for a society that was industrializing and advancing technologically. A century later, pollution control was added to the list in recognition that industrialization and urbanization are beginning to poison the environment. Then, in the 1970s, came evidence that intensive human use of physical resources threatens the biosphere and the basic life-support system of the biogeochemical cycles. During that same period, growing scarcities and rising prices of raw materials and energy raised new questions about the adequacy of world reserves (Meadows and others, *The Limits to Growth,* 1972).

Cyclical variations in the level of economic activity complicate the analysis of these changing relationships between population growth and resource use; they also confuse public perceptions of these problems and hamper governmental responses to them. Periods of prosperity cause consumption to rise, straining available supplies of physical resources and intensifying environmental pressures. This heightens the general awareness of resource limitations, prompts greater research on such problems, and leads to official measures to minimize the impacts of shortages and rising prices. Succeeding times of economic recession reduce the demand for basic commodities, causing prices to fall and bringing relief from the scarcities that had earlier prevailed. Officialdom and the general public lose sight of resource problems, and long-term research and development suffer.

This vacillating response to resource questions is much greater at those times when business cycles converge worldwide. The evidence suggests that such coincidences of global prosperity and hard times have occurred at intervals of roughly 50 years ever since the Industrial Revolution in the eighteenth century. The latest such "long wave" crested in the 1980–1981 stagflation crisis, temporarily enhancing the bargaining power of raw material- and energy-exporting nations and providing the conditions for the commodity price shocks and other global economic crises of the 1970s (see Chapter 14 for a discussion of their effects upon international trade). The wave thereupon collapsed, leading to the worldwide recession of the early 1980s and subsequently to a new upturn. Chapter 11 traces the history of earlier long waves and offers a theoretical explanation for them.

The Nature of Resources

Just as alternating periods of scarcity and abundance affect attitudes toward the relative importance of resources, so does technology alter perceptions of what actually constitutes a resource. Even at a particular level of technology, conflicting views on this subject may be held by those with differing professional perspectives.

Changing Conceptions.   In a real sense, the term *resource* refers to the supply of anything that may be regarded as useful or necessary to human beings, a store upon which we can draw as we need it. This does not imply anything absolute or constant about a resource; indeed, it does not actually become a resource until human beings conceive it as such. Thus, what we class as a resource changes as our perceptions of it change, or as new technology or rising prices make its exploitation feasible. Oil bubbling from the ground in ancient Persia was a nuisance to some of its earlier inhabitants, but it is a vital source of energy and export earnings to modern Iranians. Uranium was a waste product of Canada's radium mining operations during the 1930s, but since then the old mine tailings have been reworked to recover the newly valuable uranium ore remaining in them. The abundant but low-grade Lake Superior taconite ores became a commercially exploitable resource only when the rich Mesabi iron deposits gave out.

At a given state of technology, the absolute supply of certain natural resources can be sustained at a given level or even increased. These are the *renewable resources*—those capable of replenishing themselves or being replenished by human beings. Most biotic resources, such as forests, animal populations, and fish, are of this type. Even soils can be made to recover from excessive use in some instances; indeed, many of the soils of Western Europe and southeastern Asia are essentially made by human beings.

Resources that cannot regenerate are referred to as *nonrenewable resources*. Most minerals fall into this category. The concentration of mineral ores in economically exploitable quantities relies upon physical processes that normally require many thousands or even millions of years. Once a given deposit has been mined out, that resource for all practical purposes ceases to exist. The accelerating demand for minerals

as a result of advancing technology spurs a constant search for new deposits to replace the old. The total known world reserves of a particular mineral therefore tend to rise and fall as new deposits are discovered and old ones exhausted.

Flow resources—such as running water, winds, ocean tides, and solar rays—represent still another type. Ordinarily these do not become exhausted, but they must be used as they appear or they are lost. Each of these constitutes a potential or actual source of energy.

Conflicting Views of Nonrenewable Resources. Ensuring an adequate supply of the earth's resources for coming generations is an urgent task, but it is one that is clouded with uncertainties, especially with respect to the nonrenewable resources. Determining the future prospects for these is complicated by both measurement and conceptual problems. Total population and total food supplies can be physically measured; total nonrenewable resources cannot. The definitions of population and food supplies are straightforward; the definition of nonrenewable resources is complex. Experts disagree not only on what constitutes a resource but also on how to measure the quantity of it that exists. One group holds an "environmentalist" view, another an "economist" view.

The environmentalist view of nonrenewable resources is that the world has a fixed upper carrying capacity of population that it can support and of resources that it can supply. Technology can raise current levels toward, but not beyond, the full potential of the world's productive capacity. The environmentalist focus is long-term. Its concern is with the results of the next doubling of the world's population and the impact of that doubling on environmental pollution and on demands for resources.

The alternative view offered by many economists is that resources are not fixed in amount but created, in response to needs, through market mechanisms. If a resource becomes scarce, its price rises and the quantity consumed drops. The price increase stimulates an increase in the supply of the product and a search for substitute products.

Both environmentalists and economists offer persuasive arguments for their viewpoints. The environmentalist view appeals to common sense. The metaphor of "spaceship earth" comes naturally to mind in this space age. There must be a fixed, finite supply of oil on this, our spaceship. Every barrel we use is one less barrel that remains. But how much actually remains and how long will it last? Estimates of ultimately recoverable reserves of crude oil from conventional sources rose sharply from 600 billion barrels in 1942 to 2480 billion in 1965 as new discoveries were made. Since then, estimates have fluctuated at or above the 2000-billion-barrel mark. Proved reserves, a more reliable measure commonly used in the oil industry, are much lower—approximately 1000 billion barrels at the end of 1989. Assuming continued world production at present levels, this quantity would last about 44 years.

The reality is much more complex, and the economist view would place little value on these figures of the reserve life of oil, preferring a much more flexible approach (Figure 5.1).

The differences dividing these two schools of thought became evident during the intense debate that followed the 1972 publication of *The Limits to Growth*, which reported on an elaborate analysis of the re-

---

BOX 5.1   Are There Limits to Growth?

The environmentalist vision of a growing population pressing against fixed upper limits of nonrenewable resources gained worldwide attention with the publication in 1972 of *The Limits to Growth*, the first report for the Club of Rome's Project on The Predicament of Mankind. The Club of Rome was formed in 1968 by prominent industrialists and scientists from around the developed world who were convinced that the major problems facing humanity are so complexly interrelated that traditional institutions and policies cannot cope with them. They felt that "systems dynamics" models were needed to make wiser decisions. These mathematical tools can be made to account for the fact that population growth, for instance, depends on trends in food production, pollution, and industrial output, and each of these in turn depends on the others.

Limits to Growth projects world population, food supplies, industrial output, and pollution over a long duration, to the year 2010, with dramatic results. World population is projected to continue its exponential growth until it overshoots the world's carrying capacity, and the world's economic system collapses. This unstable pattern of overshoot and collapse is projected to occur even if the constraints on population growth are successively reduced. Doubling natural resource reserves, cutting pollution to one-fourth of its present level, increasing agricultural productivity, and introducing birth control were each added as assumptions in the model simulations, but the general results remained the same. The precise sequence of events that triggers the catastrophic fall of population numbers differs according

to the specific assumptions, but the basic pattern is always the same: overshoot and collapse, as illustrated by Figure 5a. The key policy conclusion of the study, therefore, is that an immediate slowdown in economic growth must be initiated so as to create an equilibrium between population and resources.

Limits to Growth was subjected to

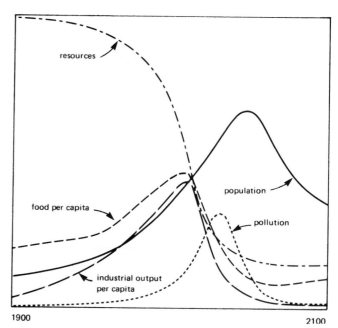

FIGURE 5a Limits to growth: a simulation of world collapse. Dennis Meadows and his colleagues projected overshoot and collapse of the world's population unless world economic and population growth slowed immediately. In this model, collapse occurs because of the depletion of nonrenewable resources, shown by the dramatic drop in the resources curve. This collapse triggers declines in *food per capita* and *industrial output per capita*. [*Source:* D. H. Meadows, D. L. Meadows, J. Randers, and W. W. Behrens, *The Limits to Growth* (New York: Universe Books, 1972), p. 97.]

source question as viewed from an environmentalist perspective. See Box 5.1 for a summary of this study and the controversy it provoked.

Political Problems.   In addition to the conceptual and measurement questions surrounding this issue, another unpredictable aspect concerns what we might call the *politics of resources.* This problem

arises from the fact that the deposits of many essential resources are concentrated in certain parts of the world and under the control of particular sovereign nation-states, whereas the principal areas of demand for these are in other regions. For instance, much of the world's most productive agricultural land is possessed by developed countries with mature, stable populations, but the largest and most rapidly growing

---

intensive scrutiny by scientists in every discipline dealing with population and resources. As a result, every facet of the work has been attacked by one critic or another, and some telling points have been made. Nevertheless, most subsequent scenarios of the future have made at least some reference to the concerns it raised. Interest was reawakened in the work of an earlier prophet of doom, the Rev. Thomas R. Malthus, whose *Essay on the Principle of Population* in the late eighteenth century similarly attracted widespread debate on physical limits to growth and on the policy consequences that followed. Indeed, one critic labeled Meadows "Malthus with a computer."

The criticisms were of four kinds and related to (1) the relationships among population and the supply of resources, (2) the use of world averages rather than specific regional data, (3) the growth of the system components and the nature of growth itself, and (4) the stability of such models under differing assumptions.

The fourth and perhaps most serious flaw in *Limits to Growth* is that quite different results are obtained if new assumptions reflecting a technological-optimist view are incorporated into the model. Robert Boyd, a zoologist, assumes, for example, that an additional key variable is needed in the model developed by Meadows and colleagues, namely technology. He further assumes that investment in technology would accelerate if there were a decline in quality of life and that this increased investment would, in turn, increase the growth of technology. He then assumes that a growth in technology would increase food output, decrease the consumption of natural resources, and decrease pollution. He also assumes that birth rates would fall with an increase in food supplies once these were above some minimal

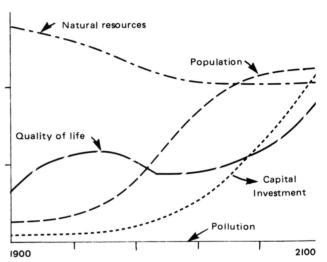

FIGURE 5b   The greening of the globe: a technological-optimist view of the future. Robert Boyd makes changes in the Meadows model by allowing changes in technology to produce optimistic results for food production, pollution levels, and quality of life. The result is a "new age" with a stable population level and improving quality of life. [*Source:* Robert Boyd, "World Dynamics: A Note," *Science,* 177 (August 1972), 516–519.]

level. The results of incorporating these assumptions into the Meadows model are that population grows to a steady-state level by the year 2000 and that, as population growth slows, the quality of life increases (see Figure 5b).

Limits to Growth demonstrates that systems modeling is limited by the assumptions used. It cannot resolve underlying theoretical conflicts. Meadows and his colleagues argue that the basic behavior of the world models appears to be so fundamental and general that they do not expect their broad conclusions to be substantially altered by further revisions. That is, world population overshoot and collapse ap-

pear inevitable if world population and economic growth continue their present course. In fact, Meadows and his associates are incorrect. Boyd demonstrates that computer simulations simply feed back the assumptions fed in. Start off with a Malthusian framework and the models make Malthusian predictions. Begin with optimistic assumptions and an optimist future unfolds; in "computerese": garbage in, garbage out (GIGO). The computer models fail to resolve the crucial difference between the two viewpoints; they merely project the consequences of the investigators' initial assumptions onto a time scale.

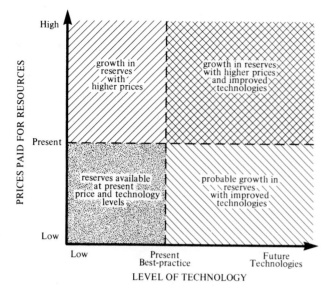

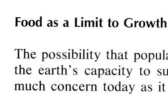

FIGURE 5.1   The economist's view of world resources. This figure is suggested by a diagram in G. Alexanderson and B. I. Klevebring, *World Resources: Energy, Metals and Minerals* (New York: W. deGruyter, 1978), p. 6. It implies that the quantity of resources available responds to prices and technology. Resource prices rise in the face of scarcity, but supplies do not run out.

populations are in countries with limited opportunities for expanding food production. Similarly, a number of countries with poorly developed industrial sectors control large reserves of minerals that are vital raw materials for factories in countries lacking these. Under these circumstances, the have-not nations run grave political risks of being cut off from these essential imports.

Another uncertainty affecting the analysis of resources on a global scale is the nature of the data, which vary in quality from country to country. Information for some Third World countries is scanty, and data for the poorest areas are often full of gaps, forcing the analyst to rely upon estimates. Projecting future world supplies therefore requires making a number of assumptions: that no major changes will be made in governmental policies; that no wars or other major disruptions will interfere with production, consumption, and distribution; and that no revolutionary advances in technology will occur. With these warnings, let us now look at the problems of providing for future populations, taking into account the various elements affecting food supply, energy, raw materials, and environmental quality.

FOOD SUPPLY

Food as a Limit to Growth

The possibility that population growth might outstrip the earth's capacity to supply enough food is of as much concern today as it was in Malthus's time, although the immediacy of this problem is much debated. Two contrary trends are partly responsible for the uncertainty. On the one hand, soil erosion, urban encroachment upon farmland, and other human and natural processes are acting to diminish the food supply; on the other, technological developments are raising the efficiency of food production by increasing output per unit of physical resources. The answer to the problem also depends upon the level of dietary quality deemed acceptable. To raise the global average of food consumption to levels now prevalent in the richer countries would be a daunting task, considering the high proportion of animal proteins and fresh green vegetables entering into such diets and the drain on basic resources such foods impose.

These matters aside, the problem of maintaining the world food supply does not appear critical in the short run. Global food production has more than doubled since World War II, and the current total is more than sufficient to feed everyone on earth. Even by the end of this century the total supply seems likely to be adequate, assuming that productivity continues to increase at current rates. The outlook beyond A.D. 2000, however, is exceedingly cloudy. Predictions for the new century depend not only upon dietary standards but also upon the possibilities for unfavorable climatic changes, containing loss of productive capacity through such factors as soil erosion, and achieving breakthroughs in food production technology.

Yet, even if total output should prove sufficient, the thorny problem remains of ensuring that all the world's inhabitants receive an equitable share of these supplies. Even now the regional differences in production and consumption are enormous: Food is just not reaching everyone who needs it and the disparities are widening. Early in the postwar era food output balanced population increase in the developed countries and even in the Third World as a whole, although particular regions were unable to keep up. More recently, North America and Europe have been overproducing—at a time when their populations have stabilized—whereas food output has lagged behind population growth in the former USSR and the majority of less-developed countries (see Figure 5.2). Meanwhile, inequities in food distribution within the Third World have continued to worsen.

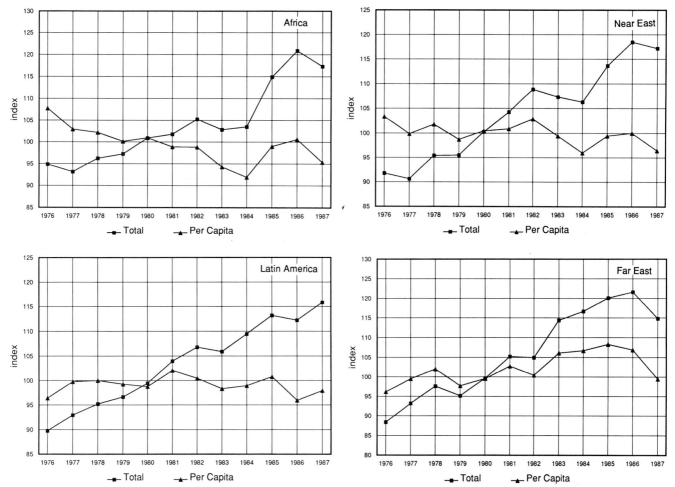

FIGURE 5.2 Food production in less-developed areas, 1976–1987, indices (1979–1981 = 100). Aided by the green revolution, total food production has generally risen in all four areas, but per capita output has lagged, especially in Africa. A temporary reversal of the upward trend in total production occurred in 1987, which was a poor crop year in three of the regions. Recurring droughts contribute to the wide fluctuations in African harvests. [*Source:* Data from *FAO Production Yearbook 1987* (Rome: Food and Agriculture Organization of the United Nations, 1988).]

Countries deficient in food output are of two main kinds. One group includes the oil-exporting countries of the Middle East and the newly industrializing countries of the Pacific rim, which are able to make up for inadequate food production by selling abroad their petroleum and valuable manufactured goods to finance imports of needed foodstuffs. The former USSR has likewise resorted to imports to compensate for its badly lagging food production.

The other group of food-deficit countries consists of the many less-developed countries too poor to buy needed food supplies abroad. Indeed, much of the Third World is suffering a food crisis at this time. Making news headlines are the famines in Ethiopia, the Sudan, Chad, and other countries of the drought-stricken region of Africa south of the Sahara; but even more common than famine today is chronic malnutrition. Hunger is a growing world problem, affecting possibly a billion people. Note from Figure 5.3 how widespread are low dietary levels throughout Africa and southern Asia and parts of Latin America.

Although the effects of hunger and malnutrition upon human beings are not fully understood as yet, we do know that they contribute to stunted physical growth, a lower resistence to disease, higher childhood death rates, and arrested mental development. Studies of this problem in Latin America have identified malnutrition as either the main or a contributing

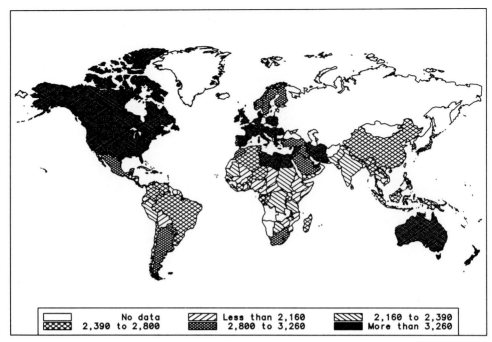

No data
2,390 to 2,800
Less than 2,160
2,800 to 3,260
2,160 to 2,390
More than 3,260

FIGURE 5.3   Daily per capita energy supply in calories. Twenty-nine African countries currently have food supplies below the 2334 calories per person cited by the United Nations Food and Agriculture Organization (FAO) as the minimum requirement for that region. Similar deficiencies are found in 10 Asian countries and 6 in Latin America. The most poorly fed nation of the Western Hemisphere is Haiti, whose population consumes only 1902 calories per capita each day. [*Source:* Based upon data from the *1990 Britannica Book of the Year* (Chicago: Encyclopaedia Britannica, 1990).]

cause of 57 percent of all deaths between the ages of one to four. In Brazil, children in this age group accounted for four-fifths of *all* deaths. In the less-developed world as a whole, according to estimates of the United Nations Food and Agriculture Organization (FAO), more than two-thirds of the present group of children will develop illnesses related to malnutrition. Upon reaching adulthood many of the survivors will remain mentally or physically handicapped to the extent that they will either be dependent upon society for their support or will be able to contribute little to it because of their reduced productivity. Hunger and malnutrition are clearly a serious drag on the economic development of impoverished nations.

The main cause of hunger in the world today is simply poverty. The world still has enough food in total, and those who can afford to buy it eat very well, including such food-deficient areas as Japan and several other Asian countries, as well as certain food-short European lands. As comparison of Figures 1.8 and 5.3 shows, the correspondence between low per capita food intake and low per capita income is very

close. In addition, wide variations in food consumption occur within countries, especially those less-developed nations with great income disparities, and even in some of the richer industrialized countries, such as the United States, where a surprising number of people go to bed hungry every night.

Regional disparities threaten to widen still further in the years to come. Although food requirements are to change little among developed countries, demand in the less-developed nations will rise steeply through the remainder of the twentieth century. Income growth will add some of the new demand in the Third World, but the greater part of it will come from population growth. World food output will therefore have to double or even treble to meet the needs of less-developed countries (LDCs) by the turn of the century. Physical limitations will make it impossible for most African and Middle Eastern countries to produce the additional food they will be requiring; hence, consumption will fall below even present inadequate levels. Moreover, it seems likely that the real price of food will double by the end of the century and pressure on current food sources will intensify, requiring ever-greater use of costly capital-intensive methods to raise productivity.

Beyond A.D. 2000 the Third World's food needs will continue to rise, but the physical limits will become even more crucial in the struggle to increase global output. What are the prospects for overcoming those limitations? Let us now consider the opportunities for meeting future food needs from conventional sources and examine the possibilities offered by certain new food technologies.

Conventional Sources of Food Supply

All types of food trace their origins to solar energy that has been captured by green plants through the process of photosynthesis. The plants are then consumed by herbivorous animals, which may be eaten by carnivorous animals, or human beings. In the sea the food chain commences with the phytoplankton, tiny one-celled plants that are eaten by certain fish, which are themselves eaten by larger ones. More than 99 percent

of the world's food supply currently comes from agriculture, and a mere 0.7 percent derives from the sea.

Agriculture and Grazing. As we approach the end of the twentieth century, only 36 percent of the world's land area is being used for the production of food, and two-thirds of this small proportion is devoted to permanent pasture, which characteristically yields a relatively meager output per hectare. This leaves only 11 percent of the world's land surface for field and tree crops. Major portions of total cropland are in Asia, North America, Africa, and the former USSR (Figures 5.4 and 5.5). The figures can be misleading, however, because these lands vary greatly in their productive capacity and in the numbers of people they must support. A more revealing measure, therefore, is the amount of cropland per person (Figure 5.6). Thus, Asia, with nearly a third of the world's cropland, has only 0.16 hectare per person, whereas North America has nearly two-thirds of a hectare per person. Because of the large quantity and high quality of its arable land, North America has been a major surplus

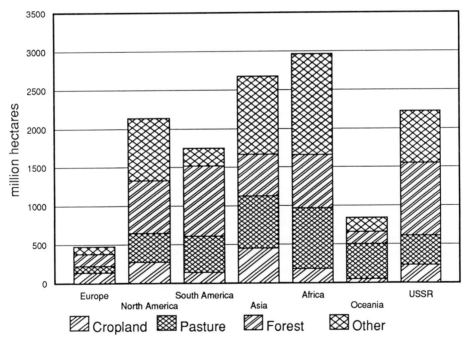

FIGURE 5.4 Land use of major world regions, million hectares. The regions vary greatly in their shares of the world's total land area and also in the ways in which this land is allocated to competing forms of land use. Immense variations likewise exist in the quality of the land and its potential for human exploitation. The "other" category includes such negative areas as deserts, arctic wastes, and mountainous terrain too rugged for human habitation. Consequently, the apparently generous land endowments of some regions are deceptive. [*Source:* Data from *FAO Production Yearbook 1987* (Rome: Food and Agriculture Organization of the United Nations, 1988).]

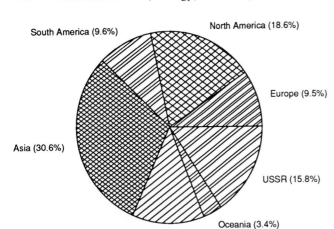

FIGURE 5.5 Regional shares of world cropland. Asia contains nearly one-third of the total global supply of cropland (arable land and land under permanent crops). North America and the former Soviet Union also enjoy large endowments. Africa, South America, and Oceania (mainly Australia and New Zealand) have much smaller shares of the world's land under crops than might be expected from the size of their total land areas. Because the regions differ greatly in population densities, a more useful indicator of their potential for food production is cropland per capita (see Figure 5.6). [Source: Based on data from *FAO Production Yearbook 1987* (Rome: Food and Agriculture Organization of the United Nations, 1988).]

food supply area from the time of the first European settlement. Despite its small overall size, Europe has the largest proportion of its land area in crops of any region (almost 30 percent); and, through intensive use, this acreage contributes more than enough to feed that continent's very large population. Though Oceania would appear to be an important source area as measured by persons per hectare, we must keep in mind that this lightly populated region accounts for only 3.4 percent of the world's cropland (Figure 5.5).

Despite the great variety of food crops grown throughout the world, a surprisingly few of these crops carry the main burden of feeding the human and animal populations. The overwhelming leaders are the grains, especially wheat, corn, and rice—in that order (Figures 5.7, 5.8, and 5.9). Being exceedingly transportable and having a multitude of uses, these commodities are staples of world diets even though they are relatively low in protein. (The millets and sorghums, another large family of grains, are locally important sources of animal and human foods in much of the world but do not figure as importantly in the world grain trade.) The world grain supply is therefore a de-

pendable barometer of the global food situation. The total output of grain has increased steadily since the end of World War II, but per capita production has risen only slowly. Population growth has effectively canceled much of the gain in total volume.

The patterns of world grain production and trade have shifted ominously in recent years (Figure 5.10). Although both South America and Asia were net exporters of grain prior to the war, both have since become net importers. Africa, never important as a source of world grain, has been a net importer since 1950. The former USSR and Eastern Europe have barely produced enough grain for their own needs, and in bad years they have had to import huge quantities. Western Europe has long had a substantial output of grain, mainly wheat, but generally had not produced enough to satisfy all of its needs. In recent years, however, the European Economic Community's Common Agricultural Policy, with its generous subsidies to farmers, has led to such an increase in output that Western Europe now faces an oversupply. Oceania (principally Australia) has relatively large grain surpluses, but these represent less than 1 percent of total world cereal output.

Although a number of countries grow enough grain to satisfy their own needs and leave a balance for export, only the United States and Canada have surpluses large enough to produce a major impact on world markets (see Figure 5.10). With only 5 percent of the world's people—and approaching zero population growth—these two countries usually account for at least one-fifth of all grain output. The critical importance of this source area was underscored by the effect on world grain supplies created by the great North American drought of 1988, the most severe in that region since the dust bowl days of the 1930s. Following a smaller-than-usual grain harvest the previous year, the 1988 crop failure reduced world food supplies and aroused fears that global atmospheric warming was at last beginning to alter the climates of critical grain-producing regions. So great was the deficit that it drew down world grain reserves to worrisome levels. Fortunately, the North American crop returned to normal in 1989 and the threat disappeared for the time being.

Meanwhile, as we saw in Figure 5.2, many less-developed regions have lost the capacity to feed themselves and have had to turn increasingly to the remaining surplus producers for help. It seems doubtful, however, that world food output will be able to keep pace with the growth of less-developed populations after the turn of the century unless important advances in agriculture production take place. What are the possibilities for these?

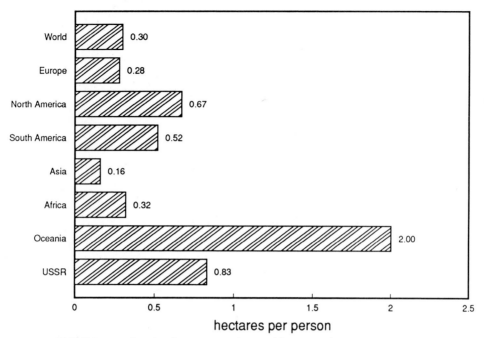

FIGURE 5.6   Cropland per capita, by world regions, hectares, 1987. On average, each inhabitant of the earth can draw upon 0.3 ha (about three-quarters of an acre) of cropland. For an Asian, the quota is only half that. Cropland per person in both Europe and Africa closely approaches the world average, but the output of that land is exceedingly different: Europeans enjoy ample diets from the output of their farms and have a surplus of agricultural goods for export; many Africans are undernourished and the continent as a whole has become a net importer of food. In most years the United States, Canada, and Australia have big farm surpluses and are leading suppliers to the world. Latin America is a region of great disparities: Argentina, Brazil, and Chile are important exporters of farm products; the three Andean countries of Ecuador, Peru, and Bolivia are unable to produce sufficient food for their citizens. Farm output in the former Soviet Union, which has 0.83 hectares of cropland per person, is highly variable from year to year. The country is therefore an unpredictable, and often major, factor in the world agricultural trade. [*Source:* Data from *FAO Production Yearbook 1987* (Rome: Food and Agriculture Organization of the United Nations, 1988).]

Two main ways exist for increasing world output of agricultural commodities: (1) expanding the cultivated area and (2) increasing the output per hectare (yield). In the modern era, however, bringing more land under cultivation does not offer an adequate solution for this mammoth problem. Some estimates suggest that the possibilities for expanding the world's cultivated land are very great, that perhaps twice the present total quantity of land in use is potentially arable. Expert opinion, however, is generally agreed that such estimates are misleading. One reason is that the unused land is generally not in the same places as the people with the greatest need for it; moreover, major economic, political, and social obstacles severely limit the wholesale transplanting of populations required to

redress the imbalance. The Food and Agriculture Organization of the United Nations (FAO) anticipates, therefore, that no more than 10 percent or 20 percent of this potential cropland will be in use by the end of the present century.

The greatest need, according to a study conducted jointly by the FAO and the International Institute for Applied Systems Analysis (IIASA), is concentrated in a group of 57 countries, all of which lack sufficient arable land, at present levels of agricultural technology, to feed the populations projected for them for the year A.D. 2000 (Shah and Fischer, 1984). Of these "critical" countries, 27 are in Africa, the one region that does not as yet show signs of significant progress toward bringing its population under control

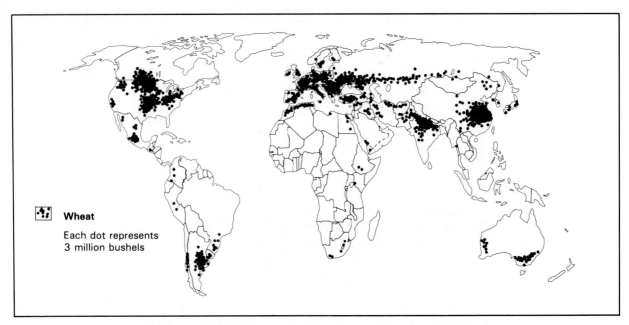

FIGURE 5.7 World wheat production. [*Source:* Data from *FAO Production Yearbook 1983* (Rome: Food and Agriculture Organization of the United Nations, 1983).]

during the twenty-first century (Figure 5.11). Most of these rank among the poorest lands on earth, with per capita gross domestic products less than $300. Ten critical countries are in Middle America: El Salvador on the mainland and nine island nations of the Caribbean. Five are in southern and southeastern Asia, Bangladesh being the most difficult case. All but four countries in the Middle East are on the list, and of these four only Turkey has substantial potential for further agricultural development. Elsewhere in the Mediterranean, and in most of Asia, reserves of unused arable land are essentially exhausted, and this

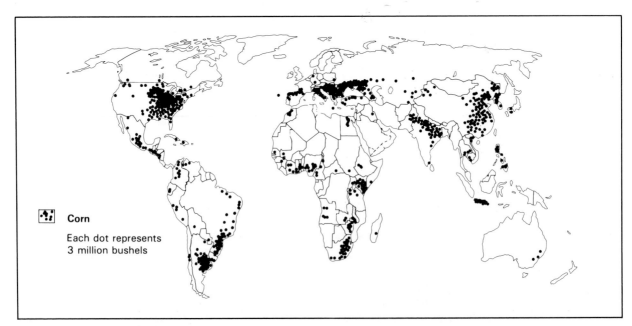

FIGURE 5.8 World corn (maize) production. [*Source:* Data from *FAO Production Yearbook 1983* (Rome: Food and Agriculture Organization of the United Nations, 1983).]

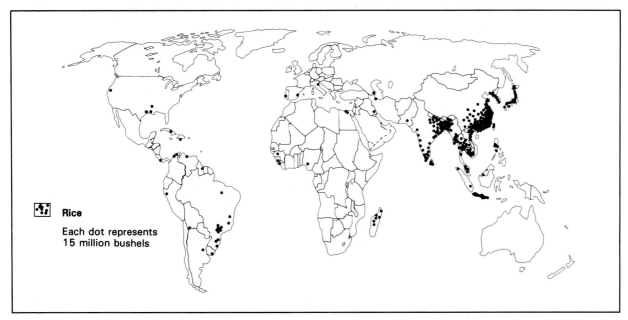

Rice

Each dot represents
15 million bushels

FIGURE 5.9 World rice production. [*Source:* Data from *FAO Production Yearbook 1983* (Rome: Food and Agriculture Organization of the United Nations, 1983).]

point is quickly approaching in many other world regions.

Another reason that estimates of unused land are misleading is that in most major areas where potential arable land is supposedly available, formidable obstacles stand in the way of its development. One such obstacle is excessive aridity. One-fourth of the earth's land surface is classified as desert—areas where rainfall averages less than 10 inches per year. Most of the unused potentially arable land of Asia is desert. Only a small fraction of such land can be irrigated.

One problem with irrigating desert lands is that many of these are covered either by shifting sands or by "desert pavement," stony surfaces devoid of soil. Equally difficult is the problem of finding enough irrigation water in the right places. Much of the irrigated agriculture in desert areas occurs along "exotic" streams, such as the Nile or the Colorado, which flow into these dry lands out of rainy mountainous regions (see Chapter 4). Many other irrigation districts make use of ground waters available through an unusual combination of geological conditions that link such areas with rainy uplands. Besides being rather uncommon, these artesian systems have an exceedingly slow rate of natural recharge—usually thousands of years. In many places, such as the American Southwest, water tables in artesian basins are falling precipitously from overuse. A further problem with irrigating deserts is the very high cost of constructing dams, canals, and roads, preparing soils, and administering these

systems. One of the most unsettling aspects of the aridity problem is the mounting evidence that some of the world's major deserts are growing, encroaching upon neighboring lands where large populations gain their livelihood from agriculture and grazing. For a discussion of this "desertification" process, see Box 5.2.

In addition to the virtually rainless desert areas, nearly one-third of the earth's surface is steppe land, where rainfall averages between 10 inches and 30 inches per year. Because of high evaporation, steppe lands in tropical latitudes are usually suitable only for grazing, but in temperate areas commercial grain farming is often possible. Although the upper-latitude steppes have some of the world's best soils—excellent for wheat or grain sorghum—the lack of dependable rainfall makes the farming of these areas highly uncertain. The tragic dust bowl conditions of the American plains during the 1930s and the failure of Premier Nikita Khrushchev's "virgin lands" project in the USSR dramatize the problems of relying upon the steppe lands for substantial additions to the earth's total arable area. Nevertheless, as we shall see shortly, many areas of uncertain rainfall in the Third World have provided important opportunities for increasing the output of existing farmlands through the introduction of new agricultural technology, including irrigation.

Many of the lands commonly classified as potentially arable lie within the vast tropical rain forests of the Amazon and Congo basins. As indicated in Chap-

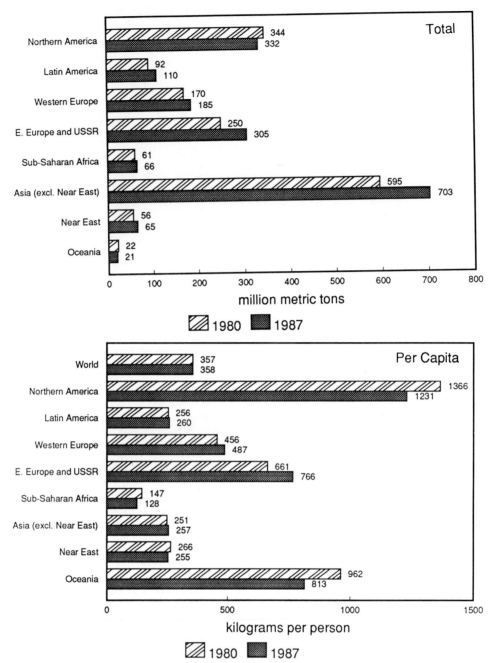

FIGURE 5.10 Total and per capita cereal production, world regions, 1980 and 1987. Total world output of all cereal crops (Figure 5.10a) rose substantially between 1980 and 1987, aided by higher yields produced by the *green revolution* in Third World agriculture, especially in Asia. U.S. grain production was held in check during this period as a result of federal farm policy. By contrast with this picture of ostensible progress by the Third World in raising total grain output, per capita figures (Figure 5.10b) show only slight gains for LDCs during the period; indeed, the average person in sub-Saharan Africa was actually worse off. Thus, when the numbers of people to be fed in the various regions are taken into account, it is clear that the world must look mainly to Northern America (the United States and Canada) for future grain supplies. Other surplus areas do not have sufficient total output to make important contributions to world supplies. [*Source:* Data from *FAO Production Yearbook 1987* (Rome: Food and Agriculture Organization of the United Nations, 1988).]

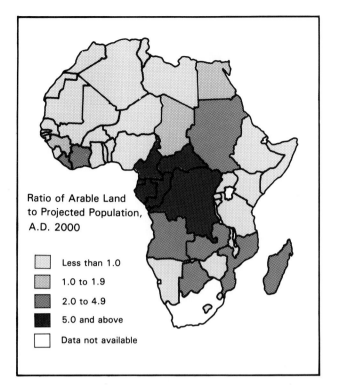

FIGURE 5.11 Land-short countries of Africa. Ratio of population-supporting capacity to projected population, A.D. 2000. Today, Africa as a whole is a food-deficit region, and many African countries depend upon food imports to sustain often-inadequate diets (compare with Figure 5.3). By the end of this century at least 29 African countries are expected to lack sufficient arable land to produce the food required by the populations they are projected to have by that date, according to a study jointly sponsored by the Institute for Applied Systems Analysis (IIASA) and the United Nations Food and Agriculture Organization (FAO). The land shortage is termed especially critical in 27 of the 29 countries. The Republic of South Africa was excluded from the study. [*Source:* Data from "People, Land, and Food Production: Potentials in the Developing World," by Mahendra Shah and Günther Fischer in *Options*, International Institute for Applied Systems Analysis (IIASA), 2 (1984), pp. 1–5.]

ter 4, the agricultural capabilities of these areas are much overrated because the heavy downpours of rain leach essential plant food elements out of the surface layers of soil, rendering them unproductive for ordinary shallow-rooted crops. Perhaps an even more serious obstacle to the use of the tropical areas of Africa, where population pressures in neighboring lands are intense, is the prevalence of dread diseases, especially river blindness (onchocerciasis) and sleeping sickness (trypanosomiasis). Great areas in the valleys

of the Volta, Niger, Congo, Gambia, and Upper Nile rivers remain unfarmed owing to fear of river blindness, which persists despite concerted efforts of governments and world organizations to eradicate it. Sleeping sickness, carried by the tsetse fly, has excluded the usual types of farming from 1 billion hectares of tropical Africa. Experiments with insecticides have been largely unsuccessful because of their high cost and because of the fly's resistance to them.

The best hope for increasing the world food supply from agriculture, therefore, does not lie in expanding the amount of arable land, but in more intensive use of existing farmlands: applying more labor and capital in order to raise yields per hectare. Recent technological advances in North America, Western Europe, and Japan—as well as in certain developing countries—point the way. The problem of transferring agricultural technology to new areas, however, is an intricate one because every locality has distinctive soil and climatic conditions and its own combination of land, labor, and capital. Plant varieties that work well in one place usually have to undergo substantial modification before they can be introduced on the farms of another locality.

The appropriate strategy for raising yields differs for a country with an abundance of farmland but a small supply of farm labor—such as the United States—and a country with a relatively large number of farm workers but a limited amount of arable land—as in the case of Japan. The situation is still different for a less-developed country with large quantities of both land and labor but lacking management skills and capital. Nevertheless, Japan's solution offers much hope for Third World agriculture because, initially at least, that country's population/food supply problems so closely paralleled those of today's less-developed countries. During the first half of this century Japan's arable land area increased by only 18 percent, but average yields rose by two-thirds and total national farm output nearly doubled.

The intensification of agriculture entails two kinds of technologies, and Japan used both: mechanization and the introduction of improved plant varieties in combination with increased fertilizer use. In addition to adopting new high-yielding seeds and making optimal use of chemical fertilizers, the Japanese developed special types of machinery suitable for use on their tiny, garden-size farms. In this way they were able to maintain and increase output even as industrialization lured more and more farm workers to the cities. Thus, in Japan, farmers substituted machinery for labor, just as their counterparts did in the United States, except at a different scale. It should be noted, however, that Japanese agriculture has also benefited

BOX 5.2 Desertification

By attracting worldwide sympathy to their suffering, the victims of famine in sub-Saharan Africa have served to focus attention upon a worsening global problem: the continuing spread of deserts into adjacent populated lands, a process called "desertification." Though a severe, prolonged drought was the immediate cause of the crop failure and resulting starvation in Africa's Sahel in the 1980s, drought is a temporary condition that has come and gone many times in that part of the world; more worrisome is the evidence that drought is merely furthering the long-term, virtually irreversible process of desertification already under way in the region. Furthermore, the deserts of Africa are not the only ones that are advancing: Desertification is also proceeding at an accelerating pace in other subhumid areas of the world, especially the Middle East and parts of northwestern Asia (see Figure 5c). Each year an additional 200,000 square kilometers are rendered useless in this manner—an area equivalent to all of New England plus New Jersey. Altogether, the threat extends to 20 percent of the earth's land surface, home to possibly 80 million people.

This destruction of productive land is largely a result of prolonged human use and misuse of a vulnerable natural environment. Soils form slowly in arid lands, and they are usually deficient in various important plant nutrients. Because of the scarcity of moisture, plant cover is sparse, and the shallow soils are susceptible to rapid deterioration through erosion and gullying. In these areas of ecological instability, the chief agents of land degradation are over-cultivation, overgrazing, and deforestation. Over the ages poor farming practices, trampling and close cropping of vegetation by goats and sheep, and stripping of woodlands for timber and fuel have so reduced the natural ground cover that the soils lie exposed to erosion from sun and wind.

Human pressures upon this fragile ecological system are intensifying, for the rates of population growth in these areas are among the world's highest. As they struggle to feed their expanding numbers, the farmers and grazers of the semiarid lands struggle to get more and more out of the land until finally the soil is so exhausted that it yields nothing. The onset of a drought therefore finds the land stripped of its natural defenses, and the process of desertification quickens. Eventually the inhabitants must abandon their farms and seek food wherever they may hope to find it.

The most recent drought in sub-Saharan Africa began in the 1970s, abated slightly in 1980, then resurged with new vigor in the following years to become the worst in a century and a half. In the process, an estimated 70,000 square kilometers succumbed to desertification each year. The band of most intense drought stretched uninterruptedly for 6000 kilometers from Dakar on the Atlantic to the Horn of Africa on the Indian Ocean, an area twice the size of the continental United States. The severest impact fell upon Chad, Ghana, Mali, Ethiopia, Somalia, and Senegal. Farther to the southeast, Mozambique was among the hardest hit in still another area of drought.

The human tragedy was immeasurable: More than 150 million people lacked sufficient food, and countless numbers died of disease and starvation. By 1983, grain output in the affected countries had fallen 35 percent below normal, a decline further accentuated by severe insect infestations of crops. Adding to the misery were outbreaks of cattle disease and brushfires, as well as wars and revolutions in Chad, Ethiopia, and Somalia.

The great African drought of the 1980s ended with the return of ample rainfall during the 1985 season. Recurrent crop failures, however, continued in subsequent years to plague the north

---

from governmental protection from import competition. This has kept domestic food prices very high, enabling farmers to continue operating despite high production costs (see Chapter 12, pages 358–66).

Though most less-developed nations have little incentive to replace their abundant rural labor with machines, they can increase farm output by introducing machinery for certain operations. For instance, at harvest time, when all workers are needed in the fields, a few trucks can transport the crop to market more quickly, economically, and with less spoilage than could any number of human porters and draft animals. Also, mechanical pumps are much cheaper and more effective in raising irrigation water than are primitive hand pumps and waterwheels.

The greatest opportunities for increasing yields, however, come from the second of these technologies: the introduction of new, higher-yielding varieties of plants, together with the chemicals and water supplies that these require for the full realization of their potential. The scientific selection and breeding of plants, which had done so much to raise farm yields in the industrialized countries since the beginning of plant genetics a century earlier, are now being applied successfully to increasing the output of wheat, rice, and other cereal crops in the Third World. International research centers have led the way by developing new plant strains and spreading them throughout the tropics and subtropics. This has required adapting these crops to an enormous variety of local soil and climatic conditions. Plant breeders have concentrated upon producing sturdy, short-stemmed plants capable of supporting the large cereal heads that yield greater output per hectare. They have also bred these plants to mature more quickly, to be resistant to pests and diseases, and to have better flavor and storage qualities.

Unlike the hardy but poor-yielding native varieties they are replacing, however, the new types re-

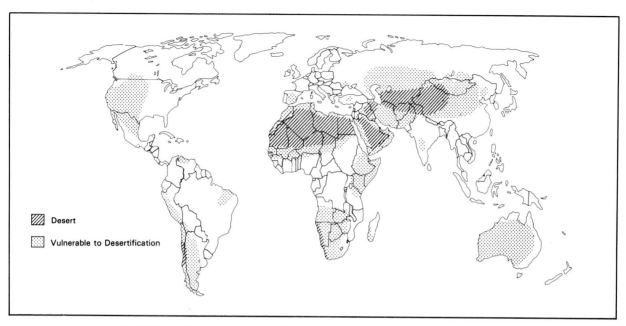

FIGURE 5c   World map of desertification. [*Source:* United Nations Conference on Desertification, 1977.]

of Ethiopia, where the loss of life from famine was exacerbated by a brutal civil war that prevented food shipments from reaching the troubled areas.

If the past is a reliable guide, the recent siege of droughts in sub-Saharan Africa will not be the last for that tormented region. The record shows that, for reasons not yet well understood, droughts in this region occur in cycles averaging seven years in length, with especially severe episodes having reappeared in each of the past three centuries. An episode of intense droughts occurred between 1820 and 1840, according to historical records; and a still earlier one took place between 1758 and 1773, as indicated by geological evidence. It seems unlikely, however, that the end of the drought of the 1980s will return the sub-Sahara to previous levels of food output. The lands most recently swallowed up in the process of desertification are probably lost for good.

quire large amounts of fertilizer. Accompanying the introduction of the new seeds, therefore, has been a large increase in the use of chemical fertilizers in developing countries, where they were virtually unknown prior to the 1960s. Indeed, half the increase in grain yields in the past three decades is attributable to greater fertilizer use. The fertilizers are effective, however, only when sufficient moisture is present in the soil to dissolve these nutrients so that they can be taken up by the plant roots. Hence, the other part of this new agricultural technology is the provision of adequate water supplies. In much of the Third World, natural rainfall is either inadequate or comes at the wrong times. In southern Asia the timing and amount of the monsoon rains have been crucial to the success or failure of harvests in the past. Supplementary irrigation has therefore been a third essential element in the drive to raise farm output in developing lands.

In some tropical and subtropical countries irriga-

tion has been the largest single contributor to improved yields. Under certain conditions it has doubled and even trebled yields during the main growing season and has made possible the growing of a second or third crop in the remainder of the year. The irrigated area has increased steadily since the 1960s until it now encompasses about a fifth of the arable lands in Third World countries. China and India alone account for half of this. Unfortunately, the extensive irrigation systems and storage reservoirs required for such projects are not feasible in many other areas, especially those parts of sub-Saharan Africa suffering from drought and famine.

On the whole, Third World agriculture has made substantial progress during the past three decades. As a result of international organized research and promotion, yields and total output of staple crops have risen markedly through the introduction of new seeds in combination with fertilizer and irrigation water. These

BOX 5.3   The Green Revolution

The dramatic development in world agriculture called the *green revolution* traces its origins to a unique international research network introduced initially in Mexico by the Rockefeller Foundation in 1943. The world first became aware of this work during the 1960s with the release of new high-yielding varieties of wheat and rice to the farmers of less-developed countries by two of these research institutes, the International Maize and Wheat Improvement Center (CIMMYT), sponsored by the Mexican government and the Rockefeller Foundation, and the International Rice Research Institute (IRRI), funded by the Rockefeller and Ford foundations. These accomplishments represented the first worldwide efforts to extend the benefits of modern plant genetics to the problems of tropical agriculture. The early successes of this program led to the establishment of 13 international research centers under the auspices of the Consultative Group on International Agricultural Research (CGIAR) in Washington.

The significance of these developments is vividly shown by their effects upon Indian agriculture. Following introduction of the new varieties in 1966, India's wheat output doubled within 6 years. Previously the world's second largest grain importer, India had become self-sufficient by the end of the 1970s, relieving its government of a drain on the national treasury and averting the tragedy of mass starvation.

Figure 5d illustrates the remarkable success achieved during those early years by wheat and rice farmers in the Indian state of Punjab, which lies on the semiarid Indo-Gangetic Plain. Although this district is subject to frequent droughts, its progressive and energetic farmers have availed themselves of local supplies of irrigation water and have applied the chemical fertilizers required by the new plan strains.

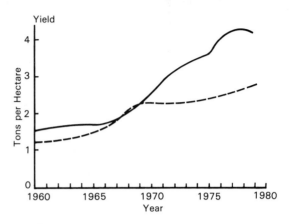

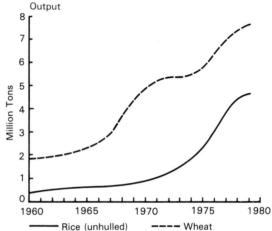

FIGURE 5d   Results of the green revolution in the Indian state of Punjab (plotted as 3-year moving averages). Dramatic increases in yields and output of rice and wheat followed the introduction of new hybrid seeds in the mid-1960s. A brief decline in wheat yields during the early 1970s, owing to the appearance of wheat rust, was subsequently corrected by the development of disease-resistant strains. [*Source:* World Bank, *World Development Report 1982* (New York: Oxford University Press).]

advances have greatly improved the lot of millions of people in some less-developed countries, where it has been termed the *green revolution* (see Box 5.3 for further discussion of the achievements and problems of the green revolution).

This revolution, however, has failed to reach all parts of the underdeveloped world. Many poorer countries have been unable to avail themselves of this new technology, and even within those countries that have profited from this development are regions that have not had access to it. Furthermore, several nations whose harvests had expanded rapidly during the

Other countries were quick to adopt these innovations, too. China, Pakistan, Turkey, and Bangladesh were among those to attain early success with the new strains of wheat. The new rice varieties likewise spread quickly throughout southern and southeastern Asia, although certain areas were unable to adopt them because of their exacting water requirements. Those districts with suitable conditions, however, enjoyed very large increases in rice output. Not only did farmers gain from the high yields but they also benefited from the short maturity times of the new strains, which make it possible to grow two or more crops within a single year.

Although the green revolution has had less impressive results with maize (corn) and grain sorghums, notable gains have occurred here as well. Maize varieties that produce exceedingly high yields in one district often fail in other areas. Nevertheless, improved types have succeeded in a number of countries, especially Argentina, China, Kenya, and Zimbabwe. Sorghums initially presented special technical problems and encountered some resistance from farmers, but they are now gaining wide acceptance in northeastern China, the drier parts of India, and some areas of Latin America.

The impact of the green revolution on Third World agricultural productivity has been striking. Mainly as a result of gains by less-developed countries, world grain output rose from only 620 million tons in 1950 to 1660 million tons in 1985, while yields increased from 1.1 ton per hectare to 2.6 tons—an unprecedented gain. Between 1970 and 1983 the area planted to the new varieties of wheat and rice expanded from 270,000 ha to 9.6 million ha. By the 1980s, half of the wheat and nearly three-fifths of the rice produced in less-developed areas came from land planted to high-yielding strains. The percentages in Latin America and China were even higher.

Despite these triumphs of the new technology, as viewed from a global perspective, it has helped some Third World farmers more than others. Indeed, the benefits have failed to reach a troubling number of these farmers altogether. The program has therefore aroused much controversy.

Perhaps 230 million rural households have been passed over by the green revolution, many of these in Africa, where only 1 percent of the grain area has been planted to new high-yielding strains. Among those overlooked are the subsistence farmers, who produce only for their own needs on marginal, rain-fed land—diverse areas ranging from the arid savannas of sub-Saharan Africa to the high altiplano of Andean America. These farmers cannot get the irrigation waters required by the new strains, nor do they have access to markets for the sale of a surplus. In many areas lacking suitable physical conditions for wheat and rice, the traditional crops upon which farmers must rely have not as yet caught the attention of agricultural research. Farmers on marginal land necessarily have a different set of priorities. For them, economic survival is the prime objective: Increasing yields is not as important as gaining security against drought and other natural calamities.

Even within those regions where the green revolution has been successful, many farmers have failed to gain from it. The main beneficiaries in these favored areas have been Western-educated farmers possessing fertile soils and the financial resources to pay for the fertilizer, irrigation equipment, and other capital- and energy-intensive inputs essential to the new technology. Such communities usually hold large numbers of illiterate, impoverished smallholders who are unable to adopt the new strains and can no longer compete when the increased efficiency of their better-off neighbors drives down commodity prices. This situation

creates a landless rural proletariate, many of whom migrate to the cities, further swelling the urban slums.

Critics also point to the environmental damage caused by the intensive use of chemical fertilizers and pesticides. These have penetrated underground water supplies and have contaminated streams and lakes, creating health hazards for adjacent populations.

The CGIAR-sponsored research institutes have responded to these criticisms by devoting more research to ways of raising crop yields without degrading the environment and by directing more attention to the special needs of small farmers. Agricultural researchers have gained a new respect for traditional farming systems and are looking for methods to improve rather than replace them in submarginal areas.

Against the disappointments of the green revolution must be weighed the very substantial contribution it has made toward global food supplies at a time when Third World populations are still mounting. It is important to note that some of the greatest successes for the new technology have occurred in the most-populous less-developed countries, particularly India, China, Indonesia, and the Philippines. As some observers have stressed, without these advances, many millions of people would have died of starvation each year. Those who developed the new high-yielding strains never regarded their achievement as the answer to all the world's food problems; their best hope was that the increased productivity would provide time for solving the central problem: bringing population growth under control. However the green revolution is viewed, few would deny that one of its most significant accomplishments has been the creation of an international network of research institutes devoted to reducing world hunger and improving the lot of farmers in less-developed areas.

early years after introduction of these innovations have since been unable to sustain those rates of increase as diminishing returns set in.

Despite the spectacular achievements of the green revolution in some countries, the overall results hardly more than offset the growth of population dur-

ing that same period. Indeed, per capia food output worldwide rose only 0.4 percent per annum during the 1960s and 1970s and it slipped to 0.3 percent in the 1980s. Moreover, the rate of increase was least in those regions with the most rapidly growing populations and lowest incomes. Thus, while per capita output was rising by 1.2 percent a year in South and East Asia during the 1980s, it remained static in Latin America and actually shrank in some other areas. In Africa, for example, per capita food output rose by 0.2 percent per annum during the 1960s but declined at an annual rate of −0.7 percent in the past decade.

As we confront the huge task of feeding future populations, the questions of time and cost arise. Enormous expenditures are required for opening new lands, building new fertilizer factories, and distributing the fertilizer and new seed varieties. Much time is needed to develop those seeds and to train farmers and technicians in their use; but time is very short. With the likelihood that the remaining supplies of potentially arable land are nearing exhaustion, and the possibility that further experiments in plant genetics will ultimately reach a point of diminishing returns, what are the prospects for supplementing future food supplies through alternative approaches?

Food from the Sea. The seas supply about one-fifth of the world's high-quality animal protein, and this source of food is particularly important to certain fishing nations such as Japan, the former USSR, China, Norway, and Iceland. Yet the nearly 80 million metric tons of food obtained from seas, lakes, and rivers provide less than 1 percent of the world's total food. Public statements on this subject often overestimate the unused potential of food from the sea: Informed sources insist that the present catch cannot be increased by much more than 15 percent on a sustained-yield basis.

This last qualification identifies the real problem, for overexploitation today means reduced catches in the future. Indeed, we have already seen stocks of many varieties of food fish greatly diminished and some species virtually depleted. Certain types, such as salmon, are especially vulnerable. Overfishing is one result of the "open seas" principle, which treats the world's oceans as common property. This means that no one is responsible for maintaining the "fertility" of fishing grounds; indeed, the open-seas concept encourages intense competition among national fishing fleets, which develop increasingly sophisticated gear to capture larger quantities of dwindling stocks of fish. Another unfortunate feature of commercial fishing is the practice among less-developed nations of exporting their catches instead of retaining this valuable protein to feed their own undernourished populations. Currently, nearly one-seventh of the world catch is exported.

The seas thus contribute only a small part of global food needs, and the supply of conventional sea foods appears unlikely even to keep pace with the rate of world population growth. This realization is one of the factors spurring the search for unorthodox forms of food.

More Radical Methods of Increasing Food Supplies

From time to time the Sunday newspaper supplements report spectacular scientific discoveries that will multiply the world's food supply limitlessly. Many such claims are mere science fiction, but certain recent developments are genuinely encouraging to a world concerned with the daunting challenge of feeding future billions. Let us explore the possibilities offered by some of the proposals now being advanced.

One of the paradoxes of world agriculture is that some of the driest deserts are adjacent to huge bodies of water; however, the salinity of these oceans and seas precludes their use of irrigation. The technology of desalination is sufficiently advanced to provide large quantities of water for household use, but the process is still much too costly for ordinary agricultural or industrial purposes. One proposal is to construct large multipurpose nuclear installations whose costs are largely borne by the sale of the electric power they generate but that have sufficient additional capacity for the production of fertilizer and desalinated water for adjacent farmlands. Another alternative for seaside agriculture in dry lands is to breed food plants that tolerate salt water. Research on this problem has already shown some promise.

A second approach to augmenting the global food supply is for the world as a whole to adopt the traditional Oriental practice of bypassing animals in the food chain. Under this plan everyone would eat the products of the soil directly rather than first converting them into animal products. These "direct calories" are much more efficient in their use of the land because at best only 14 percent of the plant food value per hectare reaches the meat eater. This would require radically altering the eating habits of most people, especially in the richer nations, but it might also subject them to the same high-starch, low-protein diets that keep so much of the Third World malnourished.

A likely solution for this nutritional problem is to develop high-protein foods from plant sources. Research has focused upon soybeans, and to some extent cottonseeds, both of which are already important sources of nutritious animal feed. An acre of land can supply 10 times as much protein in the form of soybeans as it can in the form of beef and at a far lower cost. One difficulty has been to make soybean and cottonseed products sufficiently palatable for human beings. Thus far these products have served mainly as additives to meat and bread. Among other radical experiments are attempts to convert alfalfa leaves, forest leaves, pea vines, and other common green plant parts into high-protein human food. Scientists have also worked at developing a palatable human and animal food from single-celled organisms cultured on petroleum.

Possibly the greatest promise lies in the discovery of a complex chemical that is the medium through which the fundamental characteristics of all living things are transmitted—deoxyribonucleic acid, or DNA as it is more commonly called. As scientists gain a better understanding of this substance, they are able to create entirely new organisms by manipulating the genes of various species.

Although genetic engineering is only in its infancy, plant scientists have already succeeded with certain experimental techniques, notably *tissue culture*. This is a method for multiplying plants starting with only a single part—a piece of root or leaf—and developing completely new and genetically identical plants. Tissue culture is a much quicker way of multiplying plants than seeding or grafting, and the resulting clones are completely uniform in all important respects, such as yield, quality, and maturing times. The technique also permits the engineering of plants that are resistant to disease and that are adapted to particular environments. Considerable success has already been achieved with various temperate and tropical tree crops. The potential for quantum increases in world food supplies through these and other recently developed techniques of plant engineering offer much hope for the next century.

Meanwhile, other scientists are seeking ways to multiply the food-producing potential of the seas. One product attracting attention is *fish protein concentrate,* a flour made by grinding up whole fish and using it as an additive to fortify low-protein diets in poorer countries. Not only does this method employ more of the fish for food but it also makes possible the use of fish not ordinarily caught for human consumption. Thus far, however, fish protein concentrate has not been well received by consumers.

Despite the sophisticated techniques employed by some fleets, commercial fishing is still essentially little different from the activities of food gatherers and hunters. Modern fishing fleets merely seek out what nature has provided, with little or no thought for cultivating or replenishing the breeding stock. For the long run at least, it would seem logical for the fishing industry to follow the example of agriculture or animal husbandry by devising methods for commercial fish farming. Oriental rice farmers have traditionally cultivated carp and other fish in their irrigation ditches, ponds,

and flooded fields as a source of much-needed protein in their starch-filled diets. In the same way, rice farmers in the lower Mississippi valley and delta successfully produce edible crayfish and catfish as by-products of their irrigated rice growing. Oyster farming is a long-established industry in the brackish waters of Chesapeake Bay and various other coastal waters of the United States. These techniques are now being adapted to the cultivation of other relatively sedentary forms of sea life, such as lobsters, clams, and crabs.

Several fishing nations of Western Europe have begun to cultivate nonsedentary species, especially certain high-quality food fish found in the open seas. Norway's fish-farming program is already far advanced: By 1984 it was earning a substantial income from trout and salmon and had begun production of cod, turbot, and flatfish. Spain, France, and West Germany have developed techniques for growing fish and shellfish in aquaculture plants and releasing the hatchlings into their coastal waters for restocking. Japan and other fishing countries have long used such methods for rebuilding their salmon fisheries.

As in agriculture, opportunities exist for short-cutting the food chain of the seas. Harvesting seaweed is already a well-established industry, especially along the coasts of Japan and Canada's Atlantic provinces. The seaweed yields products widely used as food additives (ice cream stabilizers, for example) and in the chemical industries. One frequently voiced proposal is to harvest plankton directly instead of concentrating upon catching the fish that feed on it. Experiments have shown that this is an expensive operation, however, and consumers find the fishy flavor of the product distasteful. Moreover, some marine biologists argue that large-scale harvesting of plankton would merely deprive food fish of their main source of sustenance.

Feeding the World beyond A.D. 2000

The problem of feeding future populations raises many complex questions that lack sure answers. Just how many people will have to be fed, and how much food will it take? Where will the greatest demand for food come from? Who will have to produce it and how? As we have seen, the world population will probably continue growing at a fairly high rate into the twenty-first century before it tapers off, and the less-developed countries will account for virtually all of that growth beyond the year 2000. Moreover, the new additions to population will increasingly concentrate in the poorest of the poor countries.

Thus, the new demand for food will be confined

almost solely to the Third World. The growth in demand will stem from two sources: (1) the increase in numbers of people to be fed and (2) greater per capita consumption as a result of rising incomes. Better diets for those Third World populations whose standards of living are improving probably mean more consumption of animal proteins, which in turn will substantially augment the demand for feed grains. This second source of demand increase—rising incomes—will center upon the middle-income less-developed countries. The poorest countries will probably continue subsisting on their accustomed high-starch diets and direct calories.

How will this new demand be supplied? The Third World as a whole is already a net importer of food: About 9 percent of current needs come from foreign sources. Only a select number of less-developed countries—notably the newly industrialized nations of the Pacific rim—could find the needed foreign exchange to pay for significant additional supplies of imported food. Many Third World countries already have burdensome trade deficits and large foreign debts. Realistically, therefore, most less-developed countries must count upon producing their new food needs themselves.

We have previously noted that future increases in food supplies will have to come predominantly from two sources: conventional agriculture and new developments in nonconventional food production. The seas currently contribute only a minor fraction of world food needs, and conventional fish catches have already leveled off. Agriculture remains the chief hope, especially with the encouraging rise in yields and output during the past two decades, which exceeded most predictions. Even so, the world food supply has little more than kept up with population growth thus far, and the task for the twenty-first century is immense. If world agriculture is to continue keeping up with population, it must achieve ever-greater technological improvements. It must also minimize future losses of arable land to competing forms of land use—urban, industrial, transportation, and so forth—and to soil deterioration from such causes as erosion, desertification, and alkalinity.

Agricultural experts concerned about the earth's future food supply have still another worry: the possibility of a major climatic change. This century has already seen unusual periods of global warming and cooling, leading some climatologists to speculate that this growing variability foretells the approach of another ice age, which they believe is about due. Others, however, note that human activities may actually be producing a countertrend that could bring a general warming instead. The combustion of fossil fuels causes carbon dioxide and other chemicals to accumulate in the upper atmosphere, where they create a "greenhouse effect" by trapping the incoming sun's rays and raising air temperatures. If either of these opposing trends were to materialize, crop production could be greatly affected, particularly in those areas that are unusually sensitive to temperature change: the higher latitudes, the upper elevations, and the semiarid regions. For instance, a 1°C decrease in mean annual temperatures, it has been estimated, would cut the potential wheat-growing area of Canada by one-third and would cause the U.S. corn belt to shift 140 km (85 miles) southward. Farmers in the South American Andes and other upland areas would have to abandon their lands at higher elevations and retreat to the lowlands.

Aside from the threat of environmental change, agriculturalists can expect additional yield increases to become ever more costly because these require larger capital outlays for irrigation and growing amounts for machinery and chemicals. Furthermore, most of the measures upon which we rely to augment world food supplies have the effect of intensifying the demand for other resources, most of which are nonrenewable. Minerals are essential for the manufacture of commercial fertilizers, for smelting metals used in making farm machinery and transport equipment, for the mechanical energy to propel this equipment, both on the farm and off, and for the construction of buildings, roads, dams, irrigation ditches, and other facilities. What are the prospects for maintaining an adequate supply of such resources?

ENERGY, MINERALS, AND OTHER EARTH RESOURCES

Resource Use and the Threat of Exhaustion

Soils can often be restored to fertility, plants and animal stocks can be replenished, and some barren wastes can be afforested; but a mineral deposit, once exhausted, is gone forever. The rate at which nonrenewable resources are being used is rising steadily throughout the world and especially in the industrialized countries. During much of this present century the United States alone has accounted for one-third to one-half of total world consumption of these resources; U.S. mineral usage increased tenfold (reckoned in constant dollars) during the first 70 years of this century while population was rising only 2.7 times. Today the United States, with fewer than 5 percent of the world's people, consumes resources at a per capita rate more than seven times the world average.

The history of U.S. consumption has somber implications for future world resource use. The U.S. experience has shown that per capita resource use rises steeply during the earlier stages of industrialization but eventually tapers off at some higher level, describing an S-shaped logistic curve similar to that of population growth (see Figure 3.3). This plateau is reached as an economy turns increasingly to the production of advanced-technology goods, which are less resource intensive in their manufacture, and as the output of services claims a larger proportion of gross national product. Although U.S. consumption had leveled off by the third quarter of the century, the world as a whole was just entering the steepest part of the growth curve. This suggests that other countries have been following the path already taken by the United States. In recent decades Western Europe and Japan have indeed substantially increased their consumption of resources, and the newly industrializing countries of the Pacific rim and Latin America have added further to the drain on global supplies. Thus, if the world as a whole were ultimately to attain the current American level of per capita production, vast quantities of energy and materials would obviously be required.

The important question to be addressed in the following pages, therefore, is whether or not the total supply of these resources will be adequate for a world consuming at the United States rate. The resources to be examined will be mainly of the nonrenewable kind; but a few are of the flow type, such as water, which are constantly being renewed by nature but are limited in total amount and subject to deterioration in quality as a result of human use.

The Nature of Reserves. Viewed in absolute terms, 88 known elements occur in the earth's crust in great amounts. Though some of these elements are indeed plentiful, others are relatively scarce (Figure 5.12). These less-abundant materials have become available to human beings only through the natural processes of concentration, which have caused comparatively large amounts of each to accumulate in a few places. This is the basis for the usual concept of a *reserve,* defined as that part of a known natural supply of a raw material that can be exploited commercially with existing technology and at current prices. A price rise makes it economically feasible to exploit deposits that are less accessible or poorer in quality. Thus, it took an OPEC crisis to add the high-cost deposits of Alaska's North Slope and Britain's North Sea to world oil reserves. Conversely, falling prices cause

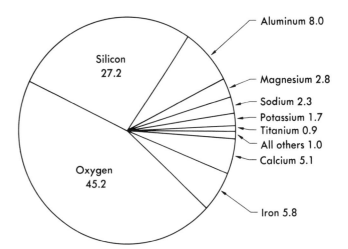

FIGURE 5.12 Elements in the earth's crust. Some of the most important industrial raw materials are included in the category "All others," which comprises only 1.0 percent of the earth's crust. [*Source:* Brian J. Skinner, *Earth Resources* (Englewood Cliffs, N.J.: Prentice Hall, 1986).]

global reserves to decline as marginal deposits become uneconomical.

Considering the erratic, seemingly capricious way in which such concentrations have formed, what is the current state of world reserves? The consumption of most resources is growing more rapidly than the rate of population growth. Not only are more people consuming resources but the average person is consuming larger quantities. According to most projections, the known resources of many vital materials would be used up within the next century, and some of the more important ones would become exhausted within only a few decades.

Rarely, however, are natural resources totally exhausted; usually their extraction is abandoned as a result of accelerating costs and prices. This does not usually happen suddenly. More often, rising prices cause the rate of use to diminish to the point where exploitation virtually ceases and substitutes are sought.

Among the variables affecting the cost of exploiting a resource are *quality* and *accessibility*. In the case of a mineral resource, accessibility includes both the depth of deposits in the ground and their distance from markets. As exhaustion of a material approaches, miners pursue reserves of increasingly poorer quality to greater depths and in more remote locations. Meanwhile, however, technological developments may slow the rise of production and processing costs, thereby postponing the exhaustion of a resource in this economic sense.

Spatial Distribution.   Most natural resources are distributed very unevenly. This erratic spatial pattern results from the nature of the physical processes that cause such concentrations to form initially. In many cases a single country, or two or three, possesses a major share of the world total. The leading producers of a material, however, are not always those with the largest reserves. The most intensive production usually takes place in the most industrialized countries, which are the principal markets for those materials and for the products made from them. On the other hand, some of the largest reserves of certain vital nonrenewable resources are in countries with economies too small—such as Canada or Australia—or too underdeveloped to make full use of what they possess. Russia and certain politically volatile areas, such as the Middle East and southern Africa, are leading producers of several essential fuels and raw materials.

This combination of spatial patterns of production and consumption holds many important implications both for world commerce and for global politics.

These concerns will underlie our discussion of the present and future status of particular types of earth resources.

Energy

Ever since the dramatic events of the 1970s, energy has been a matter of intense international concern. When the Organization of Petroleum Exporting Countries (OPEC) seized control of global oil supplies and pricing late in 1973, it abruptly halted an era during which the world had come to believe that energy would remain cheap and abundant forever. Subsequent oil crises in 1979–1980 and 1990–1991 again brought soaring prices and renewed fears of energy shortages. These episodes have posed two urgent questions: Will the world have enough energy for continued economic growth? If so, will those who control these supplies share them with the rest of the world—and at what political and economic price?

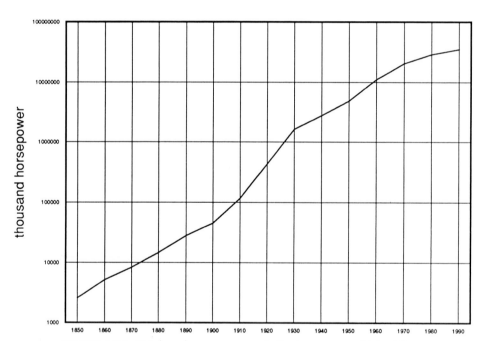

FIGURE 5.13   Total nonhuman energy of all prime movers, United States, 1850–1990 (horsepower). Except for a slight slowing in the depression years of the 1930s, the capacity for mechanical energy use in the United States more than doubled in every decade of this century until the 1970s, when the first Middle Eastern crises threatened foreign supplies of oil and raised its price. Since then the growth of consumption has lagged, mainly as a result of increased energy efficiency in transportation, industry, and housing and a shift in the economy toward less energy-intensive forms of production. [*Sources:* U.S. Bureau of the Census, *Statistical Abstract of the United States: 1990 (110th edition)*. Washington, D.C.: U.S. Government Printing Office, 1990; and *Historical Statistics of the United States* (Washington, D.C.: U.S. Government Printing Office, 1960).]

Accelerating Demand. Considering the central role of mechanical energy in modern technology, this concern for future supplies seems warranted. Indeed, the spread of industrialization throughout the world has called for ever-growing amounts of energy. Although some of the poorest lands may still depend upon human porters, hand laborers, and crafts workers for power, this is no longer true—or even possible—for those countries where modernization is well advanced. A little more than a century ago, for instance, the United States still relied upon human labor for 94 percent of its industrial power; today less than 8 percent derives from this source.

As in other forms of resource use, the United States has led the way in the enormous expansion in energy consumption. How rapidly this growth took place in the United States is apparent from Figure 5.13, which shows the increase in total horsepower of the country's main prime movers (that is, the various devices for harnessing mechanical energy, such as electric motors and steam and gasoline engines). Between 1870 and 1970, U.S. nonhuman energy capacity more than doubled in almost every decade. This means that in 1870 the average resident of the country could draw upon only 0.4 horsepower, but a century later each American had access to 100.6 horsepower. Note, however, that the growth of energy consumption slowed sharply following the oil crises and economic recessions of the 1970s and slipped further during the 1980s.

The United States still leads the world in energy use, consuming 24.1 percent of the total in 1987, followed by the former Soviet Union (19.3 percent), but it no longer has the highest per capita use. The current leaders in per capita terms are Canada and two small Persian Gulf states—Bahrain and the United Arab Emirates—all surplus energy producers. Although total world energy use has tripled since 1960, consumption rates vary greatly among countries at different levels of development. The relationship between en-

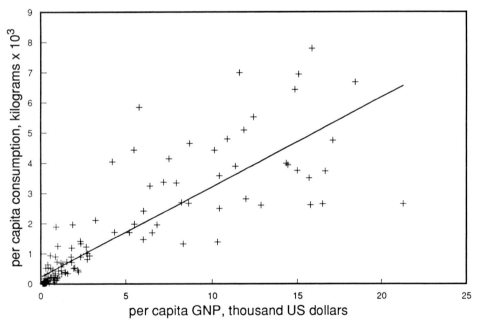

FIGURE 5.14 Per capita energy consumption and level of development. On the whole, a strong association exists between the amount of energy used per person and a country's per capita GNP ($R^2 = 0.724$), but the relationship weakens at higher levels of development. In this diagram, Japan and most of Western Europe form a cluster of energy-conserving nations in the lower right, below the regression line. To the right above the line is another group of prosperous countries that are more profligate in their use of energy, including Canada and the United States and a few oil-exporting countries. The former Soviet Union and the nations of Eastern Europe, with their economic emphasis upon energy-intensive heavy industry, also appear above the line, but at intermediate levels of per capita GNP. [*Sources:* United Nations, *Energy Statistics Yearbook 1987* (New York: United Nations, 1989); and *Encyclopaedia Britannica Book of the Year 1990* (Chicago: Encyclopaedia Britannica, Inc., 1990).]

ergy use and economic development arises from the fact that the development process requires quantum increases in labor productivity. This is possible only through the replacement of human and animal power with inanimate energy. The closeness of this relationship is apparent from Figure 5.14, which shows how per capita energy consumption rises with increases in per capita national product. The world map of energy consumption (Figure 5.15) offers further confirmation of this.

During the 1960s and 1970s, per capita energy consumption climbed in Europe, Japan, Australia, and New Zealand but it never reached Canadian and U.S. levels, owing in most cases to a lack of domestic oil supplies and high energy taxes imposed under government policies designed to restrain demand for costly imports. In the aftermath of the energy crises, per capita consumption actually lessened somewhat in most of those countries during the 1980s. Therefore, except for the former USSR, all other major world regions continue to lag well behind North America in per capita energy use (Figure 5.16).

Consequently, the regions differ markedly in their shares of total energy consumption (Figure 5.17). Thus Europe's 498 million people consume only 23 percent of the world's energy while only 275 million Americans and Canadians use 27 percent. As could be expected, the sharpest disparity exists between the developed and less-developed regions. With 77 percent of the world's population, the less-developed countries account for only 25 percent of all energy use. Except for the relatively few oil exporters among them, the majority of LDCs must spend the greater part of their export earnings for energy imports, even as their industrialization efforts call for ever-larger amounts of energy.

The various forms of inanimate energy upon which the world increasingly relies are drawn from five storage banks, all ultimately derived from that basic source, solar energy. The first of the five to be used by human beings was the *living-plant bank,* which was tapped through the domestication of herbivorous draft animals and the burning of wood. Exploitation of the *water-storage bank* came next, followed by develop-

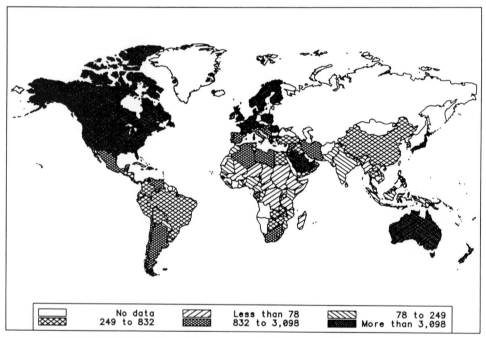

No data	Less than 78	78 to 249
249 to 832	832 to 3,098	More than 3,098

FIGURE 5.15 World energy consumption per capita (kilograms petroleum equivalent), 1987. The countries with the least mechanical energy consumption per person are in Africa south of the Sahara, southern Asia, and Andean Latin America, all areas at generally low levels of development. Several OPEC members, notably those on the Persian Gulf, rank with the industrialized countries in per capita energy consumption. Those nations at the highest levels of development differ substantially in their rates of energy consumption, depending upon a variety of economic, political, and cultural considerations. [*Source:* United Nations, *Energy Statistics Yearbook 1987* (New York: United Nations, 1989).]

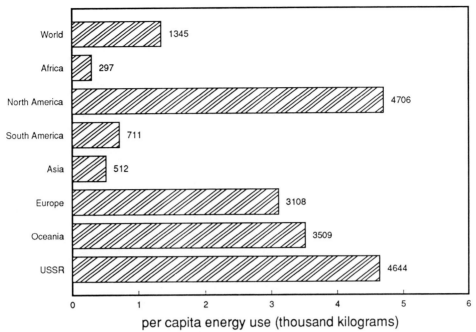

FIGURE 5.16 Per capita energy use (thousand kilograms of petroleum equivalent) of major world regions, 1987. The average earth inhabitant used the equivalent of 1345 kg of oil in 1987. A typical Latin American, however, consumed only half that much and an African less than a quarter. Canadians and Americans, on the other hand, consumed energy at three and one-half times the world average, and the former Soviets, with their energy-intensive heavy industry, were close behind. Europeans were much more restrained. [*Source:* United Nations, *Energy Statistics Yearbook 1987* (New York: United Nations, 1989).]

ment of the *fossil-fuel bank,* consisting of decayed and buried plant remains in the form of coal, oil, and gas. More recently the world has begun to draw upon the *nuclear-fuel bank* through the harnessing of the products of nuclear decay. In some favored localities, heat generated deep in the earth itself is providing the basis for commercial development of *geothermal power,* and in other places the power of ocean tides and direct solar energy are subjects of experimentation.

Since the middle of the nineteenth century, major changes have occurred in the relative importance of the different energy banks. In 1850 draft animals supplied the largest share of nonhuman animate energy in the United States, and these remained important well into the twentieth century. Fuel wood, however, was the leading source of inanimate energy in 1850, accounting for 87 percent of the total (Figure 5.18). In the latter part of the nineteenth century elec-

FIGURE 5.17 Regional shares of world energy consumption (petroleum equivalent), 1987. The less-developed countries account for only one-quarter of the energy consumed in the world as a whole (note that Asia's share falls to only 14.4 percent if prosperous Japan is excluded from the amount shown here). [*Source:* United Nations, *Energy Statistics Yearbook 1987* (New York: United Nations, 1989).]

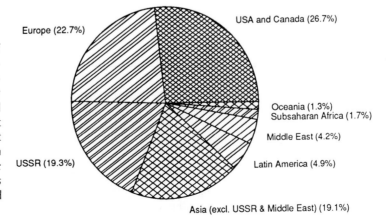

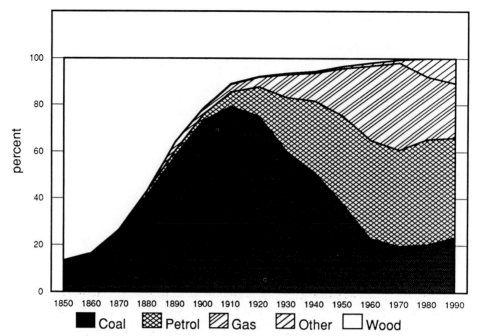

FIGURE 5.18 Percentage production of energy in the United States, by major sources, 1850–1990. ("Other" consists mainly of hydro, nuclear, solar, and geothermal power.) Wood supplied 87 percent of the country's inanimate energy in 1850, but it is little used for that purpose in the United States today. Its place has been taken mainly by fossil fuels—first coal, then oil and natural gas. The impact of the energy crises since the early 1970s is seen in the arrested growth of petroleum and gas output and the relative gains made by coal and such alternative sources as nuclear, geothermal, solar, and wind power. Falling crude prices in the 1980s engendered complacency and oil consumption began to edge upward again, until another Persian Gulf crisis in the second half of 1990 reminded the country once more of its excessive dependence upon uncertain foreign sources of supply. [*Source:* U.S. Bureau of the Census, *Statistical Abstract of the United States: 1990 (110th edition).* (Washington, D.C.: U.S. Government Printing Office, 1990); and *Historical Statistics of the United States, Colonial Times to 1970* (Washington, D.C.: U.S. Government Printing Office, 1976).]

tricity came into general use, followed quickly by the internal combustion engine. This meant increasing dependence first upon the water-storage bank for electric power generation and then upon the fossil-fuel bank, which subsequently gained overwhelming dominance. During this present century, however, the relative importance of the various fossil fuels has changed greatly. Coal was the principal fossil fuel prior to 1910, but oil and gas have since overshadowed it. Today our mounting needs force us to turn to the remaining energy banks.

In view of the accelerating demand for mechanical energy, we need to ask just how good are our reserves in each of the principal energy-storage banks, where these reserves are located, and who controls them. Considering our present heavy dependence

upon fossil fuels, let us begin by reviewing the status of each of these and examining the possibilities for maintaining a future supply.

The Fossil Fuels. Today the United States obtains nine-tenths of its mechanical energy from the fossil fuels. The figure was even higher prior to the early 1970s, when the sudden crisis in global oil supplies and prices gave added urgency to the search for alternatives. As Figure 5.18 shows, the share of other forms of energy (hydroelectric, nuclear, geothermal, and solar) edged slowly upward during the late 1970s and 1980s. Nevertheless, the fossil fuels offer so many advantages in cost and convenience that they continue to dominate the short-run U.S. energy picture.

This is equally true in the world at large; indeed,

some regions rely upon fossil fuels to a degree even more extreme than that of the United States (Figure 5.19). This is especially true for that large group of resource-poor less-developed countries dependent upon imported fuels for all their energy needs. For them the energy of choice almost invariably is oil, because of its transportability, ease of storing, and versatility.

The fossil fuels are derived from the fossil remains of plants and animals and represent the energy products of organic decay. Normally these decay products escape into the atmosphere through radiation, but under certain special conditions they may be trapped and stored. This occurred ordinarily in swamps and bogs, where these materials later become preserved and concentrated under the pressure of lay-

ers of rock. The resulting hydrocarbons assume the form of solids (coal), liquids (oil), and gases. Although these formed in minute quantities each year, their total accumulation eventually became exceedingly great during the millions of years of the Carboniferous era (between 280 and 350 million years ago). Considering their slow rate of formation, the fossil fuels are essentially nonrenewable, which poses grave problems for future supply.

Oil and natural gas are more highly prized as fuels and as chemical raw materials than is coal because they are more easily transported and stored, have higher caloric content, and give more nearly complete combustion. Although oil is cheaper to transport than gas, which requires pipelines for overland shipment and specially designed vessels for movement

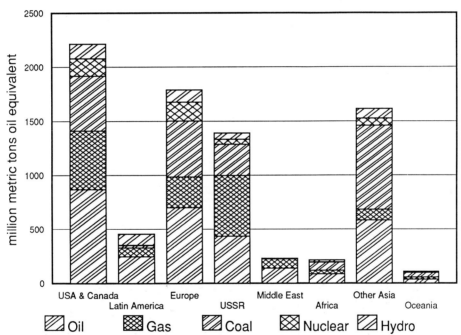

FIGURE 5.19   Primary energy consumption by fuel, world regions, 1989. By comparison with the rest of the world, the United States and Canada have a relatively balanced distribution of primary energy sources. The particular mix of energies in each region is attributable not only to availability of domestic supplies but also to the relative costs of imports and considerations of public policy. The European consumption pattern, for example, shows a preference for oil, found in and around the North Sea, and coal, mined in a number of European countries. In addition, hydroelectricity is abundant in Scandinavia and the Alpine lands. Nuclear energy is unusually well developed in Europe also, a result of government policies designed to reduce dependence upon unreliable foreign sources of energy. The former Soviet Union's consumption pattern reflects that country's large domestic reserves of all the fossil fuels, especially natural gas. The unusually large consumption of coal in Other Asia (which excludes the former USSR and the Middle East) shows the influence of China, which has huge deposits of coal. [*Source:* Based upon data from *BP Statistical Review of World Energy* (London: The British Petroleum Company plc, 1990).]

by water, gas has the advantage of burning more cleanly. By contrast, because it is solid in form and has a high ratio of bulk to heating value, coal is expensive to ship, and its combustion creates many pollutants.

Much of the crude oil (a liquid) and natural gas (mainly methane) occurring in nature are found in association, both apparently having been derived from decayed organic matter in ancient sea basins. Crude oil is a complex mixture of hydrocarbons—hydrogen and oxygen chemically combined in many ways. It therefore occurs in many grades, some light and others very heavy. The lighter grades are naturally richer in gasoline and other valuable fractions, but modern refining technology makes it possible to "crack" the heavy fractions into lighter forms. Unlike coal, oil and gas often migrate from the rocks in which they originated. Moving upward toward the surface, they become caught in "traps," rock formations that act as barriers. There they accumulate in pools, with the gas partly dissolved in the liquid and partly resting on top. Oil and gas are also capable of lateral migration, sometimes moving many miles from their origin. As the lightest fraction, natural gas often migrates still farther and may become entirely separated from the oil. In addition, some natural gas is derived from organic ma-

terials that are incapable of yielding oil. Hence, some countries lacking the geological conditions for oil have sizable reserves of gas.

Today, every barrel of crude oil brought to the surface is used completely. Not only does it yield gasoline, kerosene, jet fuel, lubricants, and fuel oil, but it also serves as a feedstock for hundreds of thousands of petrochemical products in direct competition with coal chemicals. Natural gas has a similarly wide range of uses. Modern urban-industrial economies have therefore grown heavily dependent upon these convenient and versatile fuels, which until recently were so cheap. As a result, these two energy sources, which have been exploited commercially for only a little more than a century, are being extracted and consumed at a profligate rate. How much is left, and where is it?

Proved reserves of crude oil are widespread, but they are unevenly distributed (Fig. 5.20). (*Proved reserves* are those quantities of a mineral that current geological and engineering information indicate with reasonable certainty to be capable of recovery from known reservoirs with existing technology and under present economic conditions.) The heaviest concentrations are in a select group of less-developed countries, most of which belong to the Organization of Pe-

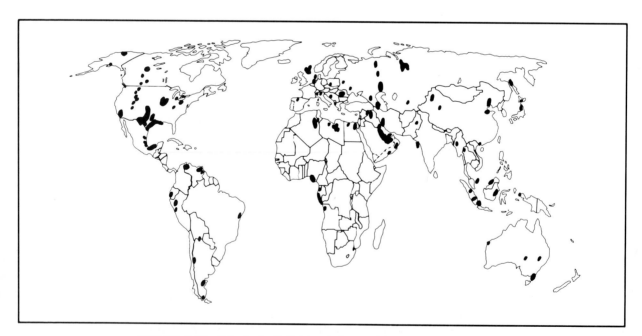

FIGURE 5.20 Principal oil fields of the world. Deposits of oil occur throughout the world and on all continents, but the reserves contained in those deposits vary greatly in size. Potential supplies for the future are therefore concentrated in only a few favored regions (see Figure 5.21).

troleum Exporting Countries. The majority of OPEC's members are in the Middle East (Iran, Saudi Arabia, the United Arab Emirates, Kuwait, and Iraq), centering upon the Persian Gulf, and in North and West Africa (Algeria, Nigeria, Gabon, and Libya), but two are in South America (Venezuela and Ecuador) and another (Indonesia) is in South Asia.

OPEC's proved reserves (1989) represent more than three-fourths of the world total, and the Middle Eastern states alone account for 65 percent of that total (Figure 5.21). Saudi Arabia possesses more than a quarter of the world's proved reserves, and Iraq and Kuwait together have another fifth. Furthermore, every year brings upward revisions of these estimates as new discoveries are made in the Persian Gulf. At present rates of production, the Middle Eastern reserves are expected to last more than a century. Not only are these deposits vast, but the average output per well is many times that of North America, and costs of discovery, development, and production are only a fraction of those elsewhere.

Latin America holds the next largest block of proved reserves, which, reflecting significant new finds, now account for more than one-eighth of the world total. Some of these discoveries have been in Mexico, which now ranks third in reserves outside the Middle East. Substantial deposits of oil occur along the Andean margins of South America, especially in Venezuela. After many years of exploitation, Venezuela's oil fields still rank first in proved reserves among non-Arab producers, as indicated by recently revised estimates. The reserve life of Latin America's oil is judged to be 51 years.

The prospects are less promising for the oil futures of the United States and Canada. After more than a century of intensive exploitation, proved re-

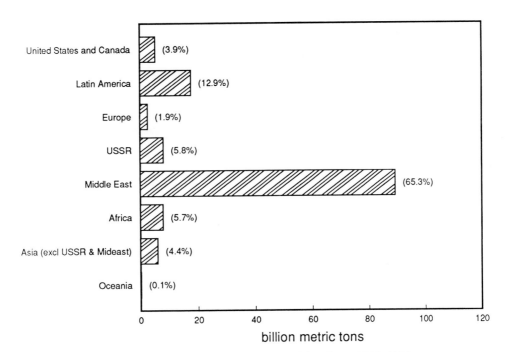

FIGURE 5.21 Proved oil reserves, major world regions, 1989. With two-thirds of the world's proved reserves, enough to last more than a century at present rates of production, the Middle East dominates world oil supplies, present and future. Latin America, which has more than one-eighth of the total, is second, bolstered by encouraging new oil strikes in Mexico and Venezuela. Former Soviet and African producers also have large reserves, with surpluses available for sale on world markets. Europe and Northern America have much smaller shares of total reserves and, at present rates of production, will have exhausted those supplies by the turn of the century. [*Source:* Based upon data from *BP Statistical Review of World Energy* (London: The British Petroleum Company plc, 1990).]

serves are dwindling, despite the development of large deposits along the North Slope of Alaska and continued exploration along the continent's Arctic margins. In 1989 the two countries had only 4.2 percent of world reserves. At current rates of exploitation, these would be exhausted by the turn of the century.

Europe's oil fields are estimated to hold 1.9 percent of the world's proved reserves, enough to last into the first decade of the coming century. Although previously considered a have-not region with respect to petroleum, Western Europe has been the scene of important discoveries in recent years. High prices, resulting from OPEC's impact upon world markets, provided the stimulus for intensive exploitation of high-cost North Sea deposits, principally those of Norway and the United Kingdom. Despite these developments, the continent must import large quantities of oil, some of it from the former Soviet Union, whose reserves are the second largest among non-Arab producers.

Asia, excluding the former Soviet Union and the Middle East, possesses another 4.4 percent of the world's proved reserves, an amount calculated to last 20 years at present rates of production. However, significant strikes continue to be made in previously neglected parts of the continent, particularly China and Southeast Asia.

The spatial patterns of global oil production and consumption correlate poorly with the locations of world reserves. With 87.9 percent of reserves concentrated in less-developed countries and another 5.8 percent in the former Soviet Union, only 6.3 percent of the total is left for the developed market economies of North America, Europe, and Oceania (Australia and New Zealand). Yet the latter continue to exploit their remaining deposits with growing intensity. As a consequence, the developed market economies still produce nearly a quarter of the world's total output (Figure 5.22). This means, however, that they are depleting their dwindling reserves at a rapid rate. Even this is not enough to satisfy the enormous demand of this group; in all, these nations are responsible for more

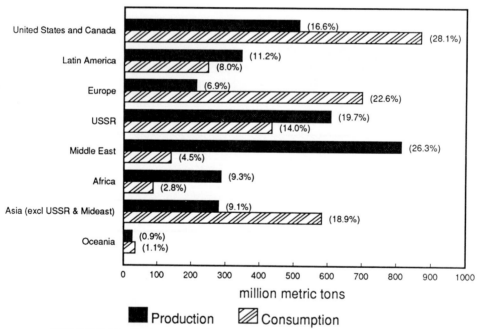

FIGURE 5.22 Production and consumption of crude oil, major world regions, 1989. The world relies heavily for its oil upon four regions of surplus production: the Middle East, Africa, Latin America, and the former Soviet Union. The developed market economies of Northern America, Europe, and Oceania, plus Japan, all consume far more than they produce. Those nations within this latter group possessing domestic oil reserves continue to exploit their dwindling domestic resources with great intensity. Nevertheless, large deficits remain between production and consumption, necessitating massive imports from the surplus regions. [*Source:* Based upon data from *BP Statistical Review of World Energy* (London: The British Petroleum Company plc, 1990.]

than half of global consumption. They must therefore make up the difference in imports from the less-developed countries and the former USSR.

By the early 1980s the United States had slipped to second place among individual producers of oil, but at the end of the decade it continued to lead in consumption. Together, the United States and Canada use more than 28 percent of world output, with the United States alone responsible for more than a quarter of world consumption. On average, an American uses oil at a rate five times that of the world as a whole, and the country must import more than 45 percent of its needs. Even so, the United States has avoided the extreme import dependence of most industrialized nations because of its generous supply of other fuels. With its smaller population, Canada produces sufficient oil to cover domestic consumption and provide a small surplus for export.

Other industrialized regions are less fortunate than Northern America. As a whole, Europe uses more than one-fifth of the world's oil (Figure 5.22) and must import 70 percent of its needs despite substantial production in the North Sea. Japan, the third largest oil user, has negligible domestic output and is therefore much worse off than other major industrial nations. The Japanese have long been acutely aware of their precarious dependence upon foreign supplies of this vital energy source and, through conservation and industrial restructuring, they reduced their oil use by one-eighth during the 1980s. During this same period, however, the rest of eastern and southern Asia increased its consumption by more than two-fifths, as the nations of that region have quickened the pace of their industrialization. Japan's dominance of Asian oil consumption is therefore much reduced from a decade earlier, when it comprised more than half the total.

Since 1983 the former USSR has been the world's largest oil producer; in subsequent years it has contributed nearly one-fifth of total supplies, making it a leading exporter. Saudi Arabia ranks third among producers, and the Middle East as a whole furnishes more than a quarter of global output. More than four-fifths of this goes into world markets. Among Latin American producers, Mexico has moved ahead of Venezuela to attain fifth place as a world oil producer. As a whole, Latin America now supplies 11 percent of the world's oil. Asia, excluding the Middle East and the former USSR, now contributes 9 percent, and Africa provides a like amount.

World oil consumption peaked at 64 million barrels per day in 1979, the year of the second big OPEC oil-price rise. By 1983 it had dropped to 58 million barrels, owing to conservation measures by consuming nations and also to the global economic recession of the early 1980s. The most highly developed countries were responsible for most of this decline; consumption actually continued to rise among less-developed countries, especially the newly industrialized members of this group. The weakening world demand for oil, together with widespread cheating by some OPEC members against their agreed-upon production quotas, subsequently caused a supply reversal—from the shortages of the 1970s to the glutted markets of the late 1980s. The accompanying fall in prices resulted in a slackening in exploration for new reserves and retarded the development of alternative sources of energy.

Relaxed pressures on oil supplies and prices inevitably led to increased use and by 1989 world consumption had again returned to the 64-million-barrel level of a decade earlier. Then, just as predictably, another Persian Gulf crisis erupted in 1990 and oil prices climbed once more on a nervous world market. This time, however, the threat was a political and military one—the *fear* of a cut in supplies rather than an actual shortage.

Further helping to ease the pressures on world oil supplies is the growing availability of natural gas, which often occurs separately from oil and therefore has a somewhat different global pattern (Figure 5.23). In all, natural gas has been found in some 30 countries that apparently have no oil. Gas is much better represented in the former USSR, North America, and Western Europe than is oil but is relatively less abundant in the Middle East, Latin America, and Africa. Indeed, the former USSR, which possesses only 5.8 percent of proved oil reserves, has nearly 38 percent of the world's gas supplies. Recent estimates have raised the Middle East's proved reserves to 30.7 of the world total, and they show a fairly equal division of the remainder among Northern America, Latin America, Europe, Africa, and Asia (excluding the former USSR and the Middle East).

Estimates of proved gas reserves have risen steadily throughout the past decade, increasing by more than one-third in that period (Figure 5.24). Although these new reserves stem predominantly from major finds in Russia, Kazakhstan and the Middle East, large discoveries have also been made in such widely scattered places as China, South Africa, and western Australia. Reserve estimates have also been revised upward in Western Europe, Latin America, and Northern America.

A comparison of Figure 5.22 and Figure 5.25 shows that natural gas also differs from oil in its spatial patterns of output and use. Some of the leading oil-producing regions—especially the Middle East and Africa—use only a fraction of their own petroleum

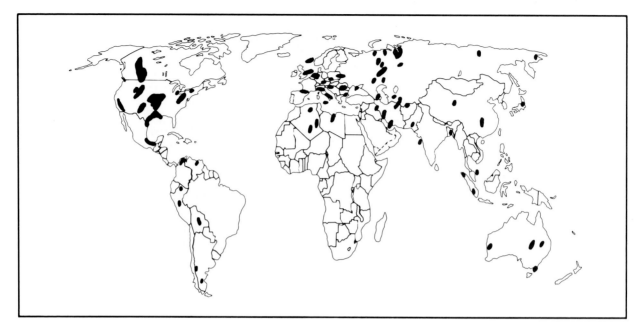

FIGURE 5.23 Principal producing natural gas fields. Natural gas is found in many parts of the world but, as in the case of oil, the most productive deposits are concentrated in particular areas. The major concentrations of gas, however, do not necessarily coincide with those of oil (refer to Figure 5.24).

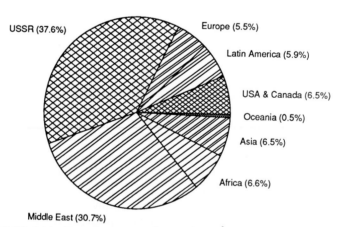

USSR (37.6%)
Europe (5.5%)
Latin America (5.9%)
USA & Canada (6.5%)
Oceania (0.5%)
Asia (6.5%)
Africa (6.6%)
Middle East (30.7%)

FIGURE 5.24 Proved reserves of natural gas, by region, 1989. Although natural gas frequently occurs in association with oil, this is not always the case. A comparison of this figure with the graph of proved oil reserves (Figure 5.22) shows a number of marked differences. The most striking distinction between the two distributions is the prominence of the former Soviet Union's gas reserves in the world picture. The political volatility of the world oil supply situation has further increased the attractiveness of this energy source and has led to an intensified search for new supplies. As a result, estimates of the world's proved gas reserves increased by 36 percent during the 1980s. [*Source:* Based upon data from *BP Statistical Review of World Energy* (London: The British Petroleum Company plc, 1990).]

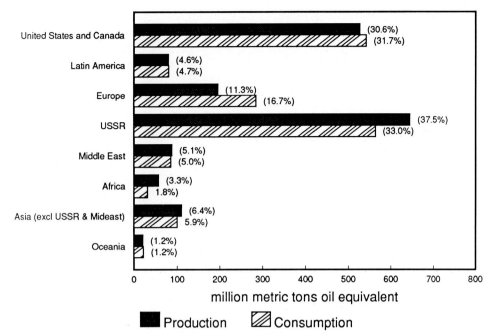

FIGURE 5.25 Production and consumption of natural gas, major world regions, 1989. Unlike oil, the pattern of natural gas production is generally similar to that of consumption, a consequence of the high cost of transporting gas by sea. Pipeline shipment between adjacent regions, however, occurs on an ever-larger scale. Thus, Europe, though a significant producer in its own right, imports large quantities of gas from the nearby Soviet Union, and the United States receives gas by pipeline from contiguous Canada and Mexico. Some natural gas is indeed exported in pressurized ocean-going vessels from Africa, the Middle East, and Southeast Asia. World production and consumption of natural gas grew by one-third during the 1980s, the greater part of this increase taking place in the former Soviet Union. [*Source:* Based upon data from *BP Statistical Review of World Energy* (London: The British Petroleum Company plc, 1990).]

output, whereas the major oil-consuming areas of Western Europe, the United States, and Japan have huge deficits. By contrast, quantities of gas produced and consumed are very similar at the regional scale (Figure 5.25). This close correspondence results mainly from the high cost of transporting gas by sea, which limits intercontinental movements. Within continental areas, however, this valuable fuel moves readily by pipeline and has become an important item of commerce between neighboring countries.

Pipeline distribution systems, however, are feasible only in high-income areas where urbanization and industrialization provide mass markets. Gas came to be widely used in the United States during the postwar years, and by the early 1970s it was supplying one-third of national energy needs. Conveniently served by an elaborate pipeline network direct from the producing fields, consumers obtained this clean, efficient fuel very cheaply because of government-regulated prices. The low prices discouraged the search for new re-

serves, however, so that the energy shortages resulting from the OPEC oil crisis of the 1970s forced a relaxation of price restraints. Higher prices thereupon caused gas consumption to slip to one-quarter of U.S. energy use (Figure 5.18), but they also stimulated new drilling. The resulting new supplies, plus imports from Canada and Mexico, have once more made gas plentiful, at least in the short run.

Meanwhile, production and consumption of natural gas have increased in other industrialized countries as new fields have been discovered and linked by pipeline to industrial and consumer markets. During the 1960s large finds were made in the British and Norwegian sectors of the North Sea and in Groningen Province of The Netherlands. As intra-European trade in this new energy source grew, the United Kingdom and neighboring lands on the continent switched from coal and oil to natural gas for many of their energy needs.

In recent years Russia has found enormous quantities of natural gas, especially in northwestern Siberia. As pipelines are built, Russia has begun converting more of its economy to natural gas and exporting the growing surplus to Eastern Europe. A further extension of these pipelines has brought a large flow of Siberian gas into Western Europe, adding to the growing domestic supply and causing gas prices to fall.

As Figure 5.25 shows, the Third World has lagged in its use of natural gas. Even the Middle East, which has nearly a third of world reserves, accounts for only 5 percent of consumption. Lacking effective consumer and industrial demand, producers in these countries merely burn off into the atmosphere much of the gas that naturally occurs in association with the oil. In the world at large about 6 percent of this valuable resource is lost in this manner, and nearly half of this waste occurs in the Middle East. Some progress is being made, however. Saudi Arabia, for instance, has constructed two great petrochemical complexes, one each on the Persian Gulf and the Red Sea, that use natural gas as a feedstock and an energy source.

New technology is also providing Third World countries with a way to export their natural gas to overseas markets. At special waterside installations this bulky product is converted to the liquid state by reducing its temperature to −259°F. The liquid natural gas (LNG) is very compact and can be transported long distances in tankers designed like thermos bottles. Algeria was one of the pioneers, exporting LNG to the United States, Britain, and other European markets. Japan, the most energy-deficient large economy, is receiving LNG from a growing number of sources. Pipeline transport is much cheaper, of course, and a number of Third World producers are finding ways to export their gas by this means. Algeria and Libya ship gas to southern Europe through a trans-Mediterranean pipeline, Mexico has direct pipeline links to its U.S. markets, and Malaysia now pipes gas to Singapore.

Although more natural gas is being used productively rather than being burned off and wasted, the rate at which it is being consumed hastens the time when global reserves of this valuable nonrenewable resource will begin to diminish, as is already occurring with oil. Later we shall look at the projected life span of this and other energy sources, but let us first consider the status of some competing forms of mechanical energy.

One form of energy that appears to face no immediate global supply problem is coal, the most abundant fossil fuel. Although coal was the energy that powered the Industrial Revolution, it has been

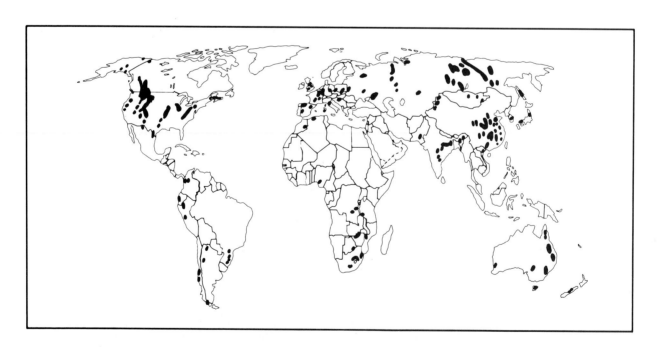

FIGURE 5.26 Principal coalfields of the world. Most abundant of the fossil fuels, coal is amply represented in several of the major world regions (see Figure 5.27).

eclipsed in this century by oil and gas, which are much more convenient to extract, transport, and use. Thus, coal accounts for 70 percent of the world's energy reserves, yet it comprises little more than one-fourth of current consumption.

Coal is a solid fuel that evolved from the burial, compaction, and aging of peat, a process that progressively increased its density and carbon content. The energy-giving qualities of coal therefore rise with increasing age. Hundreds of coal types exist, ranging from the highest-quality anthracite (hard coal) and bituminous (soft coal) to the lowest-grade lignite (brown coal). Although the major coal basins of the world have apparently been identified, the full extent of these is only now being determined with any accuracy. The projected life span of world reserves is estimated to be several hundred years at current rates of use. Very likely, however, the continuing preference for oil and gas will delay the final exhaustion of world coal supplies for some time. For this reason, and because they are much less plentiful, oil and gas will probably be exhausted first, after which coal will increasingly be converted into liquid and gaseous fuels until it too is finally used up.

Not only is coal more plentiful than the other fossil fuels but it is more evenly shared by the major world regions (Figures 5.26 and 5.27). Furthermore, as better information has raised estimates of proved global coal reserves, these new additions have been fairly well distributed across the world. Northern America is the leading source area with a quarter of the total, and the United States alone accounts for 24.1 percent. The former Soviet Union is second with 22.1 percent, though its largest deposits are inconveniently located in Siberia. Close behind is Asia, most of its reserves being in China (which ranks third behind the former USSR) and India. Europe, too, is well endowed with coal, despite continuous heavy use of this energy source since the eighteenth century. Less than 15 percent of the estimated supply is found south of the equator, but this is substantially more than had earlier been thought. Both Australia and South Africa have large amounts—indeed, Australia's reserves rank fourth in the world.

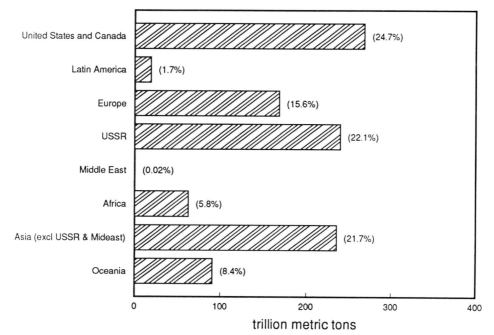

FIGURE 5.27 Proved coal reserves, major world regions, 1989. Estimated world reserves of coal have risen by nearly one-quarter during the past decade, and these increases have occurred in most major regions. By comparison with the other fossil fuels, coal is found in substantial amounts in most world regions. The only region lacking significant deposits of coal is the oil-rich Middle East. The calculated life of world coal reserves, at present rates of extraction, is nearly three centuries. [Source: Based upon data from BP Statistical Review of World Energy (London: The British Petroleum Company plc, 1990).]

Because of high transport costs, coal consumption has always been greatest in those regions where it is mined (compare Figure 5.27 and Figure 5.28). Changes are beginning to take place in the world patterns of production and consumption, however. Several major coal-producing areas are either developing other fossil fuels or are gaining better access to them, and high oil prices have brought a resurgence of coal use in certain other regions. At the same time, intensified exploitation of coal deposits is occurring in some places in response to industrialization and in others because of export opportunities.

Figure 5.28 shows the resulting patterns of production and consumption. The prominence of Asia (excluding the former USSR and the Middle East), for instance, stems from the surge of coal use by China, which ranks close behind the United States in coal output. Both China and India have had substantial growth in energy-intensive heavy industries that draw upon their large coal reserves. Although the United States and Canada have more coal reserves than do

the Asian lands, they rely more upon other fuels. As oil and gas have become more expensive, however, their dependence upon coal has risen somewhat. The same is true in Western Europe, which is not only a large producer of coal but also a major importer. The growing availability of natural gas, however, has prevented an even greater increase in Europe's coal use. Coal consumption in the former USSR and Eastern Europe has always been very great, but during the past two decades it has been declining because of increased availability of gas and oil. Another country that has relied heavily upon coal is South Africa. A pariah nation, isolated from the world community because of its racial policies, South Africa has intensively exploited its sizable coal reserves as a way of achieving energy independence. To make up for its lack of oil, it has successfully synthesized liquid fuels from coal and has even become an exporter of its synfuel technology, as well as an important supplier of coal.

The United States still leads in coal exports, although its share of the world market is shrinking. Aus-

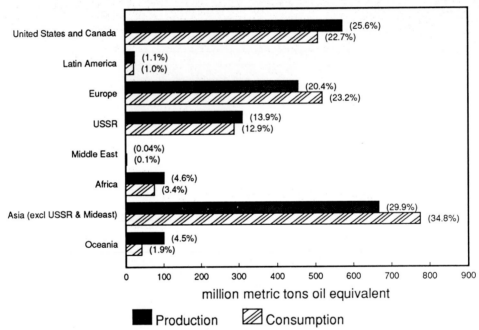

FIGURE 5.28 Production and consumption of coal, all types, major world regions, 1989. Because it is so costly to ship, most coal is consumed in the areas where it is produced. The spatial pattern of world production and consumption therefore corresponds to some degree with that of world reserves (Figure 5.27). China and some European countries lacking domestic oil supplies, however, rely upon coal to a greater extent than their reserves might suggest. The former Soviet Union has reduced its previous dependence upon coal, much of which is located in remote areas, in favor of abundantly available natural gas and oil. The chief exporters are the United States, Australia, and South Africa. [*Source:* Based upon data from *BP Statistical Review of World Energy* (London: British Petroleum Company plc, 1990).]

tralia, whose northeastern coalfields are well located near major sea lanes, ranks second. Other major suppliers to the world are the Ukraine, Poland, and Canada.

Coal production and use in the industrialized world would be still greater were it not for the harmful effects of coal combustion upon the atmosphere. Newly developing countries that rely upon coal, such as China and India, have yet to become concerned with this problem. Ironically, with all its problems as a pollutant, coal is the leading fuel for the generation of electricity, which is the cleanest form of energy.

Electricity. Of the conventional forms of energy, electricity has experienced the steadiest growth in demand during the modern era. Indeed, electric energy requirements have at times risen so fast that new generating capacity could not be installed quickly enough in some areas to avoid power shortages at peak periods of use. The popularity of electricity stems from its many special advantages. One of these is its mobility, which has given a new locational freedom to its users, especially light industry. It is clean to use, even though generating it can create a great deal of pollution. It also can be used in precisely the quantities needed, unlike the big steam engines that supplied power for factories in earlier times.

Because it is so flexible and versatile, electricity is ideal for an infinite variety of energy applications. In the United States 35 percent of all electricity is consumed by residences, 27 percent by commercial establishments, and the remainder by industrial and other users. In many parts of the world the percentage used by manufacturing is much larger. Electric motors account for much of the industrial consumption, but electrometallurgical and electrochemical companies also require great amounts of power.

Electricity is difficult to categorize, for it is really a hybrid. An electric current is essentially a movement of electrons and it therefore has many characteristics of a flow resource, except that it is used up. Also, unlike other flow resources, electricity is hard to store and most of the output, except for transmission losses, is consumed as it is produced. It is easy to transmit over short distances, but long-range transmission entails higher costs and greater losses. The difficulty of storing electricity requires that the power industry attempt to anticipate demand, which can vary seasonally, daily, and even hourly.

Electricity is a derived form of energy rather than a primary source in itself. It is produced by generators that are powered by other (primary) energy forms. Thus, the force of falling water drives turbines, which generate hydroelectricity. In the production of thermoelectricity, heat from the burning of coal, oil, or gas is used to raise steam, which in turn drives the turbines. Generators may also be powered by internal combustion engines, which may burn either gasoline or diesel fuel. More recently, new types of primary power for generating electricity have appeared. Two thermal sources—nuclear and geothermal energy—are in commercial use, whereas solar and tidal energy are still experimental.

Per capita consumption of electricity varies widely (Figure 5.29), and so does the source of primary energy employed to produce it. The richer countries use far more electricity per person than do the poorer ones. For instance, in 1987 Ethiopia used only 18 kilowatt-hours per person, Chad only 10, and Haiti 65, whereas semi-industrialized Argentina consumed 1681 kilowatt-hours per capita and the United States 11,204. In most less-developed countries, per capita electricity use is considerably lower than total energy consumption, much of which is in the form of motor fuels for transportation.

The correlation of electricity consumption and level of development is not perfect, however, mainly because advanced countries differ so greatly in their use of power. How much electricity a high-income country uses depends upon its industrial structure, whether or not a particular cheap source of power is available, and the frugality of the populace. Thus, Canada uses 56 percent more electricity per person than does the United States, and Norway uses more than twice as much. Both Canada and Norway have small populations and unusually abundant supplies of inexpensive hydroelectricity, which has attracted large electrometallurgical and electrochemical manufacturers requiring huge blocks of power.

In the world at large, nearly two-thirds of the primary energy for generating electricity is from thermal sources—mainly coal and petroleum (fuel oil and diesel) (Figure 5.30). Nearly a fifth of the world's electricity comes from falling water, and another one-sixth is from nuclear energy. Geothermal and other forms of primary energy provide the remainder, less than 1 percent of the total.

Of the thermal sources, the preferred fuel in much of the world is coal, despite the environmental problems it creates. Because of the cheapness and availability of this form of primary energy, the United States and the majority of Western European countries rely upon coal for three-fourths or more of their generating capacity. The proportion is much higher in Eastern Europe, Australia, and South Africa.

Petroleum is a leading fuel for electric generation in many places, especially the Persian Gulf countries, which rely almost entirely upon this locally abundant

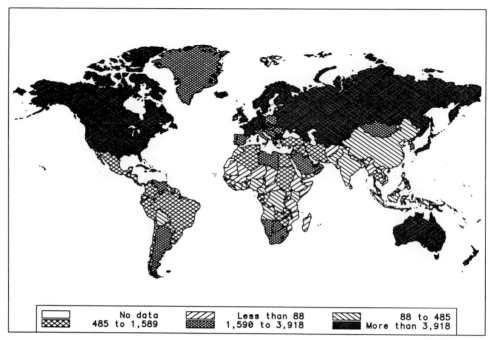

FIGURE 5.29 Annual electric power consumption per person, 1987. Northern America and Scandinavia have very high levels of per capita electricity use, and the other industrialized countries are close behind. The lowest consumption rates are in sub-Saharan Africa, southern Asia, and the Andean Americas, where annual usage levels are generally less than 100 kilowatt-hours per person. [*Source:* Data from *1990 Britannica Book of the Year* (Chicago: Encyclopaedia Britannica, 1990).]

resource for their electricity. Moreover, Japan produces three-fifths of its electricity with oil-fired generators; and the United Kingdom, which obtains four-fifths of its electric power from fossil fuels, uses dual generators designed to burn either coal or oil, depending upon availability and market conditions.

Water power is a main source of electricity in those countries fortunate enough to have the requisite physical conditions and the large supplies of capital needed to develop such resources. Norway obtains 99.5 percent of its electricity in this way, Switzerland 60 percent, Iceland 94 percent, and Canada 64 percent. Hydroelectricity is especially important in certain parts of the Third World. A prominent example is Brazil, which, to reduce its burdensome dependence upon imported energy, has embarked upon an ambitious dam-building program; at present the country relies upon falling water for 92 percent of its electricity. Brazil's latest major project is the world's largest hydroelectric dam, Itaipu on the Paraná River, which began delivering power in 1984. Among other large hydroelectric facilities in the Third World are Zambia's huge dam on the Zambezi River and Egypt's Aswan Dam on the Nile. Africa as a whole has 27 percent of the world's hydroelectric potential but only a tiny propor-

tion of that has been harnessed. This is true also of Southeast Asia, which has 16 percent of the potential, and Latin America with 20 percent. In each region the problems are lack of necessary capital and lack of a present market for the power. In the industrialized countries, on the other hand, the largest and most accessible sources of hydroelectricity have mostly been used up, especially in Western Europe, North America, and Japan.

In those countries lacking fossil fuels or water power, the second most common primary source of energy is uranium. At present levels of technology, nuclear energy appears to offer the greatest potential for satisfying the rising demand for electricity in future years. The power of the atom is harnessed in two ways: nuclear *fission* (the process used by the atomic bomb), and nuclear *fusion* (the hydrogen bomb method). The former entails capturing the energy released by fissioning radioactive elements, a process that can be controlled to release study amounts of heat for generating electricity. One pound of nuclear fuel can produce as much electric power as 5900 barrels of oil. This fuel is uranium 235, a rare and costly element with the potential to create dangerous levels of radioactivity in the environment. Nuclear fusion, on the

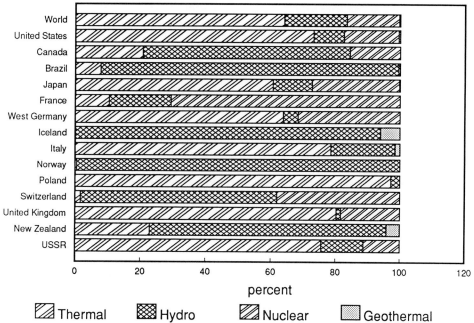

FIGURE 5.30 Production of electricity by type of primary energy source, selected countries, 1987. As a derived form of energy, electricity relies upon various primary energy sources for its generation. Of these, thermal generation (chiefly from coal, petroleum, or natural gas) leads in the world as a whole. Because of the growing trend toward dual generators, which can be switched quickly from one fossil fuel to another, the world statistics do not distinguish among thermal sources. Countries that depend upon thermal generation to a high degree include Poland (97 percent), Italy, the United Kingdom, the former USSR, and the United States. Hydroelectricity predominates in countries with large supplies of falling water, especially Norway (99.5 percent), Iceland, Brazil, New Zealand, Canada, and Switzerland. Nuclear energy has its greatest development in France (71 percent), Switzerland, Germany, and Japan. A few countries are able to generate electricity from geothermal sources (the earth's heat), notably Iceland (6 percent), New Zealand, Italy, the United States, and Japan. [*Source:* Data from United Nations, *Energy Statistics Yearbook, 1987* (New York: United Nations, 1989).]

other hand, relies upon cheap and plentiful raw materials, and the process is nearly pollution free. Fusion reaction presents formidable technological problems, however, and it is therefore unlikely to become a commercial source of energy before the twenty-first century.

Despite its high cost and the hazards it poses, nuclear fission is gaining widespread use throughout much of the world. By 1984 France had taken the lead in fostering this energy source, upon which its state-operated utility system now relies for 71 percent of its electricity. The United Kingdom, which pioneered in the commercial development of atomic power, depends upon this source for 18 percent of its electricity. Indeed, atomic energy has become a major supplier of electric power to nearly all parts of Europe, both West

and East. Even Japan, the only country to experience wartime atomic destruction, depends upon nuclear power for 27 percent of its electricity. Among Third World countries with atomic power installations are India, South Korea, and Taiwan. The former USSR obtains 11 percent of its electricity from this source, and the United States, despite its many problems with nuclear power, generates 17 percent of its electricity in this manner.

Still another new technology that contributes significant amounts of electricity in several countries is *geothermal* energy. This method of generating power relies upon heat that occurs naturally inside the earth; temperatures rise with increasing depth, reaching 5000°C at the core. Over most of the earth's crust this heat remains too deep for it to be tapped in any useful way, but in a few areas abnormally hot rocks approach the surface. Where groundwater comes into contact with these rocks it forms geothermal pools, which overflow as hot water or steam to create hot springs and geysers. Among countries successfully harnessing this earth heat to generate commercial quantities of electricity are Iceland, Japan, Mexico, New Zealand, and the United States (in California).

Today, increasing amounts of electricity are traded among countries as power-surplus nations sell their excess supplies to power-short neighbors. Regional and national power grids link adjacent countries in order to balance differing peak loads and to provide extra reservoirs in case of emergency. The continental countries of Western Europe have interconnected power systems of this sort, and a two-way cable linking the United Kingdom and France under the English Channel is nearing completion. The leading exporting country is Canada, which sends large amounts of its cheaply produced hydroelectricity to nearby power-deficient areas of the United States. In Western Europe the chief exporters are Switzerland, Norway, and Austria—all with great surpluses of hydroelectricity—and France, which is rapidly expanding its supply of nuclear-generated power for export. A similar exchange of electricity takes place in Eastern Europe, the former USSR being the largest supplier. Some trade in electricity is even taking place among less-developed countries. Zambia, for example, finds sizable markets for its abundant hydroelectricity in neighboring Zimbabwe and South Africa.

Noncommercial Energy.

In the Third World as a whole, much of the inanimate energy comes from noncommercial sources. Ironically, it is in these lands that perhaps the most critical energy shortages of all are taking place, threatening not only local economies but also the physical environment itself, along with all those people who depend upon it for support. The amount of energy obtained from fuel wood, agricultural wastes, animal dung, and other noncommercial fuels is immense. For instance, in India and Indonesia, two of the most populous less-developed countries, these sources contribute almost as much to total energy consumption as do commercial sources. In all, possibly 1.5 billion people rely solely upon firewood for heating their water and cooking their food. Most have no access to alternative forms of energy and could not afford them even if they did. The total amount of firewood used in a year is likely more than a billion metric tons.

Although noncommercial energy constitutes a diminishing proportion of total energy consumed in the Third World—a result of increasing industrialization in some developing countries—the number of people still relying upon traditional fuels remains very great because of the high rates of population growth in these lands, especially the poorest ones. Indeed, severe population pressure is a prime cause of the worsening energy crisis now facing major parts of the Third World. With growing numbers of people scavenging for wood, the forest cover is disappearing at an alarming rate over vast areas. Wood gatherers have to range farther and farther each day in search of wood, and in some countries they are forced to take every sapling and twig and even the litter on the ground. As the forest floor becomes denuded, trees and shrubs are no longer able to reseed themselves and the bare soil is left to erode in the wind and rain.

When the firewood disappears altogether, as it has in much of Africa south of the Sahara and in southern Asia, the population must turn to the dried dung of their livestock for fuel. This deprives their fields of vitally needed animal fertilizers and thus reduces crop yields. Hence, the crisis in noncommercial energy adds to the crisis in food supply of poorer lands. This Third World energy problem is little noticed in the general effort to ensure future supplies of commercial energy for the industrialized countries.

The Energy Future.

Having examined the characteristics of conventional energy forms, and the spatial patterns of their reserves, production, consumption, and exchange, we now turn to the most pressing question: Is the supply of energy adequate for future needs? Public complacency on this subject gave way to deep concern after the oil price shocks precipitated by the Arab oil embargo of 1973–1974 and the Iran-Iraq War beginning in 1979. As oil prices rose, the prices of gas and other competing fuels rose in sympathy, introducing a new era of more costly energy and greater uncertainty. It brought with economic recession and slower economic growth and it aggravated income and social inequities.

Considering the immense transfer of wealth from oil-importing to oil-exporting countries that took place during the 1970s and early 1980s, the world as a whole made a surprising adjustment. Energy consumption declined in response to higher prices and slower economic activity. And new sources of petroleum were vigorously sought and found in the North Sea, Alaska, Mexico, and other non-OPEC areas. Indeed, the adjustment was sufficient to lull many people, and their political leaders, into a false sense of security.

This illusion was abruptly snapped by Iraq's August 1990 invasion of Kuwait and the ensuing United Nations embargo, which deprived world markets of one-fifth of their usual supply. Crude oil prices soared, again reminding the world of its dangerous reliance upon a vital resource tightly concentrated within a politically volatile region.

Looking to an uncertain energy future, therefore, we may ask: What can be done to avoid these recurring crises? And, even if further oil-supply interruptions can be averted, how long are the world's stocks of this and the other conventional forms of energy likely to last? What can we do to postpone the ultimate exhaustion of these nonrenewable resources? What are the prospects for replacing them with new kinds of energy? Before taking up these questions of future supply, however, we must first see how much energy the world can be expected to need.

Anticipating future world demand is difficult because countries at various levels of development use energy differently and react differently to price changes. Less-developed countries generally spend a higher proportion of their gross national products on energy than do advanced countries, and this proportion continues to diminish at the highest levels of development. Though per capita energy consumption is very low among the least-developed countries, this climbs steeply with rising GNP (refer back to Figure 5.14).

The effects of price on energy demand are complex. In the short run the price-elasticity of demand for energy is low in advanced countries; that is, a rise in price is not immediately reflected in reduced consumption (see Chapter 6, pages 180–82, for a more detailed explanation of price-elasticity of demand). Consumers do not instantaneously trade in their gasoline-wasting big automobiles for more energy-efficient ones when fuel prices rise, nor do factories immediately install new machinery or homeowners insulate their houses. More likely, a quick, sharp rise in energy prices will merely precipitate an economic recession. In the longer run, however, the price-elasticity of demand is much higher: The next car purchased gets much better gasoline mileage, and so forth. On the whole, citizens of the richer countries have many opportunities for saving energy merely by making discretionary changes in lifestyle—living closer to work and recreation, traveling less, and turning off electric lights and appliances. The effects of price rises on the economic growth of advanced countries are generally less, too, because a larger part of GNP is derived from the services and high-technology industries that consume little energy.

The cost of energy and its availability have a severe impact on the economic growth of less-developed countries, however, because of the nature of their industrial and transport needs. Any rise in their level of development is directly reflected in increased demand for energy. High rates of population growth add further to this demand.

Projections of future energy needs therefore suggest that a doubling of total energy demand in the industrialized nations would likely be accompanied by a five- to sevenfold demand increase in the less-developed countries. Nevertheless, current levels of energy use in the LDCs are so low that even this gain in total amount would leave their per capita consumption six or seven times smaller than that of the richer ones. Thus, if in some manner all the world's nations could achieve the levels of prosperity now enjoyed by the industrialized countries, enormous increases in the total demand for energy would result.

Finding sufficient additional quantities of energy to supply this growing demand raises still other uncertainties. Although reserve estimates such as those appearing in Figures 5.21, 5.24, and 5.27 give some indication of near-term prospects, the more distant future is clouded by questions of data quality and changes in costs. Added to this is the problem of uneven world distribution and the political risks this poses for energy-importing countries, all of which carry great potential for future price fluctuations.

Based upon what we know now, and assuming a minimum of political intervention in world commerce, we may expect oil production to peak during the final decade of this present century. Therefore, supplies will likely diminish gradually and production costs and market prices will rise accordingly. Because such a large proportion of known reserves is concentrated in the former USSR and the politically volatile Middle East, however, the political uncertainties surrounding this current prime energy resource are especially troublesome.

Natural gas production should rise substantially toward the year 2000, reaching a peak within the first two or three decades of the new century. Gas supplies are thus likely to last a little longer than oil. As in the case of oil, however, a major part of the world's natural gas is in the former USSR and the Middle East (although this time the former USSR has the greater share). North America and Western Europe are relatively better off in gas reserves than they are in oil, and the United States has a very large potential from high-cost sources. As we have seen, however, the sharing of this resource between have and have-not nations is more difficult than oil because gas is so costly to ship by sea.

As the most abundant fossil fuel, coal should be plentiful throughout the next century. Moreover, its reserves are more widely distributed, including very large stocks in the United States and China, as well as the former USSR, Europe, and Australia. This pattern is therefore much more favorable for the industrialized nations than other conventional fuels. Yet, those countries lacking coal are at a disadvantage because of its high shipping costs. Widespread future use of coal also requires finding an economical solution to the problem of atmospheric pollution now associated with coal combustion.

The remaining energy sources now making a significant contribution all pose problems for future expansion. With current technology, nuclear fission is unlikely to last beyond the turn of the century because of limited supplies of low-cost uranium. Environmental constraints are also a serious deterrent, especially in the United States. Hydroelectricity has a limited future among developed countries, where most of the existing waterpower potential has been exhausted. A very large unused potential remains in parts of the Third World, but obtaining the capital required to develop this resource will continue to be a great obstacle.

Beyond this present century, projections of energy demand and supply become increasingly uncertain. The distant energy future is easier to foresee in the case of the present group of industrialized nations because their populations have stabilized and their levels of resource use appear to have peaked and even to have begun a decline. The less-developed countries present an entirely different set of problems. We cannot be sure of their future demand for energy without knowing how far their development will proceed and what form their industrialization will ultimately assume. What we can be sure of is that the potential demand will inevitably rise as Third World populations continue to climb before peaking in the latter part of the twenty-first century. At that point, the number of potential users of energy will probably have reached 10 or 12 billion. With the output of today's preferred forms of energy expected to dwindle soon after A.D. 2000, the search for new kinds of energy is already pressing. This is especially so because of the long lead time required for a new form of energy to supersede an older one; in the past this has usually required about 50 years.

Experience gained from the energy crises of the 1970s demonstrated that one sure way of gaining additional time for developing radically new kinds of energy is to stretch out existing supplies of conventional energy. Conservation is now generally recognized as the cheapest and quickest method of obtaining energy in the short run. The OPEC crises slowed the rate of energy use far more than the most optimistic predictions of the time. The reaction was almost worldwide; between 1979 and 1983 consumption in the noncommunist industrialized countries actually fell by one-tenth, reversing the steady rise in energy consumption that had prevailed for decades previously (Figure 5.31).

This reversal in consumption trends was especially dramatic in the United States, long a profligate user of energy. By 1983 the country was using less energy than it had in 1973 on the eve of the first OPEC crisis, yet gross national product had risen at an average annual rate of 2.5 percent during that 10-year period. The United States achieved its 1983 GNP with 22 percent less energy than if 1973 levels of energy efficiency had continued unchanged.

The trend toward saving energy acquired a momentum of its own when people discovered that unlimited future supplies of cheap oil were no longer assured. As a result, energy efficiency has assumed a built-in quality. Purchasers of home furnaces and household appliances now expect these to be energy-efficient, and builders routinely insulate new residential and commercial structures. In the United States, federally mandated standards for new automobiles had raised the average fuel efficiency from only 14 miles per gallon in the 1970s to 28 miles per gallon by the late 1980s. Though both consumers and government officials had grown increasingly complacent during that era, the Persian Gulf crisis of 1990 brought a return to realism. Following this event, the U.S. Congress imposed much stricter fuel standards upon vehicle manufactures for future model years.

During the 1980s industrial users intensified their efforts to improve energy efficiency. By 1982 industrial use of all types of energy was one-third less in the United States than would have been the case if 1973 consumption trends had persisted. Continuing this persuit, industries have reduced their share from 40 percent of total U.S. energy use in 1983 to only 36 percent by 1990. This has been achieved in part by installing better equipment, but it has also reflected slower industrial growth associated with structural changes in the economy. At a time when service activities have been contributing a larger share to GNP, older energy-intensive industries have been declining—replaced by new high-technology enterprises with far lower energy requirements. Nevertheless, the potential remains for even greater improvement: The Department of Energy has declared that American industries could actually turn out the same amount of product with 50 percent less energy than at present.

In its conservation efforts, the United States continues to lag behind Japan and Western Europe, where energy has always been more costly. Even the Europeans and Japanese, however, had been lulled by the cheaper petroleum of the 1980s and had relaxed their vigilance. Jolted by the 1990 Iraqi invasion of Kuwait into renewed awareness of their vulnerability

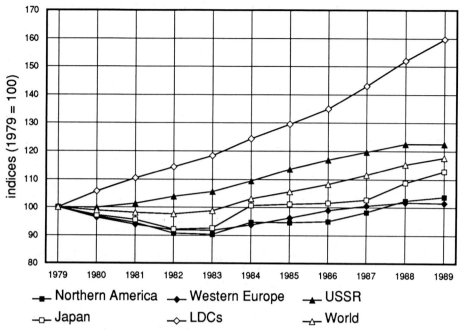

FIGURE 5.31 Changing consumption of primary energy, selected areas, 1979–1989, indices (1979 = 100). The sharp run-up in energy prices following the 1979 Persian Gulf crisis prompted a worldwide drive to conserve energy. Reinforced by the 1982 global recession—itself a product of escalating fuel costs—the conservation effort produced much better results than any had anticipated. By 1983 total energy consumption in the noncommunist industrialized countries had dropped by a tenth. The former Soviet Union, however, with its abundant domestic supplies, continued to increase its energy consumption throughout the period. Energy use also continued to rise in the Third World, which lacked the opportunities for fuel savings enjoyed by the richer countries. At the end of the decade, on the eve of the 1990 Persian Gulf crisis, total world consumption was 18 percent above its 1979 level. Western Europe's energy use, however, had risen only 2 percent during the 10 years, and Northern America's consumption had gone up only 3.8 percent—a decline in per capita terms. Japan's energy use was 12.8 percent higher in 1989 than in 1979, but this represented a marked decline in relation to its GNP, which had expanded by more than 40 percent in that time. [*Source:* Data from *BP Statistical Review of World Energy* (London: British Petroleum Company plc, 1990).]

to oil-supply interruptions, these countries once again revived energy restrictions of the kinds imposed during earlier emergencies.

Viewed globally, some of the greatest opportunities for energy conservation are in the former Soviet Union, whose per capita consumption is 50 percent greater than Europe's (refer to Figure 5.16) despite a far-lower standard of living. Soviet energy use continued to rise steadily throughout the 1980s at a time when noncommunist countries were cutting consumption (Figure 5.31). The reasons for this high rate of energy use are to be found mainly in Soviet industry, which emphasized heavy, energy-intensive forms of production and relied upon outdated plants and equipment.

Although in the short run conservation has proved unexpectedly effective, in the longer run substantial new supplies will have to be found. One way of doing this is to intensify exploitation of existing reserves and exploration for new ones in order to extend the life spans of conventional fuels. Those producing countries that are net importers of energy are already pursuing this policy with considerable effect. Thus, the United States, which has only 3.4 percent of the world's proved oil reserves, accounts for 14 percent of total production, whereas the Middle East, with 65.2

percent of the reserves, yields only 26.3 percent of world output. Additions to U.S. production now come mainly through horizontal and vertical expansion of existing fields, that is, drilling new wells on the margins and going to greater depths.

The only truly important U.S. finds in recent times were in Alaska, and that region (which holds one-third of U.S. reserves) continues to be the country's main hope for new supplies to replace the now-dwindling output at Prudhoe Bay. An equally intensive and costly search for oil and gas is under way in the Canadian Arctic. Elsewhere in the world the effort to locate new supplies has continued since the first OPEC crisis, yielding important finds in the North Sea, southern Mexico, China, Australia, and Colombia. The USSR, though known to have some of the world's largest energy resources, has had to put massive new investments into oil exploration to compensate for declining output. The USSR's main problem is that thus far the country has been relying upon only the richest and most accessible deposits, thus skimming off the cream of its huge energy wealth. As these older fields decline, new exploration has led ever deeper into remote and frozen areas of Siberia, where high costs and technical difficulties have slowed development. Meanwhile, the Middle East maintains its status as the richest area of all: Recent additions to Kuwait's reserves, for example, alone equal all the known reserves of the United States. The net effect of all this intensified exploration since 1973 is that the world has located more oil than it has used since the first oil crisis. In 1979 the world's proved oil reserves were calculated at 650 billion barrels; in 1989 they were estimated at 1012 billion barrels, a 44-year supply at current levels of production and use.

The success of this feverish search for new energy has temporarily reduced the oil cartel's hold on world markets and has postponed the time when fossil fuels will become exhausted. Nevertheless, the experts consider it unlikely that any new "Middle Easts" will appear to provide a quantum rise in world reserves. Given the long lead time for developing new types of energy, where do our best hopes lie for the more distant future?

All the options for other energy sources involve the development and refining of new technologies. One such option concerns the perfection of techniques for recovering the great amounts of oil left underground in an oilfield after the usual extraction methods have ended. When pumping of an oil pool ceases, as much as 60 percent to 70 percent of the oil remains behind, trapped in pockets and holes in the rock. The industry has developed secondary recovery tech-

niques that can bring up some of the remaining oil, and so-called enhanced recovery contributes additional amounts; but these methods still leave possibly half of the total behind. The remainder represents an enormous resource, but finding ways of tapping it poses great technical difficulties yet to be solved.

Another huge resource that awaits further technological development before it can be fully utilized is coal. Its combustion releases into the atmosphere dangerous impurities that pose serious environmental hazards, but a truly effective treatment is costly because of the number and complexity of the pollutants that must be driven off. Present techniques—washing, fluidized beds, scrubbers—add 20 percent or more to the cost of generating electricity and therefore place this valuable fuel at a competitive disadvantage with respect to other forms of energy, especially in locations remote from coalfields. Developing an economical method that would give clean-burning coal should be of highest priority to the United States, which has very large reserves. Although such techniques appear within grasp, this type of research has been unable to attract the funding needed for a quick solution.

On the other hand, during and immediately after the energy crises of the 1970s a great deal of attention focused upon synfuels. These are produced by converting solid fuels to gaseous or liquid forms suitable for use in internal combustion engines. The most common raw materials are coal, oil shales, and tar sands. For at least 150 years coal has been used for generating a low-grade fuel called "coal gas," or "town gas," which was common in Europe and North America until it was superseded by cheaper, hotter natural gas. More recently, attention has turned to obtaining liquid fuels from coal, to be used as substitutes for oil and gasoline. Processes developed in Germany during World War II are the bases for existing methods, which South Africa has adopted and further refined for its drive to achieve energy independence as described earlier. Several experiments with these techniques were undertaken in the United States in the late 1970s but languished with the decline in world oil prices in subsequent years.

North America is likewise well endowed with two other resources used for making synfuels—tar sands and oil shales. So plentiful are these that they have the potential for nearly doubling the world's fossil fuel stores. Tar sands contain large-molecule hydrocarbons like those of crude oil, but they do not migrate as do oil and gas. Instead, this thick bituminous material adheres firmly to the sand grains among which it has lodged. Tar sands occur in limited quantities in several parts of the world, but the most important known deposits are in western Canada. The Athabaska tar sands of northern Alberta are 200 feet thick and extend over 30,000 square miles. Other large occurrences are the Orinoco deposits of Venezuela and the Olenek deposits in Russia. Recovery of this resource requires mining the sands and then heating them to cause the asphaltic hydrocarbons to flow. Commercial extraction of the Canadian deposits is already well under way.

Oil shales are rock formations that contain concentrations of bitumen that can be converted into valuable petroleum products. Vast reserves of rich oil shales occur in the Rocky Mountains of the United States, extending over much of Colorado, Utah, and Wyoming. These Green River shales can be made to yield from 0.5 to 1.5 barrels of oil per ton; in total the country's oil shales probably exceed the amount of its conventional oil reserves. Pilot plants have proved the technical feasibility of mining oil shale, but it is too costly to exploit at present price levels. In addition, current processing techniques threaten the vulnerable western environment with atmospheric pollution, water contamination, and problems of waste disposal. Nevertheless, both tar sands and oil shales represent potentially important supplements to future energy supplies.

To many experts, the ultimate answer to the world's energy needs lies with nuclear power—but not necessarily the form now in commercial use, nuclear *fission*. Though it is the basis of expanding power programs worldwide—by 1989, 429 commercial reactors were operating in 25 countries—fission poses such complex, and frightening, issues that its long-term prospects are in doubt.

Perhaps most serious of all are the grave environmental concerns that the commercial use of nuclear fission provokes. The siting of nuclear power plants in populated areas arouses fears of horrible nuclear accidents such as the 1986 Chernobyl disaster in the Soviet Union; controversy also surrounds the search for safe ways to dispose of radioactive waste products. Debate over these environmental issues has become so heated that atomic energy development has stalled in the United States and existing generating plants are being closed down in Sweden.

Also clouding the long-term future of fission is the prospect of rising costs. High-grade ores of U-235 are severely limited in occurrence, and continued exploitation of this scarce resource will therefore become increasingly costly. Solution of this supply problem depends upon perfection of the fast-breeder reactor, which uses a lower-grade fuel and creates new fuel at the same rate or greater than the fissioning

atoms are used up. However, the breeder reactor further heightens safety concerns; countering these would require elaborate measures that could make this form of energy prohibitively expensive.

Nuclear *fusion* promises a longer-term solution to the environmental safety problems surrounding atomic power. If and when research on this technology succeeds, nuclear fusion could supply limitless amounts of electric energy using one of the cheapest and most plentiful raw materials, hydrogen—and it would present no radiation dangers. Unlike fission, however, nuclear fusion has not yet been controlled to permit its use for generating electricity, despite intense research.

The energy emergencies of the 1970s precipitated a concerted worldwide drive to find commercially feasible alternative energies that would liberate the world from dependence upon fossil fuels and the vexing political, environmental, and long-term supply issues that surround these. Though public financing for U.S. energy research was sharply curtailed during the 1980s, strong government-sponsored energy programs continued in other countries, especially Japan and Germany. These, together with privately funded research in the United States, have made important progress in several directions. See Box 5.4 for a list of the more promising alternative forms of energy now emerging.

Clearly, then, we have many options for keeping the world supplied with mechanical energy in the future. This present period appears to be one of transition, a time when the end of the familiar and conventional forms of energy is approaching and newer forms are not yet ready to replace them fully. The transition is filled with uncertainties relating to consumption trends, investment levels, technical questions, and politics.

In the short run, we must contend with crises. Political crises in the form of wars, revolutions, and embargoes may suddenly cut off supplies, although presumably these would create only relatively brief interruptions. Crises could also arise if producing countries and companies fail to make the necessary investments to sustain necessary levels of output. Some exporting countries, for instance, could decide that it is in their own best interest to keep their surplus oil in the ground for future sale. Finally, we may encounter crises of reserve supply, occurring when the physical supplies of nonrenewable resources are finally exhausted. Some predict that this crucial transitional period could continue through the first quarter of the next century.

The long-run situation is another matter. After

BOX 5.4   *Promising Energy Alternatives*

Among all the new forms of energy proposed as alternatives to the familiar types now in use, a select few appear to have at least some of the characteristics required of an eventual replacement for fossil fuels. A viable alternative energy would have to be (1) competitive in cost with existing types, (2) in abundant supply, and (3) widely available or cheaply and easily transported. Ideally, it should also be (4) nonpolluting and (5) safe to transport, store, and use. The present candidates tend to fall into two somewhat overlapping categories: (1) primary energies for generating electricity and (2) energies designed to propel motor vehicles.

GENERATING ELECTRIC POWER

A derived form of energy, versatile and convenient, electricity is indispensable to modern technology and society. Though the main uses for electricity are nonpolluting, the fossil-fuel-burning plants that generate it are among the worst of environmental offenders. Important advances have recently been made in the search for ways to make electricity cleanly for primary

sources that promise energy independence of foreign monopoly control.

Fuel Cells. The technology that supplies on-board electricity for U.S. space shuttles has now become commercially available for use in apartment complexes, office buildings, factories, public utilities and, eventually, homes and motor vehicles. A fuel cell works much like a battery: Hydrogen atoms diffuse through an anode that strips off electrons, producing an electric current. Extracting the hydrogen from natural gas or coal entails no burning and is therefore an appealing way to use these fuels without creating pollution. Fuel cells are very efficient, converting up to 60 percent of the energy in natural gas into electricity as opposed to 30 percent for conventional boiler-fired generators. The early fuel cells had two disadvantages: high operating temperature and cost. Improved designs have now reduced temperatures, however, and unit costs are falling as larger numbers are produced for commercial installation.

Solar Energy. One of the most tempting energy alternatives involves extracting energy directly from its very

source—the sun's rays. For some time solar collectors have been heating water and generating electricity in regions with cloudless skies, such as the Middle East and the American Southwest. By means of solar (photovoltaic) cells, made from silicon wafers, it is also possible to use incoming rays of the sun to generate electricity. Photovoltaic research has now raised the efficiency of solar cells to the point where they are close to being economically competitive with conventional methods of generating electricity.

Wind and Sea. A number of areas with sustained winds of high velocity have experimented with using wind turbines to generate electricity. Thousands of these are in operation in California, where they feed current into the state grid, sufficient to power a city of 350,000 (California gets 45 percent of its electricity from renewable sources). The ocean tides and currents also represent immense potential sources of energy. Several experimental efforts have been undertaken to harness these inexhaustible flow resources, but commercial applications remain in the more distant future.

---

the transition is past, the world energy supply is not likely to be limited by an insufficiency of resources. After the oil and natural gas are gone, large amounts of coal, tar sands, and oil shales remain to be used as environmental problems with these fossil fuels are solved. Meanwhile, radical new forms of energy are already becoming commercially feasible.

Industrial Materials

If the long-run outlook for energy is optimistic, the situation is less secure for another class of nonrenewable resources, the industrial new materials. The future is especially doubtful for continuing supplies of certain metallic ores that must be teamed with mechanical energy if the modern economic system is to function.

The Metals.   Metals are a class of elements that are hard, heavy, and opaque, have a "metallic" luster, and are capable of being drawn into fine wire (ductil-

ity), hammered into thin plates (malleability), and melted by heat. Moreover, they are able to conduct both electricity and heat (conductivity). Each metal, however, possesses these qualities in different combinations and degrees and therefore has its own set of uses. The versatility of many metals is enhanced by a capacity for *alloying*, that is, for combining with other metals in varying proportions. This multiplies the already extensive range of special purposes that these elements are able to serve.

An intimate relationship exists between metals and the consumption of mechanical energy. Indeed, metals are indispensable to all sectors of the modern economy. Although obvious in the case of manufacturing and transportation, this is equally true of the extractive industries, including modern agriculture. Not only do the metals contribute to high agricultural yields through their use in farm tools, machinery, and transport equipment but also in the production of agricultural chemicals. A great many metals are required by an increasingly complex modern technology, in

MOTOR VEHICLE PROPULSION

For any country that seeks to reduce its dependence upon foreign energy, the prime targets for savings are its motor vehicles. At a time when the United States imports 50 percent of its oil (at a cost of $50 billion in 1990), the transport sector accounts for two-thirds of national consumption. Raising the average fuel efficiency of the country's automobile fleet to 40 miles per gallon would save 2.8 million barrels of oil per day. While this political issue is being debated, however, another option would be to convert cars and trucks to alternative fuels that are available domestically—and are less polluting than gasline and diesel. Motor-vehicle manufacturers now recognize that the days of oil-dependent vehicles are numbered and are concentrating their research efforts on new forms of propulsion. Several alternative fuels now offer viable options.

Ethanol.   Existing internal combustion engines work very well on grain alcohol. Alcohol made from corn and mixed with gasoline to produce "gasohol" has become a popular motor fuel in the grain-producing American Midwest. Brazil uses pure alcohol distilled from its plentiful, cheap sugar cane to fuel its motor vehicles.

Methanol (Wood Alcohol).   The nonpetroleum fuel that currently leads in contention for commercial use is methanol, which can be made from coal, natural gas, or even garbage. These are so abundant in the United States that they could soon completely emancipate the country from dependence upon imported oil. Although methanol is corrosive and therefore requires some modification of the fuel system, it is powerful and cheap. American manufacturers expect to introduce several thousand methanol-burning cars into the California market by 1993.

Electricity.   Pioneer motorcars that ran on electricity were so sluggish and restricted in cruising range that they soon lost out to gasoline models. Recent developments, especially in battery design, have now yielded electric cars with rapid acceleration and greater range. For the future, one of the likeliest prospects for electrically powered vehicles is the fuel cell (see previous discussion). California has mandated zero emissions by A.D. 2009, a standard that only electric cars can presently meet, and the state now has 10,000 of these on order.

Hydrogen.   The cleanest energy of all is hydrogen, which is the staple fuel for rockets. One of the most abundant elements, it is made by passing an electric current through water. Vehicle engines run perfectly well on hydrogen, but it is still much too costly for commercial use. Steadily rising efficiencies of solar cells, however, offer the possibility of producing hydrogen in desert regions and piping it to markets at competitive prices.

Compressed Natural Gas (CNG).   Compressed natural gas is cheaper than gasoline and it is abundant in the United States and several other industrialized countries. It is also cleaner than methanol. The only major problem of CNG is the huge pressurized tank that must be installed in the vehicle, making it costly and impractical for passenger cars. Nevertheless, CNG-powered trucks and buses are competitive in price, and half a million of these are currently operating in California, Florida, Alaska, and around the world.

which subtle differences in metallic qualities can be vital. Although some substitution of materials is possible, no feasible substitutes have been discovered for certain key metals.

For these reasons, a continuing supply of metals is vital. But how good is this supply? The answer is different for each metal: Some are still plentiful whereas others are nearing exhaustion. But all are nonrenewable. One of the first things we discover when examining our metallic reserves is that some of the most "common" metals are not really common at all. Of the so-called common metals only iron and aluminum are among the first 10 elements in the continental earth crust, and these 10 represent 99 percent of the total crustal weight. Relatively speaking, therefore, the other commercially important metals exist in only small quantities. Considering the great mass of the earth's crust, however, the absolute amounts are in fact much greater than this would seem to indicate and a realistic dividing line between the abundant and the scarce metals is nearer the 0.01 percent level. The most plentiful metallic elements, therefore, are iron, aluminum, manganese, magnesium, chromium, and titanium, whereas the least plentiful include such familiar metals as copper, lead, zinc, and nickel. In many cases, the scarce elements are being extracted in large quantities despite severely limited reserves.

Some metals are much more widely distributed over the earth than others. In some instances this results from a generally greater crustal occurrence, but in others it reflects the essential character of the ores from which they are extracted. Certain ores—such as iron, aluminum, and copper—have a metallic content that varies continuously from very rich to very lean. This variability is a boon to the mining industry, for the limits to practical exploitation are set simply on the basis of cost and available technology. Many other metals, however, are discontinuous in concentration; they either occur in a place or they do not. This is true of such important metals as lead, zinc, tin, nickel, tungsten, mercury, manganese, gold, and silver. Certain of these are concentrated in only a few places.

Still another problem of world mineral supply is the fact that the countries consuming the largest quantities are not necessarily the ones that are best endowed with resources. The United States is the outstanding consumer of metals, but it lacks many vital metallic resources. Similarly, most European industrial nations are conspicuously deficient in metallic ores. Some of the largest reserves occur in less-developed countries and in those advanced nations with large territories and small populations, especially Canada and Australia.

Among those metals required by world industry in very large quantities are iron and its close partner, manganese. Of the metals, iron is the overwhelming leader in total annual tonnage of output—constituting 95 percent of all metals extracted—and the quantity rises each year. One reason for the heavy production and consumption of iron is that it is plentiful and very cheap (only a few cents per pound). Another reason for its popularity is its great strength and its readiness to form alloys with many other metals. When added to iron in even minute quantities, these elements can cause it to assume a variety of desirable properties that contribute still further to the versatility of this metal. Iron technology is relatively easy, too, for the metal can be removed from its oxides (the most common occurrence in nature) by means of chemically simple processes.

Since the first discovery of a technique for making iron, about 2000 B.C., this metal has been one of the most important materials, used by virtually every society today. Nevertheless, per capita consumption of iron is closely related to level of development. Usage is exceedingly low in such underdeveloped countries as Somalia or Bhutan, but it climbs steeply with rising per capita income. Ultimately, however, per capita use reaches a saturation point, and consumption rates among the most industrialized countries are fairly similar.

Production rates of iron and steel likewise correlate fairly closely with level of development ($R^2 = 0.633$), but the relationship is changing. Though the former USSR, Japan, and the United States still lead in steel output, many newly industrializing countries in the Third World are now installing their own steel. With new facilities using the latest technology, and with abundant cheap labor and ample domestic supplies of raw materials, China, Brazil, and Mexico, among others, are challenging the leaders in world markets (Figure 5.32). Altogether, 76 countries were producing their own raw steel by 1988, up from 50 in the early 1970s.

Many leading steel-making nations, however, have little iron ore of their own, notably Japan, Ger-

many, and most other European producers. Even the United States, which originally had large reserves, now imports much of its ore and rising amounts of finished steel. The richest Lake Superior deposits have long since been exhausted and lower grades of American ore are now being developed. Indeed, low-grade taconite iron deposits now contribute a major part of the ore mined in the United States. Prominent among today's largest producers of iron ore are such LDCs as Brazil, China, India, Venezuela, Liberia, Mauritania, and Mexico, as well as two advanced nations that have large areas and low population densities—Australia and Canada (Figure 5.33). Many of these are major exporters of ore.

Because iron is the second most plentiful metal in the earth's crust, and because nearly all types of iron ore are now successfully treated by iron technology, total reserves of this element are enormous. Consequently, iron is cheap for its bulk. Transportation costs and accessibility to market are therefore important determinants in the selection of deposits for exploitation, more so than for any other metal. But the smelting of iron ore also requires great tonnages of other ingredients, especially coal for fuel and for driving off oxygen, and limestone to carry off other impurities. Hence, transportation costs and accessibility of these other materials are likewise important locational considerations for the steel industry. For these reasons many large known deposits in remote areas remain ignored, whereas ores of indifferent quality but close to market and to other iron-making materials are actively pursued.

The projected life of world iron ore reserves is thus much greater than that of most mineral resources. In addition, vast resources of lower-grade iron ore are available. The main effect of future iron ore usage, therefore, will be to cause prices to rise as richer, more accessible reserves become exhausted. Because iron resources are in no immediate danger of depletion, the basic supply problem for iron becomes the adequacy of companion resources upon which its production and use depend, namely energy and alloying elements.

Manganese is a vital alloying metal for steel manufacture. It serves a dual function in the steel industry: (1) a process material acting as a "scavenger" to carry off sulfur and oxygen, an essential use for which there is no known substitute, and (2) an alloying element that imparts toughness to the metal. Although manganese has other industrial applications, they are minor. Because manganese is a relatively plentiful element in the earth's crust, its total world supply presents no immediate problem. Indeed, so large are current supplies that the metal tends to be overused.

The main difficulty of manganese supply is the

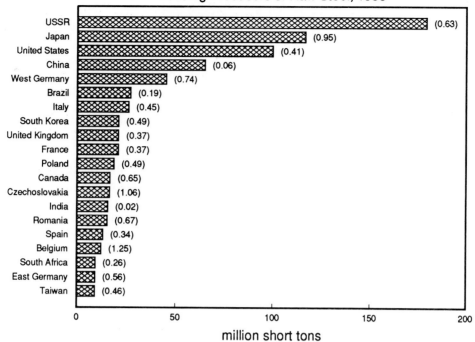

Leading Producers of Raw Steel, 1988

Country	Per capita (short tons)
USSR	(0.63)
Japan	(0.95)
United States	(0.41)
China	(0.06)
West Germany	(0.74)
Brazil	(0.19)
Italy	(0.45)
South Korea	(0.49)
United Kingdom	(0.37)
France	(0.37)
Poland	(0.49)
Canada	(0.65)
Czechoslovakia	(1.06)
India	(0.02)
Romania	(0.67)
Spain	(0.34)
Belgium	(1.25)
South Africa	(0.26)
East Germany	(0.56)
Taiwan	(0.46)

million short tons

FIGURE 5.32 Largest producers of raw steel, with per capita output, 1988. Leading the world was the former Soviet Union, with 21 percent of global production. Many of the principal steel-making nations must import all or most of their raw materials. Second-place Japan (14 percent) and most of Europe fall into this category. Longtime makers of steel, the European countries currently supply a combined 28 percent of the world total. Joining the leaders in recent times are third-ranking China, fifth-place Brazil, and a number of other newly industrializing countries such as South Korea and Taiwan. On the basis of per capita output, however, the more populous LDCs rank very low. For instance, China's per capita production is only 0.06 short tons and India's is a mere 0.02 tons. Compare those figures with Luxembourg's 10.8 tons and Belgium's 1.25 tons per person. [*Source:* U.S. Bureau of Mines, *Minerals Yearbook 1988* (Washington, D.C.: U.S. Government Printing Office, 1990.]

FIGURE 5.33 Major producers of iron ore, 1988. Iron ores are plentifully available and widely distributed around the world; hence the prominence of countries with large land areas, such as the former USSR, Brazil, Australia, and Canada in this diagram. Several of the less-developed countries in the group are also leading manufacturers of raw steel (see Figure 5.32). [*Source:* U.S. Bureau of Mines, *Minerals Yearbook 1988* (Washington, D.C.: U.S. Government Printing Office, 1990).]

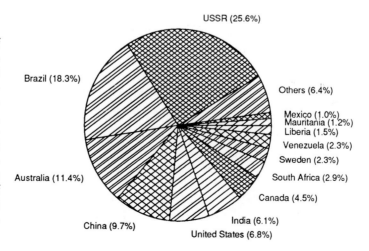

USSR (25.6%)
Brazil (18.3%)
Others (6.4%)
Mexico (1.0%)
Mauritania (1.2%)
Liberia (1.5%)
Venezuela (2.3%)
Sweden (2.3%)
South Africa (2.9%)
Canada (4.5%)
India (6.1%)
United States (6.8%)
China (9.7%)
Australia (11.4%)

spatial distribution of reserves: The best deposits are not always in the places where the metal is most needed (see Figure 5.34). The United States, in particular, has virtually no domestic reserves of high-grade manganese ore and an inadequate supply of low-grade ore. Other big industrial nations also lack manganese, except for the former USSR, which has one-third of the known world supply. Except for Australia, the remaining reserves are mainly in the less-developed nations of Africa, Latin America, and Asia. Consequently, a major part of the world output of manganese moves between continents. Fortunately for the United States, very large quantities of manganese occur on the ocean floor. Nodules of manganese have been found at depths of 500 feet to 3000 feet off the southeastern coast of the United States and at depths of 5000 feet to 14,000 feet in the eastern Pacific. Commer-

cial extraction, using dredges and vacuum devices, has proved feasible. Thus, the supply problems of iron and its close companion, manganese, are not immediately pressing.

The prospect is less promising for a second class of high-volume metals, the nonferrous group. Several nonferrous metals essential to technologically advanced countries are in relatively short supply. The members of this group—aluminum, copper, lead, and zinc—are widely used and consumed in very large quantities, often with little relationship to the total reserve supply available. Moreover, the rate of consumption of each of these four metals has steadily risen. All the nonferrous metals normally occur in low-grade ore, except aluminum. These elements are also erratically distributed in the world, resulting in a large volume of world trade both in the metals and their

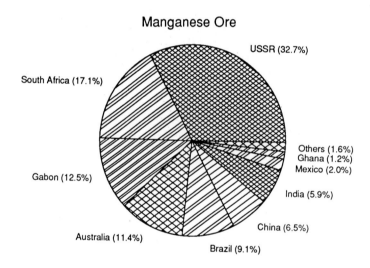

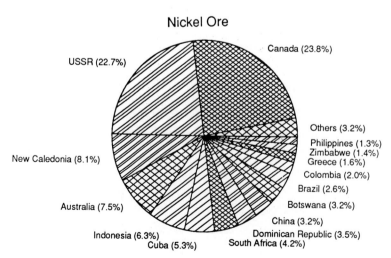

FIGURE 5.34 World production of manganese and nickel ores, 1988. Both of these elements are essential to the steel industry and both are erratically distributed in the world, as are most alloying metals. The former Soviet Union produced one-third of all manganese, and much of the rest came from Africa and other less-developed areas. Canada is the largest source of nickel, followed by the former USSR and the South Pacific island of New Caledonia. Australia is an important producer of both metals. [*Source:* U.S. Bureau of Mines, *Minerals Yearbook 1988* (Washington, D.C.: U.S. Government Printing Office, 1990).]

ores. All four metals are more costly than iron, owing to the complexity of their ores, intricate technology of extraction, and expensive processing methods.

Aluminum is an exception in this group in several respects. First, it is the only nonferrous metal that appears abundantly in the earth's crust (8 percent of the total). Moreover, it is the only one of the four that occurs in high-grade ores, mostly over 32 percent metallic content (see Figure 5.35 for the leading producers of bauxite, the chief ore of aluminum). Although consumption of this metal grew very rapidly throughout the postwar period, demand has slackened in recent years, lessening worries about its long-term prospects. Very large supplies of low-grade aluminum ore exist, but these are not commercially feasible to exploit with today's technology.

The other nonferrous metals are rare in crustal occurrence, copper being only 0.0058 percent, lead 0.0010 percent, and zinc 0.0082 percent. These three have become sufficiently concentrated for commercial extraction only through fortuitous acts of nature. Their world supply, though adequate for the near term, is cause for concern in the more distant future. Of the three, only copper occurs in continuously variable concentrations, which means that lower grades may be mined. Copper is already being extracted from exceedingly lean ores: only 0.9 percent metallic content in the United States, 1 percent to 2 percent in Canada and Chile, 4 percent in Zambia, and 6 percent in Zaire. Moreover, turning to still lower grades appears feasible, in view of the cheap open-pit mining that prevails in the copper industry. But this alternative does not

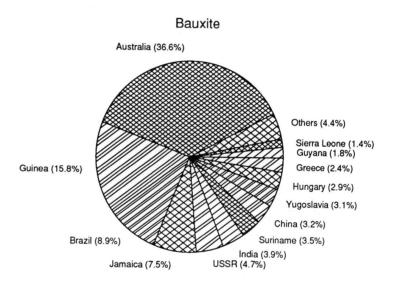

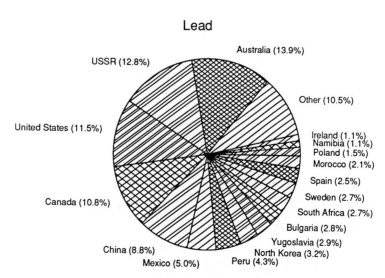

FIGURE 5.35 World production of bauxite (the chief ore of aluminum) and lead, 1988. These nonferrous ores differ substantially in crustal occurrence and in the nature of their deposits. Aluminum is one of the most plentiful elements, being a main constituent of many common rocks, but only four countries account for more than two-thirds of the bauxite mined. Though the crustal occurrence of lead is relatively small, it is extracted commercially in many parts of the world. [*Source:* U.S. Bureau of Mines, *Minerals Yearbook 1988* (Washington, D.C.: U.S. Government Printing Office, 1990).]

apply to lead and zinc, which usually occur together. Their ores are generally much richer than those of copper, but their deposits are small and require costly underground mining. This cost tends to be partially offset by the valuable by-products, such as copper, gold, and silver, that are frequently obtained in lead and zinc mining operations.

Unlike many minerals, a substantial proportion of the nonferrous metals comes from advanced nations, especially Canada and Australia (Figure 5.35 and Figure 5.36). Even so, consumption rates in those lands are so great that domestic output must be supplemented with imports from certain less-developed countries. Australia has more than one-third of the known reserves of the chief aluminum ore, bauxite (aluminum hydroxide), and the industrialized coun-

tries as a whole have about one-half of the total. Africa and Latin America have most of the rest. Nearly half of the world's copper reserves are also in the developed countries, particularly the former USSR and the United States. The rest is mainly in South America (principally Chile and Peru) and Africa's rich copper belt (Zambia and Zaire). Most of the world's larger deposits of zinc and lead are found in Australia, the United States, Canada, and the former USSR.

Although these metals cost more per pound than iron, they are surprisingly cheap, considering their relative scarcity. Nevertheless, their cost has risen as reserves have declined in size and richness. The pressures on these supplies continue to grow as more and more vital uses appear for the nonferrous metals. Copper and aluminum are virtually indispensable in elec-

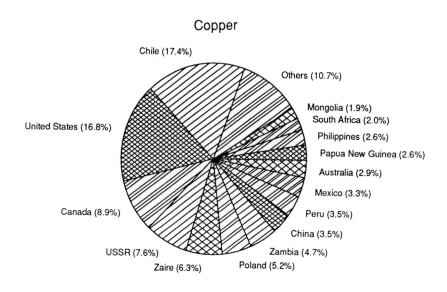

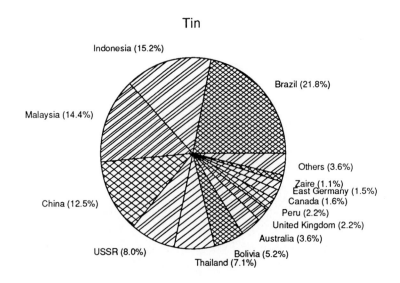

FIGURE 5.36 World production of copper and tin, 1988. Both of these elements are relatively scarce in the earth's crust. Copper is mined in many parts of the world, whereas most tin comes from two major source areas: a narrow belt extending from north to south through Asia and another zone in South America. [*Source:* U.S. Bureau of Mines, *Minerals Yearbook 1988* (Washington, D.C.: U.S. Government Printing Office, 1990).]

trical applications because of their high conductivity. All four metals are used variously in the manufacture of important alloys such as bronze, brass, monel metal, solder, bearing metal, type metal, casting metal, and special alloys for aircraft applications. Aluminum, because of its lightness, is valuable as a structural metal. Copper and aluminum are much used for cooking utensils, owing to their heat-conducting properties. Copper, lead, and zinc each have their special applications because of their resistance to corrosion: sheathing, storage batteries, and galvanizing, for example. All four have essential uses in the production of chemicals.

The nonferrous metals thus have a multitude of vital applications and have become interwoven into modern production in a variety of ways. With the possible exception of aluminum, their supplies are limited, however. Some substitution is possible, as, for example, the increasing use of aluminum in the place of more expensive copper in applications requiring conductivity; unfortunately, such substitution is not always feasible. Note also that the production of nonferrous metals is a drain on other resources. In particular, a great deal of mechanical energy is used in their extraction and processing. Zinc processing requires much heat, and copper and aluminum refining use large amounts of electricity.

Most of the metals produced and consumed in small volumes are also limited in crustal occurrence, and all are relatively expensive. Several of these low-volume metals are obtained as joint products of mining operations designed to obtain simultaneously other metals occurring in the same ores. Despite their low levels of use, these metals are essential to modern industry. Among the many elements fitting this description, two categories are especially prominent: the alloying metals and the precious metals.

The alloying metals have many individual characteristics and a multitude of uses, but they all share one kind of application: their use in combination with other metals, especially steel, to give special properties to the finished product. For most of them this is their main application. Because this is a derived use, their demand structures and price levels are usually derived also. If the price of one of the alloying metals should fall, for example, it is unlikely that any additional amounts of it would be consumed, for the quantity required depends upon the current level of steel production. Pricing is further complicated for those alloying metals obtained as joint products. Because their output is tied to that of other metals with different demand conditions, changes in price have little effect on quantities produced. Although the alloying metals are often used in minute quantities, they have such an

essential function that they are often referred to as *vitamin elements.* Some substitution among them is possible, but in many cases it is not.

Although a few of the alloying elements are plentiful in the earth's crust, others are rare. It is important here to distinguish between *rarity,* which is determined by an element's relative physical abundance in the earth's crust, and *scarcity,* an economic concept that refers to the costs of acquisition at a particular time and place. Three alloy metals appear to present no immediate problems of scarcity: chromium, titanium, and magnesium.

Because chromium helps steel to keep a sharp cutting edge even at high temperatures, it is employed in high-speed steels, a use for which chromium has no satisfactory substitute. Together with iron and nickel, it is also one of the principal constituents of stainless steels, a large and particularly important family of alloys. Chromium is fairly plentiful, four-fifths of total output coming from South Africa, the former USSR, Turkey, Rhodesia, and the Philippines. Another abundant alloying element, titanium, comprises 0.86 percent of the earth's crust, and most of its current output is in Canada, Japan, the United States, Australia, and Brazil. It is a lightweight, high-strength, corrosion-resistant metal used as an alloy of steel as well as in aerospace applications and in paint pigments. Magnesium is the lightest of all the metals, yet it is very strong. It is used to produce lightweight, corrosion-resistant alloys and in chemical production. It, too, is widespread in occurrence. Magnesium is consumed in only small amounts and total output is not great. At present, most of the world supply is obtained through electrolysis of seawater. At current levels of demand, therefore, magnesium poses no supply problems.

Supply is more critical for most of the other alloying elements, especially nickel, molybdenum, tin, and tungsten. Shortages of tin and tungsten are possible in the near future. Occasionally these four elements occur separately; but these individual occurrences are in special metallogenic provinces—regions that have undergone a rare combination of geological events. More often they occur as by-products or joint products with other elements, which means that a shift in demand and price may have little effect on the supply.

Most of the nickel that is mined is used in stainless steels and high-temperature and electrical alloys. Its crustal occurrence is small and it is found concentrated in only a few places: Canada, the former USSR, New Caledonia, Australia, Indonesia, and Cuba (Figure 5.34). Molybdenum imparts toughness and resilience to steel, and this is its chief use. Like nickel, its occurrence is highly erratic. Some of it is obtained as a by-product of copper, but most comes from a metallogenic province that extends north and south through the Canadian and U.S. Rocky Mountains.

Tin, long valued for its corrosion-resistant properties, is used for plating iron and steel and as an alloy of copper in the production of bronze. Most of its output comes from two metallogenic provinces—one in Southeast Asia and the other in South America (Figure 5.36). The tin supply from these sources is dwindling, however. Tungsten often occurs together with tin in its main source region, which extends from Korea to Malaysia in East Asia. It makes exceedingly hard alloys with steel and is also used to manufacture tungsten carbide for cutting tools.

The precious metals—silver, gold, and the platinum group—are another important class of elements whose supply is diminishing. Since ancient times silver and gold have been prized for their beauty and indestructibility. The precious metals have always been rare but they are becoming increasingly scarce today as their demand grows. Silver has a number of very useful properties, and much more would be used if it were less costly. Its principal applications are in coinage, household silver, and jewelry, but industrial applications constitute its greatest market. Silver is the main ingredient of photographic film, and it is also used in critical electrical applications because of its conductivity, which is even greater than that of copper.

Silver is naturally rare (only 0.000008 percent of the earth's crust by weight). The world's major source area is the Great Cordillera of the western Americas; smaller amounts are found in the former USSR and Australia. Today, most of the newly mined silver is obtained as a by-product of lead, zinc, and copper operations. Very little is mined for its own sake, as the ore is rarely rich enough. Because of its growing scarcity, silver has risen in price in recent years; yet its output has increased but little in response, so inelastic is its supply.

Because it occurs in the native state and is easily worked, gold was used for coinage and shaped into jewelry by the earliest civilizations. The antiquity, beauty, and rarity (0.0000002 percent of the earth's crust) of gold have endowed it with a mystical aura. This esoteric quality of gold is apparent in the tenacity with which modern governments cling to it as a basis for their currencies in the face of a steadily dwindling natural store of the metal. One of its principal commercial uses continues to be in jewelry making, where it is highly regarded for its lustrous appearance and great value. However, gold's inertness and resistance to corrosion account for many of its growing number of industrial applications. Although some gold is produced in 71 countries, 90 percent of the total output comes from South Africa (two-thirds), the former USSR (one-eighth), Canada, the United States, and Australia.

In modern times, gold and silver have been joined by another group of precious metals, the platinoids. In addition to platinum, the main member of the group, these include five other closely related metals that invariably occur together in nature. They are not quite as rare as gold, and the world supply seems fairly secure at present rates of consumption. The platinoids are acquiring a growing number of industrial applications, in addition to their use in jewelry, and current projections could prove excessively optimistic. The former USSR, South Africa, and Canada are the principal sources.

Another valuable element that does not fit into any of these categories is the industrial metal mercury, which appears in the liquid state at ordinary temperatures. Although mercury is generally regarded as indispensable to any number of industrial applications, its supply is dwindling. The ancient Spanish mines remain the leading source but their expected life is limited.

Other Nonrenewable Resources. Two other classes of nonrenewable resources remain to be considered: (1) the mineral raw materials used for the manufacture of fertilizers and other chemical products, and (2) the nonmetallic-mineral building materials. Both of these are essential to the functioning of a modern economy, and they affect every member of society either directly or indirectly. Will the supply of these be adequate to support a growing population?

As we noted earlier in the section on food supply, the best hope for feeding the expected additions to the world population is to increase the yield of land currently under the plow. Chemical fertilizers are essential to achieving this increase, along with improved seeds and more water. Although every plant type has its own particular combination of requirements, all crops must have nitrogen, phosphorus, potassium, calcium, and sulfur. These are natural constituents of some soils but not all. Moreover, some plants make unusually heavy demands on certain elements and quickly deplete them from the soil. These nutrients must be replaced for subsequent plantings.

Farmers have traditionally restored plant food elements to the soil either by *fallowing*—that is, resting the soil so that it can recuperate naturally—or by *crop rotations* that alternate soil-depleting crops with soil-restoring ones such as the legumes. But these practices are not always effective and they are too extensive in their use of land under conditions of increasing population pressure. One way of restoring nutrients to the soil is through the application of organic fertilizers, especially animal manures and, in the Orient, "night soil," or human wastes. This is inadequate for today's needs, however, and the use of manufactured fertilizers is accelerating rapidly.

The mineral raw materials for manufacturing fertilizers are also used to produce other chemical products and have a variety of other industrial applications. However, fertilizer manufacture is the largest single market for these materials. The United States is still the leading producer and consumer of chemical fertilizers, but other parts of the world are catching up.

The original source of nitrogen for fertilizers was from naturally occurring compounds, the most important deposits being those in Chile's Atacama Desert. Today, Chile supplies only minor amounts. Much of the remainder is extracted directly from the atmosphere, of which nitrogen is the largest constituent element. In addition to large quantities of electricity, the other major requirement for synthesizing nitrogenous fertilizers is hydrogen, with which the nitrogen is combined to produce a water-soluble ammonia compound that plants can readily assimilate. Ammonia is also obtained as a by-product of coke-oven operations, most of which are associated with the steel industry.

Phosphorus is essential to plant growth, but it is easily exhausted by intensive cultivation. The chief commercial source of phosphorus is phosphate rock (apatite), which is treated with sulfuric acid to make it water-soluble and thus accessible to plants. The resulting superphosphate is very concentrated. Phosphorus is an abundant element, constituting 0.1 percent of the earth's crustal weight, but most phosphate rock is found among the marine sediments of old sea beds. Despite the large global reserve of this mineral, deposits of commercial size and quality occur in only a few places (Figure 5.37). The United States produces 27 percent of the total world output, most of the rest coming from the former USSR and North Africa. One consequence of the unequal distribution of this vital material is the large quantity of it that moves in international trade.

Another abundant element that produces a vital fertilizer is potassium, which comprises 1.68 percent of the earth's crust. Potassium is widely distributed throughout the world, but not in a readily usable soluble form. Most of it is obtained commercially from saline residues formed by the evaporation of inland seas that existed in previous geological eras. Total reserves are very great, but the chief source areas are the former USSR, Canada, various European countries, and the United States. Israel and Jordan also extract this chemical, among others, from the Dead Sea salts. See Figure 5.37.

Calcium is important to certain crops, especially corn and other grains. It is a natural constituent of certain soils in sedimentary regions and it reaches high levels of concentration in subhumid lands, such as the plains and prairies of western United States and Canada and the steppes of Russia. These are all extremely productive soils. The calcium content of many other soils is inadequate, however, and easily exhausted by intensive cultivation in humid areas. Lime needed for replacement of this lost element is easily obtainable in many parts of the world wherever limestone is available. Calcium is one of the most plentiful elements, and processing is simple.

The most basic chemical raw material is sulfur, which has an endless number of uses in chemical production and manufacturing in general. The largest single application, however, is fertilizer production, which consumes two-fifths of total output. Sulfur is used both in the manufacture of superphosphates and ammonia sulfates. In addition, much of the chemical industry's use of sulfur goes eventually into agricultural applications, including insecticides and herbicides. Sulfur is widespread and abundant, being united in nature with many other elements (Figure 5.37). Relatively pure elemental sulfur is also available in limited quantities and in specific places. Volcanic cones in Japan, Sicily, and the Chilean Andes provide a certain amount, but the largest sources are coastal salt dome deposits along the margins of the Gulf of Mexico. Native sulfur reserves cannot be expected to last long, however, and increasing output is coming from fossil fuels, where it is obtained in the purification of oil and gas and collected from coal smoke. It also constitutes a by-product from the processing of sulphide metallic ores. These and other similar occurrences assure an ample supply of sulfur, though possibly at rising costs.

Total reserves of all the principal fertilizer raw materials are thus very large. No world shortage is apparent for the foreseeable future despite increasingly heavy demands for agricultural, chemical, and general industrial applications. The resource problem resulting from consumption of these minerals concerns the drain that their use imposes indirectly upon other resources. Because the nations of the world are unequally endowed with fertilizer materials (except for atmospheric nitrogen), much long-range transporting of bulky commodities is required, thereby consuming much energy and other resources. Moreover, fertilizer production involves large inputs of capital and draws heavily upon fossil fuels, electric power, and other chemicals.

The rocks and earthen materials that are used for building purposes are so common that their true importance is often overlooked. In volume of output they

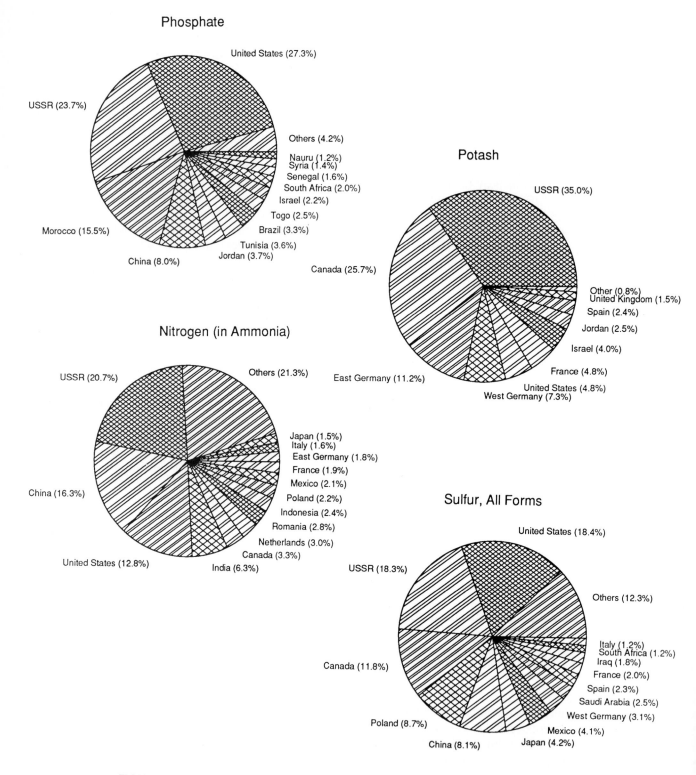

FIGURE 5.37 World production of mineral fertilizers. Three of the four principal fertilizer raw materials are mineral products; the fourth, nitrogen, is extracted mainly from the atmosphere, then combined with hydrogen to form ammonium nitrate. Only one-fourth of the world's sulfur now comes from native sulfur deposits. The remainder is extracted from mined pyrites or is obtained as a by-product of the oil and natural gas industries, coal treatment, and metal smelting. [*Source:* Bureau of Mines, *Minerals Yearbook 1988* (Washington, D.C.: U.S. Government Printing Office, 1990).]

lead all the minerals, and in value they are second only to the fossil fuels. Some of the building materials—such as sand and gravel, crushed stone, and dimension stone—are used directly with almost no further treatment after extraction. Others—including asbestos, clays, and the raw materials for glass and cement—receive considerable processing before final use.

Some of these commodities are among the most plentiful natural resources, and, with special exceptions, tend to be found in a great many places. As in the case of the fertilizer raw materials, therefore, the main long-run supply problem that the mineral building materials present is their effect on other resources. Their extraction is highly mechanized, using power machinery made of metals and burning fossil fuels. Most of the building materials are heavy and bulky, and their transportation makes further demands on the mechanical energy supply. Their processing, too, in some instances consumes large amounts of heat. Any projections of future use of these commodities must therefore take into account their substantial effects upon the energy supply.

Solutions for Mineral Supply Problems. Every mineral resource has its ultimate limit, yet the demand for minerals continues to grow steadily. In the past, the Americas, Africa, Asia, and Australia quickly yielded up fabulous finds of rich ores occurring in deposits at or near the earth's surface. Today, exploration must proceed more painstakingly in the search for hidden deposits. Ultimate exhaustion of particular nonrenewable resources would thus appear to be inevitable.

How, then is the end likely to come? For a given mining operation the final day may appear very suddenly, but it is not likely that all mines will fail simultaneously. Rather, they will probably give out one by one and the total amount of the commodity appearing on the world market will gradually diminish. For this reason, noted earlier in the cases of silver and gold, it is probable that the life spans currently being predicted will actually be exceeded as annual output falls and as the amount demanded is reduced by accelerating prices. Approaching exhaustion will be signaled well in advance when growing shortages force prices upward until they finally become prohibitive.

If eventual depletion of reserves thus seems unavoidable, do we have any way of postponing that final day? The optimists answer yes to this question and some confidently predict that technology may prevent that day from appearing at all. Those who place their trust in technology cite the impressive accomplishments of the past, when one spectacular breakthrough often followed on the heels of another. Let us con-

sider, therefore, some of the ways in which technology may come to our aid, either by stretching out the life spans of resources or by conserving the existing supply.

Among the new developments that are helping to keep known reserves from dwindling too soon are new methods for discovering, mining, extracting, and refining minerals. In the past, such technological advances have had the effect of reducing costs (or at least preventing prices from rising unduly). They have also made feasible the exploitation of materials that had not previously been classified as resources because of their remoteness or poor quality.

Some optimists are predicting that technology will eventually provide such an abundance of very cheap electricity from new sources that it will become feasible to use this to extract and process minerals from sources now considered unorthodox. One such source, it is suggested, could be the oceans, which cover 71 percent of the earth's surface to an average depth of nearly 2.5 miles. This great volume of salt water contains much dissolved material—as much as 160 million tons of solids per cubic mile. Salt, magnesium, sulfur, calcium, and potassium constitute 99.5 percent of this. Other, more valuable, elements in a cubic mile of seawater include 47 tons of zinc, 14 tons of copper, 14 tons of tin, 1 ton of silver, and 40 pounds of gold. Sodium, chlorine, magnesium, and bromine are already being extracted electrolytically from the sea and the idea of removing some of the others is very tempting. One of the problems with the proposal is that the disposal of the enormous tonnages of waste materials would make this a formidable undertaking. Even more serious is the fact that the valuable metals are contained in extremely dilute solutions, which would require that huge quantities of water be treated. The most serious problem of all is the amount of energy needed to do the job.

Fanciful as such ideas may appear, certain other radical methods are being actively pursued with some success. One is the development of techniques for seeking out ores deep beneath the earth's surface and for determining the most promising areas in which to concentrate exploration. Many people insist that more resources are yet to be found, both in areas that have already been explored and in some that have not yet been thoroughly surveyed. These individuals believe that better exploration techniques and an improved knowledge of regional geology will substantially expand reserves of many commodities. Remote sensing of the earth's environment from orbiting satellites has had some success in accomplishing these ends.

Even the most confident of the technology optimists, however, are coming to agree that we should take better care of the mineral resources available now. The recent success in conserving energy described above has stimulated interest in this approach to enhancing other earth resources. A promising place to begin is the reduction of waste in extraction and processing. Indeed, surprisingly large quantities of valuable mineral materials are lost in the earlier stages of production. Underground mining is especially wasteful. Pillars left to support mine roofs are often rich in minerals, but these have traditionally been left behind after the mine is abandoned. Many minerals are overlooked, owing to ignorance of irregularities in the shape of the ore body; others are ignored because the ores are considered too lean for economical extraction. Although improved techniques may subsequently allow these residues to be of use, reopening an abandoned flood mine is usually difficult.

Open-pit or strip-mining operations are ordinarily far more efficient in extracting most of the valuable mineral. Perhaps the best example of this is the mining and processing of porphyry copper ores, which result in virtually 100 percent recovery of the copper from ores averaging below 0.9 percent in the United States. In addition, these techniques yield valuable by-products, such as gold and silver.

Several techniques permit resources to be used more efficiently in manufacturing. The quantity of a metal that is required for a given application can often be reduced, for example, by producing the metal to closer tolerances or by adding alloys to increase its strength. Today, a ton of steel gives about 43 percent more structural support than the same amount would have provided a few years ago. Because of this, it is possible to make structural members and sheets thinner than before. This is one reason why the United States produces relatively less tonnage of steel than does the former USSR, where steel products tend to be heavier than necessary in order to fulfill official quotas specified in terms of total weight.

In addition to these advances, certain others are equally feasible but require changed social attitudes and goals. Thus, one way to husband large quantities of valuable resources would be to increase the durability of manufactured products. This is desirable not only for goods employing scarce materials but even those using abundant ones, for valuable energy resources are required for their manufacture in either case. Most advanced societies have innumerable opportunities for changes in lifestyle that would deemphasize high per capita levels of resource use.

The idea of reusing valuable metals and other materials has received much attention recently, but the notion is by no means a new one. Today, approximately 40 percent of the copper consumed each year

has been reclaimed from discarded objects, as has a high proportion of the tin. Nearly half of the lead is recycled, most of it from old automobile batteries. Far more reclamation of metals and other materials is desirable and possible, especially the reusable materials from abandoned vehicles and household wastes.

It must be accepted, of course, that these and other conservation techniques may raise resource costs. Recycling of most materials is expensive, and so are improved product designs and more intensive mining methods. Moreover, the recovery of metals is only partial after each cycle of use. Some metal is essentially lost altogether, and all of it is therefore due to be permanently consumed in the long run.

To an ever-increasing extent the substitution of one material for another has been forced upon us by growing scarcities and rising costs of certain commodities. More aluminum is replacing copper in electrical applications, and aluminum is substituting for tin-plated steel in the container industry. Tinplated cans are also being replaced by lacquered ones. Undoubtedly the most significant progress toward substituting new materials for old, however, is the accelerating development of novel advanced engineering materials such as fiber optics, composites, and ceramics. See Box 5.5 for some of the innovative products now reaching world markets.

Although past achievements may seem to justify continued faith in the ability of technology to bring salvation, previous experience is no longer a reliable guide to the future. As more and more developing nations join the ranks of the industrialized lands, and as levels of prosperity rise still further in the richer countries, global consumption steadily rises. Many authorities therefore recognize that excessive optimism diverts attention from the real problem of ultimate exhaustion of nonrenewable resources.

What will the final depletion of our natural resources mean to us as individuals and citizens? Ultimately it will touch each of us, but in the near term, people living in industrialized lands will be affected differently from citizens of less-developed countries. High levels of consumption affect advanced countries in several important ways. They show up first in the intensive exploitation of domestic reserves, such as the Lake Superior iron ores, followed in time by depletion, or the threat of it. Even prior to exhaustion, consumption may greatly exceed the resource endowment and the country will begin to rely more and more upon imports. The United States used to be a net exporter of minerals, but since World War II it has been a net importer. By 1970 the country was importing five-sixths of its nickel, three-fourths of its bauxite, nearly half of its zinc, more than a third of its iron ore, and

---

BOX 5.5 Nonmetallic Substitutes for Scarce Metals

One of the most encouraging solutions for the imminent depletion of crucial metallic elements is the trend toward substituting new classes of nonmetallic materials for these. Intensified efforts to develop *advanced engineering materials* have yielded a variety of synthesized substances with properties that match or even exceed those of conventional metals now in use. The success of this work is suggested by the degree to which plastics are replacing metals in a growing variety of uses, from plumbing pipes to automotive parts. Further augmenting the usefulness of these advanced plastics has been the recent development of *composites,* products in which high-strength fibers of such materials as graphite or glass are embedded in a plastic matrix. Worldwide demand for these extraordinarily strong, light materials has burgeoned as their technical merits and cost effectiveness in automotive, aerospace, and other industries have come to be appreciated.

Another group of engineered materials that holds great promise for advanced applications is *ceramics*—a type of production that is rooted in one of the most ancient of human technologies, the making of pottery and bricks. Ceramics are products manufactured from a nonmetallic mineral by firing at high temperatures. One of their prime attractions is that they are made from some of the commonest, cheapest, and most widely available earthen materials, such as clay and silicon.

Advanced ceramics have quickly forged a global market, totaling $12 billion in 1990. An early triumph of advanced *electronic ceramics* was fiber optics, which, because of their superior efficiency, are replacing copper and aluminum cables in communications. Equally bright are the prospects for advanced *structural ceramics,* whose applications include automotive heat engine components, cutting

tools, and wear- and corrosion-resistant industrial components. The first ceramic-intensive auto and truck engine (containing at least six ceramic components) is scheduled for the Japanese market in 1995 and for the United States in 1999. The Japanese now dominate the world market for advanced ceramics with 57 percent of the total in 1988, as against 31 percent for the United States and 12 percent for Europe.

Despite the recency of these radical new human-made materials, they appear destined to relieve much of the pressure on conventional metallic elements, especially the increasingly scarce alloying metals. The fact that their raw ingredients are so widespread and cheap is an obvious boon to Japan and other resource-poor industrialized countries on the Pacific rim. Advanced engineering materials would thus seem to be a case favoring the technological optimists.

---

almost all of its tin and manganese. As world reserves of a particular resource diminish, however, those countries still possessing reserves may be unwilling to export to deficit countries. Some mineral-rich nations in the early stages of development may prefer to retain their raw materials for use in domestic industries.

With a few exceptions, the known world reserves of even the most abundant mineral resources would not be sufficient for global consumption at per capita rates now prevailing in the richest lands. Burdened by large and growing populations, the Third World as a whole can hardly expect to attain the current rate of United States consumption. It thus follows that the possibilities for industrialization of many underdeveloped nations are dim. Already some voices in the Third World are expressing concern that the industrialized lands are using up their heritage, and they wonder what resources will be left when the time comes for them to need them.

Contrary to common belief, growth can actually increase inequality. And as the gap between the rich and poor widens, high rates of population growth exacerbate this difference. With increasing numbers and rising consumption, distribution may become less equitable; those who have anything of value hang onto

it. Because dwindling resources ultimately affect everyone, the need for a coordination of resource policies is becoming clearer.

ENVIRONMENTAL QUALITY

Thus far our attention has focused upon the quantitative results of the increasingly intensive exploitation of our physical environment. The main question has been whether sufficient resources exist to support large numbers of people at ever-higher levels of per capita consumption. Now we consider the qualitative aspects: How are rising levels of human activity affecting the world as a place in which to live?

The Physical Environment

Pollution is a problem with many facets. At the least, it concerns aesthetics; at the most, it poses a threat to the ecosystem involving the survival of human life itself. Pollution wastes important resources during the process of contaminating the air and water. Thus, the compounds of mercury and lead entering the atmosphere and water supplies are serious pollutants, but they also represent the loss of critically scarce metals. And just as resource use is growing even more rapidly than the population, so also is pollution rising at ever-increasing rates. This is evidence of the relationship that pollution bears to agricultural activity and industrialization.

The impact of pollution tends to be delayed, raising the danger that it will exceed the limits of safety before we become aware of the problem. Many long-lived toxic substances travel great distances and accumulate in unforeseen places. Besides the problems of mercury and lead poisoning, chemicals such as DDT pose serious threats. DDT evaporates and is carried long distances in the air, precipitating out of the atmosphere, entering the food chain, and persisting in the tissues of living organisms. At least two decades may be required for it to lose its potency.

Contamination of the Atmosphere

Air pollution occurs when waste gases and solid particles enter the atmosphere and spread. In the form of smog (smoke plus fog) it hangs visibly over large industrial cities, so thick at times that it shuts out much of the sunlight. It assails the other senses too, irritating the eyes and lungs and issuing repulsive odors. Some other common effects of air pollution are corrosion of paint, steel, rubber, nylon stockings, and statuary.

To a major extent, air pollution is a product of the consumption of energy, especially the combustion of fossil fuels, and of many industrial processes. Among the greatest offenders are the internal combustion engines that power passenger cars, buses, trucks, and aircraft, all of which emit great quantities of noxious gases: carbon dioxide, carbon monoxide, sulfur oxides, nitrogen oxides, particulate matter (soot), and tetraethyl lead. The most serious industrial offenders are pulp and paper mills, iron and steel mills, petroleum refineries, smelters, and chemical plants, which contribute enormous tonnages of carbon monoxide, sulfur dioxide, nitrogen oxide, and fly ash to the atmosphere.

Oddly enough, the cleanest form of energy, electricity, is the source of some of the worst pollution. Thermal generating plants contribute one-fifth of all the particulates and nitrogen oxides and half the sulfur oxides sent aloft from the United States annually. Sulfur compounds emitted from coal-burning plants become dissolved in particles of moisture within the upper atmosphere to form sulfuric acid. Drifting with the prevailing winds from its industrial source, this airborne moisture subsequently falls as "acid rain," which is accused of destroying forests and other vegetation and of killing water life in ponds and lakes. In-

creasingly, this is becoming the subject of international disputes. Canadian provinces downwind of the Ohio River Valley's coal-burning industries protest the environmental damage attributed to this source, and several Western European countries are in contention over the acid rain that crosses their borders from elsewhere to kill forests and water life. Nuclear power plants, which contribute a growing proportion of the world's electricity, avoid the atmospheric pollution problems of conventional power plants but add new environmental hazards of their own.

A further source of atmospheric pollution is *space heating*. The use of fossil fuels to heat homes, offices, and factories adds much to the total load. The burning of trash by householders and also by municipalities, commercial junk dealers, and others is an additional source.

Each of the principal contaminants of the atmosphere is capable of becoming extremely hazardous to human beings. These toxic substances in the atmosphere tend to be slow-acting with people of normal health, but they may affect with tragic suddenness the very old, very young, or those with respiratory ailments.

Evidence is mounting that atmospheric pollutants may even affect the weather and perhaps alter climatic patterns. Because all energy is ultimately dissipated as heat, the cumulative effect of energy consumption on a large scale is to warm the atmosphere. It has been estimated that by the year 2000 the amount of heat released by human activities may be equal to 18 percent of incoming solar energy. This may eventually impose a limit to the amount of mechanical energy that can be safely used.

Probably the most valuable resource of all is water. The total amount on the earth's surface, below it, or above it, is vast; but 99.35 percent of this is in the oceans or locked in the polar ice caps and thus not directly accessible for human consumption. The remaining 0.65 percent is all that we have to use (except for navigation); this occurs as ground water or is in lakes or streams. When viewed on a global scale, water is a renewable resource; at the local level it can be a vanishing resource.

During its stay on earth, water is often used and reused many times for municipal purposes, industrial cooling, process water, or irrigation. Almost every time that water is used, contaminants are added to it. Flowing water has natural recuperative powers, but these can easily be exceeded under intensive use. It must usually then be treated before reuse, but much of the water that contains municipal and industrial wastes is incompletely treated, and some is dumped into streams with no treatment at all.

The Cost of Growth

The accelerating pace of modern living has thus brought with it a multitude of problems whose dimensions we are only now beginning to comprehend. Increasing numbers of people and rising volumes of industrial production have resulted in contamination of the atmosphere, pollution of water, disfiguration of the landscape, and deterioration of human relationships within an environment that is being used with ever-greater intensity. These are the complications that have accompanied our efforts to reach successively higher levels of material well-being measured in terms of more and better transportation, housing, appliances, clothing, recreation, medical care, and other specialized services of a proliferating variety—in other words, all that is contained in that familiar measure called the gross national product (GNP). More formally defined, GNP represents a country's total annual output of goods and services.

Today, some people are saying that the GNP has been misleading us, that it does not take into account hidden costs exacted by problems of the kinds just described. Such costs, it is said, actually reduce the total benefits gained from rising output. As a more realistic index of how well off a population may be, economists William Nordhaus and James Tobin have proposed a Measure of Economic Welfare, MEW. This is derived by adjusting the GNP to allow for the costs to a society resulting from environmental deteri-

oration and the problems of contemporary urban life. More euphoniously, and perhaps more accurately, Paul Samuelson has relabeled this measure Net Economic Welfare, or NEW.

Figure 5.38 illustrates the relationship between GNP and NEW as this evolved during a four-decade period. Note how steeply per capita GNP climbed following World War II. On the other hand, NEW rose much more slowly, owing to the cumulative effects of modern urban problems. Because the two curves are rising at different rates, the gap between them is widening. If effective steps should be taken to solve the problems caused by growth, NEW would begin to rise more steeply; however, the costs of such remedial measures—for example, sewage treatment plants and devices for precipitating pollutants in factory stack gases—would reduce the slope of the GNP curve. In this way the gap between the two would begin to close and GNP would thereby gain increased reliability as a measure of a society's well-being.

HUMAN NEEDS IN THE TWENTY-FIRST CENTURY

Our assessment of the problems of supporting an increasing population at higher levels of material comfort, while attempting to minimize the distorting effects of growth, has reinforced our impressions of a world system that is intricately interrelated. We have seen that an increase in population requires larger supplies of food, clothing, shelter, transportation facilities, services, and an ever-expanding array of other needs. Satisfying these enlarged demands in turn calls for heavier investments of capital. Greater allocations must be made for the production of fertilizer, farm machinery, and chemicals; for the construction of irrigation works and farm-to-market roads; for building textile and clothing factories; for constructing dwellings and so forth. But these uses of capital make rising demands upon nonrenewable resources: fertilizer and chemical raw materials and other metallic and nonmetallic minerals, as well as fuels.

Some of these resources, we have learned, are plentiful; but a great many others are not. Yet exploitation and use of even the abundant resources makes demands on other resources more limited in supply. Iron is plentiful, but steel production requires carbon and heat, provided by fossil fuels, together with a variety of scarce alloying metals. The raw materials of cement are abundant, but their manufacture consumes much heat. The ultimate solution to the energy problem appears to be electricity obtained from unconventional sources, but scarce nonferrous metals are needed to transmit and use this electricity.

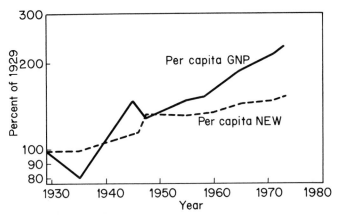

FIGURE 5.38 Differential growth of net economic welfare and gross national product. Note that as per capita GNP dropped during the Great Depression, net economic welfare (NEW) remained little changed. When war production brought a sharp rise in GNP during the 1940s, NEW lagged behind until the period of postwar readjustment. Since that time GNP has continued to rise more rapidly than NEW. (Drafted from trends suggested by Paul Samuelson.)

Moreover, the consumption and final discarding of resources results in pollution, which adversely affects both population and production. Not only does pollution present severe health hazards but it also imposes a mounting cost burden on the economic system. Its ultimate effects we cannot anticipate with accuracy because of the time lag in its impact. Yet it is most certainly a grave problem that cannot be avoided, because both the United States and world populations are now too large to survive without intensive and mechanized agriculture, industry, and an integrated transportation system. It is no longer possible to retreat entirely to a simpler era. There are too many of us.

All projections thus point to continued growth in population, investment, resource use, and pollution, at least in the near term. Yet, considering the ultimate limits to the total supply of food and resources and to the amount of contamination the environment can absorb, where will these projections of growth take us? How long can the world system continue to expand without tempting disaster?

Before we can reasonably address this question, we must examine more closely a variety of important facets of the world economic system as it is structured and functions. These will be the subjects of the next several chapters, and the information presented there should enable us to think more analytically about the issues of growth and change.

TOPICS FOR DISCUSSION

1. Explain the general trends affecting the numerator and denominator of the Malthusian resources/population ratio. What do these trends tell us about the future spatial pattern of resource use? Why are government policy-makers and the general public unable to sustain a long-range view of resource problems and to adopt the necessary measures to solve them?

2. What is meant by the term "resource," and why must any given resource be regarded as a changing concept? Define the various categories of resources. Why do the spatial patterns of supply and demand for most resources differ, and what political and economic problems arise from these differences?

3. Most experts no longer fear that the global food supply will be exhausted before the end of this century. What has happened to allay those fears? Why, then, do 1.5 billion people nevertheless remain hungry? Discuss the nature and spatial pattern of world hunger.

4. Give the reasons why many estimates of the world's potential cropland are misleading. Describe the process of "desertification" and examine the various dimensions of the food problems of sub-Saharan Africa. Where must the world look for additional supplies of food that will be required beyond the year 2000?

5. Discuss the relationship between resource use and development, and suggest the implications this holds for future supplies of nonrenewable resources. Define "reserve," indicate why reserve estimates fluctuate from time to time, and describe the process of resource exhaustion.

6. How do oil, natural gas, and coal differ in their spatial patterns of occurrence, exploitation, consumption, and trade? Account for these differences. How was OPEC able to gain command over world oil markets, and what caused this control to slip by the mid-1980s?

7. Where is future demand for energy likely to be greatest and why? What sources of energy are likely to predominate in the short-run future? In the longer run? Explore the various measures available to us for extending current supplies of energy and for ensuring future supplies. Should we be optimistic or pessimistic about the short-run and long-run prospects for energy?

8. Why are many observers more worried about world supplies of industrial raw materials than they are about energy? What classes of industrial materials give the greatest cause for concern and why? Discuss the political and economic implications of the erratic spatial distribution of minerals. Why have OPEC-like cartels failed to develop in the case of industrial materials?

9. Not only does pollution poison the physical environment and threaten human health but it also constitutes a waste of scarce and valuable physical resources. Explain. Discuss the implications of pollution for international politics and for economic development. Interpret Samuelson's concept of Net Economic Welfare.

FURTHER READINGS

DARMSTADTER, JOEL, HANS H. LANDSBERG, and HERBERT C. MORTON, with MICHAEL J. COADA. *Energy Today and Tomorrow: Living with Uncertainty.* Resources for the Future. Englewood Cliffs, N.J.: Prentice Hall, 1983.

This concise review and analysis of contemporary energy issues is based upon the authors' work at the Center for Energy Policy Research at Resources for the Future. Included is a useful examination of the contrasting views of "limitationists" and "expansionists" on resource questions.

GLAESER, BERNHARD (Ed.). *The Green Revolution Revisited.* London: Allen & Unwin, 1987.

An assessment of the economic, political, and social effects of the technological revolution in Third World agriculture. The contributors, experts in tropical farming methods, report their observations of the green revolution in the field. Some are critical of the widening income disparities that result from the tendency for the benefits of innovative techniques to favor the educated, more prosperous farmers to the competitive disadvantage of the others. They urge increased research on ways to improve upon traditional farming methods and to reduce the vulnerability of Third World farmers to periodic crop failures.

KATES, ROBERT W. *The Human Environment: Penultimate Problems of Survival.* Natural Hazards Research and Applications Center, Special Publication No. 6. Worcester, Mass.: The Center for Technology, Environment, and Development, Clark University, 1983.

Thoughtful analysis of three related sets of issues: the Malthusian question regarding the adequacy of resources for a growing population, the problems of growing income disparities and their potential for widespread unrest and conflict, and the contrast between the growing technological capability for change (and destruction) and the meager ability of society to control it.

MEADOWS, DONELLA H., DENNIS L. MEADOWS, JØRGEN RANDERS, and WILLIAM W. BEHRENS III. *The Limits to Growth: A Report for the Club of Rome's Project on the Predicament of Mankind.* New York: Universe Books, 1972.

A very influential study commissioned by the Club of Rome, an international group of prominent industrialists, scientists, and economists. Using a dynamic world model linking population, pollution, resources, land, and capital generation, Dennis Meadows and coworkers at MIT predict that exponential growth will ultimately result in global collapse.

SHAH, MAHENDRA, and GÜNTHER FISCHER. "People, Land, and Food Production: Potentials in the Developing World." *Options,* International Institute for Applied Systems Analysis (IIASA), 2, 1984, pp. 1–5.

Assesses the output of particular food crops and their population-supporting potentials in the Third World. Synthesis of a study conducted by IIASA in collaboration with the Food and Agriculture Organization of the United Nations. This work finds that, of the 117 countries analyzed, 57 do not have sufficient land resources to feed the populations that have been projected for them A.D. 2000.

SADIK, NAFIS. *The State of World Population 1990: Choices for the New Century.* UNFPA United Nations Population Fund. New York: United Nations, 1990.

Declaring that the world's population has arrived at a critical stage in this final decade of the twentieth century, the executive director of UNFPA contends that the ultimate check on population growth in the coming era may not be merely the earth's capacity to feed growing numbers of people but rather the poisoning of the physical environment that overcrowding would cause. Heedless overuse of material resources by great masses of humanity could render the planet uninhabitable.

SKINNER, BRIAN J. *Earth Resources,* 2d ed. Englewood Cliffs, N.J.: Prentice Hall, 1976.

Succinct discussion of the geology of existing and potential sources of energy and industrial raw materials. Describes the spatial pattern of their occurrence in the earth crust, and provides estimates of reserve size and relative scarcity.

WOLF, EDWARD C. *Beyond the Green Revolution: New Approaches for Third World Agriculture.* Worldwatch Paper 73. Washington, D.C.: Worldwatch Institute, 1986.

A concise, informative, and balanced examination of international research in tropical agriculture. The author describes the evolution of the current worldwide system of research institutes and reports on the differing effects of technological innovations in various regions. He discusses the constructive responses of these research programs to criticisms of earlier phases of the green revolution and he proposes further steps that need to be taken to relieve the worsening circumstances of farmers living in remote areas under adverse physical conditions.

6

Price and Other Mechanisms for Regulating Exchange

OVERVIEW

This chapter deals with one of the central issues raised in the previous chapters: the mechanisms by which limited supplies of resources and products are shared among the growing demands of an escalating world population. Two sets of mechanisms are described: traditional and modern. In traditional, smaller-scale, preindustrial economies, sharing is based on social rules, established rights, and customary obligations. In modern economies, exchange occurs in response to the profit motive and is regulated by a price mechanism. In both traditional and modern economies, distinct variations on the basic mechanism exist.

The chapter is introduced by a preamble on the relationships among economics, geography, and economic geography. This preamble describes a gap in theory that results from the divergent goals of economics and geography. Economists deal with an abstract, homogeneous world in which space is collapsed to a point, whereas geographers ignore economic fundamentals. This chapter helps to bridge this gap by explaining the basic economic concepts of price and applying them to the geography of price found in modern economies.

OBJECTIVES

- to describe the householding, redistribution, and reciprocity mechanisms for regulating exchange in preindustrial economies
- to discuss differences in exchange mechanisms among the principal types of contemporary political economies
- to explain the mechanisms by which price regulates exchange in market economies
- to define and interpret the basic economic concepts underlying price theory and illustrate how they can be extended to apply to actual data and the real world
- to provide a foundation for the discussion of theories of location, exchange, and interaction

ECONOMICS, GEOGRAPHY, AND ECONOMIC GEOGRAPHY: A PREAMBLE

Divergent Disciplinary Goals

Economics is concerned with how scarce resources are allocated among competing users, with how prices are determined and incomes distributed, and with policies for promoting economic growth. Geography also is concerned with humanity's use of resources, but from the perspective of spatial distribution, patterns of spatial interaction, and the regionalisms that result.

Historically, economic geographers disregarded the contributions that economic principles might have made to their disciplinary goals. Some elementary probes into the economic fundamentals of the subject were made by G. G. Chisholm (see Chapter 2). Geographers abandoned these attempts, however, when they espoused environmental determinism. The subsequent rejection of determinism led to highly descriptive study of areal differentiation rather than to the pursuit of more satisfactory economic principles.

This failure of economics and geography to integrate their theory has clouded the thinking of social scientists and policymakers on many world issues. One example is the conflict between the environmentalist and economist views on resources. Are resource shortages an indication of underpricing (the economist viewpoint) or of real, absolute shortages (the environmentalist view), or a bit of both? And are the most crucial world problems those of limits to growth or disparities in distribution? Unfortunately, we cannot even begin to examine these problems adequately, much less resolve them, until we have developed an integrated approach involving both geographic and economic fundamentals.

It is this interdependence of economic life and environment to which Erich Zimmermann referred in his classic study titled *World Resources and Industries* (1933, 1951, p. xi). There is, he argued, a need for economists to incorporate physical realities into their theory, and for geographers to incorporate basic economic theory into their explanations of areal differences.

The Role of Theory

The objective of theory, whatever its content, is to reduce a hodgepodge of details to an intelligible pattern of consistent relationships among phenomena. The development of theory requires preselection of which characteristics are to be examined, which relationships are to be explored, which aspects of total reality are to be explained, and what assumptions are to be made.

The first beginnings of theory may be prompted by casual observation and experience. In these first probes toward theory, description of fact makes up the preponderant share of the effort. Increasing sophistication and rigor leads to a growing concern with testing tentative theories using carefully selected data and a variety of statistical techniques. In these later developments, the subject matter of a discipline becomes increasingly theoretical and deductive, rather than empirical and descriptive.

The objective of theory in modern economic geography is to explain the geography of economic systems using a relatively small number of variables. Among the items to be explained are the spatial distributions of production and consumption, the spatial interactions evidenced by data on communications and trade, and regional differences in growth and development. The economic geographer's concerns begin at the individual level, for ultimately it is individual decisions and behavior that create spatial systems and that change them. Humankind is both producer and consumer. As producers we engage in employment that results in the creation of materials and services and yields income. As consumers, we have needs. Our values, embedded within a culture, translate these needs into *wants* for materials and services that we obtain with the income we earn. To develop these concerns, however, economic geographers must devise theoretical structures that can be applied to economic planning as well as to the satisfaction of individual and social needs.

TRADITIONAL AND MODERN ECONOMIES

The question of *scale,* one of the most fundamental questions in economic geography, arises out of this need to establish a bridge between the individual and society. For some individuals, the relationship between production and consumption is local. For example, an individual in an isolated village in the highlands of New Guinea may be part of a local, essentially closed, and self-sustaining system. On the other hand, the spatial domain of Westerners is worldwide: The global economy is a complex network of flows of people, money, energy, goods, information, and ideas, and changes in any part affect the whole. Between these two extremes of local and worldwide systems, a whole range of types and scales of social groups and socioeconomic systems can be identified, many of which will be discussed in detail in later chapters.

Sociocultural Bases of Traditional Economies

This variety of socioeconomic systems is, of course, a product of the long period of sociocultural evolution of humanity. Recently, American anthropologists have tried to develop a classification of cultures that charts this evolutionary process. They argue that change has been expressed in two fundamental ways: (1) a steadily rising level of sociocultural development throughout human history, expressed in increasing economic and social control of the environment; and (2) progressively more complex development of organizational resources to permit larger and larger groups to work together to mutual advantage. Furthermore, they argue that, up to the modern transformation of the world beginning in the Industrial Revolution, human social systems evolved through four stages, examples of which have persisted to the present:

1. Hunting and gathering societies
2. Seminomadic groups engaging in simple slash-burn agriculture without animal husbandry
3. Settled villages of tropical agriculturalists with animal husbandry
4. The larger-scale Eurasian plow agriculture dominated by urbanized central governments and complex forms of social stratification

Organizational Bases of Modern Political Economies

Fundamental transformations in these basic cultural systems occurred in the past three centuries as the result of a succession of industrial, political, and social revolutions. As a result, global economic organization should be described today in terms of five basic types of *political economies,* among which there are significant differences in how growth takes place, and how locations and land use are determined, as we saw in Chapter 1:

1. *Free-enterprise, decentralized, market-directed systems.* In such systems decisions are made by individuals, groups, and corporations. These decisions interact in the market through the interplay of the forces of demand and supply. Economic power and political power, vested in the claims of ownership and property, are widely dispersed and competitively exercised, leading to pluralistic societies in which many groups exercise influence. Collective or government action protects and supports the central institutions of the market and maintains the decentralization of power. In the last four decades, these market systems have first moved toward Types 2 or 3, discussed next, and then back as economies have been deregulated and privatized.

2. *Organizational market-negotiated systems.* Modern postindustrial societies are one recent outgrowth of the decentralized free-enterprise systems in the West, and also have emerged under the force of "Confucian capitalism" (discussed in Chapter 1) in the East as well. In these systems developmental decisions are made by negotiation among large-scale organizations. Pitted against each other, these organizations, which are profit-oriented but not necessarily maximizers, bargain together and exist in a context of negotiated relationships. Decision-making power is determined as a matter of policy or is agreed upon by the counterbalancing power of corporations, labor unions, special-interest groups, and governments. Listing the characteristics of these systems, we obtain the following:

(a) Organization of production is by large corporations run for the benefit of stockholders. Labor negotiates wages through large-scale unions.

(b) Consumption of end products is determined partly by individual choice, partly by special interests working through the courts, and partly by governmental policy.

(c) The power of organizations, the collective power of the government, and the free choice of individuals are all part of the system. A classic case is the alliance in Japan among business, labor, and government in what is often called "Japan Incorporated."

3. *Redistributive welfare states.* In such states, the free-enterprise system has been modified by government action to reduce social and spatial inequities, to provide every citizen with minimum guarantees of material welfare—medical care, education, employment, housing and pensions—usually achieved through differential taxation and welfare payments, but sometimes, too, by nationalization of industries and by direct governmental investment. Throughout the world, but particularly in Western Europe, there was a progressive increase in the welfare functions of governments after World War II, with an associated extension of more centralized decision making designed to make the market system satisfy social as well as traditional economic goals. Since 1980, the inefficiencies associated with such centralization have led

to a countervailing move to "privatize" state-run enterprises, however.

4. *Socialist economies.* An outgrowth of twentieth-century political revolutions, this group consisted of single-party political systems, in which there was state operation of nonagricultural industries (in some, agriculture too), centralized direction of the economy (with experiments in decentralization), semi-industrialized production structures, per capita incomes more variable than in the West, and strong commitment to economic growth. This group included the former USSR, and Eastern Europe, and still includes China, Cuba, Vietnam, and North Korea (although the latter countries share many features with Type 5, discussed below). In such systems

(a) The *plan* rather than the free movement of market prices controls production, consumption, and distribution,

(b) The essence of the plan is centralized decision making; the few decide for the many, and the activities of the many are carried on under the directives of the few, and

(c) Centralized action requires a complex apparatus for gathering basic data needed for decision making, for formulating goals and alternatives, and for enabling the feedback necessary to adapt processes and expectations to changing circumstances.

Central direction has proved incapable of guiding increasingly complex economies, however, resulting in lagging growth, continuing poverty, and mounting environmental degradation. Former Soviet President Mikhail Gorbachev recognized that socialism had to be replaced by free-enterprise markets and began a reform program in 1985 that led to the elimination of socialism in Eastern Europe and the collapse of the Soviet Union. At the end of 1991 Russia and other newly-independent states such as Ukraine and Kazakhstan began to introduce market reforms and private property, starting a wrenching process of economic and political transformation.

5. *Authoritarian political economies of the developing countries.* A collection of partly preindustrial and partly modernizing societies, this group is characterized most commonly by one-party governments or military dictatorships, political instability, with limited capacity for public administration, small public sectors, fragmentation of the economy along geographic and modern-versus-traditional lines, imperfection of markets and limited development and continued predominance of agriculture, lower per capita product,

and market dependence on foreign economic relations. This group comprises many nations in the Americas, Africa, Asia, and many small island economies.

No single theory can bridge the fundamental differences between the several kinds of traditional socioeconomies and the equally diverse range of modern political economies. Indeed, the shift from traditional to modern economies has been called by Karl Polanyi "the great transformation." In traditional economies, the economy was submerged in social relationships. Laboring was motivated by social mores and custom, and it was not for cash income. Trade was not primarily undertaken for economic gain, but to acquire prestige items. Life was not directed by principles of economic efficiency or distinct economic institutions. The great transformation changed all this. Market economies developed in which price regulated exchange, and social motivations yielded to economic imperatives. These two groups of systems will be discussed separately, after first introducing elementary concepts in a "Robinson Crusoe" case.

ROBINSON CRUSOE: A SIMPLE CASE

Consider Robinson Crusoe before his man Friday came along. He was responsible for satisfying all his own demands. That meant he had to decide what he wanted, *extract* his raw materials and crops, *transport* them to his workshops, *process* them to create desired products, *store* the products at some convenient place until the need for them arose, and finally *distribute* them in the proper proportions to wherever they were to be consumed. His *productive process* (embodying the stages of extraction, processing, and distribution, and the attendant operations of transportation and storage) thus led to final satisfaction of his needs in *consumption.*

Crusoe was a complete *economic system* unto himself, for he originated the *demands,* created the *supplies,* and so organized his work that his demands and supplies were maintained in overall *equilibrium,* consistent with his needs and capabilities and the resources available to him. Clearly, equilibrium was in his best interest, because to produce too much would be wasteful of time and effort, and to produce less than he needed would be dangerous, and potentially fatal.

Both historically and in the less "Westernized" parts of the world today, examples may be found of small groups of people subsisting in communities with simple, self-sustaining "Crusoe-like" economies in which the proper quantities and varieties of products are distributed among the members without the need for markets, money, or prices. In many of these communities, a primitive form of affluence also may be seen: Many hunters and gatherers, for example, satisfy their needs with only a two- to four-hour workday. To the extent that there is production above subsistence levels, this is elicited by kinship organization and the institution of chieftancy, which serves to generate effort, output, and movement of goods in excess of the limited desires of the domestic group.

In Crusoe's case the decision as to how much to produce and how to distribute the output was his own *individual* one. In Crusoe-like economies the decision is *social*; the rules, obligations, traditions, and group decisions of the community determine who shall produce what and how it will be distributed. Three such patterns of social control have been identified: *householding, redistribution,* and *reciprocity.*

HOUSEHOLDING, REDISTRIBUTION, AND RECIPROCITY IN SMALLER SCALE SOCIETIES

Householding

Householding is a literal translation of the Greek word *oeconomia,* the etymon for our word "economy." Householding means "production for one's own use." The economic historian Karl Polanyi has described householding in his book *The Great Transformation* as follows:

> Whether the different entities of the family or settlement or the manor form the self-sufficient unit, the principle is invariably the same: that of producing and storing for the satisfaction of the wants of the members of the group. . . . Production for use as against production for gain is the essence of householding.[1]

The householding unit is a self-sustaining entity. The medieval *manor,* the Roman *familia,* and the South Slav *zadruga* are all comparable examples of such householding economic systems. Large numbers of these independent economic units were the basis of feudal society in Europe.

The householding unit is closest to the Robinson Crusoe example in both pattern and organization. Instead of a single consumer, there are several, with division of labor based upon age, sex, social standing, and tradition. Only when kinship or political organization demanded it was *Chayanov's rule* overridden.

[1] Karl Polanyi, *The Great Transformation* (New York: Octagon Books, 1975).

This rule states that "the greater the relative working capacity of the household, the less its members work." The rule indicates that householding production is designed to meet the household's needs, and nothing more.

Thus, the medieval manor consisted of a series of families who worked cooperatively in cultivating their communal fields, woods, pastures, and ponds. Each family had an established right to the output from certain strips of land, to pasture a certain number of animals, to use a certain amount of wood, and so forth, but it also had the responsibility to produce a surplus for the feudal lord, who in turn was responsible for security. Equity was maintained by these rights. Local demands and supplies were kept in balance.

Redistribution

In some societies equity is maintained through the institution of a strong central authority, whose function is *redistributive.* Products are delivered to this head person, or chief. They are then parceled out by this person to members of the social group as determined by custom.

Many of the ancient empires, such as the New Kingdom of Egypt, were founded upon this principle of redistribution. It is also common among many of the cattle-raising tribes of East Africa. One interesting manifestation was found in the *potlatch* of the *Kwakiutl* Indians of the Pacific Northwest, in which the chief assembled the wealth of the tribe and redistributed it by giving to others in elaborate gift-giving ceremonies.

Redistribution by government is, of course, also the fundamental difference between modern market and socialist societies, and it was the organizing principle of the now defunct communist state.

Reciprocity

The third pattern of exchange is *reciprocity.* Needs are met by exchange between complementary producers. In the Trobriand Islands of Western Melanesia, for example, inland communities are paired with coastal villages in a pattern of exchange of inland breadfruits for coastal fish. The pairing extends to particular individuals being responsible for the direct exchange, in symmetrical arrangements of remarkable regularity and persistence. Many such exchanges are disguised in the form of reciprocal giving of gifts, but the principle is the same.

Karl Polanyi (1975), who has contributed greatly to our understanding of small-scale, self-sustaining, preindustrial societies by his pioneering work, draws the following conclusions about them. Most important is the subordination of economic life to social rules and tradition. All economic systems known up to the end of feudalism in Western Europe were organized either on the principles of reciprocity, redistribution, or householding, or on some combination of the three. The orderly production and distribution of goods were secured through a great variety of individual motives disciplined by general principles of behavior. Gain was not prominent among these motives. Custom and law, and magic and religion cooperated in inducing the individual to comply with the rules of behavior that, eventually, ensured one's functioning in the socioeconomic system. Further, Polanyi argues that as long as social organization ran in the ruts of tradition, no individual economic motives needed to come into play. Nor was the shirking of personal effort to be feared. Division of labor was automatically ensured. Social and economic obligations were duly discharged. Material means for an excellent display of abundance at all public festivals were guaranteed. Such are the basic considerations guiding the simplest forms of exchange, not simply in feudal Europe, but in all societies in which the market-place is absent.

BARTERING AND HIGGLING IN PEASANT SOCIETIES: A STAGE IN THE EVOLUTION OF MARKETS

The gradual emergence of both local and long-distance trade between social groups was responsible for the transition of many self-sustaining groups into peasant societies and, in turn, the transformation of peasant societies into full-fledged exchange economies. A *peasant society* is one in which the household or local social group remains relatively self-sustaining with respect to necessities such as food and shelter, but trades a surplus or a specialty product for outside manufactured goods or luxuries. A full *exchange economy* is one in which the principles of the division of labor apply to every producer. In an exchange economy, very few producers, even farmers, consume more than a small part of their own specialized output, for they come to produce only that for which they have a comparative advantage, not everything.

Perhaps the earliest long-distance trade was exploration beyond the limits of the local area. Such exploration might involve warlike forays or irregular trading, often for ritual goods associated with the temple, the early focus of society, and the god-king who maintained social controls. As long as the resulting exchange of goods was sporadic, market centers did not develop. Only when regular trade connections emerged was there justification for the establishment of permanent market places.

One regular form of long-distance exchange was between complementary production zones, for example, between plains dwellers and hill folk, each trading surpluses of their own specialty for those of the other. Market sites would often develop along the territorial boundary zone, on neutral ground. At the appropriate season, often in conjunction with religious festivities, people from surrounding areas would converge upon the market sites to barter surpluses. Where relations between the different groups were strained, a truce would be called and the market site would constitute neutral ground.

Local trade emerged on the basis of regular intercourse between peasants, local craftsworkers and specialists, and town merchants and intermediaries. Local surpluses would be traded for such necessities as salt, iron, or durables, and merchants would have available some luxuries and trinkets obtained from the great fairs. To fit in with work on the land, the markets would be held periodically. Links connecting long-distance trade, great fairs, and local periodic markets were provided by the town merchants, whose travels would transport the goods from one place to the other.

It was only with the emergence of local and long-distance trade that market sites and trading posts became widespread in peasant societies. For example, in Yorubaland in West Africa, the earliest markets were located along the contact zone between forest and savanna, along coastal lagoons and creeks, or at the boundaries between different peoples. The larger markets were situated along the chief trade routes, and changed in importance with these routes. One important origin of Yoruba markets was the resting place where local populations provided services to passing groups of traders. If such resting places became popular, a market into which farmers brought their wares sprang up, and periodic market days developed. Extra-large meetings would be held less frequently, when large numbers of traders converged.

Initially, at these meeting-places *bartering* was the dominant means of exchange. But gradually, some form of *money* took over as the medium of exchange, and goods began to move at prices determined by *higgling,* that is, face-to-face bargaining between buyer and seller with both trying to maximize their advantages, ultimately agreeing upon mutually satisfactory payment. Under such conditions prices are highly variable and flexible from time to time and place to place, although in each case they reflect a balance or agreement between buyer and seller that transfers a commodity or a service from one to the other.

THE GEOGRAPHY OF PRICE
IN FREE-ENTERPRISE SYSTEMS

Basic Economic Concepts

Now consider the problem in a much larger-scale free-enterprise economy in which there are many buyers and sellers who cannot meet face to face to bargain, yet for whom some type of balance between demands and supplies ultimately must be achieved. It is to this case that the classic microeconomic price theory applies. Three important concepts drawn from this theory will enable us to develop a *geography* of price. These three concepts are the nature of *price* itself, the relationship of *supply and demand* to price, and *market equilibrium*, the price at which supply equals demand. The concept of *elasticity*, the rate at which supply and demand change with price, also is introduced.

Price. According to *price theory*, price is the rate at which a good, service, resource, or factor of production can be exchanged for any other good, service, resource, or factor of production in a manner that clears the market of available goods and satisfies consumer demand at that price. Goods have prices because they are *useful* and *scarce* in relation to the uses to which people want to put them. When something has no use, it does not command a price; when it is useful but available to all in unlimited amounts, like air, it cannot command a price.

Whether or not a good is useful is determined by consumer demand. Scarcity, on the other hand, is determined by the capacities and willingness of producers to generate the supplies needed at the prevailing price. Price, then, is determined by the demands and supplies of many consumers and producers jointly interacting in a market where goods and services are exchanged for each other.

The most fundamental characteristic of such free-enterprise markets is that, because there are large numbers of equally small producers and consumers, the individual buyer or seller is a "price-taker," having no control over the price he or she must pay or can receive. The prices are determined competitively in the market, and the actions of any particular individual cannot change them. Indeed, very elaborate legal safeguards (antitrust legislation) have been developed in free-enterprise societies to preserve this situation as the way of conducting business. In some types of businesses, because of the possibility of achieving economies of scale, there has today been the transition to market negotiation, while markets continue to work best in agriculture, the precious and nonferrous metals industries, the stock exchanges, and the markets for land, homes, and other kinds of property.

Demand and Supply. The relationship between demand and price is quite simple. The theory of demand postulates that, *as the price of a product falls, more of it will be bought*. This is because some people who could not buy at the higher price will begin to make purchases as prices fall and because many buyers are likely to increase their purchases of the cheapening commodity in place of alternative goods that have become relatively more costly. In addition, if nothing else changes, the price decline will increase people's real incomes, and they will consume more because they are relatively better off.

The theory of supply postulates that *the higher the price is, the more of a good that will be offered for sale* because existing sellers are eager to sell while conditions are good, and rising prices will make it attractive for more producers to enter the market. If prices fall, supplies will be withheld in the hope that prices will rise again, and marginal producers may go out of business. Supply is also affected by the relative efficiency of different producers and production units. If prices are low (or demand drops) only the more efficient, lower-cost mines, power-generating plants, railroad rolling stock, and so forth will be used. When prices are high, less-efficient products and facilities will be brought into use because the higher prices will cover the higher costs.

Demand and supply can be represented in tables (or schedules) or by graphs. Hypothetical data are given in Figure 6.1 to illustrate how the demand and supply for "thingamabobs" might react to price changes, and the typical downward-sloping demand curve and upward-sloping supply curve that result.

An example, using real data, may help to emphasize that demand, even of such basics as specific food items, can be very sensitive to price. The U.S. Department of Agriculture, for example, attempted to estimate demand for a variety of meats, based on prices for 1948–1962. In the case of chicken, there was a fairly progressive drop in price throughout this entire period. As prices fell, demand increased, apparently tracing out a smooth downward-sloping demand curve (Figure 6.2). Chicken consumption doubled in just 15 years in response to a halving in price (adjusted for cost of living). This change could be observed because the demand curve for chicken remained constant over the entire study period, whereas the supply curve shifted progressively.

Figure 6.3 provides a second example, the estimated demand curve for gasoline using data for 21 countries 1970–1971. In this case, countries' supply

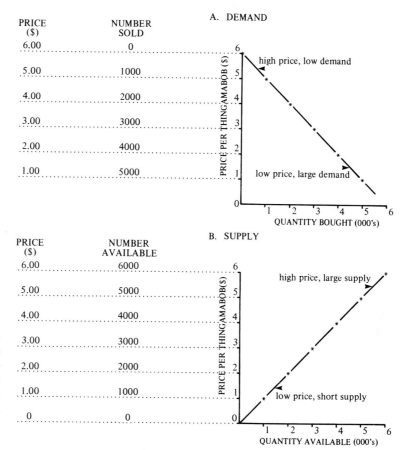

PRICE ($)	NUMBER SOLD
6.00	0
5.00	1000
4.00	2000
3.00	3000
2.00	4000
1.00	5000

PRICE ($)	NUMBER AVAILABLE
6.00	6000
5.00	5000
4.00	4000
3.00	3000
2.00	2000
1.00	1000
0	0

FIGURE 6.1 Demand, supply, and price. Demand has an inverse relationship to price: the higher the price, the lower the demand. Supply has a direct relationship to price: the higher the price, the greater the supply. These relationships are illustrated in table form (the demand and supply schedules) and by graphs.

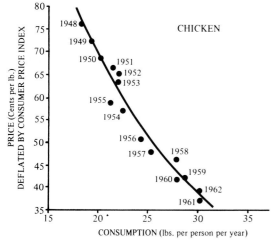

FIGURE 6.2 The demand curve for chicken, United States, 1948–1962. The demand curve for chicken remained constant in the United States over the study period: 1948–1962. The supply curve, however, kept shifting, because producers were able to produce more chicken at lower prices (in constant dollars) as the years went by. The demand curve is traced out as a sequence of market equilibrium points (see Figure 6.4). [*Source:* U.S. Department of Agriculture, Economic Research Service, Neg. ERS 2147-63(7).]

curves vary because of differences in industrial organization and tax policy, but the 21 market equilibria trace out the demand curve.

Market Equilibrium. In order to understand how demand and supply are brought into balance to produce equilibrium, it is helpful to plot supply and demand curves back to back on a single graph. The results for the "thingamabob" example are shown in Figure 6.4.

If suppliers are prepared to increase the quantity of a good they market as price increases, and if consumers reduce the amount they buy as price increases, then there should exist a *price at which supply equals demand*. This price, which "clears" the market of available supply and also satisfies demand, is the point of *market equilibrium*. Market equilibrium is identified on a graph of back-to-back supply and demand curves as the point of intersection (*E* on Figure 6.4).

Price will tend to fluctuate around the market equilibrium in a free-enterprise economy. If the price rises above the equilibrium, price reductions will be needed to clear the market of excess supply resulting from the price rise. If demand rises above supply, disappointed customers will scour the market, offering

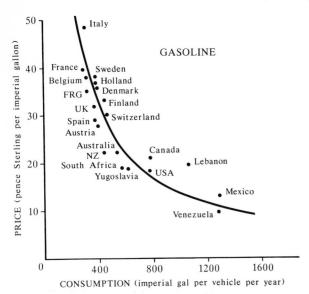

FIGURE 6.3 The demand curve for gasoline. Given the relatively small changes in gasoline prices that had occurred in Canada and the United States, Dennis Reynolds used data for some 21 countries to estimate the demand curve for gasoline. The data are for 1970–1971. Reynolds notes that the results may be affected by substantial differences in incomes, geography, history, demography, and road layout. [*Source:* D. J. Reynolds, "Consumer Expenditures on Auto Use: Income, Price Elasticities of Demand and Gasoline Rationing." Role of the Automobile Study, Working Paper No. 17. Transport Canada (January 1979), p. 17.]

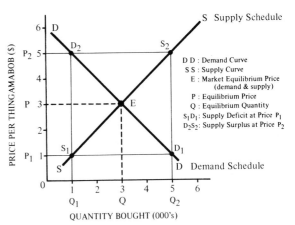

FIGURE 6.4 Market equilibrium. The market equilibrium is the point of intersection of the supply and demand curves (*E*). The market equilibrium determines the price (*P*) of the good, the quantity (*Q*) bought and sold, and total demand (*P* × *Q*). At price *P*, buyers and sellers match purchases and sales and are just able to clear the market of available supplies. In the case of thingamabobs $P = \$3.00$ and $Q = 3000$, so that total demand is $9000. If the price were $1.00, demand would rise to 5000, and supply fall to 1000, leaving a deficit (S_1D_1) of 4000 thingamabobs. Disappointed customers would bid up the price. If the price rose to $5.00, demand would fall to 1000 and supply would increase to 5000, leaving a surplus (S_2D_2) of 4000. The market glut would force down prices. Thus, the market price will tend to remain at the market equilibrium level.

higher prices. Any deviation from the market equilibrium price thus triggers corrective action that pushes the price back toward the market equilibrium level.

The natural tendency of prices to hover around the market equilibrium level makes it difficult to observe the full demand-and-supply schedules in real market conditions. Hence, the chicken and gasoline examples are of special interest. Actually, what Figure 6.2 shows is a series of market equilibria, one for each year! These market equilibria join to pick out the demand curve because the shifting supply curves intersected an unchanging demand curve at a progression of different price-and-quantity equilibrium levels. Similarly, what Figure 6.3 shows is a series of 21 market equilibria for each country that trace out the demand curve because supply conditions vary across countries, whereas the responsiveness of demand to price changes is much more consistent.

Elasticity. The magnitude of response in demand or supply to changes in price can vary a great deal depending on the good. For some items, such as tobacco, there is little drop in demand with increase in

price. But consumers are conscious of the seasonal swings in the prices of fresh fruits and vegetables and are highly responsive to these changes (see Tables 6.1 and 6.2).

Elasticity (e) is a measure of response to price changes. *Elasticity of demand* is the percentage fall in demand for a product that results from a 1 percentage point increase in price. *Elasticity of supply* is the percentage increase in supply of a product that results from a 1 percentage point increase in price. If there is no change in demand with a change in price, the elasticity of demand is zero. If small changes in price produce massive shifts in demand, the elasticity of demand approaches infinity, as is shown in Figure 6.5. An elasticity of 1.0 means that a 1.0 percent change in price results in a 1.0 percent change in quantity.

Some examples for goods in low- and high-income countries illustrate the factors affecting price elasticity of demand (Table 6.3). Luxuries tend to have higher elasticities of demand than basic goods. Meat is much more price-sensitive than rice in a low-income country. Big-ticket items such as automobiles are

TABLE 6.1

Seasonal variations in apple prices

Oct.	Nov.	Dec.	Jan.	Feb.	Mar.	Apr.
5.00	4.25	4.25	4.38	4.35	4.38	4.60

Source: U.S. Department of Agriculture, *Prices and Spreads for Apples, Grapefruit, Grapes, Lemons and Oranges Sold Fresh in Selected Markets, 1962/63-1966/67* (Washington, D.C.: USDA Economic Research Service, Marketing Research Report No. 888, 1968).

Note: Prices are *shipping point price (FOB)*, the simple average of the midpoint range of daily prices for a specified container of apples of specified grade and size received by a broad sample of shippers in representative shipping districts during a specified week. FOB means *free-on-board*, and signifies that the price excludes transportation charges.

TABLE 6.2

Retail price variation of selected food items, New York City, 1936–1940

	Average Monthly Variation in Prices (percent)		Average Monthly Variation in Prices (percent)
Fresh beets	31.0	Fresh milk	4.0
Fresh tomatoes	28.7	Butter	3.5
Cooking apples	17.5	Dried navy beans	2.0
Grapefruit	14.3	Canned tomatoes	1.2
Potatoes.	12.0	Canned peaches	.7
Large white eggs	9.7	Rice.	.5
Oranges.	8.3	Dried prunes	.5
Fresh carrots	6.2	Cheese	.2

Source: 738, Department of Agricultural Economics, Cornell University, June 1950.

Note: What is the relationship between (1) price variation and length of season?, (2) perishability and price variation?

much more price-sensitive than cheap items such as matches in high-income countries. The availability of substitutes is important too. Fresh foods can be replaced by dried foods (in low-income countries) or canned and frozen foods (in high-income counries) and so are price-sensitive. Liquor and tobacco, lacking ef-

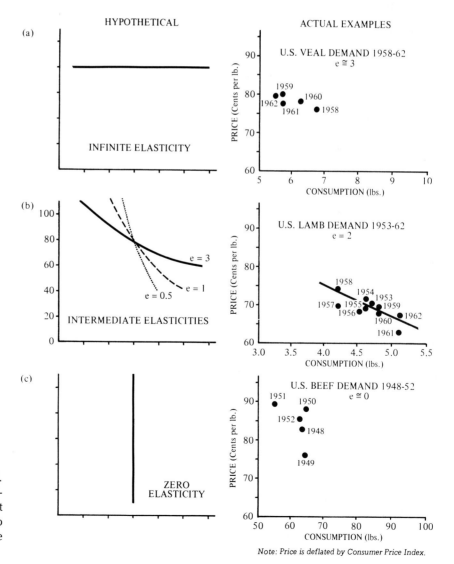

FIGURE 6.5 Elasticity of demand. This figure shows a variety of elasticities from zero to infinity. Note that the more sensitive consumers are to price, the higher the elasticity and the gentler the demand curve is.

Note: Price is deflated by Consumer Price Index.

TABLE 6.3

Elasticity of demand in high- and low-income countries

| Elasticity | | Result of a Price Increase on | | Examples For | |
		(a) Total Amount of Good Purchased	(b) Total Amount Spent on Good	Low-income Countries	High-income Countries
High	−2.0	Decrease is more than proportional to price increase	Decreases		Automobiles Furniture
Unitary	−1.0	Decrease is exactly proportional to price increase	Stays the same	Vegetables Meat Fruit Maize Fresh fish Wheat	Clothing Gasoline Food
Low	−0.5	Decrease is less than proportional to price increase	Increases	Rice	Liquor Tobacco
	−0.2				Matches

Note: The high-income countries' elasticities are drawn from many different sources. The low-income countries' elasticities are adapted from Angus Deaton, "Price Elasticities from Survey Data—Extensions and Indonesian Results," Washington D.C.: World Bank, 1990.

fective substitutes, are not and have low elasticities of demand.

To be useful in economic geography, each of the basic economic concepts (supply and demand, price, elasticity, and equilibrium) has to be extended by introducing ideas of the market as a *place,* of location relative to this place, and of transportation costs. The result is a *geography* of supply, a *geography* of demand, and a *geography* of market equilibrium in free-enterprise economic systems.

The Geography of Supply

Basic Concepts. The supply curves of the economist ignore the systematic impact of transportation charges on the delivered cost of any good. Transportation costs can be expected to increase directly with the distance a good has to be transported. Because price therefore increases with distance from the point of production, the result is a *supply-price funnel* as can be illustrated with the example of "thingamabobs" (Figure 6.6).

August Lösch (1954), who introduced the term *price funnel,* has provided maps and data to illustrate such price variations in space for a wide variety of goods. Agricultural products were cheapest, he found, in the centers of production and increased in price outward from these centers. Potatoes in 1936 were 18 cents a pound on Prince Edward Island, for example, but 25 cents a pound in Toronto. Orange prices were 16 cents a pound in California, but 37 cents a pound in Chicago. Lösch also examined nonagricultural goods and found significant price funnels for newspapers

with large market areas, automobiles, and soap, for example. Similarly, and quite surprisingly, given the large number of small producers and the short distances milk is transported, even for milk, there was in 1957–1958 a single, countrywide price funnel centered on Eau Claire, Wisconsin, at the heart of the dairy belt (Figure 6.7).

The Role of Central Markets in Setting Prices Received by Suppliers. Lösch's price funnels, upward and outward from supply regions, do not tell us what individual suppliers receive for their output, however. Within the supply region there will be one or more *central markets,* and the price received by a given supplier will be the price established in that market *minus* the costs of transporting the product to that market. The farther the supplier is from that central market, the lower the price, as shown in Figure 6.8.

Suppliers have a choice of selling to consumers in their local market, or disposing of their supplies in the central market. The supplier will sell to local consumers only if the price they are willing to pay exceeds the central market price less transportation costs. Prices in the central market minus costs of transportation therefore set a *producer's price floor,* the price that may be obtained by selling in the central market when local demand is weak.

Each central market has its own *supply area.* Individual producers will sell to the central market that offers them the greatest *on-site return* (on-site return is another way of saying central market price minus transportation costs). The supply area boundary is located where the producers' price floor gradients inter-

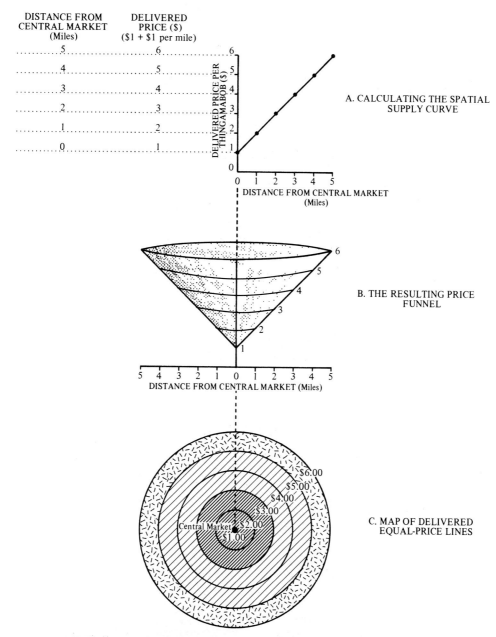

DISTANCE FROM CENTRAL MARKET (Miles)	DELIVERED PRICE ($) ($1 + $1 per mile)
5	6
4	5
3	4
2	3
1	2
0	1

A. CALCULATING THE SPATIAL SUPPLY CURVE

B. THE RESULTING PRICE FUNNEL

C. MAP OF DELIVERED EQUAL-PRICE LINES

FIGURE 6.6 The spatial supply-price funnel. The price of a thingamabob is $1.00 at the market plus a transportation charge of $1.00 per mile. The result can be shown in four equivalent ways: table, graph, price funnel, and map. Becoming familiar with all four is helpful in understanding the economic fundamentals of economic geography. Note that a price funnel shows price against distance, whereas an ordinary supply curve shows price against quantity.

sect, as at X and Y in Figure 6.9. The boundary between the supply areas of competing central markets traces out the locus of minimum on-site returns. How low that minimum is depends upon the locations of the central markets, the prices in those markets, and how rapidly the price floor falls with distance. Compare the prices at boundaries X and Y in Figure 6.9.

Why Did Central Markets Emerge? Why did central markets emerge to set the spatial patterns of prices? Central markets are a creation of modern economies and transportation systems. In the United States until the 1850s, agriculture was characterized by small production units. Transportation, communication, and marketing were local, and trading was very

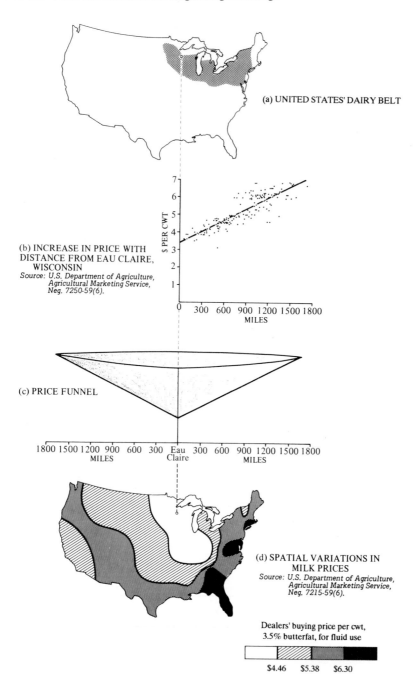

(a) UNITED STATES' DAIRY BELT

(b) INCREASE IN PRICE WITH DISTANCE FROM EAU CLAIRE, WISCONSIN
Source: U.S. Department of Agriculture, Agricultural Marketing Service, Neg. 7250-59(6).

(c) PRICE FUNNEL

1800 1500 1200 900 600 300 Eau 300 600 900 1200 1500 1800
MILES   Claire   MILES

(d) SPATIAL VARIATIONS IN MILK PRICES
Source: U.S. Department of Agriculture, Agricultural Marketing Service, Neg. 7215-59(6).

Dealers' buying price per cwt, 3.5% butterfat, for fluid use

$4.46 $5.38 $6.30

FIGURE 6.7 Milk prices in the United States, 1957–1958. The center of milk production in the United States is Eau Claire, Wisconsin. Milk prices increase regularly with increasing distance from Eau Claire, creating a price funnel. Prices climb from less than $4.00 per hundredweight (cwt) to more than $5.00 in California and nearly $7.00 in Florida. Prices increased on average by 2.2 cents per 10 miles. [*Source for (d):* U.S. Department of Agriculture, Agriculture Marketing Service, Neg. 7215-59(6).]

often a face-to-face matter between producer and consumer in a weekly market. In the last half of the nineteenth century, many changes took place that led to the development of a nationwide, commercial marketing system. Cities grew rapidly, western lands were brought into production, railroad mileage expanded quickly, and communications improved. These developments facilitated the long-distance flow of commodities from specialized production regions to food-deficit areas, but required that some other institution replace

weekly face-to-face trading (see Chapter 11, The Second Wave of Industrial Revolution).

Trading therefore progressed from the informal weekly markets to formal clubs that provided a common meeting place for traders. The next step was for *commodity exchanges* to emerge and provide organized trading. Commodity exchanges are nonprofit associations of persons acting as principals or agents in the transfer of ownership of agricultural or other primary commodities. *Futures* markets are the major part

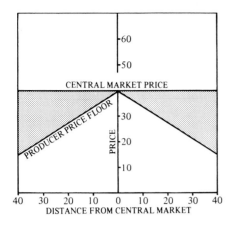

Transportation Costs to Central Market

FIGURE 6.8 Producer price floors. For many agricultural products and industrial raw materials, a base price is competitively determined at one or more central markets. The supplier receives the central market price *minus* transportation and related charges, but may be able to sell locally at a price higher than this price floor.

of most exchange activities, trading contracts for future deliveries at agreed-upon prices. *Cash* or *spot markets,* where available commodities are sold and delivered within a few hours, also are part of the commodity exchange function.

What do such commodity exchanges do? Both spot and futures markets provide continuous market trading for those who wish to buy or sell. They involve large numbers of buyers and sellers, maintain quality standards, and permit a free flow of information, so that competitive prices can be determined. In effect, they are the prime example of "the market" in classical free-enterprise economies.

Commodity exchanges functioning as central markets exist for many products including livestock, grains, fruits and vegetables, wool, cotton, hides, and tobacco. For example, in the United States, corn prices are set by the price of No. 3 Yellow Corn on the Chicago Board of Trade. The prices of oats and soybeans are also set there. Barley prices are set by the quotations for No. 3 Barley in Minneapolis. Sorghums are based on No. 2 Yellow Milo at Kansas City. American cheese at factories in Wisconsin is priced at the Wisconsin Cheese Exchange. On the world scene, many metals are priced on the London Metals Exchange. Rotterdam now functions as the world's spot market for petroleum.

Chicago and London are examples of the large *terminal markets* where products from wide areas were concentrated, and it is for this reason that they developed their market concourses. Another example is that of Liverpool, which prior to 1940 was the major international market for wheat. Wheat prices regis-

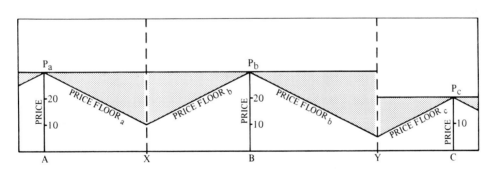

A, B, C : Locations of Central Markets

X, Y : Supply Area Boundaries

AX : Primary Supply Area of A

XBY : Primary Supply Area of B

YC : Primary Supply Area of C

P_a, P_b, P_c : Prices at Central Markets

: Transportation Costs to Central Markets

FIGURE 6.9 Supply areas of central markets. The boundaries of supply areas were set by the intersection of producer price floors from competing central markets. The boundaries are thus lines of indifference along which producers receive the same price from competing central markets. The lower a central market's price is, the smaller its supply area will be. Thus, C's primary supply area (CY) is reduced and B's (BY) is extended.

tered on the Liverpool market were looked upon as the world price. The United Kingdom was the largest single importer of wheat, and Liverpool was an ideal world market as prices were little affected by special conditions in one or another of the world's producing areas, but reflected the general tendencies in all producing areas.

Logically, of course, the world price of wheat should be determined chiefly by the world supply of wheat and the general level of world commodity prices. From 1924 to 1938, virtually all the variation in the price of wheat at Liverpool, commonly referred to as "British parcels," was tied to variations in the world supply of wheat and British wholesale prices. A 1 percent change in supply in this period was associated with a 1.4 percent change in the price of wheat in the opposite direction. A 1 percent change in the index of prices was associated with a 1.2 percent change in the index of wheat in the same direction.

United States wheat prices tended to depend directly on British wheat prices. Thus, from 1922 to 1939, three-quarters of the variation in the price of wheat in the United States at the domestic wheat-price basepoint, Kansas City, was associated with variations in the price of British parcels of wheat at Liverpool. Prices elsewhere in wheat-producing areas of the United States reflected transportation charges to Kansas City. In most years since then, however, U.S. domestic prices have been determined chiefly by the level of price support established by the government or by other governmental policies.

Role of the Market Traders. It is the market traders who make the whole process of balancing demands and supplies work. To illustrate, consider a trader who has been put in charge of a grain "desk" at the Continental Grain Company. A cable arrives from one of Continental's overseas offices—say, Paris. A buyer has bid for 10,000 tons of soybeans for July delivery in Rotterdam. Before accepting or countering with an offer, the trader considers future prices, world news, freight quotations, vessel bookings, the crop outlook, and the competition.

Then the trader makes a simple calculation. The basis for the final price is the "futures" quotation on the Chicago Board of Trade for July soybeans. The trader adds in the barge freight to New Orleans, the cost of handling at Continental's grain elevator there, and the ocean freight to Rotterdam. Then the trader cables the Paris office with a CIF price offer—cost, insurance, and freight.

If the trader gets an "accept" from the other side, the trader begins the task of seeking out a profit. First, the trader "hedges" by buying July futures in Chicago. Because the futures price is the basis for the actual soybean sale, the trader can limit losses this way. Then the trader tries to find cheaper soybeans. If he or she does, the trader can sell his or her July futures, and the trader's speculative profit will be the difference between the Rotterdam contract price and what the trader paid for the cheaper soybeans, less any cost of reselling the July futures.

The chartering department, meanwhile, will be speculating on shipping, trying to get the best deal possible for the July delivery in Rotterdam. It may take a section of a ship under charter by another company. Or it may charter a tanker for the 10,000-ton sale; 30,000 tons excess may be filled by another sale, or it may figure on selling the space later to a competitor at a profit.

All these facts, and more, determine what Continental's profit on the sale will be. At any rate, it will be months before the trader will know if the sale to Rotterdam was a success, but it is the possibility of making speculative gains that motivates the traders who keep the free-enterprise system of buying, selling, and price determination operational.

The Geography of Demand

Under perfect competition, the price paid by a *consumer* increases with distance from a central market, in the manner of Lösch's price-funnels (Figure 6.6). Central market price plus transportation costs from the central market sets a ceiling on the price that local consumers have to pay. They can always buy from local suppliers if prices are lower, but they need never pay more than the ceiling price determined by the central market plus transportation (Figure 6.10).

Where goods or services are available from competing central markets, consumers will buy from the market offering the lowest ceiling price if they do not buy locally. Market prices plus transportation costs thus lead to ceiling price gradients that trace out *market area* boundaries where they intersect (as at X and Z in Figure 6.11). Such boundaries trace out the locus of maximum ceiling prices between adjacent central markets, leading to the conclusion that there is a direct relationship between welfare and distance: The most distant consumer pays the highest prices (Figure 6.11), just as the most distant producer receives the least (Figure 6.9). Those on the periphery are doubly disadvantaged!

The Spatial Demand Cone. Demand for a good sold at a central market can be expected to drop progressively outward from that market as transportation

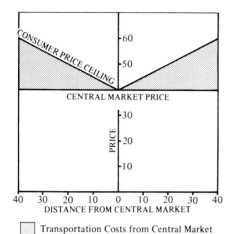

Transportation Costs from Central Market

FIGURE 6.10 Consumer price ceilings. Under perfect competition, the maximum delivered price equals the central market price plus transportation. This price sets a *consumer price ceiling*. The consumer may be able to buy locally for lower prices, but will not pay more. Figure 6.10 can be thought of as the top half of Figure 6.8. Combined, they show two price gradients fanning out from central markets, a consumer price ceiling and a producer price floor.

costs add to the price of the good. This relationship follows from the basic relationship of demand to price (see Figure 6.1). Using the demand schedule, which indicates the amount bought at each given price, and the delivered price at each distance band from the market, one can draw a *demand cone* centered on the market. The outer perimeter of the cone, where demand drops to zero, would be the market area boundary in the absence of competitive centers, and is called the *range of the good*. (See Figure 6.12.)

Consider the case of thingamabobs discussed earlier (Figures 6.1 and 6.12). The price of these delicate widgets increases from \$1 at the central market to \$6 at a radius of 5 miles. Each dollar increase in price produces a decline in demand of 1000. Demand drops from 5000 at the central market to zero at 6 miles distance.

A map of the market area can be drawn showing the demand contours for thingamabobs. The demand at the market boundary itself is zero. A succession of contours at \$1000-thingamabob intervals can be drawn with a spot height of 5000 at the central market itself. The table, graph, demand cone, and map are equivalent. They all show the same information, but in different forms.

Incomes and Demand. Demand for most goods is sensitive to income. Purchases of many items increase with higher income (Table 6.4). Exceptions are food stuffs such as dried beans, which are cheap but take time and trouble to prepare and which are replaced by more convenient substitutes as incomes rise. These exceptions are called *inferior goods*. By

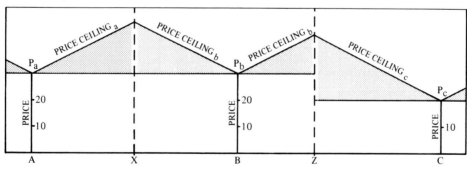

A, B, C : Locations of Central Markets

X, Z : Market Area Boundaries

AX : Primary Market Area of A

XBZ : Primary Market Area of B

ZC : Primary Market Area of C

P_a, P_b, P_c : Prices at Central Markets

Transportation Costs from Central Market

FIGURE 6.11 Definition of market areas. The market area of a central market is the area in which central market price plus transportation is less than (or equal to) the delivered price from competing central markets. The lower the price at the central market area, the larger the primary market area. Thus, C's primary market area (CZ) is increased at the expense of B's (BZ).

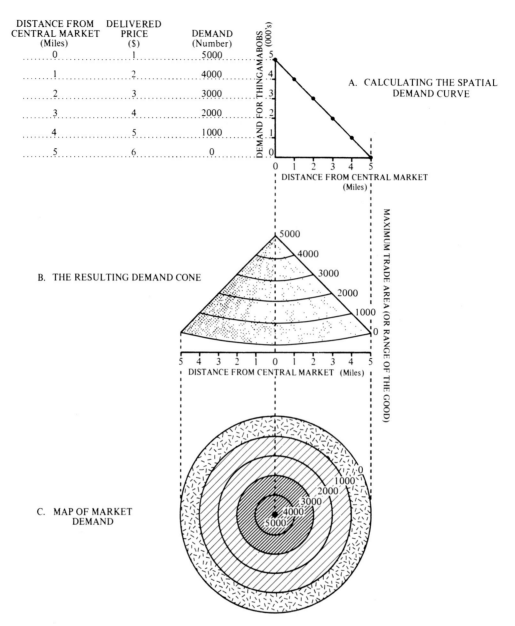

DISTANCE FROM CENTRAL MARKET (Miles)	DELIVERED PRICE ($)	DEMAND (Number)
0	1	5000
1	2	4000
2	3	3000
3	4	2000
4	5	1000
5	6	0

A. CALCULATING THE SPATIAL DEMAND CURVE

B. THE RESULTING DEMAND CONE

C. MAP OF MARKET DEMAND

FIGURE 6.12   The spatial demand curve, or demand cone. The construction of a demand cone requires data on the delivered price with increasing distance from the market (the price funnel) and the quantity bought at each price (the demand schedule). Delivered price at each distance band is then translated into demand at each distance band. The maximum market area in the absence of competition (called the *range of the good*) is set by the radius at which demand falls to zero. It is important to understand that the table, graph, demand cone, and map are four equivalent ways of presenting the same information. Compare this figure with Figure 6.6.

contrast, expenditures on luxury items such as women's clothing increase very rapidly as income increases.

The sensitivity of consumers to price changes for any good also differs with income level. It is believed that, in general, lower-income families are more sensi-

tive to price than higher-income families. Demand curves can, therefore, be drawn according to income. An example using our familiar "thingamabobs" is provided by Figure 6.13. In this example, the demand curve for low-income families, D_L, has a greater elasticity than that for high-income familes, D_H. The total

TABLE 6.4

Variation in food expenditure by income level

	Income Level in $ per Annum						
	Under 5000	5000 to 9000	10,000 to 14,999	15,000 to 19,999	20,000 to 29,999	30,000 to 39,999	40,000 and Over
Household characteristics							
Age of householder (years)	44.2	51.8	59.6	45.4	42.5	41.5	43.7
Children < 18 years per household	0.29	0.58	0.57	0.61	0.77	0.97	0.90
Vehicles per household	0.6	0.9	1.1	1.4	1.7	1.9	2.3
Home ownership (%)	26.0	39.0	48.0	48.0	63.0	71.0	85.0
	Average Weekly Expenditure in Dollars						
Food eaten at home							
Flour	0.05	0.07	0.06	0.04	0.03	0.03	0.03
White bread	0.30	0.32	0.32	0.31	0.27	0.25	0.24
Doughnuts	0.10	0.11	0.13	0.15	0.13	0.16	0.18
Sirloin steak	0.07	0.04	0.06	0.10	0.11	0.10	0.16
Lamb	0.04	0.05	0.04	0.08	0.07	0.05	0.05
Fresh whole chicken	0.15	0.21	0.17	0.17	0.16	0.14	0.16
Sugar	0.15	0.16	0.15	0.15	0.11	0.10	0.10
Candy	0.22	0.19	0.26	0.22	0.31	0.40	0.44
Roasted coffee	0.23	0.22	0.26	0.23	0.26	0.24	0.27
Instant coffee	0.19	0.20	0.17	0.14	0.17	0.11	0.14
Food away from home							
Dinner	2.63	2.08	2.82	3.37	4.33	4.15	6.42
Wine	0.14	0.09	0.13	0.14	0.17	0.17	0.28
Total Food Expenditure	20.19	19.09	20.83	22.08	25.44	24.95	31.15

Source: David M. Smallwood, "Food Spending in American Households, 1980–1986," Statistical Bulletin No. 791, Encomic Research Service, U.S. Department of Agriculture (March 1990), pp. 69–71. Table is for urban households, 1986.

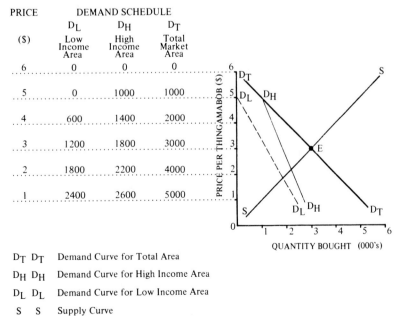

FIGURE 6.13 Income level and market demand. Aggregate demand schedules, such as those presented in Figures 6.1 and 6.2, ignore differences in income level among consumers. Disaggregating the schedule for low- and high-income areas reveals in this hypothetical example that low-income areas are more sensitive to price. They stand to gain most with any fall in price (as in Figure 6.2), but conversely to suffer most with any increase in price. Note that the market equilibrium remains at *E* as in Figure 6.4 with the low-income area purchasing 1200 and the high-income area 1800 thingamabobs, to make a total of 3000 as before.

PRICE	DEMAND SCHEDULE		
($)	D_L Low Income Area	D_H High Income Area	D_T Total Market Area
6	0	0	0
5	0	1000	1000
4	600	1400	2000
3	1200	1800	3000
2	1800	2200	4000
1	2400	2600	5000

D_T D_T Demand Curve for Total Area

D_H D_H Demand Curve for High Income Area

D_L D_L Demand Curve for Low Income Area

S   S   Supply Curve

E   Market Equilibrium Price

demand curve is formed by adding up the quantities demanded at each price by high- and low-income families.

These differences also may reveal themselves spatially. Suppose the market for thingamabobs is divided into high- and low-income sectors. The demand cone is steeper and the market area smaller in the low-income sector (Figure 6.14). This example demonstrates the general principle that the higher the income level is, the farther out the market area can extend.

Demand is affected by many other factors, too, besides price and income. The demand for food in Canada, for instance, has been shown to be affected by the aging of the population (older people spend less on food); the increasing proportion of women who work and smaller families (resulting in more restaurant

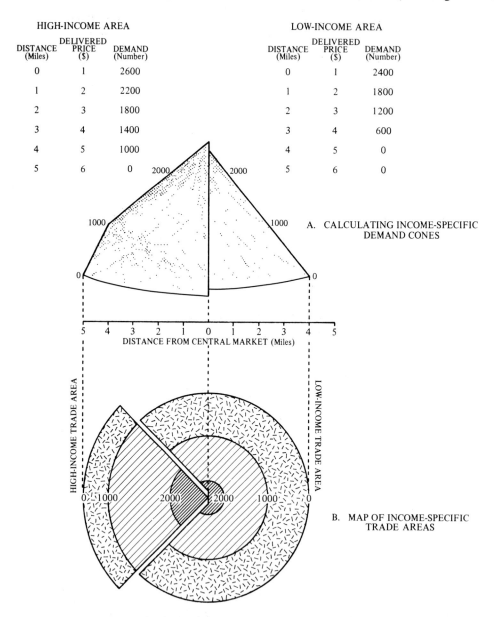

HIGH-INCOME AREA

DISTANCE (Miles)	DELIVERED PRICE ($)	DEMAND (Number)
0	1	2600
1	2	2200
2	3	1800
3	4	1400
4	5	1000
5	6	0

LOW-INCOME AREA

DISTANCE (Miles)	DELIVERED PRICE ($)	DEMAND (Number)
0	1	2400
1	2	1800
2	3	1200
3	4	600
4	5	0
5	6	0

A. CALCULATING INCOME-SPECIFIC DEMAND CONES

DISTANCE FROM CENTRAL MARKET (Miles)

HIGH-INCOME TRADE AREA

LOW-INCOME TRADE AREA

B. MAP OF INCOME-SPECIFIC TRADE AREAS

FIGURE 6.14 The demand cone for high- and low-income market areas. The demand schedules differ between high- and low-income areas (Figure 6.13). Therefore the demand cone will be different for high- and low-income areas. The trade area is larger for the high-income area and smaller for the low-income area. Aggregate demand for a good within any given distance-band of the central market equals the sum of the demand in the high- and low-income areas shown separately in this figure. The market boundaries occur at the price where demand falls to zero.

meals and less spent on grocery food), and the increasing ethnic diversity of the population (so more food is bought in speciality food shops) (Johansen et al., 1989).

Spatial Market Equilibrium

The balancing of supply and demand in the economic textbook case depicted in Figure 6.14 is a straightforward exercise. The supply and demand curves are drawn back-to-back and the equilibrium price and quantities indicated by the point of intersection. This exercise is repeated every day in central markets throughout the world (Figure 6.15a). Suppliers can expect to receive, at the minimum, central market price *less* transportation costs (Figure 6.15b). Consumers can expect to pay, at the maximum, central market price *plus* transportation costs (Figure 6.15c).

The total supply and demand curves at the central market (Figure 6.15a) are, however, an amalgam of many individual supply and demand curves. If you wish to understand how a combined supply curve is derived, refer to Figure 6.16. Suppose there is a central market at *M*. In the manner of Figure 6.15a the right-hand side of the graph in Figure 6.16 shows how the combined supply curve of two producers is derived at the central market. The producers are shown at *A* and *B* on the left-hand side of the graph (Figure 6.16), which corresponds to Figure 6.15b. The problem is one of combining the two producers' individual supply curves, taking into account transportation costs. This

process is described in the caption accompanying Figure 6.16.

MANAGED PRICES IN IMPERFECTLY COMPETITIVE SITUATIONS

The foregoing discussion refers to free-enterprise dynamics. But what about less-competitive situations? A market is imperfectly competitive when the actions of individual buyers or sellers can affect the equilibrium price. Such individuals are not ''price-takers'' forced to accept the price collectively determined by the free play of market forces. On the contrary, in the extreme case just one or two sellers or buyers set the market price themselves.

A situation of *monopoly* exists where a single *seller* sets the selling price, and a situation of *oligopoly* exists where relatively *few sellers* determine the price. This may be the case where a large proportion of total output of some product is accounted for by just one, or a few, manufacturing firms. *Monopsony* is where a *single buyer* dominates the market for the product and so dictates the purchase price. *Oligopsony* is where a *few buyers* dominate. A firm may be both monopsonist and monopolist. It may dominate the market for some raw materials, or components, hence setting the purchase price for them. It may also dominate the market for the finished product and so set the selling price. An automobile manufacturer, for instance, may dictate the price to parts manufacturers at which components such as tires will be bought, and, as a price leader, the

FIGURE 6.15 Spatial market equilibrium: simple case. Under perfect competition, buyers and sellers are price-takers. The equilibrium price is set by the equation of demand and supply at the market. Suppliers receive this price minus transportation. Buyers pay this price plus transportation. There is not, however, a one-way determinism of price at the marketplace without regard to transportation costs. Instead, the spatial market equilibrium price reflects the transportation costs of buyers and sellers as a whole, as well as setting their individual price ceilings and price floors.

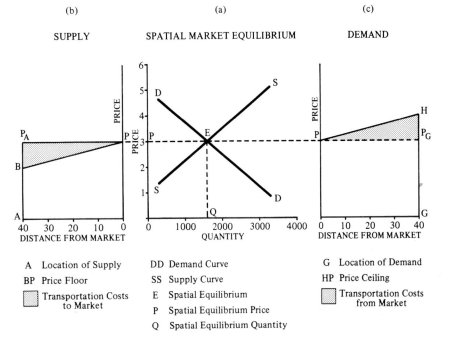

(b) SUPPLY   (a) SPATIAL MARKET EQUILIBRIUM   (c) DEMAND

A   Location of Supply
BP   Price Floor
▨   Transportation Costs to Market

DD   Demand Curve
SS   Supply Curve
E   Spatial Equilibrium
P   Spatial Equilibrium Price
Q   Spatial Equilibrium Quantity

G   Location of Demand
HP   Price Ceiling
▨   Transportation Costs from Market

FIGURE 6.16   Spatial market equilibrium: a more complex case. The spatial market equilibrium price must take into account transportation costs of all suppliers and consumers as a whole. To simplify, imagine there are just two producers, at *A* and *B*, respectively. The local price at which *A* is able to start production is *AE*. At *B* it is *BC*. Notice that although *A* is more distant from the market, it can supply *M* more cheaply (*ME'* rather than *MC'*).

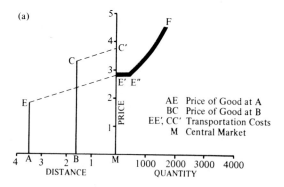

(a)

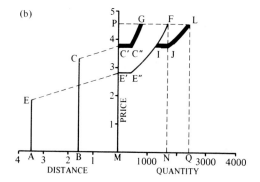

(b)

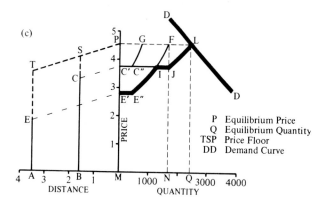

(c)

(a) As price increases above *ME'* and *MC'*, each supplier will be willing to produce and ship more to the market. Assume that the supply curve for producer is *E'E"F*. (This takes into account transport costs from *A* to *M*. At *A*, the supply curve would be lower because no transportation costs need be added in at the point of supply.) As the price at *M* increases, a level will be reached at which *B* becomes willing to supply the market, in competition with *A*. That price is *C'*.

(b) Once the price at *M* exceeds *C'*, *B* begins to supply the market. *B*'s supply curve is shown in (b) by the upward-sloping line *C'C"G*. Since both *A* and *B* supply the market at prices above *C'*, their *combined supply curve* in the market has to be derived. This is *EE" IJL* and it is formed by adding *B*'s supply curve *C'C"G* to *A*'s supply curve *E'E"F* horizontally, to show the total amount the two producers are willing to supply at each price level. *EE" IJL* is the combined supply curve.

(c) The combined demand curve in the market is *DD* (note: *DD* can be derived in a manner analogous to the foregoing). The point of equilibrium is *L*. The resulting market price is *MP*. The total quantity *MQ* will be supplied. *PST* is the local producer's price floor. At the price *MP*, *A* supplies the quantity *MN* (given by the intersection of *A*'s supply curve *E'E"F* and *PL*) and *B* supplies the balance, *NQ*.

price at which cars will be sold on the market. Or one large firm acting as a monopsonist may *countervail* the power of another large firm, as where a retail chain accounts for a large proportion of sales of household appliances and is thus able to bid down the manufacturer's price of these items.

In conditions of imperfect competition the industry may follow a price leader, or engage in price collusion or in other discriminatory practices. Smaller firms

with a local market must follow the price lead set by a dominant firm with a national market. To do otherwise would be to invite lethal retaliation, because the large firm can wipe out local competition by undercutting prices in that local area. Large firms in competition with each other realize they must restrain competition or be ruined by it. But whatever the precise circumstances, the general objectives are always the same, namely, to maximize returns either by manipulating the firm's sale price or negotiating its purchasing prices, and to stabilize the prices and volumes of goods bought or sold.

The Basing-Point System

The most common form of noncompetitive pricing is the *basing-point system*. Consumers pay a price set at a given place, the *basing-point*, plus a transportation charge from that location—even if the good is produced and shipped from a nearer and lower-cost site. The purpose of the basing-point system is, of course, to entrench the advantages of the site selected as the basing point, and the producers whose facilities are concentrated there.

An example may be used to clarify the details of basing-point pricing. We have selected the British cement industry as described in a study by A. Moyes (1980). Prices are administered by the Cement Maker's Federation (CMF), an industry association to which all producers of any consequence belong. The price at the nominated basing-points varied in March 1978, from £22.51 to £26.90 per ton, reflecting to some degree differences in production costs. Delivery charges were added to the basing-point using a standard formula based on 5-mile steps. The first four steps cost 20.7 pence each. The next three cost 18.1 pence, after which all steps cost 12.9 pence each. The result was a regular concentric pattern of delivered prices radiating out from each basing point (Figure 6.17).

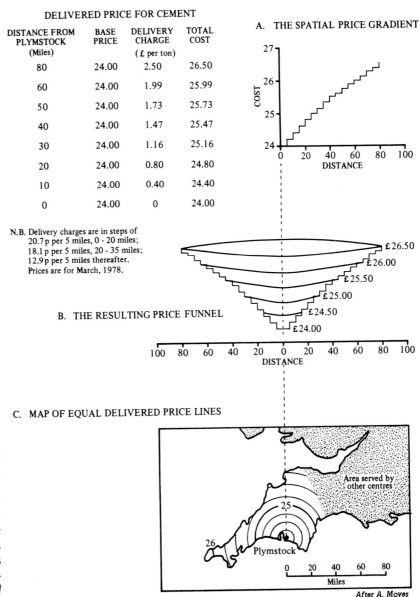

DELIVERED PRICE FOR CEMENT

DISTANCE FROM PLYMSTOCK (Miles)	BASE PRICE	DELIVERY CHARGE (£ per ton)	TOTAL COST
80	24.00	2.50	26.50
60	24.00	1.99	25.99
50	24.00	1.73	25.73
40	24.00	1.47	25.47
30	24.00	1.16	25.16
20	24.00	0.80	24.80
10	24.00	0.40	24.40
0	24.00	0	24.00

N.B. Delivery charges are in steps of 20.7p per 5 miles, 0 - 20 miles; 18.1p per 5 miles, 20 - 35 miles; 12.9p per 5 miles thereafter. Prices are for March, 1978.

A. THE SPATIAL PRICE GRADIENT

B. THE RESULTING PRICE FUNNEL

C. MAP OF EQUAL DELIVERED PRICE LINES

FIGURE 6.17 The delivered price of cement in southwest England. The price of cement was £24 a ton in Plymstock in March 1978. Delivery charges were based on distance from Plymstock. The result was the regular concentric pattern of delivered prices shown in the map. For more details see: A. Moyes, "Can Spatially Variable Prices Ever Be 'Fair'?," *Regional Studies*, 14 (1980), 37–53.

After A. Moyes

These results look very similar to the base-point pricing of central markets discussed in the previous section. The two should not be confused, however. They differ significantly in the way in which prices are set. In basing-point systems the price level at the basing point, the transportation cost schedule, and the number of basing points are all preset by the industry. With the free-enterprise base-point system, these three elements of delivered cost—the price level at the central market, freight rates, and the number of central markets—are all determined by the free play of supply and demand.

Industry-determined basing-point price systems were used as early as 1880 in the United States, but they did not come into widespread use until after 1901, when such a system was applied to steel by the U.S. Steel Corporation.

The U.S. Steel scheme was known as "Pittsburgh plus." Under it, delivered prices for steel and steel products were quoted throughout the United States as the sum of a basing-point price at Pittsburgh plus a transportation charge from Pittsburgh, regardless of the actual plant price or freight costs incurred from the actual producing point. Nearer or lower-cost plants, which could actually deliver at lower cost than Pittsburgh plus, thus were able to earn extra profits. These profits were called "phantom freights" (Figure 6.18). The overall effect was to raise prices, reduce demand, and protect U.S. Steel's Pittsburgh investments.

Soon after the adoption of the basing-point plan by the steel industry, the practice was extended to the cement industry. Then, after 1912, the single basing-point practice spread rapidly to a variety of other industries; for example, cast-iron pipe, glucose, malt, maple flooring, welded chain, zinc, lead ("St. Louis plus"), and copper ("Connecticut Valley plus"). The practice became worldwide. In Russia, for example, before the communist revolution, steel was priced according to a "Chelyabinsk plus" basing-point system.

In some industries multiple basing points were established. The principle is the same, except that two or more producing centers are quoted as bases, and the market was divided among them according to base-price-plus-freight charges. Some of the industries adopting multiple basing points have been iron and steel (in 1924, following U.S. government antitrust action declaring a single basing point illegal), cement, hardwood lumber, gasoline, sugar, chemical fertilizers, milk and ice cream cans, asphalt roofing material, small-arms ammunition, corn products, gypsum products, hard-surface floor coverings, linseed oil, rigid steel conduit, firebrick, lubricating oil, and plate glass.

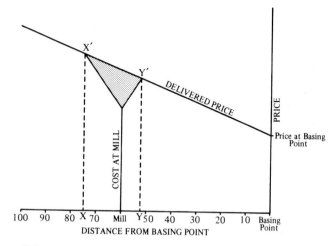

▨ Phantom Freight

XY   Distance from Basing Point over which Delivered Cost from Mill is less than Quoted Delivered Price.

FIGURE 6.18 Phantom freight with basing-point pricing. Under the basing-point price system, customers pay price at basing point plus transportation costs from that point. A local mill may not undercut basing-point price structure. Its delivered price is boosted to the basing-point price level, yielding it a "phantom freight." The phantom freight negates any locational advantage of the mill. Thus, the market area XY is shared between the local mill and mills at the basing point. Under FOB pricing, the local mill at M could expect to dominate the market area XY.

An example of basing-point pricing on the international scale is provided by petroleum (Melamid, 1962). The United States was the largest petroleum exporter at the turn of the century and its major producers set world prices on a "Gulf-plus" system. Delivered prices anywhere in the world equaled the price at the Gulf of Mexico plus transportation costs, regardless of the origin of the oil. Iranian oil shipped to the United Kingdom was priced at the U.S. Gulf price plus transportation rates from the Gulf of Mexico to the United Kingdom. Today, the world petroleum price is set by OPEC on the basis of Saudi Arabian light crudes at Dhahran, on the Persian Gulf, plus transportation.

Uniform Pricing

Under basing-point systems, consumers may be quoted prices FOB (free on board), meaning they pay the basing-point price and whatever they can arrange for transportation charges, or CIF (cost, insurance, and freight), in which case the supplier guarantees the delivered price at the consumer's location.

Another form of price quotation is *uniform pricing*, according to which suppliers quote consumers the same delivered price regardless of location. Such pricing is much more common than is generally realized. A number of good reasons exist for its use. Transportation costs are often a very small fraction of total delivered price, and improvements in transportation make the scheme more logical (see Figure 6.19). Uniform pricing is also sensible when a commodity is moved in very small quantities to a large number of places, if transportation costs themselves vary little or not at all with distance, and if the administrative costs of determining the proper transportation charges are high.

Uniform pricing may also be used to extend the market area. Customers near the plant are charged more than FOB prices to subsidize customers beyond the FOB market area. Industries sometimes argue that advertising campaigns are more effective where a uniform price can be quoted, and that the additional sales achieved permit economies of scale. The practice is widespread in, for example, the United Kingdom, even in cases where transportation costs are substantial. British Oxygen, which accounts for virtually all oxygen and acetylene sales in the United Kingdom, charges uniform prices even though transportation costs average one-fourth of total delivered price. Studies have shown that the practice is becoming more widespread, especially as improvements in transportation and communications reduce the share of delivered price accounted for by these factors.

PRICE REGULATION BY GOVERNMENT

Regulation by Western Governments

Strengthening Perfect Competition. Governments as well as industry associations try to influence prices. Western governments intervene in the marketplace under two opposite circumstances: (1) to strengthen the free play of market forces where free-enterprise is considered beneficial, if the prices resulting from perfect competition are appropriate; and (2) to modify the ordinary price mechanism where perfect competition is deemed inappropriate. The result of the latter intervention has been a growing body of government regulations that may have the detrimental side effects of adding significantly to the cost of doing business and weakening the effectiveness of market signals. The goals of all these regulations are often summarized in broad policy objectives such as encouraging economic growth, stabilizing prices, increasing productivity, and guaranteeing social welfare. But virtually all government regulation explicitly or indirectly affects the supply and demand for goods and the prices at which they trade as well as the size and even the location of supply and market areas.

Governments strengthen market forces by three sets of policies. First, all Western governments are concerned with the degree of concentration of production or purchasing of goods, and the danger of price-fixing (as in basing-point systems) that may result. Where there is sufficient evidence of price-fixing, governments may seize company documents and initiate legal proceedings against the companies involved.

Second, governments strengthen the competitive market mechanism by increasing market information. Labor exchanges provide both employed and unemployed persons with job information. A wide array of information is made available to industrialists, ranging from technical, to general management, to trade information. One function of census-type surveys is to provide information on labor and markets that can be used to improve the working of the economy.

Third, special attention is given by governments to ease adjustment to secular (long-run) change. Indus-

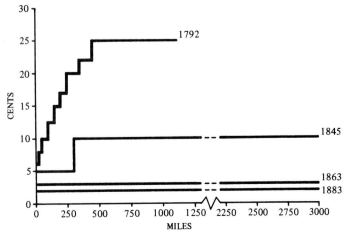

FIGURE 6.19 Toward uniform pricing: The example of postal rates. *Note:* National postal rates tend to be uniform, which makes delivery costs for industries shipping smaller goods by post also uniform. [*Source:* Ronald Abler, "What to Do While the Isolines Converge," paper prepared for the first Conference on the Geography of the Future, London, Ontario, Canada, October 15–18, 1970.]

try may be locked into obsolete technology, regions over-reliant on declining industries, and workers immobilized in declining regions. Government may offer industry investment incentives to retool. Research and development incentives are also sometimes available. Labor-retraining programs and relocation benefits may be introduced. Rural land-use programs may be developed where farmers have locked into inefficient practices. Such programs are intended to substitute long-run gain for short-term pain.

In each of the above cases, the objective of government intervention is to bring market prices closer to what they would be under perfect competition, free from oligopoly and oligopsony, and to ensure more perfect knowledge and an economy that adjusts freely to market changes. Such government intervention strengthens the working of the price system as a mechanism for regulating production and exchange.

Economic Problems with Market Prices.

Governments may, however, want to modify the free play of market forces where these fail for reasons that are economic, social, or regional. Economic issues arise: in pricing goods with a high social cost; in paying for collective goods; where maintaining quality takes priority over minimizing price; and in countervailing seasonal and cyclical fluctuations for particular commodities or for the economy generally. Governments find that free-market prices are undesirable under these circumstances.

The clearest case is where producers can pass some production costs onto society. One example is what Hardin calls the "tragedy of the commons." The market price does not include the costs of industrial pollution or resource depletion. Government may then regulate pollution levels or set production levels, or it may tax the industry to recover part or all of the social costs involved. A particular problem arises in transportation. Subsidies for public transportation are justified because road and fuel taxes may fail to recover the full social cost of private travel to work. Similarly, subsidies for rail haulage are justified because rail companies must build and maintain their own lines, whereas road haulage companies do not. In each case, the concern is that optimizing on the basis of private plus social costs may lead to different decisions and prices than optimizing on the basis of private costs alone.

Some goods are collective and are not purchased in individual market actions. Examples are national defense forces, police and fire protection, meteorological services, city parks, and the cost of government itself. The cost of collective goods cannot be recovered effectively on a "user" basis. Thus, governments are elected in part on the level of such services that they promise to provide and they pay for them by taxes and public borrowing. The cost of these services to the individual is based on ability to pay (where taxes are progressive, that is, increase with income) and not on use or need. The price is determined by the level and quality of the service set by government policy.

Government also establishes the quality of service and regulates price when consumers cannot be expected to judge quality of service for themselves, as in the case of goods and services for which minimum standards are essential for consumer protection. Many regulations come under this third category, whether government-imposed or industry-controlled: fire protection, building codes, and zoning ordinances; regulations controlling foods and drugs; transportation services and equipment, whether automobiles, airlines, or ships; professional services and trades, whether medical, legal, insurance, electrical, or plumbing.

The fourth economic circumstance where free-market prices are considered inappropriate is where there are serious fluctuations in supply or demand, with concomitant fluctuations in price. To stabilize welfare in face of recessions or booms, the government may, for example, set minimum prices for farm products and store surpluses. Countercyclical measures also may be taken: These may be *fiscal,* as when tax rates are reduced to stimulate demand, or *monetary,* as when interest rates are raised to curb excessive demand and to relieve inflationary pressures.

Social Needs versus Economic Efficiency.

In certain cases governments may conclude that the ordinary price mechanisms are inappropriate because they put economic efficiency above social need. Governments identify three broad cases of such social priority: the provision of minimum living standards and of social security; the distribution of benefits and responsibilities; and the maintenance of cultural levels. As Western countries industrialized, they found that the existing mutual-aid schemes failed to meet the needs of urban, industrial workers. Five basic sets of welfare policies were introduced in country after country, and generally in this order: for (1) injury related to employment; (2) sickness and maternity; (3) old age; (4) unemployment; and (5) family income supplements. Governments have added regulations on working conditions, housing, education, and health and welfare, all of which affect the supply and cost of labor. Location decisions in the case of labor-intensive industry may well be influenced by the level and cost of such regulations in regions competing for the industry.

Social equity may also override market considerations where goods are in short supply. In times of war, particularly, governments and the public are not prepared to accept the allocation of food and other supplies on the basis of the ability to pay. A rationing system then is used to hold prices below their free-market level and to allocate supplies equitably, without regard to income. Duties such as military service are parceled out on the basis of ability, and individuals are not permitted to buy out. At such times even the most free-enterprise country is prepared to abandon the very economic principles on which its society is based and argue instead, "from each, according to one's abilities; to each, according to one's needs."

Governments also feel a need to support cultural activities that could not survive the rule of the market place. The young writer seeking the wherewithall to write her first novel, the symphony orchestra that has established an international reputation, and live theater groups are all dependent on public funding to some extent. They give artistic expression to the sentiments of a nation and add to its culture and traditions in ways that cannot be measured in the market place. In such cases, it is agreed that support should be based on excellence and not commercial viability.

Regional Goals. Finally, the free play of market forces may be incompatible with the desires of Western governments for balanced regional growth and development. This set of goals may take three forms. Initially, in the case of New World countries, the concern may be with the spread of settlement and the development of resources across the entire national territory. Governments are sensitive to the dangers of large empty tracts of national territory and historically have encouraged immigration, settlement, and the building of railways. We saw in Chapter 2 how Griffith Taylor got into trouble with the Australian government over the settlement potential of the outback by returning World War I veterans. Canada is very sensitive about the presence of any foreigners in its Arctic regions and concerned that oil and gas developments there involve a much higher degree of Canadian ownership and control than in previous Canadian oil developments.

More recently, governments in all Western countries have become concerned with the problems of lagging or depressed regions. Until the 1930s or even later, governments believed that if they maintained strong national economic performance, then the regions would be able to take care of themselves. The reality of severe and persistent regional disparities forced a change in this attitude and the adoption of

policies, often tied to the location of manufacturing activity, to diminish regional disparities. As with social policies, the argument is one of equity, not efficiency.

In other cases, governments are concerned with locational aspects because of the nature of the specific activity. In wartime, governments may give higher priority to security than to economic efficiency in the location of industry. In peacetime, the recreation needs of the population may dictate the setting aside of lands for park use that may have a much higher economic value as industrial or commercial land. Beaches, cross-country ski trails, camping grounds, and adventure playgrounds are all established by government on the basis of geographic supply and demand rather than economic laws. Governments are finding that they must be even more sensitive to location issues when dealing with hazardous or potentially hazardous activities. The location of nuclear power stations close to, and upwind from, large urban concentrations is hard to justify on grounds of cost efficiency. The regulation and control of the dumping of industrial waste products is another example where safety must be given precedence over convenience and cost.

Augmented Government Impact. The impact of government regulations on the economy and its regions is augmented by direct involvement of governments in the economy. Three measures of this direct involvement are the amount of spending by all levels of government in a country; the percentage of labor force employed in the civil service; and the surface area of the national territory owned by government. Usually the first measure is employed, with government spending quoted as a percentage of gross national product or of total consumption expenditures. Western governments usually account for about a fifth of consumption expenditures and about a quarter to a third of gross national expenditures. Shifts in government expenditure patterns can therefore have a very significant impact on the economies of the regions affected, and indeed on the national economy as a whole.

The direct impact of government is further augmented and complicated where industries are owned by the government. Such industries are generally considered to make some special contribution to the nation, over and above their direct economic worth. Hence, their survival may not depend entirely on profitability as in private enterprise. In the United Kingdom, for example, most nationalized industries, including steel, ship building, automobiles, and rail transportation, lost great sums of money and would not have survived at the scale they did without the umbrella of government ownership coupled with heavy subsidies. There were major restructurings when Prime Minister Margaret Thatcher's Conservative government returned them to private ownership in the attempt to restore efficiency to British industry.

Diminished Effectiveness.

Both public and governmental attitudes on the effectiveness of government regulation of the economy underwent rapid change in the 1970s. Theoretical analysis and actual experience suggest that government regulation is far less effective than was previously thought. Far from correcting economic failures in the market-place, government regulations can suffer their own failures. Far from achieving a wide range of economic, social, and regional goals, these goals can sometimes conflict with each other and policies can sometimes prove countervailing rather than reinforcing. And far from improving the working of the economy, government regulations can sometimes run into jurisdictional and administrative problems, consume resources, and sap enterprise.

The economic failures of government regulations are drawing increasing attention. The basic economic problem is that government regulations to control price inevitably affect quantity or quality, and regulations to control quantity or quality affect price. Economists have discovered that such regulations create a *transitory-gain trap*. The regulations create advantages or disadvantages that are quickly identified and capitalized. The advantages (or disadvantages) are temporary, or "transitory." Three examples, taxi regulation, housing policy, and transportation regulation, illustrate how this trap undermines government efforts to achieve economic, social, and regional goals in cases where free competition was considered inappropriate.

In many cities, local governments regulate the taxi business and limit the number of taxis by use of permits or medallions, to protect users and provide some security for drivers. But the number of permits issued is usually below the competitive level, giving them a scarcity value. As a result, taxis can earn an extra income. That extra income can be converted into a capital value (based on current interest rates), or "capitalized." The price of a license is then equal to the city fee plus this capitalized value. The price varies from city to city depending on the level of undersupply. Thus, one study of the Canadian taxi industry found 1972 going prices of $18,000 in Toronto, and $30,000 in Vancouver. The extra profits accrued to the original holders of permits (often taxi companies). The taxi driver, burdened with the cost of renting a licensed vehicle, or of buying a license, may find it as hard or harder to earn a living than it was before the regulations were introduced. The advantage was indeed transitory. But to deregulate the business would cause unfair losses to those who paid high prices for permits in good faith that the regulations would remain in force. On the contrary in 1980, Montreal taxi drivers, misunderstanding the nature of the problem, complained that there were too many taxis to make a decent living and wanted a reduction in the number of licenses granted.

The same fundamental supply relationship between price and quantity has triggered a transitory-gain trap in rent controls. Government attempts to help low-income families by imposing rent controls create increasing distortions in the marketplace. In the short run the supply of rental housing is inelastic, although rent controls do reduce supply as apartments are converted into condominiums and sold, and as construction rates fall. The frequent market response to price controls where supply is inelastic is to allow quality to fall. Thus, profit levels can be redressed by postponing or eliminating customary maintenance. The demand for rental accommodation, however, can be expected to increase as rental controls make home ownership less attractive. In this case families must vie with one another for possession of apartments on grounds other than rent. These grounds may include paying key money, offering to buy or rent furniture from the owner at high prices, agreeing to paint the apartment or provide other work at no income, or at less than market wage, or simply waiting in a long queue with little hope of success. Where key money is the principal factor, the amount paid will be related to the capitalized value of the subsidy. It is thus equivalent to the medallion price paid by prospective taxi drivers.

The transitory-gains trap also afflicts regional policy, and has become a particularly contentious issue in the case of statutory grain rates in Canada. The development of western Canada after confederation of the British North American colonies in 1867 was based on a National Economic Policy of railway building, agricultural settlement, and tariff protection for industry. The railways were granted land rights and subsidies, but in return promised to accept government-imposed freight rates for wheat. These statutory rates, often called *Crow rates* after a pass through the Rocky Mountains used by the railways, are the same today as when they were first set at the turn of the century. A temporary increase imposed by the federal government during World War I was rolled back by order of the Supreme Court of Canada in 1925.

The result of Crow rates on wheat shipments is

that it costs a farmer less to ship a bushel of wheat to Vancouver or Thunder Bay than to post a letter. Controlled prices have reduced the quality of service as the railways are understandably reluctant to invest in rolling stock or line maintenance for shipments that pay about a quarter of their real transportation costs. But farmers resist any attempt by the Canadian government to raise rail rates, even if new rates are coupled with major improvements in speed and quality of service.

The problem is that the price of farmland in the Canadian prairies is related to yield, to wheat prices at central markets, and to the costs of shipment to those central markets (formerly dominated by Liverpool, as we saw earlier). The value of the Crow rate has already been capitalized and included in the price of farmland. The subsidy has thus created a sort of "key money" that farmers have to pay to gain access to the land. If the freight rate for wheat is increased, the capital worth of farmers will be reduced, perhaps seriously. The failure of grain freight rates to keep in step with inflation created capital values that were captured primarily by the original farm owners. The gain was transitory and imposed the trap of increasing government subsidies to the railways and diminishing quality of service to the present farmers.

These examples of government regulations suffering market failures of their own are very specific, but the principle of the transitory-gains trap is very broad. It applies, and has geographic implications, whenever quotas are set on farm acreages for specific crops, or minimum prices are established for commodities. It applies when industries are subsidized with grants or special loans, or protected by tariffs. It applies within cities where development is regulated by zoning or other controls. And it applies as well to all regulation of transportation and of fuel charges. Regulations tend to create special profits that can be capitalized, sometimes by the owners of the resource, sometimes by labor and sometimes by a third party. The benefits cannot always be held by those intended to gain from the regulations. They can end up serving private interests rather than the common good.

Regulation in Socialist States

The economic theory and political objectives that govern prices in socialist states have been quite different from those in Western countries. Even the definition of economics presented in this chapter is not relevant to socialist economies. Recall how these "command" economies were described at the beginning of the chapter. Monolithic, authoritarian governmental systems were dominated by a single party. The state owned the means of production, operating nonagricultural industries, and in some socialist countries, agriculture too. There was centralized direction of the economy. In the classic socialist scheme, each industry was supposed to produce according to preset physical targets. Performance—at least until the late 1960s—was measured by output rather than sales, which meant that commodity movements were managed through rationing systems rather than the interplay of demand and supply. Prices played little, if any, role in economic management. Socialist economies were geared to ensuring rapid growth above all else.

Strong central direction did prove effective in running high-priority projects, such as space exploration and weapons development, which demand considerable concentrations of skills and resources regardless of cost. It failed in the ordinary economic management of where to invest resources, how to identify and exploit each competitive economic edge, how to achieve quality as well as quantity, how to balance supply and demand, and, in short, how to run efficient and productive economies. For years, Western economists assumed that the growth rates of gross domestic product (GDP) in socialist states matched or exceeded that in the West. The reality was quite different. Productivity growth (GDP per man hour) lagged increasingly behind the Western countries. The Soviet Union reduced its productivity gap with the United States in GDP per worker hour until 1973, but retrogressed thereafter. Energy consumption per unit of output increased after 1973, and there was negative total factor productivity after 1984 (i.e., there was decreasing output, notwithstanding increasing inputs). As Russian workers jibed, "We pretend to work, they pretend to pay us."

The extent and the causes of the economic failure of socialist economies are now being discussed openly in the Russian press. This discussion is similar to that made in the past by economists who fled to the west, such as Ota Sik in his *Czechoslovakia: The Bureaucratic Economy* (1972). The economic problems arose from the huge party-controlled bureaucracies needed to devise plans for economic growth, to enforce economic planning decisions, to determine the allocation of resources and set production quotas, as well as to fix prices on millions of categories of goods, determine their distribution, and conduct all foreign trade.

How Prices Were Set. Prices in socialist economies were set without any reference to demand or supply, but only to production costs (themselves reflecting administered prices for inputs) and to some concept of "social value." Basic foodstuffs and rents were heavily subsidized. In the case of manufactured goods, retail prices were ultimately related to the pricing of labor and of industrial materials, taking into account standard markups and a turnover tax that varied between commodities to reflect social desirability. Industrial materials were, in turn, priced so that the return equaled the average production cost plus a limited planned profit. Because average costs change with the scale of output, this pricing policy had the effect of ultimately relating all prices back to the nature, scale, location, and efficiency of production—all of which were set by the command structure of economic planning in the state. Demand played no role whatsoever in price determination in this scheme.

In the 1960s, Soviet economic planners relied increasingly on mathematical programming methods to estimate more-efficient relationships among planned targets, output levels, and commodity flows. They thought that mathematics could substitute for the free market's prices. The methods produced what the Soviet planners called "objectively determined values" for products. Similar values are called "shadow prices" by Western scholars; if charged, these prices would ensure that the economic relationships sought are achieved. Such shadow prices can be calculated in ways that reflect both scarcity and productivity, and if they had been so estimated some of the problems of shortages and surpluses that exist in the former USSR would have been avoided. However, because consumption targets were preset by the planners before the mathematical methods were used, Soviet shadow prices still reflected only production-and-supply considerations. The free play of consumer preferences and demands that characterize Western societies played no role in determining the mix of things produced. Persistent problems of deficits of items desired by the Soviet citizenry and surpluses of inferior-quality, unwanted goods that merely met production quotas were central to the decision to restructure and let market prices serve as the thermostat controlling the economy.

East Europhoria.   In the "East Europhoria" that has followed the dramatic moves toward political democracy and economic reform, there has been great optimism that Eastern Europe and the former USSR will repeat the rapid recovery achieved by Western Europe with the help of Marshall aid after World War II. By 1990, the World Bank committed $7.5 billion over a 3-year period to Poland, Hungary, Yugoslavia, and Romania. The French have proposed the establishment of a European Bank for Reconstruction and Development modeled after the World Bank (the full name of which is The International Bank for Recon-

struction and Development). This European Bank is planned to have initial capitalization of up to $12 billion. The International Monetary Fund is also making substantial credits available. Multinational corporations, too, are investing in Eastern Europe, hoping to benefit from the highly skilled labor force and to gain a foothold in this newly opened market. General Electric, for example, paid $150 million for a half-ownership of a Hungarian light bulb company.

Restructuring Socialist Economies.   The capital needed to rebuild the former socialist world's neglected infrastructure, to modernize backward technologies, and to deal with the environmental consequences of uncontrolled pollution presents, however, a daunting challenge. East Germany alone may need some $300 billion over the 1990s. These capital requirements will need to be accompanied by comprehensive economic restructuring. Massive state enterprises need to be broken into manageable companies, overstaffing must be eliminated, and the rights to private ownership need to be legally entrenched. Financial and stock markets need to be established and an efficient banking system must be created to channel savings into investment. Drastic currency reforms are crucial to deal with the huge overhang of worthless currency. Perhaps even more challenging are the changes needed in the attitudes of management, workers, and the population generally, first to forgo the privileges bestowed party members, second to accept the rights, responsibilities, and risks of running businesses competitively, and third to permit the accompanying inequalities in the distribution of wealth and income that are related to business success and failure to occur.

Furthermore, the transition from socialist to free-market-oriented economies involves a number of immediate issues. Should the change be gradual, as in Hungary, or sudden as in Poland? How does one place a market-economy value on socialist state assets? How are these assets to be allocated among the employees, the public, and foreign investors? How do the new governments deal with the transition costs, which may include severe inflation, unemployment, trade deficits, and government budget deficits? The long-term benefits of the economic changes are not in question. Unfortunately the price of bad economic management in the past has yet to be paid in full.

SUMMARY

Human beings regulate the exchange of goods and services that they require by mechanisms that are primarily social, economic, or political (Figure 6.20). *Social*

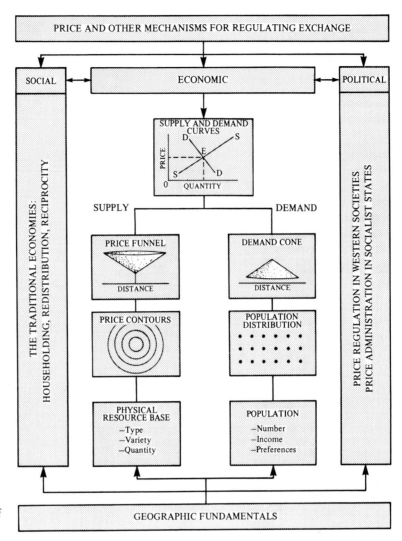

FIGURE 6.20 The geography of price: a synthesis.

mechanisms were dominant in the traditional small-scale economies before the Industrial Revolution. These economies were largely self-sufficient, either at the level of the household, the region (with *redistribution* among households), or a set of regions (with *reciprocity* between regions). Reciprocity involved trade, often disguised as gift-giving. The expansion of trade to include more goods shipped over greater distances was associated with the gradual emergence of *peasant economies*. Peasant economies are intermediate in nature. Necessities are home-produced and are distributed according to social custom. Surpluses and specialty goods are traded on economic principles.

Full-exchange, *free-enterprise economies* use price to regulate exchange. Goods command a *price* when they are both useful and scarce. The *market equilibrium price* attracts just enough output to meet demand and just enough buyers to clear the market of output. *Supply* and *demand* come into balance because they have opposite relationships to price. Sup-

ply increases with price; demand decreases. If supplies are short, the price tends to rise, augmenting supplies and cutting demand. The rate of response of supply and demand (or elasticity) varies for different goods, and for market conditions such as income levels and consumer and producer preferences.

Price, supply, and demand vary systematically across supply and market regions because of transportation costs. Prices increase outward from production or market centers generating *price funnels*. The price funnel is the consumer *price ceiling*. Consumers pay central market price plus transportation costs unless local producers can sell at lower prices. Demand drops, in step with price increases, producing corresponding *demand cones*. The outer limit of the market area is the base of the cone, where demand falls to zero. The *price floor* for producers is the central market price minus transportation costs. The limit of the central market supply area is where the price floor is too low to attract supplies. The spatial market equilibrium price brings aggregate demand and supply over the market and supply areas into balance. The economic principles and resulting geographies can be severely distorted, however, in conditions of imperfect competition. Producers or consumers can distort prices at a market and across its region using basing-point price systems or uniform pricing.

Government regulation of free-enterprise economies has risen sharply since the 1930s, either to strengthen the competition or, conversely, to modify it, as deemed appropriate. Some regulations have explicit regional goals, such as diminishing income disparities and high unemployment in lagging regions. All other policies, though not explicitly regional, have regional impacts, because of the regional concentrations of the target commodity or population of any policy.

Government regulation of the economy, intended to correct failures in the pricing mechanism, falls victim to failures of its own. Prominent among these is the *transitory-gains trap*. All regulations give advantage to some group at the expense of others. Often, that advantage can be converted into a value capitalized by some group. This group is not necessarily the group intended to benefit from the legislation. Examples are premium prices paid for taxi medallions, apartment key money, inflated land values. Regulations then become entrenched in the price system.

Political administration of the economy reaches its extreme in socialist countries. In principle, socialist economies have no private ownership or profit. The economic principles applying under perfect competition are irrelevant. Prices are set by a central authority on the basis of some assumed average costs, without taking demand or market equilibrium into account. The emphasis is on the achieving of production levels set by planners rather than satisfying the demands expressed by consumers.

No comparative assessment of various mechanisms of regulating exchange has yet been offered. Different mechanisms reflect different goals. Traditional societies were not oriented to growth, producing only what was needed. Chayanov's rule applied; the greater the productivity, the less the hours worked. Socialist economies produced more social equity than economic growth, albeit at low levels, and to achieve some growth they neglected the environment with disastrous consequences. Market economies and welfare states, to encourage innovation and stimulate economic growth, reduced governmental intervention and privatized state-run enterprises, but this had adverse consequences too: Inequality increased, and there were growing complaints about "fairness."

What is increasingly clear is that different types of political economies deliver different mixtures of growth, equity, and environmental integrity. What also is clear as the world approaches the twenty-first century is that cultural traditions are less constraining than they have been in the past. Societies can make explicit choices about the values that are important and the goals that are to be achieved. Selection implies choice of a self-image and of the belief systems and the theories that are to serve as the guides to action.

TOPICS FOR DISCUSSION

1. Plot the demand curve for a selected commodity. (You may use annual data on price and quantity in the U.S. Department of Agriculture (*Annual Statistics*).) Is the demand relatively elastic (that is, greater than 1.0) or inelastic (less than 1.0)?

2. Draw a map of regional variations in price for some commodity. (One good data source is the table in Lösch, p. 487; see Further Readings.) What is the relationship between the spatial price pattern and centers of production?

3. Draw a graph showing the relationship between prices for beans and kerosene and distance from Kano, Nigeria, on the basis of the maps in Figure 6.21. How do spatial variations in price relate to areas of surplus and deficit?

4. The greater the costs of transportation, the less important are differences in central market base prices in determining the boundaries of market areas. Demonstrate this assertion by redrawing the consumer price ceilings for central markets B and C in Figure 6.11 with slopes at 10°, 25°, 40°, and 55°. Note the location of the supply market boundary at each of these gradients.

5. Continue to test the assertion in Topic 4 by determining the boundaries of the supply areas for central markets B and C given producer price floors at slopes of 10°, 25°, and 55°, on the same diagram in Figure 6.11.

6. How low can transportation costs get before central market C, with its lower prices, loses all its supply area to central market B? At this price, which central market loses its market area, B or C? Evidently a central market can attract supplies from a competing central market, paying higher prices, only if the transportation costs are greater than the price difference between them. What is the corresponding conclusion regarding the existence of separate market areas?

7. Assume that demand within the market area of central market C in Figures 6.9 and 6.11 increases. What happens to the price at C? How does this price change

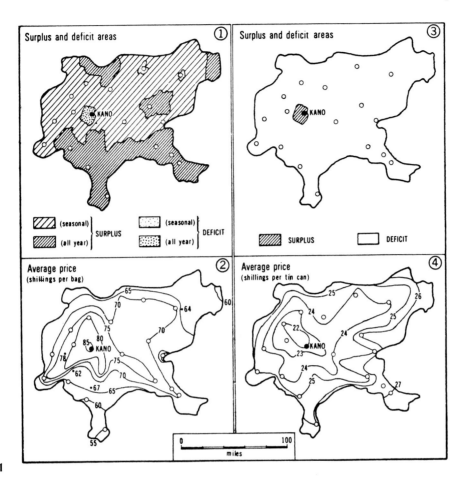

FIGURE 6.21

affect the supply and market areas? Now describe the reverse process where there is a large surplus at central market *C*. How might this affect prices at central market *B*? Where central market prices are in spatial equilibrium are they then dependent of one another?

8. Explain how a price funnel results where a market is in spatial equilibrium, even when there are no formal central markets, as in milk. (You may wish to consult the map of optimum interregional dairy product movements in Bressler and King, p. 191, see Further Readings, as well as Figure 6.7.)

9. Draw demand cones for two hypothetical goods that have very high and low elasticities, respectively. Assume that a very large area must be supplied with both goods. What is the approximate spacing needed for plants producing these goods, assuming FOB pricing? Why might a plant wish to use CIF pricing to market a good with high elasticity?

10. Describe the problems and the progress of the shift of socialist economies toward a market system.

FURTHER READINGS

The *Banker, Business Week, Business Monthly Fortune,* and *The Economist* are useful sources of current information on the rapid economic changes in Eastern Europe and the USSR.

Also see:

BRESSLER, RAYMOND G., and RICHARD A. KING. *Market, Prices, and Interregional Trade.* New York: John Wiley, 1970.

A description of economic development and regional specialization in the United States from colonial settlement to mid-twentieth century is provided (pp. 3–70), as an introduction to an advanced theoretical treatment. See Figure 102, p. 191, for a map of optimal interregional movements of dairy products in the United States and compare it with Figure 6.6 in this chapter.

CHISHOLM, MICHAEL. *Geography and Economics.* London: G. Bell & Sons, 2d ed., 1970.

Provides a key reading on the economic fundamentals of economic geography. For this chapter, see "Relations

Between Geography and Economics," pp. 4–7, and "Pricing Policies," pp. 163–194.

DEATON, ANGUS. *Price Elasticities from Survey Data—Extensions and Indonesian Results.* Living Standards Measurement Study. Working Paper No. 69. Washington, D.C.: The World Bank, 1990.

Deaton has written numerous papers on price elasticities in low-income countries that make clear the methodological problems involved. This paper is based on surveys of rural households in Java in 1981.

GREENHUT, MELVIN L. "When Is the Demand Factor of Location Important?" *Land Economics,* 40 (1964), 175–184. Reprinted in *Locational Analysis for Manufacturing,* Gerald J. Karaska and David F. Bromall (Eds). Cambridge, Mass.: MIT Press, 1969, pp. 339–348.

Greenhut has published extensively on location theory and the theory of spatial pricing, often at a very advanced level. This article presents a basic nonmathematical treatment of the three industrial pricing systems: CIF, FOB, and basing point. A recent mathematical treatment is provided in M. L. Greenhut et al.: *The Economics of Imperfect Competition: A Spatial Approach,* Cambridge: Cambridge University Press, 1987.

JOHANNSEN, E., L. ROBBINS, G. HEWSTON, M. ZAFIROU, and L. HUNT. "Demography and Socioeconomic Bases of Food Demand—What Does the Future Hold?" *Food Market Commentary,* 11, No. 2 (July 1989), 27–44. Canada: Dept. of Agriculture. Policy, Planning and Economic Branch Food. Markets Analysis Division.

A very readable account of the ways in which demographic, ethnic, social, and economic factors affect the demand for food in a country where immigration is becoming increasingly important in population growth.

LÖSCH, AUGUST. *The Economics of Location* (Translated from the 2d rev. ed. by William H. Woglom). New Haven, Conn.: Yale University Press, 1954.

This great classic always makes rewarding reading. See particularly Chapter 26 on "Price Levels in Space," pp. 452–495, which demonstrates the continuing importance of regional differences in prices, notwithstanding reduction in freight rates and many cases of uniform pricing.

MELAMID, ALEXANDER. "Geography of the World Petroleum Price Structure," *Economic Geography* (October 1962), 283–298.

A most interesting account of the basing-point price system from before World War II (Gulf plus) and the changes made following World War II.

MOYES, A. "Can Spatially Variable Prices Ever be 'Fair'? Some observations on the Price Commission's Judgements on British Cement Prices," *Regional Studies,* 14 (1980), 37–53.

Not only an excellent case study of the basing-point price system, but also an exemplary geographic analysis.

POLYANI, KARL. *The Great Transformation.* New York: Octagon Books, 1975.

An impressive and wide-ranging work of synthesis that emphasizes the social and economic changes wrought by the Industrial Revolution and the fundamental differences between traditional and modern economies. See particularly Chapter 4, "Societies and Economic Systems," Chapter 5, "Evolution of the Market Pattern," and Chapter 6, "The Self-Regulating Market," pp. 43–76.

RADFORD, R. A. "The Economic Organization of a P.O.W. Camp." *Economica,* XII (1945). Reprinted in *Readings in Economics,* Paul A. Samuelson et al. (Eds.). New York: McGraw-Hill, 7th ed., 1973, pp. 21–29.

As a prisoner of war in World War II, Radford saw in microcosm the emergence of a price system based on cigarettes. Samuelson notes that, "The very simplicity of the story he tells has made this article a minor classic in economics. To understand its full flavour is to know the world around us better."

WAGNER, PHILIP. *The Human Use of Earth.* London: The Free Press of Glencoe, 1960.

This book is primarily concerned with the ecological expression of different cultures and social arrangements. Chapter 5, "The Economic Bond" (pp. 60–87) restates and develops Polyani and presents a geography of economic forms. The themes of the text are summarized masterfully in Chapter 10, "A Geographic Outlook," pp. 228–237.

WARNTZ, W. *Toward a Geography of Price.* Philadelphia: University of Pennsylvania Press, 1959.

As innovative study of supply and demand in space and time, which links physics, economics, and geography. The concepts are illustrated with four crops (wheat, potatoes, onions, and strawberries) in the United States, 1940–1949.

7

Costs and Output: Economies of Scale

OVERVIEW

*Economies of scale are the reduction in unit costs that result from an increased level of output. These cost reductions may be **internal** economies of scale, gained within a **single plant** in the manufacture of a single product such as shoes. They may be **internal multi-plant** economies achieved by a chain of bottling-plants, shops, or hotels in many different locations. They may also be **external** economies of scale achieved by the agglomeration of many **different firms** at a **single** location, thereby attracting specialist services and knowledgeable customers and gaining a na-tional or even international reputation. However achieved, economies of scale are important to the sur-vival of firms and essential to achieving an interna-tional competitive edge. Understanding the various ways in which economies of scale can be achieved, why diseconomies of scale set in, and how they can be measured for production in a single plant, thus helps to explain the location and growth of economic activ-ity and patterns of trade, both regional and interna-tional, in goods and services.*

OBJECTIVES

- to identify and describe the various kinds of internal and external economies and diseconomies of scale
- to explain the relationships among scale, industrial concentration, and barriers to entry in oligopolies
- to differentiate between short- and long-run cost curves
- to incorporate the effects of transportation costs into the measurement of economies of scale

THE IMPORTANCE OF ECONOMIES OF SCALE

Economies of scale are the reductions in unit costs of production that result from an increased level of output. These cost reductions are easiest to identify and to measure in the case of internal economies of scale, which involve the increased output of a single good or service in a single establishment. But internal economies of scale can also be achieved by a multiestablishment enterprise, perhaps producing a variety of goods and services in a number of different locations. And cost reductions can be achieved, too, by a number of different enterprises operating in the same location and thereby benefiting from external economies of scale in their inputs and marketing.

Economies of scale were considered at one time to be of secondary importance in the location and growth of industry and services. Because competition was assumed, it was thought until the 1950s that firms would maximize profits if located where the joint transportation costs of assembling raw materials and marketing the finished product could be minimized. Under competitive conditions all firms receive the same price for their product. Firms were expected to group together at a different place where external economies of scale could be achieved only in the special case of such economies exceeding the additional transportation costs incurred at that place. Because competitive industries are made up of similarly sized cost-minimizing firms, internal economies of scale were not usually considered in industrial location theory.

Increasing importance is now being attached to economies of scale in understanding the location, survival, and growth of industry and, to a lesser extent, of services. Michael Porter (Chapter 1) remarks on how frequently international competitive advantage is restricted to a narrowly defined set of industries, such as the manufacture of printing machines or ceramic tiles, in a particular region or even a particular city. The (external) economies of scale generated by this spatial concentration provide a cost advantage that makes it possible to export to international markets, even in the absence of comparative advantages in the costs of labor or raw materials. Scott and Angel made similar observations about the U.S. semiconductor industry some years earlier. Just why the industry should have developed in Santa Clara County (Silicon Valley), California, in the 1950s is open to question. But once the process of growth had begun, the accumulating external economies of scale created a privileged location for the industry. More recently, the United Nations Industrial Development Organization noted in 1989 that Japan was able to capture virtually the entire world market for 1-megabyte DRAMS by undercutting American producers with the price advantage obtained through mass production. The battle between the United States and Japan to capture the world markets for the next generation of computer chips will again depend on which country gains the critical economies of scale.

The pervasive importance of the subject has stimulated a continuing flow of research with detailed studies of a wide range of industries and with instructive international comparisons. These studies have sought to identify the factors responsible for economies of scale, to measure the minimum efficient size (MES) for various industries, and to evaluate the economic, geographic, and policy consequences that follow.

This chapter begins, therefore, by identifying the economies of scale that occur in manufacturing and other economic activities, dealing first with economies internal to the firm, and then with external economies of scale. Next, the chapter reviews the *measurement* of internal economies of scale for the production of a single good. It then identifies the complicating factors in measuring such economies of scale, including the effects of transportation costs (which are, in effect, diseconomies of scale) and of the age of equipment. It also notes the distinction between short and longer-run costs.

IDENTIFYING INTERNAL ECONOMIES OF SCALE

Unit production costs usually decrease with increasing output until a minimum average cost is achieved. This output level is the minimum efficient size (Figure 7.1). Unit production costs rise, in the short run, if production is increased above this level. Hence, if all firms are operating at or near their MES and their selling prices are set accordingly, they will increase the supply only if prices increase.

Internal economies of scale include all increases in efficiency and improvements in productivity that occur with increasing output within a single firm. These efficiencies may result, for example, from better, faster production; the use of specialized machines; concentration on the production of a single, standard item; and longer production runs. A distinction must be drawn, however, between economies of scale and *pecuniary advantages*. A large corporation may be able to obtain special rates for raw materials, energy, transportion, advertising, and bank loans as a result of the bargaining power bestowed by size. Where such price advantages involve no physical resource saving or change in productivity but only a redistribution of

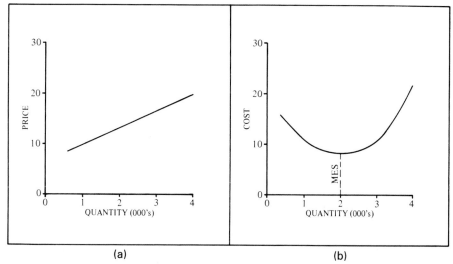

FIGURE 7.1 The industry's supply curve and the firm's unit cost curve. (a) The supply curve. Supply curves such as were used in Chapter 6 show how industries respond to price changes by offering more or less goods. Higher prices are needed to cover the increased costs of additional output by existing firms, and to attract new producers into the field. (b) A unit cost curve. Unit cost curves show the relationship of production costs to scale of output. Initially, increasing output is accompanied by economies of scale, and unit costs fall to a minimum efficient size (MES)—in this case at an output level of 2000. Thereafter, costs per unit of output may rise if diseconomies of scale are incurred.

income between buyers and sellers, the advantage is *pecuniary,* rather than a *real* economy of scale.

Internal economies of scale are pervasive and can be cross-classified in a variety of ways. They are sometimes distinguished by the level in the corporate hierarchy at which they are achieved. That is, economies of scale can result from the concentration of resources on the manufacture of particular *products,* within specialized *plants,* integrated in a single *corporation.* Economies of scale are often described according to the function involved: labor, technical, managerial, marketing, and finance. Economies of scale for these functions are achieved largely at some given level of the corporate structure. The corporate hierarchy thus generates a functional hierarchy of economies of scale (Figure 7.2).

Product-Specific Economies

Product-specific economies are associated with spreading start-up costs over a large output, with product standardization, with improved labor efficiency as production runs increase in *length,* and with technical efficiencies as production runs increase in *rate* of output.

Product Development Costs. The production of any good requires initial development and design costs. These may be very small, as in the case of shoes, or may be an important element of total cost, as in aircraft manufacture. Economists call these costs *indivisible* with respect to output. That is, the cost required for development and design cannot be reduced by reducing output. Development and design costs can be averaged out, however, and the larger the output, the smaller the average will be (Figure 7.3). The economies of averaging such fixed costs over increasing scale of output are tending to increase in importance over time, as products become more sophisticated. However, such economies quickly become insignificant at the output levels involved in most industries. The semiconductor industry is an important exception. Fixed overhead costs can run up to 75 percent or more of the total costs of manufacturing microchips.

Labor Economies. Specialization of production on a single good permits *labor efficiencies.* These efficiencies arise from the division of labor. The division of labor was described by Adam Smith over two centuries ago in his *Wealth of Nations* (see accompanying box). If instead of each worker making the entire good,

Adam Smith on Producing a Pin

A workman not educated to this business . . . could scarce, perhaps, with his utmost industry, make one pin in a day, and certainly could not make twenty . . . but it is divided into a number of branches. One man draws out the wire, another straightens it, a third cuts it, a fourth points it, a fifth grinds it at the top for receiving the head; to make the head requires two or three operations; to put it on is a particular business, to whiten the pins is another; it is even a trade by itself to put them into the paper. . . . I have seen a small manufactory of this kind where ten men . . . could make among them upwards of forty-eight thousand pins in a day. Each person, therefore, . . . might be considered as making four thousand eight hundred pins in a day.

The Wealth of Nations, 1776.

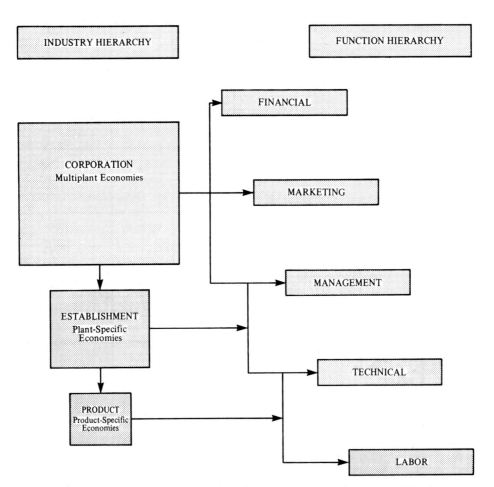

FIGURE 7.2 The dual hierarchy of economies of scale. Economies of scale can be arranged into two hierarchies. Industries have a three-level hierarchy: the corporation, the establishment, and the product. Functions within industry can be ranked from financial, to marketing, management, technical, and labor according to the industry level where they apply. Labor and technical economies of scale are exhausted first, and at the lowest level. Marketing and financial economies persist longest, and at the highest level.

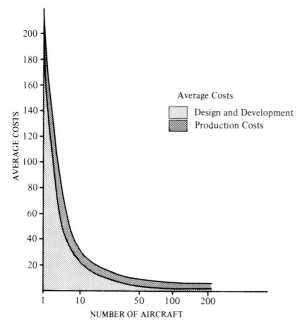

FIGURE 7.3 Economies of scale in the aircraft industry. Development costs include research and development, and the cost of special tools. These figures are representative of aircraft costs in the early post-World War II period. Development costs quickly fall to a small fraction of total production costs. [*Source:* After C. F. Pratten, *Economies of Scale in Manufacturing Industries* (London: Cambridge University Press, 1971), p. 152.]

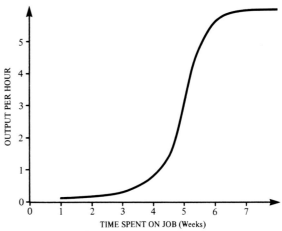

FIGURE 7.4 The learning curve. The longer a worker remains on the job, the higher is his or her productivity. Productivity tends to rise at an accelerating rate to the average level of efficiency, and from then on at a decelerating rate. The importance of experience is dramatic in highly technical activities. In the manufacture of large-scale integrated circuits, fewer than 2 in a 100 made by an inexperienced worker may function properly. With experience this proportion may rise to 80 out of 100.

production is divided into particular processes, output can be substantially increased. There are three reasons for this. First, there is increased dexterity in performing the work. Second, time is not lost in passing from one process to another. Third, machinery can be specialized, adding technical economies of scale to labor economies.

Practice makes perfect. Experienced workers gain a rhythm and an economy of motion. Output tends to follow a *learning curve* (Figure 7.4). Labor costs in aircraft production during World War II were found to fall by 20 percent for each doubling of output. The British Textile Council reported that output per worker increased by 167 percent when average rayon clothweaving runs increased from 3800 to 31,000 yards. The most dramatic examples of increased output are in highly technical industries such as integrated electronic circuits, where much experience is needed before good parts exceed rejects. And, of course, division of labor facilitates the allocation of workers to jobs at appropriate skill levels.

The second economy in the division of labor is the time saved in passing from one job to another. The manufacture of a relatively simple product like a pair

of shoes requires a hundred or more distinct operations, divided into five sets. First is "clicking"—the highly skilled work of cutting the uppers. Decoration, stitching, and cementing of the uppers takes place in the "closing" room. The bottoms are made in the "preparation" room. Twenty different machine operations are employed in the "making" room, completing the shoe. The final shoe process is inspection and packing. The work is passed from room to room on conveyor belts, or on trolleys or trays (Pratten and Dean, 1965).

Third, the division of labor, concentrated on the production of a single commodity, justifies the development of special machines that would be quite uneconomic unless kept continuously in production over long periods of time. For instance, the decoration of the uppers in the closing room of a shoe factory may involve a pattern of perforations. Where a small number of shoes is to be made, this work must be done by hand. Press stamping is much faster, but the machine cost can be justified only for long production runs.

Ball-bearing production provides an example of three technology levels according to output volume. On the largest runs of standard size bearings (perhaps a million a year), a computer-controlled, fully automated process is justified. At intermediate levels (about 10,000), simpler automatic equipment can be used, but unit costs may be double. Even so, unit costs are much less than for very small runs (of perhaps a 100). These small runs must be done on general-purpose lathes by skilled operators because the eight hours it takes to set up an automated machine cannot be justified.

Plant-Specific Economies

It is at the level of the establishment, or plant, that most economies of scale can be attained. Many *fixed costs* are incurred at the plant level and can be averaged down, the greater the scale of the output. Major technical economies come into force, involving a number of different principles. These technical economies produce concomitant labor economies. Management economies are achieved with larger operating scale as well.

Averaging Down the Fixed Costs. Operating a factory incurs *fixed costs.* The magnitude of these costs is unaffected by the volume of output. Fixed costs include property taxes and rents, interest payments, depreciation of buildings and equipment, maintenance costs, and insurance. All functions, from labor and maintenance, to marketing and finance, involve some component of fixed costs (Table 7.1). The larger

TABLE 7.1

Examples of fixed costs in manufacturing industry

Type of Cost[a]	Partly or Wholly Indivisible with Respect To
Financial	
Issuing a prospectus to raise capital	Size of issue
Marketing	
Preparation of advertisements	Size of area over which advertisement is shown, and number of times used.
Calls by salespeople	Number of lines carried, and amount sold.
Managerial	
Office records on product specifications	Output
Management personnel	Output
Technical	
Capital cost of equipment	Output
Labor	
Maintenance	Output

Source: C. Pratten, *Economies of Scale in Manufacturing Industries* (London: Cambridge University Press, 1971), p. 11.

[a] Fixed costs are organized by industry function. Product-specific fixed costs (research and development) and some plant-specific costs (building-related costs) are not shown.

the factory output, the lower are the average fixed costs per unit.

Economies of Scale on Variable Costs. Plant-specific economies of scale are also achieved for *variable costs.* Variable costs are those costs that vary in magnitude with the level of output. These economies of scale occur when an increase in variable cost is less than proportional to the increase in output. Most of these economies are technical and involve three principles. These principles are the *cube-square law, the principle of multiples,* and the *principle of reserves.* A fourth principle, *bulk transactions,* may also apply.

The cube-square law states a simple and obvious relationship between the volume of a container and its surface area. Surface area increases as the square of the dimensions. Volume increases as the cube of the dimensions. Double the dimensions and the area is four times larger (2^2), but volume is eight times greater (2^3). The "container" may be a blast furnace, a storage tank, a compressor, a turbine, or even a ship (see Box 7.1). The cube-square law (or *two-thirds rule* as it is sometimes called) still holds. If costs increase in proportion with area, as they can be expected to do, and output increases in proportion with volume, then significant economies can be achieved by scaling up equipment. Thus, chemical engineers often apply "the 0.6 rule," which states that if equipment is scaled up, capital cost increases at a rate of 0.6 (rather than the 0.66 of the cube-square, or two-thirds rule). The same rule applies to breweries. Of course the figure (whether 0.6 or 0.66) is only a rough guide and the specific characteristics of the industry modify the actual economies of scale substantially.

The *principle of multiples* is also straightforward. The design of special equipment for each specific process in making a commodity raises a problem. The machines are not all likely to run at the same rate. Those that complete their step in the production chain at the slowest rate will hold all faster machines back to their speed unless a principle of multiples is applied. This principles states that the minimum efficient scale (MES) at the technical level is the lowest common multiple (LCM) of the individual machines. If three steps are involved, with machines processing 4, 3, and 6 units per hour, the LCM is 12. The MES requires three of the 4-unit, four of the 3-unit, and two of the 6-unit machines, respectively, to produce 12 units per hour (Box 7.2).

The actual output figures are rarely as convenient as in our preceding example. In the making room of the typical shoe factory, 20 different machines are used, capable of producing anywhere from 480 pairs of shoes in a day to 2400 pairs (Box 7.2). Furthermore,

BOX 7.1   The Cube-Square Law: Economies of Large Machines

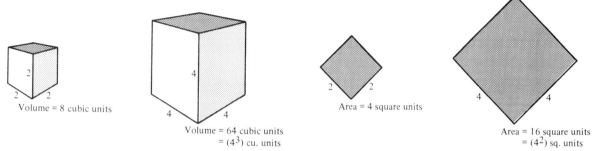

Volume = 8 cubic units

Volume = 64 cubic units
= (4³) cu. units

Area = 4 square units

Area = 16 square units
= (4²) sq. units

FIGURE 7a *The cube-square law.* This is also called the *two-thirds law.* It states that area increases at a rate of two-thirds the increase in physical volume of the equipment. In industries where output is proportional to volume, and capital costs are proportional to area, substantial economies are offered by scaling up equipment. Chemical engineers thus sometimes use a "rule of 0.6" to estimate the ratio of capital cost increase to volume increase when scaling up equipment.

FIGURE 7b *The cube-square law in action.* Adding a deck to this British Columbia Ferries Corp. ferry doubles its car capacity from 192 to 400. The ferry was cut horizontally, and the top deck, weighing 2500 tons, was raised by using 108 jacks. The job cost about $10 million, compared with $29 million for a new ferry. The cube-square guideline suggests that doubling capacity increases capital costs about 60 percent. The additional capacity in this case cost only 30 percent, because the equipment and engines remained unaltered, apart from extra stabilizers, new bulbous bow, and extra bow thruster and new generators.

BOX 7.2   *The Principle of Multiples*

The problem of balancing output in the making room of a shoe factory

Type of Machine	Output per Day per Machine (pairs of shoes)	Machine Utilization to Produce 1200 Pairs of Shoes per Day
1	1800	0.7
2	1440	0.8
3	1260	1.0
4	1800	0.7
5	1260	1.0
6	480	2.5
7	600	2.0
8	1440	0.8
9	1860	0.6
10	1980	0.6
11	840	1.4
12	1860	0.6
13	1320	0.9
14	1860	0.6
15	1200	1.0
16	1200	1.0
17	720	1.7
18	1200	1.0
19	960	0.7
20	2400	0.5

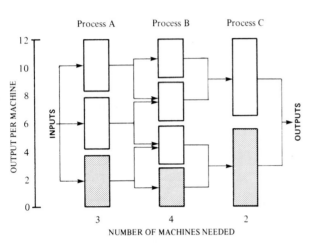

FIGURE 7c   *The principle of multiples.* Given a number of processes involving machines operating at different rates, the technical minimum efficient size is the lowest common multiple of the rates.

Source: C. F. Pratten and R. M. Dean, *Economies of Large-Scale Production* (Cambridge, U.K.: Cambridge University Press, 1965), p. 49.

Note: The making room is where the uppers (which have been through the clicking and closing rooms) are combined with the bottoms (made in the preparation room). Twenty different machines are used, with many different output rates. Technical and labor economies are achieved by increasing output toward the lowest common multiple of the different rates. This is the principle of multiples (or balance of processes). Without such economies at the plant level, the economies of the division of labor can be seriously offset.

The principle of multiples at work in the making room of a shoe factory

Expensive Operations	Output Rate	Possible Combinations of Machines and Operatives at Different Outputs					
		600	800	1000	1200	1500	2400
4	1800	1	1	1	1	1	2
6	480	2	2	3	3	4	5
8	1440	1	1	1	1	2	2
17	720	1	2	2	2	3	4
Total no. all operatives		21	23	25	26	37	48
Average output per operative		29	35	40	46	41	50

Source: Pratten and Dean, 1965, p. 49.

Note: One operative is required for each machine. The figures apply to both the number of machines and the number of production workers in the making room. Output figures are in pairs of shoes per day. Average output rises steadily to output levels of 1200 pairs per day, and then falls until production is doubled to 2400 pairs.

some of the machines with very high output rates are very expensive and therefore should be kept running as much as possible. It is not feasible to reach a full multiple of every machine; what is important, however, is to approach an output level approximating the lowest common multiple of the *expensive* machines—numbers 4, 6, 8, and 17 in Box 7.2. This minimum is 1200 pairs of shoes a day, and costs fall at each multiple of this output level (Table 7.2).

The third explanation of greater efficiency at higher output levels is the *principle of reserves*. The smooth operation of a plant, including production and marketing, requires maintaining some minimum level of stock, raw materials, fuel, spare parts for equipment repair and maintenance, and perhaps even spare machines. These economies are harder to document although their existence is easy to understand. They are most evident where equipment must be taken out of service at regular intervals for maintenance. A basic oxygen furnace in the steel industry must be relined with refractory bricks every 25 to 40 days. Two furnaces are needed to keep a steady flow of steel. Adding a third furnace, however, increases output by 50 percent for a 33 percent increase in cost.

A special case of the scale economies of reserves occurs when plant size permits a just-in-time delivery of stock. Very substantial sums are tied up in manufacturing industry stock: Interest and other costs of holding stock have been estimated to be as high as a quarter of the purchase (Estall, 1985). Chrysler Corp. saved $1 billion in the first year it adopted a just-in-time inventory, which was more than its reported profits.

Finally, a *principle of bulk transactions* sometimes applies. Economists distinguish between the case where size is used to bargain for better rates, which is a pecuniary advantage, and where real increases in efficiency occur. Shoe manufacturers often sell their shoes through their own outlets. A complete range of sizes in each color for each style must be carried. Where sales are large, the size distribution of the stock can more nearly approximate the size distribution of the market. Volume sales thus reduce overhead costs and the risks of being left with extreme sizes at the end of the season.

Management costs, not all of which are fixed, also rise less than proportionately with size. Management economies at the plant level are very much like labor economies at the product level. Division-of-management tasks permit allocation of duties according to aptitude. The principles of the learning curve, specialization of duties, and development of specialized management aids become feasible in larger plants. Management economies are thought to continue beyond the scale where technical economies are exhausted and continue on up to multiplant firms.

Multiplant Economies

The organization of industry into multiplant firms permits production economies over and beyond those attributable to the sizes of the individual plants. These economies of scale for multiplant firms involve primarily the financial and marketing functions.

Production Economies. Multiplant firms can allocate particular products to specific plants, increasing product-specific economies. The 1969 merger of three British companies manufacturing antifriction bearings provides an example of just how great such economies can be. Two of the companies had manufactured overlapping lines of general-purpose bearings. The merger permitted production assignments that ended duplication and permitted longer production runs. Output per employee jumped 50 percent in one year, and even greater improvements in productivity were expected with the introduction of new equipment justified by longer runs. Two Canadian companies, each making broad lines of home appliances, merged in 1971, ending duplication and achieving major, if less spectacular, economies.

Marketing Economies. Multiplant firms can also achieve important marketing economies. Companies sometimes spend large amounts on advertising to hold or extend their share of sales, or to market a new product. Advertising costs are particularly high in the case of soaps and detergents. A new enzyme detergent that cost £200,000 to develop was launched on the British market in the mid-1960s with a £1-million advertising campaign. A similar sum would have been

TABLE 7.2

Average costs at various output scales in the shoe industry

Output Capacity (pairs per day)	Labor and Equipment	Total Production Costs Including Materials
300	100	100
600	94	97
1200	90	95.5
2400	87	94
4800	85	93

Source: Pratten and Dean, 1965, p. 52.

Note: These estimates, based on British factories making women's medium-priced shoes in the 1960s, are representative of economies of scale in the shoe industry generally.

needed for any new company to launch its product. That is, some threshold level of expenditure must be made on advertising before the product catches public attention, word spreads, and sales take off.

An effective sales campaign can reshape an industry, as it did in the case of the United States brewery industry. After the repeal of Prohibition in 1933, a few breweries chose to set their prices high relative to local and regional beers, and to promote a national image as "premium" Milwaukee beers. The big three, Anheuser-Busch, Schlitz, and Pabst, captured an increasing share of the market. The consequent economies of scale then enabled them to reduce their prices and to start driving out smaller-scale local producers, thus enlarging their market share still further.

Financial Economies. Multiplant firms also achieve important financial economies of scale. They can concentrate their financial resources on the expansion of each plant in turn as the market grows. This strategy is impossible for single-plant firms. Where an industry is composed largely of single-plant firms, all firms will try to expand competitively, usually resulting in initial overexpansion and then of failure by the least efficient.

Multiplant firms can also raise capital through stock issues at lower interest rates because the financial community views them as better risks. Many of the costs of negotiating a loan are fixed, and it has been found that costs can vary from as little as 5 percent of share value to as much as 44 percent according to the size of the corporation.

Underlying these multiple economies are the same set of principles as in the plant-specific and product-specific cases, and they apply to all functions. First is the principle of averaging down the fixed costs over larger volumes. Next are the sets of principles applying to variable costs: the cube-square law, multiples, massed reserves, and bulk transactions. The last two are particularly important. The economies of scale at the firm level depend in part, however, on the relationship among the plants. This relationship in turn depends on any mergers by which the plants were acquired.

The Merger Movement in the United States. Multiplant corporations dominate most industries in most Western countries. A 1963 U.S. survey of 417 industries revealed only 22 industries in which the four leading sellers operated only single plants. This dominance of the market by multiplant firms is the result of three great merger periods. The first period was dominated by horizontal integration, the second by vertical

integration, and the third by conglomerate mergers. Let us look at each of these in turn.

The first period, which lasted from 1887 to 1904 in the United States, saw the consolidation of thousands of firms into relatively few multiplant corporations dominating the market they supplied. The mergers were triggered by changes in transportation, communications, manufacturing technology, and legal institutions. Standard Oil captured 90 percent of the petroleum market by acquiring competitors. U.S. Steel was formed in 1901 by the merger of 785 plants accounting for 65 percent of the country's steel capacity. The American Can Company, organized the same year, involved 120 firms with 90 percent of the national market. Other leading corporations established during the great merger wave are U.S. Rubber (Uniroyal), Pittsburgh Plate Glass (PPG Industries), International Paper, United Fruit (United Brands), Eastman-Kodak, and International Harvester. Almost all industries were affected: copper, lead, railroad cars, tobacco, chemicals, and shoe machines among them. The first great merger period was halted only by a combination of a depression and the enactment of antitrust laws, but some significant mergers still occurred. IBM was established in 1911. General Motors was formed from Buick, Cadillac, and Oldsmobile, added Chevrolet a few years later, but was unable to raise the cash to buy out Ford when Henry Ford offered to sell out in 1908 and 1909.

The second great merger period, from 1916 to 1929, involved more companies but created fewer industrial leaders. It did, however, create important "number two" firms, such as Bethlehem Steel and Continental Can. One authority distinguished this second period as "mergers for oligopoly" as compared with first-wave "mergers for monopoly." In addition, the second merger period saw much more *vertical integration* of industry than the first, during which *horizontal integration* predominated.

Horizontal mergers (integration) involve the combination of firms producing similar items and selling in the same market. Industry concentration is involved. The leading firms may account for most of the sales in a given industry. Competition is reduced as former competitors become integrated partners in a single firm.

Vertical mergers (integration) combine successive production activities into a single firm. The firm's plants now serve each other in sequence as the product is carried through a progression of processes. In steel, the succession of steps involves making pig iron, converting it to steel, and shaping the steel into semi-finished products. In other cases, vertical integration involves separate components of a good, as when a soft-drink producer buys out a bottle manufacturer. Vertical integration is *backward* when a firm buys out its suppliers. A steel company may acquire coal and iron ore mines, to secure raw materials. Vertical integration is *forward* where the purpose is to secure markets and outlets for the production of the dominant partner in the integration. Breweries in Britain own their own pubs, the film industry operates its own cinema chains, automobile companies sell through franchised dealerships.

The impact of vertical integration on competition is more subtle than in the case of horizontal integration, and it can involve clear economies where the production steps are technologically complementary, as in the steel industry. Mergers that produce sizable shifts in market shares are increasingly frowned on, however. As a result, the post–World War II period has witnessed a third wave of *conglomerate mergers,* in which the firms that join together have no obvious complementarities other than those of financial and tax manipulation. A case in point is the 1982 acquisition of Marathon Oil Co. by U.S. Steel (renamed USX). Where some small complementarities do exist, the mergers are described as *lateral integration.* The British aircraft industry has thus moved into a variety of engineering ventures.

The urge to merge springs from a variety of motives. Among these are the search for financial security, the instinct to jump at a good business opportunity, tax advantages, and hoped-for economies of scale. Horizontal integration increases security by reducing competition, vertical integration reduces vulnerability by controlling supplies and markets, and conglomerate mergers spread product and financial risk by diversity. Integration may be good business where another company's stock is underpriced, where new management can revitalize a lagging corporation, or where its physical plant can be acquired at a low price. But mergers also offer economies of scale. These are most obvious in horizontal mergers. Vertical integration can improve the flow of output through the sequence of processes and facilitate the management of quality and design of components, and size always bestows financial and marketing advantages. Indeed, a company may be acquired for its good will, even if the physical plant is not needed. An extreme example is in the case of U.S. breweries when the G. W. Heileman Co. paid $10.7 million for the Blatz trademark, 32 trucks, and the Blatz marching band. In the case of commodities with high transportation costs, where the market area that can be served by any one plant is as a result restricted, horizontal integration offers nationwide sales: Several factories in different market areas produce and sell the same nationally

advertised product. This is an important factor in cases like beer (not all "Milwaukee" beers are produced in Milwaukee), cement, petroleum refining, and the soft-drink industry. Coca-Cola, Pepsi-Cola, and others are bottled in a myriad of small plants serving particular urban-regional markets.

EXTERNAL ECONOMIES OF SCALE

In addition to the internal economies of scale that a firm obtains through the scale of output of specific products, the size of individual establishments, or of the firm itself, *external* economies of scale may contribute to lower average production costs. External economies of scale are the gains in efficiency and productivity resulting from the concentration of different firms in a single location. External economies derive from *spatial association* rather than corporate integration. They may be *industry-specific* and depend on the concentration in one location of different firms involved in the manufacture of similar products (called *localization economies*), or they may be *place-specific* and result from efficiencies in the provision of services to industry that are dependent not on the particular nature of the industry, but on the local scale of output of all kinds (called *urbanization economies*).

Localization Economies

Localization economies arise from the clustering of plants engaged in similar activity in a restricted geographical area. The local scale of the industry that results benefits individual plants within the group and tends to perpetuate the localization of the industry. Several kinds of economies exist:

1. The reputation acquired by goods produced in a given locality leads to *product differentiation.* Goods produced in some localities, whether or not they meet the standards of that locality, carry with them the aura of high standards of workmanship and quality. A typical case is that of the cutlery and steel produced in Sheffield, England; others are Brussels lace, Irish linen, and Milwaukee beer. Whether or not the products are superior, the image is that they are and their product is therefore differentiated from the same goods produced elsewhere, giving a distinct market advantage.

2. The consequences of the industrial atmosphere pervading the localized area stemming from the close association of manufacturers who meet frequently. Rivalries among these manufacturers breed innovation; at the same time there can be interchange

of personnel and information and, where necessary, cooperative action to preserve or enhance the locality's reputation. Knowledge under such circumstances is more rapidly diffused among firms located within the cluster. Firms in the same industry but outside the cluster operate at a disadvantage. This factor of geographic association was, of course, more important during the nineteenth century than the twentieth. It is of less importance today because of the growth of nationwide selling organizations and of a trade press that diffuses ideas rapidly. Nonetheless, it has been of real significance in the localization of computer chip–making firms in California's Silicon Valley and of high-tech firms around Boston's Route 128.

    3.   The creation of a pool of skilled labor, which thereby strengthens localization economies, results in the local labor force becoming uniquely adapted to the needs of the local industry, which enhances local productivity.

    4.   The adaptation of local utilities and services to the particular needs of the industry also produces efficiencies that reduce costs. Banks, insurance agencies, and transportation companies supplying special facilities appropriate to the needs of the industry dominate the kinds of service provided in the locality, and their costs are lower because they become expert in the problems and needs of the industry.

    5.   Most important, the local scale of industry permits the subdivision of operations between plants. Auxiliary specialists emerge, meeting the requirements of several firms. The specialists provide components or needed services more cheaply than if the individual firms had to provide their own. With a localized industry, then, vertical *dis*integration is important. It arises from the close geographical association of firms, short hauls, speedy delivery, and the lessening of stock requirements. The resulting interdependence facilitates those real economies of subdivision that are exhibited by the most localized activities. The outstanding historical examples have been the clothing industry and the cutlery trades. Examples include the garment districts of New York and the East End of London. In the metal trades of the West Midlands of England, three main types of activity constituted the localization: (a) a large number of firms performing common metal processes, but not producing finished goods; for example, the foundries, rerollers, forgers, welders, galvanizers; (b) a large number of firms making common components, screws, bolts, nuts, tools, springs; and (c) service trades; for example, small establishments making wooden patterns or machine tools, the scrap merchants, and so on. These three main types of activity supported the highly localized metal goods manufacturers who engaged in assembly

and the further processing of the components made by the three main types of activity. Good examples were motor vehicles, bicycles and motorcycles, guns in Birmingham, locks at Wolverhampton, and so on. Localization economies thus accomplish through geographic juxtaposition the same kinds of linkages as those achieved through corporate integration in internal economies of scale.

Urbanization Economies

Urbanization economies derive from the close association of many different kinds of industry in large cities. The cost advantages derive from several sources, the most important of which are:

    1.   *Transportation costs.* A large city usually has superior public transportation facilities offering significantly lower transportation costs to regional and national markets. A city located at a focal point on transportation networks is especially suited for easy assembly of raw materials and for ready distribution of products. There are thus market advantages for speedy and cheap distribution that may be accentuated by the advantages arising out of the size of the local consuming market. The local population may in fact form a large part of the total national market. Greater London, for example, has one-fifth of the British consumer market, and the New York metropolitan area was called "one-tenth of a nation" in the 1960s. In both cases, these markets account for a significantly larger proportion of the higher-quality and fashion-oriented demands. Thus, the large city may be the ideal plant location: Local demands are substantial and the rest of the plant's output is easily distributed.

    2.   *Labor costs.* The large city labor market is diverse and dynamic, and the labor demands of single firms are only a small part of the total demands for labor. This labor pool is especially important where firms have seasonal variations in labor needs. The big-city labor market also offers a wide range of skills. Facilities for workers that are readily available in the large city may also have to be provided by the firm in the small town, which raises the real labor costs.

    3.   *Quality of services.* The larger the city the higher the scale of services it can supply. Services such as firefighting, police, gas, electricity, water, waste disposal, education, housing, and roads are generally better in the larger city than in the small town, and they are provided publicly. Firms located in otherwise unindustrialized areas may be forced to spend much more of their capital on infrastructure and social facilities. These kinds of advantages first came into play in the industrial development of the largest metro-

politan areas in the period following World War I. Service economies had a magnetic effect on industries in which coal was replaced as motive power by electricity, and in which rail and water transportation was replaced by the truck. Light industry, manufacturing consumer goods, was attracted to large cities not only by their markets and marketing facilities but also by their services. In turn, the accumulation of light industry in large cities further enhanced the attractiveness of the cities, creating positive conditions for further growth. In this way, urbanization economies have fed on themselves in a process of "circular and cumulative causation."

DISECONOMIES OF SCALE

Average costs of production tend to fall with increased scale of output because of economies of scale, but there is reason to believe that once a minimum efficient size of production has been reached (the MES), costs may not fall any further, and may rise, at least in the short run (see Figure 7.1).

Internal Diseconomies of Scale

Labor Diseconomies of Scale. The reductions in labor costs per unit of production end when all the economies of the division of labor have been achieved. As workers become skilled in operating their equipment, the learning curve flattens out and no further economies can be expected from this source (Figure 7.4). There is a one-time savings in keeping workers at a single specific task using specialized equipment. Overspecialization of jobs makes the work repetitive and boring. As workers find their jobs less satisfying and challenging, they must be paid higher wage rates. As a result, many industries have been reorganized to make work more varied and interesting. The sales offices of Rowntree & Co. in York, England, reintegrated the handling of correspondence and the granting of credit into a single division, thus giving wider responsibilities for fewer customers to each section head. Their tasks thereby became less monotonous, and as section heads became familiar with their own batch of customers, the time lost on consulting records was reduced. In Sweden, long assembly lines have been replaced in some industries by smaller work groups carrying the product through to completion, resulting in greater worker commitment and higher-quality products.

The sheer size of the labor force in a single plant also produces problems. Workers in large plants tend to find their work less satisfying than workers in small plants for reasons not yet properly understood by psychologists. Large plants find they must therefore pay a wage premium. Furthermore, as the size of the labor force grows, it must begin to attract workers from greater distances. The added transportation costs faced by workers are reflected in wage rates. A point will be reached when increases in wage rates associated with increasing size of plant cannot be offset by increased efficiency. At that point, labor economies of scale give way to labor *dis*economies of scale.

Technical Diseconomies of Scale. In the case of technical factors, many firms find that a size is reached where technical economies of scale are exhausted. The cube-square law faces sheer size limits beyond which technical problems and costs exceed possible economies. Cement lime kilns experience unstable internal aerodynamics above 7 million barrels per year capacity. Machines and equipment become increasingly unwieldy. Parts may have to be strengthened in proportion to volume rather than size once strength limits are approached, offsetting any possible scale economies. Where the size of a new plant is above the usual size range for the industry, there may also be substantial design costs and initial difficulties in getting into production.

The principle of multiples confers fixed rather than continuous economies of scale. Costs are a minimum where the product of output per machine times number of machines is the same for each step in a process. If output is increased beyond this level, costs rise until production reaches a new multiple of machine capacity. But the average costs per multiple may be the same unless increased scale permits larger and more efficient machines to be introduced.

The other principles underlying technical economies of scale also run into diminishing returns. The *principle of reserves* may not apply fully if several smaller production lines are replaced by a single large production line. In the chemical industry, for example, continuity of production is essential. Supplies are more vulnerable for a large single-stream plant than for many small ones. The danger of disruption can be reduced by storage, but the storage costs reduce the economies of scale of a larger plant.

A firm may run into actual technical difficulties in increasing scale of output. Limited physical space available for expansion may cause increasing congestion. There may be physical limits imposed by availability of water for production or cooling processes from nearby rivers and lakes. Environmental pollution may become more difficult to cope with at larger output levels. In sum, technical considerations tend to set a minimum efficient scale of production, but once this scale has been reached, further technical economies of scale may be hard to win. Technical diseconomies of scale can be avoided by operating a number of separate plants. In this case, however, the firm is still faced with management diseconomies of scale.

Management Diseconomies of Scale.
Management diseconomies of scale occur because of the increasing difficulty of coordinating larger firms. These management diseconomies have been described in different ways and from different viewpoints. One writer has argued that the cube-square law works against economies of scale in management (Haire, 1959). Using a simple biological analogy, Haire argued that supervisory and management personnel grow disproportionately with output, in fact, at a $\frac{3}{2}$ power of the growth in production. Many functions that can be taken care of informally in small plants must be organized formally in larger organizations. Parking, eating facilities, medical care, and security are examples. Coordination becomes more complex with increasing size and division of labor. What was managed by a worker as part of the job routine becomes a new and wholly separate function. Hierarchies of management control evolve, with the attendant danger that top management becomes increasingly remote from day-to-day production problems. Decision making becomes more difficult, takes longer, and becomes less flexible. Bad decisions are harder to detect but may be more damaging and difficult to reverse. One need only to look at the giant corporations in difficulty today to see examples of this.

Marketing Diseconomies of Scale.
The most serious diseconomies of scale may be in marketing. More output requires more sales. Advertising can be used to promote additional sales, but too much advertising can backfire. Budweiser found that advertising increased its sales of beer up to a maximum, beyond which further advertising appeared to reduce sales. Scherer (1980) notes that consumers deluged with Budweiser ads asked their liquor dealers to give them anything *but* a Bud (Figure 7.5).

Sales may be increased by extending the market area, but more distant sales incur greater delivery costs. Beyond a certain distance, these increased costs can be expected to exceed the economies of scale.

Of all the factors contributing to internal economies of scale, only finance appears to be immune to diminishing returns, and hence to diseconomies of scale.

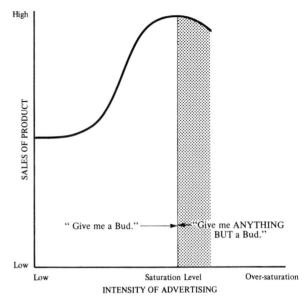

FIGURE 7.5 Diseconomies of advertising. Saturation advertising of a product beyond consumer tolerance levels can turn off potential buyers, as Budweiser found. [*Source:* Suggested by F. M. Scherer, *Industrial Market Structure and Economic Performance* (Chicago: Rand McNally, 1980), p. 109.]

External Diseconomies of Scale

External diseconomies of scale set in once the costs of urban congestion begin to exceed the benefits of industrial concentration. Precise definition is more difficult than in the case of internal diseconomies of scale. The general nature of these diseconomies is not, however, difficult to understand. Some cause industries to seek lower-cost regions, as when big-city wage rates force labor-intensive industries such as textile producers to exploit lower-wage labor forces elsewhere. Others produce a shifting of activities between central and suburban locations. High land values in inner-city areas, cramped and restricted sites, parking difficulties, deficiency of light and air, and environmental pollution lead industries that seek space, light, and air to go to the periphery of the big city, to smaller towns, or to nonurban areas; often a relocation is planned to bring the plant closer to the owner's or manager's preferred place of residence. The peripheral area avoids the diseconomies of centrality while retaining the advantages of proximity. There the best of both worlds can often be obtained.

This movement to the fringe took place slowly in the industrial areas of the United States and Western Europe before World War II. Despite more widespread use of electric power and the development of road transportation and of improved highways, reducing the locational pull on industrial locations of rail terminals and docks in central areas, a long period of economic depression prevented wholesale relocation or many new suburban plant locations, although new outlying planned industrial estates were pioneered in many countries. The great change came after World War II: Highways were further improved, and new large-scale trucks came into operation, often in combination with rail transport (''piggyback''). Rapid decentralization of industry from the central cities began in force.

It operated selectively. For some kinds of activities, central locations remained so crucial that they outweighed the disadvantages of congestion. Industries decentralizing were those using road transportation and preferring single-story facilities or expansive sites. Industries moving out of big cities altogether have done so in sequence: First were those seeking low labor costs (especially textile producers and a variety of assembly operations), next were the machine tool industries serving those that left first, then integrated production complexes that were capable of standing alone, and then a variety of new computer- and communications-based industries that were relatively immune from the pulls of the central city but highly dependent on being able to attract skilled scientists and technicians to attractive residential environments.

MEASURING SCALE ECONOMIES

The Theoretical Approach

The many ingredients contributing to economies and diseconomies of scale can be usefully melded into a composite picture by focusing on the relationships of costs to output. Costs can be measured in various ways, but if these various measures of cost can be identified for a particular industry, then the most efficient size can be identified very precisely. Actual cost data for a comprehensive range of outputs and industries are not generally available. Even if they have such comprehensive data, industrialists are naturally reluctant to part with information that might help competitors. The cost curves shown in most books are, therefore, based more on the theoretical understanding of economies of scale than on actual cases. In this text, too, the data are hypothetical and employed only to illustrate the key relationships between cost, output, and economies of scale.

Costs can be classified in two distinct ways. First, there is the distinction between *fixed costs* and *variable costs:* This distinction was noted in describing plant-specific economies. Second, there is the distinction between *total, average,* and *marginal costs.* It is this second classification that is crucial to the theoretical approach to understanding economies of scale.

Total costs of operating a plant at a given output level are equal to the fixed costs plus the total variable costs. If fixed costs are $100, and total variable costs are $180, then total costs are $280. Fixed costs do not change with output. However, variable costs must always *increase* with output (Box 7.3). If they did not, an industry could find itself in the enviable but bizarre position where it cost less to produce more.

Economies of scale are easier to identify from average costs than total costs. Average costs are simply total costs divided by output. Average fixed costs always decrease with higher output (Box 7.3). Average variable costs decrease until diseconomies of scale come into play. Diseconomies in variable costs may be offset by continuing economies in fixed costs. Thus, the output level with minimum average total costs may be higher than for the minimum average variable costs. It is the output level with *minimum average total costs* that marks the point of *maximum economies of scale.*

There is a simple test of whether output has reached the point of maximum economies of scale, which depends on calculating *marginal cost.* Marginal cost is the added cost of producing just one more unit of output (Box 7.3). As long as the marginal cost is less than the average total cost, producing more will lower the average. For example, if the average cost of six units is $50, and the marginal cost of producing one more unit (the seventh) is $42, it pays to do so. The average cost for seven is less than for six. But it turns out in the example that the marginal cost for the eighth unit jumps to $60, which is higher than the average. Hence, the average cost starts to rise. The rule is, therefore, that *average total cost is a minimum where it equals marginal cost.* At lower output levels, marginal cost is less than average cost and pulls average cost down. At higher levels, it pulls average cost up (Figure 7.6). Thus, economies of scale are maximized where average total cost equals marginal cost.

In summary, costs can be classified into fixed, variable, and total costs, and further classified into total, average, and marginal costs (Figure 7.6). The behavior of the cost curves in this two-way classification identifies the point of maximum economies of scale. This point is the MES (minimum efficient scale). The point occurs *after* marginal costs have started to rise, and *after* average *variable* costs have started to

BOX 7.3   *Measuring Internal Economies of Scale*

OUTPUT	TOTAL COSTS ($)		
Number of Units	FIXED	VARIABLE	TOTAL
0	100	0	100
1	100	50	150
2	100	90	190
3	100	123	223
4	100	152	252
5	100	180	280
6	100	210	310
7	100	252	352
8	100	311	411
9	100	405	505
10	100	550	650

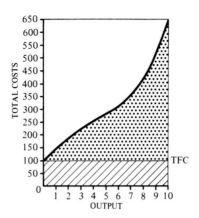

FIGURE 7d   Change in total production costs with scale. Total production costs comprise two components, fixed costs and variable costs. These figures are entirely imaginary and are chosen to display, first, increasing economies of scale and then increasing diseconomies of scale in the figures that follow.

OUTPUT	AVERAGE COSTS ($)		
Number of Units	FIXED	VARIABLE	TOTAL
1	100	50	150
2	50	45	95
3	33	41	74
4	25	38	63
5	20	36	56
6	17	35	52
7	14	36	50
8	13	39	52
9	11	45	56
10	10	55	65

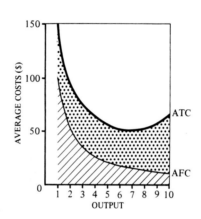

FIGURE 7e   Change in average production costs with scale. These figures are obtained simply by dividing the totals in Figure 7d by the output levels involved. The total fixed cost for five units is $100, so the average is $20. Total variable for five units is $180, so the average is $36. The average total cost for five units is then $56. Thus, average cost is cost divided by output.

OUTPUT	TOTAL VARIABLE COSTS	MARGINAL COSTS	INCREASE IN OUTPUT
Number of Units	($)	($)	from
0	0		
1	50	50	0 to 1
2	90	40	1 to 2
3	123	33	2 to 3
4	152	29	3 to 4
5	180	28	4 to 5
6	210	30	5 to 6
7	252	42	6 to 7
8	311	60	7 to 8
9	405	93	8 to 9
10	550	145	9 to 10

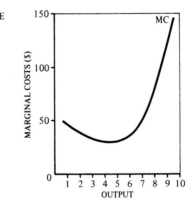

FIGURE 7f   Change in marginal production costs with scale. Marginal cost is the additional cost of producing one more unit. It can be calculated as the difference in variable costs, in increasing output by one unit. The result is the same if total cost is used. These figures are derived from Figure 7d. The marginal cost of increasing production from five units to six is $30. The marginal cost is $210 in variable costs for six units minus $180 for five. Equally, it is $310 in total costs for six minus $280 for five.

▦ Variable costs	ATC Average Total Cost	TFC Total Fixed Cost	
	AFC Average Fixed Cost	TC Total Cost	MC Marginal Cost
▨ Fixed costs			

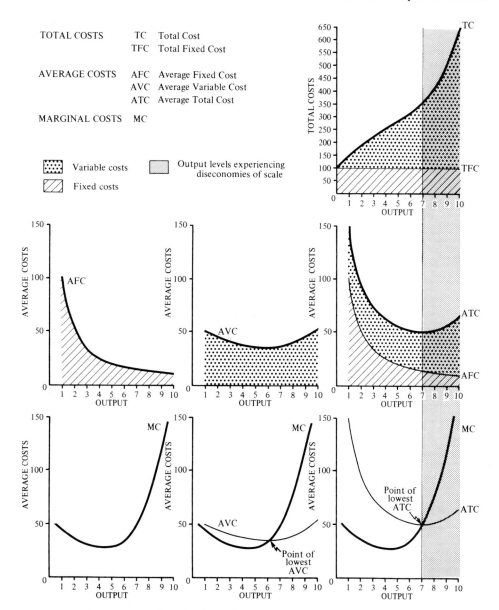

FIGURE 7.6 Finding the divide between economies and diseconomies of scale. This figure essentially brings together the figures shown in Box 7.3. Note that the marginal cost curve *MC* for a product always intersects the average variable cost curve *AVC* where *AVC* is a minimum. It also intersects average total costs *ATC* where these costs are a minimum. The divide between economies of scale and diseconomies of scale is at this point of intersection, where *ATC* is a minimum and where there is an inflection in total costs. Total costs are rising at a decreasing rate if there are economies of scale, and at an increasing rate if there are diseconomies of scale.

rise. The MES occurs where average *total* costs are minimized.

Complicating Factors: Transportation Costs. A number of complications need to be considered. Increased output may require a larger market area and involve higher transportation costs. If transportation costs are substantial, they can reduce the MES. Each marginal unit sold involves higher and higher transportation costs, forcing up average total costs (Box 7.3). Another layer of costs is added to production so that average costs comprise average fixed, average variable, and average transportation costs (Box 7.4). Comparing the output levels with and without transporta-

BOX 7.4 *Adding in Transportation Costs*

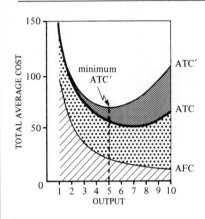

Average transportation costs

Average variable costs

Average fixed costs

ATC′ Average Total Costs
plus Transportation

ATC Average Total Costs
not including Transportation

AFC Average Fixed Costs

Average costs of:

Output Number of Units	Transportation	Production	Transportation and Production
		ATC	ATC′
1	0	150	150
2	3	95	98
3	5	74	79
4	9	63	72
5	14	56	70
6	20	52	72
7	26	50	76
8	33	52	85
9	40	56	96
10	48	65	113

Marginal costs of:

Output Number of Units	Total Transportation Cost	Transportation	Production	Transportation and Production
0	0 > . . .	0 . . .	50 . . .	50
1	0 > . . .	5 . . .	40 . . .	45
2	5 > . . .	10 . . .	33 . . .	43
3	15 > . . .	20 . . .	29 . . .	49
4	35 > . . .	35 . . .	28 . . .	63
5	70 > . . .	50 . . .	30 . . .	80
6	120 > . . .	65 . . .	42 . . .	107
7	185 > . . .	80 . . .	60 . . .	139
8	265 > . . .	95 . . .	93 . . .	189
9	360 > . . .	120 . . .	145 . . .	265
10	480			

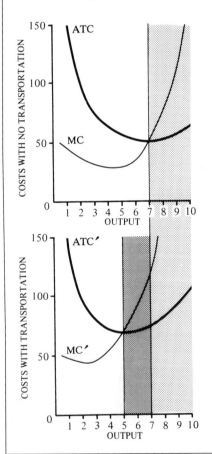

MC Marginal Costs

ATC Average Total Costs

MC′ Marginal Costs plus
Transportation Costs

ATC′ Average Total Costs plus
Transportation Costs

Diseconomies of scale

Impact of transportation costs:
diseconomies of scale if
transportation costs incurred

Note: Total transportation costs are given and assume that increasing production levels require a growing sales area and increasing transportation costs. The average and marginal costs are both calculated from total costs as before. Then total average costs plus transportation (ATC′) equals the total average production cost from the top figure plus the average transportation cost. Marginal production cost and marginal transportation cost are summed to give the combined marginal cost (MC′).

Average total costs plus transportation are given in the accompanying table. This figure adds one more layer of costs to the average production costs presented in Box 7.3. Note that the minimum average costs occur at an output level of 5 units when transportation costs are added in.

The middle figure, repeated from Figure 7.6, shows the output level at which diseconomies of scale set in without transportation costs. The lower figure shows that diseconomies set in at a lower production level if transportation costs are incurred. The difference between the two levels indicates the impact of transportation costs on economies of scale.

tion costs thus permits an exact determination of the impact of transportation costs on the point of maximum economies of scale (Box 7.4).

Hoover's Margin Lines. Edgar Hoover introduced the concept of *margin line* to deal with the effect on economies and diseconomies of scale of extending the marketing area and incurring transportation costs. The concept is fairly straightforward. At each distance from a plant a calculation is made of what the delivered price would be at that point when transportation costs are added. As long as economies of scale outweigh transportation costs to each given distance, the margin line slopes down and it pays to extend the market area. Once the transportation costs outweigh the

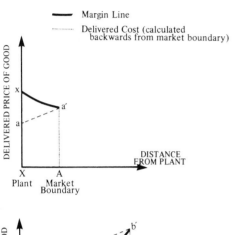

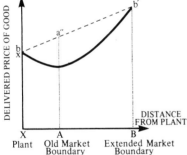

FIGURE 7.7 Diseconomies in extending the market area. Edgar M. Hoover introduced the concept of *margin line* to deal with the economies and diseconomies in extending the market area. The margin line shows what the delivered price would be at each distance from a plant taking into account the economies of scale given the market available within that distance, and the transportation costs of shipping the good that distance. Given a plant at *X*, which ships as far as *A*, the delivered price at *A* is *Aa'*. If the market is extended to *B*, transportation costs outweigh economies of scale. The price at *B* is *Bb'*, and the price at *A* rises to *Aa''*. The price at any location is the price at the market boundary minus the transportation costs from that boundary.

economies of scale, the margin line begins to slope up (Figure 7.7). The actual delivered price at each location is determined by the margin line at the actual market boundary. The price paid at each location is this price at the boundary, less the savings in transportation.

The Age and Scale of Equipment

Actual calculations of operating costs are affected by the age, or *vintage*, of equipment used and the scale of the operation. The age of factory equipment affects capital costs for a variety of reasons. Newer equipment tends to be relatively expensive because of inflation and added controls (whether for pollution, safety, or comfort). New equipment sometimes runs into teething problems, which can take years to correct. And the impact of these costs may be aggravated by accounting practices of heavily depreciating equipment in the early years. On the other hand, old equipment may be inefficient, raising labor costs. Based on his survey of British industry, C. F. Pratten thus found the structure of industry varied with the age of equipment in a characteristic way (Table 7.3; Figure 7.8). Moreover, the characteristic change between labor and capital costs with age of equipment was the same whether the equipment had a short life, as some machine tools and textile equipment, which can wear out within 10 years, or a long life, as in the case of cement or soap where machinery can continue to operate for over 40 years.

The newer the equipment is, the lower the average total costs tend to be, and the higher the output at which minimum average costs are achieved (Figure 7.9). Thus, the vintage of equipment affects not only the structure of operating costs but also the average

TABLE 7.3

Vintage of equipment and structure of costs in brick production

	Old Works (percent)	New Works (percent)
Clay	2.6	2.6
Fuel and power	31.5	28.6
Wages and salaries	41.4	20.1
Repairs	9.6	10.5
Rates (local taxes)	2.6	2.8
Office expenses	5.5	5.6
Depreciation	6.8	30.0
Total	100.0	100.2

Source: Pratten, 1971, p. 97.

Note: Costs include depreciation but exclude interest on capital. Total costs are approximately the same for the two works. The new works has a capacity of about three times the old works, which is 40 years old.

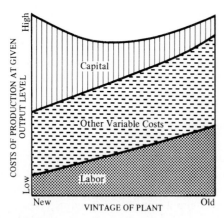

FIGURE 7.8 The effect of age of equipment on the structure of costs. New plant involves heavy capital costs, which in economic terms are incurred when it is installed, but which, for accounting purposes, may be depreciated over a number of years. Older plant is likely to have higher variable costs, for a given level of output. The structure of costs, therefore, varies according to the vintage of the equipment. [*Source:* Adapted from Pratten, 1971, pp. 306–307.]

TABLE 7.4

Cost flexibility in heavy commercial vehicle manufacture

Proportion of Total Costs Variable Within		
1 week	*1 month*	*6 months*
5	35	80

Source: D. G. Rhys, "Heavy Commercial Vehicles: The Survival of the Small Firm," *Journal of Industrial Economics,* XX (1971–1972), p. 233.

Note: Cost flexibility is not symmetric. If orders increase in a six-month period, then 80 percent of costs will increase directly in proportion with output. If orders fall, the manufacturer may become locked into some costs.

level of operating costs, and the minimum efficient scale.

Long-Run versus Short-Run Unit Costs

Most of the previous discussion refers to the shape of *short-run* unit cost curves. *Long-run* average cost curves (also called *planning curves*) differ from these, because the assumption of a fixed investment in a given plant is dropped; all costs can be considered variable. In the short run, it is assumed that one is dealing with cost variations from operating a *given* farm or factory at different levels of output. In the long

run, the business can be modified or sold, or a new unit with a different amount and configuration of investment can be planned and built for a different scale of output.

In actual practice the distinction between short run and long run is not as clear and simple as the foregoing might indicate, however. For example, Rhys (1971–1972) has estimated that in heavy commercial vehicle manufacturing only 5 percent of total costs are variable within a week's time, but in a six-month period 80 percent may be variable (Table 7.4).

One way of looking at the long-run average cost curve is by comparing average cost levels for a variety of different facilities, as in Figure 7.10, which deals with the costs per patient per day for hospitals in Chicago in the late 1960s. But each of the individual facilities representing different investment "packages" will have its own short-run cost curve, and the relationship between the two is more properly expressed by a relationship in which the long-run cost curve appears as an "envelope" embracing the many possible short-run curves, as in Figure 7.11.

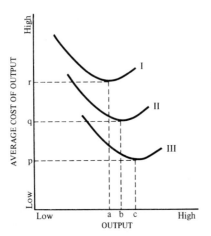

I	Oldest Equipment
II	Newer Equipment
III	Newest Equipment

a	MES of I
b	MES of II
c	MES of III

r	Minimum Average Cost of I
q	Minimum Average Cost of II
p	Minimum Average Cost of III

FIGURE 7.9 Vintage of equipment and economies of scale. Newer equipment tends to achieve its most efficient scale at higher output levels than older equipment. Thus the vintage of equipment affects not only the structure of operating costs but also economies of scale. [*Source:* After Pratten, 1971, p. 5.]

FIGURE 7.10 Cost data for hospitals in metropolitan Chicago. Each point in this graph shows the average patient-day cost for a hospital in the Chicago region. The solid line shows the average relationship for all the hospital averages. The dotted line is an envelope tracing out the silhouette of the best possible long-run average cost curve suggested by the data. The degree to which a hospital's costs lie above this silhouette is an indication of that hospital's relative inefficiency. [*Source:* Adapted from Gerald F. Pyle, "Heart Disease, Cancer, and Stroke in Chicago," Department of Geography Research Paper No. 134, University of Chicago, 1971.]

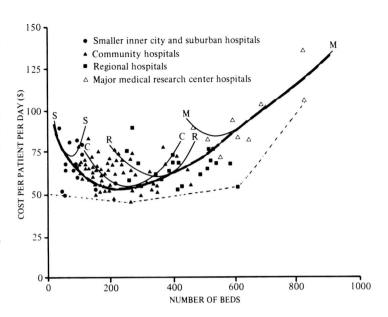

The "Lazy-J" Long-Run Unit Cost Curve. An outstanding feature of Figure 7.11 is that it shows that the long-run returns to scale of investment may not be U-shaped, but rather that the envelope may take the shape of a reverse- or "lazy-J." The graph in Figure 7.11 shows the short-run cost curves for each of several types of dairy farms in Minnesota and the characteristics of the least-cost farm are described in each case. For example, the least-cost three-person dairy farm (farm D) is one with an investment of $325,000, working 623 acres of land with a 100-head herd, and producing a net return of $16,925 per annum on a gross income of $80,000. The long-run curve traces out the best achievable cost per unit of output at each scale of production by forming an envelope beneath each of the short-run curves. Note how the long-run curve continues to slope downward to the right, indicating continuing cost advantages of increasing farm size. Each individual type of dairy farming has short-run unit cost curves that are U-shaped, with economies and diseconomies of scale, and an MES where costs are minimized. The long-run curve does not reveal any

FIGURE 7.11 Short-run and long-run cost curves in dairy farming. The cost curves are a "lazy-J" shape in this example rather than the "U" shape of the earlier discussion of economies and diseconomies. The principles are the same, however. For each investment package there is an optimal output, as shown by the short-run unit cost curve. Alternative farm sizes reveal that the long-run unit cost curve favors larger farms. Farms of 100 acres operate at a net loss. [*Source:* After Buxton and Boyd, Minnesota Dairy Farming, Fig. 4, p. 20.]

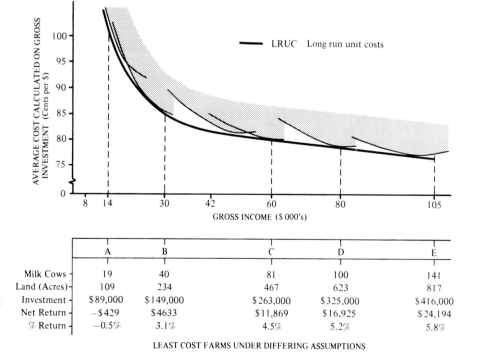

	A	B	C	D	E
Milk Cows	19	40	81	100	141
Land (Acres)	109	234	467	623	817
Investment	$89,000	$149,000	$263,000	$325,000	$416,000
Net Return	−$429	$4633	$11,869	$16,925	$24,194
% Return	−0.5%	3.1%	4.5%	5.2%	5.8%

LEAST COST FARMS UNDER DIFFERING ASSUMPTIONS

diseconomies of scale when farm sizes and management practices can be changed, however. Similar behavior of the long-run curve has been observed in many industries (Table 7.5).

Agriculture is pursuing these long-run cost advantages, resulting in rapid decline of smaller farms and a progressive increase in numbers of larger operations. Such results of cost advantages to larger-sized farms, accruing as they did throughout most of American agriculture, were responsible for the decline in the U.S. farm population from 15 million in 1960 to 10 million in 1970 and to 5 million in 1990 as the small-scale farmers moved into urban occupations.

Returns to Scale and Threshold Size. Lazy-J long-run cost curves indicate a particular pattern of returns to investment. First, for the reasons cited in the case of short-run curves, there will be economies of scale, and the long-run unit cost curve will fall with increasing output. But only if there are long-run constraints will there be diseconomies of further increases in scale, producing a U-shaped long-run unit cost (LRUC) curve. What occurs with the lazy-J is that the zone of increasing returns to scale terminates at a critical *size threshold,* the minimum size at which the lowest attainable unit costs are achieved. There is no onset of decreasing returns beyond this point because of the flexibility of different investment configurations that may be designed and built. Instead, beyond the threshold, average costs per unit of output tend to be relatively stable, and there is no apparent cost advantage of operating at either one scale or another. The *threshold size* sets the *condition of entry* for new firms to be able to compete. Entry at smaller scales means higher costs, lack of competitiveness, and ultimate failure, but firms may grow to several multiples of the threshold without cost penalty.

The Relationship of Threshold Scale to Industrial Concentration

Measurement of Scale Thresholds. One economist, J. S. Bain (1956), has identified the size thresholds associated with lazy-J cost curves in a variety of industries in North America. By expressing the scale of individual manufacturing plants as a percentage of the total national capacity of an industry, costs were shown to decrease with increasing scale, and then to level off. This enabled threshold size to be measured in relation to the proportion of national industrial capacity contained in one plant of minimal efficient size, by selecting as the threshold the point at which costs leveled off. It also enabled the capital requirements for a new plant to enter the industry at the minimum efficient cost threshold to be calculated. The threshold conditions for entry in many of the industries that Bain studied were substantial.

Emergence of Oligopolies and Administered Prices. There are several consequences of such reverse-J long-run cost curves with high conditions of entry. Generally, high conditions of entry limit potential new competition and tend to create oligopolies in which the industry is controlled by a small number of multiplant firms.

An example of a typical oligopoly in which a few firms have consistently controlled a large share of the market is that of the sulfur industry, in particular the Frasch sulfur industry, which produces sulfur from brimstone deposits found in the salt domes of the United States and Mexican Gulf coasts.

The Frasch sulfur industry is oligopolistic because of the high conditions of entry, and the LRUC is reverse-J. The difficulties faced by potential new competitors in gaining entry to the industry are threefold:

TABLE 7.5

Long-run economies of scale: Cement industry

Item	Capacity (1000 tons)	100	200	500	1000	2000
	Number of kilns and mills	1	1	2	2	2
Fuel, power, and materials		100	98	97	96	95
Wages and salaries		100	70	55	40	35
Depreciation and return on capital		100	80	70	58	47
Overhead		100	90	82	75	70
Average total costs		100	85	77	69	62

Source: Pratten, 1971, p. 92.

Note: Costs are given as an index of production costs in the smallest plant (100,000 tons per annum). Costs of transportation and selling are excluded. All plants are new.

1. *Absolute cost barriers.* Established firms control existing Frasch sulfur deposits, and there is great competition for new deposits when discovered. A new sulfur firm enters this arena by having to raise capital for the cost of entry at the same time that it competes with existing producers owning less costly deposits. The effect is to raise the price that must be paid for the new deposits.

2. *Product differentiation barriers.* Firms who have an established reputation with their customers have a sales advantage over new competitors.

3. *The economy of scale threshold.* The minimal scale at which a new firm may achieve the lowest attainable cost is a significant fraction of the total capacity of the industry. The entry of an additional firm may induce established firms to lower their price to preserve their market share. In this case, the newcomer must compete against a price that is even lower than the prevailing price when the firm entered. This discouragement is often sufficient to turn away potential new entrants.

Relatively free from new competitors, Frasch sulfur producers let their prices be determined by administrative decisions rather than allowing them to fluctuate with market conditions. First, prices were determined by the industry in response to long-run criteria, rather than with respect to short-run economic changes. Second, the industry practiced price discrimination, charging one price in domestic markets and a second, higher basing-point price for foreign markets. The higher price was quoted FOB vessels, Gulf port through the Sulfur Export Corporation, to which all Frasch producers belonged. The domestic price was established competitively by producers; the foreign price, however, was an arranged one producing a world pattern of Frasch sulfur prices rising with transport costs from U.S. Gulf ports.

Product Differentiation as a Barrier to Entry.

In most such oligopolistic circumstances, product differentiation is as powerful a force in restricting entry as is the condition of entry itself. The most obvious sources of product differentiation are differences in quality of design among competing outputs. For example, one brand of shoes may have better materials and workmanship than another, or one make of clothes may be fashionable whereas another may not. In either case, different buyers may rank the competing products differently. One buyer may be fashion conscious, looking for the latest styles. Another may be quality conscious, willing to pay a considerable premium for quality shoes. Yet another may be price conscious, accepting the lower quality if there is only a relatively small price concession.

A second source of product differentiation is the ignorance of buyers regarding the essential characteristics and qualities of the goods they are purchasing. This is likely to be an important consideration particularly with durable consumer goods, which are infrequently purchased and complex in design or composition. In this situation, the buyer is likely to rely on the "reputations" of the various products or their sellers—on popular lore concerning the product's performance and reliability, or on whether or not the seller has successfully remained in business for a long time.

Third, buyer preferences for certain products are developed or shaped by the persuasive sales-promotion activities of sellers, particularly by advertising of brand names, trademarks, or company names.

J. S. Bain has classified industries according to degree of product differentiation. He concludes that product differentiation is generally negligible in the producer-good segments of the agricultural, forestry, fisheries, and mining industries. Because goods produced by these industries are likely to be standardized at various grades and qualities, the sellers' efforts to introduce product differentiation have generally been unsuccessful. Moreover, these industries have many small sellers, thus providing a close approximation to the theoretical "pure competition."

On the other hand, in manufacturing and processing industries—particularly those producing consumer goods—product differentiation becomes very important. The consumer-buyer tends to be poorly informed, especially when faced with choosing among goods with complex designs. Even when the goods are not complex, buyers are susceptible to persuasive advertising campaigns that emphasize the sometimes nominal differences among products. In addition, producers can purposely vary the designs or quality of their goods in ways whose significance is not easily understood by consumers.

In some consumer-goods manufacturing industries, however, product differentiation is relatively unimportant. This seems to be especially true of basic necessities—food, clothing, and household supplies. In these industries the efforts of competing sellers to differentiate their products significantly have not been too successful. Thus, the establishment of brands and their support by advertising has not been automatically efficacious in creating strong product differentiation within a consumer-goods industry.

In manufacturing industries making producer goods, product differentiation is most frequently slight or negligible, and for the usual reasons—expert buyers, and goods that may be produced to standards or specifications. Basic industrial chemicals, for example, clearly come under this heading. Buyers purchase to specification or rely on established grades and generally do not prefer one seller's output to another sufficiently to induce them to pay a higher price for it. The slight buyer preferences that do introduce some product differentiation generally depend on ancillary services that the seller performs for buyers, such as promptness in filling orders or making deliveries. But with producer goods for which the provision of services by the manufacturer is an important element of the transaction (often when the producer-buyers represent rather small firms) and with large, complex producer goods (specialized machinery of various sorts), product differentiation may become as important as it is in consumer-goods categories. This would be true, for example, of farm machinery and business office machines of various sorts.

Other sectors of the economy may be characterized more briefly with respect to the incidence of product differentiation:

1. Wholesale and retail trade (groceries, clothing stores, pharmacies, and so on). In retail distribution, product differentiation based on type and quality of service offered by the retailer and on the convenience of location to the buyer is generally quite important. Product differentiation is evidently less important in wholesale markets in which retailers purchase from wholesale distributors.

2. Service trades (barber shops, dry cleaners, entertainment enterprises, and so on). Product differentiation is again important, for the same general reasons as those that apply to retailing.

3. Contract construction. On large-scale construction for industry or government where contracts are awarded after a process of bidding to specifications, product differentiation is a minimal factor. In residential construction, product differentiation based on design and location is generally quite important.

4. Finance (real estate firms, insurance companies, banks, and so on). Product differentiation is important in some cases and not in others.

5. Public utilities and transportation. In most utility industries, including suppliers of electricity, gas, and communications services, local monopoly by a single firm typically forestalls the emergence of product differentiation. In the transportation field, product differentiation among the services of competing types of carriers and between competing carriers of the same type is present, but is evidently more important in passenger transportation than in freight transportation.

Conditions of Entry and Pricing Behavior. The degree of difficulty that a new firm has in entering a field of industry determines how much the already established firms can raise their prices above the defined competitive level without attracting new competition. In effect, the established firms administer a geography of price, with their selling prices restrained according to the barriers of entry. In industries where the conditions of entry are not difficult, the established firms can exceed only slightly the competitive selling price before new competitors will enter; if entry conditions are difficult, the established firms can perhaps attain a monopolistic price—substantially higher than the competitive level—without attracting competitors; if entry conditions are moderately difficult, the established firms can only raise their prices moderately to keep out new competitors.

Thus, J. S. Bain found in his studies that

1. When barriers to entry are either high or moderate, then
   a. among industries of high seller concentration, *limit pricing* to exclude entry is likely. This will result in higher prices and greater monopolistic output restriction according to the height of the barriers to entry.
   b. among industries of moderate to low seller concentration, the preceding tendency is likely to be modified or obscured because intra-industry competition will frequently keep price fairly close to the competitive level.

2. When barriers to entry are low, then
   a. among industries of high seller concentration, periodic high prices and monopolistic output restriction are likely to emerge, followed by induced entry, and further followed by excess plant capacity. The ultimate result may be a significant decrease in seller concentration, an increase in intra-industry competition, and a lessening or elimination of monopolistic tendencies.

b. among industries of moderate to low seller concentration, the pressure of entry plus the inherent tendencies toward strong intra-industry competition are likely to produce close approximations to competitive pricing and output.

Costs, prices, and the degree of concentration of production are thus closely interdependent.

THE CONTINUUM OF ECONOMIES OF SCALE

Economies of scale have become very important in influencing where industries survive, grow, and compete internationally. One conclusion to emerge from Michael Porter's *The Competitive Advantage of Nations* (1990) is that firms that achieve world class are likely to have built their international competitive edge on the continuum of economies of scale from internal to external. The process of accumulating these economies of scale to create a privileged location for a particular industry may begin with the location of a single firm, as when K&B (Koenig and Bauer) moved from England to Oberzell, Bavaria, Germany in 1818 to manufacture printing press machines (Porter, p. 182). The firm grows, achieving internal economies of scale: product-specific, plant-specific, and firm-specific, step by step (Table 7.6). The firm may then promote technological developments among local supply industries to enhance its competitive position, as when K&B helped local paper producers to develop the stronger papers needed by the printing machines, and the German chemical industry to develop synthetic printing

inks. Spin-off companies are created as employees leave the firm to set up business on their own, as when an ex-K&B foreman set up Helbig and Muller in Vienna in 1836, which after various mergers, again become part of K&B in 1921. The growing importance of the industry in the region may lead to the establishment of specialized apprenticeship programs and vocational schools. The industry may gain an important voice in regional and even the national government, ensuring that attention is given to its public infrastructure needs and ensuring public funding of industry-related research in regional universities, to help it maintain its technological and quality advantages. The growing international reputation of the region attracts world-class suppliers to move to the region—as when Linotype moved its headquarters from the United States to Germany in the 1980s. The external economies of scale achieved by the industry in that location now begin to constitute a barrier to the entry of competing firms in different regions. Germany has maintained a competitive edge in the manufacture of printing presses for 160 years. It accounts for half the world's exports of these machines. The explanation for that dominant position does not lie in the local availability or cost of raw materials, or in cheap labor. Instead, it depends on the created advantages of internal and external economies of scale mutually reinforcing themselves in an increasingly privileged location. The fundamental ingredients of the success story of the German printing press industry can be replicated for many different industries in many different countries, and it serves to underline the importance of economies of scale as a primary factor in the survival and growth of economic activity.

TABLE 7.6

Internal and external economies of scale: The continuum

	Type of Economy of Scale	Economy of Scale Depends on	Example of an Economy of Scale Achieved
EXTERNAL (Different firms)	Place-specific (urbanization)	Size of city	Range of urban services
	Industry-specific (Localization)	Size of industry	Research and development
INTERNAL (Same firm)	Firm-specific	Size of firm	Advertising and marketing
	Plant-specific	Size of plant	Larger machines (cube-square law)
	Product-specific	Length and volume of production run	Division of labor

Note: External economies are in part a continuum on the range of economies of scale. They are industry- or place-specific, rather than specific to a particular firm, or to a plant or product within that firm. Sometimes they are a partial substitute for internal economies. Firms internalize economies of scale by integration, and they externalize them by disintegration.

TOPICS FOR DISCUSSION

1. How do the principles of multiples, bulk transactions, massing of reserves, and the engineering principle apply to a particular local industry?

2. Distinguish between the economies of scale owing to large plant size and economies of scale relating to large firm size.

3. Prepare a questionnaire that would be appropriate for the study of economies of scale of a local industry.

4. What advantages does joining a franchise offer to the entrepreneur of a small firm?

5. What are the external economies of scale that accrue to a firm as a result of locating in or near the central business district?

6. What are the external economies of scale offered by industrial parks?

7. What do the size and spacing of plants in different types of industries reveal about the tradeoffs between increasing economies of scale and increasing transportation costs? Does Hoover's margin line help in understanding these tradeoffs as a basis for intrafirm location policy?

8. What are the relationships among the following: minimum efficient scale of operation of an industry, the number of plants in a country, the ubiquity of the industry, and the urban hierarchy?

9. What are the implications for public policy of increasing firm size?

10. If economies of scale are so important, how do you explain the growing relative prominence of small firms?

FURTHER READINGS

BAIN, JOE S. *Barriers to New Competition.* Cambridge, Mass.: Harvard University Press, 1956.

A pioneering work that laid an intellectual foundation for much that followed on the engineering approach to measuring minimum optimal scale as a percent of national capacity, and on product differentiation and other barriers to entry.

ESTALL, R. C. Stock Control in Manufacturing: The Just-in-time System and its Locational Implications. *Area* 17 (1985), 129–133.

Examples from the U.S. automobile industry of the cost of inventories in business and the important economies that can be achieved with the Just-in-time system.

GORECKI, PAUL. *Economies of Scale and Efficient Plant Size in Canadian Manufacturing Industries.* Toronto: McGraw-Hill Ryerson, 1980.

A comprehensive description of economies of scale and the tariff is provided (pp. 67–90) for a country that is concerned about the inefficiencies of an industrial structure that is a miniature replica of the United States.

HAIRE, MASON. "Biological Models and Empirical Histories of the Growth of Organizations." In *Modern Organization Theory,* Vol. I, M. Haire (Ed.). New York: John Wiley, 1959, pp. 272–306.

HOOVER, EDGAR M. *Location Theory and the Shoe and Leather Industry.* Cambridge, Mass.: Harvard University Press, 1937.

One of the great classics on location theory, this book is in two distinct parts: Part I, pp. 3–111, provides a systematic review of location theory within the framework of Alfred Weber (with the developments of Wilhelm Launhardt and Tord Palander). The rest of the book is devoted to two case studies. Economies of scale, discussed in Chapter VI, "Economies of Concentration," pp. 39–111, focuses upon Hoover's concept of the margin line and on the balance of additional production economies less additional delivery costs.

MUND, V. A., and R. H. WOLD. *Industrial Organization and Public Policy.* New York: Meredith Co., 1971.

Like F. M. Scherer's *Industrial Market Structure,* this book is a text for economics courses in market structure, conduct and performance, and their implications for public policy. The authors discuss many topics of interest to economic geographers, such as pricing policies and how prices are set in central markets, in addition to economies of scale.

PORTER, MICHAEL E. *The Competitive Advantage of Nations.* New York: The Free Press, 1990.

A widely reviewed book by an economist. Its numerous case studies show how localization economies improve the cost and quality performance of industry.

PRATTEN, C. F. *Economies of Scale in Manufacturing Industries.* London: Cambridge University Press, 1971.

A detailed study of some two dozen industries, which, together with the 1965 study below, describes the production process, the structure of the industry, cost components, and economies of scale. An excellent source book to use as a foundation for further field study.

PRATTEN, C. F., and R. M. DEAN. *The Economies of Large-Scale Production in British Industry: An Introductory Study.* Cambridge, U.K.: Cambridge University Press, 1965.

An exemplary study of economies of scale in four industries: book printing, footwear manufacture, the steel industry, and oil refining.

RHYS, D. G. "Heavy Commercial Vehicles: The Survival of the Small Firm." *Journal of Industrial Economics,* XX (1971–1972), pp. 230–252.

A well-documented case study of economies of scale.

ROBINSON, E. A. G. *The Structure of Competitive Industry* (rev. ed.). Chicago: University of Chicago Press, 1958.

A lucid statement of economies of scale and their impact on industrial structure, written for the layperson.

SCHERER, F. M. *Industrial Market Structure and Economic Performance* (2d ed.). Chicago: Rand McNally, 1980.

See Chapter 4, "The Determinants of Market Structure," pp. 81–150. A readable, well-referenced book intended for courses in industrial organization and public policy. Chapter 4 covers economies of scale and mergers, providing many examples and brief reviews of key articles on the subject.

SCHERER, F. M., ALAN BECKENSTEIN, ERICH KAUFFER, and R. DENNIS MURPHY. *The Economics of Multi-Plant Operation*. Cambridge, Mass.: Harvard University Press, 1975.

See Chapter 2, "The Economies of Multi-Plant Operation: Interview Evidence," pp. 237–355. A thorough and systematic discussion, enriched with a continuous stream of examples that bring the topic alive. A useful supplement to the industrial market structure chapter (above).

SCOTT, A. J., and D. P. ANGEL. "The U.S. Semi-conductor Industry: A Locational Analysis." *Environment and Planning A*, 19 (1987), 875–912.

A case study of how localization economies create privileged locations for specific industries and enable them to achieve a competitive edge.

8

Preference Structures and Uncertain Environments

OVERVIEW

In Chapter 2 we introduced the concept of an omniscient and single-minded rational being, the Economic Maximizer, who—with perfect knowledge of present circumstances and future alternatives—is able to maximize utility by building an optimally scaled factory in an ideal location, or to combine resources and technology to achieve the "highest and best" land use.

A second image is of rational decision-makers who, facing uncertainty, become strategists. Strategists optimize their outcomes and control risks, perhaps using game theory. Current research by social scientists points increasingly to a third image, decision-makers as satisficers. Satisficers do not correctly evaluate their information; they cut their problems down to size, and they follow simple heuristic rules of thumb in making their choices. Each of these three different kinds of decision-maker produces a different geography of economic activity.

OBJECTIVES

- to describe decision-makers as economic maximizers, optimizing strategists, and heuristic satisficers
- to learn about preference maps and principles of choice among alternatives by an economic maximizer
- to explore ideas of bounded rationality and satisficing behavior
- to explain strategic choices when the "law of requisite variety" holds and the theory of games can be utilized to control uncertainty

THREE IMAGES OF DECISION-MAKERS

Classical economic theory tells us what decisions will be made and the economic landscapes that will result if decision-makers know all the answers and act rationally to maximize profits. At the microscale, for instance, the optimal mix of crops needed to maximize income on an individual farm can be calculated. We can even calculate how that optimal mix progressively changes with the distance that an imported farm input such as grain has to be transported, as we shall see. At the macroscale, Chapter 9 explains how land is allocated to various urban uses within a city, and to competing rural uses beyond, in such income-maximizing fashions.

This profile of economic maximizers assumes that decision-makers have perfect knowledge of all alternatives available; know exactly the payoffs, outcomes, and consequences of each alternative; possess a consistent order of preferences of the alternatives; and have a rigorous set of rules and procedures that enable them to act rationally to achieve the best results.

Decision-makers are not omniscient, however. Information is never complete. Judgments about uncertain environments are often nothing more than "guesstimates." But researchers have come up with a startling conclusion: *Risk and uncertainty do not necessarily rule out maximizing profits.* They do make decision making a little more interesting. The rule is that each risk can be neutralized by a counterstrategy. Is it sometimes too dry? Then irrigate. Too wet? Then drain. Insects bad? Spray. Cold? Get out the smudge pots. Each environmental risk is a strategy that must be regulated and controlled by a counterstrategy. The greater the variety of strategies played by the environment, the greater must be the variety of strategies available to the decision-maker.

"For only variety can destroy variety and nothing else can."[1] Provided that this *law of requisite variety* is satisfied, an optimal solution exists to counter any set of risks. That solution can be found by applying the *theory of games.* Without the requisite variety, the decision-maker stands to lose. Nature and the market can combine to play strategies for which there are no satisfactory replies. And such cases do occur: Witness all the uninhabited regions of the world shown on the population maps. With requisite variety, variety in the environment can be controlled by changing the structure and organization of production, however: Observe the map of world agricultural regions where

each change in climatic type is countered with a change in land use and farming type. Here then is a second image of the decision-maker, the decision-maker as *strategist*, controlling and regulating the risks and uncertainties of the environment, whether physical or human, to optimize output.

Current research in the social sciences points increasingly towards a third model of decision-makers as *satisficers* whose rationality is limited by (1) systematic biases in how they weigh up the information available to them; (2) the complexity of situations they face and their need to cut problems down to size; (3) the incompleteness and inadequacy of their information and their need to develop simple rules of thumb.

These three models of decision-makers are then quite different. The economic maximizer model, the first of the three to be developed, was one of the great intellectual achievements of economics in the first half of the century. This first model is very mathematical and makes rigorous assumptions, but it does suggest how the geography of price creates spatial rhythms of income effects and substitution effects. The second model relaxes the assumption of perfect knowledge and springs from the theory of games first published in complete form in 1944 by the mathematicians Von Neumann and Morgenstern. Coupled with Ashby's Law of Requisite Variety, the second model suggests a stimulating way of viewing the geography of agriculture.

The third model of decision-makers began to emerge in the 1950s, from the work of Herbert A. Simon. Simon was awarded the Nobel prize in 1978 for his contribution of the concept of the decision-maker as a satisficer, acting without either perfect knowledge or perfect reason. Satisficers create a third economic geography, which is affected by the spatial pattern of information flows as well as cultural and other factors.

THE DECISION-MAKER AS ECONOMIC MAXIMIZER

The decision-maker as economic maximizer is most easily demonstrated by a detailed case study of farm management. Consider the case of Farmer Jones, engaged in dairying in the state of Iowa. He wants to know what combination of grain and hay he should feed his cattle to maximize milk output and he wants to be able to determine how to crop his land to feed his cattle in an optimal manner. He decides to ask Professor Smith, an agricultural economist at the Iowa State Agricultural Experiment Station, for advice. Professor Smith suggests an experiment. Farmer Jones has a herd of larger-sized Holstein and Brown Swiss cows, each of which has an expected output capacity of 300

[1] W. Ross Ashby, *Introduction to Cybernetics* (London: John Wiley, 1956), p. 207.

to 400 pounds of butterfat annually. The professor suggests that Farmer Jones feed the cattle different combinations of legume hay, corn silage, and grain, and chart the resulting variations in milk output.

This Farmer Jones does, and later on he brings the results to Professor Smith for analysis. The professor begins by plotting Farmer Jones's data in a graph, as in Figure 8.1. The two axes record amounts of grain and hay fed to the cows. Each dot represents one cow, with the milk output noted beside each dot. The next step is to interpolate contour lines showing combinations of feeds resulting in identical levels of output. For example, the 8500-pound contour traces out those combinations of grain and hay that yield 8500 pounds of milk per cow. From a production standpoint, the professor tells Farmer Jones that if he wants this level of output per cow he can feed each of his cows 6000 pounds of grain and 5000 of hay or 3000 pounds of grain and 9000 pounds of hay, or indeed any combination of feeds along the line between. What is important, the professor says, is that Farmer Jones should be *indifferent* to these combinations of feedstuffs from a milk-production standpoint along any particular indifference curve. Each combination on a given curve works equally well, yielding equal milk outputs. The contours can therefore be called *equal-product curves,* or *indifference curves.*

Indifference Curves and the Preference Map

In Figure 8.1, a second indifference curve has been drawn at a higher level of output (9500 pounds).

Clearly, many such curves could be interpolated in the graph, and one thing Professor Smith calculated was the mathematical equation describing the shape of the curves so that he could visualize them on the figure. This equation appears in the caption for Figure 8.1. A whole set of curves in a tradeoff graph, such as Figure 8.1, describes Farmer Jones's *preference map*, with higher levels of achievement moving upwards to the right. The curves are all convex to the origin because grain and hay are not perfect substitutes for each other in feeding the cattle. For example, if a cow is producing 8500 pounds of milk, and it is being fed 5000 pounds of hay and 6154 pounds of grain, 1 pound of hay can be substituted for 1.55 pounds of grain and the milk output will remain the same. At the other extreme, however (reading along the indifference curve), if 11,000 pounds of hay and 2281 pounds of grain are being used to produce 8500 pounds of milk, 1 pound of hay only does the same job as 0.26 pounds of grain. When a great deal of any one item is being used or consumed, its relative worth is much less than if a little of it is being used (the principle of decreasing marginal utility of resources as the amount used increases).

The Production-Opportunity Line and the System of Isoquants

The preference map is the first ingredient that Professor Smith needs to answer Farmer Jones's question about feed mixtures and cropping patterns. The second ingredient relates to what Farmer Jones can produce on his land. Let us suppose that he has 100 acres

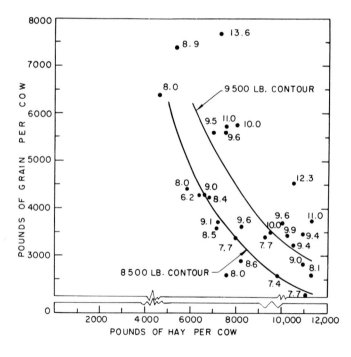

FIGURE 8.1 Equal product contours (feed combinations), at 8500 and 9500 pounds of milk per cow. Contours interpolated using the production function, $Y = 3.56 X_1^{0.5035} X_2^{0.4}$, where Y is the output of milk and X_1 and X_2 are hay and grain, respectively. Thus, for 8500 pounds of milk, the input combinations yielding the 8500-pound contour are given by $X_2 = (8500/3.56 X_1^{0.5035})^{2.5}$. [*Source:* Earl O. Heady and Russell O. Olson, *Substitution Relationships, Resource Requirements and Income Variability in the Utilization of Forage Crops* (Ames, Iowa: Research Bulletin 390, Agricultural Experiment Station, Iowa State University, 1952).]

at his disposal to grow hay, grain, or some combination of the two feedstuffs. He might be able to produce, say, 200,000 pounds of grain (2000 pounds per acre) or 500,000 pounds of hay (5000 pounds per acre) by using the land entirely for one or the other, or he could grow some combination of the two.

What should he produce, he asks Professor Smith, to maximize milk yields if he restricts his herd to 8500-pound milk-yielders? And what size herd should he maintain? Professor Smith makes some rapid calculations. Ten times the figures that can be read off the 8500-pound contour in Figure 8.1 shows feed needed for 10 cows; adding a zero to that obtains the input requirements for 100 cows.

The professor then draws another graph—Figure 8.2—with the results of these calculations in it. First, he plots Farmer Jones's *production-opportunity line,* which shows what feeds he can produce on his 100 acres: either 200,000 pounds of grain, or 500,000 pounds of hay, or some combination of the two, depending on how much land he uses for one or the other. Second, he plots contours for the results of his calculations showing total input requirements for different herd sizes. These contours are called *isoquants,* and they were the ones produced by the calculations described above. Each isoquant records the input combinations that will produce an equal quantity of output. Thus, the lowest isoquant in Figure 8.2 charts the varying combinations of inputs required to support a 25-cow herd of 8500-pound milk-yielders. The highest isoquant is for double that herd size, and the middle one is for 30 cows, which will together yield 255,000 pounds of milk.

The professor then shows Farmer Jones why it is

impossible to feed a herd of 50 cows and expect 8500 pounds of milk per cow. The highest isoquant in the graph requires far more feed than can be produced on 100 acres of land. Similarly, although the farmer could crop his land in a way that would just feed a 25-cow herd of 8500-pound producers (point A in Figure 8.2), he can do better than that. The production-opportunity line extends above the 25-cow isoquant in places, so that by producing somewhat more hay and less grain on his 100 acres he can still get 8500 pounds of milk per cow and support a herd of 30 cows (point B in Figure 8.2). At this point—the highest isoquant reachable with the production-possibility line—some 270,000 pounds of hay and 90,000 pounds of grain are produced on the farm and result in a total output of 255,000 pounds of milk. This, Professor Smith tells Farmer Jones, is the way to maximize milk output in any *given* year.

The Effect of Complementary Production Relationships over Time

But Professor Smith points out that Farmer Jones can do even better than this if he grows his crops in rotation, managing his farm properly over a *period* of years. In Figure 8.2 it was assumed that the crops were *competitive,* that is, that any increase in acreage of one resulted in a correspondingly proportional decrease in acreage—and therefore in output—of the other. But crops grown in rotation may be *complementary* in that growing one may increase the yields of the other in the following year. Grasses and legumes, for example, accumulate nitrogen and therefore increase yields of the subsequent year's crops. Professor Smith provides a

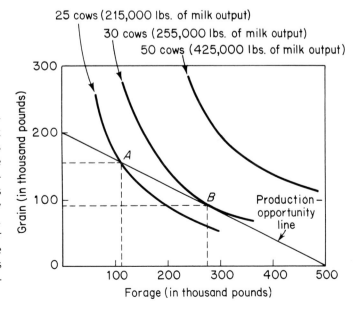

FIGURE 8.2 Determination of cropping pattern and herd size. The milk output contours are isoquants: lines of equal output from each possible combination of inputs. The maximum possible combination of inputs the farmer can produce is given by the production opportunity line. Hence the largest isoquant the farmer can sustain is indicated at B, where the isoquant for 30 cows just touches (is tangent to) the production-opportunity line.

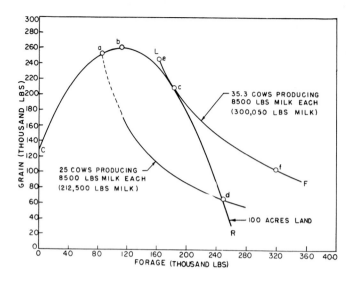

FIGURE 8.3 Substitution of forage for grain in crop production and milk production. Without crop rotation the farmer could support a herd of 30 cows. The larger output made possible by rotation is indicated by the curve abcd. This larger output makes possible a herd of 35 cows, with the amounts of grain and forage given by the coordinates of c. [*Source:* Heady and Olson, 1952.]

simple example to Farmer Jones (Figure 8.3). This was drawn from experimental data he had previously obtained from rotations grown on Marshall silt loam soil at the Page County Experimental Farm in Iowa. In Figure 8.3, the curve *CabcdR* indicates the output of grain and forage derived from 100 acres of land when the two crops are grown in rotation. The production-opportunity line is not straight, but convex upwards, indicating that the farmer might be able to crop his land and support a 35-cow herd of 8500-pound pro-

ducers, giving a total output of 300,000 pounds of milk, if he practiced proper crop rotations. Farmer Jones, seeing that point *c* is higher up in his preference map than, for example, points *a* and *d*, at either of which he could only support a herd of 25 cows, readily agrees that he should find the right crop rotation for his soils and climate.

What rotation scheme should then be used? Farmer Jones inquired next. The professor provided a series of examples of three-, four-, and five-year rota-

TABLE 8.1

Complementary and competitive relationships in forage production for two soil types (data for 100 acres of land)

Rotation[a]	Acres of Land out of 100 in		Total Production (pounds)		Pounds of Grain Sacrificed for Each Pound of Hay Added over Previous Rotation
	Grain	Hay	Grain	Hay	
Wooster and Canfield silt loams, Wooster, Ohio, 1937–1943[b]					
C	100	0	217,840	—	
C–C–C–W–A	80	20	229,776	128,800	Complementary
C–W–A	67	33	215,480	203,200	0.19
C–C–W–A–A	60	40	190,672	316,000	0.22
C–W–A–A	50	50	165,928	363,000	0.53
Clarion-Webster silt loam, Ames, Iowa, 1945–1948[c]					
C	100	0	180,320	—	
C–C–O–Cl	75	25	217,360	85,000	Complementary
C–O–Cl	67	33	182,333	132,660	0.71

Source: Earl O. Heady and Russell O. Olson, *Substitution Relationships, Resource Requirements and Income Variability in the Utilization of Forage Crops* (Ames, Iowa: Research Bulletin 390, Agricultural Experiment Station, Iowa State University, 1952).

[a] C, corn; O, oats; W, wheat; Cl, clover; A, alfalfa.

[b] See R. E. Yoder, "Results of Agronomic Research on the Use of Lime and Fertilizers in Ohio," Ohio Agr. Exp. Sta. Agron. 96 (Mimeo), 1945.

[c] From unpublished data, Dept. of Agronomy, Iowa Agr. Exp. Sta., Ames, Iowa, 1915–1948.

tions, compared with single-cropping corn (Table 8.1). From such data, he and the farmer quickly determine an appropriate cultivation plan. Farmer Jones has the information he needs to make the best choices among the alternatives available to him.

Price Changes and the Price Consumption Curve

If Farmer Jones operated a feed lot instead of cultivating the land, and bought his forage and grain on the open market, his herd size and feed mix would be determined by the funds available to purchase feeds, rather than the cropping capability of his land. Herd size and feed mix would also be subject to fluctuations in grain and hay prices. The effects are illustrated in Figure 8.4. The graph shows a succession of isoquants. For purposes of this example, it is assumed that the farmer spends a fixed sum on forage and grain. If all the money is spent on forage, OF can be purchased

Now, let forage prices remain constant, but grain prices change. When grain prices are high, only G_4 can be bought, and the farmer's *price-possibility line* is G_4F. This line, in a manner analogous to the production-possibility line discussed earlier, describes what can be purchased with the funds (or resources) available. The optimal herd size and mix of input purchases is given by point A. If the grain price falls, however, purchases of grain can be increased to G_3, G_2, etc. The equilibrium moves from A to B, C, and D on higher isoquants. Because grain prices are lower, more milk can be produced, and relatively larger shares of grain will appear in the feed mix. The line charted by the successive points A, B, C, and D is a *price-consumption curve* (or "satisfaction path").

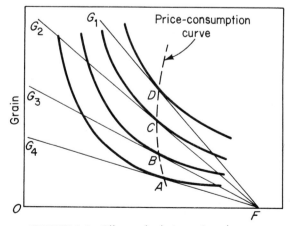

FIGURE 8.4 Effects of relative price changes.

Price Effects, Income Effects, and Substitution Effects

Movement along the price-consumption curve as prices fall is called a *price effect*, which has two parts:

1. An *income effect;* that is, as price falls, the farmer moves on to a higher isoquant, main-

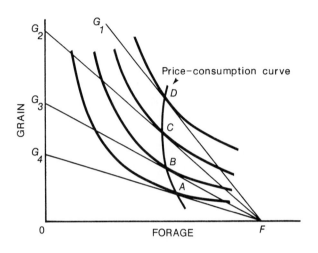

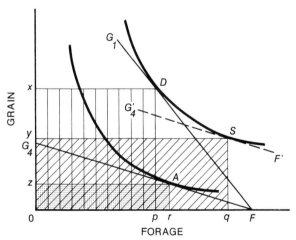

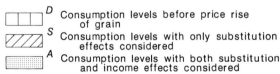

D Consumption levels before price rise of grain
S Consumption levels with only substitution effects considered
A Consumption levels with both substitution and income effects considered

FIGURE 8.5 Separating the income and substitution effects. The increase in grain price from G_4 to G_1 changes the ratio of grain to forage crops from G_4F' (parallel to G_4F) to G_1F. The substitution effect moves consumption from D to S (on the same isoquant), reduces grain consumption by yx, and increases forage consumption by pq. The income effect takes the farmer from S to A, on a lower isoquant, reducing grain consumption by zy and decreasing forage consumption by rq.

tains a larger herd, produces more, and becomes better off.

2. A *substitution effect;* that is, because the relative price of grain and forage changes with a move along the curve, the farmer tends to use more of the input that has become relatively cheaper, substituting it for the other in his input mix (see Figure 8.5).

Construction of Demand Curves

It is from the price-consumption curve that the farmer's *demand schedule* or *demand curve* can be constructed. For example, each of the points, *A*, *B*, *C*, and *D* in Figure 8.4 shows how much grain will be purchased at different grain prices. If this information is plotted in a price-quantity graph, the farmer's demand schedule for grain will be apparent: As the price falls, the quantity consumed increases.

CONSEQUENCES OF SPATIAL VARIATIONS IN PRICES

In Chapter 6 we saw how many prices increased with increasing distance from market centers because of the effect of transportation costs. What are the consequences? Restricting ourselves for the moment to the agricultural example presented above, if grain is shipped in from some central market, the more distant farmers

1. Use more forage, substituting the cheaper input for the more expensive one;

2. Have smaller herds, and produce less on a given acreage, that is, they are less intensive;

3. Earn less.

Because there are both income and substitution effects of price changes, as prices increase with distance, quantity consumed decreases, producing as a result, *spatial demand cones* of the kind discussed in Chapter 6.

Regional Variations in Welfare

The price effects of increasing distance include both income effects (people are less affluent) and substitution effects (activities are less intensive). The resulting regional variations appear and reappear in a variety of aspects of life throughout the world, where one of the most marked spatial differences is between affluent, growing activity in core regions where prices are de-

termined, and lagging peripheries, less advanced, with greater poverty populations, and with far more extensive production patterns.

To illustrate, Figure 8.6 presents a series of graphs constructed as part of a study of regional development in the United States using data from the 1960 census. The horizontal axis in each of the 12 cases covers the 270 miles from Dallas to Houston-Galveston, Texas. The vertical axis of each shows how different characteristics vary from place to place along this 270-mile stretch. The first graph on the second row shows that income levels drop with increasing distance from Dallas, rise around Bryan, fall again, then rise toward Houston. This is the income effect described above. Similar patterns will be found in each of the other graphs. In each case the *distance-gradients* reflect spatial adjustments resulting from the income and substitution effects of price increases. For example, as the extent of commuting to jobs in the metropolitan centers declines with distance from the metropolises (top left-hand graph), population densities, the proportion of the population classified as urban, the value of land and buildings, income, amount of schooling, rate of population increase, and percent change in the population through migration all decline. The percentage of the population classified as *rural nonfarm* rises and then falls. Both the percentage of families with incomes less than $3000 (the 1960 poverty line) and the unemployment rate increase with distance from the central city.

The repeating patterns of change create a spatial rhythm which symbolizes a *regional welfare syndrome*. The lowest levels of welfare are to be found at the peripheries of major metropolitan regions, where prices are highest and economic opportunities are least.

That the population is responding to these systematic variations in welfare is also implied, for population is generally decreasing at the outer edges of the metropolitan regions, responding to differences in incomes and opportunities by migrating from areas of low opportunity to the metropolitan centers that are perceived to offer greater advantages.

FIGURE 8.6 Socioeconomic gradients along a 270-mile traverse from Dallas to Galveston, Texas. The graphs have been plotted using U.S. census data from 1960. Each graph illustrates the same 270 miles from Dallas through Bryan, to Houston and Galveston. Locations of the towns are indicated at the bottom of each column. Note how incomes rise and fall in relation to the intensity of commuting to urban centers. Other characteristics rise and fall in the same manner.

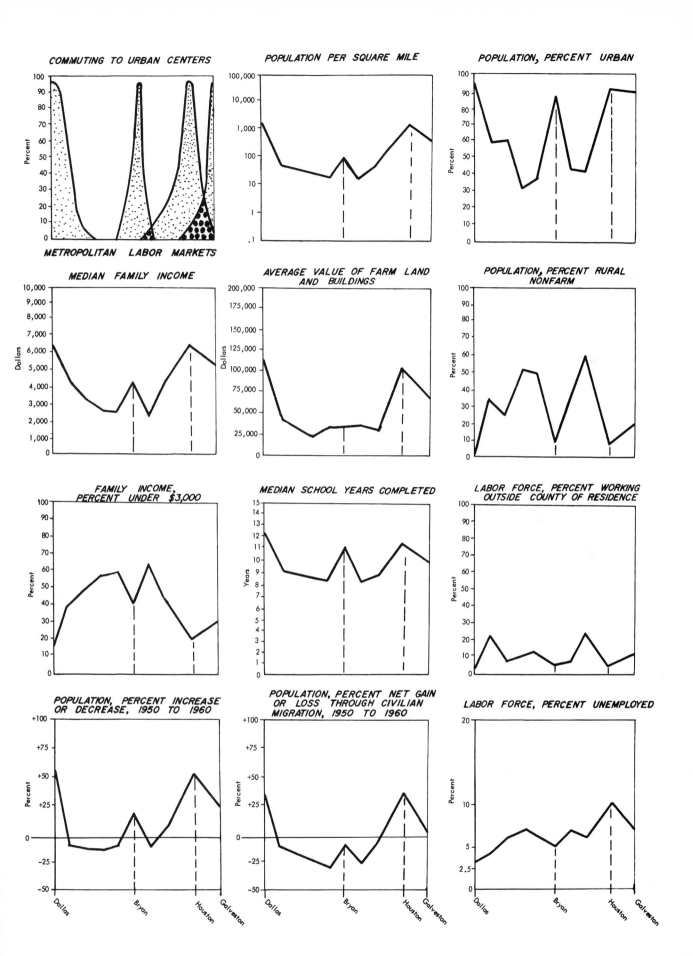

COMMUTING TO URBAN CENTERS

POPULATION PER SQUARE MILE

POPULATION, PERCENT URBAN

METROPOLITAN LABOR MARKETS

MEDIAN FAMILY INCOME

AVERAGE VALUE OF FARM LAND AND BUILDINGS

POPULATION, PERCENT RURAL NONFARM

FAMILY INCOME, PERCENT UNDER $3,000

MEDIAN SCHOOL YEARS COMPLETED

LABOR FORCE, PERCENT WORKING OUTSIDE COUNTY OF RESIDENCE

POPULATION, PERCENT INCREASE OR DECREASE, 1950 TO 1960

POPULATION, PERCENT NET GAIN OR LOSS THROUGH CIVILIAN MIGRATION, 1950 TO 1960

LABOR FORCE, PERCENT UNEMPLOYED

239

OPTIMIZING OUTPUT
IN UNCERTAIN ENVIRONMENTS

Environmental Uncertainty

The economic maximizer described in the preceding section rarely fits the reality of geography. Geography, by its very nature, is concerned with interrelationships between human beings and their environment. The environment is thought of as being primarily the physical environment: climate, soil, vegetation, and physiography. For the economic geographer, economic environment is important, too, including sources of raw material, location of markets, availability of labor, transportation facilities, and price levels. But whether the environment affecting production is primarily physical or economic, environmental conditions inevitably vary from time to time and from place to place, and these variations can create risks for the producer. Climate, for instance, has been described as average weather conditions. Average rainfall is just that, and the variability tends to increase the lower the average is. But the lower the average is, the smaller the margin may be between adequate and inadequate rainfall and the greater the risk to crops and livestock posed by any shortfall.

Risk and uncertainty may appear on first consideration to reduce decision making to a blind game of chance. The reader may well argue that if we cannot be certain of environmental conditions we cannot determine an optimal decision. Decisions based on average conditions may be wrong more often than right as actual conditions constantly fluctuate. To base decisions on averages is to ignore variety. And what if the data are not adequate to provide meaningful averages? What, in fact, if the environment is quite unpredictable? Surely that spells an end to rational decision making. Not really. A way of taking account of such risk, predictable or otherwise, is provided by the *theory of games*. This approach, first brought to the attention of geographers by Peter Gould (1963), provides a powerful tool for optimizing decisions in the face of uncertainty. This theory and the *law of requisite variety* on which it is based call for a second model of the decision-maker as a strategist optimizing output in uncertain environments. This approach also calls for a number of changes in the way that environmental uncertainty is viewed.

First, implicit in the theory of games and the law of requisite variety is the idea that the *number* of types of uncertainty is more important than any single quantitative measure of the aggregate *level* of risk. The distinction between number and level of variations in the environment is therefore critical. Variations in environmental conditions are viewed qualitatively, not quantitatively. For example, if the minimum rainfall for a successful wheat crop is 10 inches, then 6 inches may be as bad as 4 inches. A miss is as good as a mile. And if the wheat needs 90 days to mature, and there was an early frost killing the crop, it scarcely matters whether it was one week or two weeks before harvest. Similarly, it is more important to know that sometimes farmers lose their crops because of drought and sometimes because of frost than to know that any one farmer has lost it on average one year in seven. If drought is the farmer's only problem, then only one set of solutions is called for. But if there is also a problem of frost, then a second, and separate, set of considerations is called for. And once environmental variety has been turned from adversity into diversity and neutralized from risk to event, then the frequency of these events loses its economic impact.

The list of environmental elements that may vary significantly is specific to the group of products, the time, and the place involved. For the farmer they may be physical factors such as drought, frost, soil conditions, and danger of hail, and economic factors such as interest rates, market prices, prices of farm equipment, and transportation rates. For the industrialist, they may be past prices and supply of components, changes in market tastes, obsolescence due to technological breakthroughs, and changes in government legislation affecting taxes, consumer protection, competition from imports, and permitted increases in wages and prices. The important thing is for the decision-maker to know which elements of the environment may vary, and to have a countervailing strategy to control and regulate the impact of each of them, whatever the risk. Only if the risk is so slight and predictable that it can be insured against, would the decision-maker ignore it in the decision making. Otherwise it should be considered and a strategy-mix developed to cover all possibilities. Strangely enough, the theory of games does offer a strategy-mix that optimizes output even when the probability of each event is unknown.

It follows that we should think in terms of environmental variety rather than environmental risk. The environment poses risks only if our decisions make certain environmental conditions a risk to our output. A particular amount of rainfall is not an intrinsic risk to agriculture. It is the actual decision as to what crops to grow that makes any particular rainfall level a potential risk. If our decisions are taken to accommodate the possibility of low rainfall, then low rainfall is one variety of environmental condition, and no more.

Time and Place in the Strategy-Mix

Variety in the environment must be regulated and controlled if we are to regulate output, wherever and whenever it occurs. In this sense variety between locations at one point in time is as important as variety at one location over time. Variety between locations in climate, mineral deposits, and market accessibility may be regulated by producing different goods. From this standpoint, economic geography is the study of how human beings take advantage of variety in the environment to satisfy the full variety of human needs and wants, by turning environmental variety into advantage rather than risk. Similarly, the decision-maker can control the impact of environmental variety over time in one location by following a mixed strategy rather than concentrating on some single product. There is, however, an important difference between the two situations. Variety across space can be countervailed by location-specific strategies tailored to the conditions at each location. Variety through time is less predictable in the short run and must be countervailed by a mixed strategy that accommodates variety at the location over time. For instance, if in one location the optimal strategy were to allocate 70 percent of the land to sheep and 30 percent to wheat, it would add up to the same thing statistically in the long run if farmers proportioned their land use each year or if farmers divided themselves into sheep specialists and wheat specialists and proportioned out the land aggregatively, or if the farmers allocated all the land to sheep seven years in 10, and to wheat the other three. Practical decision-makers, concerned with the here and now rather than long-term statistical averages, are likely to opt for an annual proportionment. The point is that diversity over time is more difficult to regulate than variety across space. It is precisely in this situation, then, that the theory of games has its biggest contribution to make.

THEORY OF GAMES

The Rules of the Game

The *theory of games* is a rigorous and sophisticated mathematical approach to decision making in the face of uncertainty. It was developed primarily by the Hungarian-American mathematician John Von Neumann. The approach received wide attention in the social sciences with the publication by Von Neumann and O. Morgenstern of their book *Theory of Games and Economic Behavior* (1944). The simplest interesting applications involve two adversaries although the theory can be applied no matter what the number.

The theory assumes that there is a specific, predetermined outcome, or payoff, for every combination of strategies used by the players. Assume two players: a farmer versus the physical environment. The farmer (and in theory the environment too), know just what the yield will be for each crop under each set of climatic conditions. For instance, I plant corn, and the climate plays its short, cool, dry summer. Result: The corn does not grow quite as high as Rogers and Hammerstein's elephant's eye. Often the loser pays the predetermined amount to the winner, but whether this is so or not, it is assumed that each player wants to maximize winnings, or at least minimize losses.

The application of the theory of games to geographic examples involving the physical environment personifies nature. Nature becomes an unyielding opponent, relentlessly trying to outwit people in the vital task of earning their daily bread. This implied personification does not invalidate applications of the theory of games to geography but it does raise questions about the meaning of the results, which are presented as a conclusion to this section.

To see how the theory of games applies let us begin with a simple hypothetical example where the producer's strategy collapses to a single dominant choice. Imagine a farmer trying to decide whether to produce wheat or corn (or some combination of the two). The choice is dependent on the growing season, which can be wet or dry. Furthermore, rainfall has proved to be completely unpredictable so that the farmer has no way of knowing which it is likely to be. The farmer, an enthusiastic fan of Von Neumann, draws up a payoff matrix (Table 8.2). The farmer observes that the yields are lower for both corn and wheat in dry years. Nevertheless, the 10 bushels of wheat is better than 1 bushel of corn. But in a wet year

TABLE 8.2

Hypothetical payoffs in farmer versus environment

Farmer's Strategies	Environment's Strategies		Row Minimum
	Wet	Dry	
Corn	45	1	1
Wheat	35	10	10
Column maximum	45	10	

Note: Figures are in bushels per acre and are hypothetical. The important point is that the highest row minimum (10 bushels) is the same as the lowest column maximum. This strategy is then the best for each player.

the 45 bushels of corn is much better than the 35 bushels of wheat. So which should the farmer choose?

Assume each player is trying to do the best one can. If the farmer consistently goes for corn, the environment would consistently go for a dry-year strategy to minimize its losses. The farmer, realizing this was a sequence of dry years, would switch to wheat. But even with this switch to wheat, the environment would be better to stick with the dry strategy. The environment's minimum maximum, namely 10 bushels, equates the farmer's maximum minimum. The strategies, given a miserly environment, will lock into this single wheat-dry strategy. It does not pay either player to change even though both players will have guessed the other's strategy. Prior knowledge does not benefit either player. One strategy dominates the others. The collapse of the farmer's corn strategy suggests the need for alternative strategies—perhaps growing millet or sorghum or perhaps introducing livestock. The single wheat strategy fails to meet the requisite variety imposed by the environment. Let us now, then, take a real example that does meet the requisite variety and where a mixed strategy has evolved.

A Jamaican Fishing Village.   The anthropologist William Davenport (1960) has provided a vivid example of how the theory of games can be applied to understanding humanity's struggle against the environment with a study of the problems faced by 200 villagers on the south coast of Jamaica. The men of this village are all fishermen and make their living entirely by fishing in the local waters by canoe and selling their catch on the island. The fishing grounds extend 22 miles out to sea with the inshore (or "inside") banks extending out as far as 5 miles to 15 miles. Beyond are the offshore (or "outside") banks. This distinction is important. Very strong currents flow at frequent intervals in either direction across the offshore banks. The seas can be much rougher too. But the rewards for successful fishing on the offshore banks are considerably greater. Is it worth the risk?

The decision of where to fish must be made by each fishing captain. There are 26 of these, each with his or her own crew. In coming to a decision, a good many factors have to be considered. The outside banks yield fish of higher grade and larger size. But if strong currents flow for several days on end, the floats become waterlogged and the pots and their catch are lost. Even short periods of currents can cause havoc by dragging pots against rock outcrops and coral and by killing the catch with sudden water temperature changes. Equipment costs for offshore fishing are higher too because, in addition to a higher rate of pot replacement, stronger canoes are needed, which after

a few years use are suitable for inshore use only and so must be replaced. The method of paying the crew also has to be considered. Two methods are employed. Either the crew are allowed to set some pots for themselves or they are given part of the catch plus a small wage. But on days when the crew with pots catch nothing, the captain is obliged to pay them a wage even if he has caught nothing himself. Now how can all this be set out in a form that will permit us to calculate their optimal strategy? The answer is to reduce the toil, risk, and heartbreak of the different outcomes to the common denominator of hard cash profit or loss. Davenport concludes that a fisherman opting to work the offshore banks exclusively for a month (in fact none do) could stand to make £20 profit if there were no currents, but to lose £4 if currents flowed throughout the month.

The exercise must now be repeated for the inshore option. Profits here are much lower, but the risks are less. This strategy yields its highest income when things go badly for the offshore fishermen. With the offshore catch lost, competition is reduced and inshore fishermen can earn as much as £17 a month. But better times for the offshore fishermen brings in a supply of better-quality fish, thus forcing their income down to a monthly equivalent of £12. A mixed strategy is also possible with captains locating pots both inshore and offshore.

The results of the alternative strategies are summarized in Table 8.3. The figures are Davenport's, and they show three separate strategies for fishermen: inshore, offshore, and mixed. We can now calculate the proper strategy for the fishermen.

First note that a 2 × 3 game should reduce to a 2 × 2 game for the fishermen should use the very best available countervailing strategy for each environmental strategy. Two environmental strategies exist. The two best countervailing strategies only should be used. A third is redundant and is included in the study by

TABLE 8.3

Jamaican fishermen versus the sea: The payoffs

Fishing Strategies	Environment Strategies		Row Minimum
	Current	No Current	
Inshore	17.3	11.5	11.5*
Mixed	5.2	17.0	5.2
Offshore	−4.4	20.6	+
Column maximum	17.3	17.0**	

Note: The figures are from William Davenport (1960) in £ sterling and are computed on the basis of a one-month period. Davenport uses the terms *inside* and *outside* rather than *inshore* and *offshore.*

+, The offshore strategy is dominated by the mixed strategy. *, The highest row minimum is different than the lowest column maximum (**). A mixed-strategy of inshore and mixed inshore-offshore fishing will be best.

Davenport only for the sake of completeness and to illustrate how one strategy can sometimes dominate another. In the case of the Jamaican fishermen, none uses the offshore strategy. Compare the offshore and mixed strategies in Table 8.3. The row minimums are £5.2 and −£4.4. If fisherman picked the mixed strategy, the worst they can do is £5.2. The column maximums are £5.2 and £20.6. The environment might have to pay out £20.6 if it picks the no-current strategy. The worst it does is a £5.2 payout with the current strategy. So given only these two sets of choices the game would reduce to a mixed/current play with a £5.2 payoff to fisherman. We shall return to the interpretation of environment in this context later. For the moment, note that the theory of games confirms the simple lesson learned long ago by the fishermen through trial and error: Offshore fishing is too risky to be practised exclusively.

Compare the inshore and mixed strategies in Table 8.3. Neither strategy dominates the other; both should be used. There are two approaches to calculating the proportions: graphical and mathematical. The graphical approach helps us to understand the basic philosophy of the theory of games. Plot to scale the payoffs from the two fishing strategies using, say, the left vertical axis for current and right axis for no current (Figure 8.7). Connect corresponding points to produce an inshore strategy line (going from £17.3 to £11.5 on the two axes) and a mixed strategy line (connecting £5.2 on the current axis to £17.0 on the no-current axis). It turns out that where the two strategy payoff lines intersect gives the optimal "minimax" strategy. Scaling the horizontal axis to provide the percentage mix for the two strategies indicates that 33 percent of canoe fishing trips should allocate some pots inshore, some offshore: the mixed strategy. The balance, 67 percent, should play it safe and put all pots inshore. The theory of games does not solve the problem for an individual fisherman on an individual day. He still has to make the decision, but on balance, the village as a whole will expect to do best if the 26 canoes are allocated in this way and, using the mixed strategy, 18 stay inshore.

This graphical solution helps us to visualize what the theory of games does. Assume the environment wants to reduce the individual fisherman's catch to a minimum. Then the minimum maximum is the best the fisherman can hope for. Using this mix, the minimum payoff will be £13.3. And if the environment turns out to be more benevolent than portrayed in the theory of games, the payoff would be higher.

The mathematical solution is not complicated; however, it is not obvious either. The formula is set out in Table 8.4. The steps are these:

1. Calculate the difference between the two payoffs. The smaller the difference the smaller the risk attached to that strategy.

2. Risk is minimized by playing each strategy more frequently the lower its risk, and the greater the risk of the alternative strategy. The ratio with which any strategy should be used is the difference in the payoff of the competing strategy, divided by the difference in the strategy itself.

Applying the formula gives the same results as the graphical, of course, with a few decimal points thrown in as a bonus. The results for the fishermen's optimal strategy mix, showing the environment and the income that results, are set out in Tables 8.5 and 8.6.

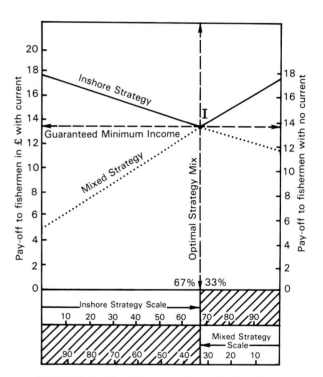

FIGURE 8.7 Graphical solution to the Jamaican fishing village strategy problem. Plot the income for each fishing strategy on the axes for current and no current, and join corresponding points. The maximum income under various mixes of current-no current conditions is given by the upper *V* above the intersection point *I*. Assume environment will force income to a minimum. Then the minimum maximum is the best obtainable solution, yielding about £13 income a month with two-thirds inshore, one-third mixed fishing. Point *I* is thus the "minimax" solution to the fisherman's problem.

TABLE 8.4

Formula for allocating competing strategies

Your Strategies	Payoff Given the Opponent's Strategies		Difference in Payoff	Proportion of Turns to Use Each Strategy
	A	B		
I	a	b	$(b - a)$	$\dfrac{(d - c)}{(b - a) + (d - c)}$
II	c	d	$(d - c)$	$\dfrac{(b - a)}{(b - a) + (d - c)}$

ratio of turns to use strategy $I = \dfrac{d - c}{b - a}$

Note: (i) a, b, c, and d are the payoffs for each combination of strategies.
(ii) The differences in your payoffs are $(b - a)$ and $(d - c)$.
(iii) Use strategy I: $(d - c)/[(b - a) + (d - c)]$ proportion of the turns.
(iv) Use strategy I: $(d - c)/(b - a)$ ratio of the turns.
(v) In calculating differences, ignore minus signs.

The Meaning of the Results. How do the results obtained by using the theory of games compare with reality? Davenport found they were very close indeed. Over the years, the fishermen have found the ideal solution to the allocation of their pots. For the village as a whole, fishermen do allocate their pots, inshore and mixed, on the two-to-one ratio predicted. And the currents do flow with about the frequency to be expected from a vindictive adversary, carefully weighing the payoffs associated with each fisherman/sea strategy, and scheming to minimize its losses. So how are these results to be interpreted?

The optimization of the mix of inshore and mixed inshore-offshore fishing by the canoe captains is not surprising. Indeed, it may well be that a good many economic systems have come, through trial and error over the years, to be guided by an intuitive grasp of the same principles that underlie the theory of games. Pro-

ducers may well have learned through experience which mix of strategies will, in the long run, provide the highest net return for their efforts. Stability of the basic production techniques over long periods of time may, in this way, confer great advantages. Lack of sophistication may be more than compensated by the simple direct links between management of production and marketing. The integration of all these functions by a small crew of fishermen in a Jamaican village, for instance, provides immediate, direct feedback on the risks and payoffs of each strategy mix.

But what of the environment? We must now drop the interpretation of environment as some animate, scheming, calculating, determined player, unremittingly struggling to reduce yields and output to a minimum. A more realistic interpretation, particularly of the physical environment as a player in the theory of games, must be sought. Are most economic systems

TABLE 8.5

Fishermen versus the sea: Optimal strategies

Fishermen	The Sea		Differences along Rows	Fishermen's Optimal Strategy Mix	Percent ($\times$ 100)
	Current	No Current			
Inshore	17.3	11.5	5.8	$\dfrac{11.8}{5.8 + 11.8}$	67.04
Mixed	5.2	17.0	11.8	$\dfrac{5.8}{5.8 + 11.8}$	32.95
Column differences	12.1	5.5			
Environmental strategy mix	5.5/17.6	12.1/17.6			
Percentage	31.25	68.75			

TABLE 8.6

Fishermen's payoff

Fishermen/Sea Strategy	Payoff Rate	Played by Fishermen (percent)	Played by Sea (percent)	Actual Payoff
a	17.3	0.33	0.31	1.77
b	11.5	0.33	0.69	2.61
c	5.2	0.67	0.31	1.08
d	17.0	0.67	0.69	7.86
Total payoff complete strategy mix				13.31

drawn to a "minimax balance" in which the environment reduces returns to the minimum maximum as exemplified in the Jamaican case study? Is it possible that necessity, the mother of invention, stimulates the development of strategies by human beings that hinge on the environmental mix of strategies? For instance, were the Jamaican fishing captains driven to experiment until they dropped offshore fishing and developed the mixed inshore-offshore fishing strategy as the only workable alternative to exclusive inshore fishing? Or is it the other way around? Does the exploitation of natural resources, for instance, drive environmental conditions back to the "minimax" balance?

Imagine that some new and improved technology were developed that allowed offshore catches on some days when currents prohibit it with existing technology. The proportion of offshore fishing would increase, thereby reducing the offshore catch in quality and size. This would in turn reduce the income line for that strategy down to some new minimax balance.

Or perhaps the relationship is one of mutual interdependency, environment influencing the ways in which we seek to earn our living, and consume the benefits of our efforts, but these in turn influencing the kinds of rewards for our efforts obtained from our environment. Or perhaps it is quite wrong to try to understand the interdependence between people and the physical environment from the models of that interdependency. It may be safest, in conditions of uncertainty, simply to meet the environment as though it were a clever adversary trying to minimize people's winnings. But the main lesson of the theory of games for the geographer may have less to do with the nature of the environment than with the law of requisite variety, which underlies all efforts to regulate systems.

The Law of Requisite Variety

The *law of requisite variety* was formulated by Ross Ashby in his book *An Introduction to Cybernetics*

(1956). Cybernetics is the science of regulation and control in all systems, animate and inanimate. Regulation and control of a system entails maintaining the performance (or output) of the system within predetermined limits by compensating for changes in inputs (from the environment). Some systems are designed to be self-regulating. Central heating systems are an example. The heating unit is switched on and off automatically by a thermostatic control. Cybernetics is concerned with how such automatic controls can, through "negative feedback," keep a system in a "steady state." Ashby's law of requisite variety draws attention to the need to compensate for greater complexity, or variety, in inputs from the environment with greater complexity, or variety, in the system's control mechanism. With a single strategy, mainly to increase the temperature, a central heating system can deal with one source of variety—cold—and it works well in winter when the environment uses this strategy with monotonous regularity.

Conversely, in summer, when it may be too hot, a different environmental input, or strategy, calls for a different countervailing strategy by the householder. If an air conditioner is added, the temperature can be regulated summer and winter. Do we want to regulate humidity as well? Then more equipment and controls are needed. For each element of variety in the environment we wish to regulate, we need one more variety of control to our system. In the words of Ashby, "Only variety can destroy variety, and nothing else can." This deceptively simple statement applies to all systems and has contributed to the solution of regulation and control problems in very sophisticated engineering systems.

Applications of the law of requisite variety are very straightforward in the case of agriculture. Agriculture must cope with a great spatial variety of climatic conditions from arctic to tropical, and from desert to rain forest. The environment cannot be significantly changed to meet the needs of any single agricultural system, so the global spread of agriculture has required the development of an equal variety of production strategies. The empty areas on the world population map indicate where we have failed. These areas are too cold or too dry, or too wet or too rugged, or perhaps too remote for existing agricultural systems.

The relationship between agricultural types and climatic types was an important theme of some earlier economic geographies. The definition of climatic types was guided by the response of natural vegetation to climate. Significant changes in vegetation suggested a meaningful subdivision of apparently unbroken gradations of climatic elements. Vegetation thus changes with changes in climatic type, and so too does agriculture.

Successful commercial agriculture has required an adjustment to variety not only in the physical environment but also in the human environment. Improvements in transportation and advances in agricultural science have changed the economic environment, opening up new areas to production, but thereby submitting older areas to new competition. The steamship and the Suez Canal helped to open up Southeast Asia to commercial plantation agriculture, including rubber, but in doing so undermined rubber production in Brazil. The facts of such developments were central to earlier economic geographers. What is being stressed here, however, is that the survival of commercial agriculture has depended on finding answers to variety in the physical and economic environment. If a solution could not be found to a new change in the economic environment, then the law of requisite variety was no longer satisfied. The margins of settlement might then retreat, as in northern Canada, or the frontier of settlement might become a hollow one, as happened in parts of Brazil.

Requisite variety applies equally to minerals and mining. The "neutral stuff," as Erich Zimmermann called the minerals found in the earth's surface, had to be converted into *natural resources* by knowledge, capital, and labor. The discovery of the limits to each development in that conversion from neutral stuff to natural resources went hand in hand with the discovery of their variety and qualities. Thus, products could be tailored to specific needs. High-speed steels that retain their cutting edge at high speeds could be achieved by adding tungsten, chromium, and vanadium. Manganese and chromium made tough steel for rail lines. Chromium makes steel resistant to corrosion. The tables are, in fact, turned. Variety becomes advantage, because controlled variety in system output helps to meet variety in market needs. The game changes. It is not so much a game of the industrialist against the physical environment as it is a game of the environment and industrialist against the needs posed by an advanced society, where they must compete with many alternative products. But however the players line up, that same law of requisite variety applies.

PEOPLE AS SATISFICERS: THE DECISION PROCESS WHEN RATIONALITY IS BOUNDED

Both the models of the decision-maker as an economic maximizer and as an optimizing strategist assume complete rationality and the astute evaluation of information. Reality tends to be different. Decision-makers

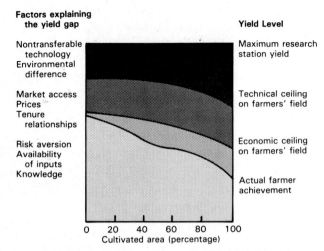

FIGURE 8.8 The yield gap in Third World agriculture.

are often satisficers, operating below the theoretical maximum or optimum. For example, farmers in the developing countries rarely achieve the record yields attained in developed countries or in the controlled research conducted by agricultural research stations. What are some of the factors that cause yields at research stations and in farmers' fields to differ? They are suggested in Figure 8.8.

First, the *technical ceiling* for on-farm yields is lower than that for research stations. The latter use technologies that are not feasible at the farmers' usual scale of production. Research stations are usually located on choice land and can depend on irrigation if it is needed. The farmers' environment is rarely as kindly.

Second, the on-farm *economic ceiling* is often much lower than the on-farm technical ceiling. Farmers' profits are often highest at input levels lower than those necessary for maximum yields, because of diminishing returns on investment in inputs.

Third, farmers' *actual yields* are usually below even economic ceilings. This may be because key inputs such as fertilizer, water, and labor are not available when needed, because farmers may not know about best cultivation practices, or because volatile output prices and unreliable rainfall reduce expected returns. These factors may force the farmer into a "safety-first" strategy, producing to assure guaranteed returns (*satisficing*) rather than risking all in a vain attempt to maximize.

Even in more-developed countries, satisficing is common. In a study of middle Sweden, Julian Wolpert (1964) compared actual labor productivity in agriculture to the theoretically optimum level of productivity calculated by using mathematical programming methods to simulate the economic maximizer. He found that, on average, middle Sweden's farmers achieved only two-thirds of the potential productivity their resources would allow, with substantial variations from place to place within the region. He concluded that the prerequisites for economic rationality (perfect knowledge and optimizing behavior) were lacking.

Lack of knowledge was one important contributor to suboptimal decision making. Wolpert discovered that information about recommended farm practices, new agricultural machinery, new seed varieties, expected costs and market prices originated in core institutions in the Stockholm-Uppsala area. From there, it was disseminated outwards, with increasing time lags, to the various local county offices, typically in the leading city in each county, from these to the larger central farms, and then finally to smaller farms in the periphery. Thus the time lag in receiving information depended on where farmers lived, and the greater the time lag, the less optimal the farming practices were likely to be. The spatial diffusion of information thus translated directly into a spatial pattern of lags in adopting best-practice farm practice.

Rather more surprising is the documentation of how inadequate decision making is in declining industries (Harrington, 1988). Over two thirds of the manufacturing industries in western economies are experiencing slow growth or less. The sales of mainframe computers in the United States, for example, peaked in 1973. This situation simply reflects the fact that all products have a life cycle and that all growth industries eventually become declining industries. Yet Harrington has found that many managers refuse to face facts. Indeed they often attempt to disguise reality by lumping together sales figures of unit shipments of no-growth products with those of growth products, or by showing only revenue trends. Alternatively, they do present the unpalatable unit sales data but attribute decline to extraordinary, temporary circumstances. The vain hope is to keep things running as they are rather than face the pain of economic adjustment. Yet, as Harrington shows, there is a range of alternative end-game strategies available. Two examples: A company can reposition itself as "the last iceman" to serve an attractive niche market; or it can exit, selling to a competitor (sometimes called "the bigger fool") and seek other, more attractive investment opportunities.

That so many captains of industry are satisficers, who are more concerned with preserving the status quo rather than with the assertive repositioning of their companies, has important implications for economic growth and for adjustment to changing technologies and markets. As Simon (1987) notes, theories that accept that managers have bounded rationality

and are satisficers lead to quite different economic conclusions than do traditional theories derived from the assumption of profit maximization. We need to know then how prevalent satisficing behavior is in industry. And we need to know too the ways in which satisficing behavior falls short of maximizing decision making.

The picture now emerging as to how most people make decisions does fall far short of the assumptions made in the economic maximizer model. People do not have the maximizer's perfect knowledge. The human attention span is too limited and most situations too complicated for people to take in all the information available. First impressions count. So does the order in which information is presented. The specialist, whether a physician, a chess grand master or a company president, may have memorized tens of thousands of pieces of information. The first symptoms, configuration or information, are seized on as indexes to access the relevant train of thought and course of action. Items that crop up later may receive diminishing attention if minor, and the response may be limited to impulse firefighting. If both major and unexpected, the later item may trigger an overreaction. Stock-market and commodity price fluctuations are typical examples of such overreaction and demonstrate inefficiency in assessing information. A Chernobyl is more dramatic, and its impact on decision making correspondingly more pervasive and lasting. Such unrepresentative major events or famous cases stick in the mind and bias future evaluations. Presented with the names of an equal number of men and women (a list that includes some famous men), people remember the famous men and believe there were more men than women on the list. The converse results when some of the women are famous but none of the men are.

Current research also indicates that people do not treat payoffs objectively and symmetrically as assumed in the economic maximizer model. Loewenstein (1988) describes experiments, for example, in which high school students were each given gift certificates that were to be honored at some future date. They were then given the opportunity to bargain for earlier or later certificates. The bargaining revealed systematic asymmetries between the forward and backward discounting. In general, students wanted two to four times more money to delay cashing their certificates than they were prepared to pay as a premium for an equal advance in the date of use. Furthermore, this result occurs regularly in similar kinds of tests and supports the view that people evaluate choices relative to a point of personal reference, not to an objective measure. This bias can be used in negotiating. A negotiator, once convinced that a settlement has virtually been reached, will make further concessions, originally quite unacceptable, to save the settlement. Equally, a subtle change in the presentation of alternatives, whether deliberate or happenstance, can change the alternative selected. Decision-makers are much more likely to pick an alternative if told it has 80 percent chance of success than if told it is 20 percent likely to fail. Credit cards are more likely to be used if cash discounts are available than if there is a credit surcharge.

And finally, people do not generally follow a rigorous set of rules and procedures that lead to the best result. Rather they are heuristic, keeping to tried-and-true solutions based on past experience. Sequential trial-and-error is too slow and probably too expensive. This bias towards positive testing leads to an overly narrow view of what works and may mean that optimal solutions may never be discovered if satisfactory solutions are in use. Where better solutions are needed, either incremental change in a process of *hill climbing* is used, or *means-ends* analysis is used. Means-ends analysis does involve a wider search for alternatives to narrow the gap between an existing situation and a required goal. But even this process falls short of Professor Smith's method of helping Farmer Jones achieve the largest herd possible on his farm.

TOWARD AN INTEGRATED MODEL OF DECISION MAKING

Three decision models have been presented to illustrate how the choices that shape the geography of economic systems can be made. *First,* the decision maker was described as an economic maximizer, aiming for the highest possible income. Location theories are built on this model. So, too, are farm management models. Whether the actual decisions observed in any given study conform to the predictions of this model or not, it can provide a norm, or yardstick, against which to compare reality. It may well be that actual decisions often fall short of income maximizing. This shortfall may be caused by uncertainty, forcing the decision maker to an optimizing strategy. It may reflect satisficing behavior, however, evidence of the bounded rationality of Simon's *third* model.

The *second* model treats the decision maker as a strategist and uses the theory of games. It treats risk as variety, and adversity as diversity, both of which must be regulated and controlled. Prior knowledge of which particular environmental conditions will occur is not required or expected, only a knowledge of what range of environmental conditions can occur. The model minimizes losses under what would be the worst possible combination of conditions in the environment, whatever the environment includes, whether physical, economic, technical, cultural, or political factors. The solution is therefore sometimes called the "minimax" solution, that is, the minimum maximum, of a set of possible maximums, assuming that the environmental forces will conspire to drive the decision maker's payoff down to this minimum of the maximums. The mathematical technique is the theory of games. This theory may appear to employ an improper personification of the physical environment. Some may prefer to think of nature as a neutral stage on which is acted out the drama of economic production, trade, and consumption. It is possible, however, that the sheer pressure of population on resources may drive the physical environment to respond as though it were a scheming opponent seeking to reduce production to a minimum.

Empirical research indicates that the reality of decision making falls far short of the assumptions made by the maximizer and optimizer models. Robert Kates (1964) wrote that the way in which people view the risks and opportunities of their uncertain environment influences their decisions on resource management. These decisions influence, in turn, the economic geographies that result. The question of just how decisions are made is now attracting tens of millions of research dollars in the United States alone. The importance of this topic is receiving growing recognition in the social sciences, business, and government. Part of the effort is directed at improving the quality of decision making and, for instance, converting managers of declining industries to being strategists rather than satisficers.

The three models of decision making are not necessarily disparate, competing models of how choices are made. The separate concepts on which each is focused apply to some extent to all comprehensive models of decision making and provide a comprehensive conceptual framework within which to set each model. In doing so, decision making is seen as a selection process influenced by different circumstances. Thus, the way in which decisions are made that shape the geography of economic systems is in turn shaped by the physical, economic, and technical environment in which those decisions are made. The approach to decision making is not autonomously determined without regard to environment, but it must take the environment into account.

All three models of decision making assume some assessment of the economic consequences of each possible choice (Figure 8.9). Whether the decision maker is a maximizer, satisficer, or strategist, the choices are listed and the income for each estimated. Thus, all choices can be ranked on an income scale

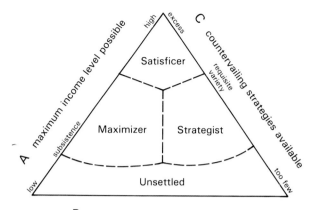

FIGURE 8.9 Decision process as a response to environmental circumstances, personal preferences, and choices available.

from high to low (scale A, Figure 8.9). If the maximum possible income in an area is below the subsistence level, that area can be expected to remain unsettled. The higher the income levels provided by the better choices, the more likely it must be that the decision maker will feel free to opt for a satisficer approach.

Likewise, all three models can be integrated according to how they are affected by environmental uncertainty and requisite variety. The ideal situation is low environmental uncertainty coupled with an excess of good countervailing strategies. Under these circumstances, the satisficer model is most likely to apply. The worst situation is a combination of high environmental variety without appropriate countervailing

strategies and a low maximum income potential. A cycle of settlement, abandonment, and resettlement may occur, but without the requisite variety needed to regulate the environment, no foundation exists for lasting settlement.

Interest focuses on the intermediate cases where requisite variety is achieved. If the environment is stable, with few variations of any significance, the decision maker can ignore risk and go for the maximum possible income. If, however, a number of environmental factors are subject to unpredictable change, decision makers must hedge their bets and opt for a mixed strategy. The game theory approach is called for, the decision maker becomes a strategist, and the highest income level achievable in the long run is the minimum maximum rather than the simple maximum.

The three different models of decision making are different aspects of a single, more comprehensive, model. Decision making in economic production ultimately involves at least three factors: (1) environmental conditions in competing locations; (2) the range of activities and technologies available to cope with environmental variety in any given location; and (3) the range of income levels promised by competing activities in the same place, or the same activity in competing places. The decision maker may play one or more different roles in different places at different times, perhaps now the strategist combatting a complex variety of environmental changes, now a simple maximizer going for the jackpot, now a satisficer prepared to sit back and enjoy the nonmonetary benefits of an alternative, satisfying activity.

TOPICS FOR DISCUSSION

1. Draw to scale the graphical solution of the Jamaican fishing village using the data provided in Table 8.3 and including the offshore option. Does your figure confirm that the fishermen should not use the offshore fishing option? What would the minimum payoff for the offshore fishing strategy with a sea current have to be to make it competitive with the mixed strategy?

2. What does the application of the theory of games to geographic cases imply about relationships between humanity and physical environment? Do these implications affect the validity of the application?

3. "Game theory is applicable only to a few highly unrealistic situations; the greater the complexity, the more difficult it is to solve the mathematics required to generate a solution" (Smith, 1981). Discuss Smith's assertion and consider whether the theory of games can make any

contributions to economic geography if the assertion is correct.

4. The Barren Middle Zone of Ghana, a belt which for environmental and historical reasons has a very low population density, has one of the most severe agricultural climates in West Africa, with heavy precipitation followed by the extreme aridity of the harmattan, which sweeps south from the Sahara. A further problem is that the high degree of variability of the precipitation makes it difficult for the farmers to plan effectively. The farmers of Jantilla, a small village in western Ghana, may use the land to grow the following crops, each with different degrees of resistance to dry conditions, as their main staple food: yams, cassava, maize, millet, and hill rice. They are faced by two different environmental conditions: dry years and wet years. Given the payoff matrix in Figure 8.10, what is the farmers' optimal cropping strategy? (Example from P. Gould, 1963.)

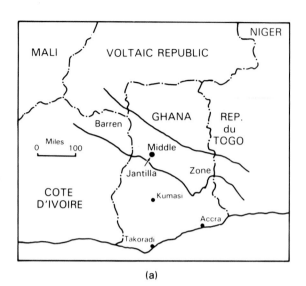

(a)

			ENVIRONMENT MOISTURE CHOICES	
			Wet Years	Dry Years
		Yams	82	11
FARMERS	CROP	Maize	61	49
OF	CHOICE	Cassava	12	38
JANTILLA		Millet	43	32
		Hill rice	30	71

(b)

FIGURE 8.10   (a) The Barren Middle Zone of Ghana of low population density and extreme variability of rainfall. (b) Payoff matrix for two-person-five-strategy-zero-sum game; crop choices against moisture choices. [*Source:* Peter Gould, "Man Against His Environment: A Game Theoretic Framework," *Annals of the Association of American Geographers*, 53, 3 (1963), 291.]

FURTHER READINGS

Ashby, W. Ross. *Introduction to Cybernetics.* London: John Wiley, 1956, pp. 202–218.

Ashby's *law of requisite variety* states simply that only "variety can destroy variety." The full implications of this powerful law have yet to be properly considered in geography.

Beer, Stafford. *Designing Freedom: Massey Lectures, 1973.* Toronto: CBC Publications, 1974.

One of the few published applications of the law of requisite variety.

Davenport, William. "Jamaican Fishing: A Game Theory Analysis." *Yale University Publications in Anthropology,* 59 (1960), 3–11.

Brought to the attention of geographers by Peter Gould, this article is the source for the theory of games example in this chapter.

Gould, Peter. "Man Against His Environment: A Game Theoretic Framework." *Annals of the Association of American Geographers,* 53, No. 3 (1963), 290–297.

Two examples from Ghana illustrate decision strategies to optimize economic decisions in the face of environmental uncertainty. A good place to begin. But ignore the mathematical calculations; they have typographical errors.

Harrigan, Kathryn Rudie. *Managing Maturing Businesses: Restructuring Declining Industries and Revitalizing Troubled Operations.* Lexington, Massachusetts: Lexington Books, 1988.

Three-quarters of the manufacturing industries in the developed world are growing slowly, if at all. Harrigan notes the frequent failure of management to address the problems and she suggests ways in which they can adopt optimizing strategies.

Kates, Robert W. *Hazard and Choice Perception in Flood Plain Management,* Dept. of Geography Research Paper No. 78, Chicago: University of Chicago Press, 1964.

Chapter 1 is a classic statement of the factors affecting the way decisions are made and it remains a valuable contribution to the subject of decision making.

LOEWENSTEIN, GEORGE F. "Frames of Mind in Intertemporal Choice." *Management Science,* XXXIV, No. 2 (February 1988), 200–214.

Decisions are influenced by how the choices are expressed. This article applies this "framing" effect to intertemporal choice to explain why discounting is asymmetrical and not symmetrical as is implied in economic maximizing.

RAPAPORT, ANATOL. "Critiques of Game Theory." In *Modern Systems Research for the Behavioral Scientist,* Walter Buckley (Ed.). Chicago: Aldine, 1968, pp. 474–489.

Rapaport gives a generally favorable review of the theory of games.

SIMON, HERBERT A. "Decision Making and Problem Solving." *Interfaces,* XVII, No. 5 (September-October 1987), 11–31.

A key reading. This paper was prepared by a panel of experts to brief the scientific advisor to the U.S. president. The selection of this topic for a special briefing highlights the increasing importance being attached to it by government.

SMITH, DAVID M. *Industrial Location: An Economic Geographical Analysis.* New York: John Wiley, 1981, pp. 121–123.

A concise, useful, and readable review of the application of games theory in industrial location.

STEVENS, BENJAMIN H. "An Application of Game Theory to a Problem in Location Strategy." *Papers and Proceedings of the Regional Science Association,* VII, 1961, 143–157.

A very clear presentation of a number of examples of strategies for locating a simple linear market under various assumptions. Stevens is able to advance the application of game theory to more realistic examples than those used in this chapter.

VON NEUMANN, JOHN, and O. MORGENSTERN. *Theory of Games and Economic Behavior.* Princeton, N.J.: Princeton University Press, 1944.

The classic study that introduced the theory of games to social scientists.

WOLPERT, JULIAN. "The Decision Process in Spatial Context." *Annals of the Association of American Geographers,* LIV, No. 4 (December 1964), 537–558.

The key reference on the decision-maker as a satisficer.

9

The Spatial Organization of Land Use

OVERVIEW

The uses to which people put the land resources available to them reflect, in part, differences in physical factors, such as soil fertility and climate in rural land use, and amenities, such as high elevation with imposing views in urban land use. Historical and cultural factors—including the timing of settlement and the cultural traditions of a population—also affect land use. But even on a homogeneous plain, where there are no physical differences, the efforts of farmers or city residents and developers to maximize their returns produce systematic land-use patterns. The exciting discovery of these spatial patterns was first presented by J. H. von Thünen in his study *The Isolated State* in 1826. The importance of von Thünen's contribution cannot be overemphasized. He provided the earliest theory of the spatial economic organization of land

use. Although the world economic geography has changed dramatically in the century and a half since von Thünen made his seminal contribution, the basic principles that he stated still apply to the zonation of land use at scales from that of the village to that of cities, regions, and even of the globe itself.

Of course, transportation costs on a featureless plain provide only a first approximation to the factors patterning land uses. Physical factors are important in rural land use, and cultural differences play a major role in differentiating urban space. Thus, in this chapter we probe not only the powerful effects of transportation in spatial organization but also explore how resources and culture add a textured richness to human use of the earth.

OBJECTIVES

- to develop an understanding of the laws of returns
- to explain the concept of rent, and why differential rents arise
- to present the problem posed by J. H. von Thünen, the deductive model he developed to solve the problem, and the application of his principles to the modern world
- to extend von Thünen's model to urban land use

We have now described the distribution of population and resources and explained some economic principles, such as optimizing scales of output and combinations of inputs. Both of these, the geographic and the economic fundamentals, help to explain the location of economic activity. Land resources and relative location are both important determinants of land use; and although the location of manufacturing industry is to some extent related to the location of raw materials, the size and spacing of industrial plants is also related to the economies of scale and the barriers to entry. In the next three chapters, therefore, we introduce formal theories of the location of economic activity, beginning with the theories of rural and urban land use.

THE LAWS OF RETURNS

J. H. von Thünen's principles rely on ideas developed in Chapter 8, particularly those of how the economic maximizer seeks to optimize production to maximize returns. We now need to develop the *laws of returns* in more detail. Recall the manner in which Farmer Jones learned from Professor Smith how to combine inputs to achieve maximum output by preparing a preference map on which were plotted isoquants and production-possibility curves. Figure 9.1 is such a preference map in which there are two inputs, X and Y, and the isoquants show the combinations of these inputs needed to produce 10, 20, or 30 units of output, respectively.

Now assume that there is a fixed supply of one of the inputs (X), so that Farmer Jones can increase output only by increasing the use of the other input (Y). Let OA be the input in fixed supply (say, land). Then AB traces out the different scales of output that may be

obtained by increasing inputs of Y (by using more capital or labor on the fixed amount of land). For example, increasing Y from 2 to 3 units enables Farmer Jones to increase output from 10 to 20 units, but the next unit increase in Y, from 3 to 4, produces a lower increase in output, as does the one following, from 4 to 5, because of the way the line AB intersects the isoquants. The increase in output that results from adding a unit of the variable input Y is called the *marginal* increase in output, or the *marginal productivity* of Y—*marginal physical productivity* if it is measured in physical units of output, such as bushels of wheat, and *marginal revenue productivity* if it is measured in the dollar value of the output. The concept of marginal productivity is central to understanding the laws that govern returns to changing scale of output. The example just given illustrates decreasing returns to scale. Refer back to the discussion in Chapter 7 and consider the example provided in Box 9.1.

The marginal revenue productivity curve can be interpreted as the demand curve for the variable factor. In Box 9.1, if labor costs $10.00 per unit, then the farmer will maximize returns by consuming 9 units of labor at a cost of $90.00. If the price of labor were to double, two things would happen. First, all the numbers in the second column of the box would change. But, second, reading down column 5, so would the point at which Farmer Jones could maximize returns: By consuming only 7 units of labor at a cost of $140.00, the resulting maximum net returns would be $6.00 ($146.00 − $140.00). In other words, the marginal revenue productivity curve also records how many units of an input should be used to maximize revenues as the price of the input changes. The relationship between quantity demanded and price is the demand curve for the input.

THE CONCEPT OF RENT

We can now use this relationship to develop the idea of the marginal revenue productivity of land (that is, the demand curve for land), and for this the concept of land rent. To do this we will turn the analysis around and treat land as a variable input and other inputs as fixed. The concept of land rent is basic to the development of theories of agricultural and urban land use, because the core idea of land use theory is that land use is determined by land rent.

Rent as a Scarcity Payment

Assume we are dealing with an island that contains a fixed amount of homogeneous land available for cultivation (OS in Figure 9.2). The first farmer settles on

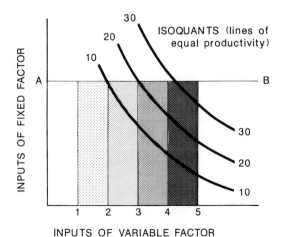

FIGURE 9.1 Production possibilities with one fixed and one variable output.

BOX 9.1 Equating Marginal Cost and Marginal Revenue

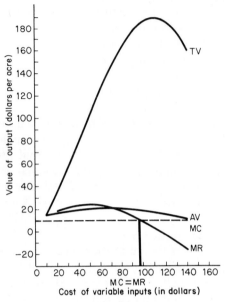

FIGURE 9a Total, average, and marginal value of output per acre under conditions of increasing and decreasing returns. This figure compares the cost of variable inputs with total value of output, the average value of output at the scale of output reached, and the marginal value of the last $10.00 increase in outputs. The data from which the graph is plotted are shown below. Marginal cost (MC) is fixed at $10.00

It is assumed that Farmer Jones has a fixed amount of land in grain production, and the output of grain can be changed by using more labor. Column 1 in Figure 9a shows the dollar value of the inputs of labor that could be used (per acre) in increments of $10.00; column 2 shows the resulting yield in bushels per acre; column 3 shows the dollar value of output per acre; column 4 shows the marginal value of output per acre for each successive $10 of inputs applied—the marginal revenue productivity of each labor unit—and column 5 shows the average value of the output per acre per $10 of inputs. The three lines in the graph show how the total (TV), average (AV), and marginal (MR) value of output per acre change as the total value of the labor inputs per acre increases. As more labor is applied to the land, the value of output first increases (that is, there are *increasing returns to scale*) and then decreases (that is, there are *decreasing returns*).

At what point should Farmer Jones stop trying to increase output? This depends upon both the marginal cost of the inputs and their marginal returns. As long as each successive $10.00 worth of labor input produces a greater marginal increase in the value of output, Farmer Jones should add inputs. But if an extra $10.00 of input produced less than $10.00 worth of output, it should not be made. The general rule is that Farmer Jones should keep on adding labor inputs to the point where *the marginal cost of the inputs equals the marginal revenue produced,* but no further. At this point, returns are maximized. Go beyond this point, and returns will decrease. Can you find this point in Figure 9a? Subtract from the total value of output the cost of inputs needed to produce that output. The resulting net returns (profits) will increase from $5.00 to a maximum of $87.00 when $90.00 of inputs are used. But the next $10.00 of input yields only $9.00 in output and, indeed, total value ($186.00) less total inputs ($100.00) produces only $86.00 in net returns.

Units of Land Used	Cumulative Cost of Inputs of Variable Factor (labor, per acre)	Yield (bushels per acre)	TV: Total Value of Output at $1.50 per Bushel	MR: Value of Additional Output per $10 Input per Acre (marginal value of product)	AV: Average Value of Output per Acre per $10 Input of Variable Factors
1	$ 10.0	10	$ 15.0		$15.00
2	20.0	22	33.0	18.0	16.50
3	30.0	36	54.0	21.0	18.00
4	40.0	52	78.0	24.0	19.50
5	50.0	68	102.0	24.0	20.40
6	60.0	83.3	125.0	23.0	20.83
7	70.0	97.3	146.0	21.0	20.86
8	80.0	109	163.5	17.5	20.45
9	90.0	118	177.0	13.5	19.67
10	100.0	124	186.0	9.0	18.60
11	110.0	126	189.0	3.0	17.18
12	120.0	124	186.0	−3.0	15.50
13	130.0	117.3	176.0	−9.0	13.54
14	140.0	106.6	160.0	−16.0	11.43

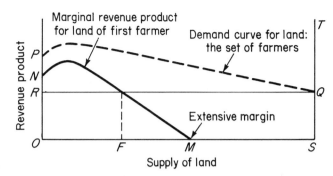

FIGURE 9.2 Marginal revenue product and the emergence of land rent.

the island, bringing a fixed amount of capital and labor. How much land will be used, and what rent will be paid?

Suppose this is a grain farmer selling wheat on the world market. Because of the nature of that market the farmer must be a price-taker, accepting a fixed world price. Let the marginal revenue productivity curve for land (demand curve) be *NM* in Figure 9.2, as output is increased by increasing inputs of land. The price paid by the farmer for the land (the land rent) and the quantity of land consumed will be determined by the intersection of the demand and supply curves for land. The demand curve is the marginal revenue productivity curve *NM*. The supply curve is the line *OST*. Thus, the farmer will use *OM* land. The rent will be zero. This is because there is land to spare. The farmer could always move if a landlord tried to charge rent.

Rent is payment to landowners for use of their factor of production, land, which arises solely because land is *scarce*. This can be seen in Figure 9.2, if we let additional farmers arrive on the island. The total demand curve increases as each individual's marginal revenue productivity curve is added to that of the others. For example, *PQ* might be the total demand curve for land of one group of farmers (the summation of their individual marginal productivity curves). *PQ* intersects the supply curve *OST* at *Q*. Since there is only *OS* land available, farmers compete for the land, balancing demands and supplies at price *OR* (= *SQ*). The marginal cost curve for land is thus the price line *RQ*, and our first farmer, maximizing profits by equating marginal revenues and marginal costs, will cut land consumption to *OF*. The other farmers will cultivate the rest of the island, *FS*.

Differential Rents Due to Productivity Differences

Although the preceding example suggests that rents are uniform across the island, in reality rents do differ. Differential rents arise because

1. The productivity of different parcels of land varies;

2. Land is located at different distances from market.

Both types of variation are central to the theory of agricultural location, in which the basic idea is that each parcel of land is used for the activity that can pay the highest rent. If we can understand the reasons for the variations, we will have gone a long way toward understanding one of the basic problems of economic geography—that of explaining land use.

First, let us take the question of productivity differences. The idea of rent variations being attributable to productivity of the soil was first discussed by David Ricardo in his *Principles of Political Economy and Taxation* (1817). Ricardo said that high rents were due to the "niggardliness of nature" (to scarcity) and were related to the "original and indestructible power of the soil" (to productivity differences). Further, he said that the most fertile lands are put to use first, with production extending to less favorable lands only as demands increase.

Why is this so? Productivity differences change the marginal revenue productivity curve for land because they change marginal physical productivity. For example, in Figure 9.3 the marginal revenue productivities of two grades of land, *A* and *B,* are shown. Assume situations in which both are in equal supply *OS.* The lower-quality land will not command a rent, whereas that of higher quality will command rent *OR.* In agricultural terminology, the lower-quality land is "marginal" because it does not pay any rent, and the rent charged for the superior-quality land is entirely due to its greater productivity.

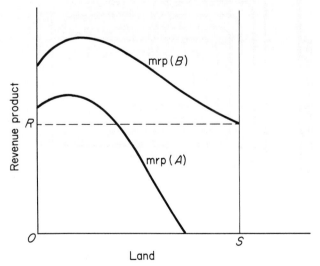

FIGURE 9.3 Marginal revenue product differences for differing land qualities.

A generalization of Ricardo's idea has been provided by geographers H. H. McCarty and J. Lindberg in the form of an "optima and limits" scheme (see Figures 9.4, 9.5). In Figure 9.4, two variables—temperature and moisture—provide the basis for their hypothesis. In some restricted area, those variables are presumed to combine ideally for producing a particular crop. That area is identified as having "optimum" conditions. Outward from it, conditions become less and less favorable until, finally, the physical limits are reached, beyond which production of that crop is impossible. In most cases, however, greater significance attaches to the "economic limits," which appear in Figure 9.5. When the productivity data of Figure 9.4 are translated into unit-costs of production and when those unit-costs are converted into rent (per unit of output), the areas of production that would appear in response to various price levels for that commodity can be estimated. Assume that a price of "7" will cover costs in the four inside zones of the model. No production will occur outside that zone (in the "no-rent" areas). Further, rent will increase toward the optimum.

What will happen if the price rises for the products of the land because of increasing demand? Marginal revenue productivity will rise, and the extensive margin of production will move into uncultivated lands. By the same token, the higher-rent land will also be used more intensively, because—recalling the earlier discussion of input substitution—if rents are higher for better-quality land, and if other factor prices

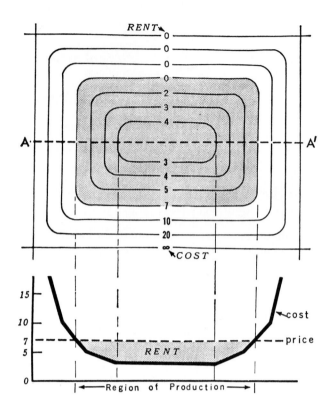

FIGURE 9.5 Rents in the productivity schema. [*Source:* McCarty and Lindberg, 1966.]

are constant, it will pay farmers to substitute inputs of the other (cheaper) factors for inputs of the more expensive land to achieve the same resulting output.

Differential Rents Due to Locational Differences

The same relationship holds in the case of rent differences due to transportation cost. Marginal revenue productivity is defined in terms of market prices. Yet as we saw in Chapter 6, the at-farm price involves market price less transportation costs. Holding land quality constant, the effect of increasing transportation costs therefore is to reduce the more distant farmer's marginal revenue productivity curve (even though marginal physical productivity remains unchanged), and thus to reduce the rent he pays for a given amount of land. See Figure 9.6, in which a farm of size OL pays OR_1 at the market, declining to OR_3 20 miles away. The difference (R_1, R_3) is accounted for by the reduction in revenues due to the cost of transporting output the 20 miles to the market.

In such a situation, rents display a pattern of distance-decay from the market center. Further, just as higher-quality land will be used more intensively, so will more accessible land. We should expect to see both farm costs and returns decline with increasing distance from markets, and this is exactly the case in

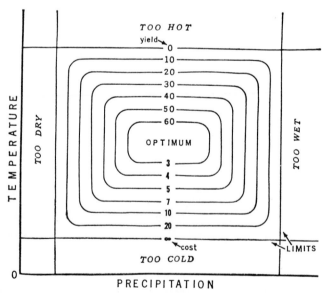

FIGURE 9.4 The optima and limits schema. [*Source:* H. H. McCarty and James B. Lindberg, *A Preface to Economic Geography* (Englewood Cliffs, N.J.: Prentice Hall, 1966), pp. 61–62.]

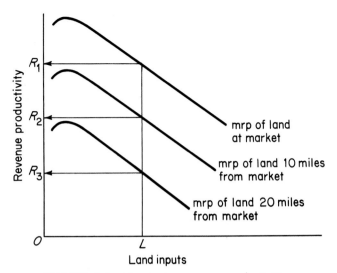

FIGURE 9.6 Marginal revenue productivities (mrp) of land of identical quality at different distances from market.

the agricultural example depicted in Table 9.1. Note that as rents fall with increasing distance, farm size increases because farmers substitute the cheapening factor of production (land) for others in their productive process.

Relationship of Land Rent to Everyday "Rents" and to Land Values

Is land rent the same thing as the rent paid to a landlord for an apartment? There is an important differ-

ence that must be clearly understood. What we call *rent* in an everyday sense is a payment to a landlord for a variety of things: land, building, furnishings and other services. Only a portion of this payment is the land rent. The rest is a "rental" for the capital, labor, and enterprise involved in constructing and maintaining the apartment. The difference is clearly seen on local property tax bills, which separate assessments for the land from those for the "improvements."

The assessor talks of land and building *values*, not rents, however. What is the difference? Land value is the price paid to purchase the land; land rent is the payment to an owner to use the land. There is a simple accounting relationship between the two: Land rent capitalized at the current rate of interest equals land value, or the price of land is the present or capitalized value of the rent the land will earn during its useful life.

VON THÜNEN'S ISOLATED STATE: THE FIRST ECONOMIC MODEL OF SPATIAL ORGANIZATION

The simple idea that rents decline with distance from market was the basis of the first economic model of spatial organization, Johann Heinrich von Thünen's 1826 classic *Der Isolierte Staat*. It is worth spending some time with von Thünen's model, not simply out of historical curiosity but because of the systematic way he linked the economic logic of rent theory to the spatial organization of land use.

Von Thünen had a university education in philos-

TABLE 9.1

Some variations in agricultural characteristics with increasing distance from Louisville, Kentucky (1918)

Distance from Louisville (miles)	Rent of Land per Acre	Value of Land per Acre	Percentage of Receipts from		
			Truck and Potato	Dairy	Other
8 or less	$11.85	$312	68%	10%	22%
9–11	5.59	110	35	12	53
12–14	5.37	106	34	20	46
15+	4.66	95	20	27	53

Distance from Louisville (miles)	Average Area of Improved Land (acres)	Operating Expense per Acre	Gross Receipts per Acre	Land Earnings per Acre	Value of Fertilizer Used per Acre
9	44	$73	$96	$23	$19.25
12	121	36	45	9	6.50
13	212	15	20	5	5.20
16	420	14	18	4	4.25

Source: J. H. Arnold and Frank Montgomery, *Influence of a City on Farming*, Bulletin 678 (Washington, D.C.: U.S. Department of Agriculture, 1918).

ophy, biology, economics, and languages, and in 1810, when he was 27, he bought an 1146-acre estate at Tellow, southeast of Rostock in Mecklenberg, Germany. As he operated and managed Tellow he kept meticulous records, and his early training led him to speculate about the best way of using his land.

Nature of the Abstraction from Reality

Von Thünen found it most helpful to develop the abstract ideas underlying the everyday operation of Tellow, pointing out to the readers of *Der Isolierte Staat* that "the reader who is willing to spend some time and attention" to his work should not "take exception to the imaginary assumptions . . . because they do not correspond to conditions in reality" since the reader will find that they allow him "to establish the operation of a certain factor, whose operation we see but dimly in reality, where it is in incessant conflict with others of its kind." This is to be said of all location theories, which are abstract because they seek to understand the basic processes at work shaping the complex reality of the everyday world, and it also explains why we spent so much time with rent theory at the beginning of this chapter.

Von Thünen was unremittingly logical. He stated his assumptions, posed his problem, deduced the consequences, and tested the deductions with empirical evidence that he collected on his estate over many years. As such, he was a model scientist.

The Assumptions

The assumptions enabled von Thünen to focus on spatial differences, and in particular upon the effects of transport costs on land use:

Imagine a very large town, at the centre of a fertile plain which is crossed by no navigable river or canal. Throughout the plain the soil is capable of cultivation and of the same fertility. Far from the town, the plain turns into an uncultivated wilderness which cuts off all communication between this State and the outside world.

There are no other towns on the plain. The central town must therefore supply the rural areas with all manufactured products, and in return it will obtain all its provisions from the surrounding countryside.

The mines that provide the State with salt and metals are near the central town which, as it is

the only one, we shall in future call simply "the Town."[1]

These assumptions are severe: a plain with complete physical homogeneity; a single market, the "Town"; a single source of food supply, the plain; transportation costs related only to volume and distance shipped; and decisions made by an economic maximizer, relentlessly organizing space in an optimal way. But these assumptions are needed in order to establish the role of distance, whose operation in reality is in constant conflict with other factors affecting land use, including variations in climate, soil fertility, management, and the transportation network with its freight-rate structure.

The Problem

Von Thünen then presented the problem that concerned him.

The problem we want to solve is this: what pattern of cultivation will take shape in these conditions?; and how will the farming system of the various districts be affected by their distance from the Town? We assume throughout that farming is conducted absolutely rationally.

It is on the whole obvious that near the Town will be grown those products which are heavy or bulky in relation to their value and which are consequently so expensive to transport that the remoter districts are unable to supply them. Here also we find the highly perishable products, which must be used very quickly. With increasing distance from the Town, the land will progressively be given up to products cheap to transport in relation to their value.

For this reason alone, fairly sharply differentiated concentric rings or belts will form around the Town, each with its own particular staple product.

From ring to ring the staple product, and with it the entire farming system, will change; and in the various rings we shall find completely different farming systems.[2]

What von Thünen is suggesting is that locational differences alone are sufficient to cause a complete system of spatial organization of land use, embodying

[1] Peter Hall (ed.), *Von Thünen's Isolated State*. Trans. Carla M. Wartenberg (Oxford: Pergamon Press, 1966), p. 7.

[2] Ibid., p. 8.

concentric circles of crop production and farm types. But he did not stop there. Once the effect of distance had been observed, the assumptions were relaxed, and other variables introduced into the model to see how they modified the "ideal" pattern of rural land use that results from distance effects alone.

Location Rent for a Single Crop at a Single Intensity

Let us proceed stepwise through von Thünen's model. He recognized that land inputs embody two different goods, *space* (physical area) and *location* (accessibility). The basic assumption in *Der Isolierte Staat* is that space is physically homogeneous, so that all variations in land quality involve the second quality, accessibility to the Town. The impact of diminishing accessibility on net income per unit land area is thus measurable as total income minus production and transportation costs. Because production costs for any single farm commodity were also assumed to be virtually invariant with distance from the Town, variations in net income could then be attributed to differences in accessibility alone. Income net of all costs von Thünen called *location rent*. The question he then asked was how location rent differences were related to transport costs.

Von Thünen essentially calculated location rents as follows. Where

R = location rent per unit of land

E = output per unit of land

p = price per unit of output

a = production expenses per unit of output (including labor)

f = transportation costs per unit of output per mile

k = miles from market

then

$$R = E(p - a) - Efk$$

To illustrate the change in rent gradient with distance, let us assume production of a crop such that E = 40 bushels per acre; price (p) = $2.00 per bushel; expenses (a) = $1.00 per bushel; and the transportation rate (f) = 2 cents per bushel per mile. For farm A, directly at the market and with no transportation costs, $k = 0$, and the equation reduces to:

$$R = E(p - a)$$

Substituting gives

$$R = 40(\$2 - \$1)$$
$$= \$40 \text{ per acre}$$

For a second farm, B, 25 miles from the market:

$$R = 40(\$2 - \$1) - 40(\$0.02 \times 25)$$
$$= \$20 \text{ per acre}$$

At 25 miles the rent has fallen to half. At what distance will it fall to zero? If

$$R = E(p - a) - Efk = 0$$

then

$$k = \frac{(p - a)}{f}$$

Substituting our hypothetical values gives

$$\frac{2 - 1}{0.02} = 50 \text{ miles}$$

Figure 9.7 shows how the components of gross farm income will vary with distance from the Town. A

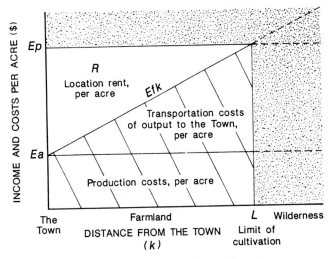

FIGURE 9.7 Components of gross farm income with increasing distance from the Town. Gross income per acre is invariant with distance from the Town. The residual amount, *R*, left after production costs, *a*, and transportation costs, *Efk*, are paid, diminishes with distance. This residual is termed *location rent* and is a measure of market accessibility

rent gradient, sloping downward with increasing distance from the Town, can be identified. Rotating the rent gradient around the Town produces a rent cone, the base of which maps out the extensive margin of farm land, as demonstrated by Figure 9.8.

Who receives the location rent? Imagine that all the farms are rented out each year on a fully competitive basis at an auction. The farmers know that net return increases with accessibility and bid up the rents for farms closer to market. It pays to continue bidding until the bid rent equals the location rent; indeed, it is necessary for the farmer who wants to occupy the land to do so. At that price the farmer just recovers production expenses (including what he expects to receive for his own labor) and transportation costs, and the landowner receives the location rent as a payment for his land. The competitive bidding eliminates the income differential to farmers that otherwise would be attributable to accessibility; and the bid rent, or contract rent, is the location rent. This bid rent produces a spatial equilibrium situation in which bid rent falls just enough from market to cover additional transportation costs so that the farmer is indifferent as to the distance from market. In essence, there is a tradeoff between transportation costs and accessibility rent.

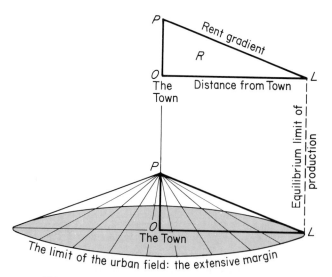

FIGURE 9.8 The rent cone and the extensive margin of production. The rent gradient is derived from Figure 9.7. Economic rent at the Town is *OP*. At *L*, the equilibrium limit of production, *O*. The △*OPL* is rotated to describe the rent cone and to map the extensive margin, where farm land gives way to wilderness.

Location Rent for a Single Crop at Differing Intensities

The higher location rent paid for land with greater accessibility is an incentive to increase output per unit of land by increasing inputs of capital and labor. Even in von Thünen's day when technology was limited, distinct intensities of grain production existed involving different proportions of the three factors of production—capital, land, and labor. As noted earlier, however, factor substitution is imperfect. The incremental output for each additional unit of input of labor and capital is not uniform. At some point in the intensification of production extra units of labor, machinery, or fertilizer add a smaller amount of product than the previous unit. Total physical product may continue to rise, but marginal physical product begins to fall.

This law of diminishing returns has important spatial ramifications. Consider the location rent formula again, $R = E(p - a) - Efk$. The difference between market price (p) and production costs (a) diminishes per bushel as intensity increases, and the transportation cost per bushel (fk) increases with distance. The optimal level of intensity occurs where the marginal addition to yield by the final increment of capital and labor just pays for the transportation of that marginal yield to market. The lower the transportation costs are, the lower that marginal addition to yield need be to pay for itself. The closer the farm is to market, the further along the marginal physical product curve the farmer can proceed and the more intensive his farming system can be.

The spatial ramifications in the case where two intensity levels reflect two different types of farming organization (the *improved* and the feudal *three-field* systems) were explored in some detail by von Thünen. The data came from the Tellow accounts for 1810–1819, but were standardized for an area of 100,000 rods, or 217 hectares, an area slightly smaller than Tellow, and for soils a little poorer. See Box 9.2.

A spatial separation of the two farming systems occurs, with an inner circle of more intensive grain farming and an outer ring of more extensive farming. This separation illustrates the principle of highest and best use, which states that land is allocated to that use earning the highest location rent.

Land Use Organization in the Multicrop Case

The most prominent contribution of von Thünen's study was the determination of land use organization for the multicrop case. Activities are ordered according to the principle of the highest and best use as measured by their location rent at each distance from the

BOX 9.2   Location Rent for a Single Crop at Two Different Intensities

The improved system yielded a gross product of 3144 bushels of grain with costs of 1976 bushels and 641 thalers. Location rent fell to zero at 28.6 miles, at which distance the 1168 bushels of grain for sale (3144 minus 1976 bushels) just fetched enough to pay the town-based costs (641 thalers).

The three-field system produced a much smaller gross product—1720 compared with 3144 bushels—but both farm-based and town-based costs were smaller. A 45 percent reduction in yield contributed a 48 percent reduction in grain costs and a 49 percent reduction in town-based costs. The economic rent was lower, but it fell more slowly with increasing distance because the ratio of the 327 thalers of town-based costs to the 696 bushels for sale at the market in the three-field system was smaller than the corresponding ratio for the improved system. Plotting these data indicates that at 24.7 miles from market the three-field system provides the same location rent as the improved farming system (Figure 9b). The improved system is better up to 24.7 miles from the market, and the three-field system from there to the extensive margin at 31.4 miles.

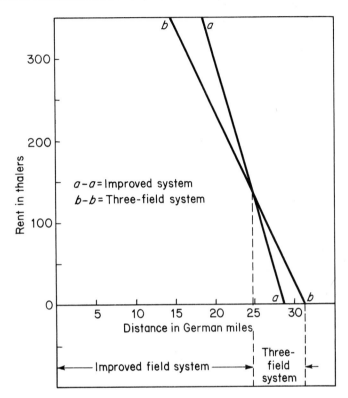

FIGURE 9b   Rent gradients for the improved and three-field systems. [*Source:* Data are derived from Peter Hall, ed., *Von Thünen's Isolated State* (Oxford: Pergamon Press, 1966), p. xxvii.]

market. Market price, transportation costs, and production expenses vary between crops so that the simple intensity law that applies to any single commodity is inappropriate. Instead, the general rule becomes that land uses are sequenced outward from the market in the order of the price spreads they achieve between market price and production plus transport costs. The

site nearest the market will be appropriated by the product that can pay the highest location rent.

The details are complex but the basic operation of these principles may be illustrated by using hypothetical data for four commodities—milk, potatoes, wheat, and wool (Table 9.2). To graph the rent gradients, only the rent at the market and the limit of culti-

TABLE 9.2

Location rent for competing crops

	Milk	Potatoes	Wheat	Wool
Annual yield, E	725 gal	150 bu	50 bu	50 lb
Market price, P	$ 0.65 per gal	$ 1.75 per bu	$ 1.70 per bu	$ 0.60 per lb
Production cost, a	$ 0.05 per gal	$ 0.25 per bu	$ 0.20 per bu	$ 0.10 per lb
Transport rate per mile, f	$ 0.05 per gal	$ 0.075 per bu	$ 0.025 per bu	$ 0.005 per lb
Location rent at town	$435.00	$225.00	$75.00	$25.00
Rent at $0.00 at	12 mi	20 mi	60 mi	100 mi

Note: The data are hypothetical.

vation need be computed. Thus, wheat commands a rent of $75 per acre at the market and can extend 60 miles from market.

The rent gradients for the four crops, based on their market rent and distance values shown in Table 9.2, are superimposed to construct the rent diagram, Figure 9.9. In accordance with the law of highest and best use, the land use with the largest location rent at any given distance from market outbids the others. The four competing land uses are sequenced outward from the market to form concentric zones of milk, potato, wheat, and wool production.

Von Thünen's Farming Systems with Relaxed Assumptions

Von Thünen's model of land use in the Isolated State had six farming systems sequenced outward from the Town (Box 9.3). In the simplest case, under the rigorous assumptions of homogeneity of fertility and transportation costs, the systems were concentric.

Von Thünen recognized that his assumptions needed to be relaxed to approximate actual conditions more closely, even in 1826. He wrote:

Actual countries differ from the Isolated State in the following ways:

1. Nowhere in reality do we find soil of the same physical quality and at the same level of fertility throughout an entire country.

2. There is no large town that does not lie on a navigable river or canal.

3. Every sizeable state has in addition to its capital many small towns scattered throughout the land.[3]

What changes in spatial organization result from taking account of these factors? And what effects do increasing prices or yields have on the pattern? The central diagram in Box 9.3 represents von Thünen's description of the effects of increasing prices and yields on crop zonation. The effects maintain the concentric zones.

An irregular pattern of natural soil fertility, on the other hand, might completely disrupt the ordered pattern of concentric land-use zones. A pocket of fertile soil beyond the limit of cultivation for low-yield soil might support the intensive crop alternation system. Such variations in soil fertility distort the spatial pattern of interaction and the simple rent gradients.

Finally, as shown in the bottom diagram of Box 9.3, substantial reorganization in the land-use pattern occurs with the introduction of a navigable river, for which von Thünen assumes a transportation rate of only one-tenth the land rate. A farm 100 miles from the Town but located on this river has the same relative accessibility as a farm 10 miles from the Town by road. A farm 5 miles from that riverside farm has the same relative accessibility as one 15 miles by land from the Town. Von Thünen pictured the crop alternation system that results extending along the banks of the river to the limit of the cultivated plain with the land-use zones changing from a concentric to a sectoral pattern. One can imagine, of course, radiating highways of superior quality producing a "starfish" pattern.

Von Thünen also raised this question: What determines the relative position of the towns in the Isolated State in respect of size and distance from each other? For example, towns of one size, distributed evenly throughout the country would support higher location rents and farm population density. But a number of disrupting factors are discussed by von Thünen. Mineral deposits, notably ore, salt, and coal, are unevenly distributed resulting in an irregular distribution of mining towns and of the manufacturing towns processing raw materials of little value in relation to their bulk. The largest town, on the other hand, as the focal center of the country, would attract those industries enjoying large economies of scale, as well as functions and amenities such as government administration, institutes of higher learning, and art collections associated with the capital city of a state.

Von Thünen was satisfied, then, to leave the Isolated State with one primary center, introducing only

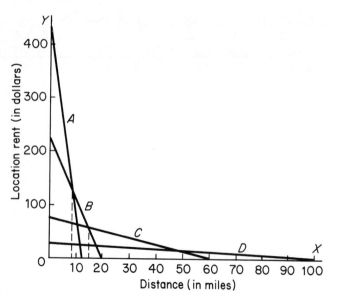

FIGURE 9.9 Rent gradients for competing crops.

[3] Ibid., p. 171.

one small town to illustrate the effect resource-oriented centers would have on land-use pattern, as in the bottom of Box 9.3. The small town would compete with the large town for food supplies, and have a region skewed away from the big town.

How might one determine the market area boundary between the large and small town? Figure 9.10 provides the answer. First, market price is lower in the small town because of lower population and, hence, demand. Rents fall with distance from each town, as in the top diagram of Figure 9.10. The spatial pattern of rents is shown in the middle figure, as is the market ''indifference'' line (that is, that line along which rents from selling in the two centers are equal). The bottom diagram thus illustrates the subdivision of the plain into market territories, and the rent patterns that result.

VON THÜNEN'S PRINCIPLES, THEN AND NOW

Great changes have occurred in agricultural and transportation technology, and world population has grown

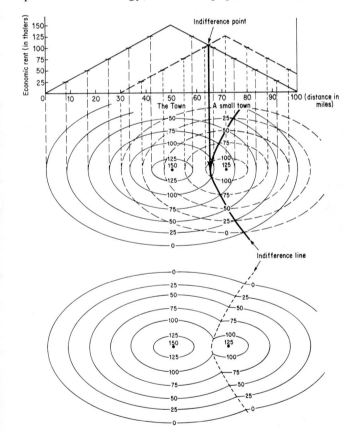

considerably since the *Isolated State* was written. At that time in many parts of the world, broad distance-related production zones could be distinguished not only in agriculture, but in other kinds of resource exploitation. W. R. Mead, for example, has described how exploitation of the forest resources of Scandinavia responded to ''the discipline of distance'' in the early nineteenth century (see Figure 9.11). The sailing vessel, with complementary horse haulage or riverboat transport, gave rise to the distinctive regional zonings of farmland and woodland use. There was a sharp gradient in softwood timber values from coast and tributary waterway to the interior, with corresponding differences in their use. In general, accessible woodlands tended to provide the bulkier, less-refined materials, whereas less-accessible woodlands produced the refined more transportable commodities. Norway, closer to Western European demand, produced relatively more of the transport-sensitive forest products than Finland.

Similar examples have been reported in many other historical instances, and at many scales, from the agricultural village to zonation of activity in the global economy itself. Even today, in those parts of the world where people still walk or use animals for their principal motive power, distance-related adjustments of land use take place. One example explored by P. M. Blaikie involves villages in north India, where minute adjustments of land use to distance have come about because self-sustaining farmers existing close to the basic survival level have to economize upon use of their own time traveling to and from their fields (Figure 9.12).

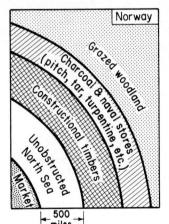
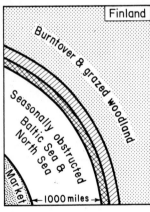

FIGURE 9.10 The impact of a second town on rent gradients and supply areas in the isolated state. The data are hypothetical and assume a single-crop, single-intensity land use with simple transportation cost-to-distance relationships.

FIGURE 9.11 Zones of softwood exploitation in Scandinavia in the early nineteenth century. [*Source:* W. R. Mead, *An Economic Geography of the Scandinavian States and Finland* (London: University of London Press, 1958), p. 95.]

BOX 9.3   Von Thünen's Farming Systems

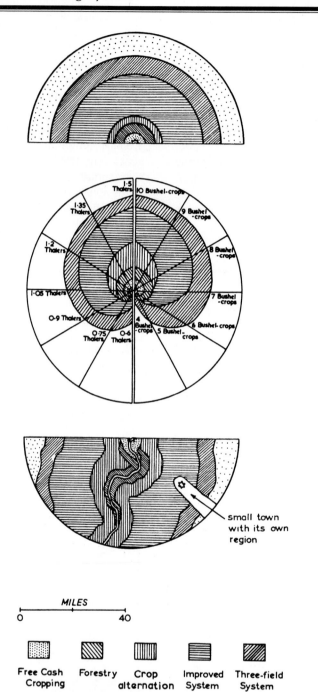

FIGURE 9c   Agricultural regions in the Isolated State, showing effects of changing prices or yields, and of a navigable river and a small second town. [*Source:* Hall, 1966, pp. 216–217.]

Von Thünen described six farming systems in the *Isolated State,* ordered outwards as follows (Figure 9c):

1. *Free cash cropping* included horticulture and dairying for which perishability dictated a location as close as possible to market. Land use is intensive, involving large labor inputs, multicropping, and heavy fertilizing; its outer limit of four miles is the maximum range of manure shipments from the city, where horses provided the principal motive power in von Thünen's day. The land is too valuable for open grazing and the milk cows are stall-fed.

2. *Forestry.* The location of forestry in the second zone comes as a surprise from the perspective of modern technology. It was logical at a time when forestry products were in great demand for both building and fuel and when transportation costs, by the primitive means available, were high so that it achieved a substantial cost reduction by proximity to market.

3. *Crop alternation system (Belgian System).* Rings 3, 4, and 5 represented decreasing intensities of crop and livestock farming modified by von Thünen from contemporary agricultural practice. The crop alternation system involved a six-year crop rotation without fallow in which a given field was devoted for two years to rye, the staple grain crop, and for one year each to potatoes, barley, clover, and vetch (a legume fed to livestock). Rye and potatoes were cash crops, and the others used for livestock production, which also provided some cash income. Soil fertility was maintained under this intensive crop system by the rotation, which included two soil-builders, clover and vetch, and by farm manure.

4. *The improved system (Mecklenburg-Koppel system).*

5. *The three-field system.* Both the improved and three-field systems were used to illustrate von Thünen's crop intensity theory earlier. The improved system involved a 7-year rotation, six of crops and one year fallow. The crops were rye, barley, and oats for one year each and three years of pasture. The three-field system commonly entailed the division of the farm area into a permanent pasture and an arable area with a rotation of winter grain, spring grain, and fallow. Production costs and yield were about halved in this system compared with the Koppel system (ring 3). Cash income in both systems came from rye and livestock products, the same commodities as the crop alternation system, with the exception of potatoes.

6. *Grazing,* the farthest zone functionally linked to the town, extended outward to a 50-German-mile radius (230 English miles). In von Thünen's day this zone was too distant for economic shipment of most grain and other crops and beyond it the land was wilderness. The grazing zone was devoted primarily to permanent pasture, although surprisingly, it could successfully market some intensive cash crops such as oilseeds, hops, tobacco, and flax.

Interestingly, zones 1, 3, 4, and 5 also tell us about economic history. The zones closest to the town were reserved for the most modern "improved" agricultures of the early nineteenth century, whereas those farthest away were the most traditional: Feudal agriculture still persisted in the more remote regions.

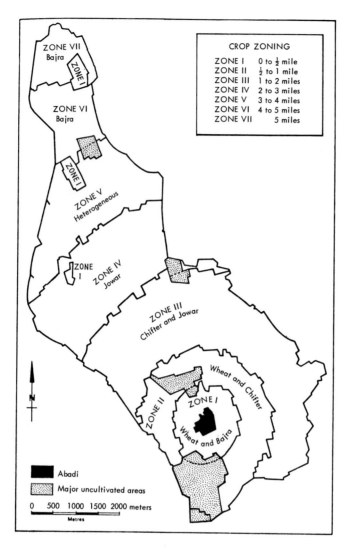

CROP ZONING

ZONE I   0 to ½ mile
ZONE II   ½ to 1 mile
ZONE III   1 to 2 miles
ZONE IV   2 to 3 miles
ZONE V   3 to 4 miles
ZONE VI   4 to 5 miles
ZONE VII   5 miles

FIGURE 9.12 Crop zoning in a northern Indian village. [*Source:* P. M. Blaikie, "Organization of Indian Villages," *Transactions of the Institute of British Geographers,* No. 52, London (March 1971), p. 15.]

Zonation characterizes dairying industries throughout the world. For example, in the United States, a hundredweight of 4 percent milk can be converted approximately into (1) 10 pounds of 40 percent cream, and 8 pounds of skim milk powder, or (2) 10 pounds of American cheese, or (3) 5 pounds of butter and 8 pounds of skim milk powder. These differences in densities cause substantial differences in the costs of shipping milk in the different forms. In addition to density, weight and perishability cause transportation costs to vary directly with the value of the product. Thus, the ratio of transportation costs of milk to an equivalent amount of cream is roughly 7 to 1, to skim milk powder 15 to 1, to American cheese 12 to 1, and to butter 25 to 1. Concentrated dairy products, whose values are high relative to their weight, can be shipped economically for longer distances than relatively bulky and perishable fluid milk. The result is a concentric

zonation of milk specialization around central markets, as illustrated in Figure 9.13.

In Western Europe, the intensive cash-cropping areas that extended only four German miles from the Town in 1826 expanded by 1950 far beyond Mecklenburg to encompass much of Europe. Some authors foresaw a single von Thünen pattern for this area (see Figure 9.14).

The stock farming belt and the extensive grain production regions have migrated largely to the New World and the Southern Hemisphere. More traditional peasant agricultures remain in remoter regions, and hunting and gathering societies only in the world's remotest peripheries. In a sense, then, the Isolated State has become the world, and the urban-industrial complexes of northwest Europe, northeast North America, and Japan great "world Thünen-Towns," albeit affected by major world-scale differences in resources.

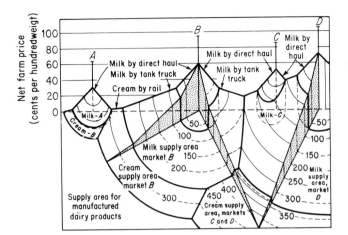

FIGURE 9.13 The net farm prices and supply areas for fluid milk, cream, and manufactured milk products, four-market model. Relative to base price for milk sold in manufacturing outlets. [*Source:* William Bredo and Anthony S. Rojko, "Prices and Milksheds of Northwestern Markets," University of Massachusetts Agricultural Experiment Station Bulletin No. 470, Amherst, 1952.]

Relaxing his initial assumptions did not lead von Thünen to anticipate this ultimate scale in the hierarchy of spatial organization, however, or the growing importance of urban centers and of manufacturing activity that have accompanied it.

Von Thünen did probe urban matters—indeed he suggested that his model was applicable to urban land use—but it was not until some 80 years ago that his principles began to be applied to an understanding of urban land use and that significant extensions to location theory were made by formulation of a theory for the location of manufacturing activity by Alfred Weber. On the other hand, it will be agreed that von Thünen's propositions—or more generally, those of rent theory—attach to every kind of resource use. Every resource commands a price, determined by scarcity commensurate with its quality and accessibility. The higher quality and the more accessible resource will be used first. Each price level calls forth a particular intensity of use. In the case of human resources, the argument extends to wages and incomes; the better educated and more skilled the worker, the higher the price (wage).

In the case of natural resources the argument is the same: As exhaustible supplies of higher quality and more accessible resources are used, scarcity pushes up the marginal revenue productivity of lower-quality and less-accessible items, but at any time, the less the accessibility and the lower the quality, the lower the price.

THE ORGANIZATION OF URBAN SPACE

Although von Thünen's study captured at best only a fleeting reality in its empirical details, his work presents principles of lasting value that today still serve as the foundations of land-use theory. His conception of economic rent as a standardized measure of accessibility was, of course, his most important single contribution. Combined with the principle of highest and best use, the concept of economic rent identifies

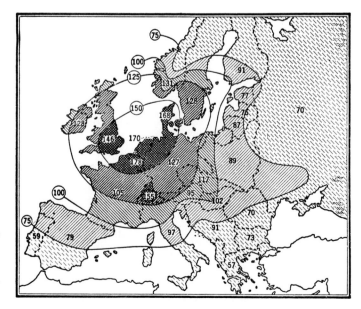

FIGURE 9.14 Intensity of agricultural production in Europe. The index of 100 is the average European yield per acre of eight main crops: wheat, rye, barley, oats, corn, potatoes, sugar beets, and hay. 1937 political boundaries. [*Source:* Michael Chisholm, *Rural Settlement and Land Use* (New York: John Wiley, 1967), p. 108, reproduced from S. van Valkenburg and C. C. Held, *Europe* (New York: John Wiley, 1952).]

the three most fundamental components of the spatial organization of economic systems:

1. *Concentric-circle arrangements* around centers of activity defining points of greatest accessibility
2. *Development axes* along major transportation routes
3. *Multiple nuclei,* with the introduction of additional points of interaction

The relevance of these components becomes more apparent when we turn to the case of urban land use.

Von Thünen noted that rural land values increase toward a large town, but that this increase is only a prelude to a far greater rise in land values within urban areas. He went on to suggest that his principles govern this determination of land values and the allocation of land use in urban areas, just as they do in rural areas.

The first applications of the principles to urban land use were not provided until the classic statements of R. M. Hurd in 1903 and of R. L. Haig in 1926, however, just 100 years after *Der Isolierte Staat* was published. Hurd wrote:

> As a city grows, more remote and hence inferior land must be utilized and the difference in desirability between the two grades produces economic rent in locations of the first grade, but not in those of the second. As land of a still more remote and inferior grade comes into use, ground rent is forced still higher in land of the first grade, rises in land of the second grade, but not in land of the third grade, and so on. Any utility may compete for any location within a city and all land goes to the highest bidder. . . . Practically all land within a city earns some economic rent, though it may be small, the final contrast being with the city's rentless and hence, strictly speaking, valueless circumference. . . .
>
> Since value depends on economic rent, and rent on location, and location on convenience, and convenience on nearness, we may eliminate the intermediate steps and say that value depends on nearness.[4]

Haig's principles, following on from Hurd, were

1. Each activity seeks the location of maximum accessibility; *rent* is the charge that the

owner of a relatively accessible site can impose because of the saving in transport costs which the use of his site makes possible.

2. The activity that can most successfully exploit the locational attributes of a given site will probably gain it through competitive bidding in the real estate market.
3. Land-use organization reflects the evaluation of the relative importance of accessibility to particular land uses.
4. The efficiency of urban spatial organization is inversely proportional to the aggregate costs of friction in overcoming spatial separation of urban functions.

A land economist, Richard Ratcliffe, succinctly restated these principles as "the structure of the city is determined by the dollar evaluation of the importance of convenience."

Concentric zones of urban land use were reported in 1923 by E. W. Burgess, who believed that these zones, illustrated in Box 9.4, developed because (1) cities grow outwards from their original center, with the newest housing always found at the edge of the developed area, and (2) socially mobile individuals move outwards geographically as they move upwards in the socioeconomic system. Thus, higher-income families build new houses on the periphery of the city where open land is available and sell their old homes to lower-income families. The market provides housing for lower-income families not by building for them directly, but by a "filtering" process, letting higher-income families absorb depreciation costs before the house is handed on. This, in turn, produces very definite patterns of urban development and community change as the city grows and as new immigrants on the lowest rungs of the socioeconomic ladder find initial residences in "ports of entry" in the oldest neighborhoods closest to the city center. The growth of the city increases the space needs of residents of each zone causing an *invasion* by each zone into the next outer zone so that at any given distance from the city center there is a "succession" of land uses. Burgess called this the *process of invasion and succession.*

Later, in 1939, Homer Hoyt advanced an axial model of urban development. He had been studying block data on rents for 64 medium to small American cities, provided by the Works Progress Administration of the United States federal government, supplemented by his own surveys of New York, Chicago, Detroit, Washington, and Philadelphia. He discovered that high-rent residential areas occupy only certain segments of an urban area, extending outward like

---

[4] R. M. Hurd, *Principles of City Land Values* (New York: The Record and Guide, 1924), pp. 12–13.

slices of a cake. The high-grade residential area has its point of origin near the retail and office center where the higher-income groups work and farthest from the industries and warehouses where the lower-income groups work. Expansion can be outward only, because other growth points having a different character also grow, thus preventing lateral expansion. Hoyt noted that higher-priced residential construction tends to expand along the fastest existing transportation lines and toward the homes of community leaders. It is also attracted toward high ground and to waterfronts and riversides free of industrial use. It tends to follow the same direction of growth for long periods but is influenced by the location of new office buildings, banks, and stores. Hoyt noted, finally, that the direction of the growth of better residential neighborhoods may be changed by estate developers.

Soon after Hoyt, in 1943, Chauncy D. Harris and Edward L. Ullman suggested that models of urban land use must recognize the existence of more than one nucleus within a city around which growth occurs. The nuclei may date from the origin of the city as in London where "The City," the center of finance and commerce, and Westminister, the political focus, were at one time separated by open country. In addition, new centers may develop with city growth, as in Chicago where heavy industry, at first localized along the Chicago River in the heart of the city, migrated to the Calumet District, serving there as the nucleus for extensive new development.

The emergence of separate nuclei and differentiated districts are related by Harris and Ullman primarily to three centrifugal and one centripetal factors. The centrifugal factors are the rent gradient coupled with space requirements, the need for specialized facilities, and incompatibilities among different land uses. The centripetal factors that convert simple dispersion to multiple nuclei are the functional convenience, magnetism, and prestige that are not entirely restricted to the central nucleus.

The number of nuclei, Harris and Ullman said, may vary according to the historical development and localization forces involved. Typically, however, five distinct nuclei occur: the central business district, wholesaling and light manufacturing, heavy industrial, specialized nuclei, and suburban and dormitory satellites. The resulting internal structure of the city is suggested by Figure 9.15.

The strongest pattern is that of the decline of land prices with distance from the city center. That population densities repeat this pattern should be no surprise: As land prices fall relative to the prices of other inputs, households will substitute land for capital and labor. Because per-household land consumption increases, there will then be less households per unit of area, and population densities must fall.

The population density gradient has a very particular shape. This was the conclusion of Colin Clark in 1951. He argued that the pattern was one of negative exponential decline from the city center and could be

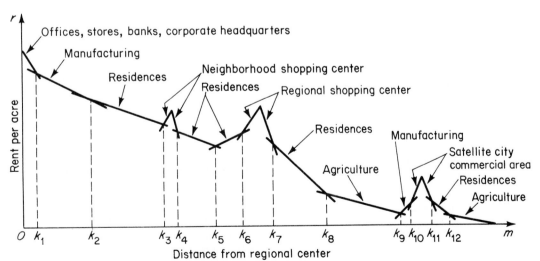

FIGURE 9.15 Hypothetical land rent profile in a multicentered urban area. [*Source:* William Goldner, *A Model for the Spatial Allocation of Activities and Land Uses in a Metropolitan Region* (Berkeley: Bay Area Transportation Study Commission, September 1968).]

BOX 9.4   The Burgess Model of Urban Social Geography (circa 1925)

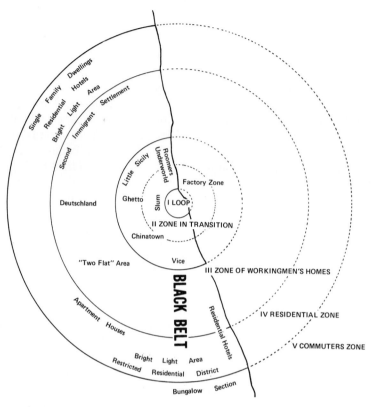

FIGURE 9d   Burgess's spatial model. [*Source:* Robert E. Park and Ernest W. Burgess, *The City* (Chicago: University of Chicago Press, 1925), pp. 41–53.]

expressed by the formula

$$d_x = d_o e^{-bx}$$

where

d = population density

x = distance from city center

d_o = density at city center

e = natural logarithmic base

b = density gradient (a measure of city compactness)

or

$\ln d_x = \ln d_o - bx$ when the natural logarithm (ln) of density is used

Clark provided 36 examples of cities for which this equation provided a good fit of population-density gradients. These examples ranged in time from 1801 to the contemporary period and from Los Angeles to Budapest. Subsequent research has added a myriad of cases, and repeated testing has not overturned Clark's basic claim that the negative exponential pattern is universally the simplest and best-fitting description of urban densities.

The five zones E. W. Burgess said characterized the internal structure of the city were

Zone I: The Central Business District. The center of the city is the focus of commercial, social, and civic life. The heart of this district is the downtown retail district with its department stores, smart shops, office buildings, clubs, banks, hotels, theaters, museums, and headquarters of economic, social, civic, and political life. Encircling this area of work and play is the less well-known Wholesale Business District with its "market," warehouses, and storage buildings.

Zone II: The Zone in Transition. Surrounding the Central Business District are areas of residential deterioration and social disorganization caused by the encroaching of business and industry from Zone I. This Zone in Transition has a factory district for its inner belt and an outer ring of retrogressing neighborhoods, first-settlement immigrant colonies, roominghouse districts, homeless-men areas, resorts of gambling, bootlegging, sexual vice, and breeding-places of crime. It has the greatest concentration of cases of poverty, bad housing, juvenile delinquency, family disintegration, physical and mental disease. As families and individuals prosper, they escape from this area into Zone III beyond, leaving behind a marooned residuum of the defeated, leaderless, and helpless.

Zone III: The Zone of Independent Workingmen's Homes. This broad urban ring of second immigrant settlement has residents who desire to live near their work. It is a housing area of two-flat dwellings, generally of frame construction, with the owner living on the lower floor and with a tenant on the other. While the father works in the factory, the son and daughter typically have jobs in the downtown area, attend dance halls, and motion pictures in the bright-light areas, and plan upon marriage to set up homes in Zone IV.

Zone IV: The Zone of Better Residences. The Zone of Better Residences contains the great middle class of native-born Americans, small business men, professional people, clerks, and salesmen. Once communities of single homes, they are becoming apartment-house and residential-hotel areas. Within these areas at strategic points are found local business centers of such growing importance that they have been called "satellite downtowns." The typical constellation of business and recreational units includes a bank, one or more United Cigar Stores, a drug store, a high-class restaurant, an automobile display row, and a so-called "wonder" motion picture theatre. With the addition of a dancing palace, a cabaret, and a smart hotel, the satellite Loop also becomes a "bright-light" area attracting a city-wide attendance. In this zone men are outnumbered by women, independence in voting is frequent, newspapers and books have wide circulation,

and women are elected to the state legislature.

Zone V: The Commuter's Zone. Beyond the areas of better residence is a ring of encircling small cities, towns, and hamlets. The Commuter's Zone contains the main dormitory suburbs, because the majority of men residing there spend the day at work in the Central Business District, returning only for the night. Thus, the mother and the wife become the center of family life. If the Central Business District is predominantly a homeless-men's region; the rooming house district, the habitat of the emancipated family; the area of first-immigrant settlement, the natural soil of the patriarchal family transplanted from Europe; the Zone of Better Residences with its apartment houses and residential hotels, the favorable environment for the equalitarian family; then the Commuter's Zone is without question the domain of the matricentric family. The communities in this Commuter's Zone are probably the most highly segregated of any in the entire metropolitan region, including in their range the entire gamut from an incorporated village run in the interests of crime and vice, to exclusive villages with wealth, culture, and public spirit.

[*Source:* Ernest W. Burgess, "Urban Areas" in T. V. Smith and L. D. White, eds., *Chicago: An Experiment in Social Science Research* (Chicago: University of Chicago Press, 1929), pp. 114–123.

TOPICS FOR DISCUSSION

1. If, when the fixed factor *Y* is equal to 1, a firm's production functions are

$$\text{total product (TP)} = 6x^2 - x^3$$

$$\text{average product (AP)} = 6x - x^2$$

   (a) What is the marginal product (MP) function?
   (b) From the three production functions, construct a table and a figure showing graphically the three production functions for six successively larger increments to the variable factor *X*.
   (c) It should be possible then to divide the figure into three stages, a phase of increasing average returns to the variable factor, a phase of diminishing average returns to the variable factor, and a phase of negative marginal returns. Give the characteristics of each function in each stage.

2. Holding land quality constant, what is the effect of increasing transportation costs on marginal revenue productivity? In such a situation, what kind of a pattern do rents display? What happens to farm size with increasing distance? Why?

3. In what sense has von Thünen's Isolated State become the world? Is there anything wrong with this interpretation? If so, what?

4. Consider the location rent formula, $R = E(p - a) - Efk$:
   (a) As intensity of land use increases, what happens to

the difference between market price (p) and production costs (a)?

(b) What happens to transportation costs per unit as distance increases?

5. *Economic rent* of a good is the portion of the price that does not influence the amount of that good in existence. Consider the following statement: "The rent for land in Chicago is not a payment that is necessary to produce that land. It is a necessary payment to obtain use of the land. From the first point of view, it is an economic rent; from the latter point of view, it is a cost." Do you agree? If so, why? If not, why not?

6. In what aspect does Hoyt's model of land use differ from Burgess's, and how do both Hoyt's and Burgess's models differ from Harris's and Ullman's model?

FURTHER READINGS

BECKMANN, MARTIN. *Location Theory*. New York: Random House, 1968.

A succinct treatment of the theories of industrial location, land use, and central places, together with the locational impact of economic growth. See especially Chapter 4, "Allocation of Land," which summarizes von Thünen's main ideas and extends these to include the effects of changes in demand, wage differentials, the appearance of urban rings, the introduction of transportation routes, and other complicating elements.

CHISHOLM, MICHAEL. *Rural Settlement and Land Use: An Essay in Location*. New York: John Wiley, 1962.

Simply and interestingly written, this introduction to the theory of rural land use is abundantly illustrated with empirical examples taken from many parts of the world.

GREGOR, HOWARD F. *Geography of Agriculture: Themes in Research*. Englewood Cliffs, N.J.: Prentice Hall, 1970.

A general treatment of the geography of agriculture. Chapter 4, "Spatial Organization," contains a brief exposition of rural land use theory.

HALL, PETER (Ed.). *Von Thünen's Isolated State*. Trans. Carla M. Wartenberg. Oxford: Pergamon Press, 1966.

This translation of von Thünen's classic work on agricultural land use theory covers the essential portions of the original. The book provides invaluable access to von Thünen's seminal writings for English-speaking students of location theory. A substantial introduction by the editor supplies revealing background information on von Thünen and his times and includes an especially helpful guide to the main features of his theory.

HAUSER, PHILIP M., and LEO F. SCHNORE. *The Study of Urbanization*. New York: John Wiley, 1966.

In this general study of urbanization, Chapter 10, "On the Spatial Structure of Cities in the Two Americas," interestingly contrasts the typical urban land use patterns of two distinct cultural realms.

HOOVER, EDGAR M. *The Location of Economic Activity*. New York: McGraw-Hill, 1984.

An influential and comprehensive statement of location theory for four decades, this very readable work remains a valuable sourcebook on the subject. See particularly Chapter 6, "Land Use Competition."

KELLERMAN, A. "Agricultural Location Theory 1: Basic Models," *Environment and Planning A* 21 (1989), 1381–1396 and "Agricultural Location Theory 2: Relaxation of Assumptions and Applications," pp. 1427–1446.

A straightforward and thorough review of von Thünen that is well illustrated and fully referenced.

10

Locational Decisions and Choice by Manufacturing Industry

OVERVIEW

The classical theory of the location of industry is concerned with the optimal location for an individual plant in a given industry. It assumes an economic maximizer seeking the plant location that minimizes transportation costs or maximizes some benefit. In practice locational decisions are the work of economic satisficers who lack perfect knowledge and who may be more concerned with retaining their share of the market than with trying to maximize profits. Significant differences occur between the locational behavior of small firms, operating a single plant, and multinational enterprises (MNEs), which may operate several firms, each with numerous plants. The location of small firms may reflect an adoption process in which surviving firms map the margins of locational choice. The location of MNEs involves an eclectic theory that includes elements of international trade theory.

An industry is simply the aggregation of firms making similar products, and the spatial distribution of an industry is simply the aggregate of the locations of all its individual firms. That distribution changes as firms expand, decline, or exit and as new firms are established. Location theory must be concerned with all these components of change in firms and their employment to understand the changing location of industry.

OBJECTIVES

- to identify the essential features of least-cost location theory as developed by Weber and others
- to present laws of the market area that can be derived from least-cost location theory
- to review other location theories that make different assumptions about the relative importance of transportation costs, market, and locational choice generally
- to describe the resurgence of small firms, the components of change in firm numbers and their employment, and the characteristics of small-firm owner-managers and their contribution to employment growth at the urban, regional, and national scales
- to distinguish between locational *adoption* and *adaption* and to suggest how far the geography of the births and deaths of firms may reflect these processes
- to outline the growth and distribution of the multinational manufacturing enterprise and the organization of mass production, and to note the contrasts with lean, just-in-time production that is beginning to replace it
- to outline employment creation, both direct and indirect, by MNEs (multinational enterprises)

THE IMPORTANCE OF LOCATIONAL DECISIONS AND CHOICE BY MANUFACTURING INDUSTRY

Locational decisions by manufacturing industry are thought to be of considerable importance to the economic growth and health of cities, regions, and even nations. Manufacturing is the dominant economic base of most large cities, and a large proportion of employment in the service industries meets the need of manufacturing workers and their families. Hence manufacturing tends to be a *city-forming* activity, and service industries tend to be *city-serving*. The distribution of the urban population in most developed countries is largely an echo of the distribution of manufacturing.

The differences in employment growth rates between cities and regions are much affected by their industry mix. Areas enjoying a disproportionate share of fast-growth industries have usually had a relatively fast rate of employment growth, as was demonstrated by Harry Jones (1940) in the Barlow *Report on the Distribution of Industrial Population*. Jones found that regional differences in the growth rates of the same industry were much smaller than the national differences in the growth rates of different industries at that time.

There is, however, a concern by government and trade unions that manufacturing can be relocated more readily than other economic activities. Employment in the primary sector is, after all, resource-based, and the resources, whether mineral, biotic, or aquatic are thought of as being locationally fixed. Oil wells are, for instance, locationally tied to oil fields. Equally, nonbasic service employment is locationally tied to the distribution of the workers in the basic industries. Shops need a location that is convenient for their customers. But what of manufacturing industry? What locational choice does it have? Manufacturing is moving out of high-labor-cost locations in developed countries to countries with lower labor costs, thereby "deindustrializing" the developed world and industrializing countries in the less-developed world. Such relocation saps the developed countries of their economic base and drains their job market of manufacturing employment. Because manufacturing provides higher-paid, more secure jobs with better fringe payments than employment in traditional service industry, fears of deindustrialization raise concerns not only about the loss of jobs both directly and indirectly, but also about income levels and the standard of living.

The deep concerns about the *global* shift of industry first expressed in the 1970s are in sharp contrast with the benefits anticipated from a *national* shift of industry that were first identified in the Barlow report of 1940. If a country's declining regions were only slightly less competitive in costs than the more fortunate regions that benefited from a concentration of fast-growth industries, then national governments could attract new industries into the declining regions with industrial incentives and prop up their declining industries with industrial subsidies.

National policies to direct the location of industry to serve the objective of balanced regional growth have raised a host of problems. How are disadvantaged regions to be defined and delimited? Do subsidies prevent or just delay closures in declining industries? Do incentives merely offer windfall profits to firms that intended to open in these regions anyway? And much more serious is the speculation that the use of manufacturing as a *national* policy lever in fact only served to delay the necessary adjustments and rationalization of industry, so that when it did finally come, it was not only more abrupt and severe, but also contributed to the *international* shift of industry.

If incentives and subsidies have failed to secure a lasting industrial base in declining regions in Western countries, what are the future prospects of export processing zones in the newly industrializing countries? Can their lower labor costs secure for them a lasting industrial base at the international scale in competition with the new "lean producers" in more favorable locations? Is deindustrialization a passing phase, with labor costs becoming less important as a location factor?

What is the role of multinational enterprises (MNEs) in this global shift of industry? They have less attachment to any single region or country than does the small single-establishment firm, and they can move production with relative ease to take advantage of global differences in production costs. So are MNEs "snatchers" (concerned with short-run profits) rather than "stickers" (concerned with building up long-term business)? If foreign multinationals have proved to be the unstable element in manufacturing location, this shift may also explain the resurgence in the Western World of small manufacturing firms. Thus, to the general question of the factors that affect location and locational mobility must be added the specific question of differences between the locational decisions and choice of large multinational manufacturing enterprises and of small owner-managed firms.

LOCATION DECISIONS AND THEIR OBJECTIVES IN THEORY

Beckmann's Classification of Optimal Location Types

An active decision by a firm to determine the optimal location for a new manufacturing plant must, in theory, take into account whether or not production costs and the factory selling price are affected by the location of the plant. Martin Beckmann has accordingly classified locations into four types (Table 10.1). The classical theory deals with Type A, which occurs when production costs of assembling raw materials and shipping the finished goods to market vary significantly with location. It is assumed that market demand does not vary with selling price, although consumers will buy from the lowest-cost supplier. The concern of the firm is thus to find the location at which the combined costs of procuring raw materials and shipping the product to market are minimized. The firm will deviate from this least-cost location only if some other advantage such as lower labor costs or economies of scale offset the additional transportation costs that some competing location entails. The iron and steel industry is a good example of a Type A industry.

In the reverse locational type, assembly costs of components or raw materials are insignificant, so that manufacturing costs are spatially uniform. Accessibility to market is crucial because demand is sensitive to selling price, and selling price is sensitive to location. So Type C industries maximize their profits by locating close to market. Soft-drink bottling plants are an example.

Some industries may combine elements of both Types A and C. Production costs and selling price may both be sensitive to location. The location solution is then to find the location that maximizes profits by making the best trade-off possible between production costs and selling price offered by each location (Type B). The New York apparel industry, for example, has to weigh the advantages of the lower labor costs that would result from moving out of New York City with the design and marketing advantages of remaining there. Men's work clothing and women's house-dresses, which are not governed by rapid style changes, were the first to move out of New York City to locations in Pennsylvania, the Southeast, St. Louis, and Kansas City. Other firms producing cheaper dresses, coats, or suits moved outside the city but within quick truck delivery time.

A locational type of growing interest, Type D, occurs where neither production costs nor market demand vary spatially. Industries in this group, which tend to be dominated by standardized production processes, are footloose. However, those with nonroutine production activities associated with a high level of innovation do tend to agglomerate, endowing particular locations with local economies of scale and a support network of services that can reduce costs, increase sales and enhance the survival chances of new firms starting up. Silicon Valley, California, is an example of such a location where such *external economies* have developed. Recall that several types of these economies were identified in Chapter 7:

TABLE 10.1

Beckmann's classification of location types

	Selling Price (FOB):	
	Locationally Variable	*Locationally Invariant*
Production costs: Locationally variable	Type B Optimal location maximizes difference between production costs and sales revenue—for example, David M. Smith, 1981.	Type A Optimal location minimizes costs to maximize profits—for example, Alfred Weber, 1908.
Locationally invariant	Type C Optimal location maximizes profits by maximizing sales—for example, Chauncy D. Harris, 1954	Type D Plants are footloose. However, theories relating to small-firm birth rates and survival apply.

Source: After Martin Beckmann, *Location Theory*, New York: Random House, 1968, p. 11.
Note: See bibliography for references to authors cited.

1. *Economies of localization,* which result from similar plants clustering together and achieving benefits from joint use of subsidiary facilities, such as a common pool of skilled labor or uniquely specialized financial institutions.
2. *Economies of urbanization,* which result from many businesses of many kinds serving a common market, drawing on a large pool of labor, and making joint use of public facilities (housing, transport, recreation).

Emergence of Beckmann's four different types may be understood historically. The earlier phases of the Industrial Revolution involved the growth of large numbers of small manufacturing firms converting raw materials to finished products that were sold in highly competitive markets. As price-takers, these firms depended upon minimizing production costs for their successful competition and long-term survival. Toward the end of the nineteenth century, scholars began to observe that survival of the fittest had produced quite distinctive locational patterns in these industries. Industrial location theory developed as these scholars codified their understanding of the market's guiding hand: The first theories sought to explain Beckmann's Type A locational choice. The first of these theories was that of Alfred Weber (1909).

As the Industrial Revolution progressed, plant sizes increased along with scale of industrial organization and the ability of oligopolies to manipulate prices in different markets. Type A locational choice was joined by Type B behavior, and then by Type C decisions in industries creating high value-added products from standardized components produced by other manufacturing industries. By the middle of the twentieth century, as a consequence of this economic evolution, location theorists such as August Lösch and Melvin Greenhut were adding demand, price, and markets to their extensions and reformulations of Weber.

Since World War II in particular, economic evolution has progressed to even higher levels of technology with the creation of products selling at uniform prices in national markets, using inputs and manufacturing processes that cost the same wherever the plant is located. Type D situations have emerged where qualitative factors not entering into the plant's cost or profit equation seem to have dominated locational choice; predominant among these have been the regions and the environments where businesspeople and their key personnel prefer to live. Some of these locations have acquired considerable industrial concentrations and developed external economies that have lowered costs for those located within the clusters.

Cost-Minimization as a Determinant of Optimal Location

A manufacturing firm must go through several stages in getting its product onto the market:

1. Procurement of raw materials
2. Processing of raw materials into finished products
3. Distribution of products to the consumer.

The first and third of these stages involve transportation costs. The second involves the productive operations—capital inputs and economies of scale—plus labor costs. Transportation costs may dictate a plant location near the sources of raw materials where:

1. The raw materials are highly localized.
2. The processing of the raw materials involves a considerable reduction in their weight.
3. Transportation costs form a significant proportion of the manufacturing costs and the value of the finished product per unit weight is low.
4. Large volumes of raw material are used per worker.

Examples are the heavy industries such as iron and steel, shipbuilding, and chemicals that formed the economic base of many towns following the Industrial Revolution.

Under the converse conditions, a plant would be more likely to locate near the market. Such industries might use raw materials that are almost ubiquitous or for which there is little or no weight loss in processing, or produce fragile goods, making distribution costs much higher than procurement costs. Other factors supporting a market location include a requirement for frequent or rapid contact with consumers, as in the high-fashion industry, or differential transportation rates that favor bulk goods and discriminate against finished products.

Weber's Theory of Plant Location.   The original theory of plant location was formulated in 1909 by a German location economist, Alfred Weber, in a book entitled *Über den Standort der Industrien* (Theory of the Location of Industries) and was basically a theory of transport orientation. Weber sought a theory of industrial location that, he believed, would represent "one of the keys to understanding the current general social phenomenon of population concentration along with a host of other social and cultural changes which characterize our period.'' Because transport orientation was, for him, the primary key, it is appropriate that we conclude this section by examining his ideas (which shaped the analysis on which the findings already presented were based).

Assumptions and Definitions.   The assumptions upon which Weber's argument is based are as follows:

1. A uniform country with equal transportation rates like that of von Thünen's uniform plain;
2. The locations of sources of raw materials were assumed to be known and available at equal cost throughout;
3. The location of points of consumption also were assumed to be known;
4. Labor was geographically fixed. Weber assumed that there exists a number of places where labor at definite, predetermined wages could be had in unlimited quantities;
5. Transportation costs were assumed to be a function of weight and distance and were the key locational determinant. Differences in topography are allowed for by appropriate additions to distance and differences in transportability by additions to actual weight.

Limited by the science of his time, Weber conceived of his model as a mechanical system of pulleys and weights.

Terms defined included the following:

1. *Ubiquities*—materials available practically everywhere, and presumably at the same price everywhere.
2. *Localized materials*—materials obtainable only in geographically well-defined localities.
3. *Pure materials*—localized materials that enter to the extent of their full weight into the finished product. Thread to be woven into cloth is perhaps an example of this category.
4. *Gross materials*—localized materials that impart only a portion of, or none of, their weight to the finished product. Fuel is the extreme type of gross material, for none of its weight enters into the product.
5. *Material index*—indicates the proportion that the weight of localized materials bears to

the weight of the finished product. A productive process which uses pure material has an index of 1.

6. *Locational weight*—the total weight to be moved per unit of product. An article made out of ubiquities would have a locational weight of 1 because only the product itself would be moved; if it were made from pure material the locational weight would be 2 because for transportation of the product an equivalent weight of materials would be required.

7. *Isodapane*—the locus of points of equal transportation cost. The meaning of the term will become clear in the discussion.

Working with these assumptions, employing these terms, and seeking in the first instance to measure the effect of transportation upon location, Weber then imagined certain cases and developed conclusions about them.

Case 1: One Market and One Source of Raw Materials.   The first case supposes a raw material to be produced at *A* and the finished product made out of the material to be consumed at *B*. The problem is to determine where the manufacture or processing is to take place. Weber states four possibilities:

1. If ubiquities only are used, the processing will occur at point of consumption *B*, because the selection of *B* will make transportation unnecessary.
2. If one pure material is used, processing may occur at *A*, at *B*, or at any point between *A* and *B*. This conclusion is based upon the fact that the weight to be transported and the distance to be covered is the same in all instances.
3. If pure material plus ubiquities is used, the processing will occur at the point of consumption *B*, because the pure material will be without influence, and the ubiquities will govern.
4. If one weight-losing material is used, processing will occur at point of production, because the weight that is lost will not have to be transported.

Case 2: One Market and Two Raw-Material Sources.   Weber's second case assumes that raw materials are available at two places, *A* and *B*, at equal prices. The finished product is to be consumed at *C*, and the problem as before is to determine where manufacture or processing is to take place. Three possibilities are now considered:

1. If ubiquities alone are used, manufacture will occur at the point of consumption for the same reasons as when only two points were involved.

2. If several pure materials are employed, manufacture will also take place at point of consumption. On this supposition, the weight of materials exactly equals the weight of the product. All weights, whether in the form of materials or in the form of product, have to be moved from their deposits to the place of consumption. They should not deviate unnecessarily; therefore each material will proceed along the straight line that leads from the origin to the point of consumption. Unless the way of one should lead, by chance, through the deposit of another, all these ways will meet for the first time in the place of consumption. Because the assembly of all materials at one spot is the necessary first condition of manufacture, the place of consumption is the location where manufacturing will be carried on; a productive enterprise, using several pure materials alone, will always locate at the place where its products are consumed.

3. The conclusion is different if several localized weight-losing materials are used. In analyzing this case Weber sets up what he calls a "locational figure." Let us suppose a process that uses two weight-losing materials produced at *A* and *B,* and let us suppose that the product is to be consumed at *C*. Manufacture will not take place at *C* because it is undesirable to transport from *A* and *B* to *C* the material weight that does not enter into the weight of the finished product. It will not, according to Weber, occur at *A* or *B* unless the importance of one material happens to be so great as to overcome the influence of all other elements. Instead, it will usually be found somewhere *within* the triangle, at that location determined by the relative balance of the locational weights.

The "Distortions."   Weber treated labor costs as "a first distortion" of the industrial locations determined by transport costs (but see Box 10.1). The sec-

ond step of his locational analysis, then, was to plot the spatial variations in transport cost away from the optimum transport-cost location in order to observe the background against which differences in labor cost operate. If, at some other place in the region, the cost of labor per unit of product is less than it is at the optimum transport location, perhaps because an established industry closed down or an unusually high rate of population growth occurred, or a pool of particularly skilled workers is available, and if the increment to transport costs at this alternative location is less than the labor savings, a "deviation" from the "optimum" least transport cost location will arise.

Weber suggested that *isodapanes* be used to determine whether deviations from an optimum least-cost location could occur. Isodapanes are curves of equal transportation cost. All places on the same isodapane thus have transportation costs equally higher than the least-cost location. A *critical isodapane* can be identified along which the additional transportation costs are equal to the savings in labor costs. A plant can move to an alternative labor-saving location only if it is within the critical isodapane.

Having combined the effects of transport and labor costs, Weber then turned to the problem of determining how that location may be deflected within the region by the tendency of firms to agglomerate. In Weber's view, there are two main ways in which a company can gain the benefits of agglomeration. First, it may increase the concentration of production by enlarging its factory, thus obtaining savings through a larger scale of operation. Second, it may benefit by selecting a location in close association with other plants. This "social" agglomeration yields benefits from sharing specialized equipment and services, greater division of labor, and large-scale purchasing and marketing.

As a "second altering force," agglomeration acts to divert manufacturing from either a least transport-cost location or a least labor-cost location, depending upon which was originally the dominant locating influence in a given instance. For an establishment that would normally be transportation-oriented, the savings from locating close to other firms may be sufficient to justify some sacrifice of transport cost. To determine whether or not such a diversion from the least transport-cost was feasible, Weber employed a similar logic to that previously used for weighing the counterattractions of transport and labor locations.

Because the attractions of agglomeration and labor-cost savings both represent deviations from the least transport-cost location, however, in Weber's view, these two influences may conflict. The decision will go to the one that provides the greater savings.

Weber indicated that the winner is more likely to be the labor location because that is a place where "accidental" agglomeration may be expected to occur as a result of a concentration of population or the presence of special transport features. "Pure" agglomeration, he felt, would prevail only with industries having very low labor requirements, such as oil refining or chemical manufacture. The main effect of the conflict, then, is to increase the tendency of industry to collect at only a few locations.

The Launhardt-Palander Solution of the Least-Cost Location

Alfred Weber was concerned with finding the least-cost location where the market was located at certain known points of consumption. A useful contribution to understanding the importance of the location of the raw materials in determining the least-cost location for a plant had already been worked out in a general way by Wilhelm Launhardt in 1882 and was elaborated by Tord Palander in 1935. The Launhardt-Palander construction is summarized in Box 10.2, and its application to the U.S. steel industry is illustrated in Box 10.3.

The Launhardt-Palander solution leads to three principal conclusions about the location of industry under Weberian assumptions. First, there cannot be as many least-cost locations as points of consumption. Indeed, the number of least-cost locations is much more limited than might be expected. So even under the strict assumptions of Weber, industry would tend to concentrate in a manufacturing belt delimited by the location of the raw materials and by the numerical value of the material index. Furthermore, the higher the material index is, the more limited the possible number of least-cost locations and the narrower the manufacturing belt will be. Second, only the raw material locations can offer the lowest transportation costs for any extensive area, and they are the only locations that can command a large market area. The advantages of a location at the raw materials is further enhanced by the economies of scale that production for a large market area make possible. Third, and perhaps most important, the Launhardt-Palander solution provides a clear demonstration of the impact of technological advances on the location of industry.

If inputs of both raw materials per unit of output are reduced, then both lose market area to the points of consumption. However, any change in the material index has the effect of changing the actual location of an intermediate least-cost location. This change occurs because the location of the pole (P) on the weight triangle (Box 10.2) changes, and hence the line from the pole to the point of consumption (PC). The vulnerability to technological change of the least-cost status of an intermediate location enhances the advantages of a location at the source of raw materials. Intermediate locations are further disadvantaged if more realistic assumptions are introduced about transportation costs involving terminal costs and line-haul economies (Box 10.4).

The evidence about the importance of source of raw materials as stable least-cost locations for large market areas is very important. It serves to correct the impression given by simple applications of Weber's principles involving ubiquitous and localized pure materials that the point of consumption may often be the least-cost location. Under the more realistic case of localized gross materials, the point of consumption loses much of its attraction as a location for industry. Conversely the evidence about the impact of technological change is very different. It helps to explain why markets have had an increasing attraction on the location of industry, and why location theory has moved away from a concern with cost minimization (Type A, Table 10.1).

Economic Laws of the Market Area under Least-Cost Location

Assuming that any given consumption point will be served from whichever plant can deliver at the lowest combined production cost plus freight, it is possible to determine laws of the market area. The principal contributors to such laws have been Tord Palander in *Beiträge zur Standortstheorie* and Frank Fetter in "The Economic Law of Market Areas" (Box 10.5).

In the simplest case of producers with identical production and freight costs, the market boundary between them will be an *equidistant straight line*. The delivered price from either producer is equal along this market boundary and consumers are indifferent as to which firm they buy from. However, the delivered price is not the same all along the market boundary. The more distant a consumer is from the production point, the higher the transportation cost is. The two plants thus deliver at an equal but higher price.

In the case where transportation costs are equal but production costs are not, then the lower-cost producer extends its market area. The market boundary then becomes a hyperbola pointing towards the high-cost producer. As in the case before, the consumer is indifferent along the market boundary as to which firm they buy from, but the price increases along the market boundary as distance and transport costs from the firms increase. If one producer were able to progressively reduce production costs, the market boundary

BOX 10.1   Types of Labor Orientation

Labor costs are dominant locational forces in certain types of industries. If transport costs are a low proportion of total costs, if the ratio of labor to total cost is high, and if labor costs vary a good deal from place to place, plants tend to be most competitive when they are located in areas in which labor cost is least. It is under such conditions that plants are described as being *labor-oriented*. In the world today, there are major industrial shifts taking place in labor orientation as part of a global scramble for cheap labor. Accelerating wage inflation in established industrial areas is pushing manufacturers into new efforts to tap the vast pool of willing and cheap labor in poorer countries. Manufacturers are farming out production of component parts, subassemblies, and even finished products sometimes for export to other areas but often for use back home. In the process they are not only cutting their own costs but speeding the industrialization of underdeveloped countries, some of which are coming to relish the role of workshops for distant, richer lands.

Trade-offs between Money Wages and Skills.

What are the bases of this movement? Clearly, the prime reason is labor costs, but studies of labor costs show how important it is to recognize that labor costs involve not only money wages. There are many situations where money wages vary apparently without effect on industrial locations because the benefits of lower wages are offset by a lack of skill and lower productivity of the lower-wage labor force. In such cases, skills are far more important in determining the least labor cost location than money wages alone. However, the importance of labor orientation to skills may be offset by technological advances that make unskilled and semiskilled workers as productive as the skilled

workers who previously dominated the industry. In such cases, an orientation to low-wage areas rather than to skills has arisen, and is apparently the source of the world trend noted above. Labor costs, therefore, vary first in terms of money wages, and second in terms of productivity and skills.

Short- and Long-Run Labor Advantages.

If the supply of labor is great relative to local demands for labor, wages will be low compared with areas where competition for labor is relatively greater. But research has shown that low wage conditions tend to be ephemeral: If industry comes to an area in search of the low wages, the very act of movement changes the local supply and demand schedules for labor and raises the price. Also, labor tends to migrate from areas of low opportunity to areas of higher opportunity, tending to equalize geographic differentials in wages for that reason, too. Thus, labor cost variations due to money wages tend to be short-run differentials that can only persist in longer periods of time either because there is a substantial immobility of labor due to ignorance, poverty, or local social ties, or political barriers between countries that inhibit the free movement of labor. But even such immobilities will tend to be eroded in longer periods of time.

Persistent long-run money wage differentials have been studied in two types of conditions. First, are those cases in which money wage differences do not represent differences in real wages; for example, in areas where the cost of living is low. Second, there can emerge those dynamic conditions described by Gunnar Myrdal in *An American Dilemma* for the United States or in his work *Asian Drama* for conditions on an international scale. Myrdal argued that processes of "circular and cumulative causation" can

be identified such that labor cost differentials, rather than being equalized in the long run, tend to increase over longer periods of time. The principal reasons that he cited were the differential nature of the migration flows from areas of low to areas of high economic opportunity. Put simply, the most able people move to find better jobs, leaving behind an older and less able population group. This migration decreases the economic viability of the home area, although it increases the quality of skills available in the reception area. These skills impart advantages for further growth, so that the reception areas gain more and more relative advantages.

Regions with Money-Wage Advantages.

Money wages have been shown to be low in four kinds of areas, which therefore represent the most attractive zones for industry decentralizing in search of low labor costs.

1. *Where the supply of labor is increasing more rapidly than the demand for labor.* This is typical in rural and backward areas where net reproduction rates are substantially greater than elsewhere. Such a condition was typical of the rural parts of the United States in which particular minority groups lived. On an international scale, this is the characteristic of the South Asian countries. In each of these cases, migration rarely tends to offset the natural increase completely, so that a persistent labor surplus develops, which keeps the price of labor at a minimum.

2. *Where economic opportunities are declining in relation to a sizable local labor force.* Such a condition is typical of any kind of economically depressed areas. The coalfields, for example, were in this position during the

peacetime between the world wars. For a long time the anthracite towns of eastern Pennsylvania have faced this situation, as have many other mining areas. This was the history of the cotton textile towns of New England when the cotton textile industry moved to the Piedmont area of the Carolinas and Georgia. Of course, where economic opportunities are declining in relation to the labor force, wage rates will drop.

3. *Where employment opportunities are available only for part of the population.* This has been a general characteristic of female labor in heavy industrial areas where the demand is traditional only for male labor—in the coalfields, in mining areas, in fishing towns, or in railroad towns. In these areas of heavy industry, female labor has traditionally been available at very low wage rates. Where the size of the local female labor pool is large, however, labor-intensive, low-wage industries have been attracted.

4. *Where the cost of living is low so that real wages are high relative to money wages.* For example, housing prices in the American South and Southwest are much lower than in the Northeast because homes in the Northeast must be protected against the very severe winters. Lower housing prices mean that people can maintain the same real level of living at lower money wage rates because they need to put less into the housing that they purchase. A similar situation is where superior residential amenities create a substantial "psychic income" that people are willing to take instead of the higher wage rates offered in areas with fewer residential advantages. In such conditions, of course, money wages will tend not to reflect the real level of living, and the money-wage differential will act to the competitive advantage of labor-oriented firms.

Technological Change and the Ties of Localized Skills. Money wages are only significant locational factors where skills are relatively insignificant. We will turn later to instances in which the advantages of certain highly localized skills lead to the long-term ties of particular industries to particular locations, and we will discuss the reasons for the development of these localized skills. What is significant is the condition under which skill factors have been shown to exert a diminishing pull on industries. Localized skills are usually relevant to only one industry and are relatively immobile. They are thus very powerful causal factors in geographical inertia. Many operations can only break out of the bonds of localization in a skilled labor area by diminishing reliance upon the skill factor. Only when higher productivity is not related to skills will lower labor cost mean lower wages.

Industry has been shown to shift into areas of lower money wages most generally only under conditions of technological change, when increased mechanization, routinized operations and processes have tended to diminish the importance of skills. The introduction of line methods of production facilitates the use of relatively "green" labor, for example, so that operations can become routinized and can be performed efficiently with only a short period of training. Thus, when semiskilled labor force requirements become increasingly uniform, decentralization of routinized operations is facilitated in the direction of low-wage areas, and a wider source of labor is available. But, of course, we have to repeat that this movement to low-wage areas is essentially a movement of routinized operations. Quality products have to stay in the traditional areas, for style cannot be routinized and the skills required for production of high style are localized. In the clothing industry, for example, ready-made clothing production has moved to cheap labor areas, but style lines remain in the world style centers—New York, London, Paris, and so on.

In routinized operations, on the other hand, low-wage areas may even have an advantage in productivity. First of all, a new plant coming into a previously nonindustrialized area can "skim the cream" off the local labor force by offering higher wages than those offered by the alternative occupations of the previously nonindustrialized area. This new labor force in general, having no previous experience in factory employment and no preconceived notions about the organization of the industry, or about work loads, is more plastic to requirements of a changed technology, and will be willing to operate with more pieces of machinery than the worker in the traditional industrial areas. Also, too, low-wage areas tend to be those areas that have the least restrictive labor codes—we are all well aware of the substantial differences in legislation relating to employment and labor conditions among the states. The areas that have the most restrictive forms of legislation also tend to be the areas in which the trade union movement is strongest. In the United States this reflects, in general, the differences between North and South and between large city and small town. The relative abundance of labor in the South and in small-town locations means the inability of trade unions to establish themselves. Smaller towns, too, will tend to be dominated by one producer, who controls whatever he or she does not own locally. There, work loads are likely to be higher, employee benefits lower, and employers much freer to adapt the productive process to their wishes.

BOX 10.2   The Launhardt-Palander Solution of the Least-Cost Location

---

1. Launhardt and Palander provided a simple geometric construction that demonstrates the market area served, given Weber's assumptions. In particular, assume that the firm must minimize transportation costs and that M_1 and M_2 are the only sources of the raw materials needed for production.

2. Construct a weight triangle $M_1 M_2 P$ in which the sides of the triangle are proportional to the weights of the raw material inputs and the weight of the finished product output.

    (a) $M_1 M_2$ is translated from a geographic distance, set by the scale of the map, to a geometric distance equal to the unit weight of output.
    (b) $M_1 P$ equals the weight of the M_2 input per unit of output
    (c) $M_2 P$ equals the weight of the M_1 input per unit of output

3. Draw the circumscribing circle through $M_1 M_2 P$.

4. Extend PM_1 to A and PM_2 to B. The least-cost location for any point of consumption above $M_1 M_2$ can now be determined.

5. Assume the point of consumption, C_1, is beyond the circumscribing circle. The manufacturing location which minimizes transportation costs is L, where the line PLC_1 intersects the circumscribing circle. Repeat for C_2 also on the line PLC_1. The least-cost location is still at L. For A, the least-cost location is M_1 and for B it is M_2.

6. Market areas can be determined that are served from least-cost locations on or within the arc $M_1 L M_2$. M_1 and M_2 have the largest areas. The arc $M_1 L M_2$ is the locus of points serving markets beyond the arc. The area within the arc is served by plants at each point of consumption.

7. To complete the map of market areas, the construction (steps 2 to 6) is repeated with the weight triangle above $M_1 M_2$. In this example, M_1 has the largest market area because it has a larger input, by weight, than M_2.

The Location of M_1 and M_2

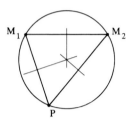

The Weight Triangle with Circumscribing Circle

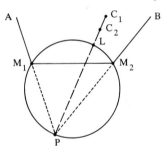

Note: the material index equals

$$(M_1 P + M_2 P)/ M_1 M_2$$

The Least-cost Location for C_1 and C_2

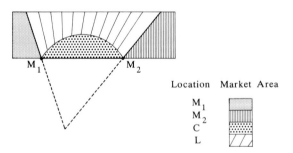

Market Areas Above $M_1 M_2$

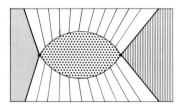

Location	Market Area
M_1	
M_2	
C	
L	

The Complete Map of Market Areas

BOX 10.3 *Locational Implications of a Reduced Material Index: The Case of the U.S. Steel Industry*

1. In 1900 the U.S. steel industry averaged 1.85 tons of coal and 1.83 tons of iron ore per ton of finished steel. The MI (material index) was 3.68 and given the primary locations of coal at Connellsville and ore at Mesabi, the market area map is easily constructed using the Launhardt-Palander construction. Pittsburgh had the largest market area and had been the leading steel producer since 1875.

THE U.S. STEEL INDUSTRY: 1900

Annual Capacity
million gross tons

25
10
1

Mesabi

Connelsville-
Pittsburgh

2. By 1960, coal inputs had dropped to 0.79 tons and iron ore to 1.10 reflecting technological advances and the greater use of scrap. The MI was 1.89. Pittsburgh had tried to retain its market share with Pittsburgh-Plus Pricing, but the industry was moving closer to the markets, particularly along the Eastern seaboard, and to Detroit and Chicago.

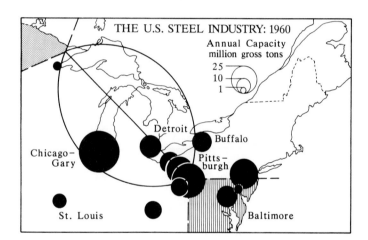

THE U.S. STEEL INDUSTRY: 1960

Annual Capacity
million gross tons

25
10
1

Detroit

Buffalo

Chicago-
Gary

Pitts-
burgh

St. Louis

Baltimore

3. Superimposing the two sketch maps illustrates the locational implications of the reduction in the MI.

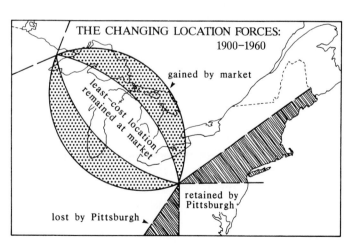

THE CHANGING LOCATION FORCES:
1900–1960

gained by market

least-cost location
remained at market

retained by
Pittsburgh

lost by Pittsburgh

Note: This example is based on an unpublished idea of Richard Lamb.

BOX 10.4   Plant Location with Line-Haul Economies and Transshipment

Consider an industry using one raw material located at *X* and serving one market located at *Y*. The farther a plant from the raw materials, *X*, the higher will be its procurement costs. So procurement costs, *ab*, increase from *X*. Conversely, the farther the plant from the market at *Y*, the higher will be its distribution costs. So distribution costs increase from *Y*(*cd*). The transport cost curves assume there are terminal or loading charges (*cY* for *Y* and *aX* for *X*), and line-haul economies so that the cost per kilometer decreases with distance.

A plant minimizes its transportation costs, under these assumptions, by locating at either the market (*Y*) or at the raw materials (*X*). At either of these locations it eliminates one set of terminal charges and gains the maximum long-haul economies.

The cost structure changes if there is a break of bulk point *T* where goods must be transshipped, say from railroad to canal. Both procurement and distribution costs jump at *T* because of additional unloading-loading charges. A plant at *T* avoids these charges, and in fact, on the freight rate scheduled as shown, *T* is a lower transportation cost point than *X*, the raw material location.

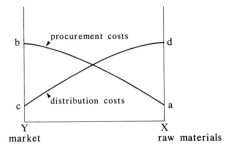

Procurement and Distribution Costs

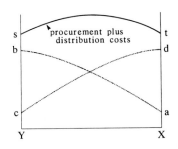

Total Transportation Costs

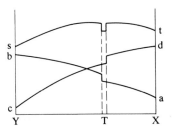

would encroach on the second producer in a succession of hyperbolas. Provided, however, that the difference in production costs remains less than the shipping costs between the two producers, then the higher-cost producer will always retain the local market together with the area facing away from the lower-cost producer. It is only where a producer has lower transportation costs than a competitor, that the competitor's market area can be reduced to an enclave. Furthermore, this can happen even though their production costs are lower.

Some excellent examples of the above cases can be drawn from Britain's Labor government's post–World War II White Papers on the sand and gravel, brick, and cement industries. These examples reveal increasing concentration of production as relative transport and production costs decline from one case to the other.

Sand and gravel are widely available in superficial deposits in Britain. They are usually worked together, because gravel aggregates are found surrounded by sand. The product has a very low value in relation to bulk: In 1948 the pit price was 5 shillings per ton, including all costs of excavation and dressing. Pit price does not vary much from one part of the country to another. Transportation costs loom large in final delivered prices: Transportation of only 2 miles increased selling prices by 30 percent (the markup being for the fixed costs of loading and the variable costs of carriage) and shipment of 13 miles doubled the pit price. Because consumers make their purchases on the basis of final delivered price it is easy to see how small sand and gravel pits multiply, each serving small market areas limited by increasing transportation costs. Few pits sold sand and gravel farther than 30 miles from the pit in Britain; the few exceptions are where cheap water transportation is available.

In 1950 there were almost 1500 brick-making plants in Great Britain. There are very few clays in the country that have not been worked for brick making. Transportation costs were lower in relation to production costs than for sand and gravel. Prices increased 20 percent with shipment of 50 miles, and doubled if shipped 150 miles. Lower transport costs imply larger market areas, and more latitude in location of the brick-making plants. Thus, plants tended to concentrate on the best brick-making clays. One-third of the productive capacity of Great Britain was found at the time of the White Paper in 46 plants at Bedford, Bletchley, and Peterborough in the Midlands where the superior Oxford clays were used to make "Fletton bricks," the familiar red bricks that characterize the English landscape. This concentration was made possible because production costs on the Oxford clays were lower than elsewhere. Peculiar advantages are thick homogeneous beds that reduce excavation costs, the fact that 5 percent of the volume of the clay is carbonaceous, which reduces the amount of coal that has to be purchased to bake the bricks, and the plastic qualities of the clay, which eliminate pretreatment, such as pulverization, normally required before bricks can be molded. The Fletton producers sold over longer distances by virtue of lower production costs.

A third case is illustrated by the British cement industry. There are two kinds of cement: (1) Portland cement, formed by burning clay and chalk together until they fuse in a clinker, which is crushed to make cement, and (2) blast-furnace cement, a by-product of the steel-making industry. The former is most common in England, and provides this third example of the joint role of transport and production costs in reducing the diffusion of industry.

Several raw materials are needed to produce Portland cement. To obtain 100 tons of cement requires 225 tons of chalk, 75 tons of clay, 60 tons of

coal, and 5 tons of gypsum. Clay and chalk are usually found close together in England, and because chalk inputs are greatest, cement plants tend to be tied to sources of chalk. But because costs of transporting cement are high, cement plants tended to be small, located centrally to small scattered markets. Price increases with overland transport are such that the cement was not sold farther than 25 miles overland from the cement plant.

In spite of such obvious pressures for diffusion, however, 50 percent of Britain's Portland cement was produced in the Thames-Medway area, southeast of London. Why should there have been this concentration? First, the Greater London market, accounting for 25 percent of Great Britain's consumption of cement, lay within a 25-mile radius of the Thames-Medway cement plants. Second, the chalk of lower Thamesside is pure, easily extracted and converted into cement so that production costs are lower than elsewhere. As in the use of Fletton bricks, this led to increases in the market area of the cement plants. Third, the plants were located by the river Thames, and cheap water transport was available to cement markets around the coasts of England. Thamesside was able to dominate the coastwise cement trade for several hundred miles. The lesson is that the size and shape of market areas, and amount produced in any area, may be modified by the size of local markets and by differentials in transportation rates.

The Market as a Factor in the Location of Industry

Chauncy D. Harris has drawn attention to the increasing importance of market as a factor in the location of industry and proposed a market potential concept to measure the aggregate accessibility of any location to all consumers within a given area (Box 10.6 and Type C, Table 10.1).

Harris's argument is fundamentally as follows. Market is growing in importance as a factor in the location of industry. But freight movements can be shown to decrease systematically with increasing distance from a market. Total shipments to a market must, of course, increase in direct proportion to the size of a market. No industrial plant is restricted to serving a single market. Hence an abstract measure is needed of possible contacts with all markets taking into account their size and their distance. Physics provides such a measure in calculating the strength of a field, whether electrical, magnetic, or gravitational. Harris calls this measure *market potential* and notes that it is analogous to population potential, which had

BOX 10.5   Laws of the Market Area Under Transport-Cost Minimization

MARKET AREA LAWS WHERE TRANSPORTATION COSTS ARE EQUAL

The Law of the Equidistant Market Boundary

Assume that equal products are made at A and B and shipped at equal transportation rates. The delivered cost will increase concentrically outwards from A and B. If consumers always buy the product sold at the lowest delivered price, then *the market boundary between A and B will be an equidistant straight line.*

1.(a)   Delivered prices from A and B and the Equidistant Market Boundary

1.(b)   The price profile along the section through AB, showing delivered price gradients A_pA_f and B_pB_f.

The Law of the Hyperbolic Line of Indifference

If the price at $B(B_p)$ is higher than the price of $A(A_p)$, and assuming goods are shipped at equal transportation rates, then the market boundary is a hyperbolic curve, which cuts into market area of the higher cost producer.

a.

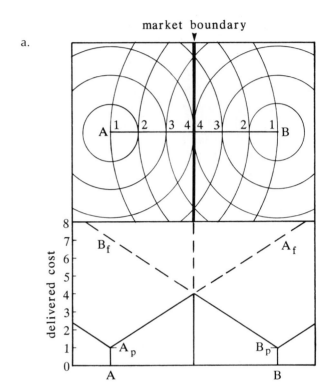

b.

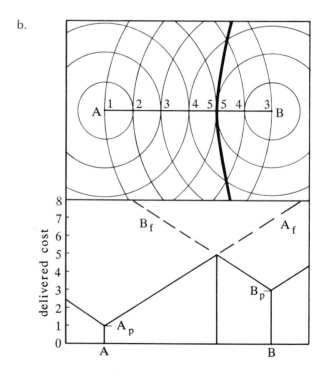

The Law of the Encroaching Hyperbolic Market Boundaries

If the price at B were to increase in progressive increments, then the market area of A would steadily encroach on B. A sequence of hyperbolic curves would result. The penultimate case is where A can deliver to B at only slightly more than B's FOB price. The market area of B then collapses to a line extending from B away from A. Finally, B exits from production, where its FOB price is higher than the delivered price from A.

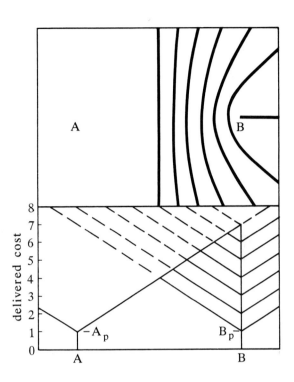

MARKET AREA LAWS WHERE TRANSPORTATION COSTS ARE NOT EQUAL

The Law of the Parabolic Market Enclave

Market areas are sensitive to differences in transportation costs. If the plant at B faces higher freight rates than A, in addition to a higher FOB price, the market area around B can shrink to a parabolic market enclave.

See Frank Fetter, "The Economic Laws of Market Areas," *The Quarterly Journal of Economics,* 38 (1924), 520–529.

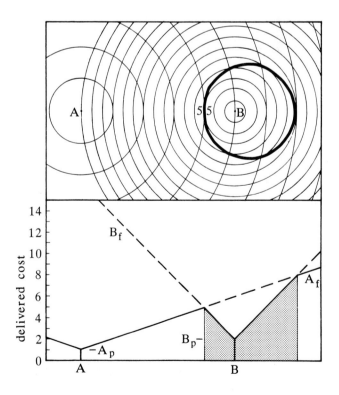

BOX 10.6   *Market Potential*

ASSUMPTIONS: Market potential makes two simple, basic assumptions:

1. Larger market centers generate more sales at a location than smaller market centers at equal distances from that location.
2. The sales made in a given market diminish with distance from that market.

DEFINITION: The market potential (P) of any location (i) is proportional to the sales (M) of every location (j) weighted by their distance (d_{ij}) from that location.

$$P_i = \sum_j \frac{M_j}{d_{ij}}$$

Market potential was defined by Chauncy D. Harris, who introduced the concept, as *an abstract measure of the intensity of possible contact with the market.* That is, it indexes each location's aggregate accessibility to the national market.

MARKET SHARE: The market share assumption of market potential is in sharp contrast to that made in Laws of the Market Area under Transport-Cost Minimization, Box 10.5.

Spatial monopoly within market area

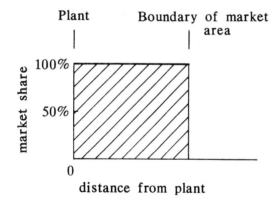

Market share under transport-cost minimization

Distance decay in market share

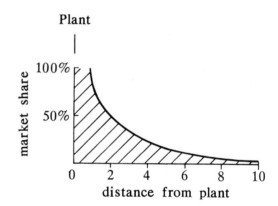

Market share with market potential

Calculating market potential

1. Data

Town	A	B	C	I	J	K	L	M	N
Sales	250	1000	250	100	500	100	250	100	100

Distances to:
From:

	A	B	C	I	J	K	L	M	N
B	5	1.5	5	5	10	15	20	25	25
J	15	10	15	5	1.5	5	10	15	15
M	30	25	30	20	15	10	5	1.5	10

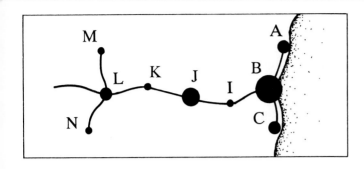

Map of Locations

2. *Calculations (sales divided by distance)*

										Total	Index
B	50	667	50	20	50	7	13	4	4	865	100
J	17	100	17	20	333	20	25	7	7	546	63
M	8	40	8	5	33	10	50	67	10	231	27

3. *Explanation*

The calculations are illustrated for an area with nine towns, three on the coast (A, B, and C), and the remainder inland (I through N). All towns are 5 miles from their nearest neighbor. Average travel distance within towns is set at 1.5 miles. The sales at B are $1000, at J $500, at A, C, and L $250, and at the rest, $100. These totally un-realistic figures facilitate the arithmetic.

The data are set out in the form of a matrix with sales in the first row, followed by the *ij* distances for each *i*th town.

The calculations are given for three of the towns: B, J, and M. For each town, the sales at every other town are divided by the distance to that town and the results recorded. B is 5 miles from A, so that contribution of A to B's potential is its $250 of sales divided by 5 miles equal 50. The sum of all B's values is 865—the highest value for the area. Indexing to a 100 on this value gives a market potential index of 63 for J and 27 for M. The indexes for the complete set of towns are as follows:

Town	A	B	C	I	J	K	L	M	N
Potential	84	100	84	83	63	47	41	27	27

The market potential index values can be plotted on the map and isolines (or contours) of equal value plotted.

Market Potential Index

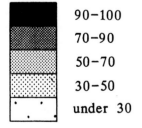

- 90–100
- 70–90
- 50–70
- 30–50
- under 30

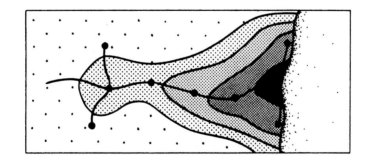

See Chauncy D. Harris, "The Market as a Factor in the Localization of Industry in the United States," *Annals of the Association of American Geographers*, 44, (1954), 315–348.

been introduced to the social sciences by John Q. Stewart. The market potential of any location is the sum of its interactions with each market (including itself). These interactions are proportional to the size of each market and inversely proportional to the distance from that market. Hence market potential (P) is defined as the summation (Σ) of markets (M_j) accessible to a point (i) divided by their distance from that point (d_{ij}).

$$P_i = \sum_j \frac{M_j}{d_{ij}}$$

There are many reasons why market has increased in importance as a factor in the location of industry. One is the technological advances that have decreased the amount of material inputs per unit of output in most industries (Box 10.3). Another is the higher productivity of labor, which frees an increasing proportion of the labor force to move from primary activities to manufacturing, and from both to move into services. That is, a shift of the labor force is taking place from activities that are raw-material oriented to those that are market-oriented. Products too are becoming more sophisticated. The horse and buggy gives way to the automobile, and the automobile incorporates over time more and more features to increase ease of driving, safety, and comfort. The icebox is replaced by the mechanical refrigerator, which also incorporates, over time, additional features. As another example, compare the amounts of materials used in a microwave oven and a conventional oven.

Not only are the material inputs being reduced in manufactured products, but the research and design, the engineering, and the sales and marketing components are all increased. These components are generally concentrated at major market centers. Furthermore, as manufacturing processes become more sophisticated, waste products become by-products, reducing still further the attraction of raw material locations for industry. In any case, manufacturing becomes vertically integrated and multistage, with the final stages comprising the assembly of components in which there is no weight loss. So as Harris notes, major agglomerations of population become self-reinforcing networks with a growing concentration of the facilities and services, management and labor force, and transportation and marketing in addition to their actual market sales.

The correlations between market potential and some aggregate measure of manufacturing activity, such as the total number employed in manufacturing, generally prove to be very high. This result is to be expected. Manufacturing provides the economic base of most large cities, and market potential will reflect

the distribution of the large urban centers. The principal contributions of the market potential concept may, therefore, be in drawing much-needed attention towards the market as a factor in the location of industry and in demonstrating the feasibility of producing what is, in effect, a demand surface.

Maximizing Profits

It is possible, conceptually at least, to combine the results of least-cost location theory (Type A) and market potential theory (Type C) to determine locations that maximize the differences between production costs and sales revenue (Type B). David Smith has developed such an approach by drawing on the idea of Weber's isodapanes, the measurement of spatial variations in demand, and E. M. Rawstron's concept of margins of profitability.

The isodapane was used by Weber simply to describe the additional transportation costs in moving from the least-cost location. It served to deal with the effects of lower labor costs and agglomeration economies on location. Its significance is far greater than this, however, for it changes the focus from the identification of a single least-cost location point to the map of production costs. From the isodapane as a contour map of transportation costs, it is a small conceptual step to a map of total production costs for any given level of output, incorporating all relevant costs. Similarly a revenue map can, in concept at least, be produced showing the revenue a producer could expect to derive at each location, given the market area such a location would confer and the sales that could be expected.

Profits are revenues minus costs. Subtract the cost map from the revenue map and the difference equals the profit map. The areas in which the industry can make a profit are a map of the spatial margins of profitability. Plants that open within these spatial margins survive. Those that open beyond it will fail.

Conceptually, this approach to location theory is more appealing than either least-cost or market-maximization approaches. But by combining these two partial approaches, it combines their measurement problems and has proved empirically intractable. Furthermore, by the time that Smith was developing this approach, a number of fundamental questions were being raised that called into question the whole search for a location theory looking for the optimal location for single plants by single-establishment firms operated by economic maximizers. These theories do continue to provide useful insights and practical solutions. But interest of location theory is now turning to a more aggregative and general level.

LOCATION CHOICES BY SMALL FIRMS

Location theory deals with the optimal location of new plants by economic maximizers without regard to the size of the firm. This approach is both much too narrow and much too general. In practice, the location of industry depends not only on where new plants are opened, but on the complete set of components of change, by firms that range from small owner-managerial workshops to very large multinational enterprises (MNEs), none of which may place profit maximization at the top of their principal objectives.

The *location of new plants* is only one of four components of change in the location of industry. Less obvious but very substantial changes in the distribution of industry can result from *increasing the size* of some existing plants (perhaps as an alternative to opening a new plant, or at the expense of production elsewhere) and by disinvestment decisions to *sell or close down* production facilities, or to *reduce their size*. Each of these components may have a different geography and the process of industrial change can have a quite different balance of components across a metropolitan area, an industrial region, and a nation.

The size of the firm making locational choices is important too, for the differences between small firms, large firms, and MNEs are qualitative, and not merely quantitative. The balance of the components of change varies with size of firm. Entries (births) and exits (deaths) account for most of the change in small firms and so geographers need to know the factors influencing entry and exit rates for small firms and how much these factors vary spatially. Large firms usually accommodate change by increasing or decreasing the size of existing plants. Small and large firms differ too in ownership and management style, in motivations and objectives, and in market share and probable stage in the life cycle of the products they manufacture. These factors can also affect locational choice. Most manufacturing firms are small when they are opened, and it is these new small firms that have been creating most of the net increase in employment in manufacturing in developed countries since the 1960s. We begin to broaden the topic of locational decisions and choice, therefore, by focusing on small firms and how they differ from large firms.

The Growing Importance of Small Manufacturing Firms

Small manufacturing firms were defined in the 1971 landmark study, the Bolton *Report of the Committee of Enquiry on Small Firms*, as firms employing 200 workers or less, having a relatively small share of the market, administered in a personalized way by their owners or part-owners, and independent and free from outside control in making their principal decisions. Most manufacturing firms in the United Kingdom and North America employ less than 20 workers and the Canadian data use this number as the upper employment limit to define small firms. In fact, the typical manufacturing firm in Canada is very small, employing less than five workers, and is only about 5 years old.

Small manufacturing firms are contributing most of the net employment growth in Western countries and are accounting for an increasing proportion of total manufacturing employment. Studies in the United Kingdom, United States, and Canada, for instance, show that net employment growth decreases with the size-class of firm. Indeed, in recent decades, all net growth has occurred in size-classes with less than 100 employees: larger size-classes than this have experienced net declines in all three countries. It is time then to revise the old rule that large firms grow larger, and small firms grow more numerous. In the last business cycle in Canada, 1978 to 1986, small manufacturing firms increased in both average size and numbers to outperform small firms in the economy generally. It was the large manufacturing firms (with more than 100 workers) that declined—in numbers as well as in total employment (Figure 10.1).

The remarkable contribution of small firms to employment growth in Western countries is not, as has sometimes been thought, due to the economic sectors

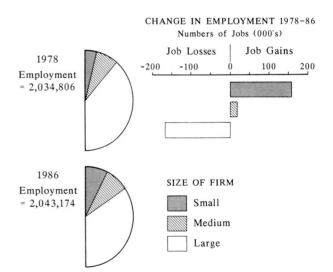

FIGURE 10.1 Employment change in manufacturing industry in Canada by size of firm, 1978–1986. [*Source:* Special tabulation by Statistics Canada. *Notes:* 1. Firm sizes are: small—0 to 19.9 employees; medium—20 to 99.9 employees; large—100 and more. 2. Firms are classified by their size in 1978.

or regions in which small firms are concentrated. On the contrary, when these other attributes are factored out in the Canadian longitudinal data, then the disparity in employment creation between small and large firms is increased, not decreased. Longitudinal data are unavailable for other countries, but such data as are available for other developed countries support the same view. For half a century, geographers have been schooled to believe that employment growth in a region is determined by the industry mix in the region and regional shifts of industry in and out of that region. However, the current resurgence of small firms is becoming so pervasive that industry performance is beginning to reflect the size-mix of firms in different industries (Box 10.7).

Some economic geographers see serious limitations in the contributions of small firms to employment growth and hence to the changing location of industry. One concern is triggered by the higher exit (or death) rates of small firms. The "churning" of small firms may create two classes of firms and jobs—temporary jobs in unstable small firms and permanent jobs in stable large firms. And even if small firms have higher net job creation rates, job loss through plant closure may involve greater dislocation and inefficiency than do layoffs from continuing plants. Furthermore, the gross employment creation by new small firms may be less than the gross employment growth by large firms. These concerns involve the components of employment change in industry, which are not always prop-

---

BOX 10.7   The Size-Mix of Firms and Simpson's Paradox

The longitudinal tracking of individual firms in Canada enables us to tabulate employment growth rates by industry. Consider the forestry, wood, and paper industries over the last business cycle, 1978–1986. Firms in the paper industry had by far the largest growth rate for all three size-classes, small, medium and large. Forestry had by far the lowest in all three. Yet when industry totals are computed, the industry rankings are completely reversed: Forestry did best, paper worst. Crude industry growth rates are biased by the heterogeneity in their size-mix.

Employment growth in the forestry, wood, and paper industries, by size-class: Canada 1978–1986

	Forestry Percent Growth	Rank	Wood Percent Growth	Rank	Paper Percent Growth	Rank
Size-Class						
Small (0–20)	52	3	80	2	179	1
Medium (20–100)	−28	3	−6	2	29	1
Large (100 +)	−40	3	−19	2	−14	1
Industry growth rate	−3	1	−4	2	−9	3
Percent employment:						
In small firms	36	1	12	2	1	3
In large firms	35	3	65	2	94	1
Industry standardized growth rate	−54	3	17	1	−7	2

Growth rates are standardized at the two-digit SIC level, by province, by size-class, and by country of control of firms. The standardized growth rate is the industry growth rate corrected for size, and regional and ownership mix. It is equivalent to the growth for each industry size–class–region–ownership group of firms multiplied using standardized weights. (D. Michael Ray, "Standardizing Employment Growth Rates of Foreign Multinationals and Domestic Firms in Canada: From Shift-Share to Multifactor Partitioning," 1990: Geneva ILO Multinational Enterprises Programme, Working Paper No. 62.)

The reversal of the rankings of the crude and standardized growth rates for the forestry and paper industries is an example of Simpson's paradox. Simpson's paradox occurs when crude rates or averages computed for two heterogeneous groups are the opposite rank of the standardized rates corrected for their heterogeneity. Other examples have been given for crude and standardized female death rates for Costa Rica and Sweden (Cohen, 1986). Observed examples of Simpson's paradox emphasize that crude rates confound true underlying rates with compositional differences. For instance, firms have many attributes that affect their growth rate such as their industry type, size-class, location, and country of control. Simply to use a crude national growth rate for an industry is to attribute to industry type all the growth that has occurred without taking any account of the other factors involved. This is rather like comparing regional growth rates, without taking into account their industry mix.

Reference: Joel E. Cohen, "An Uncertainty Principle in Demography and the Unisex Issue," The American Statistician, 40, (February 1986), No. 1, pp. 32–39.

erly understood (Box 10.8). These concerns are not without some foundation.

The Components of Change in Manufacturing Firms and Their Employment

Almost half the 1978 stock of small manufacturing firms in Canada had gone out of business by 1986, just 8 years later (Table 10.2). More new small manufacturing firms were established between 1979 and 1986 than existed in 1978, but about 40 percent of these new firms also had closed by 1986. The net result was that each addition to the stock of small manufacturing firms was the balance of four new firms opened, and three closed. The rate of firm entry and exit diminishes with size-class of firm: Larger firms are more likely to decrease employment than to close. But the proportion of firms that either closed or reduced their employ-

---

BOX 10.8 *Components of Change in Firms and Their Employment*

An industry begins a period with an existing stock of firms **(A)**. Existing firms either grow **(P)** or decline in employment **(Q)** or they exit **(R)** during the course of a period. Whether they grow or decline, they are called continuing firms **(P + Q)**. The stock of firms at the end of the period equals continuing firms plus new firms **(B)**, opened during the period, that survive to the final year **(I)**. New firms that open and close during a period **(J)** are not usually tabulated and their employment impact is not included in job turnover.

Gross job gains occur from continuing firms that grow **(P)** and new surviving firms **(I)**. New surviving firms have, by definition, grown: They had zero employment in the initial year.

Gross job losses occur from continuing firms that decline **(Q)** or existing firms that close **(R).**

The net employment record of all continuing firms is **(P)** + **(Q)**. This record is sometimes compared with the net employment created by (surviving) births **(I)** and (continuing firm) deaths **(R)**. Such comparisons may have little meaning. Strictly, the employment records of existing firms **(P, Q, and R)** should be compared with that of new firms **(I and J)**. The data on new firms is incomplete: **J** is not tabulated. The net employment contribution of new firms which close is zero. But they did create jobs and those jobs were lost and they are part of the job churning caused by the entry and exit of firms.

Job turnover is the sum of the absolute value of (tabulated) jobs gained or lost **(P + Q + R + I**, with sign ignored).

Job losses from declining firms can be divided into temporary or permanent. Temporary layoffs are sometimes defined as lasting two years or less. Temporary layoffs cause fluctuations in the employment of continuing firms. Job gains from surviving firms must increase, the longer the period is. Hence the relative importance of employment creation by continuing firms and new firms is not independent of the length of period.

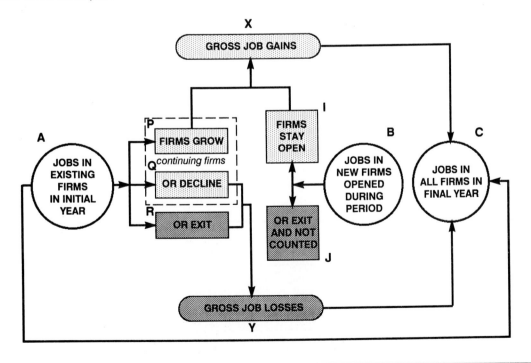

TABLE 10.2

The components of change in manufacturing firms and employment: Canada, 1978–1986

Life Status of Firms	Number of Firms			Change in Jobs 1978–1986, in 1000s		
	Small 0–19.9	Medium 20–99.9	Large 100 +	Small 0–19.9	Medium 20–99.9	Large 100 +
Existing firms 1978	31,076	7463	2724			
Continuing firms 1978–1986	16,104	4930	2003	67.6	54.8	−85.8
Increased jobs	9,737	2607	933	85.0	92.5	196.1
Decreased jobs	6,367	2323	1070	−17.4	−37.8	−281.9
Exits of 1978 firms	14,972	2533	721	−53.0	−98.4	−176.6
Net job change, 1978 firms				14.6	−43.6	−262.4
New firms 1979–1986	43,320	1144	248			
Exits 1978–1986	18,121	387	68			
Entries (surviving in 1986)	25,199	757	180	144.0	61.0	81.6
TOTALS						
Net growth	10,227	−1776	−541	158.7	17.4	−180.7
Gross job turnover				299.4	289.7	736.2
Job creation efficiency				0.53	0.06	−0.25

Source: Special Tabulation, Statistics Canada

Note: Data: Employment figures are in standardized labor units. Employment losses from exits are tabulated only for firms operating in 1978. Firms opening after 1978 and closed by 1986 are not included in employment tabulation for the period.

Reading the table: There were 31,076 small firms in 1978, of which 16,104 survived (were continuing firms 1978–1986). Of these continuing firms, 9737 increased their employment 1978–1986. Some 6367 small continuing firms decreased their employment and another 14,972 of the 1978 firms closed.

During the period (1979–1986), 43,320 new small firms opened, of which 18,121 closed in 1986 or earlier, so only 25,199 firms survived past 1986. The new small firms that closed are not usually included in components of change tables.

The employment consequences of this considerable firm churning is that *net* changes are small compared to the underlying components of employment change.

The gross turnover in employment serves as an indicator of the ability of manufacturing to adjust to change.

Job creation efficiency is the quotient of net growth in jobs divided by gross job turnover. The maximum value is +1.0 when there are no job losses from decreasing firms of exits. The minimum value is −1.0 when there are no job gains from firms increasing or entering.

ment is about the same for all size-classes of manufacturing firms (Table 10.3).

The proportion of jobs lost through firm declines and exits combined is higher for smaller firms than for larger ones, according to the Canadian data. But size-class differences in gross job losses are very much less than differences in gross job gains. The better performance of small manufacturing firms in net job creation and in the efficiency of job creation can be credited to

their much higher gross job-creation rates bought at the cost of somewhat higher gross job-loss rates.

What of the quality of jobs created? Smaller firms tend to pay lower wage rates and fringe benefits than larger firms. Some of the increased employment in small firms may also represent a shift of jobs from large firms subcontracting production as a means of evading labor standards. But tracking individual workers by industry in Canada demonstrates just how high

TABLE 10.3

The proportion of manufacturing firms that decreased employment or closed: Canada 1978–1986

Employment size-class in 1978	Less than 4.9	5 to 19.9	20 to 49.9	50 to 99.9	100 to 499.9	500 or more	Total
Percent decreased	17.8	28.3	31.3	33.2	36.7	54.2	24.8
Percent exits	50.7	35.7	32.1	32.8	27.3	13.3	41.4
Total decreases and exits	68.5	64.1	63.4	66.0	64.0	67.5	66.2

Note: There is a remarkable symmetry in the table. The figures for the percentage of firms that closed is almost the reverse series of the figures for firms that decreased. And the sum of the two is always equal to about two-thirds of the firms in the size-class.

worker turnover is even in industries dominated by large firms (Boxes 10.9 and 10.10). The general evidence in Canada is that worker turnover is heavily concentrated among young workers with no evident reduction in average length of job tenure by the work force as a whole.

Comprehensive longitudinal data on manufacturing firms and employment are not available for other developed countries. Such data as are available for Western Europe, the United States, and Japan point to a shift in production and in employment in all these countries to small manufacturing firms, so that a recent report of the International Labor Office is entitled *The Re-emergence of the Small Firm* (1990).

The Location of Small Firms

Where small firms open and where they survive are becoming increasingly important both for the location of industry and for regional variations in industry mix. The factors influencing their birth and death rates do not, however, point in any simple or direct way to a geography of industrial change. The geographic consequences of firm births and deaths arise indirectly from the factors involved. A Darwinian process of economic adoption occurs in which the surviving new firms map the margins of locational freedom and firms become concentrated in those regions best able to meet their prerequisites for births and survival.

No published surveys of the motivations of entrepreneurs have ever found that they are driven by a single, dominant goal of profit maximization or that they explicitly locate on the basis of location theory. Some, the "classical entrepreneurs," may include profits and growth high on a list that includes many other motivations. The most typical case is the "artisan" or "craftsperson entrepreneur," setting up a business close to home with the help of loans from family and friends, because of the personal satisfaction they derive from autonomy and quality workmanship. These craftsperson entrepreneurs are probably prepared to work longer hours for a lower return on their investment than would be acceptable to a large firm. They may also have less formal education than senior executives in large firms and hence feel socially marginalized. They may want to keep their business small, concerned that growth would threaten their independence. A third group, "management entrepre-

---

BOX 10.9   *Worker Turnover in the Canadian Steel and Automobile Industries: 1978–1983*

Worker turnover is very high even in industries dominated by large firms as this example of the steel and automobile industries shows. Individual workers in these industries were tracked from 1978 to 1983. Both industries reduced their actual number of workers by about 10 percent, but in each case about one-third of the 1978 labor force had left 5 years later (which would include voluntary quits and retirements as well as permanent layoffs).

Workers	Steel	Automobiles
Actual number		
1978 total	97,270	116,667
Indexed numbers		
1978 = 100	100	100
1978 workers		
Left (1978–1983)	34	38
Remained	66	62
New workers (1979–1983)		
Total hired	n.a.	79
Left	n.a.	51
Net additions	23	28
1983 Total	89	90

Note: These special tabulations from Statistics Canada are for iron and steel mills (SIC 291), steel pipe and tube mills (SIC 292) and wire (SIC 305); and for motor vehicle manufacture (SIC 323) and motor vehicle parts and accessories (SIC 325). The numbers are for individual workers (full-time, part-time, or temporary) and are not converted to average labor units as in earlier tables. Some tabulations for the steel industry are not available (n.a.).

BOX 10.10   The Industry Shift of Workers Who Leave Their Jobs

What happens to workers who separate—that is, voluntarily or involuntarily leave a job in manufacturing? Box 10.9 shows that 34 percent (actually 21,093 workers) of the 1978 work force in iron and steel in Canada left the industry 1978–1983. Tracking these workers showed that most of them had found a job by 1983 at incomes slightly lower than they had previously earned, but only about a third stayed in manufacturing. The same proportion held for all Ontario workers who left the independent automobile parts industry 1981–1982. And for Ontario autoworkers, the figure was lower—only one-fifth.

Percentage distribution of workers out of steel and automobiles who found another job

To:	From:	Canada Steel (1978–1983)	Ontario Auto Parts (1981–1982)	Ontario Motor Vehicle (1981–1982)
1. Primary (+ mining)		6	5	3
2. Manufacturing		32	36	19
3. Construction		8	6	12
4. Transportation		7	2	4
5. Retail and wholesale trade		14	19	13
6. Finance, insurance, and real estate		6	10	9
7. Services (community, business, and personal)		19	18	32
8. Public administration		8	4	8
Total		100	100	100

Source: Special Tabulations, Statistics Canada.

neurs'' may have a superior education and industrial experience, setting up their own business perhaps with a contract from the firm where they previously worked, to supply it with components previously made in-house. Or perhaps they have identified a new product that fills a neglected need.

Entrepreneurs vary in background, objectives, and motivations, but whatever their profile, their failure rate is high. Probably a third of small new manufacturing firms will close down within 3 years, and one-half will fail within 5 years. As with the reasons for their entry into business, so too the reasons given for their exit lack any obvious geographic logic. Some of the reasons given for closing are unique to small firms, such as the death of the managing director or owner-manager; fire; end of lease on premises; or voluntary liquidation. By contrast, large firms cite a less varied list of causes; most common are a fall in demand, uneconomic production, or concentration of production elsewhere.

Whatever the specific reasons given for closing down a firm, one underlying cause is the locational imperative. Firms that have failed to pursue an active policy of economic ''adaption'' (making rational and correct decisions on product, location, and technology) will be subjected to a process of economic ''adoption'' (selection by the ''guiding hand'' of the market).

Locational Adoption. All new firms must compete for venture capital, workers, premises, equipment, supplies, and customers. This competition for survival ensures the survival of only the fittest. The location pattern of the beginners may be haphazard and random. The process of adoption has a large enough cohort of new firms each year, and high enough death rates, to produce a residual pattern of rational location for the survivors. For survival depends on competitiveness in product, price, and marketing, and these in turn are influenced by location.

The longitudinal tracking of firms in Canada makes the point emphatically. Establishments or firms that close are less productive and less profitable on average than either surviving firms, or the new establishments of existing firms that are opened. Economic adjustment and locational adoption are continuous processes, relentlessly transferring resources from less-productive and less-profitable uses to firms that are more competitive. The rapid turnover of firms and the churning in the job market that is generated exist on a much larger scale than was imagined from simple net change data, and they emphasize the major role played by locational adoption in the economy.

Locational Adaption. The opposite of locational *adoption* is locational *adaption*. Locational adaption is the rational selection of an optimal location for a firm, or for a new plant of an existing firm, based on the evaluation of competing locations. Firms enhance their chances of success by a careful analysis of market trends and locational factors. The result is that the initial location pattern is rational and consistent with location theory.

In principle, it is to be expected that small firms with more limited resources and more complex motivations are subjected to locational adoption, and that large firms with more to lose and more comprehensive management structures achieve economic adaption. The longitudinal tracking of manufacturing firms in Canada by initial size does provide indirect support for this dichotomy of adoption of small firms and adaption by large firms, though the distinction is blurred:

1.   The differences in death rates between small and large firms is greatest during the first 3 years after start-up (Table 10.4). After the high death rates in these early years, the death rates for small firms fall to the steady low level experienced by large firms right from their start-up. The concentration of firm deaths among small firms in their infancy points to a swift process of economic and locational adoption.

2.   The death rates of large firms are much more sensitive to this stage in the business cycle than small firms are. New small firms fail at a high rate even when the economy is booming, suggesting that causes other than the general business climate are responsible for their failure. Among these other causes is locational adoption.

3.   The simplest evidence of adoption among small firms is the sheer number of births and deaths involved (Table 10.1). Half the existing small manufacturing firms in Canada in 1978 made it through to the end of the business cycle in 1989. For every 10 firms that did survive, another 25 had opened between 1979

TABLE 10.4

Exit rates of small and large manufacturing firms: Canada, 1978–1986

	Total Firms	Total Deaths		Year in which Firms Died as Percent of Total								
	No.	No.	%	1978	1979	1980	1981	1982	1983	1984	1985	1986
Existing firms 1978												
Small	31976	14972	48	10	7	6	6	5	4	4	3	4
Large	2724	721	26	2	2	2	2	3	4	3	4	3
Firms starting up in:												
1979												
Small	5462	3196	59	—	11	13	11	8	5	4	3	4
Large	37	15	41	—	0	14	5	5	3	5	5	3
1980												
Small	5052	2816	56	—	—	10	15	10	6	5	5	4
Large	24	14	58	—	—	33	0	0	21	0	0	4
1981												
Small	4906	2454	50	—	—	—	10	14	9	7	6	5
Large	25	11	44	—	—	—	8	12	8	8	0	8
1982												
Small	4208	2068	49	—	—	—	—	11	13	11	8	7
Large	14	6	43	—	—	—	—	14	14	0	7	7
1983												
Small	5399	2466	46	—	—	—	—	—	12	15	10	8
Large	21	7	33	—	—	—	—	—	14	5	10	5
1984												
Small	5655	2198	39	—	—	—	—	—	—	13	15	12
Large	47	10	21	—	—	—	—	—	—	6	9	6
1985												
Small	6106	1859	30	—	—	—	—	—	—	—	14	16
Large	35	5	14	—	—	—	—	—	—	—	9	6
1986												
Small	6532	1064	6	—	—	—	—	—	—	—	—	6
Large	45	0	0	—	—	—	—	—	—	—	—	0

Source: Special Tabulations: Statistics Canada

Note: The recession years, 1981–1983, affected large firms more severely than small. The difference in death rates between large and small firms tends to narrow after the first three years. For the complete set of new firms opened 1978 to 1986, the period death rate was 42 percent for small firms and 27 percent for large, a difference of 15 percentage points: almost all that difference was accounted for by the difference in the death rates for the first three years (for which the rates were 32 percent and 19 percent).

and 1986. But 10 of these new firms closed by 1986. Nevertheless, the 1986 cohort of small manufacturing firms was made up of 15 new small firms for every 10 survivors established 1978 or earlier. For large manufacturing firms three-quarters survived. For every 10 that survived, one more opened and it too probably survived. The 1986 cohort was thus made up of one new large firm for every 10 survivors. These figures allow for locational adoption to be a powerful force among small firms, but not among large ones.

Adoption and adaption are two extremes marking the limits of a continuum. In reality, the locational decisions of firms are some mixture of the two, with the balance favoring adoption in the case of most small firms, shifting to adaption by most large firms. But whichever the dominant process, surviving new firms reinforce the locational advantages and strengthen the economic support network of their region. The survival of new firms, particularly new small firms, depends on the network of voluntary associations, trade associations, venture capital groups, public agencies, university research centers, and informal meeting places where information and ideas are exchanged, production problems solved, venture capital raised, and markets identified. Such networks build very slowly. Case studies (such as Silicon Valley in California, the Cambridge phenomenon in England or Sassuolo in Italy) suggest several decades are needed before a high density of ties is established where actors and decision-makers know each other and influential persons have emerged with an established reputation for reliable opinions and judgments. It is this regional network that selects which new firms will survive. But the surviving firms add new competence to the region's pool of management and technology and new products and industries to its economic base. So while new firms must be adopted by the region in which they locate, they can serve to enhance the competitiveness of that region and help it to adapt to increasing world competition.

The Consequences of Small Firm Reemergence for Location Theory and Regional Development

The reemergence of small firms has important consequences both for location theory and for regional development. Location theory can no longer confine itself to identifying the specific location that optimizes some requirement of an economic maximizer. Instead, it must seek to understand the processes that enable an entrepreneur to start up a small business, to survive and to grow, as well as the processes that cause firms, large or small, to fail and to exit. Consequently, the location of raw materials and markets, which are read-

ily mapped, are becoming less important. Conversely, the emergence and intensification of networks of influential people who support selected entrepreneurs is becoming increasingly important to understanding shifts in industry. Economic geographers no longer map location triangles, isodapanes, and market potential surfaces and are turning their attention to the components of change of industrial firms, jobs and workers.

There has been a corresponding change in the thinking about regional development. Traditionally, geographers have identified two components to regional employment growth: an industry-mix effect and a regional shift. The mix of industries has become less important as the capital-goods industries have declined to the point where they have few jobs left to shed. Regional effects, considered relatively unimportant at the time of Barlow *Royal Commission on the Distribution of the Industry Population* (1940), are probably becoming more important as regions establish supportive networks, achieve industrial growth, and enhance their regional advantages.

A number of additional factors now need to be added to this traditional two-factor approach. The size-mix of firms in a region is of increasing importance because small firms generate much of the net employment growth and because birthrates of small firms are highest in regions with a high concentration of small firms. Very important, too, are changes within the urban hierarchy. British geographers have identified large net shifts of employment outwards from metropolitan centers to suburbs, and down the urban hierarchy from large cities to small towns. Such a shift is contrary to what would be expected if economies of scale were the single dominant factor, and it suggests the importance of special factors such as urban congestion and high land costs as significant diseconomies of scale, coupled with a growing preference for "greenfield" locations to avoid the poor labor relations in older industrial regions. Evidence for Canada shows a rather different pattern. Small and medium-sized firms are disproportionately concentrated in large cities, and the differences in components of change show rather small differences with size of city. Another factor in countries like Canada with a significant proportion of foreign ownership is the locational impact of multinational enterprises.

MULTINATIONAL ENTERPRISES: TRENDS IN LOCATION, ORGANIZATION, AND EMPLOYMENT

Multinational enterprises (MNEs) are probably the dominant economic organizations in the world today, and they have a significant direct and indirect impact on employment, trade, and technology transfer and hence on the location of industry. MNEs may open a branch plant in a foreign country as an alternative to foreign trade. Therefore, a full understanding of MNEs requires an eclectic approach involving elements of both location theory and international trade theory. Furthermore, classical location theory may explain why an industry is located where it is; it does not attempt to explain whether the industry will be run by a domestic firm or a foreign multinational. We return again to the subject of MNEs after a discussion of international trade theory, but will introduce here some elements of an eclectic theory on why firms locate production in foreign countries to become MNEs.

The Importance of MNEs

There are many different measures of the extent and importance of MNEs, although surprisingly, all of them pose considerable conceptual and measurement problems, and data are very incomplete even in the developed countries. For example, an MNE, whether foreign or domestic, may exercise effective control over another enterprise with far less than majority ownership. That MNE may in turn be controlled by another MNE of a different nationality. Most data are highly confidential, and only limited aggregated data are released by government agencies using definitions that vary from country to country. These data are for the direct effects of MNEs, but MNEs have important indirect effects because of their linkages with other firms and where and how they source their inputs, which are not measured on any systematic basis.

The largest MNEs have sales of up to $100 billion, which is comparable to the GNP of entire countries. Indeed, if MNEs and countries are ranked on the basis of sales or GNP, then half of the top hundred are nation-states and the other half are MNEs. In total, it is possible that MNEs account for one-quarter of the goods produced in the world's market economies. From quite small beginnings in the late nineteenth and early twentieth century, MNEs grew rapidly in the interwar years (1918–1939) and after World War II until 1973. After that, high interest rates, severe inflation, and a general slowdown in economic growth served to depress direct foreign investment and the growth of MNEs, particularly in the less-developed world. But after 1981 MNEs began to expand again at least as rapidly as the world economy.

The sheer scale of MNE production gives MNEs a dominant share of international trade, part of which is simply intrafirm transfers of components, investments, profits, and services among their plants in various countries. Combining all MNE shipments, for operations within their home country and foreign countries, they account for more than 80 percent of trade from some of the developed countries, including the United States. MNEs play a major role in the international transfer of technology, whether it is "hard" technology, such as microelectronic information technologies, or "soft" technology, such as Japan's just-in-time inventory organization. Indeed, direct foreign investment is one mechanism by which firms can obtain profits from the foreign use of their *own* technologies, by operating that technology in foreign-based plants that they *own* or *control*.

One of the simplest and most useful measures of the importance of MNEs, and of their impact on location, is the employment that they generate. The International Labor Office estimates the direct employment in MNEs to be at least 65 million. Of this total, 43 million work in the home country of the MNE and 22 million in foreign branch plants. These figures, although absolutely large, are a relatively small proportion of the world's paid work force. The proportion is 3 percent of the world total, rising to 10 percent in the developed world and falling to well below 1 percent in the less-developed world. For individual countries, the proportions have reached very high levels, including Canada, where in the 1960s, more of the mining, petroleum, and manufacturing sectors were owned or controlled by foreign MNEs than by domestic firms. Foreign MNEs also play a dominant role in other developed countries such as Belgium, France, and Italy. Foreign MNEs employ more than one million workers in Canada, France, Germany, the United Kingdom, and Brazil.

An Eclectic Theory of International Location

Why do companies open up branch plants in foreign countries? John Dunning has identified three specific requirements:

1. The host country must offer the MNE some advantage specific to the country. These assets may be raw materials or domestic markets. But these *country-specific endowments* or advantages are presumably more readily accessible to domestic firms in the host country than to the MNE. Therefore, there is a second condition.

2. The MNE must have technologies, patents, or some other *firm-specific advantages* that are relevant to the country-specific endowments of the host country. But the MNE could sell these assets to a domestic firm in the host country.

BOX 10.11   Why Do Firms Invest Abroad?

A distinction is made between an investment by a firm in another firm in a foreign country, without gaining control of that firm (this is termed a portfolio investment), and direct foreign investment. Direct foreign investment includes opening a new, greenfield branch plant or gaining a controlling interest in an existing firm in a foreign country. In general, the following three conditions must be met before a firm will make a direct foreign investment.

1. The foreign country must offer specific advantages, or *country-specific endowments*, such as raw materials and growing markets.
2. The firm must have relevant assets, called *firm-specific advantages*, and
3. There must exist *market imperfections* that make it better for the firm to use its own assets in its own foreign branch plant rather than to sell them to a foreign firm.

See Chapters 12 and 13 for additional foreign trade conditions relating to barriers to trade that lead to foreign direct investment.

There are three classes of firm-specific endowments:

TYPES OF FIRM—SPECIFIC ADVANTAGES	EXAMPLES OF INDUSTRY TYPES
1. *Barriers to entry by domestic firms.* MNE has patents and trademarks and has established significant product differentiation.	Brand name consumer goods such as soft drinks, breakfast cereals, and automobile tires.
2. *Branch plant advantages over new firm.* MNE offers a convenient, market-tested package of product, technology, and capital with costless access to MNE's research and development, advertising, and marketing know-how, and to product-specific economies of scale.	Product with high fixed costs and large economies of scale such as automobiles (although trade barriers are a key additional factor). Capital-intensive resource industries such as the oil industry, and R & D–intensive products such as computers.
3. *MNE's access to international markets.* MNE can take fuller advantage of country-specific advantages in costs of materials and labor because of its knowledge of international market conditions and international marketing network.	Manufacture of components or goods in a foreign branch plant largely to serve export markets, taking advantage of host country low labor costs.

3. There must exist, therefore, some market imperfections, which make it difficult for the MNE to capture the true market value of its firm-specific endowments, and which drive it to internalize these assets by operating a branch plant in the host country.

There are further conditions relating to barriers to international trade, discussed in Chapters 12 and 13, which make it better for the firm to establish foreign production facilities rather than shipping goods to that country.

MNEs can have three different kinds of firm-specific endowments: (a) endowments that constitute barriers to entry by domestic firms, (b) advantages of an existing firm over a new firm attempting to set up operations, and (c) advantages of a multinational with internal connections over a domestic firm (see Box 10.11).

The most obvious firm-specific advantages of MNEs are assets such as patented technologies, trademarks, economies of scale, and their international experience and networks. One asset that may be less obvious is the soft technology advantage of superior management and organization, which endows a firm with decisive cost and sometimes quality advantages. Soft technology advantages proved most telling in the changeover of organization from craft production to mass production at the turn of the century, as they are in the contemporary changeover from mass production to lean production. New production organization has pervasive implications for the management and labor force of a firm, its suppliers, and its distribution network. These changes take much longer to incorporate and assimilate than might be thought, and meanwhile, during their diffusion, they can give lead firms a clear advantage over laggards, providing them with an unequalled opportunity to capture larger market

In addition to firm-specific advantages that foster the establishment of a foreign branch plant, there are general advantages to multinational operation that apply to all MNEs regardless of their firm-specific advantages. These advantages are:

- Protection from trade barriers and currency shifts. The weak U.S. dollar from 1987 to 1989 badly hit the profits of luxury European car exporters such as Jaguar, for example, and underlined the competitive advantages of global enterprises.
- Achieving cross-regional product flows. The three major world markets, Europe, North America, and Japan, tend to demand different types of products and to have different images of what constitutes luxury. So an MNE can produce regionally for the region volume markets and export to the other two regions serving their luxury niche markets. An example is the Honda Accord, marketed as a middle-range, high-volume automobile in the United States, and sold as a luxury product in Japan.
- The sophistication and knowledge of market and product trends gained by MNEs in comparison to local firms.
- Further, while all regional markets experience business cycles,

they are not necessarily synchronic. The Japanese and North American business cycles, for example, are often at different stages with respect to each other. MNEs can alleviate the effects of fluctuations in demand by use of cross-regional product flows.
- Finally, producing in the foreign country should increase local knowledge of the firm, recognition of the firm's commitment to the local market, and acceptance of the quality of its products. This enhanced reputation of the MNE should boost the sale of the MNEs products, whether locally produced or imported.

There may be additional advantages that apply to all MNEs from a particular home country and which support their expansion abroad. These include:

- A large, stable home market
- Superior education facilities providing R & D facilities, quality business school graduates, and engineers and scientists, as well as a generally skilled and productive labor force
- Highly efficient services, including financial markets and transportation and communication facilities
- A generally supportive and stable government with a liberal attitude

towards mergers and industrial concentration.

Alternatively other factors such as high labor costs and an unfavorable home-currency exchange rate may push a firm to seek a foreign location for production.

The host country may also offer a number of general attractions to MNEs, including

- A rapidly growing market
- Comparatively few competitors
- Export processing zones where manufacturing is free of duties and taxes
- Access from that host country to a larger regional market forming a free-trade area.

See:

U.N. Center on Transnational Corporations, *Transnational Corporations in World Development,* New York: United Nations, 1988.

John H. Dunning, ''Trade, Location of Economic Activity and the MNE: A Search for an Eclectic Approach,'' in *The International Allocation of Economic Activity,* edited by B. Ohlin, P-O Messelborn, and P. M. Wijkmann, London: Macmillan, 1977, pp. 395–418, and

———, Towards an Eclectic Theory of International Production: Some empirical tests, *Journal of International Business Studies,* II (1980), 9–31.

shares and expand production internationally at the expense of lagging firms. The expansion of lead firms has important consequences for subsequent location of industry. The automobile industry provides a graphic example.

The Evolution of Automobile Production

Craft Production. The dramatic improvements that industrial organization can have on productivity and quality and hence on competitiveness and location of industry have been documented by James P. Womack and his colleagues in *The Machine that Changed the World* (Macmillan, 1990). A key-points summary of their findings about the history, objectives, principles, achievements, and problems of craft production, mass production, and lean production, all of which coexist today, is provided in Box 10.12.

Automobile production began in the late nineteenth century as a small-scale, made-to-specification, custom industry. There was no standard product. One company, Panhard et Levassor, established the *Système Panhard,* with the engine in front driving the rear wheels, and passengers placed in rows in the middle. Technical problems with the cutting of steel parts meant that skilled fitters were required to file down adjacent parts, one after the other, to fit them together, producing dimensional creep. The amount of dimensional creep varied from car to car—no two were identical even if produced using the same blueprints. Craft production did achieve pioneering advances in technology, such as the development of the gasoline engine. It did demonstrate the usefulness and practicality of the product and tested market reaction. But it did not solve the problems of replacement parts, reliability, large output volumes, and cost, the essence of the ''American system'' of manufactur-

BOX 10.12   Competing Production Methods of Automobile Production

Attribute	Craft Production	Mass Production	Lean Production
General Characteristics of Production Method	Small-scale craft producers relying on highly skilled work force to produce a low volume of output	Use of specialized machines to turn out high volumes of interchangeable parts that can be assembled by unskilled workers, eliminating need for craftspeople	Flexible batch production by multiple-skilled workers using flexible machinery and just-in-time inventory delivery
History	Developed in late 19th century with innovations such as the high-speed gasoline engine of Daimler (founder of Mercedes-Benz)	Production technique developed by Henry Ford with Model T after 1908. Management and marketing by Alfred Sloan of General Motors after 1920	Developed by Toyota Motor Co. in Japan after World War II, based on analysis of problems with Ford plant at Detroit
Objectives	• High-quality • Innovativeness • Customized features	• Ease of manufacture • Low price • High volume • "Good enough" quality	• Eliminate waste • Reduce capital equipment costs • Achieve flexible cost-effective batch production • Constant improvements
Principles	• One at a time, even one-of-a-kind customized products	• Standardization of parts • Division of labor and reduction of task cycle time • Economies of scale • Vertical integration to regulate inputs and control sales	• Just-in-time inventory • Identify and solve assembly line problems immediately • Component suppliers organized into tiers • Decentralized design and decision making
Achievements	• Pioneered basic technology • Demonstrated usefulness of product • Tested market reaction • Established basic design features of product	• Reduced product costs—Model T fell in price steadily from 1908 • Easier to drive and maintain than craft-produced vehicles • Helped to make automobile production the largest industry in the world	• Assembly time halved • Design effort halved • Design time reduced by a third • Assembly faults almost eliminated • Much higher quality level
Problems	• No standard gauge—so dimension creep in fitting parts together • Problems of reliability and replacement parts • Averaging down the cost of R & D • Tradition versus new technology	• Labor problems frequent layoffs and worker boredom • Long product development times • Lack of flexibility • Quality control and waste	• Requires great commitment and acceptance of responsibility by all workers and management • Requires paradigmatic shift in management thinking

ing that began in the mid-nineteenth-century gun industry.

Some cars are still made today on a craft production basis. Aston Martin, for instance, turns out only one car per working day. The aluminum panels are shaped by skilled panel beaters who pound them onto the dies with wooden mallets. But Aston Martin has produced less than 10,000 cars in its 65 years compared with a current industry total of 50 million cars made each year. And even Aston Martin has had to link up with Ford to gain specialized technical information at reasonable cost on a range of subjects from emission controls to crash safety.

Mass Production. It was Henry Ford who spelled out the end of craft production as the dominant organization of car production, sensing the essential ingredients of mass production and laying the foundation of what is today the world's largest industry.

A key principle of mass production is the standardization of parts achieving simple fitting of adjacent parts, and complete interchangeability of corresponding parts (the American system). This principle could be realized because of Ford's introduction of standard gauges to measure part sizes, and of advanced machine tools that could cut hardened steel. A second key principle was the reduction of the task cycle and moving the assembly line at an optimal speed, based on time and motion studies pioneered by F. M. Taylor. In 1908 Ford's task cycle (the time required by an assembler to complete one set of operations) was 8 h 56 min. By 1913, parts were delivered to workers and with further division of labor the task cycle had been reduced to 2.3 min. That year Ford introduced the moving assembly line and reduced the task cycle to 1.2 min. A third principle of mass production is economies of scale. Ford built his first car, the Model A, in 1903, and it was not until he reached his twentieth model (and the twentieth letter of the alphabet) with his Model T in 1908 that he had a car that was easy to assemble, drive, and repair. Production soared, reaching over two million in 1923. Prices fell continuously throughout the company's production history. The increases in industry efficiency were extraordinary. Between 1913 and 1914 alone, the time to assemble a vehicle fell from 12 h 30 min, to 1 h 33 min. Because of the productivity increase, Ford was able to double wages to an unheard of $5 a day.

The achievement of economies of scale and the efficient use of very expensive, highly specialized equipment required that production lines be kept moving without interruption. Consequently, buffers had to be built in: extra supplies and parts, extra workers, and extra space. Vertical integration was used to control the flow of parts with closer tolerances and tighter delivery schedules than ever before thought possible.

There was one key ingredient of mass production and the large corporations it created that was introduced not by Ford, but by Alfred P. Sloan, Jr., president of General Motors: the concept of the multidivisional company with decentralized divisions. Five of the divisions were each allocated one of the product ranges, from Chevrolet to Cadillac; others were given responsibility for component groups such as steering gears and generators. The divisions reported to the senior executive on sales, market share, inventories, profit and loss, and capital budgets. This organizational decentralization was crucial for combining the economic advantages of mass production with the product diversity demanded by the market.

Given the willingness of Henry Ford to show European carmakers around his Highland Park plant and to explain his system, the clear cost and productivity advantages of his system, and the establishment by Ford of European subsidiaries, beginning with Trafford Park, Manchester, in 1911, it might have been expected that mass production would have diffused quickly and smoothly to Europe. It did not. The story of Europe's failure to emulate American mass production and productivity is long and involved. One fundamental cause was the resistance of European skilled craftspeople, who saw nothing in mass production to benefit them, versus the unskilled immigrant workers in the United States, many of them barely able to speak English, used by Ford in Highland Park. Another was the endemic weakness of British management, who, unable to cope with operational routines, surrendered these to "shop stewards" (themselves often skilled craftspeople) who were deeply suspicious of mass production. Indeed, it was not until the financial crisis of the 1990s that Rover, successor of the original Austin and Oxford Motor Companies, adopted standard hourly rates (rather than the craft piece rates) and set out explicitly to match U.S. productivity. But by 1990, U.S. productivity and quality had long since been overtaken by Japanese lean production. On the European continent, it was the 1960s before Detroit-style mass production was mastered and European carmakers could successfully challenge U.S. producers.

Lean Production. Womack and his colleagues use the term *lean production* to describe the revolutionary management system first introduced by the Toyota Motor Co. of Nagoya, Japan, after World War II. One important aspect of the system is the "just-in-time" (*kanban*) delivery of parts to the assembly line, which contrasts to the "just-in-case" buffer of spare parts in mass production. The organizational revolution triggered by Toyota is fully comprehensive, however, affecting the organization and management of labor, design, and production at the intrafirm and interfirm levels. The approach appears to contradict the logic and principles of mass production, the division of labor, and the economies of scale. It seems to revert to some of the ideas of craft production in its use of multiple skilled labor responsible for the quality as well as the quantity of output, in the level of commitment it requires of all workers in the assembly plant and in part supplies to track down the causes of any faults, and to eliminate them, and in its concern with flexible batch production rather than long uninterrupted production runs. The most important attributes of lean production are the contrasts in its productivity with those of mass production. Lean production enables Japanese cars to be designed in about two-thirds of the time, with about half of the engineering design input as the U.S. and European cars. The products are universally ranked highest in ease of assembly and take only about half the time to assemble. Lean-produced cars have a much lower incidence of defects than do mass-produced cars, with virtually no reworking at the end of the assembly line, even though fixing assembly line faults accounts for up to one-quarter of their total production time. So not surprisingly perhaps, the United States lost 20 percent of its domestic market to Japanese cars in just 8 years. Moreover, as lean production techniques spread to other Japanese industries, the success story of Japanese cars was repeated in motorcycles, machine tools, consumer electronics, and others in which the firm-specific advantages were not hard technology, but organizational superiority.

Toyota began its organizational changes with rethinking the process by which mass production uses hundreds of extensive, highly specialized presses to stamp the individual parts of cars and trucks. It takes up to a day to change the dies on these machines to produce a part with a different shape, so typically very large quantities of any one part are stamped out and stockpiled before the dies are changed. Toyota redesigned the presses so that the assembly line workers could change the dies in just a few minutes and make the parts on an as-required basis. The results were surprising. Flexible batch production was achieved at lower costs, without the space and carrying costs of large inventories and with very quick feedback on stamping mistakes, eliminating the waste of large numbers of defective parts. Capital costs were reduced too, because only a few presses were needed for an entire car. This kind of lean principle was carried through the entire automobile manufacturing chain, from assessing the wants of customers, design, development, engineering manufacturing of components, assembly, and distribution.

Lean production depends on and promotes quality work. For instance, inventory in a mass production system is several weeks' supply. Under lean production it may be several hours'. Lean production is hand-to-mouth: A string of defective parts would halt production. Workers have to be concerned constantly with quality, to anticipate problems and to devise solutions. And they must do these things themselves. Under lean production there are no supervisors or shop stewards to turn to.

Lean production does not accept the "move the metal" mentality of mass production under which the assembly line is kept running with a rework area at the end to correct errors. Lean production treats rework areas as a waste that should be made redundant. Workers are expected to stop the production line if they detect an error they are unable to correct. It is argued that it is better to correct defects before they become embedded in the vehicle and at the point where they occur so that the ultimate root causes responsible for the defect can be solved. (Workers are taught to ask the "five why's"—"And why did that go wrong?" is asked and answered five times.)

Lean production began in Japan, but not all Japanese producers are equally lean, and the worst have lower plant productivity than the average in North America. North America has been improving its productivity, but in two cases, General Motors and Chrysler, this has come from closing the least-efficient plants. It is Ford Motor Co., the pioneer of mass production to the world, that is the first Western automobile company to begin incorporating the lessons of lean production. Just how far North American and European car producers still have to go in catching up with a continually improving Japanese industry is illustrated by Womack's figures on the average assembly hours needed per vehicle in the three major world markets (Table 10.5).

The Impact of Lean Production on the Location of the Automobile Industry

The impact of lean production on cost, quality, and upgrading of product range achieved by Toyota and subsequently by other Japanese carmakers has resulted in a shift of automobile production from North America to Japan, and of North American and European production from domestic companies to Japanese companies. The locational impact is most visible in the list of domestic assembly plants closed and of foreign branch plants opened, but it goes beyond the components of industrial change to include indirect effects as well.

The direct locational effects of lean production are startling. The Japanese share of world motor vehicle production rose from a couple of percent in 1955 to 30 percent in 1980. The world recession and the Japanese shift of production offshore reduced Japan's share in the 1980s. Nevertheless, about one car in four is now made in Japan. That figure is about equal to the current North American share of world production, but North America dominated world output in 1955 with about three-quarters of world production.

The loss of their world market share by U.S. producers is even worse than the North American fig-

TABLE 10.5

Car industry productivity in major world regions: Assembly time in hours per vehicle

Market	Japan	North America		Europe		NIC
				Japanese and		
MNEs	Japanese	Japanese	United States	United States	European	All
Best	13.2	18.8	18.6	22.8	22.8	25.7
Average	16.8	20.9	24.9	35.3	35.5	41
Worst	25.9	25.5	30.7	57.6	55.7	78.7

Source: Data are from James P. Womack et al., *The Machine That Changed the World,* New York: Macmillan, 1990, p. 85.

Note: The data are for volume producers: GM, Ford, Chrysler, Fiat, Peugeot, Renault, Volkswagen, and all Japanese producers. The assembly time is based on gross number of vehicles produced and total hours of plant labor, and standardized for variations in size and equipment. The category NIC (newly industrializing countries) includes Mexico, Brazil, Taiwan, and Korea.

ures suggest. Japanese branch plants now account for almost a quarter of North American production, and beginning with their first American branch plant in 1982, they have established in less than 10 years an industry in the U.S. Midwest that is larger than Britain's or Italy's and almost the size of the French car industry. As the list of Japanese branch plants in North America grows, so too does the list of U.S. plants closed. As of 1990, 11 Japanese assembly plants have been opened, and 10 U.S. assembly plants closed. General Motors has opened one new plant, Saturn, at Spring Hill, Tennessee, based on lean production, and plans in 1991–94 to close most of its "Rustbelt" assembly plants.

The lesson is clear. Firms with obsolete technology, whether relating to product or management, cannot survive, and in an increasingly competitive world, such firms face extinction. Yet firms find it very hard to adjust to new ways of making things or of managing production. It has been said that GM acts as though it prefers progressive self-liquidation and sequential abandonment of market segments to changing from a mass production, move-the-metal, mentality to competitive, quality lean production. Neither GM nor Chrysler have been able to apply the lessons they have learned from their associations with Toyota and Mitsubishi, respectively. Nor do the employment impacts and locational shifts end with the loss of market share by domestic firms. To the direct losses must be added the indirect losses.

Assessing the Direct and Indirect Impact of MNEs

The immediate reaction by host country governments and labor organizations to foreign direct investment (FDI) and to the opening of branch plants tends to be enthusiastic. But if foreign direct investment grows rapidly or if foreign subsidiaries are sold or closed, then serious concerns begin to be expressed about their effects. Assessing the direct and indirect effects of MNEs is difficult, but a framework for doing so has been developed by the International Labor Organization (ILO) (Box 10.13).

It might be thought that the direct effects of foreign branch plants are simply the new employment created by those plants. But is the contribution of a foreign branch plant to employment growth and industrial output the same when the MNE buys out a going concern as when it builds a new factory at a greenfield location? The new Nissan plant at Washington, England, would appear to contribute more to the British car industry than did Chrysler's ill-fated buy-out of the British Rootes group. However, Rootes was in trouble when Chrysler bought a controlling interest in it in the 1960s. The new Rootes small car, the Hillman Imp, had smaller sales than expected and was not generating the profits needed to update the aging product line or the outdated inefficient engines. Had Chrysler not bought in, Rootes probably would have closed: No other corporation had shown an interest. In 1978, after Chrysler found it was unable to turn the losses around and was facing mounting financial difficulties in the United States, it sold out to Peugeot. Again, had Peugeot not bought out Chrsyler's European interests, the former Rootes' factories would have had to close down. Indeed, Peugeot did close one assembly plant in 1981 at Lynwood, Scotland, which had been newly opened at the time of the Chrysler takeover. Even if it is argued that the Chrysler and Peugeot buy-outs did not directly create employment, they did save employment and preserved industrial locations. So considerations of employment effects, direct or indirect, are always bedeviled by the "alternative hypothesis": What would have happened if the direct foreign investment had not taken place?

BOX 10.13   The Direct and Indirect Employment Effects of Branch Plants of MNEs in Host Country

Type of Effect	Definition and Example
A. Direct	Total labor force in all plants in the host country owned or controlled by MNEs.
B. Indirect	Employment generated in the country as a result of spending by the MNE (for parts and services from enterprises in that country) and by its employees on domestically produced goods and services.
1. Horizontal	Employment displaced from similar industries in host country that may be locally owned, labor-intensive.
2. Vertical	
(a) Backward linkages	Employment generated by the MNE among domestic suppliers of raw materials, parts, components, and services.
(b) Forward linkages	Employment generated in the distribution and service networks.
3. Macroeconomic	Second-round employment generated by the spending on domestic goods and services by MNE workers and reinvested MNE profits.

See N. Jéquier, "Measuring the Indirect Employment Effects of Multinational Enterprises: Some Suggestions for a Research Framework," Geneva: ILO, Multinational Enterprises Programme Working Paper No. 56, 1989.

Even if the direct employment effects are accepted, three concerns have been raised about the limitations of the direct contributions of direct foreign investment. First, branch plants are often truncated firms, performing a number of the production and assembly operations, but seldom involved in the full hierarchy of corporate activity. Strategic planning, research and development, and design and engineering tend to remain in the MNE's home country. Japanese foreign investment typically begins with an assembly plant, followed later by a plant to assemble engines. Nissan, Honda, and Toyota each now have an engine plant both in the United States and United Kingdom. The design and engineering are still all performed in Japan. One concern with MNEs is then that they export the production jobs, but keep the best jobs at home.

A second concern is with exports. An MNE may expressly locate a branch plant in a country to serve a free-trade area to which the host country belongs. More usually the branch plant is limited to serving the host country market. Even when the branch plant secures export orders, these shipments may be contrary to government policy in the MNE's home country. Problems of "extraterritoriality" may then occur in which the branch plant finds itself subject to laws of the MNE's home country. This problem has occurred in Canada, for instance, where one Canadian subsidiary planned to export buses to Cuba. Exports are job-creating and when they are restricted, the growth of the branch plant is limited.

A third concern is whether foreign branch plants are "snatchers," concerned mainly with seizing a quick profit and ready to close if profit levels fall. Certainly the exit barriers (that is, the costs of closing down operations in a host country) are lower for MNEs than for domestic firms. They can transfer equipment to another country rather than liquidating. Intangible assets, such as good will and proprietary knowledge, which can be of considerable value, need not be lost in an MNE transfer of production as they usually are in the closing down of a domestic firm. Furthermore, MNEs may be under political pressure to maintain employment levels at home during a recession, whatever the employment cost to branch plants in other countries.

The evidence on the strategies of MNEs regarding foreign branch plants is complex, but does not generally support the "snatcher" argument. MNEs tend to follow a long-term strategy such as portfolio adjustment based on their share of market and the growth expectations of that market. Mark Casson argues that where an MNE closes a branch plant as opposed to selling it as a going concern, the most likely reasons are these.

1. The facility may be in the wrong location.
2. The plant is obsolete.
3. The plant has incorrigible management and working practices.
4. The plant may have high costs in an industry faced with falling demand.

A plant may be in the wrong location for many reasons. The sources of inputs may have changed, leaving the plant stranded. Tariff and nontariff barriers may change, opening the plant to new sources of competition. Transport costs and facilities may have changed. Manufacturers located in older industrial districts may be disadvantaged by traffic congestion. Or the plant may be a victim of government policy that has lured the plant to the wrong location or left it unable to compete with plants benefiting from incentives in another location.

The Lynwood plant in Scotland, closed by Peugeot, is an example of a plant in a wrong location selected to obtain government subsidies. Lynwood did have poor industrial relations too, but the decisive factor in its closing was high transportation costs. Engines were cast at Lynwood, then shipped to Coventry in the Midlands, England, to be bored. The completed engines were transported back to Lynwood for final vehicle assembly. The vehicles then were shipped south again to their main markets. It seems unlikely that Lynwood could have survived regardless of country of control. The investment-divestment sequence fits more closely to the portfolio strategic planning explanation than to any "snatcher" hypothesis.

The indirect employment consequences of MNE direct foreign investment are more difficult to sort out. In general, the horizontal indirect effects are likely to be negative. The opening of a new branch plant, perhaps using state-of-the-art technology and able to draw on the resources of the parent company, may lead to closure of domestic plants making similar goods. The closure of U.S. automobile assembly plants in North America is an example of such negative horizontal effects. Once established, branch plants may constitute barriers to entry by domestic firms.

Vertical indirect effects are likely to create jobs, though probably less than had the plant been domestically owned. The vertical effect depends on the local content of the product made in the branch plant. Japanese car plants in North America had only 20 percent North American content in the early 1980s. That figure

has now reached 60 percent and may reach 75 percent by the late 1990s. The many individual case studies point to a wide array of factors that influence the vertical effect of MNEs on employment. They vary with the industry type, the home country of the MNE, the industrial policies in the host country, and the length of operation of the MNE in the host country. Capital-intensive industries tend to create more indirect employment. So do export industries that are growing rapidly. European countries, particularly the smaller ones like The Netherlands, Sweden, and Switzerland, do better than the United States, which in turn does better than Japan. But Japan's poor performance may reflect the recentness of its direct foreign investment. It takes time for a branch plant to establish linkages, and so longer-established branch plants tend to generate more indirect employment than new ones.

In addition to the industry-specific horizontal and vertical indirect employment effects, MNEs have broad macroeconomic effects on employment. The wages spent by branch plant workers help to create more jobs. And retained profits reinvested in the host country can stimulate the economy. But there are concerns that these macroeconomic effects can be reduced by repatriation of profits and by transfer pricing. Transfer pricing can occur because the dealings of a branch plant with sister plants in other countries are not at arm's length so that prices are not determined in the marketplace. An MNE can, therefore, set the prices so as to transfer the apparent profits of its various operations to those countries where corporate tax rates are lower, for example. If an MNE transfers profits out of a host country, it reduces the macroeconomic benefits of its operations. Transfers of declared profits can also have implications for the macroeconomic contributions of the branch plant, for exchange rates, and for balance of payments.

All these employment effects, direct and indirect, affect the amount, the type, and the location of industry. MNEs affect the distribution of industry on a global scale through their investment policies. In addition to the country-specific endowments that attract branch plants mentioned by Dunning in his eclectic theory, it is clear that in the initial stages of foreign direct investment, MNEs exhibit a strong preference for similar cultures in nearby countries. For U.S. branch plants, the most frequent order of investment is Canada, United Kingdom, Mexico, West Germany, Brazil, France, Columbia, Spain, Japan, and Italy. Compare the global distribution of U.S. MNE manufacturing activity in the 1950s when it first began its major expansion, with that for Japan in the 1980s at the onset of its major expansion. In 1955 U.S. foreign direct investment in manufacturing was concentrated in

Canada (45 percent), Europe (30 percent) and Latin America (15 percent). For Japan in 1983 the distribution was quite different: North America (27 percent), Asia (33 percent), Latin America (20 percent), and Europe (7 percent). It takes experience before foreign direct investment by a country's MNEs is an efficient response to global economic opportunities and conditions, rather than reflecting a mix of economic opportunity, cultural similarity, and geographic proximity. With growing experience, then, initial contrasts in the geographic distribution of direct foreign investment by different countries should narrow. Meanwhile, the rapid growth of Japanese foreign direct investment is an important force for change in a pattern previously dictated by U.S. MNEs.

LOCATIONAL CHOICE AND DECISIONS: A NEW PERSPECTIVE

The real world of location decisions and choice by manufacturing industry thus is in stark contrast to the narrow picture presented by early theorists. They

---

BOX 10.14   The Cycle of Manufacturing: A Schematic Collage

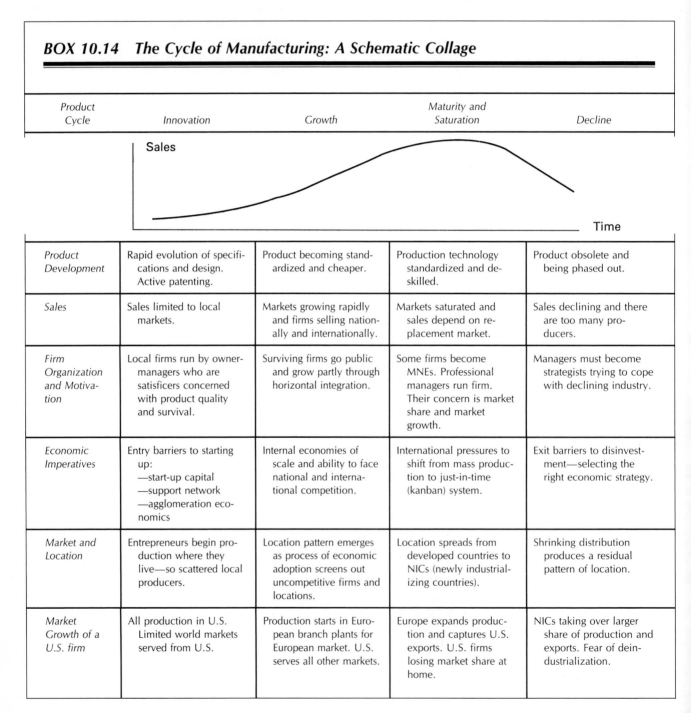

Product Cycle	Innovation	Growth	Maturity and Saturation	Decline
Product Development	Rapid evolution of specifications and design. Active patenting.	Product becoming standardized and cheaper.	Production technology standardized and de-skilled.	Product obsolete and being phased out.
Sales	Sales limited to local markets.	Markets growing rapidly and firms selling nationally and internationally.	Markets saturated and sales depend on replacement market.	Sales declining and there are too many producers.
Firm Organization and Motivation	Local firms run by owner-managers who are satisficers concerned with product quality and survival.	Surviving firms go public and grow partly through horizontal integration.	Some firms become MNEs. Professional managers run firm. Their concern is market share and market growth.	Managers must become strategists trying to cope with declining industry.
Economic Imperatives	Entry barriers to starting up: —start-up capital —support network —agglomeration economics	Internal economies of scale and ability to face national and international competition.	International pressures to shift from mass production to just-in-time (kanban) system.	Exit barriers to disinvestment—selecting the right economic strategy.
Market and Location	Entrepreneurs begin production where they live—so scattered local producers.	Location pattern emerges as process of economic adoption screens out uncompetitive firms and locations.	Location spreads from developed countries to NICs (newly industrializing countries).	Shrinking distribution produces a residual pattern of location.
Market Growth of a U.S. firm	All production in U.S. Limited world markets served from U.S.	Production starts in European branch plants for European market. U.S. serves all other markets.	Europe expands production and captures U.S. exports. U.S. firms losing market share at home.	NICs taking over larger share of production and exports. Fear of deindustrialization.

thought that the distribution of an industry was decided by the incremental additions of firms that made once-and-forever decisions on where to locate. In reality, the distribution of industry is constantly changing and the locational decision of a firm is a continuing one that begins with where it starts up, but extends throughout its life as it grows or declines at that location, moves production to other locations, and finally sells out or closes down. Indeed the evidence shows that, of the various components of employment change in the life status of a firm, births may be the smallest and have the least immediate impact on the distribution of industry. It follows that all the components of change are integral parts of locational choice, and that in order to understand the changing distribution of industry, we need to understand the processes generating the individual geographies of firm births and expansions, and of firm declines and exits.

Furthermore, classical location theory assumed that the optimal location varied according to the type of industry, but not with the size of the firm. *There is now a growing belief that locational decisions vary more with size of firm than with type of industry.* This remarkable change in thinking is prompted in part by the declining importance of raw-material procurement costs and the growing importance of market. Different industries use different raw materials and components but all industries ultimately serve the same sets of markets. A raw-material orientation produces different geographies for different industries. A market orientation draws all industries to a common geography.

However, even in the same industry, small firms differ from large firms in their motivations for starting up a plant, their locational needs, and their survival chances. Most small firms are located where the entrepreneur happens to live. Their establishment tests the margins of locational choice and their survival depends on their adoption by the support network in the area. Those that do survive may broaden the area's industrial base, contribute to its management experience, and enhance its external economies of scale. The branch plant of an MNE is, on the other hand, a self-sustained package of product, technology, and capital. The locational choice of such plants is evaluated initially on the country scale, and the MNE may use its locational autonomy to select a greenfield location within the selected country where new technologies are not biased by old ways of doing things. The consequence of these changes in location is that the intrinsic advantages of a location, including its raw materials, or geographic position, are becoming less important than the acquired attributes such as markets and the calibre of suppliers, skilled labor, and support services.

Where industries survive and grow has come to depend increasingly on their competitive edge in technology—both "hard" technology, as in product design, and in the "soft" technology of management and organization. It is the successful firms that come to control investment and location decisions. Ultimately then, location theories must be embedded within a much broader intellectual framework that takes into account product development and sales, firm organization, and motivation, as well as locational choice and market areas served. Understanding the changing location of industry requires understanding how these characteristics change during the profit life cycle. Such a schema, presented in Box 10.14, involves a less deterministic approach to location theory, recognizing instead that the location of industry can be the indirect result of many factors. This chapter has sketched some of new directions which a rapidly changing field of industrial geography is taking. The details have yet to be worked out.

TOPICS FOR DISCUSSION

1. The accompanying table shows the results of a survey undertaken by Mueller and Lansing in 1960 in an attempt to explain given plant locations in Michigan. How can one reconcile what industrialists say *they do* with what researchers say *they see?* Can anything be inferred from the different responses larger firms gave from the responses of smaller firms? If so, what?

2. In the world today, major industrial shifts are taking place in labor orientation as part of a global scramble for cheap labor, yet there are many situations where money wages vary apparently without effect on industrial locations. Why? Why do labor cost variations due to money wages tend to be short-run differentials? In what circumstances can these differentials persist in longer periods of time?

3. What kind of industries tend to remain localized within the boundaries of the central business districts (CBDs) of America's cities? Do these industries tend to conform with a hierarchy of land usage in the city? What is the basic principle involved in this land usage in the city? What is the basic principle involved in this land-use hierarchy? Explain with an example.

4. What were Weber's formal assumptions in his theory of plant location? What were his two "distorting" or "altering" forces in industrial location? Explain each.

Explanations given for location of plant by number of plants operated by firm (percentage of employment represented)

	All Michigan	Number of Plants Operated by Firm		
		One plant	2–4 plants	5 or more plants
Main Reasons for Locating Plant in Michigan[a]				
Personal reasons; chance	50%	63%	52%	32%
Opportunity-found good site, etc.	19	23	20	14
Proximity to customers; central location . . .	15	17	20	4
Proximity to auto industry	8	14	4	4
Labor advantages	7	c	12	14
Proximity to materials	6	3	8	9
Local concessions and inducements; encouragement by groups or persons	2	c	c	4
Better tax situation	1	c	c	4
State already established as a center for the industry	1	c	4	c
Total	d	d	d	d
Main Reasons for Locating Plant at Particular Site[b]				
Personal reasons; chance	33%	55%	32%	20%
Opportunity-found good site, etc.	18	27	16	14
Proximity to customers; central location . . .	15	16	15	14
Proximity to auto industry	13	7	14	12
Labor advantages	7	4	9	7
Proximity to materials	12	7	6	15
Local concessions and inducements; encouragement by groups or persons	4	2	4	7
Better tax situation	3	4	6	2
Area already established as a center for the industry	2	1	2	4
Total	d	d	d	d

Source: From Eva Mueller and John Lansing, "Location Decisions of Manufacturers," *American Economic Review,* 502 (1962), 204–217.

[a] Asked only at plants that started operating at present location after 1940. The question was: "What were the main reasons for locating the plant in Michigan?"

[b] The question was: "What were main reasons that operations were set up here in [name of town]?"

[c] Less than 0.5 percent.

[d] Totals differ from 100 percent because some respondents mentioned more than one reason, and for some others the reasons were not ascertained.

5. Select a case that has received attention by government and labor of a decision by an MNE to buy, sell, or close a branch plant. How well were the direct and the indirect effects on employment discussed? What effects were missed altogether?

6. How much attention is being given in your area to employment creation by small firms and to job loss (or gain) by large firms? Are all the components of change receiving attention? If not, are the conclusions reached biased?

7. What kinds of organizations are there in your area to assist small firms? Find out what assistance you could get in starting up your own manufacturing business.

FURTHER READINGS

BIRCH, D. L. *The Job Generation Process.* Cambridge, Mass.: M.I.T. Program on Neighborhood and Regional Changes, 1979.

This study sparked North American interest in the role of small firms in employment creation.

BURNS, PAUL, and JIM DEWHURST (Eds). *Small Business and Entrepreneurship.* London: Macmillan, 1989.

Written for practical guidance as well as academic study, the combination of literature review and case studies makes this book fascinating as well as instructive.

CASSON, MARK. *International Divestment and Restructuring Decisions (with special reference to the motor industry)*. Geneva: International Labor Office, Multinational Enterprises Programme, Working Paper No. 40, 1984.

One of a series of working papers dealing with individual countries in the industrialized and developing countries, and with special topics such as export-processing zones, indirect employment effects, and the employment effects of technology choice. It is a key source of information. Casson is useful because he provides a detailed typology of divestment decisions as well as the Chrysler-Peugeot case study.

DICKEN, PETER. *Global Shift: Industrial Change in a Turbulent World*. London: Harper & Row, 1986.

A comprehensive survey of the growth of MNEs and their role in the major industries, and an assessment of their costs and benefits to host countries. Essential reading.

FOTHERGILL, S., and G. GUDGIN. *Unequal Growth: Urban and Regional Employment Change in the UK*. London: Heinemann, 1982.

A key reading on the changing factors in regional development, particularly employment creation by new small firms.

HARRIGAN, KATHRYN RUDIE. *Managing Maturing Business, Restructuring Declining Industries and Re-vitalizing Troubled Operations*. Lexington Mass: Lexington Books, 1988.

Harrigan is a seminal contributor to the extension of Bain's structure, conduct, and performance paradigm to include exit barriers and suboptimal decision making in declining industries.

HARRIS, CHAUNCY D. "The Market as a Factor in the Localization of Industry in the United States." *Annals of the Association of American Geographers,* 44 (1954), 315–348.

The seminal statement that led location studies on from a preoccupation with least-cost location.

MASON, COLIN M., and RICHARD T. HARRISON. "The Geography of Small Firms in the U.K.: towards a research agenda." *Progress in Human Geography,* 9 (1985), 1–37.

A useful review of a rapidly growing literature and some unanswered questions.

ROTHWELL, R., and W. ZEGVELD. *Innovation and the Small and Medium Sized Firm*. London: Francis Pinter, 1982.

Chapter 7, SMEs and Employment, is particularly interesting, but the whole book provides pithy summaries of the literature, a good bibliography, and the general economic context for employment trends through the 1970s.

SMITH, DAVID M. *Industrial Location, An Economic Geographical Analysis*. 2d ed. New York: John Wiley, 1981.

The most authoritative source on traditional location theory.

UNITED NATIONS CENTER ON TRANSNATIONAL CORPORATIONS (UNCTC). *Transnational Corporations in World Development: Trends and Prospects*. New York: United Nations, 1988.

The most comprehensive yet of these regular reports from UNCTC, with detailed chapters on MNEs in world development, their growth, technology, and organization (including a box, p. 45, on just-in-time) and their employment impact.

WATTS, H. D. *Industrial Geography*. Harlow: Longman Group U.K., 1987.

The first of the new-look textbooks on the subject. Makes an interesting contrast with R. C. Riley's *Industrial Geography* of 1973 and exemplifies how rapidly the field is changing.

WEBER, ALFRED. *Theory of the Location of Industries*. Translated by Carl J. Friedrich. Chicago: The University of Chicago Press, 1929.

Where location theory begins, it is far more comprehensive in its scope than can be portrayed in a textbook summary.

WOMACK, JAMES P., DANIEL T. JONES and DANIEL ROOS. *The Machine that Changed the World*. New York: Rawson Associates, 1990.

The book that attracted world attention, spelling out more forcefully than ever before why mass production can't survive. Is lean production the beginning of a new Kondratiev wave?

11

Location Theory in Historical Context: Long Waves in Economic Evolution

OVERVIEW

The Industrial Revolution, by which a world composed of largely self-sustaining agrarian societies was transformed into a progressively more interdependent global economy, was neither gradual nor continuous. Key innovations came in a succession of bursts at roughly 50-year intervals: in the 1770s and 1780s, the 1820s and 1830s, the 1870s and 1880s, and the 1920s and 1930s. Each swarm of innovations introduced new industries and transformed older ones, signaled the end of a period of "stagflation," and precipitated decades of new growth. Each wave of growth ended in a major depression in which there was a collapse of former growth industries that had overshot needs and were overbuilt. New types of industry, new industrial

regions, and new forces affecting industrial location emerged in each period of growth. Depressed areas suffering from the collapse of their base industries appeared in each depression.

This chapter, which begins with an excursion into economic history, will enable you to understand the waves of growth and the industrial types, industrial regions, and location factors that emerged. It then presents the theory of "long waves" or "Kondratiev cycles" in economic evolution, and it concludes by exploring the nature of present-day high-technology and service-based growth—the Fifth Kondratiev—that has followed the 1980–81 stagflation crisis..

OBJECTIVES

- to understand the nature of the "long wave" phenomenon, and the theories that explain Kondratiev cycles
- to learn about Mensch's "metamorphosis model," and of the triggering mechanisms for the clusters of innovations that drive new long waves
- to appreciate current changes in the United States and the global economy: growth of "thoughtware" economies, advanced services, flexible automation, and "economies of scope"

A PREAMBLE ON ECONOMIC HISTORY

Porter's categories of national development discussed in Chapter 1 presume the globalization of production, trade, and markets. How was this globalization achieved? Barely 250 years ago the world was largely agricultural, and the circuits of trade and specialization were quite limited. The transition came in a series of waves of 50 to 60 years each, named after the man who first theorized about them, Russian economist Nikolai Kondratiev.

The First Industrial Revolution (1770–1820s)

The first Industrial Revolution, described by Arnold Toynbee as a period of accelerated change that transformed a people with peasant occupations and local markets into an industrial society with worldwide connections, occurred in Great Britain from the 1770s to the 1820s. The major technologies triggering the change were in the textile industry, first using the power of falling water, but ultimately enabling exploitation of the potential of coal and of steam power.

Textile production was a cottage craft at the beginning of the eighteenth century. Technological changes later in the century laid the groundwork for its transformation into a factory industry in the early years of the nineteenth century. The cottage craft produced a rough cotton cloth for women's dresses and men's shirts. In its original form a single hand loom operated by a skilled male weaver was supplied with hand-spun yarn by as many as six women or children. John Kay (of Bury) invented the *flying shuttle* (1733) to make the weaver's job easier. It doubled the productivity of a weaver, but placed great strains on the capabilities of the household's hand spinners, a problem solved by James Hargreaves's *spinning jenny* (1770), which enabled one woman to supply all the yarn for a hand loom by spinning up to eight threads at a time. Initially this was a great boon to the cottage weavers, because a husband and wife became a self-sufficient combination; the 1780s and 1790s were years of great prosperity for the cottage hand-loom industry, scattered throughout rural areas. Although the jenny was adopted very rapidly, it only produced soft yarn suitable for the weft, however. Cottage weavers in the 1770s still used linen for the warp, which had to be stronger.

The solution for this problem was the *spinning frame* developed by Richard Arkwright and another John Kay (of Warrington) in 1769 and 1775. The water-powered frame produced cotton yarn strong enough for the warp and made it possible for English weavers to manufacture cheap, high-quality calicoes and mus-

lins comparable to those imported from India. Warp production was concentrated where the power of falling water could be used. Later spinning machines such as Samuel Crompton's 1779 *spinning mule* (a hybrid of the *jenny* and the *frame*) also were too much for unaided human muscles. As a result, the handicraft cottage industry gave way to cotton mills located where water power could be tapped to drive the new spinning machines. By 1812 the water-powered spinning mule enabled a single worker to produce yarn 200 times faster than the pre-1770 spinner could. Because power was required for the spinning it might as well be applied to the loom, as Edmund Cartwright saw in 1785. Thus, the key inventions involved in the mechanization of spinning and weaving and the replacement of the cottage craft by a factory industry were in place by 1800.

The transformation in weaving, lagging behind spinning, came between 1810 and 1830. In 1813 there were only 2400 power looms in England (against a hundred times as many hand looms), but by 1830 the number of power looms had grown to 85,000 in England and 15,000 in Scotland, and many mill towns had developed around sources of water power. In these towns the productivity of a single worker was orders of magnitude greater than in the cottages, resulting in a rapid decline in the price of cotton products, especially fine muslins. Rising demand had created a short-lived prosperity in the 1780s and 1790s for all weavers, including cottage hand-loom operators, but this period of prosperity ended as the supply from mechanized factories caught up. One of the sad episodes of history was the brief revolt of technologically unemployed cottage weavers under the banner of "General Ned Ludd." The Luddite revolt was put down brutally with a series of hangings at York in 1813.

At the same time, Britain deliberately set about destroying the prosperous competing Indian cotton-weaving industry of Bengal, converting India into a captive market for British cotton goods. Unemployment and declining income for cottage weavers and colonial abuses were not the whole story, though. Factory operatives, on the whole, received wages better than the cottage pieceworkers of earlier generations. Employment in the cotton industry rose from less than 100,000 jobs in 1770 to 350,000 jobs in 1800 as former cottage weavers and agricultural laborers displaced by the enclosure of the common fields moved into the mill towns. The *Penny Magazine,* a publication of the Society for the Diffusion of Useful Knowledge in the mid-nineteenth century, observed: "Two centuries ago, not one person in a thousand wore stockings—now not one person in a thousand is without them." Production and export of cotton textiles soared. In 1764

Britain imported 4 million pounds of cotton; by 1833 the figure was 300 million pounds. In 1835, Britain produced 60 percent of all cotton goods consumed in the world, compared with 16 percent from France and 7 percent from the United States.

During the same period of time, key innovations also took place in the metal industries. These involved the substitution of coke (from coal) for charcoal (from progressively scarcer wood) in iron smelting, and Henry Cort's (1784) development of the "puddling furnace," which was used to convert crude pig iron into vastly superior wrought iron. Production and consumption of iron in Britain had been 25,000 tons in 1720 and 68,000 tons in 1788, but this rose to 1,347,000 tons in 1838. The small furnaces of the old iron industry had been scattered in forested areas where charcoal could be produced; the new furnaces that used coke were located on the coalfields to minimize the costs of transporting that bulky raw material.

Coal mining expanded rapidly to meet the demand for the cheap alternative to charcoal, using the method of producing coke from coal discovered by Abraham Darby in 1709. But more coal could only come from deeper mines, mines that were often waterlogged (as were Cornwall's tin mines). An initial solution was Thomas Newcomen's (about 1705) pump, of which 100 were installed in Britain's coal and tin mines by the 1760s. These pumps were cumbersome, inefficient, and expensive, problems solved by James Watt's (1769) steam engine and his succeeding improvements to it, including the "sun and planet" gear system (1781), the double-acting engine and parallelogram cranking mechanism (1784), and the steam governor (1788). Watt's basic patent expired in 1800, by which time he had built 500 engines, and unlicensed imitators had built another 1000. The steam engines burned coal and when, later, they were used instead of water power in new factory industries, they produced relocations of those industries from the scattered sites where falling water was available to the coalfields or to other spots where cheap water transport for coal was available. Mill towns developed around these locations. Indeed, the new spinning factories, with their central source of power, their batteries of expensive machines, and their large permanent working force, moved out of the hills into the lowland towns—towns that were close to market, to sources of supply, and to labor. Manchester had its first steam mill in 1787. By 1800, dozens of great mills were in operation, and Manchester had already become the prototype of the modern industrial city, along with the rapidly growing iron-making towns of Birmingham and Sheffield in Britain's "Black Country."

The results of the exploitation of the new sources of industrial power and heat were indeed profound. The factory and the industrial town spread rapidly in Great Britain bringing with them an enlarged urban middle class, an industrial bourgeoisie, and a much larger working class—an industrial proletariat. It was the view of Manchester (with side glances to Birmingham) that provided Karl Marx with his inspiration. Moreover, as the new coal-powered factories made Britain the workshop of the world, the course of international trade was transformed. Before the 1790s one of Britain's most important imports was cotton goods from India. Quickly the reverse became true as India came to be a major market for British textiles.

The economy of the recently formed United States was even more fundamentally altered. The new nation quickly became the largest customer for British textiles and hardware and by far the largest supplier of the basic raw material for the spinning and weaving mills of Lancashire. Prior to 1786, the year before the first spinning mill was built in Manchester, no cotton was grown commercially in the United States. At first it was grown commercially only on moist sea islands of Carolina and Georgia, the only areas suitable for the production of smooth-seed, long-staple cotton. The burry, prickly seeds in short-staple upland cotton made its cleaning too costly for commercial production. By 1792, however, farmers were planting short-staple cotton in the uplands in anticipation of the invention of an engine that could efficiently remove the burry seeds. The following year Eli Whitney obliged, thus providing a classic example of an induced invention. His cotton gin and the others that followed made possible the rapid spread of cotton culture, and with it slave labor, throughout the lower South. Because climatic and soil conditions prevented the production of other crops suitable to cultivation by slaves—rice, sugar, and tobacco—in this vast area of the South, historians have often maintained that the cotton gin, by spreading slavery into these regions, was at least partly to blame for the American Civil War.

The spread of the Industrial Revolution beyond Britain was at first surprisingly slow. (See Box 11.1, Diffusion of the Railroads.) The great wars of the French Revolution and Napoleon and the then-existing economic, political, and social structures delayed its spread to the Continent. But when it came, it came fast, as Britain moved into the Second Wave of Industrial Revolution. In the United States, where economic, political, and social barriers to change were less formidable, the reason for the delay is clear. The first industrial revolution reached the U.S. in force only after canals had been built to open up the anthracite fields in eastern Pennsylvania, during the second wave of Britain's industrial transformation. As coal began to course through the economy in the 1840s, the textile industry reached maturity by the building of steam mills in the port cities of New England, a modern American iron industry boomed in eastern Pennsylvania, and once the railroad reached Pittsburgh, that city became America's Birmingham. Then in the 1850s a brand-new machine industry grew rapidly in Philadelphia and in southern New England. By the 1850s the American Northeast was undergoing as profound an economic and social transformation as Britain had a half-century earlier.

The Second Wave of Industrial Revolution (1820s to 1870s)

The second wave of industrial revolution came after 1820, again largely in Britain, but with France and Germany as the principal partners. Perhaps the key technological innovations were the application of steam power to water and land transportation, but there were also fundamental organizational inventions, as well as the pioneering of the mechanization of production in the United States. The latter force was not, however, to have its full impact until the third wave of growth and change coming after the early 1870s. The principal results of the second wave were increased regional specialization and trade, the rapid growth of coalfield-, waterside-, and railroad-oriented industry, and the acceleration of urbanization and rural-to-urban migration.

High-pressure steam had been added to Watt's engine by Richard Trevithick in 1800, setting the stage for using coal-powered steam engines in place of increasingly scarce water power for factory production, as well as a power source for boats and to haul a train of cars on iron rails. Robert Fulton's steamship *Clermont,* designed to be able to travel upstream on the Hudson River under its own power, was built in 1807. George Stephenson's Stockton and Darlington Railway was opened in 1825.

In the United States, as John Borchert has pointed out, the real buildup of steamboat tonnage on the Ohio-Mississippi-Missouri system began in the 1830s, and the main period of increase in the tonnage of general cargo vessels on the Great Lakes also began in the 1830s and 1840s. Rail mileage, likewise, grew rapidly after initial development in 1829. By the end of the decade the major mechanical features of the American locomotive were established, boxcars had been introduced, regular mail routes were in operation on the railroads, and the first transatlantic steamer had arrived in New York. Soon thereafter the telegraph lines were built, and a transatlantic cable was laid from the American side.

The introduction of steam power created major transportation corridors on the western rivers and the Great Lakes and resulted in enlargement of the hinterlands of ports on both the inland waterways and the Atlantic. It made possible the development of a national transportation system through the integration of these major waterways and regional rail webs. These changes favored the growth of ports with relatively large harbors and proximity to important resource concentrations.

Steam power was also applied in manufacturing in the United States, but its impact was apparently more localized because of the impracticality of long hauls of coal or other bulk commodities with the comparatively light equipment and iron rails of the time. As a result, local water-power sites continued to dominate industrial location. By 1870 waterwheels were still providing roughly half of the inanimate energy for manufacturing, especially in the major northeastern manufacturing region that was developing. About half of the entire inanimate power for industry was in the five states of Massachusetts, Connecticut, New York, Pennsylvania, and Ohio. Steam was not universally used in cotton mills in the United States until the railroads were sufficiently developed to transport coal cheaply. That ability came generally in the 1870s.

As steam was being applied to rail and water transportation, the United States also was pioneering the "American System of Manufactures" (a phrase coined by British observers in the 1850s) based on interchangeable parts, building a successful machine tool industry and, simultaneously, exploring notions of mechanical and press production. The United States was very short of both machine tools and skilled machinists, and Britain refused to export machine tools until after 1843. Manufacturers in Philadelphia and New England therefore concentrated on simplifying product design and rationalizing the production process to minimize the need for "fitting" parts together. The use of interchangeable parts was perfected in the gun-manufacturing industry. Whereas Britain's key eighteenth-century inventions had been in response to progressively more serious shortages of charcoal, in the United States the key shortage was skilled labor, out of which emerged each of the country's principal nineteenth-century innovations, the American System of Manufacturers in the 1830s and both agricultural mechanization and labor-saving consumer products in the 1870s.

Hired farm labor was unavailable, in practice,

BOX 11.1   Diffusion of the Railroads

Diffusion is the term used to describe the spread of innovations outward from centers of innovation. The time sequence involves a small band of "early adopters," followed by accelerated acceptance as a "bandwagon effect" takes hold, succeeded by a slowing rate of adoptions as laggards finally join in, and the potential market is saturated. The spatial pattern involves two elements: *hierarchical diffusion* and *spread effects*. Hierarchical diffusion is the tendency for inventions to be adopted in larger cities and markets first, and to diffuse down the urban hierarchy. A spread effect is the wavelike pattern of acceptance outwards from an urban center into a surrounding rural area. Together, time-space sequences incorporate the following features of geographical diffusion:

1. Outwards from heartlands where circular and cumulative causation occurs into progressively more remote hinterlands
2. From large cities to small, down the urban hierarchy
3. From urban areas into their rural hinterlands

In each case the laggards benefit least.

An example of a typical time-space sequence is provided by the diffusion of the railroads, without which industrialization probably could not have run its course. Railroads represented the fastest means of transportation in the century preceding World War I. During the period that railroads were the best means of transportation available, railroad mileage grew in a logistic fashion of increasing then of decreasing rates of construction. The logistic increase of railroad mileage was accompanied by a lagged outward spread from the original center of the innovation, Great Britain, at an accelerating growth rate (Figure 11c). The sequence was from the original heartland of the Industrial Revolution, outwards into the world's hinterlands.

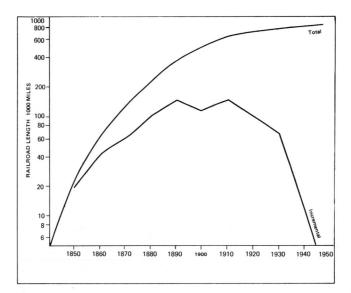

FIGURE 11a   World railroad building, 1840–1950. Most railroad mileage was built in the period when railroads enjoyed a speed superiority over other modes. [*Source:* Alfred J. Lotka, "Population Analysis as a Chapter in the Mathematical Theory of Evolution," in *Essays on Growth and Form*, W. E. Le Gros Clark and Peter P. Medawar, eds. (Oxford: The Clarendon Press, 1965), p. 380.]

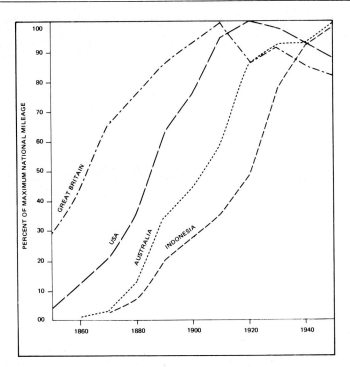

FIGURE 11b The logistic curves of railroad building for selected countries. [*Source:* W. S. Woytinski and E. S. Woytinski, *World Commerce and Governments: Trends and Outlook* (New York: Twentieth Century Fund, 1955).]

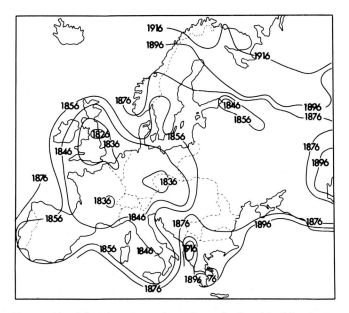

FIGURE 11c The diffusion and growth gradient of railroad building in Europe, 1826–1916. [*Source:* Sven Godlund, "Ein Innovationsverslauf in Europa, dargestellt in einer vorläufigen Untersuchung über die Ausbreitung der Eisenbahninnovation" (Lund, Sweden: Department of Geography, Royal University of Lund, Series B in Geography, Human Geography No. 6, 1952).]

because land in the west was so cheap in the period 1800–1850 that any able-bodied person with appropriate skills could buy an acre of land for as little as a single week's wage—as contrasted to the situation in England where an acre of farmland cost as much as a *year's* wage. In the northern United States the only choice for a farmer was to breed as many children, horses, and mules as possible, and whenever possible to mechanize. In the south the solution was to breed or import more slaves.

Similarly, skilled "mechanics" (machinists) and metal workers were very scarce in America, whereas the market for metal products such as hand tools, farm implements, guns, clocks, wagon wheels, and axles was burgeoning. There was a societal need for more efficient, less-skilled labor-demanding methods of manufacturing, particularly of metal products. The American system of standardized interchangeable parts was the solution, replacing the need for skilled "fitting" of parts into products.

Finally, there was a shortage of household servants in the northern states. Any middle-class family in Europe could have several live-in female servants (daughters of agricultural laborers and peasants) to undertake labor-intensive chores such as food processing and preserving, sewing, laundry, and cleaning. In the United States such servants were much scarcer and more expensive, and a middle-class housewife in a small town or rural area readily utilized mechanical assistance of all kinds. This led to a host of labor-saving inventions from apple corers and ruffle ironers to the sewing machine, washing machine, and vacuum cleaner. Indeed, the Model T car was essentially a utility vehicle for the rural middle class. But many of these inventions did not come until the third or fourth wave of the Industrial Revolution.

As noted earlier, it was during the second wave that basic organizational invention took place, and reinforced the structure and spatial pattern of urban hierarchies. See Box 11.2. The coming of the steam-powered "iron horse" running on iron rails and the coal-fired iron steamship led to the formation of the modern multiunit enterprise with its hierarchy of salaried managers. This happened because the new forms of transportation and communication made possible a speed, regularity, and certainty in the movement of goods, messages, and people that simply was not available as long as transportation and communication depended on the vagaries of wind and water current and on the limited power of horses and mules. In the first place, the new speed and volume forced the railroads to build centrally controlled managerial organizations, if only to prevent trains from running into each other. Then much larger hierarchies became absolutely essential to guide the flow of millions of tons of a vast variety of goods over distances of hundreds and even thousands of miles, to thousands of different destinations.

In the second place, the new speed, regularity, reliability, and the massive volume of flow of transportation and communication resulted in institutional innovation in the processes of distribution by making possible mass marketing of goods, and in continuing change in the process of production by greatly expanding the possibility of mass output. In distribution, completely new types of enterprises—department stores, mail-order houses, and chain stores, all operated through managerial hierarchies—quickly came to market an unprecedented volume of goods at very low prices.

In production came the almost simultaneous inventions of continuous and large batch processes—all voracious users of energy from coal for heat and power. These included the Bessemer and open-hearth processes for the mass production of steel; the new superheated and catalytic techniques in refining sugar, vegetable oils, and then petroleum; the mass producing of machinery by the fabrication and assembling of interchangeable parts; and the creation of new milling, canning, and packaging techniques in the processing of food.

The modern industrial enterprise first came into being by integrating the new mass production with the new mass distribution. In those industries where the existing wholesalers and the new mass retailers were unable to sell the output of the new processes in the volume that they were able to produce, enterprises began to build their own national wholesaling, and occasionally retailing, networks and their own extensive purchasing organizations, which often included control of raw materials. This strategy of vertical integration occurred where independent marketers were unable to satisfy manufacturers' requirements in several areas: the complex scheduling essential to producing and distributing annually millions of packages, tins or cans of cigarettes, soap, soup, kerosene, pills and the like, or tens, even hundreds, of thousands of sewing machines, typewriters, harvesters, or other mass-produced machinery; or specialized distribution facilities such as refrigerated warehouses, train cars, and ships; or specialized marketing services such as demonstration, after-sales service and repair, or extensive consumer credit.

In those industries where wholesalers were unable to meet the manufacturer's distribution and marketing needs, the giant, multiunit, multifunctional firm appeared with suddenness in the 1880s in the United States in the production of food, rubber, kerosene, consumer chemicals, and light and heavy machinery. Large integrated enterprises came more slowly in Europe. In Britain they were formed in some number in packaged, branded consumer goods like foods, soap, paint, and proprietary drugs. In Germany they came in producers' goods, particularly in electrical machinery and chemicals. In the United States and in Germany, but to a much lesser extent in Britain and France, such firms quickly came to be operated through large managerial hierarchies—hierarchies that were organized along functional lines with major departments for production, distribution, purchasing, and finance. It was within the organizational framework of these new managerial hierarchies that the third wave of the Industrial Revolution took place.

The Third Wave (1870s to 1920s)

The third wave of industrial revolution, shared by Germany and the United States, took place in the 1880s, building upon innovations introduced as the economic crises of 1865 (U.S.) and 1871 (Europe) waned. In this period, too, industrial growth spread to new centers in Eastern Europe, Western Russia, and Japan. The key innovations were those permitting low-priced steel production (Bessemer, 1860; Gilchrist Thomas, 1879), the harnessing of electric power, the invention of the internal combustion engine, the emergence of the modern chemical industry, and the introduction of the mass-production assembly line. Geographically, the consequence was the heartland-hinterland pattern of regional development within the United States and within the European nations' colonial empires. See Box 11.3. An equally important ingredient was the creation of institutional arrangements that permitted the systematic application of science to the improvement of existing processes and products and to the development of new ones. By the 1890s successful technological innovation was beginning to require more than just an individual innovator to develop the product and, with one or two entrepreneurs, to build the organization to mass produce and to distribute it to national and world markets. In a few industries technological advances became increasingly dependent on people trained in science and working in well-equipped laboratories to do the innovating, and then on teams of professional managers and engineers to bring the new product into full-scale production and widespread use.

Steel was produced only in very small quantities in the United States in 1870. Output was only 70,000 tons in that year, but demand was rising fast, especially for rail, where steel was far superior to iron because of its superior wearing qualities. Bessemer steel rail cost $170 per ton in 1867, when only 2500 tons were made, compared to 460,000 tons of iron rails at $83 per ton. Bessemer's discoveries increased output and cut prices sharply. By 1884, the last year of iron rail manufacture, production of steel rail was up to 1,500,000 tons at $32 per ton. The price dropped to a low point of $15 per ton in 1898 when output reached 10 million tons.

The consequences were dramatic. Steel rails replaced iron on both newly built and existing lines. Heavier equipment and more powerful locomotives permitted increased speed and the long haul of bulk goods. Rail gauge and freight car parts were standardized (there had been 11 gauges among the northern systems in 1860), so that both interline exchange and coast-to-coast shipment were possible. Refrigerated cars made their entry, ushering in a new era of regional specialization in agriculture, and centralization of the packing industry at major rail centers. Other ramifications favored industrial, hence urban, centralization. The practical length of coal hauling was extended and the cost reduced. The effort was to open vast central Appalachian bituminous deposits and to facilitate the movement of coal to the great ports whose growth had been launched four decades earlier. The greater availability of coal was soon supplemented by the availability of central-station electric power, which followed in the 1880s.

For the first time massive forces were arrayed that favored market orientation of industry and the "metropolitanization" of America. At the same time there were negative impacts. The long rail haul spelled the doom of most passenger traffic and cargo movement on the inland waterways, especially the rivers. Small river ports were destined to become virtual museums. It is noteworthy that general cargo shipping capacity on the western rivers peaked not on the eve of the Civil War but in the 1870s; thereafter it fell precipitously for half a century. The easier availability of coal and central-station electricity doomed the small water-power sites that had yielded to the centralizing force of the metropolitan rail centers, their giant markets, and their superior accessibility.

As important in the long run as the introduction of steel rail were inventions in electricity and magnetism. Michael Faraday's work had been in the 1820s and 1830s, but it was commercially minded inventors such as Werner Siemens, Thomas A. Edison, Frank Sprague, Charles Brush, Elihu Thomson, and George Westinghouse who spawned great industrial firms in the late nineteenth century in Germany and the United States. From Edison's first electric generating plant in 1882 (Pearl Street, New York City), electrification in the United States proceeded rather slowly for a decade as alternative technologies for power transmission—

BOX 11.2   The Concept of Urban Hierarchies and Central-Place Theory

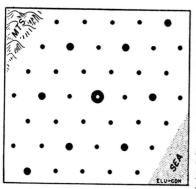

Theoretical distribution of central places. In a homogeneous land, settlements are evenly spaced; largest city in center surrounded by 6 medium-sized centers that in turn are surrounded by 6 small centers. Tributary areas are hexagons, the closest geometrical shapes to circles that completely fill area with no unserved spaces.

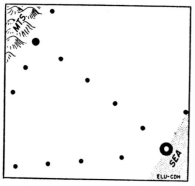

Transport centers, aligned along railroads or at coast. Large center is port; next largest is railroad junction and engine-changing point where mountain and plain meet. Small centers perform break-of-bulk principally between rail and roads.

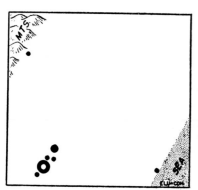

Specialized-function settlements. Large city is manufacturing and mining center surrounded by a cluster of smaller settlements located on a mineral deposit. Small centers on ocean and at edge of mountains are resorts.

There are many reasons for cities. *Transportation centers* perform break-of-bulk and allied services along transportation routes and tend to be arranged in linear patterns with respect to railroads, highways, coastlines, and rivers. *Specialized-function cities* perform services such as mining, manufacturing, or recreation. Because the principal localizing factor is often a particular resource such as a coalfield, or a sandy beach and a warm sunny climate, such cities occur singly or in clusters. *Central places* organize retail and service business into *urban hierarchies,* which involve

1. A system of cities, arranged in a hierarchy according to the types of business provided by each;
2. Corresponding areas of urban influence or urban fields surrounding each city.

The size and functions of a city and the extent of its urban field are proportional. Each region within the national economy focuses upon a center of metropolitan rank. A network of intermetropolitan connections and interregional trade-flows links the regions into a national whole. The spatial incidence of economic growth within these regions is a function of distance from the metropolis. Troughs of economic backwardness lie in the most inaccessible areas along the intermetropolitan peripheries. Each major region is, in turn, subregionalized by successively smaller centers at progressively lower levels of the hierarchy—smaller cities, towns, or villages that function as market centers for the distribution of

FIGURE 11d   Differing patterns of urban location. [*Source:* Chauncy D. Harris and Edward L. Ullman, "The Nature of Cities," reprinted from *Annals of the American Academy of Political and Social Science,* CCXLII (November 1945), 7–17, in Harold M. Mayer and Clyde F. Kohn, eds., *Readings in Urban Geography* (Chicago: University of Chicago Press, 1959), pp. 278–279.]

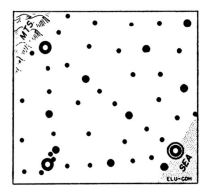

Theoretical composite grouping. Port becomes the metropolis and, although off center, serves as central place for whole area. Manufacturing-mining and junction centers are next largest. Railroad route in upper left has been diverted to pass through manufacturing and mining cluster. Distribution of settlements in upper right follows central-place arrangement.

goods and services to the region's consumers. The theory relating to urban hierarchies is called *central-place theory*.

Although many antecedents can be cited, the first explicit statement of central-place theory was made by the German geographer Walter Christaller in 1933 in a book entitled *Die Zentralen Orte in Süddeutschland* [*The Central Places in Southern Germany*]. The essential features of Christaller's argument may be summarized in six points.

1. The main function of a market town is to provide goods and services for a surrounding market area. Such towns are located centrally within their market areas, and hence they can be called "central places."

2. The greater the number of goods and services provided, the higher is the *order* of the central place.

3. Low-order places offer convenience goods that are purchased frequently within small market areas and hence the *range* of low-order convenience goods (that is, the maximum distance consumers are willing to travel) is small.

4. Higher-order places are fewer in number and are more widely spaced than lower-order places, providing goods with greater ranges. Generally, the greater the range, the greater is the *threshold* (that is, the minimum sales level necessary for the seller to make a profit).

5. A *hierarchy* of central places exists to make as efficient as possible the arrangement of convenience and shopping goods opportunities for consumers who have a basic desire to travel as little as possible to obtain the goods and services they need to maintain their households and persons, and for producers, who must earn at least a minimum "threshold" to survive.

6. Hierarchies have three spatial forms, organized according to
   a. A marketing principle,
   b. A transportation principle, and
   c. An administrative principle.

Christaller proceeded, in the manner of von Thünen and Weber, to a case in which extraneous variables were controlled by simplifying assumptions. Assume, he said, identical consumers distributed at uniform densities over an unbounded plain on which access is equally easy in any direction. Under such circumstances the range of any good has a constant radius. How can centers be located so as to provide for the most efficient marketing of the goods? Given the homogeneity of the plain, Christaller concluded that each good should be supplied by a uniform net of equidistant central places, close enough together so that no part of the plain is left unsupplied.

The resulting distribution is one in which the central places are located at the apexes of a network of equilateral triangles, with each set of six centers forming a hexagon. This organization permits the maximum packing of central places into the plain.

BOX 11.3   Heartlands, Hinterlands, and Polarized Growth

Harvey Perloff, an American planner, together with several associates, has described the process by which *heartland-hinterland organization* emerged within the United States. They point out that North America's oldest cities were mercantile outposts of a hinterland resource area whose exploitation was organized by the developing metropolitan system of Western Europe. The initial impulses for independent urban growth came at the end of the eighteenth century when towns were becoming the outlets for capital accumulated in commercial agriculture and the centers of colonial development of the continental interior. Regional economies developed a certain archetype: a good deep-water port as the nucleus of an agricultural hinterland well adapted for the production of a staple commodity in demand on the world market.

New resources became important from 1840–1850 onward, and new locational forces came into play. Foremost was a growing demand for iron, and later steel, and along with it rapid elaboration of productive technologies. Juxtaposition of coal, iron ore, and markets afforded the impetus for manufacturing growth in the northeastern United States, localized both by factors in the physical environment (minerals) and by locational forces cre-

ated by prior growth along the East Coast (linkages to succeeding stages of production, in turn located closer to markets). The heartland of the North American manufacturing belt therefore developed westward from New York in the area bounded by Lake Superior iron ores, the Pennsylvanian coalfields, and the capital, entrepreneurial experience, and engineering trades of the Northeast. This heartland became not only the heavy industrial center of the country but remained the center of national demand, determining patterns of market accessibility through the 1960s. The heartland had initial advantages of both excellent agricultural resources and a key location in the minerals economy. With development, it grew into the urbanized center of the national market, setting the basic conditions for successive development of newer peripheral regions by reaching out to them as its input requirements expanded, and it thereby fostered specialization of regional roles in the national economy. The heartland experienced cumulative urban-industrial specialization, while each of the hinterlands found its comparative advantage based on narrow and intensive specialization in a few resource subsectors, diversifying only when the extent of specialization enabled the hinterland region to pass through that

threshold scale of market necessary to support profitable local enterprise. Flows of raw materials inward, and of finished products outward, articulated the whole.

Perloff concluded that the American economy could be divided into

> . . . a great heartland nucleation of industry and the national market, the focus of large-scale national-serving industry, the seedbed of new industry responding to the dynamic structure of national final demand and the center of high levels of per capita income . . . .[1]

and, standing in a dependent relationship to the heartland,

> . . . radiating out across the national landscape . . . resource-dominant regional hinterlands specializing in the production of resource and intermediate outputs for which the heartland reaches out to satisfy the input requirements of its great manu-

[1] Harvey S. Perloff, Edgar S. Dunn, Jr., Eric E. Lampard, and Richard F. Muth, *Regions, Resources and Economic Growth* (Lincoln, Nebr.: University of Nebraska Press, 1960), p. 51.

---

alternating current (AC) versus direct current (DC)—competed. Electric street railways and lights were the first major applications, followed by such things as electric elevators, which permitted the development of the modern steel-framed skyscraper.

After 1895 progress in electrification was extremely rapid. Niagara Falls was tapped for hydroelectric power in that year. In 1899, there were 16,891 industrial electric motors in the United States with a capacity of under 500,000 hp. But 10 years later the number of industrial motors had grown twentyfold to 388,854 and installed capacity had risen tenfold to 4,817,000 hp. Meanwhile, the cost of electricity was dropping rapidly as generating plants grew larger and increased in efficiency. By 1910 the major cities of Europe and the United States were electrified. Many

urban homes had electric lights, and some had other electric appliances such as electric sewing machines (Singer), electric carpet sweepers (Hoover), electric washing machines (Hurley), and electric talking machines (Edison). However, the spread of electric appliances into the average home took place mostly in the 1920s.

Another important new technology was the telephone, an outgrowth of research to improve the telegraph. An unsuccessful telephone was developed in Germany in 1860. The successful version was invented virtually simultaneously by Alexander Graham Bell and by Elisha Gray, of the Western Electric Co., living a hundred miles apart in New England. Each inventor accused the other of pirating his work. Both men filed with the U.S. Patent Office on the same day in Febru-

facturing plants . . . in the hinterlands, resource-endowment is a critical determinant of the particular cumulative advantage of the region and hence its growth potential.[2]

Others have argued similarly with respect to both the European and the global case. V. I. Lenin, for example, presented a *colonial model of world spatial organization* in which he argued that since the early nineteenth century the economic geography of the world has been organized by and for the benefit of the industrial countries. The German location economist Andreas Predöhl gave the notion more substance when he described how, during the early nineteenth century, Britain became the focus of a unicentric world economy which, with the growth of new industrial core regions, has now become multicentric, with the rest of the world organized to produce raw materials for and to consume the products of the industrial heartlands. Europe was divided into an industrial heartland and agricultural hinterland by F. Delaisi in 1929 in a book with the graphic title *Les Deux Europes: Europe industrielle et Europe agricole* (*The Two Europes: Industrial Europe and Agricultural Europe*). Subsequent

[2] Ibid.

researchers have identified a regular pattern of distance-decay in agricultural productivity and per capita income from the European heartland, as was noted in Chapter 9, so that agricultural productivity is actually higher in "industrial" Europe than in "agricultural" Europe.

More recently, international heartland-hinterland contrasts have been identified by Raul Prebisch, who divides the world into an industrial center and a primary-producing periphery, and who blames much of the economic difficulties of the periphery on what he considers to be a long-term deterioration of the periphery's terms of trade. John Friedmann, in turn, attempted to elaborate the heartland-hinterland model as a *general theory of polarized growth* applying at all geographic scales.

Friedmann's paradigm was presented as an intellectual framework for the study of the processes—economic, social, and political—that act to create heartland-hinterland contrasts. *Heartlands* are defined by Friedmann as territorially organized subsystems of society possessing a high capacity for generating innovative change. *Hinterlands* are all the regions beyond the heartlands whose growth and change are determined by their dependency relationships to the heartlands. Heartlands share in common a heavy con-

centration of their labor force in manufacturing (secondary) activity and advanced (quaternary) services, representing a shift from development based on natural resources to development based on human resources.

At both national and global scales, heartlands set the developmental path for the hinterlands, stimulating economic growth in the peripheries differentially according to the resource needs of heartland industries and consumers. Complementarities in the availability of factors of production between heartland and hinterland lay the foundations for interaction. Improvements in transportation and the organization of trade increase the transferability of staples from hinterland to heartland. Intervening opportunities impose spatial regularities in the timing of hinterland development and sequence the order in which unsettled areas and areas with a subsistence economy are drawn into the heartland's sphere of influence.

Friedmann saw the diffusion of innovations from the core as controlling system growth and the form of the heartland-hinterland relationship affecting economic activity and settlement patterns, sociocultural traditions and values, and the organization of power not only in the core, but also in the periphery. The periphery is thus dependent on the core in all respects.

ary 1876 and the legal battle for priority went on for years and ended in the Supreme Court. Bell finally prevailed. Telephone service was initiated almost immediately after the invention was demonstrated. The first switchboard went into operation in New Haven in 1878, and by 1880 over a thousand customers had signed on. Acceptance was much faster in the United States than in Europe. By 1900 there were 1,500,000 phones in the United States, or 8 phones for every 100 persons, compared to 4 in Canada, 3 in Sweden, 2 in Switzerland, fewer than 1.5 in Germany and the United Kingdom and only 0.5 in France.

The culminating features of the third wave of industrial growth derived from basic French and German inventions of the late nineteenth century. New chemical industries were created, and a new world

arose out of the internal combustion and the diesel engines, particularly when combined in the twentieth century with the distinctively American idea of mass production and consumption.

From the founding of Baron Justus von Liebig's famous laboratory at Giessen (in 1825), Germany pioneered in organized research supported largely by government grants. In addition, Germany invested in a high-quality public school and university system. What drove Germany to do these things was lack of land and natural resources. One of Liebig's major concerns, for example, was how to make Germany's scarce farmland more productive so that the country could be more nearly self-sufficient in food. The addition of mineral fertilizers to supplement needed elements in the soil began in Germany. A long quest to learn how to "fix" atmospheric nitrogen to replace depleted soil nitrates culminated at last in the famous Haber-Bosch process to synthesize ammonia (1914). The quest itself strengthened the German chemical industry still further. The innovativeness of the German chemical industry enabled Germany to produce synthetic rubber and gasoline from coal in World War II, despite almost total lack of petroleum.

In 1895 the United States still lagged several years behind European automotive technology, perhaps because roads were poor and distances were so great. But a growing, prosperous, and dispersed population needed more flexible means of transportation than railroads could provide. Moreover, petroleum was being discovered in vast quantities in Texas and liquid fuel was rapidly becoming cheaper. In short, conditions were ideal. In 1900 the census reported that 4292 "horseless carriages" were produced in the United States. The biggest manufacturer that year was Stanley Motors, in Maine. Average price of a car was $1000, and vehicle performance was poor. By 1908, the year of the introduction of the Ford Model T and the founding of General Motors, production rose to 65,000 units.

Scores of small manufacturers abounded, but Henry Ford had already begun to change the structure of the industry. His contribution to technology was minor. His innovation was the *assembly line* and *mass production,* enabling the widespread realization of the potentials of the American System of Manufactures. From 1910 to 1920 prices declined by 62 percent in real terms. When the Model T was finally discontinued in 1926 its price was down to $300. Yet annual output rose more than tenfold in 10 years and employment in the industry increased from 37,000 to 206,000 in that period. Automobiles were cheap enough and reliable enough to be practical personal transportation for virtually anyone. Road surfacing and petroleum production began their steep climb in the 1920s. The need for a national system of highways was recognized in 1916 with the first federal aid for road construction.

The impact of the internal combustion engine on American cities needs little review. But some of the most profound changes affecting the city occurred in agriculture. True, the new technology put the farmer in an automobile and thus encouraged the centralization of urban growth at the larger, diversified centers in all the commercial farming regions. But also, by putting farmers on tractors, it multiplied the land area they could work alone, initiated a revolution in family farm size, and hastened the urbanization of much of rural America. The age of mass production and marketing had arrived. This idea has since become deeply embedded both in U.S. national economic policy and national mythology. The United States became—and remains to this day—the exemplar of the *consumer society*.

The United States is also the exemplar of another force that is even more important today, namely organized research and development. (See Box 11.4.) The process began in electricity. The development, production, and marketing of machines to generate and transmit electricity were from the very beginning much more complicated. The most notable innovators, Thomas Edison and Werner von Siemens, worked in large, carefully organized laboratories. And soon the giant multifunctional organizations such as Edison General Electric and the Siemens Company in Germany, which had been created to make and sell their innovations, were relying, as were their competitors, on large research facilities to improve existing products and processes and to develop new ones.

Enterprises in other scientifically based industries quickly adopted the same strategy. In the chemical industries the Germans led the way. Bayer, BASF, AGFA, Hoechst, and other firms built their research laboratories in the 1880s and 1890s. In the United States Du Pont and General Chemical followed suit in the first years of the new century. By the 1920s laboratories in large chemical companies in the United States and Germany were turning out a stream of new synthetic products—dyes, pharmaceuticals, fertilizers, fabrics, plastics, detergents, paints, and films. By the 1920s comparable laboratories were appearing in metals and machinery industries. By 1929 two-thirds of the personnel employed in industrial research in the United States were concentrated in five technologically advanced industries—50 percent were in just two of these, electrical machinery and chemicals. And in these industries, by far the largest numbers were working in large, multifunctional corporations.

However, if science was to be applied to the processes of production and distribution, the laboratory by itself was not enough. Its activities had to be carefully integrated with those of the rest of the organization. Unless the work of the laboratory was coordinated with the technicians responsible for the final design of product and processes, with the factory managers, and with the engineers in marketing, efficient, low-cost production and distribution were rarely realized. Moreover, as Harold Passer has pointed out in describing the fast-moving technology in electric traction (streetcars and subways) of the 1890s, the constant interaction among marketing, production, design, and research departments became in itself a powerful force for continuing technological innovation.

Research normally accounts for only 10 percent

BOX 11.4   R & D and Economic Growth

In an article entitled "Why Growth Rates Differ" in Giovanni Dosi et al., *Technical Change and Economic Theory* (London: Pinter Publishers, 1988, pp. 432–438), Jan Fagerberg provides startling graphic evidence of the relationship between per capita GDP, R & D expenditures as a percentage of GDP, and the magnitude of patent ap-plications. His data, which deal with 27 North American, European, Central and South American, and East and South Asia industrial or industrializing nations for the period 1973–1983 are presented in the two graphs. The R & D percentage goes up at an increasing rate with higher levels of economic de-velopment (the GDP data are in thou-sands of dollars). The relationship is even sharper for levels of patenting ac-tivity, the results of R & D, indicating that increases in the magnitude of a nation's research effort stimulate even greater increases in the volume of use-ful (that is, patentable) inventions.

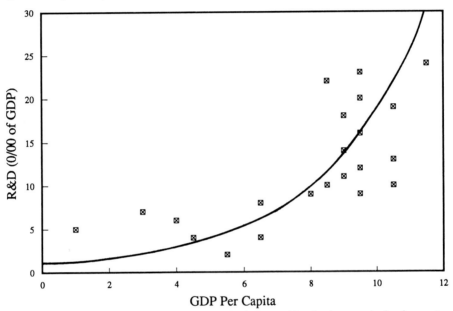

FIGURE 11e   Relationship between R&D expenditures and levels of economic development.

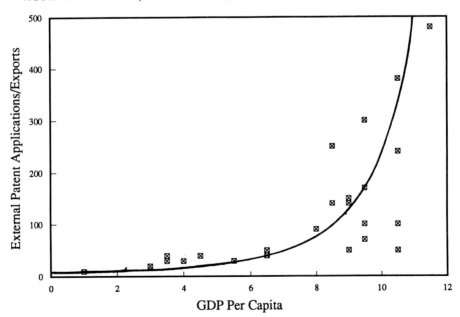

FIGURE 11f   Relationship between patenting activity and economic development.

of the cost of putting a new product in the stream of commerce. What takes the time and money, and what makes the critical difference in whether a product is widely used, is the work involved in building prototype models and pilot plants, in fashioning distribution channels, in locating and contracting with suppliers who can deliver on schedule to specification, and, finally, in making the necessary financial arrangements for fixed and working capital.

The Germans and Americans, leaders in the application of science to industry, adopted quite different arrangements to achieve this essential internal coordination. Because the Germans normally concentrated their production in massive plants along the Rhine, in the Ruhr, or near Berlin, and operated their enterprises in a highly centralized fashion, they turned to committees of middle managers responsible for each function involved in the production and distribution of a major product line—committees that had their own permanent staffs, secretarial forces, and facilities. In the United States, where plants were smaller and more scattered and where, domestically at least, more sales branches existed, a new office—the development department—became responsible for all the activities involved in bringing a new product on stream. At Du Pont this change came in 1912, when the laboratories were instructed to concentrate on research and the development department became responsible for coordinating the work of the laboratories with the other functional activities.

In these same industries technological innovation called for the devising of external linkages as well as internal arrangements. One reason for Werner von Siemens's industrial success was that, from the start, he and his managers maintained close personal ties with the leading physicists and other scientists in Germany. In the early 1880s, Siemens endowed chairs in physics at leading universities and then became the driving force in the founding of the government-supported National Physical Technical Institute—an institute that became a model for similar ones in physics and later in chemistry in Germany and other countries. In Germany by World War I comparable close ties between the enterprise and the academic world had been created in the chemical and metallurgical industries.

In the United States, Thomas Edison, a self-taught man, felt little need to reach out to the universities, but those companies founded to produce his inventions did. General Electric had ties with the Massachusetts Institute of Technology (M.I.T.) even before a member of its faculty, William A. Whitney, went to Schenectady in 1901 to set up its laboratory for basic research. Other faculty members and graduates

soon followed Whitney. In working out their research problems, Whitney and his associates checked closely with their former colleagues. They and their company also continued to look to the institute as a vital source for young managers. The story was much the same at Du Pont, for the three cousins who created the modern company all attended M.I.T. The later relationship between Standard Oil of New Jersey and other oil companies and M.I.T.'s "Doc" Lewis, a founder of modern petroleum engineering, was of a similar nature. Other American corporations in technologically advanced industries quickly developed similar ties to universities, technical institutes, and later to business schools.

What happened in Germany and the United States must not, however, be taken for granted. These institutional innovations were not inevitable responses to technological needs, for they rarely occurred in Britain or France. There the entrepreneurs who began to mass-produce for volume markets after the coming of the railroad and the steamship rarely created managerial hierarchies on the scale of those in Germany and the United States. Larger enterprises continued to be family-owned. These families preferred, where possible, to continue to buy from and sell through agents. They employed plant superintendents and one or two sales and purchasing supervisors, but far fewer middle and top managers. There were valid economic, geographic, and historical reasons for this choice. The principal reason, however, appears to be simply that the families wanted to remain in full control of their enterprises. They did not want to turn over so much of their business to outsiders.

This preference did not seriously affect the performance of firms producing low-technology products such as food, soaps, paint, and other consumer chemicals, or even textiles and steel. It was, however, disastrous in the new technologically advanced industries. The families rarely set up research laboratories. When they did, they did not create committees or departments to coordinate research with the other functional activities. British and French innovators, both within and without the industrial firm, often came up with impressive inventions; but these were rarely brought into volume production and distribution by British and French firms. Nor did the British and French enterprises build ties to the universities. Because they did not form linkages similar to that of Siemens with the academic community in Germany, or General Electric with M.I.T., they rarely called on the universities or institutes to assist in solving technical problems. Nor did they use them as a source for trained managers.

Because of their failure to create institutional arrangements comparable to those of the Americans and

Germans, the British and the French missed out on central developments of the third wave of the Industrial Revolution. Once behind, they only continued to get further behind. Of the four largest electrical manufacturers in Britain in the years before World War I, only one was British-owned, and that one, originally in the retail trade, did not set up a laboratory until 1919. The others were subsidiaries of General Electric, Westinghouse, and Siemens. The London subway system was, for example, equipped by General Electric. The British continued to rely on German dyes and synthetic drugs until the 1930s. They obtained the new plastics, paints, detergents, and other synthetics from the United States. The story appears to be much the same in France. It was not until after World War II that British and French enterprises began to fashion institutional arrangements similar to the ones the Germans and Americans had devised before World War I. Only then did they and their national economies begin to benefit fully from that systematic application of science to industry that was the centerpiece of the third wave of industrial revolution.

The Fourth Wave of the Industrial Revolution (1920s to 1980s)

Following World War I, but interrupted by the Great Depression and the disruptions of World War II, came another spurt of growth that finally ended in the stagflation crisis of the early 1980s. The greatest impulse came after World War II with the rapid growth of a group of new industries based on new technologies that had emerged during the previous 20 years. The rapid development of these technologies was facilitated by the establishment of production line technologies, and forced by the political conditions prevailing in Europe in the 1930s and especially by the 1939–1945 war. The industries that emerged on a significant scale during the 1940s and 1950s—electronics, synthetic materials, solid-state devices, petrochemicals, agrichemicals, composite materials, and pharmaceuticals—created rapidly growing new markets. At the same time there was a rapid growth in demand for capital equipment, often of a new kind. The wealth generated by the emergence of these new technology-based industries caused an associated boom in demand for consumer durables, leading to the rapid growth of the automobile and consumer goods industries, of superhighways, shopping centers, and suburbs.

What was at the heart of the fourth wave? The spread and continued improvement of institutional arrangements and the exploitation of vast new sources of fossil fuels were probably the very factors making possible the unprecedented economic growth following World War II. Among these, two fundamental institutional developments that influenced the continuing application of science to industrial activities were critical. One was the rapid spread of the multidivisional form of corporate organization. This form, by replacing the centrally controlled functional departments with autonomous, self-contained product or regional divisions, permitted the enterprise to move rapidly into new products and new markets. Facilitating product diversification, the M Form, as economists have come to call it, greatly enhanced the potential value of the industrial research laboratory and further institutionalized the continuing flow of new products into the economy. The M Form, invented by Du Pont shortly after World War I, began to be widely adopted in the United States only in the 1950s, and in Europe only in the 1960s. By the 1970s this organizational form, or variations of it, had become the standard operating structure for the large industrial enterprise in all advanced market economies. With some justification, Oliver Williamson has called the M Form the most important invention of American capitalism in the twentieth century.

The other basic institutional development was the creation of new formal and informal ties between corporations and universities and the government. In the United States these arrangements were the product of World War II. The prototype was, of course, the Manhattan Project, where the technology of the atom bomb was developed in the universities, and the facilities for production as well as the product itself were built and operated by industrial contractors such as Du Pont, with the federal government funding and coordinating the project as a whole. As the war moved on, the armed services set up a multitude of relationships with corporations and universities to develop a wide range of military products.

The continuing military demands of the cold war and the new postwar industrial needs (many of them generated by the application of war-inspired technologies) stimulated other forms of institutional linkages among business, government, and the universities. In rapidly moving technologies, faculty members and Ph.D.'s from places like M.I.T. and Stanford built their own enterprises to meet highly segmented specialized markets, a phenomenon exemplified in Massachusetts by Route 128 and in California by Silicon Valley. However, once these technologically advanced products were mass produced for national and international markets, the large enterprise took over, as IBM demonstrated in computers and Xerox in copying machines.

These institutional developments provided one pillar for postwar economic growth: The coming of cheap oil was another essential pillar. Because oil and gas were less costly to extract, transport, and deliver than coal, and because they were more concentrated and flexible fuels, they had already begun to replace coal in the interwar years. Nevertheless, it was only after World War II that oil became the instrument that caused advanced industrial economies to become totally and possibly fatally addicted to fossil fuels. In 1945, coal still accounted for 53.4 percent of the energy consumed, and the United States was still an exporter of crude oil. Then the oil fields of the Persian Gulf came into full production. As the supply poured out, the price dropped. Suddenly everyone was converting to oil. The utilities did so massively. By the 1960s the diesel locomotive had made the steam locomotive an historic relic. Chemical companies that had relied almost entirely on coal for the feed stocks in the rapidly growing production of synthetics turned to oil, and oil companies integrated forward into chemicals. By the mid-1950s coal had become a sick industry. By 1960 it produced only 28 percent of the nation's energy. The figures for the transformation in Europe are even more striking.

The results of the unprecedented abundance of cheap oil and gas and the spread and perfection of the new institutional arrangements were indeed impressive. In the United States the annual rate of growth of the GNP per capita reached just over 20 percent a decade, a very high figure in historical context. In other industrial countries the rates were higher: 63 percent in Germany and 128 percent in Japan. The German and Japanese miracles also were based on improved institutional arrangements and cheap oil. The amount of energy required to maintain the rates was staggering when compared to earlier periods when the total GNP was, as it was early in this century, one-twentieth to one twenty-fifth the size of that of the postwar years. Moreover, such unprecedented growth meant that each year billions of dollars went into investment in industrial plants, transportation facilities, housing, and household equipment that was geared wholly to the ever-continuing supplies of cheap oil. Cheap energy, like water, was taken for granted.

The pattern of evolution in the years after World War II has been summarized schematically by Ray Rothwell, using British evidence, in the manner depicted in Table 11.1. The early situation (which appears to have been characteristic of the early phases of each wave of industrial revolution) was of rather small firms, or units, operating in fast-growing, new, and relatively undefined markets and concentrating on product-related technological innovations; this *dynamic growth phase* lasted from 1945 to about 1964, during which many new manufacturing jobs were created.

TABLE 11.1

A model of post–World War II industrial evolution

1945 to approximately 1964—dynamic growth phase

Emergence of new industries based largely on new technological opportunities.
Production initially in small units.
Emphasis on product change and the introduction of many new products.
Rapidly growing new markets.
Some market regeneration in traditional areas; for example, textiles.
New employment generation (output growth greater than productivity growth).
Competitive emphasis is mainly on product availability and nonprice factors.

Mid- to late 1960s—consolidation phase

Increasing industrial concentration and growing static scale economies.
High dynamic economies.
Introduction of organizational innovations.
Increasing emphasis on process improvement.
Some major product changes, but based mainly on existing technology.
Rapid productivity growth.
Markets still growing rapidly.
Output growth and productivity growth in rough balance (manufacturing employment more or less stable).
Competitive emphasis still mainly on nonprice factors.

Late 1960s to mid-1970s—maturity and market saturation phase

Industry highly concentrated.
Very large production units, often vertically integrated.
Some product change, but emphasis predominantly on production process rationalization.
Increasing organizational rationalization, including foreign direct investment in areas of low labor cost.
Growing automaticity.
Stagnating and replacement markets.
Productivity growth greater than output (demand) growth.
Rapidly growing manufacturing unemployment.
Where products are little differentiated, the importance of price in competition is high.

Source: Roy Rothwell, "The Role of Technology in Industrial Change: Implications for Regional Policy," *Regional Studies*, Vol. 16 (1981), 361–369.

A *consolidation phase* followed from the mid- to late 1960s in which markets became better defined, organizational rationalization took place, mergers occurred, and there was increased emphasis on process improvement. While productivity increased rapidly during this phase, so did demand. A rough balance between the two meant that manufacturing employment remained unchanged.

Beginning in the late 1960s, a *phase of industrial maturity and market stagnation* was reached. By this time the new industries were highly concentrated, production was centered on very large units, and development was aimed primarily at process rationalization and productivity increase. Price became a much more significant factor in competition. Productivity growth outstripped demand growth in largely saturated markets, and many jobs were lost. At the same time firms increasingly relocated production of mature product lines to areas of low labor cost.

Subsequently, very high rates of inflation, accompanied by high interest rates, further effectively depressed the real level of demand. A *recessionary trend* thus became established. This cycle from dynamic growth to "stagflation" and recession took about 50 years and involved roughly the same time span and sequence as in the three preceding waves of industrial revolution.

THE EXPLANATION OF LONG WAVES

Kondratiev Long Waves

Speculation about the existence of approximately 50-year cycles in modern market economies dates at least from Dutch economist J. van Gelderen's writings in 1913, but the idea is now generally attributed to the Russian economist Nikolai D. Kondratiev, who wrote about the phenomenon in the 1920s. Kondratiev put forward the hypothesis in 1925 that the industrial nations of the world, when looked at collectively, have experienced successive cycles of growth and decline since the beginning of the Industrial Revolution with a regular periodicity of between 50 and 55 years. To

traditional Marxists who believe only in short-term business cycles and in the long-term growth and decline of capitalism, Kondratiev soon became something of a heretic, and he died in the Soviet Union's "Gulag Archipelago"—committed there for daring to suggest that capitalist economies could recover after disastrous depressions, rather than being doomed to collapse as Marx had argued. However, his ideas were taken up in the 1930s by several economic historians in the West, most notably Joseph Schumpeter, who pointed out that each Kondratiev wave coincided with a spurt in technological innovation and by Simon Kuznets, who undertook painstaking statistical research on the long-wave phenomenon.

The first three Kondratiev long waves were described by Kuznets as involving successive periods of recovery, prosperity, recession, and depression, as depicted in Table 11.2. The new technologies of each epoch (for example, in transportation, the first centering on water transportation and use of wind and captive water power, the second on coal use for steam power in water and railroad transportation and in factory industry and later for the generation of electricity, and the third on petroleum use in the internal combustion or diesel engine for road and air transportation) each saw their peak development immediately preceding a major economic collapse. In the wake of this collapse, a new set of replacement technologies emerged and prevailed, as depicted in Figure 11.1c and d. All shaded columns depict the periods of depression.

TABLE 11.2

Long waves of economic growth

Phase of Growth[a]	Kondratiev Long Wave:				
	I	II	III	IV	V
Recovery	1770–1786	1828–1842	1886–1897	1940–1954	?
Prosperity	1787–1800	1843–1857	1898–1911	1955–1969	
Recession	1801–1813	1858–1869	1912–1924	1970–1980	
Depression (and new innovation)	1814–1827	1870–1885	1925–1939	1981–	

[a] Macroeconomic characteristics of long-wave phases are as follows:

Characteristic	Recovery	Prosperity	Recession	Depression
Gross national product	Increasing growth rates	Strong growth	Decreasing growth rates	Little or no growth
Investment demand	Increase in replacement investment	Strong expansion of capital stock	Scale-increasing investment	Excess capacity rationalization
Consumer demand	Purchasing power seeks new outlets	Expansion of demand in all sectors	Continued growth of new sectors	For a while continued growth at the expense of savings

Source: Adapted from Simon Kuznets, *Economic Change*, New York: W. W. Norton & Co., 1953.

Mensch's Metamorphosis Model of Economic Evolution

Kondratiev and Kuznets simply described the phenomenon we have just discussed. It was an Austrian economist, Joseph Schumpeter, who in the 1930s emphasized the key role of technology in long-wave formation, introducing the idea of *technological revolutions* as the central driving force. More recently another German economist, Gerhard Mensch, has built on Schumpeter's notions and advanced a *metamorphosis model of industrial evolution* as the essential explanation for Kondratiev's long waves.

Mensch distinguished *scientific discovery and invention*—both of which, as S. C. Gilfillan pointed out in the 1930s, appear as a more or less steady stream in response to well-articulated social needs—from *innovation,* the practical application of the invention or idea. Innovations, Mensch discovered, tended to come in clusters or surges. Charting the dates of inventions and the basic innovations that followed them in the early nineteenth century (examples: rolled wire invented 1773, innovation 1835; steam locomotive invented 1769, innovation 1824), he discovered a clustering in the period 1814–1828. Likewise, there was a clustering of innovations in electricity and chemistry in the period 1870–1886, and of early twentieth-century innovations in the years 1925–1939. Surprisingly, the periods of innovation (pre-1787, 1814–1828, 1870–1886, 1925–1939) coincided with periods of depression that accompanied world economic crises.

Two questions therefore emerged: Why do innovations cluster? Why have the clusters coincided with depressions?

Mensch's important contribution has been to cast light on these questions, tying together in an explanatory framework the empirical observations of Kondratiev and Kuznets and the technological innovation hypothesis of Schumpeter. His key concept is that of a *technological stalemate,* out of which an economy is ultimately eased by clusters of innovations that are implemented within a society, out of a reservoir of investment opportunities formed by a continuing stream of scientific discoveries and practical inventions, producing a *structural metamorphosis* as old activities are cast off and replaced by revolutionary new ones. See Figure 11.1.

Mensch's metamorphosis model postulates the following causal sequence:

1. A cluster of *basic innovations* introducing new branches of industry, and *radical improvement innovations,* which rejuvenate existing branches, occurs in response to a technological stalemate. Venture

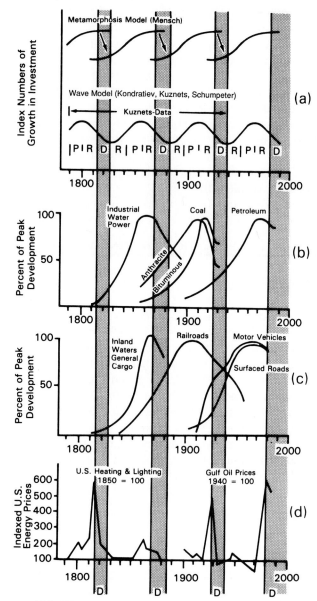

FIGURE 11.1 Long waves: Theories compared with major epochs of energy use, transportation development, and energy price inflation. [*Source:* Adapted from John R. Borchert, "American Metropolitan Evolution," *Geographical Review,* 57 (July 1967), 301–332; and Gerhard Mensch, *Stalemate in Technology* (Cambridge, Mass.: Ballinger Publishing Co., 1978).]

capital is attracted to the new lines of business. New demands are awakened.

2. Parallel S-shaped *product growth cycles,* perhaps substituting for older goods or services, characterize the new branches of industry. Initial entry is followed by rapid upswing, and then by accelerated growth until market saturation is reached.

3. During the new product upswing, invest-

ment, employment, and incomes increase rapidly, well ahead of prices and inflation, and lifestyles may well be revolutionized.

4. The revolutionary pioneering innovations are then followed by *routine improvement innovations* that rationalize production and increase capital intensity. But they find themselves subject to diminishing returns on the demand side and diminishing marginal utility on the supply side. The growth curve grades over from acceleration to deceleration. This is a natural phase of the *product life cycle of manufactured goods,* as discussed by Raymond Vernon in 1966. As Vernon saw it, new products will tend to be introduced and produced initially in the biggest, richest market, but as the market grows, the basis for competition gradually shifts from *performance* to *price*. This evolution requires standardization of the product and (to exploit economies of scale) of the production technology. When the latter is sufficiently standardized, the optimum location for mass production facilities moves away from the rich market to areas with lower labor or material costs. (We should note that the United States has provided the *initial* large market for *most* major new consumer products since the late nineteenth century. Examples include the telephone, typewriter, camera, sewing machine, automobile, washing machine, vacuum cleaner, airplane, radio, record player, tape recorder, TV, videotape, and so on.) The predicted emigration of production (and jobs) is clearly visible in the case of textiles and shoes, cameras, watches, consumer electronics, steel, autos, bulk chemicals, and many other standard products. As the jobs are transplanted, so is the purchasing power of the workers. Thus, unless the emigration of older industries is more than compensated for by growth in newer, more innovative industries, economic stagnation is an inevitable consequence. It cannot be reversed by increased capital formation per se because the capital itself—being mobile—will also tend to move where returns are higher. The stagnation can only be reversed by the creation of new, more dynamic industries. In this view, the fundamental problem is a technological one.

5. But *corporate growth tends to overestimate domestic markets and produces excess supply and heated competition*. Almost inevitably, an industrial economy tends to overinvest in any new technology—capital goods industries in particular. For example, the latest wave of overinvestment began in the 1960s and now is obvious in worldwide overcapacity in steel, autos, diesel engines, chemicals, shipbuilding, machine tools, and even semiconductors. The auto industry is the best recent illustration of how overinvestment occurs. In the postwar period, autos not only became one of the nation's biggest industries but also helped spur the growth of highways and spawned suburbs, which created new markets for homes, shopping centers, schools, and hospitals. Automobiles also influenced the location of plants and distribution centers. Today, however, with the stock of cars near a saturation level and with consumers keeping them longer, autos have become primarily a replacement market in which sales will grow slowly if at all. And the influence of cars and trucks on population shifts and business location will be minimal. Meanwhile, the nation has spent the past 25 years building up an enormous investment in industries—steel, machine tools, cement, glass, forest products—needed to produce cars and the many other products they helped create. But as the auto industry wanes, and its economic influence shrinks, much of this investment will be unusable. The long decline in capacity utilization reached its peak in the late 1960s and dropped to 43 percent in steel and 63 percent in nonelectrical machinery by the end of 1982.

6. There are two responses to excess supply:

a. Attempts to reduce competition by market segmentation and industrial mergers.

b. Attempts to segment domestic and foreign markets, "dumping" excess output.

Overinvestment breeds *pseudo-innovation* that benefits neither buyer nor seller, reflecting rather the attempt on the part of existing industries to protect their market shares by *product differentiation* in which the "image" or "packaging" of the product is changed, but no longer any of its basic qualities. The pace of change means that individual products have limited life cycles. This results in

a. Rapidly vanishing returns for a given product;

b. Intense competition to substitute new products;

c. Ultimately, after repeated attempts to substitute new products by packaging "pseudo-innovations," the opportunities for further technological improvement are exhausted—the usable fund of ideas runs out.

The economy enters a period in which output stagnates and industry leaders merge with other firms to create *oligopolies* that try to maintain their revenue growth by increasing prices. Definite *limits to growth* are encountered, markets are often flooded, key resources may be scarce, there is a slowdown in income and employment growth, and spreading stagnation. Rates of return decline, and capital is therefore not reinvested in existing lines of business: A huge money and capital market builds up instead. Funds move into currency speculation and paper investment: *"Stagflation"* results—a standstill in industrial investment, with money flowing into capital markets where returns are greater than in existing industries, but ceasing with rapid price inflation.

Mensch notes that satiated markets and stagflation are accompanied by a *"dinosaur effect"* because the largest companies are the least innovative. "Pseudo-innovations" are a device by which producers seek dominance over a market segment. Consumers' choices become more limited as production concentrates in a few oligopolies. Producers can maximize profits and keep prices increasing by eliminating price competition. The attempt is to secure the bastions of established producers, because diminishing returns in existing branches of industry first lead to capital being used to protect markets via pseudo-innovations/market segmentation and acquisitions to limit competition. Mancur Olsen (see Box 11.5) sees such protectionism as the principal reason for the decline of nations.

7. The end result is a *technology stalemate* in which growth is replaced by stagnation, and in which large-scale organizations seek to maintain the appearance of growth by controlling output and raising prices, inducing stagflation—the apparently antithetical conditions of simultaneous recession and inflation—and then by the collapse of a depression. It is during this period that one sees increasing protectionism, yet it is overconcentration in leading industries that sets the price spiral into gear. Large-scale organizations that grow in the period of pseudo-innovation require and promote conservative patterns of investment: Risk-taking in new ventures is minimized.

BOX 11.5   Mancur Olsen on The Rise and Decline of Nations

Mancur Olsen argues that in societies that permit free trade and free organization, coalitions form around marketable goods and services. Groups of producers, like those who grow wheat or own oil, organize to protect their assets and, if possible, boost profits by raising prices. Physicians and lawyers do much the same in joining professional societies. Labor unions organize workers to bargain for wages.

In the early stages of this coalition-building process, there are relatively few interest groups, and their memberships are small compared to the society in which they operate. As they develop, they try to impose a variety of specialized rules on the economy that supports them. By law or collusive contract, they make penalties for those who would market the same goods or services outside the group. They also offer selective advantages to those who join and cooperate. Because these groups are small (Olsen says they typically include no more than 1 percent of the people in their state), they have no incentive to boost members' welfare by boosting the state's welfare. Instead, they concentrate on promoting their own narrow interests, even at the cost of retarding the general economy.

A modest effort at self-aggrandizement may bring great rewards.

In time, tariffs, price supports, monopoly prices, wage guarantees, and business codes grow more numerous. All are intended to channel commerce into areas that benefit the special groups that fought for them. The combined effect is to create obstacles to trade and to prevent innovation. The economy suffers. In the past, nations suffering from this affliction have enjoyed renewed growth after a cataclysm has intervened to wipe out existing trade barriers, or when new territory has been opened for development. Sometimes the power of a domestic group is undercut by low-cost imports, if the imports are not blocked. Rarely has any nation abolished special-interest codes voluntarily.

Inflation may be a common symptom of nations in a sclerotic condition, because it offers a brief measure of relief from economic stagnation. Special-interest groups, being run by committee rule, generally maneuver slowly. For this reason, they cannot always adjust their demands upward as rapidly as the nominal value of goods and services increases. This is particularly true if inflation appears suddenly,

without warning. Thus, inflation may be tolerated because it temporarily devalues the cost of products within the control of special interests. In time, this form of relief fails because the special interests soon catch up and raise their demands in pace with inflation.

In the contrary case, during periods of sudden price decline, the advantage held by interest groups is intensified. Those who operate outside the protection of a group may be forced to lower prices or wages. But the interest groups, again moving slowly, haggle over proposals while the storm rages around them. They may not reduce their demands until a recession has already damaged the economy. After a period of negotiation, they may begin to adjust, but by then investment in new projects will have been cut short, worsening the prospects for recovery. Thus, there is a real risk that the inflexibility of special-interest groups can lead in bad times to a vicious downward spiral.

Source: Mancur Olsen, The Rise and Decline of Nations: Economic Growth, Stagflation, and Social Rigidities (New Haven, Conn.: Yale University Press, 1982).

8.   But as returns in older established industries are eliminated during stagflation and vanish in the ensuing depression, new *venture capital* becomes available, seeking high-growth investment opportunities. The appearance of venture capital at this time results in a rush of attempts to convert many of the speculative inventions that had appeared since the preceding period of basic innovation into useful techniques or products, that is, into a rush of basic innovations that precipitates another long-term growth upswing. During the upswing, dormant basic innovations will attract capital and, via entrepreneurship, begin to diffuse into economic use. Resulting new industries attract capital and labor from stagnant sectors, circumvent older resource scarcities, stimulate demand for new kinds of goods and services, and generally introduce the reinvigorating effects of a *structural transformation* of the economy.

This key idea that basic innovations produce structural changes in the economic system and drive the business cycle has, as we noted early, been most closely associated with the German economist Joseph Schumpeter, who wrote that the fundamental impulse that sets and keeps the capitalist engine in motion comes from the new consumers' goods, the new methods of production and transportation, the new markets, and the new forms of industrial organization that the capitalist enterprise creates.

Mensch's contribution was to identify the precise circumstances when these "fundamental impulses" occur. He noted that "they do not simply fall from heaven." What determines them is the degree of stagnation of old technologies and the attractiveness of new alternatives. Stagnation reduces the usefulness and profitability of labor and capital in overgrown traditional business fields and induces the implementation of cost-saving and product-adding innovations. Labor is displaced and older privileged groups lose self-confidence. Sociopolitical conflict increases, and a variety of groups look to revolutionary change in the period of temporary instability—not only innovators looking to profit from new ventures, but also radical political reformers, because conditions of instability offer the opportunity for talented individuals to circumvent established social and power structures. Meanwhile, existing governments are pressured to create jobs through new large-scale technologies with military or civilian applications or both. Conservatism and radicalism, arms races and New Deals, are products of their times, as are attitudes and lifestyles. The cycle appears to be approximately 50 years, or two generations; grandchildren thus think and act in ways more similar to their grandparents than to their parents!

THE FIFTH WAVE: EMERGENCE OF THE THOUGHTWARE ECONOMY

Consider the characteristics of a technological stalemate: Old industries collapse and unemployment soars; stagnation is accompanied by rapid inflation; and then new venture capital becomes available, seeking high-growth investment opportunities in innovations that produce new industries, stimulating demand for new kinds of goods and services, and generally introducing the reinvigorating forces that promote a structural transformation of the economy. Are we on the verge of such a structural transformation? Certainly, the last decade has seen stagflation and recession and, throughout the industrial world, collapse of overbuilt basic industries such as steel and coal, shipbuilding, and the manufacturing of automobiles. But there also have been accompanying signs of the new: rapid growth of venture capital availability, and the emergence of new growth sectors. This section will deal with these indicators of an incipient fifth Kondratiev wave.

Growth of Venture Capital

Availability of venture capital has soared since the late 1970s in the United States. Once restricted to a few families with immense personal wealth, the venture capital industry now has a wide variety of participants, both private and corporate. The funds that have become available have been of a variety of kinds, with each kind having its accompanying funding specialists:

1.   EARLY-STAGE FINANCING
    a. *Seed financing*—a relatively small amount of capital provided to an investor or entrepreneur to prove a concept. It may involve product development but rarely involves initial marketing. This kind of investment is sometimes referred to as "adventure financing."
    b. *Start-up financing*—used for product development and initial marketing. Firms may be in the organizational process or in existence a short time (usually less than one year).
    c. *First-stage financing*—for companies that have expended their initial capital and require funds to initiate commercial production and sales.
2.   EXPANSION FINANCING
    a. *Second-stage financing*—provides working capital for the initial expansion of a firm which is producing and shipping and

has growing accounts receivable and inventories. The firm may not yet be showing a profit.

b. *Third-stage financing*—allows for the major expansion of a growing firm which is breaking even or profitable. These funds are utilized for plant expansion, marketing, working capital or further product development.

c. *Fourth-stage (bridge) financing*—for a company expecting to go public or be bought out within six months to one year.

3. ACQUISITION/MANAGEMENT BUY-OUT FINANCING

a. *Management-leveraged buy-out*—funds to permit operating management to acquire a firm or division for the purpose of entrepreneurial expansion.

b. *Acquisition.*

That this venture capital contributes to new economic development is now becoming abundantly clear. Recent research can be summarized as follows:

1. Venture capital stimulates the growth of small, innovative firms

a. By providing long-term equity financing

(1) Small, young, innovative firms need equity capital because their product development costs are relatively high and their capacity for asset-based debt is limited. Young firms may not be able to generate cash flow sufficient to support the amount of debt required.

(2) Because their asset base is small and the risk involved with developing a new product is relatively high, traditional debt sources, such as banks, have demonstrated a reluctance to provide the amounts of debt that are needed.

(3) Long-term financing allows the firm a margin for error if the product or processes takes longer to develop than anticipated. A reliable base of funds lowers the risk that initial setbacks will prove fatal to the firm, encouraging the entrepreneur to continue.

b. By providing managerial assistance

(1) Managerial deficiency is thought to be a leading cause of business failure.

2. Small, innovative firms are the leading sources of growth and change in an economy, because

a. They are responsible for a disproportionate number of the new jobs created: 87 percent of all new private sector jobs created between 1969 and 1976 came from firms with fewer than 500 employees; 77 percent from firms with fewer than 50 employees; and 66 percent from firms with 20 or less employees (Table 11.3).

Nature of the Structural Transformation

The question then is: What kinds of industry will these new, innovative firms introduce? As the old manufacturing economies have collapsed, the principal contributor to employment growth has been the advanced services sector (Figure 11.2). Simultaneously, manufacturing is being transformed by the adoption of new technologies, revealed dramatically by the growth of high-technology products with substantial research and development inputs.

The services that have been growing have not been services in the traditional sense at all, but central administrative activities, their supportive producer services, and health and education (Table 11.4). Their defining feature is that they are *creating and using knowledge-products* in exactly the way that manufacturing industry transformed raw materials into physical products. They are the driving forces of the modern "thoughtware" economy.

Table 11.5 gives some indication of how one observer expects the advanced service industries to expand by the year 2000 in seven major industrial countries. Many observers believe these projections are conservative.

The important feature of the growth of advanced services is that these activities are the sources of most of the productivity increase in U.S. manufacturing: technological innovation, better resource allocation, and better education (Figure 11.3).

They provide the thoughtware that permits business to be conducted more efficiently and effectively,

TABLE 11.3

Net new jobs created by size of firm, 1969–1976

Number of Employees in Each Firm	Total New Jobs	
	Number	As Percentage of Total
20 or fewer	4,459,815	66.0
21–50	759,509	11.2
51–100	288,997	4.3
101–500	353,201	5.2
501 or more	897,381	13.3
Total	6,758,903	100.0

Source: D. L. Birch, "Who Produces the Jobs?" *The Public Interest,* Fall 1981.

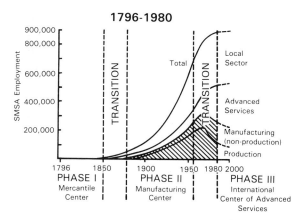

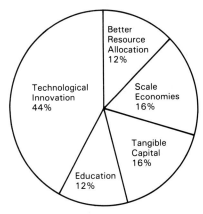

FIGURE 11.2 The evolution of the Cleveland economy. [*Source:* Richard V. Knight, *The Cleveland Economy in Transition* (Cleveland: Regional Development Program, Cleveland State University, 1977), p. 37.]

FIGURE 11.3 Contributions to U.S. productivity increases. [*Source:* The Brookings Institution.]

TABLE 11.4

Advanced services sector

Industrial Corporations[a]	Specialized Technical and Business Service Firms	Public and Not-for-profit Organizations
Corporate headquarters	Law	Federal agencies
Research and development	Engineering	State agencies
Regional offices	Accounting	Universities
Divisional offices	Finance	Musical arts
Computer center	Advertising	Hospitals and clinics
Training centers	Public Relations	Cancer center
	Insurance	Professional associations
	Seminars and conventions	Federal Reserve Bank
	Communications	Museums
	Airlines	Consultants
	Consultants	
	Business information	

[a] Includes publishing and transportation.

TABLE 11.5

Percentage labor force distribution by industry sectors for seven industrialized countries, 1970, and projected to year 2000

Industry Sectors	United States and Canada		England and West Germany		France and Italy		Japan	
	1970	2000	1970	2000	1970	2000	1970	2000
Extractive	7	5	5	4	19	10	20	5
Transformative	32	28	47	40	41	35	34	40
Traditional services	32	26	25	21	22	20	31	25
Advanced services	29	42	23	35	19	35	15	30

Source: Adapted from Singelmann, Joachim. *From Agriculture to Services: The Transformation of Industrial Employment.* Beverly Hills: Sage Publications Inc., 1978, Table 5.3.

bringing resource use closer to the theoretical maximum. They include research and development activities in the broadest sense of the term; management and management support; analysis; activities that seek to identify and reduce risk, to assure health and safety, to simplify products, to assure performance, and to increase both quality of product and of life.

The fruits of industry are in "high-tech": microprocessors, robots, genetic engineering, and space, together with better information processing and management built around computers and cheap electronic communicators.

Particularly important is the growth of flexible manufacturing systems (FMS), which complete a process of factory automation that began back in the 1950s. First came numerically controlled machines according to coded instructions on paper or Mylar tape. Then came computer-aided design and computer-aided manufacturing, or CAD/CAM, which replaced the drafting board with the CRT screen and the numerically controlled tape with the computer (Table 11.6 summarizes the principal technologies).

The new systems integrate all these elements. They consist of computer-controlled machining centers that sculpt complicated metal parts at high speed and with great reliability, robots that handle the parts, and remotely guided carts that deliver materials. The components are linked by electronic controls that dictate what will happen at each stage of the manufacturing sequence, even automatically replacing worn-out or broken drill bits and other implements.

Measured against some of the machinery they replace, flexible manufacturing systems seem expensive. But the direct comparison is a poor guide to the economies that flexible automation offers. Flexible automation's greatest potential for radical change lies in its capacity to manufacture goods cheaply in small volumes. Ever since the era of Henry Ford, the unchallenged low-cost production system has been Detroit-style "hard automation" that stamps out look-alike parts in huge volume. There is little flexibility in hard automation's transfer lines, which get their name from the transfer of the product being worked on via a conveyor from one metalworking machine to another. But such mass production is shrinking in importance compared with "batch production" in lots of anywhere from several thousand to just one. Flexible manufacturing brings a degree of diversity to manufacturing never before available. Different products can be made on the same line at will.

The strategic implications for the manufacturer are staggering. Under hard automation the greatest economies were realized only at the most massive scales. But flexible automation makes similar economies available at a wide range of scales. A flexible automation system can turn out a small batch or even a single copy of a product as efficiently as a production line designed to turn out a million identical items. Enthusiasts of flexible automation refer to this capability as *economy of scope*.

Economy of scope shatters the tenets of conventional manufacturing. The manufacturer will be able to meet a far greater array of market needs, including quick-changing ones—even the needs of markets the company is not in now. Manufacturers can keep up with changing fashions in the marketplace—or set them themselves by updating their products or launching new ones. Many more options are available for building a new plant: FMS frees manufacturers from the tyranny of large-scale investments in hard automation, thus allowing construction of smaller plants closer to markets.

Flexible manufacturing is the ultimate entrepreneurial system: It will allow fast-thinking manufacturers to move swiftly into brand new fields and to leave them just as swiftly if need be—at the expense of less agile and older producers.

Central to this flexibility that lies at the heart of the emergent thoughtware economy is *information*. What microelectronics does is to process, and eventually generate, information. What telecommunications does is to transmit information, with a growing complexity of interactive loops and feedbacks, at increasingly greater speed and at a lower cost. What the new media do is to disseminate information in a way potentially more and more decentralized and individualized. What automation does is to introduce preinformed devices in other activities. And what genetic engineering does is to decode the information system of the living matter to try to program it. Equally important is the fact that the outcome of the change is *process-oriented*, rather than *product-oriented*. *High technology is not a particular technique but a form of production*

TABLE 11.6

Principal programmable automation technologies

I. Computer-aided design (CAD)
   A. Computer-aided drafting
   B. Computer-aided engineering (CAE)
II. Computer-aided manufacturing (CAM)
   A. Robots
   B. Numerically controlled (NC) machine tools
   C. Flexible manufacturing systems (FMS)
   D. Automated materials handling (AMH) and automated storage and retrieval systems (AS/RS)
III. Tools and strategies for manufacturing management
   A. Computer-integrated manufacturing (CIM)
   B. Management information systems (MIS)
   C. Computer-aided planning (CAP) and computer-aided process planning (CAPP)

---

and organization that affects all spheres of activity by transforming their operation in order to achieve greater productivity or better performance, through increased knowledge of the process itself.

The new technologies are revolutionizing economic geography because, first, the new industries are playing a major role in the rise and decline of regions, and second, because traditional location factors have been replaced by a new set of locational forces and choices. Out of recent research on the spatial behavior of the new industries, M. Castells (1985) has proposed a model of the location of high-tech manufacturing. Five characteristics are involved:

1. Because high-tech industries are science-based and knowledge-intensive, they need a close connection to major universities and research units as well as to a large pool of technical and scientific labor.

2. Given the dependence on government markets, particularly on the military and space programs, especially until the late 1960s, high-tech activities tend to cluster historically in regions where the military has established its testing sites.

3. High-tech companies are generally characterized by a strong antiunion feeling in their management, not so much because of traditional economic reasons, such as wages or benefits, but because of the fears of bureaucratization and slowness in an industry that requires constant flexibility and innovation. Thus, areas with a strong union tradition will tend to discourage high-tech location, all other elements being equal.

4. The risk (and promise) of investment in this new field requires the existence of venture capital in the region that is a function of both a high level of wealth and an entrepreneurical culture oriented toward nontraditional financial markets.

5. The process of production in high-tech in general, and in microelectronics in particular, is highly discrete and can be easily separated, in time and space, among its research and design, fabrication, assembly, and testing functions. Given the very different requirements of each function, especially for labor, it follows a hierarchical division of labor across space and the need for all activities to be located in a good position in a communications network.

Castells believes that this model explains high-tech location better than the vague opposition between the Snowbelt and the Sunbelt or the very subjective notion of the "quality of life." For instance, Santa Clara County (Silicon Valley) possesses all the five characteristics cited; the *second* high-tech nest (in spite of having been the first until the mid-1960s), Route 128 (Boston), has almost everything, *but* it was somewhat limited in development by its strong union influence and the lack of military settlements; Texas and Arizona occupy an intermediate position, largely due to the absence (until recently in Texas) of major research centers, and, to some extent, to the fact that their financial markets were less well structured than those in San Francisco or Boston; New York–New Jersey offers the counterexample of how the concentration of giants such as IBM or RCA could not generate a milieu of innovation outside the companies themselves in spite of such assets as Bell Laboratories, Princeton, Cold Spring Laboratory, and so on, the largest financial center in the world, and the proximity to the largest information market. The absence of the military factor and the prounion environment in New York were powerful obstacles to the development of a high-tech milieu, whereas the large firms, such as IBM, were actually quite happy in building their empire inward, in isolation from potential competition and in prevention of threatening spinoffs.

The current sprawl of high-tech activities, Castells continues, modifies the geography of their location, but not the logic of their spatial relationships. New high-tech centers have developed (in Southern California, North Carolina, Texas, Colorado, Utah, Washington State, Arizona, Pennsylvania, Florida, and Maryland) along with three complementary tendencies for the location of assembly lines: offshore production (Pacific rim, Mexico), isolated rural communities in the western United States (Oregon, Arizona, Colorado, Texas) and, recently, fully automated plants closer to the high-tech nests.

Going beyond Castells's scheme, research at the Fantus Company of Chicago, perhaps the major location research firm in America, provides additional insights into this spread. Fantus believes that locational determinants for high-tech plants are not static but fluid, depending on the developmental stage of the high-tech product. Three developmental steps are recognized: theory, product, and market.

Theory-driven firms are usually embryonic, involved in advanced theoretical research. These firms are at the advanced cutting edge of ideas, innovations, and inventions. For them, the key criteria for selecting a plant location are

1. Availability of venture capital;
2. Ease of technological transfer;
3. Ease of start-up.

Product-driven firms are the second stage of high-technology development. At this stage the product is viable, but must be closely monitored for quality and must often be modified before sale. Companies at this stage employ a blend of research and manufacturing personnel. The location requirements are

1. Availability of technicians and skilled workers;
2. Demonstrated high worker productivity;
3. Accessibility to theory-driven R & D facilities;
4. Attractive living conditions;
5. A favorable business climate, such as low business and personal taxes.

Market-driven facilities emerge as the product becomes routinized, imitators enter the market, and price competition enters the selling process. Location requirements for competitive facilities switch dramatically, emphasizing

1. Cost, availability, and attitude of labor;
2. Cost, availability, and dependability of utilities;
3. Incentives, inducements, and exemptions.

Labor costs will rise to exceed 50 percent of all locationally variable costs at this stage, but where labor costs and available utilities are approximately the same, it is often special local inducements and giveaways that dictate the final locational choice.

The speed with which new innovations move from theory to product to competition is producing an increasingly fluid world economic geography.

TOPICS FOR DISCUSSION

1. What were the leading industrial sectors and the types of organizational change that characterized the first four Kondratiev cycles? In which regions did the changes occur first? What were the sequence and timing of the diffusion of the changes to other regions?

2. Why are clusters of innovations typically associated with the depths of depression in a technological stalemate?

3. What are the product cycle and the learning curve? How do they relate to concepts of industrial filtering?

4. What is the role of "thoughtware" in an advanced services economy?

5. How do locational choices of modern high-tech firms differ (if at all) from those of earlier industries whose seedbed was based on localization or urbanization economies?

6. What are the key differences likely to be in the long-run cost curves of traditional assembly-line industry and modern industries for which the economy of scope applies?

FURTHER READINGS

CASTELLS, MANUEL. "High Technology, Economic Restructuring, and the Urban-Regional Process in the United States." In *High Technology, Space and Society*, pp. 11–40. Edited by Manuel Castells. Beverly Hills, Calif.: Sage Publications, 1985.

CHRISTALLER, WALTER. *Central Places in Southern Germany*, trans. C. W. Baskin. Englewood Cliffs, N.J.: Prentice Hall, 1966.

FREEMAN, C. (Ed.). *Technological Innovation and Long Waves in World Economic Development*. London: Frances Pinter, 1984.

FRIEDMANN, JOHN. *Urbanization, Planning, and National Development*. Beverly Hills, Calif.: Sage, 1972.
    Includes an exposition of Friedmann's theory of polarized development.

HALL, P., and A. MARKUSEN (Eds.). *Silicon Landscapes*. Boston: George Allen and Unwin, 1985.

KONDRATIEV, N. D. "The Long Waves in Economic Life." *The Review of Economic Statistics*, 17 (1935), 105–115.

MYRDAL, GUNNAR. *Rich Lands and Poor: The Road to World Prosperity*. New York: Harper, 1957.
    Offers a classic extension of ideas of cumulative causation to the world economy.

STANBACK, T. M., P. J. BEARSE, T. J. NOYELLE, and R. A. KARASEK. *Services: The New Economy*. Totowa, N.J.: Allanheld and Osmun, 1981.

VAN DUIJN, J. J. *The Long Wave in Economic Life*. London: George Allen and Unwin, 1983.

VERNON, R. "International Investment and International Trade in the Product Cycle." *Quarterly Journal of Economics*, 80 (1966), 190–207.

12

Theories of International Trade

OVERVIEW

The growing interdependence of countries has meant an ever-increasing reliance upon the global system of international trade and locational decision making. Over a long period of time, theories have evolved in response to the need for a clearer understanding of these complex processes of international interaction. Modern trade theory holds that the types, quantities, and prices of goods traded among countries depend upon the relative amounts of the factors of production—land, labor, capital, and enterprise—with which those countries are endowed. These are the elements that determine the outcome of the interaction between supply and demand.

Citing the results of empirical studies, critics of contemporary trade theory have pointed to a number of weaknesses in this theory. In particular, they note the omission of certain features that are capable of substantially modifying the spatial pattern of commodity flows produced by the simple interaction of supply and demand. Chief among these missing items are two imposing barriers to trade: the time, effort, and cost of overcoming distance, and the intervention of sovereign governments in foreign economic affairs.

Although conventional theory explains the trade among countries in terms of factor endowments, the realization has grown that, in turn, trade has important effects upon the factors. The opening of trade may cause rents, interest, and wages to rise or fall, and it can alter the quantities of factors held by trading countries. Another recent discovery is the degree to which the factors—capital, enterprise, and labor—can move internationally, aided by the activities of multinational enterprises.

OBJECTIVES

- to demonstrate the relationship between the location of production and the flow of goods, services, and factors of production among countries
- to trace the development of modern trade theory, to describe the various elements that help to explain international commodity flows, and to consider the criticisms of modern theory
- to examine the effects of distance and governmental intervention as barriers to international trade
- to show how the introduction of trade among countries alters the prices and quantities of the factors of production

INTERNATIONAL TRADE AND LOCATION

As the end of the twentieth century draws nearer, nations are becoming increasingly interdependent. Contemporary standards of living call for such a variety of goods and draw upon a technology so complex that no country can by itself supply all the necessary ingredients; a retreat to self-sufficiency would so impoverish a people that no country would find such a course politically feasible. To supply its diverse needs, therefore, modern civilization relies increasingly on a global system of trade. The resulting international flows consist not only of commodities but also a great variety of services. Within the past quarter-century a growing volume of capital, technology, and management has also followed these international movements of goods and services. Trade among countries has thus laid the basis for an internationalization of the locational decision-making process.

That trade is indeed intimately bound up with the location of production and consumption was noted by Alfred Weber and later developed theoretically by Bertil Ohlin in his book *Interregional and International Trade* (1933, 1952). As Walter Isard stated later, "Location and trade are as the two sides of the same coin. The forces determining one simultaneously determine the other."

For a variety of reasons, in this chapter we emphasize international rather than domestic trade. First, it will enable us to discuss the role that national governments play in determining or controlling their foreign trade flows, and thereby influencing the international location of production. International trade and domestic trade take place for many of the same reasons, yet governments have customarily interfered to a greater extent in their trade with other countries than with movements inside their own borders. Furthermore, conditions of doing business within a country tend to be fairly uniform from one place to another, whereas commercial practices vary considerably among countries. National governments often differ in their fiscal policies and in their systems of subsidies and taxes. Legal frameworks vary in such important matters as the rights, liabilities, and obligations of firms and individuals. Countries differ in their social and cultural environments, which in turn significantly affect the nature of their production, consumption, and commerce. The existence of such differences among countries has contributed to the large amount of theoretical literature on the international aspects of trade.

Theories of international trade have evolved in response to an effort to gain a better understanding of the basic forces at work in this complex form of spatial interaction. By classifying the various parts of the international system into meaningful categories and studying their interrelationships, theorists have sought to interpret their functions and predict the consequences of any changes that may be introduced. We begin by examining the way in which the existing body of theory came into being.

EVOLUTION OF TRADE THEORY

International trade theory emerged as an independent body of thought at a very early date. Although this theory arose initially in response to specific practical needs of the times, it has subsequently reached high levels of abstraction. In large measure the character of the trade theory we have inherited reflects the way in which it has evolved, particularly in its form and emphasis.

It is customary to separate the history of international trade theory into three or four periods. The first is the preclassical or *mercantilist* era, which followed the Middle Ages and reached its zenith within about a century prior to the 1750s. Mercantilism did not actually attain the status of a true theory, however. The beginnings of trade theory as we know it today came with the *classical* period, which appeared coincidentally with the English Industrial Revolution in the middle of the eighteenth century and continued for at least another 150 years. Contemporary trade theory, or the *modern* period, has formed during this present century and has largely superseded the more simplistic notions of earlier eras, although some of the ideas of mercantilism and of the classical period persist in some national policies even today.

Mercantilism

Those who wrote on trade topics during the mercantilist era were mainly political pamphleteers who were less concerned with producing theory than with promoting policies of national self-interest. This economic nationalism was a natural element of a period when strong central governments were forming. These writings fall within a number of distinct national groupings and cannot be generalized very satisfactorily, but the various mercantilist policies share certain common features.

First, the mercantilists considered it essential that a country's merchandise exports exceed its imports, thereby producing a "favorable" balance of trade, that is, one that would contribute a surplus of money or gold to the royal treasury. Second, they emphasized foreign trade rather than domestic trade, manufacturing rather than agriculture, and the desirability of plentiful cheap labor. They favored manufacturing because it could support a denser population and because its output yielded exports of higher value. They regarded a large population of low-wage labor to be a source of national strength. Finally, the mercantilists promoted the use of various administrative measures by which countries could enforce these aims. Despite their antiquity, many of these notions sound surprisingly contemporary: Even today many national policies are at least implicitly mercantilistic. Although modern trade theory emphatically rejects most mercantilist ideas, it continues to stress the *normative:* that which ought to be.

Classical Theory

The classical period was an era of brilliant theorists, such as Adam Smith and David Ricardo, who reacted sharply to the errors and excesses of the mercantilist philosophy. The basic normative premise of classical theory was that free trade is beneficial to all trading partners. The questions raised by classical theorists were these: Why is international trade mutually advantageous? What determines the goods to be exchanged? What decides the amounts of goods to be traded (and thus the international price level)? The emphasis, therefore, was on the gains from trade. Trade among countries, these writers argued, results in an increased international specialization of production, a division of labor like that which accompanies domestic trade. To measure the effects of trade, classical theorists developed the *labor theory of value*. This was the notion that all costs can be reduced ultimately to units of labor, which in turn are directly related to the prices that must be charged for the products.

Throughout the nineteenth century and during the early years of the twentieth century, theorists continued to refine classical theory. Near the close of the classical era a number of new concepts and analytic techniques appeared, giving rise to what is sometimes called the *neoclassical* period.

Modern Theory

Modern theory began to take form with the appearance in 1933 of Bertil Ohlin's work *Interregional and International Trade*. Ohlin abandoned the classical labor theory of value, replacing it with a new theory that acknowledged the effects of all factors of production—land, labor, capital, and management—as determinants of international trade. Further extending the earlier ideas of Eli Heckscher, Ohlin based his work upon these premises: (1) countries differ in their pro-

portions of factors, that is, their *factor endowments,* and (2) commodities differ in the combinations of factors they require in their production, that is, in their *factor intensities*. Assuming that factor intensities of particular commodities remain the same in different countries, the *Heckscher-Ohlin model* states that each country will export those goods whose production is relatively intensive in the country's abundant factor and import those that are intensive in the factors it lacks. Thus Hong Kong, Taiwan, and South Korea all have large supplies of cheap labor and export labor-intensive goods such as low-priced shoes, garments, and small appliances. The Swiss, with much capital and skilled labor but little land, produce and export watches and scientific instruments. Having vast land resources, Canada exports primary goods such as wood pulp, paper, potash, and wheat to a greater extent than do most industrialized countries. At the same time, land-short Hong Kong and Switzerland import raw materials and foodstuffs, whereas Canada tends to import goods that are intensive in labor and capital. It is from the perspective of modern theory that we examine some of the basic elements of trade theory and see how these operate in world commodity trade.

THE DETERMINANTS OF TRADE

Geographers' efforts to understand better the form and nature of trade flows raise issues that have been central to trade theory ever since the classical era. The most basic question is why trade should occur at all. An obvious answer would be that trade serves to reconcile limited productive capacities with widely ranging needs and wants. The solution is not as simple as this would imply, however, nor are the gains from the exchange of goods the only benefits enjoyed by participants in trade. Pursuing this idea further will also help us to find out what commodities will be traded and in what quantities, and who will do the trading. In addition to the bases for trade, therefore, we shall be looking at its structure and its direction of movement.

The forces affecting trade fall into two broad classes. Under the ideal conditions assumed by classical theorists the principal determinants of trade are those relating to supply and demand. In reality, however, other influences distort the ideal pattern by acting as impediments to trade. The latter make trade more difficult, or even impossible, at the same time altering the commodity mix and price structure. It is mainly because of this second group of influences that international trade is more complicated than interregional trade.

Comparative Advantage

To isolate the effects of demand and supply conditions upon trade, we begin with a set of simplifying assumptions; later we can relax these as we consider other elements that influence trade. Let us assume (1) that no transport costs are required to move goods among countries, (2) that no artificial barriers to trade (such as governments might impose) exist among countries, (3) that the factors of production in each country are homogeneous (have identical characteristics throughout), (4) that perfect competition exists, (5) that production technology is identical among countries, and (6) that no international movement of factors of production (labor, capital, and so forth) can take place. Given these conditions, the Heckscher-Ohlin theory holds that countries can benefit from trade if they differ in their factor proportions (and, hence, differ in their abilities to produce particular goods), if they have unlike patterns of consumption, or if they vary in both of these respects. Two examples will show how trade can beneficially take place between countries on the basis of differing supply conditions (the effects of demand differences will be discussed in a later section).

Example 1. Absolute Advantage in Both Countries. Take two countries with economies of equal size, France and Germany, which are isolated from the rest of the world and initially have no commercial relations with each other. Both produce and consume the same two commodities, potatoes and wheat, devoting to these enterprises all their resources—land, labor, capital, and management. Because of the dissimilar nature of their resource endowments, however, the two countries differ in the quantities of these commodities that they are able to produce per unit of input.

As Table 12.1 shows, France would be capable of producing 90 bushels of potatoes per unit of resource input if she were to devote her resources entirely to this crop; alternatively, she could use these same resources to produce 60 bushels of wheat (per unit of input). This implies that French resources are better suited to potatoes than to wheat. In the absence of foreign trade, the French exchange the two goods domestically at the rate of $1\frac{1}{2}$ bushels of potatoes for 1 bushel of wheat, or, conversely, $\frac{2}{3}$ bushel of wheat for 1 bushel of potatoes. Thus, in France wheat has the higher price of the two commodities because it is more costly to produce and hence is scarcer.

Figure 12.1a shows all the possible combinations of potatoes and wheat that France is capable of producing. The French production possibilities curve, *YT*, ranges from the extreme case where all resources are allocated to potatoes, *Y*, to the other extreme, *T*, where everything is put into wheat. Between these two extremes of specialization lie the various other possible combinations of these two crops. In the example given here, the French have chosen to produce and consume the combination of potatoes and wheat given by point *M* in Figure 12.1a. This amounts to 45 bushels of potatoes and 30 bushels of wheat per unit of resource input (see Table 12.1).

In Germany the cost relationships are just the reverse. If the Germans were to specialize completely in potatoes they would be able to grow 50 bushels per unit of input, or they could use that same resource unit to produce a total of 100 bushels of wheat (Table 12.1). In the absence of foreign trade, therefore, the Germans would exchange 0.5 bushel of potatoes for 1 bushel of wheat or 2 bushels of wheat for 1 bushel of potatoes (Table 12.1). Figure 12.1b shows the full range of possibilities for German production. Note that, from the range of possible combinations, the Germans have elected to produce and consume potatoes and wheat in the proportions given by point *Q*, that is, 25 bushels of potatoes and 50 bushels of wheat.

A comparison of the production possibilities of the two countries (Table 12.1) reveals that France would have an *absolute advantage* over Germany in potatoes and Germany would have an *absolute advantage* over France in wheat if they were to enter into trade with each other. These are the conditions for trade cited by Adam Smith. When they discover this situation, the French find that they could receive up to

TABLE 12.1

Production possibilities, domestic exchange ratios, and production and consumption of potatoes and wheat in France and Germany before trade

	Production Possibilities		*Domestic Exchange Ratios*		*Production and Consumption*		
	Potatoes	Wheat	Potatoes/wheat	Wheat/potatoes	Potatoes	Wheat	Total
France	90	60	1.50	0.67	45	30	75
Germany	50	100	0.50	2.00	25	50	75
Total	140	160			70	80	150

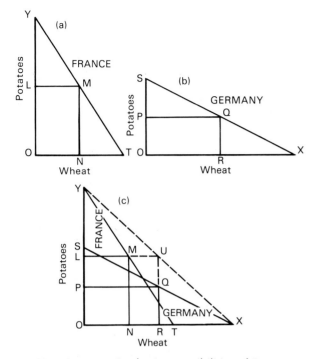

FIGURE 12.1 Production possibilities of France and Germany, exchange possibilities, and gains from trade.

2 bushels of wheat in Germany in exchange for a single bushel of their potatoes instead of the $\frac{2}{3}$ bushel of wheat they have been getting at home. Similarly, the Germans learn that in France they could get up to $1\frac{1}{2}$ bushels of potatoes for 1 bushel of wheat rather than the mere $\frac{1}{2}$ bushel obtained in their own country.

The resulting trade benefits both countries as French potatoes move eastward into Germany and

wheat makes the return journey westward. So beneficial is this exchange that French farmers begin to specialize in potato production and transfer their resources out of wheat; conversely, German farmers turn their emphasis to wheat at the expense of potatoes. Obviously, the initial exchange ratios for potatoes and wheat do not last long after trade begins and as specialization increases.

Ultimately, specialization becomes complete and trade closes the gap in prices entirely. France allocates all her resources to potatoes (OY in Figure 12.1c) and supplies this commodity to consumers of both countries; Germany puts all her productive capacity into wheat (OX in Figure 12.1c) and shares the output with France. Figure 12.1c also gives us the final *equilibrium* price at which the potato-wheat trade takes place between the countries. The *international exchange ratio* (Table 12.2) is given by

$$\frac{OY}{OX} = \frac{90}{100} = 0.90$$

Thus a bushel of wheat exchanges for 0.90 bushel of potatoes. This ratio is also referred to as the *international terms of trade*. The dashed diagonal line, XY, in Figure 12.1c is the *exchange possibilities curve*, which indicates all the various proportions of potatoes and wheat that are now available to the French and Germans at this new combined level of output.

The two countries are now using their productive resources to full efficiency. The benefits of this new arrangement are apparent from a comparison of Tables 12.1 and 12.2, where we see that total potato output

TABLE 12.2

International exchange possibilities, international exchange ratios, and production, exports, imports, and consumption of potatoes and wheat in France and Germany after trade

		International Exchange Possibilities		International Exchange Ratio	
		Potatoes	Wheat	Potatoes/Wheat	Wheat/Potatoes
	France	90	100	0.90	1.11
	Germany	90	100	0.90	1.11

	Production, Trade, and Consumption								
	Potatoes				Wheat				Total
	Production	Exports	Imports	Consumption	Production	Exports	Imports	Consumption	Consumption
France	90	45	—	45	—	—	50	50	95
Germany	—	—	45	45	100	50	—	50	95
Total	90	45	45	90	100	50	50	100	190

(all contributed by France) is now 90 bushels (per input unit) (Table 12.2), whereas the combined output of the two countries had formerly been only 70 bushels (Table 12.1). Likewise, total wheat output has gone from 80 bushels (Table 12.1) to 100 (all produced by Germany, Table 12.2). Of the 90 bushels of potatoes (per unit) produced by France, domestic consumption continues to take 45 bushels and exports to Germany take the remaining 45 bushels. Germany concentrates all her resources in wheat production, retaining 50 bushels for her own consumption and supplying the other 50 to France (Table 12.2). Total consumption in the two countries thus rises as a result of this exchange. By importing wheat from Germany instead of producing her own on lands not well suited to this crop, France is able to increase wheat consumption from 30 bushels (Table 12.1) to 50 (Table 12.2). Similarly, Germany can raise consumption of potatoes from 25 units to 45. Hence, international specialization and trade have raised consumer welfare in both countries.

Up to this point we have been assuming that the structure of demand is the same in both countries, that French and German consumers want potatoes and wheat in the same proportions. But are French consumers really content to continue consuming the same amount of potatoes as before, and do they actually want all that wheat that is coming from Germany? And are the Germans satisfied to consume potatoes and wheat in the same proportions as the French? It is very possible that the citizens of these two nations have different structures of demand. Over the centuries each population may have grown accustomed to its traditional diet and now merely wants more of each commodity. (Other influences that may affect a population's demand characteristics will be discussed later.)

Figure 12.2 shows the possible effects of such contrasting consumer preferences. Note that even in this case consumer welfare rises with the introduction of trade and specialization. Let us say that the actual demand patterns of the two countries are as shown by the families of *indifference curves* appearing in Figure 12.2, French consumption being given by those curves labeled I_F and German consumption by those labeled I_G. The indifference curves indicate the various proportions in which the French or German consumers are willing to substitute potatoes for wheat or vice versa. Each curve corresponds to a given level of consumption in a country. Thus I^0 refers to one level, I^1 to the next higher level, and I^2 to a higher level yet. Clearly a people will wish to reach the highest curve possible, thereby raising the standard of living. The point where an indifference curve is tangent with the

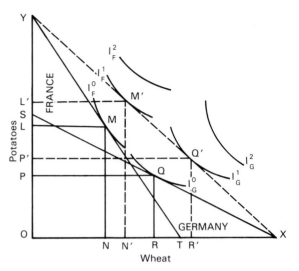

FIGURE 12.2 Gains from trade: different demand structures.

production possibilities curve indicates the actual quantities of the two commodities consumed prior to the opening of trade. M represents the amounts consumed before trade by France and Q the amounts consumed by Germany.

After trade, consumption shifts upward to the point where some higher indifference curve becomes tangent with the exchange possibilities curve. In Figure 12.2 the advent of trade causes France's consumption to move from M to M' on the next higher indifference curve (from curve I_F^0 to I_F^1). Thus, trade makes it possible for the French to consume OL' potatoes instead of OL and ON' wheat instead of ON. German consumption likewise moves up from Q to Q' (from indifference curve I_G^0 to I_G^1). Germany is then able to increase her consumption of potatoes from OP to OP' and her consumption of wheat from OR to OR'. Thus, trade permits both countries to attain greater consumer satisfaction.

Complete specialization of the kind described here is uncommon in the real world, although several less-developed countries come close to it. One reason that specialization does not reach its ultimate limits is the tendency for unit production costs to begin increasing after a certain level of inputs is reached. Underlying our discussion thus far has been the assumption that unit costs remain constant at all levels of production, as suggested by the linear shape of the production possibilities curves in Figure 12.1 and Figure 12.2. This is not realistic: Under normal conditions we would expect unit costs to increase. Figure 12.3 shows the effect of increasing costs on the production possibilities of France and Germany. As the limits of efficiency are approached for either type of farming,

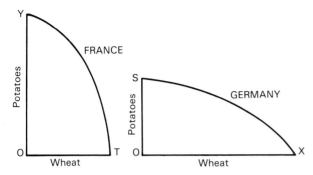

FIGURE 12.3 Effects of increasing costs upon production possibilities curves.

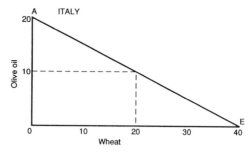

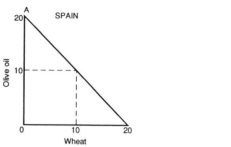

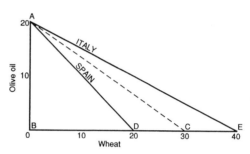

FIGURE 12.4 The opportunities for trade in a case where only one country has an absolute advantage but the other has a comparative advantage.

the application of additional resources yields diminishing returns, and output declines as a consequence. This results from the fact that rarely are all of a country's resources equally suited to a particular line of production. As farmers allocate new resources to wheat or potatoes, they eventually reach a point where each additional new unit of input (machinery, fertilizer, labor) no longer yields a proportionate gain in output. In the present example, therefore, it is likely that France will continue to grow small amounts of her own wheat and that Germany will not entirely give up potato production.

Example 2. Absolute Advantage in One Country Only, Comparative Advantage in the Other. According to Adam Smith, if trade is to take place between two countries, each must have an absolute advantage, as in Example 1. But what of the situation illustrated in Figure 12.4? Here, Italy has an absolute advantage over Spain in the production of wheat, but the two countries are equally efficient in producing olive oil. Does this offer any incentive for trade? Adam Smith would have said No. His successor, David Ricardo, would have said Yes.

As Ricardo found, all that is required for trade to be mutually beneficial to both parties is that the two countries differ in the *relative* efficiencies with which they produce the two commodities. In the present example, Spain's disadvantage in the production of wheat is relatively greater than it is in the production of olive oil (where Spain actually matches Italy's efficiency). Although Spain may lack an *absolute* advantage in olive oil production, she nevertheless has a *comparative* advantage in olive oil. That is to say, by comparison with Italy, Spain is relatively less efficient in producing wheat than she is in producing olive oil.

For confirmation of this, examine the relationship as it is shown in Table 12.3. Here we see that before trade, Italy is able to use the same set of resources to produce either 40 units of wheat or 20 units

of olive oil (per resource unit) but actually produces 20 units of wheat and 10 units of olive oil. On the other hand, Spain is capable of producing either 20 units of wheat or 20 units of olive oil (per resource unit) but actually produces 10 units of wheat and 10 units of olive oil. Their combined total output, therefore, is 30 units of wheat plus 20 units of oil—which is the maximum possible as long as each country produces solely for its own needs.

When the two countries enter into trade, however, each specializes: Italy now produces 40 units of wheat (per unit of resources), Spain produces 20 units of olive oil, and the two exchange surpluses. As a result, the combined total output rises to 40 units of wheat plus 20 units of oil, a gain of 10 units of wheat over their pretrade total.

How the two countries share the additional 10 units of wheat between them is decided by the conditions of demand in the two countries, a subject to which we shall return in a subsequent section. For the

TABLE 12.3

Production and exchange ratios of wheat and olive oil, Italy and Spain

Before trade:

| | Production Possibilities | | Domestic Exchange Ratios | | Production | |
	Wheat	Olive oil	Wheat/oil	Oil/wheat	Wheat	Olive oil
Italy	40	20	2.00	0.50	20	10
Spain	20	20	1.00	1.00	10	10
Total					30	20

After trade:

| | | | International Exchange Ratios | | | |
| | Production | | Range of potential ratios | | Ratios at point C | |
	Wheat	Olive oil	Wheat/oil	Oil/wheat	Wheat/oil	Oil/wheat
Italy	40	—	2.00 Max.	0.50 Min.	1.50	0.67
Spain	—	20	1.00 Min.	1.00 Max.	1.50	0.67
Total	40	20				

moment, however, we may note the range of potential prices (*international exchange ratios*) as given in Table 12.3. Here we see that if Italy is to benefit from specializing in wheat, she must receive a price for wheat that is higher than her pretrade price (*domestic exchange ratio*), which was $\frac{1}{2}$ unit of oil for one unit of wheat. Similarly, Spain must receive more than 1 unit of wheat for a unit of her olive oil. Thus, as the table shows, Italy's minimum exchange ratio for wheat is equivalent to the maximum price Spain can afford to pay for wheat, and vice versa for olive oil.

These minimums and maximums define the range within which the final price is to lie. They are shown graphically in Figure 12.4c, where Italy's minimum acceptable price for her wheat is given by the ratio of *AB/BE* and Spain's minimum price for her oil is *BD/AB*. The equivalent *exchange possibilities curves* are *AE* for Italy and *AD* for Spain. The ultimate price must fall somewhere between the two extremes, perhaps *BC/AB* for wheat/oil (or *AB/BC* for oil/wheat) (the new exchange possibilities curve would be *AC*). At this price Italy would receive $\frac{2}{3}$ unit of oil for a unit of her wheat, whereas before trade a unit of wheat bought only $\frac{1}{2}$ unit of oil in Italy, and Spain would receive $1\frac{1}{2}$ units of wheat for a unit of her oil as against only 1 unit before trade (Table 12.3). Thus each country would enjoy a higher price for her specialty crop and pay less for her imported good than prior to trade.

The Gains from Trade: A Summary. The introduction of trade between countries with different production possibilities theoretically leads to a number of desirable results for the participating parties. These benefits are of two kinds: (1) those that stem from the exchange of goods in and of itself, and (2) those that result from the international specialization of production that trade causes.

The preceding discussion has revealed some of the first type of gains, those from trade per se. As Figures 12.1, 12.2, 12.3, and 12.4 demonstrated, the introduction of trade permits a country to adjust its commodity mix in such a way as to move its population to a higher level of consumption than was possible in isolation. Because of trade, therefore, the production pattern no longer needs to coincide with the consumption pattern.

Over and above these first benefits, however, trade confers a second set of gains. The increased specialization of production that follows trade offers important opportunities for more efficient production, for a greater output from each unit of resources. If the inhabitants of a country concentrate their efforts upon producing a limited number of goods, they are able to use more effectively those skills and resources that are best adapted to the purpose. Then, as they continue to accumulate experience along these lines, they acquire new and even greater skills. A fertile environment for invention and innovation arises as research and development come to focus along narrow channels and as specialists in the field live and work in close association with one another.

Business enterprises gain in competitive strength from operating in such a climate. These benefits are both *internal* and *external,* as was seen in Chapter 7. Among the internal benefits are economies of large-scale production: more efficient use of machines and workers, lower prices for raw materials purchased in bulk, reduced transport rates for assembling materials and distributing products in large quantities, and lower unit operating costs as a result of spreading output over longer model runs. The external economies enjoyed by businesses located in an area of specialization include the opportunities to share ideas and information with others engaged in the same type of production and the access to a large pool of labor with the requisite skills. Important also is the availability of many specialized facilities. These may consist of auxiliary or related industries with which a company has direct ties, such as those that link steel mills with suppliers of fire bricks for lining furnaces or with customers who use steel in fabricating bridges. Such areas of concentration often acquire a variety of specialized service agencies. Associated with the cotton textile industry, for example, are cotton brokerage and exchange activities as well as banking and insurance firms having a knowledge of the peculiar needs and problems of that trade.

In this way areal specialization further enhances a country's initial comparative advantage. Once it has gained sufficient momentum, the specialized area increases its competitive edge over other areas that might wish to enter the market. Indeed, even if it had previously possessed no resource advantage at all and had merely developed its specialty through historical accident, the area might have acquired a comparative advantage by reason of the kinds of economies described here. Such considerations help to explain the existence of many industrial concentrations around the world whose original reason for location may now have vanished. Examples are Britain's clay products industry at Stoke-on-Trent, France's textile manufacturing in Le Nord, and the U.S. optical instrument specialization at Rochester, New York.

In sum, if trade is truly free, it should result in optimal use of the world's resources through greater efficiency and thus smaller resource use per unit of output. This means that the world would produce a greater supply of goods from the same resource base, thereby raising standards of living generally.

Effects of Supply Conditions

We have seen that comparative advantages arising from differences in production cost can provide the bases for profitable trade among countries. This raises a further question: How do particular combinations of natural and human assets affect the ability of countries to produce and compete in the international marketplace? These resource endowments can be grouped into four categories, referred to as factors of production—*land, labor, capital,* and *entrepreneurship*—which interact in a variety of ways. As we examine these, we shall emphasize two related aspects: (1) the factor requirements of particular industries and (2) the ways in which countries differ in their possession of these factors.

Factor Proportions and Intensity. All four factors of production enter into every type of commercial production, whether it be farming, mining, manufacturing, or any other economic activity, although different activities may require these factors in varying proportions. Most primary activities, such as farming or forestry, make heavy demands on the factor of land are thus said to be *land-intensive.* Some types of manufacturing, such as cotton textiles, need much labor; other industries, such as oil refining, need much capital and relatively little labor. Thus, *factor intensity* differs widely from one type of production to another.

In many economic activities it is possible, within limits, to substitute one factor for another. In agriculture, labor and capital (in the form of equipment or fertilizer) can usually be applied to a unit of land in varying proportions. Manufactured goods, in many cases, can be made either by hand or by machine; in the latter case, capital is substituted for labor. Sometimes, however, the factors of production occur in forms that are so specialized in their applicability that they are difficult to shift out of one use into another. This is true of certain kinds of land. For instance, acidic soils good for growing potatoes or blueberries would be poor for wheat, which requires alkaline soils.

Even labor may be difficult to transfer from one activity to another, especially if the skill requirements differ greatly. Quick shifts of labor are often difficult to effect because workers may be reluctant to learn new skills or may be incapable of being retrained. A farm worker could not immediately gain employment as a petroleum chemist, and a lathe operator could not quickly go to work as a crane operator or dairy farmer. Even some forms of fixed capital are highly specific. It would hardly be feasible, for instance, to convert an oil refinery to the manufacture of textiles. In all cases, time is the important element: Factors that cannot be shifted instantaneously to other uses may be converted over longer periods. This is especially true of labor, which, given a sufficient number of years, may be able to acquire new skills.

Scale of operations is still another consideration in determining the allocation of factors. A combination of factors appropriate at a low level of production may not be suitable at a higher level. This is apparent in two contrasting forms of European agriculture. Peasant farming, still found in the more isolated parts of France, Germany, Switzerland, and certain other countries, generally takes place on very small holdings with scattered, fragmented fields. Because large farm machinery would be useless in such limited space, peasant agriculture is labor-intensive. On the other hand, though they may produce the same crops as the peasant farms, commercial agricultural enterprises in Europe have large acreages and big fields suitable for mechanization and have thus become capital-intensive. Likewise, a given type of manufacturing activity may take place in small, labor-intensive establishments, or it may occupy large plants employing labor-saving machinery and mass-production methods. The same company may be labor-intensive during its formative years and then become capital-intensive as the firm grows and matures.

The factors of production are present in different countries in widely varying proportions. Australia and Canada occupy large land areas containing immense, diverse stores of natural resources, but they have comparatively small populations to go along with those resources. Both countries therefore lack the supplies of labor, capital, and entrepreneurship necessary to exploit fully their natural endowments. At the other extreme are Belgium, Switzerland, and several other small European countries with well-developed capital markets, relatively large pools of skilled labor, and an abundance of experienced managerial talent but lacking sufficient natural resources to match these superior human resources. Several less-developed countries—India and Pakistan, for example—are oversupplied with workers, most of them uneducated and untrained; yet these countries lack the capital and managerial requirements for putting their masses to productive activity. What are the trade effects of these factors of production?

Land as a Factor. The quantity and characteristics of *land* have much to do with determining the size and nature of world trade flows. By land we mean the territory of a country, region, district, or other areal unit, together with its particular attributes. The properties of land of particular interest are its physical re-

sources that are useful to human beings. A significant aspect of these resources as they relate to trade is that they are distributed throughout the world in a most uneven fashion (see Chapter 5). For this reason the resources of most countries are "skewed," that is, these countries may have large stores of some resources—perhaps more than they can use domestically—but inadequate supplies of many others.

Mineral resources are distributed in a particularly erratic manner. Only a few of the metallic minerals, such as iron ore, are abundant in the earth's crust and found in many places; yet even these common minerals are concentrated in commercial quantities in a limited number of areas. This resource skewness is partly responsible for the voluminous and growing interregional and international trade in minerals. Much of the world's ocean tonnage is engaged in transporting oil from Venezuela, North Africa, and the Middle East to Western Europe, Japan, and the United States.

Biotic resources are spread inequitably too, partly because of climatic and other physical reasons but also because of the destructiveness of human beings. Today the forested areas of the Pacific Northwest of Canada and the United States, together with northern Ontario and Quebec, send their wood products to the more populous parts of North America. Large flows of these commodities also converge upon central and Western Europe from Scandinavia and the former USSR. At the same time, tropical hardwoods move from equatorial regions to industrialized areas of the temperate latitudes.

The widespread trade in agricultural commodities clearly reflects world variations in *climates, soils,* and *relief.* The Mediterranean basin and similar areas in California and elsewhere are able, by reason of their long growing seasons, to specialize in growing fruits and winter vegetables for populations in colder areas thousands of miles away. The agricultural commodities that enter world trade in the largest volumes are the temperate-land grains, particularly wheat, which are exchanged for the sugar and tropical fruits of warmer areas. One of the most prominent characteristics of the wheat trade, however, is its unpredictability from one year to the next. This results mainly from the variability of harvests in the leading wheat-growing areas, where rainfall patterns are very uncertain. Thus, although the former USSR (principally Ukraine) is the world's leading wheat producer in most years, it must import enormous quantities of grain during periods of crop failure.

Differences in soils likewise affect world trade, for many crops such as grapes, tea, and sugar cane have exacting requirements. Regions with special kinds of soils, such as the Lake Okeechobee district of southern Florida, produce large quantities of vegetables for export. Another attribute of land is its physical relief. Regions with great expanses of low-lying, level terrain often produce and export foodstuffs to mountainous areas unable to grow sufficient quantities of food for themselves. The exchanges of The Netherlands and Denmark with the Alpine countries of Austria and Switzerland illustrate this element in the world food trade. On the other hand, the scenic beauty of the Alpine lands attracts thousands of freely spending tourists, who contribute ample amounts of foreign exchange to pay for the needed food imports.

The patterns of commodity movements described here are continually changing. One reason for this is the dynamic nature of physical resources; even the view of what constitutes a resource changes over time (see Chapter 5). Technology can greatly alter the production and trade of land-intensive goods, and the discovery of new resources may reshape world trade patterns, as occurred with the oil discoveries in Alaska, beneath the North Sea, and in Mexico. Resources can become exhausted, too. Witness the worn-out cotton lands of the southern United States and the depleted reserves of high-grade iron ore in the Lake Superior region. Shifts in trade flows have followed each of these events.

The *physical dimensions* of countries affect world trade in many ways. Obviously, the larger the country the more likely that it will have a wide range and ample supply of resources and, therefore, a more diversified output of goods. Thus, the United States and China are more nearly self-sufficient than are smaller countries, and their dependence upon foreign trade is correspondingly less. Because of the size of its economy the United States is the largest single trading country, but it usually exports no more than 8 percent of its gross national product. By contrast, The Netherlands, which is only slightly larger than Massachusetts, exports from 35 percent to 40 percent of its total output. A small country is also less likely to produce goods in sufficient quantity to influence international terms of trade, and it must therefore accept whatever prices world markets dictate for its goods.

Even the *shapes* of countries can affect their trade, especially in agricultural commodities. If a country's growing areas have a greater north-south extent, they will experience a wider climatic variation and thus yield a wider variety of farm products. Because Canada's agricultural lands are confined to a long narrow strip extending east-west just north of the United States border, they are able to grow only a limited number of temperate-land crops. Long borders between countries, however, are conducive to trade. Thus, whereas Ontario relies mainly upon coal im-

ported from the nearby eastern coalfields of the United States, British Columbia in the far west supplies that same fuel to the adjacent Pacific states of the United States. One of the prime physical attributes of a country is its relative location, a matter so central to the topic of international trade that we shall be treating it separately later.

It should be stressed again that neither land nor any other factor of production is sufficient of itself; all the factors are required in some combination for every economic undertaking. Land becomes economically useful only when capital, labor, and enterprise are applied to it. We have seen that such land-rich countries as Canada are unable to make full use of their physical resource endowments when they lack adequate supplies of the complementary factors. This case also demonstrates the fact that physical extent alone is not an accurate indicator of a country's economic size. Note that this imbalance in the factors of production tends to have a trade-creating effect for Canada, which exports large quantities of land-intensive commodities that a larger economy would absorb internally.

Labor as a Factor.   Historically, the factor that most interested theorists was *labor*. Indeed, they originally posed the law of comparative advantage in terms of the labor theory of value, according to which the values of all commodities can be measured by their labor inputs, such as workdays. Implicit in this theory is the assumption that the output of a unit of labor is constant everywhere and for all economic activities. In other words, laborers can shift from one industry to another with no effect upon total labor costs. The theory either ignores the other factors or treats them as stored-up labor. Except for Marxists, modern theorists no longer accept the labor theory of value, but they readily acknowledge the considerable influence that labor has upon trade. Two aspects of labor are of special significance: (1) its relative abundance or scarcity and (2) its productivity.

Countries (and regions) vary greatly in the *size* of their labor forces; many have inadequate numbers of workers to run their farms and factories while others have more workers than they can employ economically. For labor-scarce economies—those having low ratios of labor to land—the Heckscher-Ohlin theory predicts resource-intensive exports and labor-intensive imports. Hence, Finland, Canada, and Australia export commodities having a large physical resource content, such as minerals, wood products, or animal products.

Contrary to the labor theory of value, labor inputs for the same goods do vary from one country to another, especially where resource endowments differ markedly. Both the United States and China produce wheat, cotton, and rice; but China uses labor-intensive methods whereas the United States employs methods that are at the same time land-intensive and capital-intensive.

In those countries where the labor-land ratio is very high, the expectation is for labor-intensive exports and land- or capital-intensive imports. A number of Pacific Rim countries fall into this category, especially the island nations of Hong Kong and Taiwan, both of which import large volumes of raw materials and foodstuffs and export finished manufactured goods. A surplus of labor usually means low labor costs, a prime attraction to those industries using large numbers of unskilled or semiskilled laborers. Most such manufacturing activities are mature industries, that is, they have passed through the innovative stages that need highly skilled workers and engineers and can now use mass-production techniques that call for many unskilled workers performing simple tasks on assembly lines. Typical of these are factories making cheaper grades of textiles, standardized types of low-priced clothing, and even the more established forms of electronics, such as the assembling of radio and television sets. South Korea, Malaysia, Thailand, and Puerto Rico have many industries of this type.

Despite plentiful supplies of labor and land, many less-developed countries are unable to compete for new industries. Usually they lack the other essential requirements of modern industrial enterprises: capital, entrepreneurial skills, an infrastructure of public utilities and transport and communications, and a variety of supporting industries and business services. Much of Latin America, Africa, and South Asia confronts this dilemma. Although plagued by chronic unemployment and underemployment, these countries are able to attract only plantation agriculture and other extractive industries, along with all the problems these entail.

In addition to labor quantity, differences in labor quality affect trade. The quality of labor is usually expressed in terms of its *productivity,* which measures the relative value of output by a unit of labor. Several studies have attempted to assess the effects of labor productivity upon trade. MacDougall (1951) tested the notion that the productivity difference between two countries in the manufacture of a given commodity should be reflected in the difference in its production cost and thus in its selling price. Countries should therefore export most successfully those goods in which their labor productivity is highest relative to other countries. A comparison of exports from the United Kingdom and the United States disclosed a direct linear relationship on a log-log scale between the productivity ratios of the two countries and their ex-

port ratios for a number of goods. British exports were relatively greater than American exports in those goods, such as textiles and clothing, where the productivity of British workers most closely approached that of American labor. Where the unit output of American labor greatly exceeded that of the British, as in the case of machinery and motor cars, American exports were relatively greater.

The productivity of a country's labor force stems from a number of influences relating to level of development, culture and tradition, and governmental policy. Affecting labor skills, for instance, is the quality of a country's educational and technical training facilities, which in turn are associated with level of development. Work habits and attitudes toward work, on the other hand, derive from a society's culture and tradition. Less-developed countries lacking an industrial tradition may require generations to acquire the skills and habits required by modern manufacturing enterprises. Folk societies, such as those found in much of equatorial Africa, often have cultural attitudes, incentives, and value systems wholly unsuited to assembly-line work. The monetary rewards for such work have had no place in their tribal past.

At the other extreme are certain Oriental cultures, where long traditions of hard work and of devotion to group achievement yield exceptionally high levels of labor productivity. The resulting cost benefits provide valuable competitive advantages for Korea, Japan, and Taiwan in modern world commerce. Some European countries excel in the manufacture and export of labor-intensive specialties that draw upon traditional labor skills or reflect specific characteristics of national cultures. Goods of this type are Swiss watches, Belgian cut diamonds, Parisian garments, and Sheffield cutlery.

The availability of complementary factors of production is essential for labor productivity. Capital, in the form of labor-saving machinery, can multiply the output of a company's work force, as recent developments in automation and robotics have demonstrated. The productivity of a labor force depends upon the presence of managers having the skills to use their workers in the most efficient manner.

Differences in labor productivity among countries are constantly shifting in response to both long-term trends and short-term cyclical events. In some part, these result from governmental policy measures, as, for instance, public programs for educating and training the work force or special inducements to foreign investors for supply technology and managerial skills. International differences in labor costs are constantly changing as workers become unionized and as less-developed countries with lower-cost labor enter their products into foreign competition.

Governmental policies leading to high inflation can adversely affect labor productivity: An increased money supply raises demand, causing managers to expand their work forces by tapping less-productive labor pools of poorly trained workers. Labor productivity also changes with the different phases of the business cycle. It is lowest at the peak of the cycle, when managers are drawing upon all available workers, including many who are poorly qualified, and during the early stages of recession, when managers are reluctant to discharge their underutilized workers until they are sure that the business downturn will continue. Productivity is highest at the trough of the recession, when only the most skilled workers are kept on the job, and in the early stages of recovery, when managers resist hiring new workers until they are certain that better times are truly on the way.

Constantly shifting international monetary rates effectively create labor-cost differences among countries. During the late 1970s the U.S. dollar declined against other major currencies, thereby reducing American labor costs in relation to those of European competitors. Then, in the early 1980s, the exchange rate of the dollar soared against other currencies, eventually becoming so overvalued that U.S. exporters were at a severe competitive disadvantage.

Enterprise as a Factor.

Although theoreticians in the past have generally neglected *entrepreneurship* as a major influence on international trade, this factor is deservedly gaining attention. As we have seen, the availability of skilled management is essential for the efficient use of the other factors of production, and the lack of this ingredient is one of the basic problems of many less-developed countries. It has become increasingly apparent, however, that the quality of management also has much to do with the competitive strength of industrial countries in the international marketplace. In addition to being able to achieve efficient production, managers must have the vision to assess foreign markets accurately and to develop those lines of production that anticipate global needs. During the Industrial Revolution, British entrepreneurs were able to foresee, and in some cases to create, world demand for textiles, iron and steel, and machinery. Growing complacent in later times, however, British management clung to declining industries and obsolescent technology, thereby contributing to Britain's present diminished position in world commerce.

Some observers insist that a similar decline has occurred in the quality of U.S. management since the 1960s. They point to the shrinking market for American exports and the growing invasion of foreign-made goods in the United States as evidence that the quality of industrial leadership in this country has deteriorated. In response, many U.S. companies have begun to copy Japanese management style, which is perceived as one of the major reasons for Japan's startling success in marketing its products abroad.

Capital as a Factor.

The other factor of production, *capital,* is of three principal types. *Financial capital* is the more intangible, fluid form available for investment in any undertaking. More tangible types are *real capital,* consisting of equipment, buildings, and other concrete instruments of production, and *social capital,* which includes educational facilities, transport and communications, and other forms of support for productive activities. Capital is sometimes difficult to treat as a separate factor because it becomes tied up with the other factors, such as improving land, educating managers, or training workers. Nevertheless, capital is clearly a powerful determinant of trade, and a country with an abundance of capital can be expected to have a comparative advantage in the export of capital-intensive merchandise.

The United States is often cited as a capital-rich country, evidenced by foreign sales of such capital-intensive goods as chemicals. The chemical industry has a high capital-labor ratio because it must invest heavily in complex plants and equipment and make large outlays for research and development but employs relatively few workers, most of them highly skilled. Yet the United States also exports large quantities of primary goods such as wheat, corn, soybeans, and cottonseed products, which are not usually regarded as capital-intensive commodities. However, capital is almost invariably a complement to other factors, and U.S. agriculture is especially capital-intensive. So successful has been this agricultural use of capital—in the form of machinery, pesticides, herbicides, and chemical fertilizers—that American farmers, who constitute less than 3 percent of the labor force, are able to support a domestic population of 250 million people and at the same time sell huge quantities of farm produce in the international market.

Capital substitution for other factors of production has been increasing throughout the world. European agriculture has closely followed the American lead in recent decades, and Japanese farmers have mechanized their small acreages. Parallel trends have simultaneously occurred in other economic sectors. Most striking of all has been the revolutionary change in Japanese manufacturing, which during the postwar years has turned to the production of capital-intensive merchandise such as cameras, machinery, electronics, and automobiles after more than half a century of specialization in labor-intensive commodities.

Financial capital is the most mobile of factors, and recent years have seen a growing trend for the substitution of capital flows for trade flows. More and more companies are building factories in foreign lands to which they formerly exported their production. Foreign direct investment of this type has been shown to have a reciprocal relationship with trade. For the source country the initial effect of foreign direct investment is to produce a drain of capital and to reduce exports. At first this also diminishes the investing company's need for domestic labor, a major concern for labor unions. But evidence shows that the ultimate effect of foreign direct investment is generally positive for the source country and its workers (see Chapter 13). Because of their shipments of components and subassemblies to their foreign manufacturing operations, and because of the overall growth in their production and sales, multinational enterprises are a country's most active exporters and among its most dynamic employers. Furthermore, in time the returned profits and other earnings from foreign operations usually more than compensate for the outflow of capital at the time of the initial investment.

Firms have a number of inducements for investing in foreign undertakings. Often the decision results from the discovery that their exports to a particular foreign market have reached a level that would successfully support local manufacturing in that area. Locating their productive facilities abroad is particularly attractive for those companies making products that tend to be market-oriented.

A second reason for sending capital abroad in the place of merchandise is to take advantage of complementary factors of production in other countries. Agricultural enterprises may invest abroad in order to gain the use of land having specific qualities, as in the case of tropical plantation agriculture; and mining companies may enter into foreign operations to avail themselves of newly discovered ore deposits in other lands. Likewise, manufacturers of labor-intensive goods may establish factories in countries having plentiful supplies of cheap labor. Evidence of this is the growing number of American-owned plants assembling radios, televisions, and auto parts on the Mexican side of the United States–Mexican border.

In many instances manufacturers are forced to invest in foreign manufacturing facilities when the governments of countries to which they had previously exported erect trade barriers to their goods (see page 355). To forego such investment would mean the permanent loss of those markets to competitors willing to make the commitments.

Contributing to the accelerating international flows of investment funds in recent years has been the growth of various institutional aids to capital movement. Prominent among these has been the multinational enterprise, which can generate large financial resources internally within the company, can borrow freely in many lands and in many currencies, and can draw upon widespread corporate information-gathering facilities. Another institutional aid is the international bank, which maintains outlets in many countries, all having access to a common pool of financial resources, and which draws upon a growing battery of techniques and instruments to serve its multinational customers throughout the world.

Governments have grown increasingly inventive and aggressive in luring foreign investment as a means for generating domestic jobs, for reducing dependence upon imports, and for increasing export earnings. Governmental incentives to corporate investors include low-cost loans and subsidies for factory construction and labor training, tax relief, and a variety of other guarantees and offers of assistance. At the same time, governments may place restrictions on capital flows, as we shall see in the section dealing with political interference (page 358).

This discussion of supply factors has disclosed one of the weaknesses of the Heckscher-Ohlin theory, namely, the assumption that a particular type of production has the same factor intensities everywhere. We have seen that capital, labor, and land are used in widely varying proportions in different parts of the world, depending upon the characteristics of those factors in each area. Another weakness of the theory is its excessive emphasis upon production. Supply conditions represent only one side of the equation; demand considerations are likewise powerful determinants of trade.

Effects of Demand Conditions

One of the main benefits ascribed to trade is that it permits a region or country to maintain a consumption pattern that differs from its production pattern. Production possibilities differ from place to place, depending upon resource endowments; but the nature of consumption also varies widely, reflecting spatial differences among human populations. One of the prime reasons for the existence of trade is the fact that the structure of demand in any one place rarely seems to coincide with production in that location.

Even so, spatial differences in production are not absolutely essential for trade to occur. Trade can arise between two regions with identical production possibilities if they have unlike structures of demand. Take the case of two countries, A and B, both of which are able to grow potatoes and corn equally well. Most of the people in country A prefer potatoes to corn, however, and those in country B like corn better than potatoes. With the opening of trade between the two, each country can produce either or both crops and exchange its unwanted surplus with the other country for the preferred commodity. Such spatial variations in demand are common despite evidence that basic human needs are essentially the same. What are the reasons for these differences in demand?

Income. Undoubtedly the most compelling influence upon a country's effective demand is its per capita income. Although rising incomes cause purchasing power to increase, however, this additional demand does not extend equally to all commodities. One reason that growing incomes create a stronger demand for some goods than others is expressed by *Engel's law,* which states that poor families (or poor countries) spend larger proportions of their incomes on food than do rich ones. An impoverished population may be able to afford only the barest necessities, and some parts of the world today are hardly capable even of this. Although a rise in income may at first cause such a people to increase their expenditures for food and other necessities, beyond some minimum level of satisfaction they will allocate further income increasingly to other kinds of goods, including nonessentials and even luxury items. Because the latter are likely to be mainly manufactured goods—for which demand seems virtually unlimited—sellers of industrial products gain a rising share of the increase. Even agricultural products benefit unequally from an enlarged purchasing power. Poor people consume mainly starchy foods, but as their incomes grow they will substitute ever greater amounts of meats, green vegetables, and dairy products for the starches (see Chapter 5). This variation in demand for different commodities at different income levels is called the *income elasticity of demand.*

In an attempt to measure variations in elasticity of demand, Houthakker (1957) found that elasticities of particular categories of goods were roughly similar from one country to the next. He observed some international variations, however, particularly for foods. Although the income elasticity of demand for food was low everywhere, it ranged from only 0.3 in some countries to as much as 0.7 in others. This low elasticity of demand means that a unit rise in income would not strengthen the demand for food by a corresponding amount. Thus, if family incomes in a country had been averaging $30 per week and $15 of this had been spent on food, a gain of $10 in average incomes would have caused food expenditures to rise by $5 if the population were to increase food purchases proportionately. With an income elasticity of demand for food of 0.3, however, the average food budget would go up by only $1.50. The study found that housing had an income elasticity of demand of nearly 1.0, meaning that expenditures for housing would grow at a rate approximating the expansion in income. Expenditures for clothing and certain other items would actually advance at rates exceeding that of income. Despite minor variations in income elasticities of demand for particular goods among countries, the study found that such variations within countries were slight.

Because commodities differ in their income elasticities, countries at different levels of per capita income have very dissimilar consumption patterns. The reason for this is that, as countries have gained in prosperity, they have stepped up their purchases of some goods more rapidly than others, thereby altering patterns of consumption. Trade flows among countries mirror these differences. Goods exchanged by North America with Western Europe are very unlike those shipped between Europe and West Africa or Southeast Asia. Differences in consumption patterns are responsible for a major part of this contrast in trade flows.

Among the wealthier countries disparities in demand patterns tend to narrow as time passes. Rising prosperity in Western Europe and Japan in recent decades has caused lifestyles among those populations to draw closer to those of North America. Linder (1961) has cited this similarity in demand structures among high-income countries as a principal reason that the manufactured goods of rich countries find their best markets in other rich countries.

Cultural Differences. International variations in cultural traits are responsible for some of the differences among countries in their demand structures. Indeed, the surprising range of income elasticities of demand for food and beverages can be attributed to religious taboos and to national attitudes and preferences. For instance, several predominantly Catholic countries, such as Portugal, Spain, and Italy, import fish to add to their own sizable domestic production of this food; prohibitions of Hinduism limit India's consumption and importation of beef, and Moslem and Jewish restrictions on the eating of pork adversely affect sales of that meat to the Middle East. The unusually large imports of tea by the United Kingdom and of coffee by the United States illustrate the substantial effects of consumption habits upon trade. Although the countries of Western Europe enjoy similarly high standards of living, the proportion of family income devoted to purchases of food and drink differs considerably from one country to the next. Topping the list are France and Denmark, whose national cultures accord a special place to their cuisines.

Domestic Consumption and Exports. The nature of a country's demand may affect not only its imports but also its exports. Although exports of primary commodities depend upon a country's resource endowments, its success in exporting manufactured goods benefits importantly from prior production of those items for the domestic market. Indeed, entrepreneurs are unlikely even to be aware of foreign opportunities for the sale of a given product if the home market does not have an active demand for it. Equally essential, thriving domestic sales permit the industry to develop economies of scale sufficient to reduce unit costs to a level that is competitive in the international market. Before World War II, Japan's large home consumption of mass-produced, low-cost textiles provided the necessary base from which to launch a successful export business in these goods. More recently, Japan's mounting prosperity has created a lively home market for automobiles and other consumer durables, thereby contributing to that country's flourishing foreign sales of such products.

Inadequacies of Modern Trade Theory

Thus, conditions of production and consumption interact to promote trade among countries. But is this the whole story? Does modern theory, which is based upon the Heckscher-Ohlin model, provide a satisfactory explanation of trade? This theory ascribes comparative advantage to differences in resource endowments, stating that a country will export goods that intensively use its relatively abundant factors of production and will import goods that intensively use its relatively scarce factors. The previous discussion, however, has implied a number of needed modifications in this proposition. How well would the theory hold up in tests using actual data?

Empirical Tests: The Leontief Paradox.   The best-known attempt to answer this question was that of Wassily Leontief (1953, 1968), who set out to test the hypothesis that U.S. trade reflects its resource endowments. The theoretical expectation was that the country's exports would be capital-intensive and that its imports would be labor-intensive. This was predicated on the widely held notion that, relative to most of the world, the United States is rich in capital and is less well supplied with labor. Leontief based his calculations upon U.S. input-output tables for 200 industries and U.S. trade for 1947. His method was to compare capital/labor ratios in U.S. export industries with those of the country's import-competing industries (U.S. industries making the same goods as those comprising the main imports).

Leontief's findings, published in 1953, were wholly unexpected: The capital/labor ratio in U.S. export industries was actually lower than in import-competing industries. This indicated that the country's exports were more labor-intensive than its imports, a

paradoxical result for an economy that was supposedly well endowed with capital. Leontief's figures showed that U.S. import replacements actually required 30 percent more capital per worker-year to produce than did its exports.

In a follow-up study published in 1956, Leontief confirmed his earlier results with an analysis of the same industries using 1951 trade figures. Subsequently, Baldwin achieved similar results using U.S. input-output data for 1958 applied to 1962 trade, and in 1979 he released equally paradoxical findings for 30 other countries.

Explanations for the Puzzle.   The flurry of works that followed Leontif's disclosure agreed on one point: His study had uncovered basic flaws in the Heckscher-Ohlin theorem. Chief among these weaknesses was the assumption that the relative factor intensity of a good is the same everywhere and that this relationship is unchanging. That factor intensities do indeed change over space and time is clear from the numerous studies since undertaken to find explanations for the Leontief paradox. The evidence shows that the costs of factors (land, labor, and capital) vary widely from country to country: Because they differ relatively in quantity and quality they are used differently. The same goods produced abroad by labor-intensive methods are likely to be produced in the United States by capital-intensive methods. As we noted earlier, American farmers emphasize the use of machinery and agricultural chemicals to grow rice and wheat, whereas Oriental farmers rely mainly upon hand labor to produce these commodities. Influencing the allocation of factors in U.S. agriculture are the high cost of labor, the relative abundance of capital, and the availability of technology.

A further explanation for the paradox is that, by concentrating upon capital and labor, Leontief neglected the substantial place of land in both U.S. exports and imports. America produces an abundance of some land-intensive commodities but is severely short in others. Large export earnings from temperate grains and subtropical fruits and vegetables are made possible by the nation's great agricultural land area and its varied growing conditions, aided by the high productivity of its farm labor. On the other hand, the United States has inadequate supplies of many vital land-intensive commodities: metallic minerals such as bauxite, iron ore, and nonferrous metals, as well as oil and natural gas (see chapter 5). These fuels and industrial raw materials are extracted overseas by capital-intensive methods, often by U.S. multinational enterprises using American capital and relying upon familiar U.S. technology.

Some writers have pointed to the nature of

American labor as one reason for Leontief's results. As we saw earlier, labor is not the homogeneous factor of production assumed by Heckscher-Ohlin; to the contrary, international variations in labor skills significantly affect trade. Indeed, Leontief's own explanation for the paradox was that superior skills multiply the effectiveness of U.S. workers and that labor productivity is enhanced by the nature of U.S. entrepreneurship and industrial organization and by education. Some observers argue that the education and training of labor essentially represent the creation of labor skills through the application of capital. Studies have confirmed that U.S. export industries employ more skilled workers than do the country's import-competing industries. Hence, the country has a comparative advantage in those manufactured goods requiring human skills. These tend to be high-technology products, which call for much capital investment in research and development.

This suggests still another explanation for Leontief's paradox: U.S. exports contain a high proportion of new products. These goods are in the beginning stages of the product life cycle, when research and development are paramount. On the other hand, the country has long imported standardized goods that are late in the product life cycle, when labor-skill requirements are low. Also implied in the product-life-cycle explanation is the notion that factor proportions change with the maturing of the technology for making a good.

Further complicating the role of factor endowments is the fact that much U.S. foreign commerce is intra-industry trade, as is true of industrialized countries generally. Two-thirds of the trade of developed countries goes to other developed countries, and most of it represents exchanges of manufactured goods for other manufactured goods. The major part of this is intra-industry trade, that is, cross-shipments of products from the same industrial category. Within product types, companies will seek out particular niches not served by others. By concentrating upon these specialties, they gain cost advantages through economies of scale and are thus able to compete favorably in foreign markets. Companies differentiate their goods from those of their competitors by means of brand names. Much of the cross-hauling of similar commodities among countries consists of such branded items, automobiles, for example. In short, the growing place of multinational enterprises in world commerce has given new meaning to the concept of comparative advantage.

Finally, the notion that international trade is merely a function of relative resource endowments must be modified by the existence of barriers to commodity flows among countries, notably the effects of transport costs and governmental interference. For instance, the evidence shows that U.S. barriers to the import of labor-intensive goods, erected to "save American jobs," significantly reduce the influx of such items. The effect is sufficient to have influenced Leontief's finding that U.S. imports are less labor-intensive than U.S. exports. Japanese restrictions on the import of capital-intensive commodities from the United States no doubt have further strengthened this effect.

The empirical evidence clearly raises serious doubts that factor endowments are a sufficient explanation for trade. Many other elements that influence trade have been excluded by the initial simplifying assumptions of the theory. The work stimulated by Leontief's paradoxical findings has uncovered a number of additional considerations, and these will be our main concern in the pages that follow. The remainder of this chapter will focus upon the effects of trade barriers, and the next chapter will consider the influence of growth and change, with special attention to the role of technology and development, of organizational arrangements, and of the multinational enterprise, which has become a prime actor in world commerce.

BARRIERS TO TRADE

In looking to differences in production possibilities for an explanation of trade, conventional theory has given little attention to the obstacles that can intervene to alter the volume, direction, and composition of commodity flows. These are of two types: *distance* and *political interference*.

Distance

Distance acts as a barrier to trade in a variety of ways, some of them subtle. The most obvious effect of distance is the burden of transport cost it imposes upon every shipment of goods between two countries. This cost does not necessarily correspond closely with the number of miles to be covered, for some routes are cheaper to travel than others. Mountainous terrain can add many miles to the apparent distance between two points, and steep grades can multiply fuel costs. Irregular coastlines prevent vessels from taking the most direct routes between ports. Hence, transport routes are often more circuitous and difficult than they might appear, resulting in extra costs to move goods over them.

The expense of transporting commodities is not limited merely to the cost of operating a motor vehicle, aircraft, or steamship. In addition, shipments to foreign destinations incur bank collection charges, freight forwarders' and customs house brokers' fees, consular charges, and cartage expenses, and they entail extra clerical costs for preparing bills of lading, customs declarations, and a variety of other lengthy shipping documents. Adding these *terminal costs* to the expense of actually moving the merchandise gives a total outlay usually called *transfer costs*. Considering all of these elements, some of which are incurred regardless of the length of haul, transfer cost is a more reliable measure of the "economic distance" between two points than is transport cost alone.

Introducing transfer costs into the conventional two-country, two-commodity model considerably alters the outcome. Instead of trade causing prices between two countries to become equalized as suggested earlier by Figure 12.2, they will always differ by the amount of the cost of transporting the merchandise. Transfer costs make goods more expensive to importers and less valuable to exporters.

Figure 12.5 illustrates this effect with a simple case involving two countries and a single product and taking into account only transport cost and production cost. The diagram shows hypothetical demand and supply curves for paper in both the United States and Canada. The demand curves, *D*, slope downward to the right, indicating that consumers in each country will take larger quantities of paper if the price drops. The supply curves, *S*, slope upward to the right because producers are able and willing to make more paper if the price goes up. Figure 12.5 shows that, in

the absence of trade, the price of paper would be lower in Canada than in the United States, reflecting Canada's comparative advantage in forest products. This difference is evident from the points where the supply and demand curves cross in each case—*p* for Canada and *w* for the United States.

Figure 12.5 shows the results of trade, first in the absence of transport cost and then with the addition of transport cost. Table 12.4 summarizes these effects. Without transport cost the price after trade in both countries—that is, the international terms of trade—becomes $49 per ton of paper, as shown by the horizontal line extending from *t* to *z* in Figure 12.5. At this price Canada produces 6.6 million tons of paper (indicated by the distance *tv*), consumes 3.1 million tons (*tu*), and exports the remaining 3.5 million tons (*uv*) to the United States. Under these conditions the United States consumes 5.1 million tons (*xz*) of paper, of which 3.5 million tons (*yz*) are imported from Canada. U.S. producers are then able to supply the other 1.6 million tons (*xy*) that the country needs.

If, however, we introduce a transport cost of $10 per ton, this causes the price of paper to rise to $54 in the United States and fall to $44 in Canada (Table 12.4). At the $54 price the United States is no longer willing to use as much paper, and consumption then drops to only 4.5 million tons (*x'z'* in Figure 12.5). Nevertheless, the higher price induces domestic producers of paper to supply a larger quantity, 2.4 million tons (*x'y'*), and U.S. imports consequently drop to

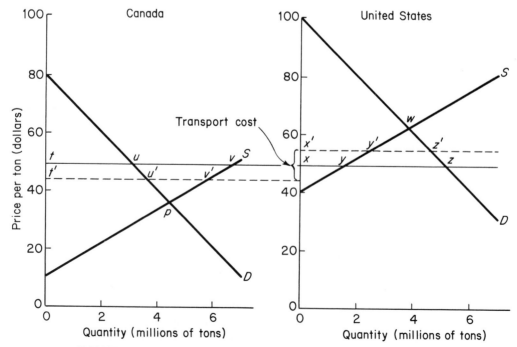

FIGURE 12.5   Price of paper in Canada and the United States and quantities traded and consumed, with and without transport costs.

TABLE 12.4

Effects of transport cost on exports of paper by Canada to the United States

	Without Transport Cost		With Transport Cost	
	Canada	United States	Canada	United States
Price per ton (in dollars)	$49	$49	$44	$54
Quantity produced[a]	6.6	1.6	5.8	2.4
Quantity exported[a]	3.5	—	2.2	—
Quantity imported[a]	—	3.5	—	2.2
Quantity consumed[a]	3.1	5.1	3.6	4.6

[a] All quantities in millions of tons.

only 2.2 million tons ($y'z'$). At the reduced Canadian price of $44 per ton, producers in that country will supply only 5.8 million tons ($t'v'$), but Canadian consumers will take a larger quantity, 3.6 million tons ($t'u'$). But the extra home consumption makes up for only a part of the lost exports to the United States, which now amount to only 2.2 million tons ($u'v'$). Note that the impact of transport cost falls with equal weight upon importing and exporting countries.

One lesson offered by this case is that transport cost does in fact decrease international specialization. The United States produces more of its own paper and buys less abroad, whereas Canadian mills must reduce total output even though the new low domestic price enables them to sell somewhat more at home. Indeed, if transport cost had exceeded the pretrade price differential, which in Figure 12.5 ranges between a low of p for Canada and a high of w for the United States, trade would not have occurred at all. Throughout the world much localized production owes its existence to the sheltering effects of a high transfer cost barrier to trade with other regions that have lower production costs. Herein lies one of the chief links between trade theory and location theory.

Transfer cost does not affect all merchandise alike, however, for some classes of goods are more cheaply and easily transported than others. Their transportability depends upon their perishability, ease of handling, and value in relation to bulk or weight. Most manufactured goods have a high degree of transportability owing to the low cost of shipment relative to value, which has been estimated at about 2 percent on the average. Such products therefore move freely over long distances throughout the world. Some primary goods are also widely traded, for instance, petroleum, which is valuable, easily handled, and cheaply transported. Likewise traveling long distances are cheese, butter, commercial fibers, and other agricultural commodities whose bulk and perishability have been reduced in processing. Grains have long been

staples of world commerce because they are nonperishable and are easily handled by bulk cargo methods.

At the other extreme are several types of goods that are so costly to ship that have traditionally entered foreign commerce much less. These include perishable foodstuffs such as fluid milk and fresh produce, and cheap, bulky building materials such as common dimension stone, sand and gravel, and bricks. Commodities of this type are often referred to as *domestic goods*.

Distance influences trade in many ways other than transport cost alone. Though often subtle, the noncost effects of distance can be substantial in some instances. Commercial relations between two neighboring countries tend to be simpler and easier than between remoter ones, if only because business people have a greater awareness of sales opportunities nearer at hand. Reinforcing the advantages of closeness are the effects of mass communication and frequent travel between two neighboring populations, as well as the personal acquaintances that arise. Constant contact between peoples usually leads to a greater familiarity with differing tastes, customs, languages, business methods, and legal systems.

Although previously neglected by trade theorists, distance has been gaining increased attention in recent studies. One example is W. Beckerman's pioneering study of the influence of distance upon Western Europe's trade. Using transport cost as a substitute for actual mileage, Beckerman compared two separate rankings of the same countries: (1) a ranking by the average amount of transport cost separating them, and (2) a ranking by value of trade with each other (adjusted for size of country). The correlation between these two rankings proved very close and tended to confirm the effectiveness of transport cost as an influence upon trade patterns in that region.

Thus, the element of distance adds a distinct new dimension to the Heckscher-Ohlin theory. It modifies the effects of a country's resource endowments by enhancing the attractions of neighboring lands and raising obstacles to commerce with remoter areas, although the force of its impact is greater for some classes of merchandise than others. It constitutes a potent advantage for a country, such as Germany, that is centrally located with respect to rich markets for its exports: Competitors in more distant locations would have to produce much more cheaply in order to invade those markets.

Distance is a dynamic influence in international trade. As we shall see in Chapter 13, technology is constantly working to reduce transportation costs. The long-term trend in those costs has therefore been downward, effectively reducing the economic distance between countries and extending the shipping range of internationally traded goods. Simultaneously, communications technology has been advancing with equal rapidity and it is steadily diminishing the noncost barriers of distance. Meanwhile, other kinds of costs are constantly affecting transportation, particularly the cost of energy: Rising and falling prices of petroleum greatly complicate the impact of distance upon world commerce. To a growing extent, these fluctuations reflect the intervention of political forces.

Political Interference

Under international law every country has exclusive jurisdiction over its territory. Governments exercise this *national sovereignty* through their police powers and taxing authority over all resident individuals and business organizations, by the physical and administrative control of their borders, and in their position as the sole legal representatives of their citizens in all relations with other national governments. These powers of the state often raise severe barriers to the movement of goods, services, and factors of production. The actions of national governments thus tend to distort the basic theoretical pattern of world commerce.

Incentives for Intervention. Why do governments interfere in foreign commerce? One reason is nationalism, an emotional attachment to the state that binds the people of a country together in the pursuit of common goals. Responding to such sentiments, a government usually acts in what is perceived to be the self-interest of its citizens. This includes the pursuit of economic policies that promote national economic growth and development so as to increase employment and raise per capita income. An essential element in this is the country's foreign economic policy, which relates to its trade, foreign investment, and external economic relations generally. Governments com-

monly intervene in market operations to further national goals that the market would supposedly fail to achieve otherwise. In particular, they engage in various actions affecting the movement of goods, services, and factors across their borders.

The ultimate in state intervention was practiced by the now-defunct Communist governments, which exercised total control over their national economies, including foreign trade, which was conducted exclusively by state enterprises under the direction of central planning agencies. Even more than elsewhere, commercial policies of Communist governments reflected not only economic considerations but also political goals tied to overall foreign policies.

Because of the importance of foreign commerce to national well-being, governments maintain a constant watch over their economic relations with the rest of the world. The usual statistical measure of this performance is the *balance of payments*. This is the sum of all economic transactions between the residents—individuals and corporations—of one country and the residents of other countries within a given time span (usually a year). These transactions include exports and imports of goods and services, gifts and other one-way transfers, investments, flows of monetary gold, and payments by central banks. The balance of payments is calculated by means of a double-entry accounting system that sets debits against credits. As in mercantilist times, when the goal was to maximize credits over debits, it is common even today to refer to a positive figure as a "favorable" balance of payments.

The most obvious contributor to the balance of payments is a country's merchandise exports, often called the *visible* trade. The difference between the total value of exports and imports of goods within a given year is the *balance of trade*. Also included in the balance of payments are the exports and imports of services—the *invisible* trade. These include transport services that residents sell to or purchase from foreigners; tourist services, which are the expenditures made by residents of one country while traveling in another country; financial services, including international banking and insurance activities; investment services that involve international transfers of interest, dividends, and profits; and technological services, represented by international payments of royalties and fees. The trade in services, currently accounting for about one-quarter of total world commerce, is the most rapidly growing part of the total and is particularly vital to certain countries. For instance, financial services are important foreign exchange earners for the United Kingdom and Switzerland; tourism is essential to the economies of Mexico, Italy, Spain, the United Kingdom, France, Switzerland, Israel, and

Egypt; and services of all kinds constitute the largest category of foreign exports by New York City.

Some countries gain much of their foreign exchange from gifts and other one-way transactions. Among such transfers are the contributions of private charities and monies sent by expatriate workers to their families back home. Both Egypt and Mexico gain substantial amounts of exchange from the repatriated earnings of their nationals working abroad. One-way governmental transfers include foreign aid, pension payments, and taxation of foreigners. Also contributing to the balance of payments are long-term capital flows. Chief among these are foreign direct investment—for example, establishing branch plants abroad—and portfolio investment—making loans to or purchasing stock in foreign enterprises. Both types of capital flows are vital to the Canadian economy, for example. A residual element in the balance of payments is the transactions between central banks, which exchange monetary gold and foreign currencies in order to balance national accounts.

Political interference in foreign commerce may have either positive or negative effects, depending upon whether it tends to create, diminish, or rechannel trade. Governments often promote their exports by sponsoring fairs and exhibits or offering subsidies, loan guarantees, tax rebates, or other financial incentives to exporters. They also enter into special trade agreements with other countries to increase sales. Most countries maintain commercial attachés in their foreign embassies in part to assist their exporters in doing business in those lands. Indeed, a study by Bruce Russett found a direct relationship between the size of diplomatic staffs and the amount of trade among countries.

Tariffs. On the other hand, a variety of restrictive measures exists for controlling the volume, composition, or direction of trade. Most governments are under constant political pressure from special-interest groups to intervene in their foreign commerce. One technique favored since early times is the *tariff,* which is a tax or duty imposed upon a particular category of merchandise entering or leaving a country. A tariff may be either an *ad valorem* duty—that is, a given percentage of the value of a good (for example, 15 percent of the invoice amount)—or a *specific* duty—a particular amount of money for a given quantity of the good (for example, $1.50 per ton). Ad valorem and specific duties may also be used in combination. Although *import tariffs* are more widespread than *export tariffs,* the latter are common among those countries specializing in the sale of primary commodities.

The two main reasons for levying tariffs are to earn *revenue* and to *protect* domestic producers from foreign competition. Governments of developing countries ordinarily rely upon tariff revenue for much of their financial support; income from import tariffs was the chief source of revenue for the United States government during its earlier years. Most countries use protective tariffs to shield their home industries against foreign producers. A common justification for such tariffs is the "infant industry" argument, which holds that newly established industries must receive this kind of special protection from foreign competitors during their early years when unit costs are still higher than those of established operations elsewhere. This argument implies that tariff protection will be lifted when the new industries reach levels of efficiency that will permit their products to compete on equal terms with imported goods. Manufacturing operations formed under such conditions are sometimes called "tariff factories." Canadian production of chemicals and household appliances began with governmental aid of this type, as did the fabricated-metal trades of Mexico and Brazil. Under pressure from industry and labor groups, governments may impose protective tariffs to save declining industries that have lost their competitiveness in world markets. In recent years, American manufacturers of textiles, clothing, and steel have agitated with increasing success for such governmental help against lower-cost foreign competitors.

Regardless of its initial purpose, a tariff ultimately produces a variety of effects, as the following example illustrates. Figure 12.6 and Table 12.5 give the case of a hypothetical tariff imposed upon United States imports of shoes from Italy (assuming that the two countries trade only with each other and in isolation from the rest of the world). Note that the changes in supply and demand resulting from the tariff are similar to those produced by transport cost as seen previously in Figure 12.5. In the absence of trade, the Italian price for a pair of shoes would have been $6.80 (shown in Figure 12.6 by the intersection of Italy's supply and demand curves at *x*), whereas the American price would have been $13.30 (given by the intersection at *y* in Figure 12.6). With trade, however, the price in both countries settles at $10 (*Oj*). At this price the United States will consume 13 million pairs of shoes (*dh*), 5 million of which are imported from Italy (*eh*).

The introduction of a tariff of $2 per pair (equal to *ia* in Figure 12.6) causes the Italian price to fall to $9 (given by *Or*) and the United States price to rise to $11 (*Oa*). Italian production thereupon drops by 1 million pairs to only 8 million and exports to the United States decline to 3.4 million pairs (Table 12.5). At the new higher price, consumers in the United States will buy only 12.4 million pairs, 9 million of which are now

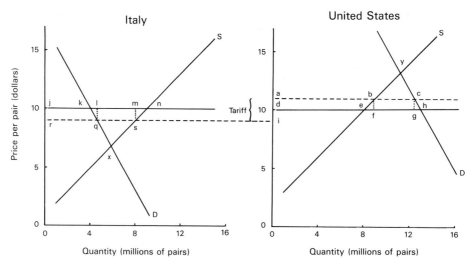

FIGURE 12.6 Effects of tariff on United States imports of shoes from Italy.

produced at home. On those shoes still imported from Italy the United States government receives tariff revenue amounting to $6.8 million ($2 times 3.4 million pairs, or *ia* times *bc* in Figure 12.6). This is equivalent to the combined areas *bcgf* and *lmsq* in Figure 12.6. Meanwhile, domestic producers (Table 12.5) enjoy an additional $19 million in receipts (on sales of 9 million pairs at $11 instead of 8 million at the earlier price of $10). Note, however, that this benefit to United States producers comes not only at the expense of foreign producers but also of domestic consumers, who now get only 12.4 million pairs of shoes for $136.4 million where they used to get 13 million pairs for $130 million. The imposition of a tariff in this case has had a *protection effect,* a *consumption effect,* and an *income-redistribution effect.* If the amount of the tariff had been set at $6.50 (equivalent to the vertical distance between *x* and *y* in Figure 12.6) or greater, the price differential between the two countries would have disappeared and the shoe trade would have

ceased altogether. Only the American manufacturers and their workers would have gained from this arrangement; the government would have received nothing.

Under the conditions shown in Figure 12.6 however, both the domestic shoe mills and the government gain income from the relatively modest tariff of $2. Although American buyers of shoes incur some additional cost, the main losers are the Italians, who are able to sell fewer pairs and get a lower price for them. This is the basis for the common observation that a tariff is a way of taxing the foreigner.

Nevertheless, a unilateral action of this kind risks retaliation from the injured party. Let us assume in the above case that Italy has been a prime customer for American farm products. If, in retribution for the United States tariff on Italian shoes, the government of Italy were to place a tariff on the import of American wheat, the effects upon the U.S.–Italian wheat trade would be like those shown for the Italian–Ameri-

TABLE 12.5

Effects of United States tariff on shoes imported from Italy

	Before Tariff		After Tariff	
	Italy	United States	Italy	United States
Price per pair (in dollars)	$10	$10	$9	$11
Quantity produced[a]	9.0	8.0	8.0	9.0
Quantity exported[a]	5.0	—	3.4	—
Quantity imported[a]	—	5.0	—	3.4
Quantity consumed[a]	4.0	13.0	4.6	12.4
Tariff revenue (in millions of dollars)	—	—	—	$6.8
Additional revenue to producers (in millions of dollars)	—	—	—	$19.0

[a] All quantities in millions of pairs.

can shoe trade in Figure 12.6, only in reverse: Italy would buy less wheat from the United States, the price of American wheat would fall, less wheat would be produced, and American wheat farmers would be hurt. Thus, where retaliation is possible both countries are harmed by tariffs; total trade declines and production and consumption diminish. Lost are the benefits of international specialization of production and exchange.

Export tariffs, under a variety of labels, are a favored revenue-raising device among less-developed countries, especially those who produce minerals and fuels in strong demand on world markets. In addition, some countries use export duties on their raw materials as a way of inducing manufacturers to increase the amount of domestic processing of such goods. Not only does this raise the value of their exports but it also serves as a means for introducing industrial development. In this way Jamaica has acquired facilities for processing bauxite ore into alumina, and Venezuela has installed refineries for her oil. Excessive export duties, however, have cost some raw-material producers their world markets when customers abroad have found new sources of supply or have developed synthetic substitutes (see Chapter 13).

Always, the effects of tariffs, whether on imports or on exports, depend upon the nature of supply and demand for the good. For instance, if consumers have a particularly strong desire for an imported good, they may continue buying it regardless of the higher price resulting from a tariff.

Quotas. An even more drastic form of governmental intervention in trade is the *quota*. A quota is a specific limitation on the *quantity* of exports or (more usually) imports that a country will permit. This device is of more recent origin than the tariff, being largely a product of the world economic depression of the 1930s. Like tariffs, import quotas serve to aid domestic producers. Quotas are especially favored as a means of protection against foreign competition for farmers and for producers of standardized manufactured goods such as textiles. Governments tend to prefer quotas where the foreign supply of a product is very great and available at particularly low prices. Under such conditions tariffs would likely be unsuccessful in stemming the flood of imports. Administrators favor quotas especially because of their sudden, drastic, and certain results and also because they are easy to impose, remove, or adjust. They can cause more friction among importers and foreign suppliers, however, because they are more difficult than tariffs to administer fairly.

A country may impose import quotas unilaterally, that is, it may do so without prior consultation with foreign suppliers; or it may negotiate with supplying countries before setting import limitations. The United States has negotiated quotas (euphemistically called "orderly marketing agreements") with Japan on the import of motor vehicles and with the European Common Market countries on specialty steel products. As this suggests, quotas may be negotiated either bilaterally (with a single supplying country) or multilaterally (with a number of suppliers). Allocation to importers under a quota system often relies upon some kind of import licensing arrangement.

Figure 12.7 illustrates the possible outcome of a hypothetical quota on Japanese rayon imported into the United States. Let us say that each year the United States has been consuming 70 million yards of rayon (*OD* in Figure 12.7) at a price of $2.50 per yard (*OE*). Of this amount, 50 million yards (*AD*) have been imported. If the government yields to the demands of domestic manufacturers and imposes a quota limiting imports to 30 million yards (*BC*), this will cause the price in the United States to rise to $3.00 (*OJ*) and total rayon consumption in the country to fall to 60 million yards. But out of this total American mills will be able to sell an increased quantity—30 million yards (*JK*) instead of the former 20 million yards (*EF*)—at the new higher price. The revenue increase to domestic producers will be $40 million (area *JKBO* minus *EFAO*). Meanwhile, American consumers will have to pay a total of $180 million (*JLCO*) for less cloth than they formerly got for only $175 million (*EIDO*). Thus, the domestic mills gain at the expense of both domestic consumers and foreign suppliers. The effects are inflationary for the importing country (as shown by the United States' experience with quotas on auto imports from Japan), and at the same time they are conducive to monopoly control of production. Quotas of this type are exceedingly arbitrary, as they freeze the volume and direction of trade into some predetermined pattern. Note also that, unlike tariffs, quotas yield no revenue to the government unless a high fee is assessed for import licenses. Because of their inherent unfairness, quotas also lead to hard feelings and retaliation.

Export quotas have also been used extensively in recent years to prop up world prices of some primary commodities. Certain agricultural products and minerals have chronically suffered from recurrent problems of oversupply and price instability. In such cases exporting countries may impose quotas in an effort to reduce world supplies and thereby raise prices abroad. In the past Brazil has tried this means for limiting exports of rubber and coffee, and the United States has attempted similar controls on cotton exports.

Export restrictions of this type have usually not been very successful. Either substitutes would be

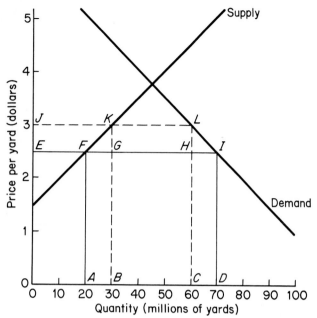

FIGURE 12.7 Effects of United States quota on imports of Japanese rayon.

found elsewhere for the country's products or new foreign sources of supply of the commodity would be developed. Thus, nitrates were synthesized to replace the overly priced Chilean natural product; plantation rubber in the South East Asia largely usurped the former markets for Brazilian rubber; Central American, Colombian, and West African growers increased their coffee output; and American price supports encouraged cotton production in Africa. Producers in different countries have attempted to cooperate in controlling foreign sales of their products, but commodity agreements of this type uniformly failed until the winter of 1973–1974, when members of the Organization of Petroleum Exporting Countries (OPEC) managed to agree on quantitative limits and prices for their oil exports.

Other Nontariff Measures. A device similar to the quota involves the use of *exchange controls:* A government buys all foreign currency brought into the country through the earnings of its exporters and then distributes these currencies to importers in a carefully regulated manner. The allocation of foreign exchange may be made through licensing schemes or auctions (as in Brazil). This is done in such a way as to control not only the volume of imports but also their composition, thereby conserving the country's money supply and assuring its most economic use. The allotments ordinarily discriminate against luxuries and favor necessities. Quota systems sometimes entail multiple exchange rates, with foreign currencies being sold to importers at higher prices for some purposes than others.

Exchange controls were common in post–World War II Europe, when shortages of foreign exchange were especially acute, and similar schemes continue in wide use today throughout Latin America.

In some parts of the world, governments go even further and participate actively in buying and selling abroad, a practice termed *state trading.* This was the standard procedure in Communist countries, but it also occurs in developing countries, and to some extent in advanced capitalistic countries. State monopolies in specific commodities such as alcoholic beverages, sugar, tobacco, cocoa, grains, and other agricultural products are fairly common. During times of war, bulk buying and selling by governments becomes necessary.

Intergovernmental relationships can alter trade patterns, as, for example, trade agreements granting special tariff concessions or generous quota allocations to favored trading partners. In general, their effects are to divert trade from the normal channels of a freely operating world market. Some of the more elaborate arrangements will be discussed in Chapter 13.

Nationalistic feelings, expressed through wars, hostile attitudes, or rivalries between populations, can influence trade. Despite the natural complementarities between the resource endowments of Israel and its Arab neighbors, their continued hostility discourages Arab-Israeli trade. Trade between Eastern and Western Europe was well developed before World War II but was much reduced when the Eastern countries became incorporated into the Communist bloc. Wars have often forced contending nations to industrialize; the War of 1812, for example, sparked early U.S. industrialization. Wars have had this kind of effect upon noncombatants, too, as in the case of Argentina, which began manufacturing many of its own needs when cut off by World War I from European sources of supply. An interruption of trade again occurred during World War II, spurring further industrialization by Argentina.

Many seemingly small governmental actions can interfere with foreign trade. Special labeling and packaging requirements may exclude goods from some markets if the cost of changing the usual practices of producers in the exporting country is excessive. Sanitary and safety regulations can have the same effect. Some European countries maintain exacting specifications for the ingredients of prepared foods; Canada requires labels in both French and English; Japan employs elaborate inspection procedures; and the United States specifies costly safety and pollution-control devices on motor vehicles. Official measures of this type may be enacted without conscious thought of their effects on imported commodities, but some are deliberately intended to exclude foreign competitors who

BOX 12.1   Spreading Protectionism: A Public Policy Problem

For the past decade or so the global community has been swept by an epidemic of protectionism reminiscent of the 1930s. In that earlier time the worldwide flurry of protectionism precipitated by the U.S. Congress's Smoot-Hawley Tariff Act of 1930 quickly caused world trade to shrink to only one-third of its former size (see Figure 12a). This swift deterioration in world commerce was one of the primary reasons for the severity of the Great Depression of the interwar years.

The parallels to that period raise troubling questions: Could today's escalating protectionism reduce the world economy to a state as perilous as that of the 1930s? Why has the agitation for sheltering domestic industries against foreign competition surfaced at this time, what reasons are given for restricting imports, and what theoretical and practical validity do these arguments have? Even more basically, we might ask why foreign competition is the target of protectionism rather than domestic competition. No one questions the economic advantages of free trade among regions of a country, yet the benefits of foreign trade are exactly the same. When we look for answers to this puzzling bias against foreigners, we find that the explanation

apparently has to do with a general spirit of nationalism, which lies within the realms of politics and social psychology rather than economic considerations.

This return to protectionism followed a long postwar era of trade liberalization, which saw global commerce soar and which brought unprecedented prosperity to much of the world. The first threats to this trend came in the 1970s, when the OPEC crises and steeply rising oil prices led to recessions in developed and developing countries alike. As international trade shrank, competition for markets intensified, imports threatened domestic industries, and a worldwide withdrawal into protectionism began. Adding urgency to the situation were rising budget and trade deficits in the United States, unaccustomedly high unemployment in Europe, and enormous foreign debts and stalled economic development among less-developed countries. The danger in all this is that widespread limitations on imports might halt world growth, reduce the efficiency of the world economy, undermine political alliances, and drive a wedge between industrialized and developing countries.

As the contagion spread, industrial-

ized countries began first to raise trade barriers to each other and then to target the less-developed countries (LDCs). Responding to a torrent of demand for protection, the President of the United States imposed 144 new quotas on textiles from 36 countries, most of them LDCs. In addition to textiles, the United States has since 1980 established quotas on apparel and motorcycles and negotiated "orderly marketing agreements" (so-called voluntary export restraints, or VERs) with European countries on carbon steel and with Japan on automobiles and computer chips. All of this has been highly inflationary: According to most estimates, the limitation on Japanese auto imports cost American consumers $15 billion in higher prices during the three-year life of the agreement. Protectionist sentiment in the United States against Japan has further intensified, however, as trade deficits with that country have mounted.

Japan itself is an inveterate practitioner of protectionism. It has long shielded its own high-cost producers of beef, rice, and citrus fruit from much cheaper products from the United States, and it has always limited imports of manufactured goods by means of rigorous inspections, intricate administrative regulations, and other subtle types of trade barriers. More recently, Japan erected new barriers to imports of textiles, apparel, footwear, and other products threatening to flood the home market from low-cost producers in Korea and other newly industrializing lands. Japan has also restricted imports of certain high-technology items in which the United States is most competitive—computer software, telecommunications gear, and communications satellites—arguing the need to develop its own industries. One prominent case was Japan's use of import protection to foster its computer memory chip industry. Sheltered by a 29 percent tariff on chip imports, Japanese chip manufacturers were able to monopolize their home market, thereby achieving important economies of scale. The resulting low unit costs allowed them to capture a major share of the world market. Under U.S. pressure, Japan signed the 1986 Semiconductor Arrangement de-

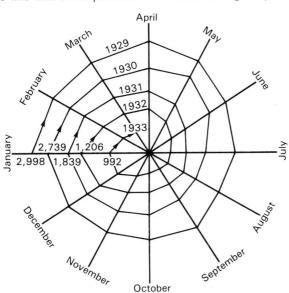

FIGURE 12a The contracting spiral of world trade, 1929–1933. Total imports of 75 countries (monthly values in old U.S. gold dollars, millions). [*Source:* Charles Kindleberger, *World in Recession* (Berkeley: University of California Press, 1973).]

(Continued on next page)

signed to halt predatory Japanese chip-marketing practices and to gain entry for U.S. chips into Japan. In the end, however, the agreement failed to accomplish these objectives and, indeed, proved counterproductive to United States interests and a boon to Japanese computer manufacturers.

Much of the trade tension between the United States and Japan, however, stems from a common failure to appreciate the inherent effects of the two countries' dissimilar resource endowments. Japan's history of mercantilism notwithstanding, studies have shown that the United States could not avoid a negative trade balance with Japan even if each country's trade were in equilibrium with the world. This can be explained by the triangular nature of Japan's world trade, which requires that this resource-poor nation earn a surplus in her manufacturing trade with industrialized countries in order to pay for essential imports of oil and raw materials from Third World countries.

Western Europe has become more protectionist, too, pressed by high unemployment, sluggish economic growth, lagging technology, and the burden of costly social programs. Because their economies depend heavily upon trade—exports generally account for a third or more of gross national product—these countries are exceedingly vulnerable to world market conditions. Yet they are losing their international competitiveness in a number of traditional industries. Low-cost textiles from Taiwan, Singapore, and South Korea began to flood European markets in the 1970s, driving hundreds of domestic firms into bankruptcy. The textile industry as a whole was saved only by "voluntary export restraints" imposed upon Asian producers by European governments. Then a tidal wave of auto imports from Japan reached European shores, seizing a quarter of the market in some countries. This resulted in still another voluntary export restraint.

The newly industrializing countries of the Third World increasingly find themselves the targets of protectionism in the older developed lands. In their drive to industrialize, these countries often used subsidies and import barriers of their own, with the tacit acceptance of the developed countries. Now they are vigorously exporting their manufactures to pay off huge international debts. Benefiting from low-cost labor and the latest technology, these Third World exporters have made serious inroads in the domestic markets of the older developed countries with their cheaper steel, ships, textiles, and electronics.

Reacting sharply to this new and unexpectedly effective competition from the Third World, the Europeans, Americans, and Japanese have restricted access to their markets. Indeed, the highest trade barriers to manufactured goods worldwide are those borne by labor-intensive manufactures—the mainstay of Third World exporters—and the class of products that incorporates one of their prime comparative advantages. Perhaps most onerous of all, because it affects many of the poorest LDCs, is the Multi-Fibre Arrangement (MFA). This is an intricate system of bilateral quotas that closely regulates the amount of textiles that each exporting country can sell to each importing country. Facing tighter restrictions on their new exports to the older industrial nations and badly needing revenue, LDC exporters have cultivated markets in other Third World nations.

Tariffs and quotas, even when euphemistically labeled "voluntary export restraints," are not the only trade barriers to gain popularity, and the rising mood of protectionism is not confined to the trade in merchandise. One favored device for protecting domestic industry is the subsidy. Agriculture is the most widely subsidized sector of all, having escaped entirely the postwar drive for trade liberalization. The extensive worldwide practice of subsidizing agriculture, the most prominent example being the European Community's costly Common Agricultural Policy (CAP), has severely distorted world commodity markets.

Rivaling agriculture as a beneficiary of government subsidies throughout the world is the transport sector. European governments, in particular, have heavily supported their aircraft manufacturers. The largest such outlays have gone to Airbus Industries, a consortium of major European aircraft makers who jointly design and build wide-bodied passenger jets in competition with American producers. In addition, most European nations maintain their own national-flag airlines, as do many countries worldwide—even some of the poorest. It is common also for governments to provide financial support for their shipbuilding and maritime industries. With the aid of heavy subsidies, for example, Taiwan has attained first rank in the constructing and operating of container ships.

Like agriculture, the services generally failed to participate in the postwar drive for trade liberalization. Today the internationally traded services constitute one of the most vigorously growing sectors of world commerce. They have also become the subject of growing national rivalry and a surge in protective measures. Many countries shelter from foreign competition such activities as banking, insurance, shipping, construction, aviation, travel industries, tourism, leisure pursuits, and real estate. Especially singled out for protection today are information services, an enormous market because of national programs to modernize telecommunications systems.

How valid are the arguments that industrialists, labor leaders, and politicians use to justify protecting favored interests? One such argument is that domestic firms have a right to their home market and that excluding imports will create jobs and help the local economy. The error in this kind of thinking is that if we buy nothing from other countries, they have nothing with which to buy our products. This costs jobs in our exporting industries and forces consumers to pay higher prices to domestic firms with assured monopolies.

Perhaps the justification used more than any other is the *infant industry* argument. This was a favorite reason given for protection in the United States and Canada during their early industrialization. According to this rationale, a new industry has the potential for ultimately becoming viable in world markets but it is vulnerable at the outset because of high start-up costs and operating inefficiencies during the initial phase. It thus cannot compete with established industries abroad that have already reached top efficiency and maximum economies of scale. As the argument goes, the industry will eventually become strong enough to compete in the world on its own and government protection can be discontinued. This argument has some validity if the industry is indeed in its start-up phase and if it truly has the potential to become self-sustaining so that government protection can be withdrawn within a reasonable time.

However, the argument is acceptable only if the country is an LDC; it has no validity for advanced countries. For instance, when Japan advances the infant-industry argument for protecting its new computer industry, this excuse meets skepticism in other countries. Furthermore, the government must indeed lift its protection after the early stages have passed; the history of protectionism is filled with cases of industries that continue to be sheltered by their governments long after the infant has become hoary with age.

An argument heard throughout the industrialized world during hard times is that protecting domestic industries will reduce unemployment at home. Its proponents insist that jobs must be preserved regardless of the cost to the country's foreign trade. The problem is that this invites retaliation from one's trading partners, which ultimately costs jobs in otherwise prospering export industries. Thus, American limitations on European steel imports induce Europeans to cut off lucrative American farm sales to them. Halting imports to preserve domestic employment means exporting unemployment to other countries and leads to an epidemic of retaliation like that which led to the Great Depression of the 1930s.

Moreover, protectionism does not solve structural unemployment, which results when a country loses its comparative advantage in a particular line of production. In the more advanced countries, many mature industries—textiles, garments, and steel, among others—can no longer compete on equal terms with newly industrializing countries that have cheaper labor and better access to high-grade raw materials. As Britain has learned, drawing upon the public treasury to preserve such declining industries is like trying to fill a bottomless pit. Retraining of displaced workers and aid to new industries are more logical uses of government funds.

The national security argument is one that nearly everyone considers legitimate. As long as wars continue to be a means for settling international grievances, countries seem justified in preserving those industries engaged in making war matériel and other goods essential to national survival in times of conflict. This argument bears close scrutiny, however, as it is frequently abused. The problem lies in the definition of just which articles are essential

to national defense. Manufacturers of all kinds of nonmilitary goods—garments, shoes, foods, and so on—tend to claim that their products should be declared essential to the national interest. High-tech manufactured goods are the subject of much recent controversy on this account.

Antidumping duties are a retaliatory technique that is generally approved. "Dumping," a predatory practice common among developed countries, consists of selling a product abroad at a price below that received for the same article in the domestic market. Under international rules, dumping is illegal: If dumping can be proved, the injured company can justifiably demand that its government impose an antidumping duty upon imports of the offending foreign merchandise. Basic metals manufacturers in the United States have obtained antidumping duties against European imports on such grounds. In theory, dumping is actually legitimate if the merchandise is consistently sold at cut-rate prices over an extended time as a form of permanent discounting operation. Dumping is wrong, however, if it is a short-run predatory practice intended to destroy domestic industries in the importing country so that monopoly prices can then be imposed by the foreign supplier. In practice, a problem with antidumping duties is that governments do not make such distinctions between legitimate and illegitimate dumping and merely apply the duties in response to political pressures. A second problem is that precise means do not exist for measuring true costs and prices in the two countries and it is therefore difficult to determine whether and how much dumping is really taking place.

Protectionism by less-developed countries is a complex issue. Until recently this has received few objections from theoreticians and governments. The infant-industry argument is clearly valid for LDCs, and almost all of them rely upon it. Most LDCs can also argue convincingly that they are entitled to some import protection because of deteriorating terms of trade with advanced countries; that is, because of imperfections in world markets, the prices of the goods they buy from industrialized countries rise more rapidly than do the commodities they customarily sell. LDCs therefore justify imposing import duties to raise revenues to help finance their own new industries.

In practice, however, many LDCs have inflicted damaging distortions and inefficiencies upon their own development programs by excessive and unwise use of import restrictions.

The validity of protectionism depends, therefore, on the grounds used for imposing it. A few of the more common arguments may be legitimate, but many are not. In practice, protective measures are subject to much abuse, and an uncontrolled proliferation of governmental interference would deprive the world of the fruits of trade. Protectionism can be very costly, too.

Some recent cases of political intrusion have carried enormous price tags. Leading the list is protection for agriculture. It has been calculated that removing all restraints on farm commodities would boost world trade by at least $100 billion annually. The cost to European governments for subsidizing just one aircraft model, Airbus A300, is reckoned at $1.5 billion. Airbus Industries lost money on this model, but the competition it created in the global marketplace also reduced profits for rival Boeing Aircraft Company. The Semiconductor Arrangement between the United States and Japan nearly doubled the price of 256K computer chips and created a global shortage of chips.

It is impossible to measure all the hidden costs of protection, but they are nonetheless very real. Among these are the lost benefits resulting from such restrictive devices as the Multi-Fibre Arrangement, which shift world production away from the lowest-cost locations. Some types of clothing covered by this measure cost twice as much to produce in Europe or North America as in less-developed countries. Diverse national technical requirements for many products result in fragmented markets, depriving manufacturers of opportunities for scale economies. Restricting entry of foreign firms into national markets erodes competition, which decreases incentives for innovation and puts a damper on research and development. Moreover, the continued proliferation of complex protective measures has made world trade less predictable for manufacturers and has caused them to be more reluctant to venture abroad. The costs of protectionism, therefore, can be measured by slowed industrial

(Continued on next page)

growth, higher unemployment rates, and inflated prices for consumers.

Theoretically, unrestricted trade creates an international division of labor that efficiently allocates the world's resources, thereby increasing total output and raising standards of living everywhere. Ideal conditions rarely exist in reality, of course: Perfect competition is not common, and the transfer of resources from one industry to another does not always take place smoothly or quickly. Yet the evidence shows that trade does bring growth and prosperity. Better forms of governmental intervention than trade restrictions are available to ensure fairness and prevent abuses of free trade by other countries. Political measures to protect local interests are clumsy at best; invariably they produce unintended and unwanted effects and deprive the world of the benefits of specialization and trade.

cannot readily comply with them. Even the mere existence of an international border crossing is sufficient to deter some trade movements. Small producers are especially reluctant to spend the time, effort, and money for complying with the red tape required for entering goods through customs. For a discussion of the growing problem of protectionism, see Box 12.1.

EFFECTS OF TRADE ON THE FACTORS OF PRODUCTION

According to the Heckscher-Ohlin theory, trade among regions and countries results from differences in their relative endowments in the factors of production. We have noted previously, however, that the introduction of trade produces feedback effects upon the factors. These effects are of two kinds: (1) trade may cause the prices of capital, labor, and land to rise or fall, and (2) it may change the relative quantities of the factors. Moreover, any interregional or international movement of factors will further alter their relative prices and quantities.

Factor Prices and Quantities

The introduction of trade may affect the prices of factors of production in both the exporting and importing regions or countries. As trade begins, country A exports the good that is intensive in the factor that is relatively abundant in that country. If the abundant factor happens to be agricultural land, perhaps corn is the land-intensive commodity and thus becomes the exported good. The first effect of trade will be to cause the domestic price of corn to rise in the exporting country, reflecting the new international terms of trade. Resources are progressively taken out of other industries in country A and put into producing more corn. But as more and more land is transferred to corn the additional land becomes available to corn production at ever-higher prices. Thus land, the intensive factor in corn production, becomes more costly in relation to capital and labor. Further reducing the return to capital and labor is the fact that these factors are not needed in such large amounts in corn production as for, say, cotton textile manufacture.

The opposite happens in the importing country, country B. Before trade took place, country B grew its own corn, even though the land was not very good for corn. When trade begins, country B's resources are taken out of corn and transferred into production of the good in which country B has a comparative advantage, namely, labor-intensive textiles. Paradoxically, trade has reduced the return to the scarce factor, labor in the case of country A and land in the case of country B. This sort of effect occurred when the importation of labor-intensive goods into Australia and Canada depressed wages in those labor-short economies.

Ultimately the returns to the factors of production should theoretically become completely equalized among trading nations. Wages paid to labor should be the same, interest rates earned by capital should become standardized, and rent received for land should be equal. Trade will have erased all differences. In reality, however, perfect conditions rarely exist and factor prices stop short of complete equalization. It is seldom possible to shift all resources from one line of production to another. Furthermore, the various barriers to commodity movements prevent full equalization: Transfer costs, tariffs, and other impediments to trade ensure that some factor-price differentials remain.

Note that not only are factor prices affected by trade but also the relative scarcity and abundance of factors in trading nations. We have seen that when trade causes the abundant factor of land, labor, or capital to rise in price, an increase in the quantity of that factor follows. At the same time, the scarce factor, being in less demand, falls in price and decreases in quantity. Thus, trade increases specialization and at the same time exaggerates the differences in factor quantities.

Factor Mobility

One of the limiting assumptions of the Heckscher-Ohlin theory is that no movement of the factors of production takes place among countries. We have seen earlier, however, that capital, labor, and entrepreneurship do indeed have varying degrees of mobility internationally. We noted that financial capital is especially mobile and can even act as a substitute for trade when tariffs or other artificial impediments interfere with commodity movements.

Another effect of interregional and international movements of factors is to produce some equalization of their prices: interest rates, wages, and salaries. For example, capital seeks the market where it receives the highest interest rates. But when the new market becomes saturated with capital, interest rates at that location will fall. Meanwhile, the drain of capital from the old area will cause its interest rates to recover. In this way the return to factors tends to become equalized. Nevertheless, the amount of equalization that can take place is limited. Because of the barriers cited earlier, complete mobility of capital and labor is seldom attained.

The suggestion that factor movements can replace trade is one that is receiving increased attention. Direct foreign investment for the purpose of making a product previously imported would appear to have a trade-reducing effect. The evidence indicates, however, that the impact of such investment upon economic growth and development can actually be to increase the propensity of countries to trade and therefore to have a net trade-creating effect. Interest is therefore focusing more and more upon the role of the multinational enterprise, that prime mover of the factors of production.

TRADE THEORY IN PERSPECTIVE

The question posed at the beginning of this chapter was: Why do countries trade with each other? Theorists have long been preoccupied with this issue and with what they see as the gains from trade. For the early classical theorists certain benefits automatically follow the opening of trade, which makes it possible for each participating country to concentrate upon making those goods for which its resources are most suited. By exchanging goods, all trading nations can use their productive capabilities to the highest efficiency, thereby increasing their combined output, raising the living standards of their citizens, and permitting consumption patterns to differ from production patterns. The end result is a more efficient use of the world's resources.

By the turn of the twentieth century theorists were discovering still another set of gains from trade. The specialization that follows the opening of trade, they noted, brings additional efficiencies as specialists accumulate experience and further enhance their skills through practice, sharing information with each other, and focusing their inventions and innovations upon a particular industry. Firms are able to reduce unit costs through economies of large-scale operation and, being able to tap large pools of specialized labor skills and to draw upon a growing body of specialized services and facilities, they can achieve external economies as well.

All of this is supposed to happen as a result of free trade, which allows all nations to make optimal use of their resource endowments. In the latter part of the twentieth century, however, the resource-endowments explanation has not stood up well under empirical tests using real-world data. The results clearly show that, although resource endowments play a big part, a number of other elements importantly affect the amount and kinds of economic flows that take place among countries. We have noted in this chapter, for instance, that the nature of demand has a significant influence, especially as it is affected by differing levels of income and cultural variations. Equally important in most cases are the barriers to trade: the impact of distance and governmental intervention. Further complicating the explanation are the feedback effects on the factors of production as a result of trade, which alter both factor quantities and prices.

One conclusion we may draw from this is that the conventional factor-endowment model of trade, as expressed by the Heckscher-Ohlin theorem, is not only incomplete but is also too static. The next chapter, therefore, focuses upon the explicitly dynamic features of world commerce. Change now is taking place much more rapidly. Moreover, it becomes increasingly necessary to extend the discussion to take into account all kinds of economic flows among countries—not just commodity movements but also internationally traded services and flows of capital and other factors. In Chapter 13 we shall be looking at the role of trade in national growth, the effects of technological change, and the inequalities among countries in sharing the benefits of international commerce. We shall give special attention to what may be the most dynamic element of all, the multinational enterprise, a preeminent agent of change in the new world economy now emerging.

TOPICS FOR DISCUSSION

1. Explain why trade theoretically benefits all participants, and discuss the two classes of benefits that trade brings to country trading partners, their citizens, and the world as a whole. How are the factor intensities of industries and the factor endowments of countries reflected in the nature of the trade among countries?

2. Under what circumstances might two countries with identical production possibilities trade with each other?

Discuss the various aspects of demand that might affect trade between two countries.

3. Compare and contrast the effects of tariffs and quotas upon the production, consumption, and trade of both the exporting and importing countries. Who benefits and who loses?

4. What are the different ways in which distance affects trade? What happens to the classical two-country, two-commodity trade model when transport cost is introduced into the equation? How are the two participating countries affected?

5. Assume that two countries produce the same two commodities but have different factor endowments. If they enter into trade with each other, how would we expect this exchange to affect both the supply of their factors of production and the prices of these factors? How may factor movements between two countries substitute for trade, and how would such factor movements affect the prices of those factors?

FURTHER READINGS

BALASSA, BELA. "The Changing Pattern of Comparative Advantage in Manufactured Goods." *Review of Economics and Statistics* (May 1979), 259–266.

Provides an analysis of the changing comparative advantage in 184 classes of manufactured goods for 36 countries. The author found that differences in commodity structure resulted from differences in physical and human capital endowments.

BALDWIN, ROBERT E. "Determinants of Trade and Foreign Investment: Further Evidence." *Review of Economics and Statistics* (February 1979), 40–48.

Employing the same approach used by Leontief in his classic input-output analysis of United States trade, Baldwin studied the trade of 30 countries with results closely paralleling those of Leontief.

BERGSTEN, C. FRED, and WILLIAM R. CLINE. *The United States-Japan Economic Problem* (rev. ed.). Washington, D.C.: Institute for International Economics, 1987.

Relying upon quantitative analyses of Japanese–United States trade, Bergsten and Cline assess the impacts of the barriers erected against each other by the two countries. They find that much of the debate on trade imbalances misses several key points, notably the contrasting fundamental structures of the Japanese and U.S. economies. The authors are, respectively, director and senior fellow of an influential Washington group devoted to the study of international trade issues facing the United States.

CORDEN, W. M. *Recent Developments in the Theory of International Trade*. Princeton, N.J.: Princeton University Press, 1965.

A succinct summary of the evolution of modern trade theory.

ELLSWORTH, P. T., and J. CLARK LEITH. *The International Economy*. New York: Macmillan, 1984.

A historical approach to the theory of international trade. Interestingly describes the economic environments prevailing at each stage in the evolution of the theory and offers useful insights into the thinking of those who contributed to its development.

HOUTHAKKER, H. S. "An International Comparison of Household Expenditure Patterns, Commemorating the Centenary of Engel's Law." *Econometrica* (October 1957), 532–551.

Houthakker measured the elasticities of demand for food, clothing, housing, and other items in the household budgets of countries at different levels of per capital income.

KINDLEBERGER, CHARLES P. *Foreign Trade and the National Economy*. New Haven, Conn.: Yale University Press, 1962.

A very readable summary of international trade theory.

LEONTIEF, WASSILY W. "Domestic Production and Foreign Trade: The American Capital Position Re-examined." *Proceedings of the American Philosophical Society*, September 1953. Reprinted in *Readings in International Economics*, R. E. Caves and Harry C. Johnson, eds. Homewood, Ill.: Richard D. Irwin, 1968, pp. 503–527.

Contains original statement of Leontief's famous "paradox."

LINDER, STAFFAN BURENSTAM. *An Essay on Trade and Transformation*. New York: John Wiley, 1961.

Linder advanced the idea that, although differences in factor endowments may explain trade in land-intensive goods, the structure of a country's manufactured exports depends upon prior production for the domestic market.

MACDOUGALL, G. D. A. "British and American Exports: A Study Suggested by the Theory of Comparative Costs. Part I." *Economic Journal*, 19, No. 2 (June 1951), 697–724.

This study evaluated the effects of differences in labor productivity on the export performances of the United Kingdom and the United States.

OHLIN, BERTIL. *Interregional and International Trade* (rev. ed.). Cambridge, Mass.: Harvard University Press, 1952.

A revision of Ohlin's classical statement of the Heckscher-Ohlin theory concerning the role of resource endowments in generating trade between countries.

SAMUELSON, PAUL A. "International Trade and the Equalization of Factor Prices." *Economic Journal* (June 1948), 163–184.

A seminal statement of the factor-price equalization theorem.

13

Dynamics of World Trade and Investment

OVERVIEW

International commerce is changing at an accelerating pace. Dynamic forces at work in today's world economy require modifications in conventional theory, which attributes trade to the factor endowments of countries but assumes that those endowments remain constant in quantity and method of use (Chapter 12). Trade plays a central role in economic growth, serving as a means for acquiring necessary technology; indeed, much world commerce is generated by the need to redress technology gaps between countries. Though trade is thus essential for development, it poses special problems for less-developed countries. Nevertheless, several LDCs with forward-looking policies have achieved rapid growth through trade.

Many groups of countries—both developed and less-developed—have established cooperative ar-

rangements for gaining the benefits of free trade. One such device is economic integration, which reduces trade barriers among members but discriminates against nonmembers. Another, broader approach, exemplified by GATT (The General Agreement on Tariffs and Trade), is to achieve agreement among a majority of the world's nations to cut barriers by stages.

The multinational enterprise (MNE) has had a great impact upon both the theory and reality of world commerce. Headquartered in one country but controlling subsidiaries in others, the MNE is an efficient agent for transferring goods and factors of production between countries. Thus, it helps to achieve a global equalization of factors and it is a prime agent of technological change.

OBJECTIVES

- to examine the relationships between trade and economic growth and the trade effects of technology
- to identify the trade problems of less-developed countries and to compare their trade strategies
- to assess the leading types of intergovernmental agreements for solving mutual problems of trade, investment, and development
- to explain why multinational enterprises have become prime agents for the transfer of goods and factors among nations

A CHANGING INTERNATIONAL SCENE

World commerce is constantly changing, and the pace of that change has quickened. Recent world developments have reinforced the inherently dynamic nature of commercial relations among countries. These relations are continuously being reshaped by changes in basic physical and human resource endowments and by the emergence of new advanced factors of the kinds described by Michael Porter. The competitive advantages of nations are undergoing fundamental shifts as a result of these new factor combinations.

Each factor is subject to many altering forces. Population age structures change, labor forces increase in size and learn new skills, capital accumulates through savings or foreign investment, new physical resources are discovered and old ones are depleted, technology is acquired through research or transfer from abroad, and managerial skills grow. These changes do not come at the same time or in equal measure to all places, however, and different rates of change can greatly alter trade and investment, creating problems for those nations that are slow to adjust. Countries have developed a variety of strategies for attacking these problems, both individually and in cooperation with others. A leading actor in this dynamic international scene is the *multinational enterprise,* which is one of the principal agents of change.

TRADE AND GROWTH

Precisely how trade affects economic growth is much disputed. But analysts generally agree that trade plays a central part in the growth process and that the relationship between trade and growth is reciprocal: Any gain for one benefits the other. This is a natural result of the close interaction between production and consumption on the one hand, and trade on the other. Growth occurs mainly in two ways. It may take place (1) through an increase in the available factors of production—additions to the supply of capital, labor, and arable land, for instance, or (2) as a result of technological advances.

In the growth of an economy trade may lead the way for the other sectors, as it so frequently did during the nineteenth century. This was clearly the case in Canada, whose rapid growth followed the expansion of its staple export industries—furs, forest products, grains—in response to rising demand in other countries. Among those countries currently in the earlier stages of their development, however, growth of the economy may precede trade growth. An example of this group is Venezuela, which has pursued a typical

Latin American policy of closely controlling its foreign trade. Note in Figure 13.1 that Venezuela's gross domestic product (GDP)—its total output of goods and services—has risen more rapidly than has its trade with the world. For many other countries, however, trade and economic growth have gone hand in hand. Still a third case is represented by several East Asian economies, which in recent decades have attained prosperity through trade-led growth. One of these is South Korea. Soaring exports have elevated that nation's economy from an impoverished state to new heights within a remarkably short time (Figure 13.1).

Growth and the Propensity to Trade

The experience of modern times has shown that countries participate in trade to a changing extent as their economies grow. At the outset, when trade is essential to its economic development, a country increases its exports and imports rapidly. Thereafter, its trade continues to expand but at a slower rate than that of the economy as a whole. In the later stages of economic growth a country's trade may decline still further in relation to its total output as the emphasis shifts from producing goods to providing services, most of the latter being consumed locally.

The world economy has expanded enormously since the Industrial Revolution, and international trade has multiplied at a corresponding rate, bringing fast growth to those countries participating in this commerce. When a country's exports first successfully enter the world market, this causes the domestic economy to expand swiftly. The rate of acceleration is all the greater if the population had previously engaged in subsistence activities, producing only for family consumption. Production for export requires specialization, which leads to an increasingly fine division of labor. As foreign sales continue to multiply, the prosperity of the export sector spreads to the rest of the economy: Money circulates more quickly and incomes rise, thereby enlarging the domestic market.

Initially, a single staple commodity may dominate a country's exports, as, for instance, cotton fiber in the early United States or cotton textiles in Britain. Growing success in this type of production soon spreads to other related industries, causing these to expand also, along with transportation and other supporting services. In some of these affected industries the rising level of output may provide sufficient economies of scale for their goods to compete successfully in world markets. This enables the country to add new classes of exports to its original staple export. All this growth creates new needs, many of which cannot be supplied locally by the still-limited productive capabil-

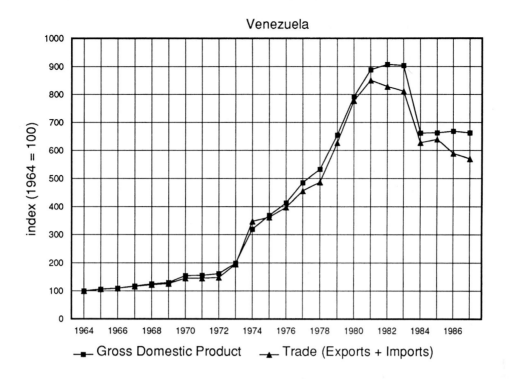

Venezuela

--■-- Gross Domestic Product   --▲-- Trade (Exports + Imports)

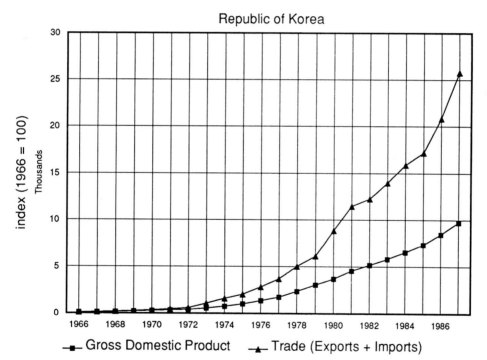

Republic of Korea

--■-- Gross Domestic Product   --▲-- Trade (Exports + Imports)

FIGURE 13.1   Growth of trade and gross domestic product (GDP) of Venezuela and South Korea. The growth of Venezuela's trade has lagged behind that of its GDP, reflecting a policy of import-substituting industrialization common to most Latin American governments in the post-World War II era. The erratic behavior of Venezuela's exports and imports since the early 1970s is a consequence of wide swings in the world market for its oil during a period of recurring energy crises and global recession. By contrast, resource-poor South Korea, in common with several other East Asian nations, has pursued a policy of export-promoting industrialization since the mid-1960s, with the extraordinary results shown here. [*Sources:* United Nations, *Yearbook of International Trade Statistics* and *Yearbook of National Accounts Statistics;* and International Monetary Fund, *International Financial Statistics Yearbook* (Washington, D.C.: International Monetary Fund).]

ities of the economy. Thus, a demand arises for an increasing quantity and variety of imported commodities, especially industrial raw materials and machinery. Meanwhile, rising incomes induce the country's inhabitants to demand a growing number of foreign-produced consumer goods. Rising incomes do not favor equally all classes of imported products, however. In accordance with Engel's law, families allocate smaller and smaller proportions of additional income to purchases of food and spend ever-larger amounts on manufactured products and services. The composition of imports therefore gradually shifts to reflect these changes in industrial and consumer demand.

As the country's consumption of certain imported goods continues to rise, entrepreneurs become aware of the opportunity these offer for local manufacture. This *demonstration effect* of imports leads to the introduction of an ever-larger number of factories making items that were previously imported. The incentive for local manufacture is especially great for goods whose production tends to be market-oriented—that is, products that can be made and sold more cheaply close to the point of ultimate consumption (see Chapter 10). *Import substitution* of this kind correspondingly reduces dependence upon foreign suppliers of such goods. Thus, both imports and exports ultimately grow more diverse even as they become a shrinking proportion of a rising total national output. Adding further to this relative decline in trade dependence with maturation of the economy is the proliferation of services and the rising share of national income spent on these.

Growth through Technology

The second kind of growth results from an improved technology, which yields greater output from the same quantity of resources. A new device such as the mechanical reaper, the cotton gin, or the self-doffing spindle frees large numbers of workers for other purposes, while at the same time expanding the volume of exportable product. A new technique that permits a larger percentage of metal to be extracted from gold ore has the effect of increasing the national reserves of that mineral. Producing a new technology involves two related processes, *invention* and *innovation*. The more fundamental process is invention, which entails the conception of a basic idea, such as the discovery that steam has the power to perform work. This is the product of laboratory scientists. Innovation, on the other hand, is the application of that idea to something directly useful to humankind, such as the development of the steam engine and the use of that device to power

pumps for raising water from mines and to run textile machinery. This is the work of engineers.

Innovation is of two fundamental types. The first of these provides more efficient and cheaper ways to make existing goods. Japanese engineers have excelled in this form of industrial technology, as indicated by their success in developing more economical and reliable techniques for manufacturing automobiles, ships, and electronic goods of all kinds. Second, innovation can result in creating entirely new products, such as fiber optics and computers. The United States clings to a dwindling lead in this form of innovation.

In recent times the pace of technological change has been accelerating at an astounding rate. Modern technology issues principally from organized programs of systematic research into which corporate, institutional, and governmental sponsors pour huge sums in an effort to gain the rich rewards of product innovation in an intensely competitive world. Innovation has always occurred more rapidly in some countries than others, resulting in a *technology gap* between the leaders and the followers. Although in the past the leadership has tended to remain with a particular country or group of countries for an extended period, the signs today point to a more rapid shift of technological supremacy among contending nations.

These international differences in technology contradict one of the basic assumptions implicit in the Heckscher-Ohlin theorem, namely that all countries are able to draw upon the same technology, and that a particular industry makes its products in the same manner everywhere. Technology not only differs among nations but it has the power to alter their resource endowments in profound ways. Technological change is thus one of the most dynamic elements in today's world trade picture.

The Trade Effects of Technology. A new production technology affects trade in a variety of ways: It can create exports for a country, it can provide substitutes for imports, and it can give rise to a new demand for imports. If the country originating a new product is able to retain exclusive control of its manufacture, perhaps through secrecy or because that country is the only one technically capable of making the product, then the effect of innovation is the creation of trade. The United Kingdom initially gained ascendency in world trade through the development of such exports as railway equipment, steam engines, and mechanical pumps and by retaining a monopoly over their production for a long time. The United States has led in producing and exporting aircraft, farm machinery, construction machinery, chemicals, and machine tools.

Technology thus yields products that people all over the world want to buy. Sometimes, however, it is possible for an importing country to use its technology to develop substitutes for goods formerly imported, thereby reducing trade. The United States has been successful in this type of invention and innovation, as shown by the many substitutes that have been synthesized to replace natural products formerly obtained from abroad. Synthetic rubber and nylon are familiar examples. Ultimately, such technology spreads throughout the world, reducing world trade in rubber, natural fibers, and other replaced commodities. In general, however, it seems probable that technology has acted to expand trade. Evidence for this is the enormous increase in high-technology goods entering world commerce.

Technology also affects international commerce through improvements in communication and transportation. Because communication is essential to business, anything that makes the transmission of information quicker, easier, or cheaper tends to facilitate the flow of goods and investment. Such developments as the overseas cable, telephone, telegraph, and radio, and, more recently, satellite communication have had powerful effects upon world commerce.

In the long run the transport rate curve has moved steadily downward, at least in relative terms. This has contributed to the gradual spread of trade to remote parts of the world. Numerous transport innovations, such as the screw propeller, steel hulls, refrigeration, containerization, and jet aircraft, have helped to bring down the cost and time required for moving both goods and people. By these means the farthest reaches of South America and Oceania have been able to join the modern world economy.

Trade Growth and the Diffusion of Innovation.
As we have seen, the emergence of one export industry in a country gives rise to others, and the effects ultimately spread through the national economy. In the United Kingdom, this diffusion began with the textile industry, then extended into other industries such as iron, metal products, and coal. This development does not remain confined to one country, but diffuses internationally as well. British investment eventually moved into France, followed by technical aid and skilled workers, enabling that country to join Britain as a supplier to the world market. The new technology quickly spread thereafter to other Western European countries, particularly Germany, Austria, Switzerland, and Italy.

The diffusion of ideas occurs in a variety of ways. Some ideas have reached new areas through the theft of technical secrets, as in the transfer of textile technology from Lancashire in Britain to New England during the early nineteenth century, thereby creating a new center from which textiles could be exported to the world in competition with the original center. The American computer industry confronts similar acts of industrial thievery today. The same result is achieved in a more open and legal fashion through licensing arrangements, the publishing of technical articles, and foreign education for technicians, engineers, and scientists. In earlier times colonization was conducive to the spread of ideas throughout the world, and the trade links that France and Britain still maintain with their former colonies testify to the durability of that avenue of communication. In recent years one of the most effective means for the rapid transfer of business and technical information has been the multinational enterprise. An innovation developed in centrally located company laboratories can be transmitted immediately to corporate branches in other parts of the world.

Another avenue for diffusion of trade has been through the foreign procurement of industrial raw materials and foodstuffs. As nineteenth-century British industrialists reached farther and farther afield for ore, timber, grains, animal products, and other needs, they brought trade to Spain, Sweden, Denmark, The Netherlands, Canada, the United States, and other foreign suppliers. Eventually such distant regions as Australia, New Zealand, South Africa, and Argentina entered the British commercial orbit, to be followed later by suppliers of rubber, vegetable oils, and other tropical goods. British investment in these foreign undertakings foreshadowed the global operations of modern-day multinational corporations.

The outward movement of particular types of production from centers of innovation tends to be selective. Raymond Vernon has explained this in terms of the *product life cycle* theory. The manufacture of a new product, he notes, usually requires proportionally large numbers of engineers and skilled workers in what is at first a highly experimental, low-volume operation. Eventually manufacture becomes sufficiently routine for the introduction of mass-production techniques yielding economies of scale. Because skill requirements are less demanding in this second phase of the cycle, production can take place in areas other than the center of innovation. When the industry becomes fully mature, still more of the production can be assigned to specialized machines that require only unskilled operators. At this point the industry shifts to areas having a surplus of cheap labor, often in less-developed countries. Thus, as an industry progresses through the product life cycle, its factor intensities become altered and its locational requirements change.

The electronics industry exemplifies this cyclical type of development (see Chapter 10). Much of the initial production of new electronic equipment occurs in such centers of innovation as eastern Massachusetts, but once production becomes standardized it does not remain in that location for long. Some of the first television picture tubes were built in the Boston area, but the mass production of television sets quickly became established in the American Midwest. In time, a major portion of the industry moved to border areas of Mexico and to Japan, Korea, and Taiwan as the industry matured. In the absence of further discoveries in the original source areas, the ultimate effect would be to reduce trade based on technology and to leave as the dominant cause of trade simple comparative advantage in the basic factors of production. This appears to be happening in the automotive industry, which is growing most rapidly in those countries with the relatively low-cost labor, capital, and large domestic markets for consumer durables required by this mature industry.

Leadership in invention and innovation has generally concentrated in one particular region or country at a given time. This has provided the leader with an important competitive edge in the exportation of high-tech goods. The principal center of innovation must strive to preserve this comparative advantage and must try to remain one step ahead of its competitors. In the past, no country has succeeded in retaining the technological lead permanently. In the beginning Britain assumed first place in technology, a position it managed to hold without challenge until about 1850. Western Europe and the United States subsequently gained ascendency, with much of the basic science originating in Europe and applied technology originating in the United States. By the time of World War II, however, the United States had attained a commanding place in both invention and innovation.

In recent decades America's lead has come under attack as the pace of technological change has quickened in other industrialized countries, most particularly Japan, West Germany, the United Kingdom, and France. As a result of this heightened activity, technology gaps have closed and new ones have opened with increasing rapidity in one line of production after another.

Thus, the United States no longer leads in many of the old technologies—textiles, steel, motor vehicles—and has become a net importer of these goods.

Now the country is struggling to maintain its long-time dominance in the manufacture and export of the newer, technology-intensive products that have become so vital to the balance of trade. The dimensions of this problem and its policy implications are discussed further in Box 13.1.

TRADE AND DEVELOPMENT

While the industrialized countries of the world vie for the lead in technology, the less-developed nations contend with the wide technology gap that separates them from the more advanced producers. The less-developed lands generally lack the research and development funds, the labor skills, and the professional, scientific, and engineering personnel required to invent and innovate. Instead, they must rely upon borrowed technology, which often is inappropriate for their needs and obsolete before it reaches them.

The technology gap is but one of the important reasons why the trade experience of less-developed countries differs so markedly from that of the industrialized countries; indeed, the circumstances facing today's poorer lands are very probably unlike those that confronted the present industrialized lands when they were beginning their own development. Many observers therefore express doubt that the benefits of trade, so obvious in the case of the advanced countries, automatically operate for the rest of the world. Why should this be so? What is there about today's newly developing countries that is so different from yesterday's? If such differences truly exist, can we be sure that conventional trade theory, with its emphasis upon free trade, is appropriate for the less-developed world?

Finding answers to these questions is complicated by the fact that the two-thirds of the world's nations that lag in their development are far from being a homogeneous group. True, they share a number of common traits that mark them as less developed—low per capita incomes, economies dominated by agriculture and other primary production, export dependence upon a limited number of commodities, high birth rates and population growth rates, low literacy, and so on—but in other respects they vary widely from each other. Even in terms of material well-being, they range from the desperate poverty of Kampuchea and Chad, whose GNP is under $150 per person, to the comparative prosperity of South Korea and Taiwan, which are becoming industrialized nations. In between lie nearly 100 other countries of varying degrees of advancement. The less-developed countries differ greatly in size, too, whether measured by territory or population, from enormous China and India to tiny Trinidad and Kiribatu.

BOX 13.1   Is the United States Losing Its Lead in High-Technology Trade?

For many years the United States has relied upon a large technological lead to sustain its balance of trade with the world, but today that lead seems to be slipping. The nation's surplus of high-technology exports over imports, which has been dwindling for some time, has finally disappeared. This comes at a time when technology gaps among countries have been opening and closing at an accelerating rate. At one time the international transfer of new technology required a generation or more, but today it takes only a few years at most.

Even the perception of what constitutes high technology is changing. In-dustrial products mature at ever-faster rates, so that a high-technology good at one time is only a medium- or low-technology good at another, later period. Thus, the product life cycle has greatly speeded up, making it difficult to compare one era with another. High-technology industries are usually defined as those making relatively large expenditures for research and development (R & D) and employing a high percentage of scientists, techni-cians, and manual workers with spe-cialized skills. Lists of high-technology products ordinarily include chemicals, machinery (including electronics), transport equipment, and professional

instruments; however, only certain subcategories of these can rightly be considered high technology at the present time. For instance, bulk chemi-cals such as acids and alkalis no longer justify this classification.

With an annual trade deficit passing the $100 billion mark, the United States has viewed with anxiety the signs that its international position in high-technology production is weak-ening. Just how vital this sector is to the country's overall trade balance is ap-parent from the accompanying figure. A big trade surplus in technology-in-tensive products has supported other major trade categories that have done

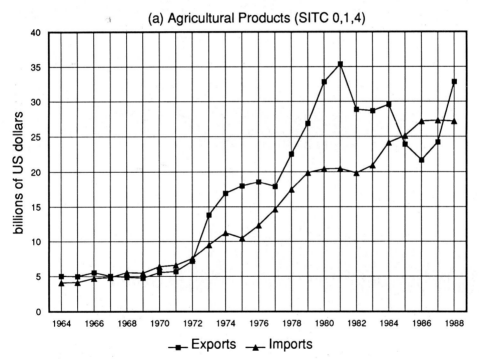

(a) Agricultural Products (SITC 0,1,4)

y-axis: billions of US dollars
x-axis: 1964 1966 1968 1970 1972 1974 1976 1978 1980 1982 1984 1986 1988

—■— Exports   —▲— Imports

Changing structure of U.S. trade. (SITC: Standard International Trade Classification) As its overall trade deficit has ballooned, the United States has relied upon a surplus in high-technology exports to compensate for trade deficits in nontechnology-intensive manufactures and in raw materials and fuels; but, as these diagrams show, the country may be losing this source of competitive strength. Such a loss would be serious because high-technology goods account for more than one-third of total exports. Moreover, the problem arises at a time when the long-time positive trade balance in agricultural goods has evaporated in the face of rising protectionism in foreign markets. [_Source:_ United Nations, _Yearbook of International Trade Statistics,_ various years (New York: United Nations).]

(Continued on next page)

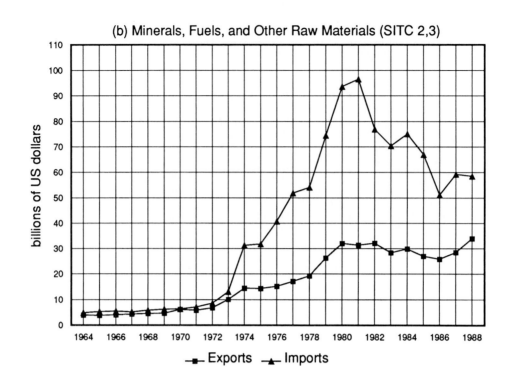

(b) Minerals, Fuels, and Other Raw Materials (SITC 2,3)

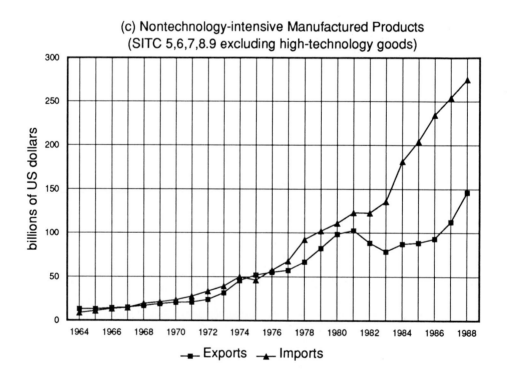

**(c) Nontechnology-intensive Manufactured Products
(SITC 5,6,7,8.9 excluding high-technology goods)**

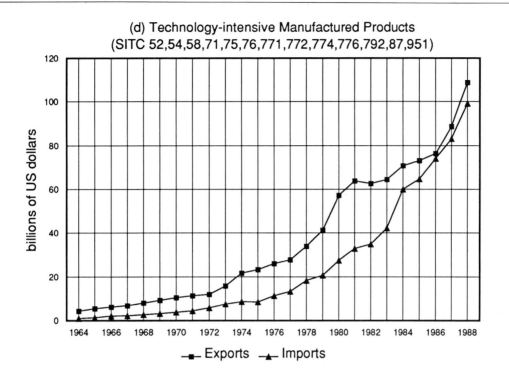

(d) Technology-intensive Manufactured Products
(SITC 52,54,58,71,75,76,771,772,774,776,792,87,951)

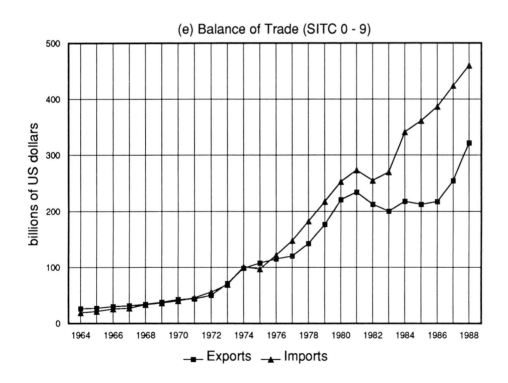

(e) Balance of Trade (SITC 0 - 9)

(Continued on next page)

less well. For many years the country has had a large trade deficit in raw materials and fuels (see Chapter 5), as depletion of domestic supplies, soaring world commodity prices (especially for oil), and rising demand have increased the country's import bill for these goods. Similarly, imports of low-technology manufactured products, such as textiles and clothing, have exceeded exports by a growing margin. A fourth category, agricultural commodities, usually has a trade surplus, although this fluctuates widely from year to year, depending upon world harvests, protectionist policies in key markets (especially Europe), the trade effects of U.S. relations with Russia, and the relative strength of the dollar with respect to other currencies.

The United States enjoyed a strong positive balance of trade in high-technology goods until 1965; since then the surplus has gradually dwindled. In the early 1960s, U.S. technology-intensive imports (as defined in the diagram below) were only one-fifth as large as high-technology exports; by the end of the 1980s, high-technology imports were almost as large as exports. Why has this turnabout occurred? It is a many-sided problem:

- To begin with, it is clear that the unusually large U.S. technology gap of the postwar era could not have been sustained indefinitely. After all, a substantial part of the U.S. lead during those years resulted from the wartime devastation of competing industrial economies. The influx of refugee foreign scientists and technicians fleeing those lands further enhanced this advantage.

- Another reason for the declining U.S. position has been the way in which the nation's multinational enterprises have responded to the accelerating product life cycle. Although new products have regularly replaced old ones in the country's export mix, the more mature forms of production now moving to other countries are high-volume operations that account for sizable shares of world trade. The newer manufactured products and services generate far lower total export earnings.

- Further reducing the U.S. trade

surplus in technology-intensive goods has been the growing trend for multinationals to transfer their latest technology immediately to their overseas affiliates in order to avail themselves of cheap labor and local raw materials, thereby forestalling potential competition. For example, Sikorsky Aircraft makes its most advanced helicopters in Brazil, and AT&T produces its latest telecommunications equipment in the south of Europe. Indeed, goods produced overseas by American companies constitute a major component of U.S. high-technology imports.

- The real crux of the U.S. high-technology problem, however, lies in U.S. manufacturers' flagging ability to translate basic scientific discoveries quickly and efficiently into useful articles that compete in world markets. The country's position in basic science remains strong, as indicated by continued American dominance of Nobel prize awards and by the large numbers of students from around the world who flock to the United States for advanced degrees in science, mathematics, and engineering. Nevertheless, American supremacy in *product innovation* seems to have begun slipping away about the time that Europe and Japan completed their recovery from World War II.

- But product innovation is not enough by itself; another essential is something called *process-oriented innovation*. This consists of refining an existing article at each turn of the production cycle and constantly looking for ways to build it more simply, cheaply, and quickly. Such an approach demands the closest intracompany teamwork. The result, however, is an incrementally better product and steadily rising productivity. The Japanese are masters at this kind of innovation. Lagging productivity has reduced the ability of U.S. enterprises to compete, even though American labor is now cheaper than Japanese or German.

- Finally, the United States is not spending enough on R & D. In recent years Japan has outstripped

the United States in its outlays for industrial research, as measured by percentage of gross national product. American expenditure for R & D represented 3 percent of gross national product in the early 1960s; by 1985 this had fallen to only 1.9 percent, about half the Japanese rate. Fortunately, outlays for R & D have begun to rise as intense foreign competition has forced American firms to automate in order to reduce costs and raise quality. Another inducement has been convincing statistical evidence from recent studies demonstrating a remarkably high correlation between levels of R & D and corporate sales and profit margins.

Some U.S. high-technology industries are faring better than others in the competition for domestic and foreign markets. American chemical companies are aggressive exporters, contributing one-tenth of the country's foreign earnings in most years. Any threat to the industry's international position would, therefore, pose a serious problem for the nation's balance of payments. During the 1950s and 1960s U.S. chemical exports soared, but they began to encounter overseas competition from European and Japanese producers during the 1970s. In the 1980s U.S. chemical imports climbed as competitors' capacity expanded, not only in developed lands but also in newly industrializing countries.

Most of the foreign competition is focused upon basic organic and inorganic chemicals, however; U.S. chemical companies hold a firm lead in high-technology chemicals. These contributed a major part of the industry's $15.8 billion trade surplus in 1990. The U.S. chemical industry safeguards this technological supremacy by maintaining a consistently high investment in research and development, even in times of recession. In the vanguard are the nation's pharmaceutical companies, which spent $8.2 billion on R & D in 1990, 16.8 percent of their total sales. The result has been a growing array of new products for world markets: Most U.S. pharmaceutical houses now sell 30 to 50 percent of their prescription drugs overseas.

Electronics has long been a positive contributor to the country's trade balance, but in 1984 for the first time imports of electronic goods exceeded exports, and by a considerable margin. This gap, which is still growing, is a serious problem because electronics is one of the country's largest manufacturing employers. It has also been a main hope for recouping some of the jobs lost by the decline of the older heavy industries, such as steel and autos. The U.S. electronics industry began to lose its international competitiveness during the early 1980s, at a time when an overvalued dollar was making American exports too expensive and imports cheap. The decline in U.S. electronics continues, even though the dollar has since fallen against other major currencies.

A more basic reason for the slippage is the inability of U.S. firms to convert their technological discoveries into competitive products. Their reluctance to invest for the future stems from the threefold dilemma facing U.S.

high-technology operating in a free-market environment:

- Steadily rising capital intensity. Developing new products now requires much time and enormous sums of money, often exceeding the resources of individual U.S. companies. The nation's capital markets are interested only in short-term results and the government is unwilling to subsidize such ventures. Today, spending power determines the outcome of competition in the industry.
- Ever-shorter product life cycles. The accelerating pace of change requires the commitment of immense human and financial resources if new-product development is to keep ahead of the competition.
- The ease with which competitors can copy new technology in an

age of instantaneous global communication and deficient international patent protection.

Illustrating these problems is the case of the computer industry. American computer makers have been locked in a competitive struggle for this crucial market with the Japanese industry, which is heavily subsidized. American companies still dominate the world market for computers, but they purchase most of their components from foreign manufacturers because they cannot make them competitively at home. The majority of computer terminals, for example, come from Japan, South Korea, and other East Asian lands.

The world market for computer chips is huge, amounting to tens of billions of dollars, and is fed by the growing trend to incorporate electronics into all kinds of products. Although computer chips were an American de-

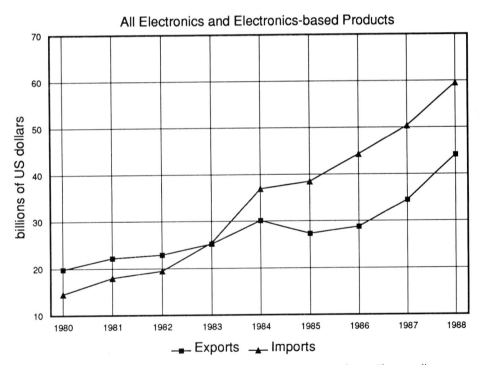

All Electronics and Electronics-based Products

billions of US dollars

—■— Exports   —▲— Imports

Deteriorating trade balance of the United States electronics industry. The overall balance in electronics has been negative since 1983, depressed by a huge deficit in consumer electronics (SITC 761, 762, and 763) and a growing shortfall in telecommunications equipment (764). Computers (752) still cling to a positive balance, though they incorporate mainly imported components (7722, 7764, 77689). [*Source:* United Nations: *Yearbook of International Trade Statistics,* various years (New York: United Nations).]

(Continued on next page)

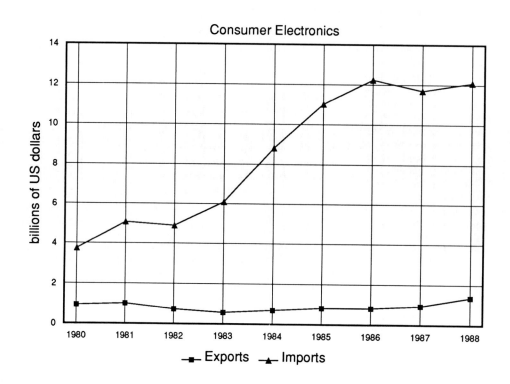

Consumer Electronics

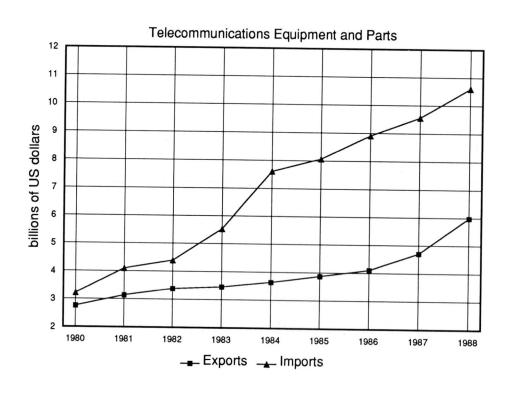

Telecommunications Equipment and Parts

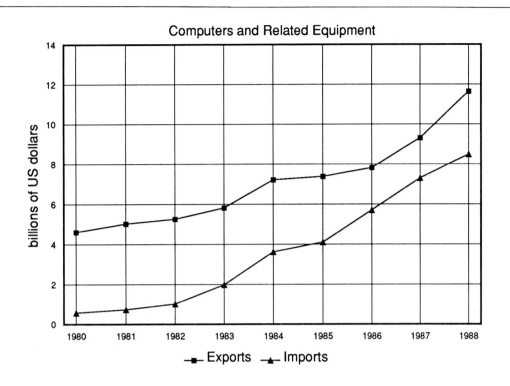

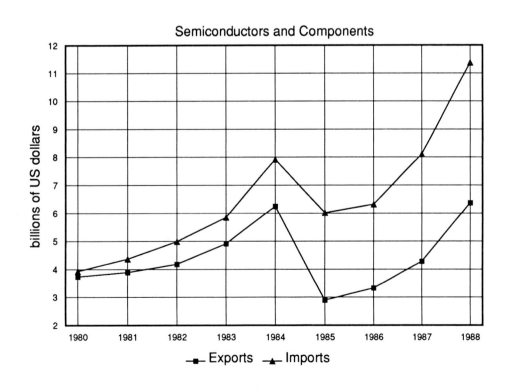

(Continued on next page)

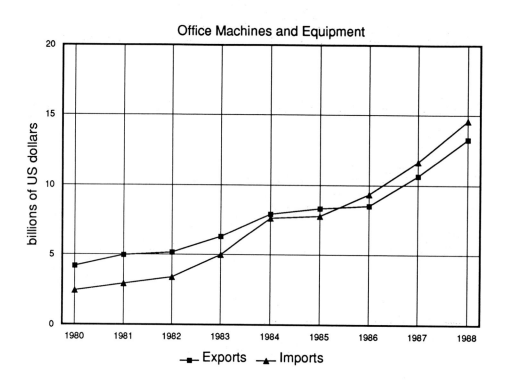

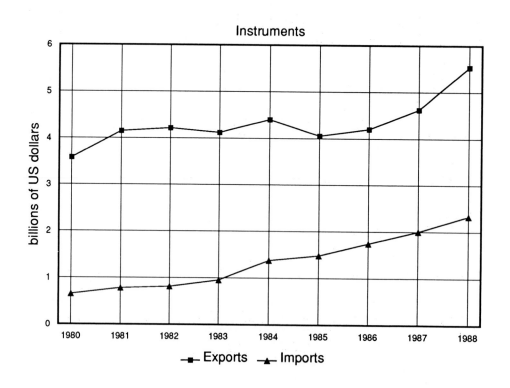

velopment, Japan quickly seized the lead in manufacture by the end of the 1970s. However, U.S. makers seem to be benefiting from the current emphasis upon chips designed for special applications, because American engineers and manufacturers still excel in devising new technologies and creative software. Furthermore, the production of custom-designed parts of this kind is locationally tied to end-users. The fragmented markets that result from this are unsuited to the Japanese, whose techniques are geared to mass production.

Telecommunications is another very large and dynamic high-technology area that is stressed by Japan's economic planners. The United States had always had a positive balance of trade in this category until the 1980s, when imports of telecommunications equipment for the first time exceeded exports. In this case the main competition comes from Canada as well as Japan.

For years, one of the keystones of the American lead in high technology has been the aircraft industry, which draws upon some of the country's greatest competitive strengths. Very large, highly capitalized companies dominate this industry, in which product development alone requires billions of dollars. American aircraft builders have benefited from enormous defense contracts from both the U.S. and foreign governments, and these have yielded valuable R & D byproducts for the development of commercial aircraft. U.S. exports of aircraft still make a large positive contribution to the balance of trade, but imports are beginning to cut into this surplus too.

How can the United States prevent further erosion of its high-technology trade? What steps should the country take to stimulate exports in this important area of comparative advantage? As foreign competition intensifies, many in the industry have agitated for government protection from imports, but a 1984 report on this subject by the President's Commission on Industrial Competitiveness (the Young Commission) offered a different set of prescriptions and stressed the need to increase manufacturing productivity.

The Young Commission urged that the United States direct more private and government money into civilian research and development. Other countries are spending much more on R & D, as a percentage of gross national product, and the United States should follow their example and in a more organized way than in the past. Half of U.S. research funding currently goes to the military, which no longer yields the civilian spinoffs that it formerly did in simpler times.

The Young Commission sternly crit-

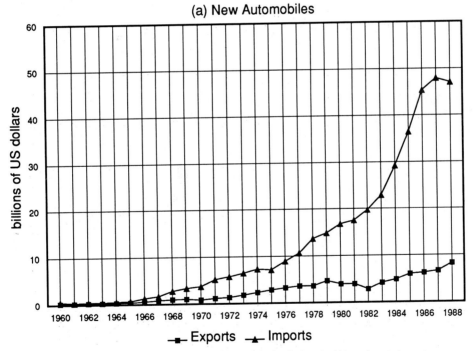

The U.S. balance of trade in new automobiles and aircraft. Although auto imports have leveled off as foreign companies manufacture larger numbers of their vehicles in the United States, the huge U.S. negative balance in this category remains a heavy drain on the country's overall trade position. A large and growing positive balance in worldwide sales of aircraft helps to offset some of this shortfall in autos. Note the effects of economic conditions on the world market for aircraft. [*Source:* U.S. Bureau of the Census, *Statistical Abstract of the United States,* various years (Washington, D.C.: U.S. Government Printing Office).]

(*Continued on next page*)

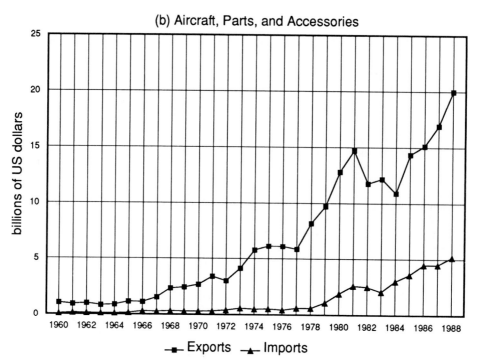

(b) Aircraft, Parts, and Accessories

icized American industry for failing to modernize its manufacturing techniques. Too often, U.S. firms are unable to gain full benefit from their newly developed products because foreign competitors soon make them more cheaply. According to the Young report, however, much of the fault lies with the U.S. government, which has created an economic environment in which capital is too costly. Japanese companies can borrow at interest rates only a fraction of those paid by American firms. The Young Commission also blamed U.S. antitrust laws and practices, which prevent the kind of inter-firm cooperation needed to compete with giant, integrated companies like those in Japan and other East Asian countries.

The international competitiveness of U.S. high-technology enterprises suffers also from the country's failure to make the best use of its human resources. The Young Commission criticized the adversarial relationship between management and labor, which is harmful to productivity and quality control. In addition, however, the country is failing to educate enough scientists and engineers and is doing too little to retrain workers at a time of rapid technological change.

Like many critics before them, the Young Commission stressed the need for the U.S. government to make a greater commitment to using the country's resources more effectively and thus increasing international competitiveness. To focus this effort, the com-

mission urged the creation of a Cabinet-level Science and Technology Department and a Trade and Industry Department. Such agencies have played key roles in the industrial development of Japan and a number of other countries.

Technology-intensive products are the most dynamic element in contemporary international commerce. The United States has long relied upon its comparative advantage in high-technology production, but its lead in this area is fragile. Whether the country can halt its recent slippage in high-technology trade in this era of intensifying competition depends upon how effectively it can mobilize its resources to that end.

For convenience, we may divide the less-developed world into three main groups. First, following Linder's (1967) classification, we may distinguish between the countries that are truly *developing,* that is, those demonstrating a real capability for the sustained growth required ultimately to join the industrialized world, and those that may be termed *backward,* nations confronting such grave obstacles to development that very little hope can be held for their future prospects. Recent events have pushed into prominence still a third group, *the high-income oil exporters,* typified by Saudi Arabia and Libya. Despite all the usual

demographic and cultural traits of underdevelopment, these lands have achieved some of the world's highest per capita GNPs because their oil revenues are very great relative to their small populations.

Trade Problems of Less-Developed Countries

Except for the high-income oil exporters and a small, select group of Asian lands, the less-developed countries (LDCs) of this present era have not found trade to be the vehicle for economic growth that it had been for those countries now regarded as developed. The great majority of LDCs encounter a host of serious problems in their commercial relations with the rest of the world. Some of these problems are of domestic origin, being inherent in the condition of underdevelopment; others, however, stem from the conditions of inequality faced by LDCs in their dealings with the industrialized world.

One of the most serious dilemmas for LDCs results from their tendency to overspecialize in export production. Most of these countries rely upon only one or two commodities, usually agricultural products or minerals, for the greater part of their export earnings. Cuba, for instance, obtains 93 percent of its foreign exchange from the sale of primary commodities, and 74 percent of the total comes from sugar alone. Coffee contributes 97 percent of Uganda's export earnings; tea and cotton supply the remainder. According to conventional trade theory, a country should benefit from concentrating its resources upon what it does best because of the efficiencies and the economies of large-scale production that specialization supposedly brings. For exporters of primary goods, however, this is not usually the case. Narrow specialization in such commodities risks heavy losses as a result of crop failures, uncertain foreign demand, and fluctuating world prices. Adding to these problems is the temptation for primary producers to increase output even during periods when the world market has become saturated and prices are falling. Seeing their incomes decline as prices drop, farmers may plant still larger acreages in the hope that the increased volume of output will help them maintain their customary incomes. This response to glutted markets is directly opposite to that of factory managers in similar circumstances.

In some LDCs the primary export industries are owned and controlled by foreign enterprises. This is common in mineral ventures and in plantation agriculture, and especially in the production of beverage crops, commercial fibers, and tropical fruits. Foreign companies supply not only the capital and technology but also the managers and skilled workers needed for a modern venture serving world markets. Only the unskilled laborers come from the local community. Surrounding these enclaves of commercial agriculture are the subsistence farms of the indigenous populations. Such a juxtaposition of the primitive and the modern constitutes a *dual economy,* a feature typical of tropical America, Africa, and southern Asia.

In the organization of their societies most of today's LDCs differ from those lands settled by Europeans, especially the British. Unlike the transplanted Europeans of the early United States and Canada, the current populations of less-developed regions lack a commercial tradition. Inherited social attitudes and value systems are often incompatible with the competitive, profit-driven viewpoints prevalent in industrialized societies. Because of this it is difficult for such peoples to adjust to the changes required for modern production. The LDCs of this present era also confront grave demographic and employment problems. Overpopulation, steadily worsening because of high birth rates, creates a surplus of labor, leading to severe unemployment and underemployment. The current group of industrialized nations did not have to bear any of these social burdens at similar stages of development.

Unequal Trade Relations with Industrialized Countries

The many economic and social problems confronting most of today's less-developed countries place them at a disadvantage in their commercial relations with the developed lands. The major exceptions to this, of course, are the high-income oil-exporting countries of the Middle East, whose membership in the OPEC cartel places them in an unusually strong bargaining position. Excluding these, the LDCs as a whole account for no more than one-sixth of total world trade. Yet, relatively small though it be, this trade is utterly essential to the developing nations. For them the industrial countries are the only source for many of their needs and the principal market for their traditional exports. These imports and exports are indispensable to the development process itself.

Among the imports required by LDCs are those consumer goods they are incapable of producing domestically. Equally crucial, however, are those commodities required for economic growth: the machinery and other capital equipment needed to modernize agriculture and build factories, the spare parts and other items to keep the machinery running, and industrial raw materials not available domestically. Many of these new industries make goods formerly imported, and this *import substitution* further alters the commodity composition of their foreign trade.

To pay for the imports they must have, developing countries have no choice other than to sell their goods in world markets. Initially, at least, these are the primary commodities for which LDCs have both absolute and comparative advantages. Their resource endowments, such as soils and climates conducive to tropical agriculture, dictate the nature of the goods they market abroad. We should stress, however, that LDCs are called primary producers solely because primary products are all they export. Several industrialized nations—notably Canada, the United States, and

Australia—actually export greater absolute amounts of primary commodities because of the immense land endowments they possess. These and other developed countries are the main sources of the grains and other temperate crops that are the major staples of world agricultural commerce.

In exporting primary goods to the industrialized countries the less-developed regions operate under severe disadvantages. For one thing, manufacturers are becoming increasingly efficient in their use of raw materials and are processing them more thoroughly than in the past, thus requiring relatively smaller amounts of these items, many of which come from less-developed areas. Moreover, industries make greater use of synthetic materials that compete with the natural substances. Again, the major exception is petroleum, the need for which grows steadily throughout the world. Otherwise, the contribution of LDCs to world exports continues to shrink relatively.

Another problem for LDCs is the nature of demand for their traditional agricultural exports. Owing to Engel's law (see Chapter 12), world markets for farm products grow slowly—at about the rate of world population growth—and demand for them responds only slightly to changes in prices. Yet, the global supply of these commodities fluctuates widely in response to the variability of harvests, causing prices to be unstable. Individually weak and disunited, LDCs are unable to influence the prices of their agricultural goods in world markets. Instead, such prices are set in the great commodity markets of London, New York, Chicago, and other commercial centers.

Developing countries as a group are becoming more active exporters of manufactured products, but many of them find it difficult to penetrate the markets of industrialized countries. Most manufactured exports of LDCs are technically simple, often the results of first-stage processing of metallic ores. Even some of the more sophisticated manufactured goods exported by developing countries pose marketing difficulties. One such problem is the technology gap, because of which the products of these countries cannot compete on equal terms with the superior quality and lower prices of similar goods produced in the industrialized countries. Furthermore, LDCs usually do not have large enough home markets to provide adequate bases for achieving the necessary economies of scale. This problem is all the greater because of the natural inefficiencies of newly started industries, which raise unit costs. Also, many entrepreneurs in less-developed lands are unfamiliar with the quality standards, delivery schedules, and customary sales channels in major world markets.

LDCs almost always have deficits in their foreign

trade, and sometimes these are relatively large. Because of the kinds of problems we have just enumerated, LDCs usually do not earn enough from their exports to pay for all the imported goods they must have to sustain their economies and promote their development. For this reason the governments of LDCs tend to interfere in their foreign trade by using a variety of devices: licensing, exchange controls, tariffs, quotas, and so on. They consider these necessary to limit the drain on their reserves of foreign exchange and to reduce the importation of "inessentials" so as to conserve financial resources needed to pay for necessary items. Tariffs help to improve the price ratio (terms of trade) with industrialized nations and provide protection for infant industries.

Among the LDCs, those that can be considered as "developing" probably have the most immediately pressing import needs, but the "backward" countries possibly have the gravest trade problems in the longer run. Trade with the industrialized world can quickly extinguish any unprotected import-competing industry that might have served as a basis for development, as happened when cheap factory-made imports killed much of the cottage textile industry of India. In some LDCs the obstacles to development are so great that even large export earnings may fail to nudge the nation toward true modernization, as shown by the experience of certain oil-exporting countries of Africa and the Middle East.

So different, then, are the less-developed countries as a group from industrialized countries that many analysts are asking whether conventional trade theory is truly relevant to the experience of today's LDCs. According to this theory, free trade invariably leads to an international specialization that is beneficial to all participants. It brings about a more efficient allocation of resources, and it spreads its effects to other sectors of the economy. The experience of the United Kingdom and other advanced countries during the nineteenth century and that of Japan since World War II would seem to confirm this. Why is it not happening generally among today's LDCs?

The main reason for the failure of these theoretical expectations to materialize widely in the Third World is that most LDCs do not have the capacity to extend growth in their export sectors to the rest of their economies. The apparent explanation for this is that in most contemporary LDCs a variety of political, social, and cultural conditions act as barriers to the linkage of export industries to the economy as a whole. It is these barriers that perpetuate the dual economies described earlier. For these barriers to be removed, development must extend to all aspects of national life. In this process public policy must establish the necessary conditions. The remarkable progress of certain LDCs that have adopted new strategies for trade and development demonstrates the importance of this.

Trade Strategies for Development

Industrialization is the overriding national goal of virtually all less-developed countries. Only industry offers the hope for achieving a level of economic growth that exceeds their rates of population growth; world demand for their traditional agricultural exports is not increasing fast enough. Only manufacturing can generate employment in sufficient quantity to absorb the flood of new entrants into their labor forces. For most LDCs, industrialization is also a matter of national pride: They depend upon it to elevate them to a status comparable to that of the present advanced lands. LDCs therefore resent the implications of conventional trade theory, which would relegate them to a permanent role as suppliers of primary goods to the richer lands.

The road to industrialization has been slow and difficult for today's LDCs, however. Most of them, especially those in Latin America, have until recently followed policies of import-substituting industrialization, that is, establishing industries to produce for the domestic market those manufactured goods previously imported from First World countries. In addition to the elaborate bureaucratic procedures these entail, policies of this sort create many new problems. Import substitution ordinarily means high-cost production for limited national markets, which leads to inflation and represents a continual drain on economies. Furthermore, industrialization of this kind soon saturates local markets and exhausts the opportunities for further import substitution. Consequently, only those LDCs with very large domestic markets—such as Brazil and Mexico—have benefited very much from this approach to development, and even these are having to find new strategies for future growth.

Some of the semi-industrialized countries of the Orient are pointing the way for LDCs that have reached the limits of import substitution. The semi-industrialized countries (SICs) are the new middle-income nations of the world community. They are the most advanced of the LDCs: Their per capita incomes are higher, their manufacturing sectors are larger and more sophisticated, and they are more urbanized. Manufactured goods represent one-fifth or more of their total output, and they constitute a quarter or more of their exports. As a group, the SICs have achieved impressive levels of economic growth, well in excess of their rates of population growth, which in

several cases are still high. Most of this growth has resulted from the effective way in which these countries have used their resources to assume new roles in the international economy.

The Four Tigers of Asia—South Korea, Taiwan, Hong Kong, and Singapore—have set the pattern for this kind of trade-led development strategy, which in turn was modeled after the celebrated Japanese example. Since the 1960s, the four have successfully followed national policies that have favored export production based initially upon labor-intensive manufacturing industries operating within a capitalistic framework. None of them is well endowed with natural resources, but each is able to draw upon an impressive array of human resources.

After nearly four decades of sustained fast growth, the Tigers have achieved per capita GNPs comparable to those of Mediterranean Europe. Realistically, therefore, they can no longer be classed as LDCs but are more generally referred to as "newly industrialized countries," or NICs. This extraordinary rise in material well-being has provided inspiration for developing nations everywhere, but especially in East Asia, where several countries have adopted similar growth strategies with promising results. Indeed, one of these, Thailand, has made such progress that it is sometimes referred to as the Fifth Tiger.

Though in detail the Tigers differ somewhat in their circumstances and approaches, South Korea's experience is fairly typical of the group. That country's economic growth, which averaged more than 9 percent per annum throughout the 1960s and 1970s, is all the more impressive when we consider its dismal state at the end of the Korean War in 1953. With the arrival of peace the country was left with only an impoverished agricultural economy: North Korea had all the mineral resources, nearly all the electric generation, and most of the manufacturing industries still remaining. The war had left South Korea devastated, most of its agricultural lands in waste, industries destroyed, a quarter of the population homeless, and per capita incomes among the world's lowest.

In the decade following the war, from 1953 to 1963, South Korean government policy emphasized reconstruction, defense, and raising the standard of living. United States aid throughout this period was substantial, amounting to 15 percent of gross national product. South Korea initially followed a typical strategy of import-substituting industrialization, concentrating upon nondurable consumer goods—mainly textiles, clothing, and foodstuffs—and giving little attention to agriculture. Though the possibilities for this kind of industrial development were exhausted by the early 1960s, South Korea had in the meantime acquired some valuable assets. Ten years of industrialization, accompanied by a drive to improve education, had produced a literate population and a corps of skilled managers and trained workers.

At this point the government abruptly shifted to a program of export-oriented industrialization, which focused upon producing nondurable consumer goods for the world market. Recognizing that the nation lacked physical resources but had an abundance of human resources, the new program offered special subsidies for exports, removed import duties on raw material imports, changed the tax structure to favor personal savings, and introduced more realistic currency exchange rates. This policy shift quickly produced remarkable results. Exports rose from only 3.3 percent of GNP in 1960 to 45 percent by 1977, a level that has remained unchanged since. Exports of manufactured goods increased during the early years at an average annual rate of 51 percent, rising from only 15 percent of Korea's exports in 1958 to 92 percent of the total by the late 1980s. The swift pace of trade-led growth has continued almost without pause: In the most 1980s Korea's GNP rose at a yearly rate averaging 9.9 percent (refer back to Figure 13.1).

The Four Tigers, and the semi-industrialized countries attempting to emulate them, have discovered, however, that an export-favoring policy succeeds only as long as world markets remain free. Because the developed countries are the best customers for SIC exports, taking about three-fifths of the total, access to these markets is very important. Yet, the more deeply SIC exporters penetrate the markets of the developed lands, the more resistance they encounter from rising protectionist sentiments in those countries (see Chapter 12, Box 12.1, for a discussion of this issue).

As quotas and other trade restrictions begin to cut their sales to the advanced countries, the SICs have discovered promising new markets for their manufactured goods in other less-developed countries. Brazil now trades more with other LDCs than it does with the United States; India is increasing its exports to the less-developed world faster than to the developed countries. The greater part of this rising trade among LDCs is from the more-industrialized countries to the less-industrialized ones; only a minor share takes place between countries at similar levels of development.

The manufactured products traded among LDCs are mainly those that rely upon economies of scale in manufacturing, have demanding skill requirements, call for relatively large capital inputs, and are produced by industries that were initially established to serve domestic markets. Note that these products ex-changed by LDCs are different in nature from the labor-intensive exports they send to industrialized countries. Furthermore, the products LDCs buy from each other are usually complementary to the kinds of goods they obtain from advanced countries, not substitutes for them.

One of the more significant recent trends in intra-LDC trade has been the rise in exports of capital equipment by certain of the more-industrialized developing countries. Producers in these countries have gained experience in designing and building machinery that is technically appropriate for their own industries, which are more labor-intensive and thus call for designs different from those of industries in Europe, Anglo-America, and Japan, where labor is more costly. Thus, Brazil, Argentina, India, and Mexico find markets for their own designs in other LDCs with labor requirements similar to their own. Argentina sells equipment for the processing and refrigeration of meats and fruits, drawing upon her own experience in the food industries. Brazil and Mexico, both well established in the metallurgical trades, export steelmaking equipment to LDCs. The semi-industrialized countries are pushing their exports of machinery and transport equipment. These are currently the most dynamic items in world trade, partly because of the growing demand among LDCs for such goods.

Attractive opportunities thus exist for trade among LDCs. They are more similar to each other in their demand and supply than they are to the industrialized countries, and they are more similar in economic size and levels of development; hence, they can compete and trade on more equal terms among themselves. The theoretical benefits of free trade are more attainable by countries at similar levels of development: Among equals, the opportunities for economies of scale and the efficiencies of international specialization are far greater. Buying from each other also permits LDCs to reduce their imports from industrialized lands, thereby saving their scarce hard currency for the purchase of those high-technology items that are as yet obtainable only from the advanced countries. Recognizing these benefits of intra-LDC trade, certain groups of less-developed countries have experimented with economic integration, a type of voluntary association pioneered in Western Europe.

INTERNATIONAL COOPERATION IN TRADE

Although the theoretical ideal of universal free trade has proved elusive, recent history has shown that the interdependence of countries is inescapable in the modern world economy. Policymakers have discovered that trying to "save jobs" by restricting imports carries excessively high costs in terms of slowed economic growth and worsened international relations. Nations have therefore resorted to intergovernmental agreements designed to give some of the benefits of free trade without sacrificing other national goals. Among the numerous approaches attempted, two main types emerge: (1) international agreements to reduce tariffs and quotas gradually and selectively among the majority of countries, and (2) arrangements that would eliminate or substantially reduce the barriers to trade among a small group of closely associated countries. The second approach, termed *regional economic integration,* has been prominent in recent decades.

Regional Economic Integration

The idea of joining sovereign nations together to form a single economic region is not new; the first experiments of this kind took place more than a century ago. Following the devastation of World War II, however, this technique seemed to offer the best hope for speeding recovery from the war and for overcoming the many problems of economic and political disintegration that had burdened Europe during the 1930s. Although trade is the main focus of economic integration, such organizations usually have other aims as well. Among the main purposes of economic integration are achieving growth through the creation of an enlarged market, raising standards of living, reducing regional disparities, enhancing the status of the group in world political and economic affairs, and finding cooperative solutions to a variety of other social and political problems. The questions raised by the postwar revival of such organizations have led to the appearance of a new body of economic integration theory, which is a subset of international trade theory and has implications for location theory. A seminal work on this subject was Jacob Viner's *The Customs Union Issue* (1950). Theoreticians and policymakers have viewed economic integration as a solution for problems of economic growth and development throughout the world.

Economic Integration in Theory and Practice.
As viewed by the theorist, economic integration is a form of selective discrimination because it combines elements of free trade with greater protection: free trade among members and restrictions on trade with nonmembers. Among other things, integration theory is concerned with the various types or degrees of economic integration, the characteristics of member countries that are conducive to successful integration, and the effects that economic integration can be expected

to have on international trade and location and on growth and development.

According to Bela Balassa (*The Theory of Economic Integration,* 1961), five levels or degrees of economic integration are conceivable (see Figure 13.2). At each succeeding stage, members surrender a greater measure of their national sovereignty. The first (and least restrictive) form of economic integration is the *free trade area,* in which the members agree to remove all barriers to trade within the group but may continue to pursue their own independent policies with respect to trade with nonmembers. The next higher degree of integration is the *customs union,* a type that has existed in Europe for more than a century. It calls for the free movement of goods among member countries but imposes a common system of restrictions on trade with outsiders. The third type is the *common market,* which, like the customs union, provides for free trade in merchandise among members of the group while maintaining uniform restraints on trade with nonmembers; in addition, however, this arrangement permits unrestricted movement of capital, labor, and entrepreneurship within the union. At a still higher level the *economic union* has all the characteristics of the common market but calls also for integrating the economies of member countries through a common central bank, unified monetary and tax systems, and a common foreign economic policy. The ultimate form is full *economic integration.* At this point the removal of all barriers to intrabloc movement of goods and factors of production is complete, unification of social as well as economic policies is achieved, and all members are subject to the binding decisions of a supranational authority consisting of executive, judicial, and legislative branches.

One of the earliest experiments, a free trade area attempted during the nineteenth century by Norway and Sweden, was unsuccessful. Certain customs unions formed at that time did survive, however. One of these was the German *Zollverein,* which joined together most of the many small kingdoms and grand duchies that eventually became modern Germany. Also still in existence are several *customs accessions.* These are customs unions that, in each case, unite a very small country with a larger one, as, for example, Switzerland and Liechtenstein, France and Monaco, and Belgium and Luxembourg.

Modern experimentation with cooperative ventures of this kind began in 1948 with the formation of Benelux, the members of which were Belgium, The Netherlands, and Luxembourg. Prior to its eventual absorption into the European Economic Community (page 390), Benelux functioned mainly as a customs union, although its founders had intended that it

A classification scheme for regional integration

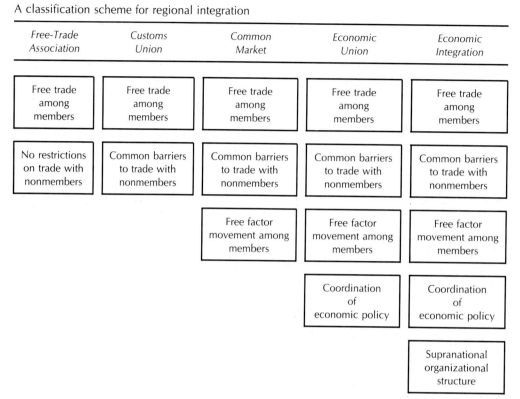

Free-Trade Association	Customs Union	Common Market	Economic Union	Economic Integration
Free trade among members	Free trade among members	Free trade among members	Free trade among members	Free trade among members
No restrictions on trade with nonmembers	Common barriers to trade with nonmembers	Common barriers to trade with nonmembers	Common barriers to trade with nonmembers	Common barriers to trade with nonmembers
		Free factor movement among members	Free factor movement among members	Free factor movement among members
			Coordination of economic policy	Coordination of economic policy
				Supranational organizational structure

FIGURE 13.2 A classification scheme for regional integration. The five categories, arrayed here in increasing order of restrictions placed upon members, should be regarded as ideal types. Though each of the existing organizations for regional integration tends in general to fall within one or more of these classes, all have distinctive features that may vary from the ideal. [*Source:* Based upon a classification suggested by Bela Balassa, *The Theory of Economic Integration* (Homewood, Ill.: Richard D. Irwin, 1961).]

evolve toward economic union. In 1952 the three members of this group joined with France, West Germany, and Italy to form the European Coal and Steel Community. The ECSC has functioned as a type of common market but with jurisdiction extending to only two sectors of the six national economies: the coal and steel industries. In view of future developments among these six countries, however, it is interesting to note that the ECSC organization was provided with executive, legislative, and judicial branches.

The immediate success of ECSC led the same six nations to extend this type of integration to all sectors of their economies, thereby creating the European Economic Community (EEC). Under the Treaty of Rome, which established this organization in 1957, the EEC ostensibly became a common market (and indeed has often been referred to as the European Common Market), but it also acquired a number of features associated with higher forms of integration (see Figure 13.2). These included an executive (consisting of the *Council of Ministers*, a policymaking body, and the *Commission*, which is charged with the day-to-day functioning of the organization), a legislature (the *European Parliament*), and a judiciary (the *Court of Justice*). Subsequently, the EEC's executive merged with the European Atomic Energy Community and the Coal and Steel Community to create a single group, now called simply the European Community, or EC.

By 1968 the EC had become a full customs union, with the lifting of all tariffs and quotas on trade between members and the instituting of a system of common impediments to trade with nonmembers. Nevertheless, certain restraints on intra-EC transactions persisted. Among these were nontariff trade barriers such as differing technical standards and government procurement policies favoring national firms and restrictions on the operations of banking, insurance, and other service activities within the union. Moreover, the surrender of individual national sovereignty implied by this arrangement was more apparent than real: Individual governments continued to exert substantial influence over EC affairs through the Council of Ministers, and the Parliament had only limited legislative functions.

Ensuing years brought some progress in forging a common market within which capital, labor, and entrepreneurship—as well as goods—could move freely. The goal remained elusive, however, and lingering restrictions on intrabloc factor movements remained. The energy crises and recessions of the 1970s and early 1980s were particularly disruptive, halting the EC's efforts to harmonize economic policies among members, except for the creation of a European Monetary Union to minimize fluctuations of currency exchange rates. Nevertheless, the EC never abandoned the prime objective of the Treaty of Rome: complete integration, political as well as economic, leading ultimately to a United States of Europe.

Largely because of this openly stated political aim for the EC and the loss of national sovereignty it would entail, seven other countries—the United Kingdom, Norway, Sweden, Denmark, Austria, Switzerland, and Portugal (later joined by Finland and Iceland)—established in 1960 a separate organization called the European Free Trade Association (EFTA). As a free trade area in industrial goods only, the EFTA is the least restrictive form of integration. Most of its members had special reasons to avoid more binding ties: prior commitments to non-European trading partners (Britain with the Commonwealth nations), long-

standing official policies of neutrality (Switzerland and Sweden), or conditions imposed under peace treaties with the former USSR (Austria and Finland).

The striking success of the EC eventually led the United Kingdom and certain other EFTA members to seek ties with the Common Market. After two fruitless attempts, the United Kingdom finally attained full EC membership in 1973, along with Denmark and Ireland. On that same date Denmark and the United Kingdom also withdrew from the EFTA, which was left with only seven members. In 1972 the new nine-member EC entered into an agreement with the remaining members of EFTA to form an industrial free trade area encompassing all 16 countries. In 1981 Greece became the tenth full member of EC, and Spain and Portugal joined in 1986 (Portugal's withdrawal from EFTA reduced the membership of that group to only seven). The map (Figure 13.3) shows the present 12 members of the EC and the effective dates of their affiliation.

In addition, the EC has entered into special arrangements with a number of other countries. It has signed association agreements with Turkey, Malta, and Cyprus and has extended preferential treatment to other Mediterranean lands, notably Israel. The group also has a trade-and-aid agreement, called the Lomé Convention, with 58 less-developed countries, all former colonies of EC members.

In 1987 the EC launched a bold initiative to

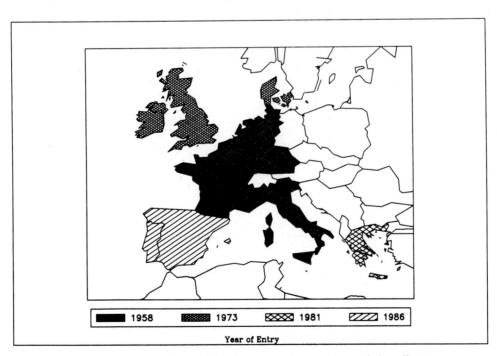

FIGURE 13.3   Members of the European Community and the effective dates of their entry into the union.

sweep away the remaining barriers to trade, migration, and capital by December 31, 1992, in a move aimed at achieving true economic and political unity. The prospect excited the imaginations of all Europeans, who dubbed it variously *Europe 1992* or *EC 92*. This project kindled a new sense of optimism in European business leaders, who initiated a flurry of corporate restruc-

turings and mergers in anticipation of unhindered access to a single market of 340 million people and a gross national product of $8.5 trillion. This prospect also revived the previously flagging interest of Japanese and American multinationals in European investment. Meanwhile, the EFTA began to seek closer links with the powerful new political and economic

---

BOX 13.2 Supereurope

Three decades after the signing of the Treaty of Rome creating the European Community, the 12 current EC members adopted the Single European Act (1986), a far-reaching program to create "an area without internal frontiers" by the end of 1992. This complex plan called for eliminating all remaining physical, political, and financial obstacles to free trade and the free movement of capital and individuals among member countries.

Following several years of economic stagnation and troublingly high unemployment, these countries had been under growing pressure from several directions to reinvigorate the EC. On one side was the threat of continued decline in the face of mounting economic competition from Japan and the United States. On the other were the tempting commercial opportunities offered by the freeing of Eastern Europe from communist domination. Lending further impetus was a special study by the European Commission, which found that establishing a single market of 340 million people would create jobs and substantially boost economic growth.

With the avowed goal of turning a unified Europe into an economic superpower, the EC mapped a three-stage approach to achieving full economic union. It called for establishing an EC central banking system, a single European currency, and supranational economic policy making. Creation of a single borderless internal market required passage of 282 pieces of legislation. The principal changes are as follows:

- Removing thousands of intricate, often invisible barriers to trade— including frontier delays, com-

plex documentation, and freight-hauling restrictions
- Eliminating restrictions on capital flows throughout the 12-nation territory
- Bringing uniformity to tax structures, especially value-added and excise taxes
- Ensuring freedom for workers to practice their professions and trades in all parts of the union
- Abolishing national government procurement deals that favored domestic firms and replacing these with Community-wide open bidding

Despite sometimes bitter controversy over details and the daunting number of practical difficulties to be worked out, support for the idea of a new "Europe without frontiers" was solid. All 12 political leaders had formally committed themselves and their governments to the venture. Polls of business leaders in every member country produced big majorities favoring a single European market; and the vision of *Europe 1992* promptly seized the popular imagination, becoming the main topic of seminars and commentary throughout the region. The mere promise of a single European market produced an immediate impact on the business climate of the entire region. The prospect of a border-free Europe forced European companies to grow bigger and stronger quickly. It produced a flurry of investment in new plant and equipment and in expanded R & D budgets, and it brought a rash of mergers and alliances among European firms. This activity was prompted not just by the anticipation of a vast communitywide market for their

goods. For innumerable small national firms long sheltered comfortably inside their home markets, the main driving force was the fear of powerful competition from other European-based companies and from Japanese and American multinationals drawn to the tempting opportunities offered by *Europe 1992*. The widespread corporate restructuring throughout the EC therefore took a clear pan-European direction.

The remaining members of the EFTA, fearful of being overwhelmed by a newly powerful neighbor, yet attracted by the business opportunities offered by this huge unified market, negotiated with the EC for creation of a "single economic space" that would include all 19 nations. In October of 1991, therefore, the two groups reached a tentative agreement to form a *European Economic Area*. Some EFTA countries began to seek EC membership and others contemplated such a move. These were in addition to an earlier application received from Turkey. Overtures also came from the newly liberated East European states. One of them, East Germany, became absorbed into the EC late in 1990 through its reunification with West Germany, and three others—Poland, Hungary, and Czechoslovakia—were granted associate membership in December of 1991.

As the target date of December 31, 1992 approached, the EC was faced with a number of urgent tasks. Most important, major amendments to the EC's constitution, the 1967 Treaty of Rome, would be required to accommodate the fundamental changes planned for the organization. After a period of intense debate, the 12 EC nations were at last forced by cataclysmic

entity taking shape in their midst. (See Box 13.2 for more on the events leading to *Europe 1992* and its consequences.)

Theoreticians have identified several characteristics of member countries that would be conducive to successful integration:

- *Parallel economies*. A union of countries whose economies are similar can be expected to achieve better results than one whose economies are dissimilar. Theoreticians reason that if several members of a union are able to produce the same goods, economic integration will

---

changes in the Soviet Union—and the potential threat these posed to European security and stability—to face this difficult assignment. Therefore, at a December 1991 meeting in the Dutch town of Maastricht they forged an agreement to create a new entity called the *European Union,* incorporating both a European monetary union with its own currency and a political union possessing the elements of a future European government. More ambitious than the earlier EC 1992 concept, these plans, if realized, would surely result in creation of a world superpower.

The new arrangement had three major components, having to do with economics, foreign affairs, and defense. A key feature was the *Economic and Monetary Union* (*EMU*), which would provide Europe with a common currency and a central bank before the end of the century. The new *European Currency Unit* (*ECU*), would replace an existing ECU (valued at about $1.28, this had previously been used only for settling national accounts). The new *European Central Bank,* which would function much as the U.S. Federal Reserve Bank, would begin minting ECUs for general distribution by 1997.

The second element of the accord was the provision for a *common foreign policy,* with rules designed to encourage foreign ministers to agree on major external issues and pursue unified policies abroad. The third part of the compact was the so-called *Western European Union,* which was to function as the organization's defense arm in coordination with the existing North Atlantic Treaty Organization (NATO). The Maastricht agreement also contained a variety of other provisions:

common citizenship throughout the European Union; increased powers for the Parliament; an assortment of "social laws" (labor regulations, consumer protection, health, education, international crime); development of trans-European networks (telecommunications, transport, energy projects); and special assistance to the Union's poorer member countries.

This last provision dealt with one of the basic problems facing the Union: the great differences in economic well-being among the 12 nations, as shown by the gulf separating Portugal (per capita GNP, $3650) and West Germany ($18,480). Even greater disparities existed at the subnational level; for example the contrasts between the affluent Dutch urban agglomerations and the impoverished Mezzogiorno of southern Italy.

The potentially powerful new economic and political Union produced by the Maastricht accord would appear destined to have a profound impact not only on Europe but on the entire global economy. When the new European Central Bank begins issuing real ECUs, it should revolutionize European finance. At the very outset, a new outbreak of inter-European bank consolidations began and stock and bond markets for all of Europe were planned. The trillions of dollars (or ECUs) attracted by these institutions could rival or even dwarf those of the U.S. and Japanese markets. Moreover, the ECU could threaten the preeminent place of the U.S. dollar as an international reserve currency.

A single currency for all of Europe would likewise benefit manufacturers, who would find it easier to finance mergers and acquisitions across borders. They would also be relieved of

the cost of dealing in 11 national currencies, thereby saving an estimated $15 billion in exchange transactions each year. On the other hand, a Union-wide discipline imposed by the European Central Bank would sharply limit the ability of individual governments to run budget deficits or indulge in inflationary practices. With all goods bearing price tags in ECUs, however, consumers would find it much easier to engage in comparison shopping.

By contrast with the enthusiasm of European business leaders for the decision at Maastricht, the American business community was wary. Many U.S. executives feared that a united Europe would become a "Europe Inc." similar to the "Japan Inc." with which they had been contending. They foresaw a host of insidious regulatory devices contrived by protectionist-minded Europeans. U.S. multinationals also disliked the social provisions of the treaty, with which they were unfamiliar.

Although the EC heads of state reached agreement at Maastricht, no treaty was signed there. The actual signing was to take place early in 1992, after the wording had been refined. It then required ratification by the various EC parliaments, as well as approval of the Danish and Irish electorates in national referendums. Final implementation was scheduled for the end of 1992.

Hard as it had been to overcome the accumulated divisions of centuries, the majority of Europeans looked upon *EC 92* as an inevitability; the process of creating a single internal market now appeared irreversible. For many this meant that the European century was at hand.

force them to become more efficient in order to survive the intensified competition.

- *Propinquity*. A union should yield greater benefits if its members are not too distant from each other. Nearness reduces transport costs, increases the likelihood that tastes of neighboring populations will be alike, and provides trading companies with a keener awareness of business opportunities across the border.
- *Contiguous countries within a compact area*. Ideally, member countries should be adjacent to one another and should form a combined land area of compact shape, thereby minimizing total aggregate transfer costs throughout the union.
- *Large combined territory*. The total area of the group should be sufficiently large to permit diverse production and a division of labor among them.
- *Small countries*. If the countries are individually small, each member will presumably enjoy relatively greater gains from union because of the enhanced possibilities for improvement that access to a large market offers a nation of limited size.
- *Best customers and suppliers*. The probability of a successful union is greater for a group whose members were previously one another's best customers and principal suppliers.
- *Major world traders*. As viewed from a global perspective, a union will be more beneficial if its members contributed in aggregate a substantial proportion of the world's output and trade.
- *High trade barriers*. The increase in intrabloc trade is likely to be greater for a group of nations that were formerly prevented from trading freely with each other because of high tariffs.

Although both the EC and EFTA countries benefited from economic integration, the EC has made the more impressive gains. At the time of its formation, observers expected the Common Market to do well because the resource endowments of member countries appeared to complement each other: France and Luxembourg offered iron ore, Germany coal, Italy surplus labor, and Belgium and The Netherlands large quantities of intensively produced food crops. In actuality, however, most of the products of Common Market countries have proved highly competitive. The members have not relied heavily upon one another's minerals or food supplies but instead have exchanged mainly finished and semifinished manufactured goods.

All make iron and steel, fabricate metal products, and produce an enormous variety of consumer goods.

The EC countries are individually small or moderate in size, but together they comprise a large part of Europe. They are mainly contiguous and are linked by well-developed transport systems. The group includes some of the world's greatest trading nations, and most are one another's best customers. All depend heavily upon trade, especially the Benelux countries, which export half or more of their output. This is a remarkable change from pre-World War II days, when high tariffs and quotas reduced intra-European trade to a minimum.

The EFTA countries are more complementary than the EC in the goods they produce. Scandinavia exports forest products and minerals, as well as manufactured goods; Switzerland and Austria are principally manufacturing nations; and Iceland is mainly a primary producer. Unlike the EC, the EFTA countries are widely separated, and several occupy locations peripheral to the European continent. Some active trading nations belong to the group, but since the departure of the United Kingdom none of the remaining members is the equal of most EC nations. Whereas the EFTA as a whole has benefited from union, it is interesting to note that the greatest relative gains have gone to the Scandinavian members, which are contiguous, highly competitive with one another, and similar in many other respects. Indeed, the four Scandinavian countries experimented for a time with a trading bloc called the Nordic Economic Union, or Nordek.

One of the theoretical tests of integration is whether it has largely created trade that did not exist before or instead has acted to divert trade out of its natural channels. This is a normative view of the problem, based upon the presumption that trade creation is "good" and trade diversion is "bad." A union has created trade if integration has caused production to shift from high-cost to low-cost sources. Trade diversion entails a shift from low-cost to higher-cost suppliers. Trade creation thus results in a more efficient allocation of world resources, whereas trade diversion has the opposite effect.

Any increase in trade among union members resulting from removal of internal trade barriers represents the creation of new trade. This comes about in the same way as in the case illustrated in Figure 12.1 (Chapter 12), where trade between two countries resulted in savings for buyers and higher incomes for sellers. Countries that do not belong to the union, however, lose some of their former export markets if these are captured by suppliers within the group. To the extent that the old sources of supply were more efficient producers than the new sources within the bloc, trade diversion has taken place. In the long run, however, integration can result in trade gains even for nonmember countries if the union causes members to enjoy accelerated economic growth and thus to demand more products from the rest of the world. Depending upon the way in which trade gains and trade losses balance each other, therefore, economic integration can result in either a net increase in total world trade or a net decrease.

These effects are to be seen in the experience of the EC, whose trade has grown enormously since union. Though the largest share of this new trade is with other EC members, trade between the EC and the rest of the world has also risen sharply because EC's prosperity has increased the general level of demand in member countries. Yet the EC has caused some trade diversion in specific commodities. This is especially true of agricultural goods, which have received a uniformly high level of protection under the EC's Common Agricultural Policy. Denmark, a long-time supplier of foods to neighboring West Germany, lost much of that trade after formation of the union and prior to its belated entry into the group. The Netherlands, a founding member that competes with Denmark in those same farm products, gained some of what Denmark lost in shipments to Germany. Sales of grain by the United States and Canada to the EC have also suffered because of the new trade barriers, whereas French farmers have been able to pick up additional sales from their protected position inside the common tariff wall. Many other farm products have been similarly affected, notably citrus fruits, as have certain types of manufactured goods.

Removing the barriers to intrabloc trade should theoretically permit each member country to concentrate upon producing those goods for which its comparative advantage is greatest. This specialization, together with increased competition and the economies of large-scale production for an enlarged market, should make producers more efficient. Reduced prices and higher incomes, together with a greater variety of merchandise on store shelves and more efficient distribution of goods, should raise levels of consumption.

The European experiments tend to bear out these theoretical expectations, but not quite in the way anticipated. Studies of trade among members of the EC and EFTA have not disclosed an increased specialization of one country in steel, another in grain, another in textiles, and so forth. Instead, these major industries have largely remained where they were before union, although certain subcategories have experienced marked changes in location. Thus, all Common Market countries make steel, but one may emphasize sheet-steel products, another may produce structural-steel members, and a third may specialize in wire and rod products.

A high common tariff wall normally discourages some imports from former suppliers outside the union. In reaction to this threatened loss of market, foreign suppliers often decide to build factories inside union territory in order to get under the tariff wall with their goods, thus substituting their flows of capital for flows of goods. The enormous investments by United States companies in manufacturing facilities in Western Europe since integration confirm this locational effect. Indeed, one study found that more than 800 new U.S. enterprises were established in the EC during the first three years of its operation.

Because it leads to a free flow of goods among member countries, economic integration is likely to result in a relocation of production within the union. Related industries tend to cluster at a limited number of the more desirable locations to avail themselves of the advantages of agglomeration. This in turn may reduce or eliminate production at those less-viable locations remaining from the preintegration period when each country protected a wide range of its industries, however inefficiently they may have operated. The centers of agglomeration emerging after integration will in turn attract additional new industries, thereby polarizing production still further.

Studies of industrial location since formation of the EC, where the freer flow of capital, labor, and management reinforces these polarizing tendencies, confirm that industrial concentration has indeed intensified in certain favored locations. Yet, the preexisting industrial centers in each member country appear to have survived, an indication of how firmly entrenched the industries of Western Europe had become prior to union. The net locational result of European integration appears to have been not only an increase in intra-industry product specialization but also an intensified regional specialization within the existing locational framework.

One of the principal purposes of economic integration is to promote the economic growth of member countries. Contributing to this growth is the increased efficiency in the use of natural and human resources that union is expected to bring about. The enlarged market provides opportunities for economies of scale to industries previously confined to limited national markets. Intensified competition forces companies to operate more efficiently, and the rising level of demand induces firms to increase in size through internal growth or mergers. As their capital resources grow, companies allocate more funds for research and development, which in turn leads to a proliferation of new products. The increased market also reduces business uncertainty and boosts profits, thereby attracting additional investment from both domestic and foreign sources. This acceleration of economic activity causes personal incomes to swell, further expanding the level of demand. The gains should be greatest for those unions with higher degrees of integration. In the EC, for instance, the combined GNP rose by more than one-half within the first decade of its existence.

The example of Europe's growth through economic integration was not lost on other parts of the world. Experimentation with such unions has taken place in nearly every part of the world, including

Oceania. There, Australia and New Zealand joined in a free trade area (NAFTA) when Britain's entry into the EC forced them to find other outlets for their goods.

In North America, the first tentative step toward cooperation of this sort was the U.S.–Canada Auto Pact of 1965, an experiment in sectoral integration. This accord created a two-nation free trade area limited to motor vehicles and original equipment parts—products of a single large industry dominated by a common set of giant companies operating on both sides of the border. The Auto Pact proved very benefi-

---

BOX 13.3 The U.S.–Canada Free Trade Agreement

The agreement creating a free-trade area between the United States and Canada became effective January 1, 1989. The FTA, as it is called, was a major achievement, reached only after 3 years of arduous negotiations to reconcile divergent interests of the world's leading pair of trading partners. Even before the FTA, commercial ties between the two had been exceptionally close: In 1988 their combined merchandise trade with each other amounted to $150 billion and their direct investments in one another's economies totaled $89 billion. The two also had a very large trade in services, $31 billion in 1987.

In some respects the FTA allowed the partners even freer access to their combined market area than the pre-1992 EC did for its members. The accord thus promised to give a significant push to the U.S. and Canadian economies. Implementation was to be fast: All elements of the pact were to be completed by 1998—10 years after the FTA's inception. As a precaution, the agreement provided a 5-year phasing-in period, during which Canadian and U.S. companies could appeal trade rulings to a bilateral panel. In addition, it offered a process by which particular industries might petition for accelerated reduction of duties ahead of the scheduled dates, if this could be shown to be mutually advantageous.

In some respects the FTA also exceeded the EC in scope of coverage. The main provisions are as follows:

- *Tariffs.* The most sweeping change in U.S.–Canadian trade relations was the scheduled removal of all tariffs by 1998. Tariffs on some goods were to be eliminated immediately, others in either 5 or 10 years, the slower schedules being mainly for agriculture and labor-intensive manufactures. On the eve of the pact, Canadian tariffs averaged 9 percent and U.S. tariffs, 4.5 percent. Dropping these duties was expected to bring a major expansion of bilateral trade, especially in those categories with substantially higher-than-average tariffs. For U.S. exporters these included furniture, textiles and clothing, electrical machinery, and fabricated metals. Chief Canadian beneficiaries were such strong export industries as steel, chemicals, pulp and paper, and brewing.

- *Services.* The U.S.-Canada FTA offered the first comprehensive international agreement on the conduct of trade in services. This is a vital element in U.S.–Canadian trade relations. Two-thirds of the U.S. gross domestic product comes from the services and nearly three-fifths of Canada's, and the services trade between the two has been growing rapidly. Though the Canadian and U.S. markets had always been relatively open to this type of activity, the FTA explicitly ensured almost

unrestricted access. In particular, it guaranteed "national treatment" of service providers, meaning that they would be treated no less favorably in one country than in the other. Specific provisions covered the rights of telecommunications services, tourist-related industries, architectural services, and banks and insurance companies.

- *Automotive trade.* FTA preserved the basic elements of the U.S.-Canada Auto Pact, but to make sure that the benefits were confined to North American producers, it specified that at least 50 percent of the value of the goods must originate in North America. The agreement eliminated Canada's tariff subsidies for car exports and its embargo on used-car imports. Canadian consumers would eventually be permitted to purchase vehicles duty-free in the United States, which they could not do under the original Auto Pact.

- *Agriculture.* The FTA eliminated all export subsidies on agricultural commodities and it specified the removal of all bilateral tariffs, and most quotas, on farm products within 10 years. It removed Canadian barriers to U.S. wine and distilled spirits. FTA set up a mechanism for reducing technical differences in health and sanitary regulations that interfere with agricultural trade.

cial to manufacturers, whose factories were able to concentrate on long production runs of individual models, thereby gaining economies of scale. Under this arrangement, too, Canadian consumers enjoyed a wider selection of models at lower prices than previously available in their relatively small market.

Then, in 1989, after long, hard bargaining, Canada and the United States signed the historic U.S.–Canada Free Trade Agreement (FTA). This produced the world's largest free-trade area, extending from the Arctic Circle to the Rio Grande and linking two countries whose bilateral trade ($150 billion in 1988) exceeded that of any other country pair. Opening the 4000-mile U.S.–Canadian border to a virtually free exchange of merchandise, the FTA also covered energy, services, and investment. See Box 13.3 for additional information on the contents of the agreement and its impact. (The U.S.–Canada FTA was actually the second such agreement for the United States, which had concluded a free trade pact with Israel 4 years previously.)

Following closely upon the U.S.–Canada FTA, the United States entered into discussions with Mexico concerning the possibilities for joining all three na-

---

- *Government procurement.* In the past, both Canadian and U.S. agencies have shown preferential treatment to their own national companies in their purchases for governmental use. FTA substantially increased the amount of government procurement that would be open to fair competition among suppliers from both countries.

- *Investment.* The FTA contained the first bilateral investment agreement between Canada and the United States. It reduced the screening of U.S. investments in Canada, eliminated most trade-distorting performance requirements, and provided guarantees for investors in both countries.

- *Border-crossing procedures.* The agreement streamlined border-crossing procedures for business visitors, professionals, traders, investors, intracompany personnel transfers, and other qualified persons.

- *Dispute resolution.* The most difficult issue facing negotiators for the FTA—and one that almost caused the talks to fail—was how to handle trade disputes. The final solution: creation of a joint panel to resolve disagreements over dumping and subsidies, which would replace review by courts. Another panel would decide the validity of future trade laws relating the dumping and subsidy questions.

Considering its range, the FTA might be expected to affect the two economies much as the EC has changed Western Europe. Though recession and other distorting events following the FTA's inception complicate any assessment, some initial impacts of the accord were apparent.

In the first 2 years of the agreement, trade between the two changed significantly. By 1990 Canada's merchandise exports to the United States had risen to more than 75 percent of its total exports. Exports of aerospace, telecommunications, and office-machine products showed impressive gains. Canada also experienced an initial import surge as its companies bought sophisticated U.S. machinery and equipment needed to make their factories more competitive.

The FTA brought a rash of expansions, consolidations, and modernizations of manufacturing operations, especially among Canadian firms. For some, as in the food-processing and the garment industries, the incentive was mainly defensive. For others, however, it was the prospect of selling into a market 10 times as large as their own. Accustomed to doing business across the immense east-west expanse of Canada, these companies began looking southward for new opportunities.

One result of these new perceptions was a rise in Canadian direct investment in U.S. production and distribution facilities. Chief beneficiaries of this new Canadian investment were U.S. border-crossing cities, such as Buffalo, which is less than 2 hours by expressway from Canada's business capital, Toronto.

Though Canadian companies were generally more alert to the potential threats and opportunities posed by the FTA, many U.S. firms reacted to these same stimuli, especially those whose businesses straddled the border. Many U.S. companies producing in both countries began to rationalize their manufacturing and sales. Rather than operating their Canadian plants independently of those in the United States, they began exchanging materials, parts, and products among their Canadian and U.S. units in the most economical way, just as car manufacturers had done previously in response to the Auto Pact.

The FTA aroused intense feelings in Canada. As with all such experiments in integration, there were winners and losers. In this case some sectors gained—Canadian exporters of gas, oil, and electricity, for example—whereas others, such as textile manufacturers, were hurt. The issue split the electorate and was the major topic in elections. Favoring the FTA were most business groups; opposing it were labor unions and those worried about preserving Canada's identity. It also divided the country regionally, the resource-rich West being in favor of the pact and the East fearful of American competition. Those who expected to lose from an open North American market drew little comfort from the prospect that the FTA would accelerate economic growth for Canada as a whole and for all of North America.

tions in a North American free-trade area. With a combined population of more than 360 million, total trade exceeding $225 billion, and GNP of $6 trillion, such a union would dwarf even the European Community. Precedent for free trade between Mexico and the United States already existed in the *maquiladora* program, which had operated for some time along the 1900-mile U.S.–Mexican boundary. Under this scheme, nearly half a million Mexicans labored for U.S. companies in more than 1800 factories on the Mexican side of the border, making products for sale in the U.S. market. In light of our previous discussion of the preconditions for successful integration, negotiating a North American free-trade agreement uniting two mature industrial economies with a newly industrializing country could be difficult, despite the potential for mutual benefits.

Economic Integration and Development. Less-developed countries in general have found inspiration in the progress that integration brought to Western Europe. With encouragement from the United Nations, LDCs in several parts of the world have turned to this solution for their many problems. Integration is particularly attractive to LDCs because it promises a larger market for their new industries. Typically, the domestic market of an LDC is severely limited by low per capita purchasing power, and this is often further reduced by the small proportion of the population that actually participates in the commercial economy. The subsistence sector of the population represents an insignificant market for most merchandise. A less-developed country therefore offers few attractions to modern industries that require economies of scale. To acquire such enterprises an LDC thus needs export outlets for its manufactured goods; union with other LDCs promises those markets.

In these circumstances, LDCs enter into integration schemes for somewhat different purposes from those of the advanced nations. Integration offers LDCs a means for simultaneously solving two trade problems: (1) it provides an opportunity for free trade with other countries that are at similar levels of development and are thus able to compete on equal terms, and (2) it offers a way to trade with advanced countries without being harmed by their superior economic power. Yet the promotion of trade is not the main reason why LDCs form integrated groups, as it is for advanced countries. Indeed, less than one-fifth of all LDC trade is with other LDCs. A more urgent goal is to generate economic growth and development.

The gains from integration are fundamentally similar for developing countries and advanced ones, but with some important differences. The less-developed nations have possibilities for proportionately greater benefits because they have so much further to go. In addition to the opportunities that integration offers for developing individual industrial specialties and trading these with other members, union can improve the allocation of resources, especially labor, which LDCs usually employ wastefully. Producers can operate their facilities at full capacity and gain instant economies of scale from the enlarged market, yet at the same time they must become more efficient in order to meet the intensified competition.

After forming a union, individual countries no longer have to strive for a full range of economic activities, which is a difficult task for LDCs. It is unnecessary for each country to acquire every major type of production as long as all the members of the union can manage this together. Within such a group the probability is that at least one member has the right combination of resources for efficient production of a given commodity.

Although the problem of trade creation and diversion is critical for unions of advanced countries, it assumes a different complexion among LDCs. For the latter, the all-important consideration is the effect of integration upon growth. Trade creation is still "good," but trade diversion is not necessarily "bad." It is true that import-competing industries divert trade from advanced countries, but these activities serve the important function of freeing foreign exchange for the purchase from those advanced countries of the high-technology capital goods essential to growth—commodities that are available only from advanced countries.

Yet, the integration efforts of LDCs encounter a number of special problems. One of the most difficult is deciding how to allocate to member countries those manufacturing specialties that are to serve as the basis for intrabloc trade. To accomplish this they must agree on the specific role of each country; but such agreement is hard to achieve because of rival national interests in obtaining these much-coveted projects. Indeed, the gravest obstacle to cooperation among LDCs is nationalism, often reinforced by longstanding antipathies between neighboring countries. Among other considerations of national self-interest is the question of basic inequalities among members. In nearly every union of LDCs certain members are at a disadvantage with respect to the others because of smaller size, fewer resources, or lagging development. Consequently, successful integration of LDCs often requires special concessions to weaker members.

Despite its difficulties, regional integration as a

cooperative approach to development has been tried by LDCs on several continents. One such venture, the Association of Southeast Asian Nations (ASEAN), linked Indonesia, the Philippines, Thailand, Malaysia, Singapore, and Brunei. Though useful as a conduit for foreign aid and investment (especially from Japan) and as a forum for airing regional problems, ASEAN made little progress toward its goal of 50 percent intraregional trade. Even less successful was the 16-nation Economic Community of West African States (ECOWAS), which was unable to develop a joint program under the leadership of Nigeria, a major oil exporter and Africa's most populous nation.

The most determined efforts to use regional integration for developmental purposes have occurred in Latin America. These grew out of an ambitious overall plan conceived by the United Nations Economic Commission for Latin America (ECLA), which sought initially to integrate all the lands south of the United States into a single Latin American common market. This grand scheme proved unworkable, largely because of the enormous disparities in size and material well-being and the diversities of cultures among the many nations in that vast territory. Ultimately, therefore, three main regional blocs (with subgroups) evolved, two in Middle America and the other largely but not entirely in South America. They were the Central American Common Market (CACM), the Caribbean Economic Community (Caricom), and the Latin American Integration Association (LAIA). The histories of these three groups typify both the objectives and the problems of integration among developing countries (see Box 13.4 for further discussion of past integration experiments in Latin American and of recent efforts to revive this movement.)

Economic Integration among Communist Countries. At the conclusion of World War II, the former Soviet Union set about consolidating its control over Eastern Europe. As an essential part of its plan for the region, it undertook to remake the East European economies in the Stalinist mold. The device used to effect this transformation took the form of an organization called the Council for Mutual Economic Assistance (CMEA, or *Comecon*). Although membership in the group shifted during the half-century of its existence, it ultimately came to include the USSR, Bulgaria, Czechoslovakia, East Germany, Hungary, Poland, and Romania, to which were later added three non-European Communist lands: Cuba, Mongolia, and Vietnam.

The Stalinist model required not only that all economic activity within individual Eastern Bloc na-

tions be placed under complete state control, but also that each country should strive for economic self-sufficiency, or *autarky*. This was in accordance with Stalin's precept that a country's national security requires it to be economically independent of other countries. Prior to World War II, the USSR had very nearly succeeded in achieving autarky for itself because of the unusually varied resources of that huge country. For the small countries of Eastern Europe, however, this goal proved elusive. Eventually, even the Soviet Union itself came to depend upon imports to make up for production shortfalls caused by planning failures. At the same time, the complex demands of a new technology forced Soviet Bloc countries to turn more and more to foreign sources for industrial inputs they were unable to make themselves.

That Comecon had failed to achieve individual national self-sufficiency for its members had become clear by 1958, at which time the EC had arrived on the European scene with its declared intention of ultimately creating a United States of Western Europe. Perceiving the EC as a threat to the East, Stalin's successor, Nikita Khrushchev, reorganized Comecon in a manner designed to strengthen the self-sufficiency of the group as a whole in order that it might compete with the EC. Toward this purpose, each member nation was assigned specific economic functions representing its contributions to the joint effort. Thus the goal shifted from autarky to something akin to economic integration.

Comecon failed in this objective, however, and it never came to rival the EC or even the EFTA. In part this failure resulted from its basic design. Unlike its Western counterparts, for example, the post-1958 Comecon relied upon bilateral agreements among its members, with the USSR remaining the dominant partner. Moreover, in a system lacking convertible currencies, Eastern Bloc countries relied mainly upon cumbersome barter arrangements and arbitrary pricing in the conduct of their trade. Other basic weaknesses included the wide disparities in size and level of development among members, together with a general unwillingness to accept assigned individual roles. Consequently, the union did little to enhance intrabloc trade. Ironically, the Eastern Bloc's economic ties with non-Communist lands grew more rapidly, especially with Western Europe. This mounting East-West trade, which relied upon natural complementarities in resource endowments, reestablished a European pattern that had existed from early times. Eventually, following the general collapse of Communism in Eastern Europe in 1990 and the disintegration of the Soviet Union in 1991, Comecon disbanded.

BOX 13.4   *Regional Economic Integration in Latin America*

The five members of the Central American Common Market (CACM)—Costa Rica, El Salvador, Guatemala, Honduras, and Nicaragua—began their experiment in integration with a unique advantage: a history of unification throughout the long period of Spanish colonial rule and for some years thereafter. These small mountainous countries have a combined territory and population about equal to California, and an average per capita GDP of $1020. Before the CACM was established in 1961, the five countries were among the world's most specialized exporters of tropical agricultural commodities, and their economies were growing slower than their populations. More than two-thirds of their work force was engaged in subsistence activities.

The CACM represented one of the highest levels of economic integration ever attempted in the less-developed world. Although basically a common market, it also had a supranational organizational structure, including a development bank and a tripartite governance arrangement. At the outset the stated goal of this group was full economic union.

During its first years the CACM made remarkable progress. By 1966 it had essentially achieved the status of a working common market, with a free flow of goods and capital among its members. Exports had become substantially more diversified. Fifteen per-

cent of foreign shipments took place within the bloc, most of this intra-CACM trade consisting of manufactured goods. Domestic and foreign investment within the union soared, and gross national product rose more rapidly than the rate of population growth.

Then trouble appeared. The long-time rivalry between neighboring Honduras and El Salvador exploded with the so-called Soccer War of 1969, which, though short-lived, interrupted intrabloc trade and communication. From that point, the CACM ceased to exist as a functioning organization. Even before the Soccer War, however, friction among members had arisen because some felt that the benefits of industrialization were being unevenly shared: Guatemala, El Salvador, and Costa Rica had attracted the greater part of this new development, whereas Honduras had received little of it. Then, bitter revolutions broke out in both El Salvador and Nicaragua, further damaging the CACM economies.

Throughout wars and revolutions, a certain amount of intra-bloc trade somehow persisted, but with great difficulty. Foreign aid helped, including the 130,000 barrels of oil per day supplied by Mexico and Venezuela on concessionary terms. By 1986 intraregional trade had fallen to its lowest level in ten years. Thus, a promising LDC experiment in integration failed to attain its potential, all because of poli-

tics—an all too common impediment to Third World cooperation.

The early 1990s, however, saw the resolution of Central America's gravest political problems. With the Nicaraguan and Salvadorian revolutions both concluded, the prospects for restoring intaregional trade rose. In 1991, therefore, the five countries agreed to revive the CACM by 1994.

A second regional bloc formed under ECLA auspices was the Latin American Free Trade Association (LAFTA), which came into effect in 1960. LAFTA's membership included most of South America (Argentina, Bolivia, Brazil, Chile, Colombia, Ecuador, Paraguay, Peru, Uruguay, and Venezuela) plus Mexico, a combined territory twice the size of the United States with a present-day population of 363 million people.

Despite its members' pressing need for solutions to their many trade problems, LAFTA generated little intrabloc trade because of many daunting obstacles. One major barrier was the great distance separating the economically active parts of these countries, which typically concentrate in coastal enclaves along the margins of the continent. Then, too, the Latin American countries tended to produce similar goods—a result of like resource endowments, historic economic isolation from each other, and independent plans for national development. Consequently, they competed with each

---

Preferential Trade Agreements

Although regional integration has received much attention in recent years, other preferential arrangements have also had significant roles. Among these are *bilateral trade agreements*, which provide for reciprocal concessions between country pairs. Though widely used, these tend to be politically risky and difficult to administer.

One of the earliest and most enduring forms of preferential agreement is the *colonial grouping*, in which a mother country and its present and former colonies grant special concessions to each other.

Prominent examples were the British Commonwealth, with its imperial preference system, and the French community. Though neither Britain nor France remains a true colonial power today, the commercial and cultural ties that developed among members of these groups over many years of close association have proved extraordinarily resilient.

Global Agreements

In contrast to these organizations based upon selective discrimination are global agreements designed to benefit all countries. This type of arrangement is rooted in

other in Northern Hemisphere markets. LAFTA did little to increase intrabloc trade because it failed to commit its members to significant duty reductions with each other.

Of all the impediments to intragroup cooperation, however, perhaps the most difficult were the great disparities among members in economic size and level of development. At one extreme were several semi-industrialized countries, especially Brazil, the world's eighth largest economy; at the other extreme was Bolivia with an economy only one seventy-fifth as large as Brazil's. When LAFTA went out of existence in 1981, only one-tenth of the group's trade was with other LAFTA members, and half of this was between adjacent Argentina and Brazil. As a replacement for LAFTA, the Latin American Integration Association (LAIA) had the same membership but an even less ambitious program.

Meanwhile, however, the steadily growing trade between Argentina and Brazil led these two large neighbors to set up a bilateral common market. In 1988 the two agreed upon a list of 524 products eligible for tariff exemption, and later they signed accords to eliminate all barriers to trade by 1998, to coordinate economic policies (including a common trading currency), and to build a pipeline to transport Argentine gas to Brazil. Trade between the two climbed rapidly, doubling to $2.1

billion between 1985 and 1990. Then, in 1991, the pact was expanded to include nearby Uruguay and Paraguay and was given the name *Mercosur* ("southern market"). The agreement called for a completely free market in goods, services, and labor by 1994.

In 1969, fearing domination by much larger LAFTA members, several countries along South America's Pacific margins set up a separate organization called the Andean Common Market (ANCOM). The five members were Bolivia, Colombia, Ecuador, Peru, and Venezuela (Chile dropped out in 1976). Although retaining their connection to LAFTA (subsequently LAIA), they attempted to increase their collective economic power by forming a much closer form of integration. ANCOM assumed many characteristics of an economic union: In addition to coordinating national policies for trade, transportation, communications, energy, and agriculture, ANCOM allocated investment among members and closely regulated the activities of multinational corporations. Its policies tended to stifle investment, however, and ANCOM discontinued these in 1987. The group made little progress in boosting intra-bloc trade until 1992, when the five signed a free-trade pact and agreed to set common tariffs with non-member countries.

Still another integration experiment undertaken under the auspices of the

United Nations Economic Commission for Latin America was the Caribbean Community (Caricom), which united 13 English-speaking island countries in the West Indies. Despite the many practical problems confronting this widely scattered group, Caricom members in 1989 agreed to establish a regional capital market, leading to a unified exchange rate, and to renew their drive to create a common market by 1993. Caricom, however, repeatedly failed to agree upon a common external tariff.

This heightened interest in trade reform came at a time when Latin American countries were shifting their development strategies toward the kinds of export-promoting policies that had proved so successful in East Asia. Trade among Latin American countries had not been growing; indeed, intra-Latin American trade had actually declined from 22 percent of their total trade to only 15 percent between 1980 and 1990. Even more important as a propelling force for this renewed activity, however, was the prospect of a North American Free Trade Area that would link Mexico with the United States and Canada (see above). Statements from Washington suggesting the desirability of free trade among all Western Hemisphere republics inspired Latin American leaders with the hope that they might gain free access for their goods in the United States market.

the ideal that nondiscrimination is best for everyone and thus follows the liberal tradition of comparative advantage theory.

General Agreement on Tariffs and Trade (GATT). Without doubt, the most effective and far-reaching of all cooperative trade ventures has been the General Agreement on Tariffs and Trade (GATT), which launched a new era in world commerce in the years following World War II. GATT is one of a trio of organizations growing out of an international conference held in 1944 at Bretton Woods, New Hampshire. Having agreed to establish an International Monetary

Fund (IMF) to bring stability to a chaotic international currency situation and an International Bank for Reconstruction and Development (IBRD, or World Bank) to foster development among less-advanced nations, the conferees saw the need for a companion organization to promote cooperation in world trade. In the winter of 1947-1948, therefore, 54 nations met in Havana, Cuba, to draft the charter for an International Trade Organization (ITO).

The ITO charter failed to receive ratification from constituent governments, however, because of its perceived threat to their national sovereignty. Thereupon, 23 countries continued their discussions at a conference in Geneva, Switzerland. There they arrived at a stopgap compromise arrangement consisting of an extensive set of bilateral trade concessions, which they then extended to all participants, in an instrument called General Agreement on Tariffs and Trade (GATT).

For what was intended as an interim measure, GATT proved remarkably durable. Though basically a contractual arrangement, GATT also became a permanent international organization, with a headquarters in Geneva and a small secretariat charged with monitoring GATT treaties. Its original 23 members have increased to nearly 100, and altogether more than 124 countries subscribe to the principles embodied in its charter:

- *Reciprocity*. If one country reduces its tariffs against another, the second country must likewise lower its tariffs.
- *Nondiscrimination*. Members must not grant one country preferential trade treatment over others. This is the *most-favored-nation rule*, meaning that every member is treated as favorably as the most favored.
- *Transparency*. Members are expected to replace nontariff barriers (whose effects are hard to detect and measure) with tariffs, which are open to scrutiny and thus more easily reduced through further negotiation.

For three decades GATT performed exceedingly well. In a series of negotiating sessions, or *rounds* (see Box 13.5), its members had slashed average tariffs on manufactured products from an initial 40 percent to less than 10 percent by the middle of the 1970s. GATT's trade liberalization measures are given most of the credit for the fivefold rise in the volume of world trade during that same period. Though tariffs continued to decline thereafter, to an average of about 5

percent by 1990, the rate of trade growth dwindled as nontariff trade barriers began to reappear (refer to Chapter 12).

It was against this backdrop of creeping violations of at least the spirit of GATT that member countries in 1986 began the Uruguay Round of negotiations (Box 13.5) in the hope of revitalizing the organization. This was a particularly ambitious undertaking because the group addressed difficult issues they had avoided in previous rounds:

- *Agricultural trade*. One of the most contentious issues, agricultural trade had been excluded from previous negotiations. Removal of all trade restrictions on farm products would swell world trade by $100 billion per annum.
- *Textiles and clothing*. The Multi-Fibre Arrangement (MFA) was a complex of bilateral export quotas negotiated in 1974, which GATT chose to overlook. Exporters were mainly very poor LDCs and the principal importers were wealthy industrialized countries. Expected gains for world trade: $50 billion a year.
- *Intellectual property*. Protection against infringement of patents, trademarks, and other intellectual-property rights was discussed.
- *Foreign investment*. Standards governing restrictions placed upon multinationals by host governments were discussed.
- *Internationally traded services*. For the first time GATT negotiators attempted to deal with barriers to service imports, the most rapidly growing segment of world commerce.

This immense assortment of complex issues proved more than GATT negotiators could resolve in the allotted time, and the December 1990 deadline passed without a new agreement. The most intractable problem proved to be the politically charged issue of

---

BOX 13.5 Gatt Negotiating Rounds

The founding session of GATT convened in Geneva, Switzerland, in 1947; the resulting initial set of agreements and the GATT charter became effective in 1948. Seven additional negotiating conferences, or *rounds*, have taken place since:

Geneva Round	1947
Annecy Round	1949
Torquay Round	1950
Geneva Round	1956
Dillon Round	1960–61
Kennedy Round	1964–67
Tokyo Round	1973–79
Uruguay Round	1986–92

agricultural protection, on which both EC and Japanese representatives were unyielding. The negotiating parties were aware, however, that failure of the Uruguay Round raised the threat of a world divided into three great continental trading blocs incessantly embroiled in paralyzing dissension. The deadline was therefore extended, and a few months later the Japanese government offered concessions that enabled talks to resume.

United Nations Conference on Trade and Development (UNCTAD). Although Article 18 of the GATT charter granted less-developed countries a broad license to use trade restrictions to protect their balances of payments, many LDCs were dissatisfied with the benefits they had gained from GATT. The rationale for GATT was based upon neoclassical trade theory and its ideal of universal free trade, which some LDCs considered inappropriate for their problems.

In 1964, therefore, the United Nations convened the inaugural meeting of a group charged with addressing the problems that LDCs face in marketing their goods in industrialized countries. The United Nations Conference on Trade and Development (UNCTAD) has operated through committees, each concerned with a particular staple commodity produced in LDCs. At conferences generally held at four-year intervals, the committees have brought together representatives of major producing and consuming nations to find ways of reconciling supply and demand for their commodities and of overcoming import barriers to these in the principal world markets.

THE MULTINATIONAL ENTERPRISE

One by one we have added modifications to the Heckscher-Ohlin factor-endowments theory of international trade, especially the barrier effects of distance and governmental intervention, the impact of technological change and development, and the role of cooperative arrangements among nations. In this present age, however, the most dynamic influence of all may well be the multinational enterprise (MNE). Often referred to as a multinational corporation, a transnational corporation, or simply a multinational, the MNE is a company that is headquartered in one country but controls productive facilities and sales outlets in other countries. Its operations involve flows of capital, goods, services, and managerial and technical personnel among its subsidiaries. Ultimately this leads the enterprise to assume a global outlook and strategy. Since World War II, MNEs have contributed a rapidly expanding share of world trade and have become the

prime movers of the factors of production among nations.

The growing prominence of the multinational enterprise lends a new perspective to trade theory. Traditional theory has viewed countries as the actors in world commerce, but in a majority of cases individual concerns are the primary agents in the international transfer of goods and factors. A theory of international economic interaction must therefore take into account the ability of multinational concerns to modify the endowments of countries, moving human and physical resources from one place to another and thereby enabling production to occur in the most favorable locations.

Although introducing this element might seem to put the principle of comparative advantage in doubt, ironically the multinational enterprise is perhaps the most effective modern-day practitioner of this "law." The MNE is able to produce in that country where the costs of materials, labor, capital, and transportation are minimized and to declare its profits in that country with the lowest tax rates. Hence, the MNE has a unique potential for making the most efficient allocation of the world's resources—the ultimate goal of the classical trade theorist!

How is the MNE able to modify the international economic environment so effectively? One advantage of such a company is the information-gathering ability afforded by its many branches and representatives throughout the world, all linked by instantaneous electronic communications. This "scanning capability" gives the firm an awareness of opportunities, problems, and other new developments in the many places where it conducts business. A second advantage is the enormous store of capital, technology, and managerial skills that an MNE can draw upon.

Considering that a corporation such as General Motors or Exxon can generate more worldwide sales in a year than the gross national products of all but 25 or so sovereign nations, it is hardly surprising that multinationals inspire such awe and apprehension. The host countries for an MNE's overseas affiliates usually suspect them of holding allegiance to the firm's home government. More likely, however, the firm's true devotion is to its own fortunes and those of its stockholders. Nevertheless, MNEs are under increased scrutiny from their home and host governments alike, and they are being subjected to a growing number of restrictions. (See Box 13.6 for a discussion of the public-policy issues raised by the activities of multinationals.)

The attention focused upon multinationals is fairly new, reflecting their recent rise to prominence. Yet their roots go deep into the nineteenth century, to

BOX 13.6   *Government Policy and the Multinational Enterprise*

Given their size and pervasive influence in international economic affairs, multinational enterprises (MNEs) receive a great deal of attention from government policymakers. Official positions on MNEs vary widely from country to country, however, largely because of their unique legal status. As yet no international authority exercises jurisdiction over them, and no country recognizes the legal existence of an entire MNE system. Under existing law, therefore, a multinational is merely a group of national companies, each subject to the laws of the land in which it is domiciled. In the absence of any international regulatory mechanism, an MNE exists in an atmosphere of uncertainty, which imposes extra costs because of the widely differing legal requirements under which its various branches function. At the same time, the absence of international constraints provides the firm with opportunities denied domestic companies. This is the basis for the common view that MNEs manufacture in those lands where costs are lowest and declare their profits where taxes are least. It also explains the frequent accusation that multinationals do not show adequate social responsibility toward the countries in which they operate.

In these circumstances, it is not surprising that both home countries and host countries tend to have love-hate feelings toward multinationals. The intensity of these attitudes varies from country to country, however, being greatest in some less-developed countries (LDCs). On the positive side, an LDC is likely to hold exaggerated expectations of the benefits it will gain from the arrival of a multinational. Government leaders expect the new company to provide a badly needed solution for their unemployment problems, to supply an infusion of managerial and scientific knowledge that will help close the technology gap, to reduce the drain on their foreign exchange, to contribute tax revenues to the national treasury, and to develop natural resources and thus relieve some of their regional disparities.

Often it is not until some time after the investment has already been made that negative attitudes toward MNEs begin to surface. Host countries—Canada, for instance—may complain that foreign-owned firms bring the "wrong kind" of employment, that citizens of the country do not receive enough technical and managerial jobs. They often charge, too, that the MNEs threaten their national sovereignty because company decisions are made in another country. Some LDCs associate multinationals with neocolonialism because these foreign-owned concerns seem to continue the pattern of economic exploitation practiced by their former colonial masters. They see the MNE draining the country's resources and begin to ask what will be left after the oil or copper or bauxite is gone. Or they may object that the country's balance of payments is suffering because the MNE is repatriating too much in profits to the home company. LDCs frequently complain, too, about the kind of technology that MNEs bring to them: They say that these firms introduce capital-intensive techniques and equipment originally designed to suit company needs in their labor-short, capital-rich homelands but which are not appropriate for poor countries needing jobs for their masses of unemployed labor.

Multinational enterprises thus find themselves immersed in a complex set of relationships that pit against each other the differing perspectives of home country, host country, and the firm itself. Many people contend, for example, that a foreign investment represents a gain for the host country and a loss for the home country. Some regard the profits repatriated by the subsidiary to its parent company as a gain for the home country and a drain on the host country. Among other questions are the possibility of political control of overseas subsidiaries by the home government (the extraterritoriality issue), government seizure of foreign-owned companies (the expropriation issue), and special performance requirements exacted of MNE subsidiaries by their hosts.

The relationships between host countries and multinationals have both economic and political sides. In balance, does a country gain or lose economically from the foreign-owned companies it hosts? Theoretically, host countries enjoy a net benefit from foreign investment, and a number of studies in Australia, Canada, and the United Kingdom seem to confirm that foreign-owned firms operating in developed countries do indeed produce a measurable rise in the gross national products of their hosts. Although the evidence for LDCs is variable, the employment-generating effects of MNEs have proved to be very great in a number of cases. In Mexico and Brazil, for example, foreign-owned firms account for half of all industrial employment. The impact of multinationals has been even more striking in the newly industrializing lands of East Asia, where electronics firms and other export-oriented, labor-intensive industries employ great numbers of unskilled workers in assembly operations.

The success of host countries in acquiring new technology from MNEs depends upon the absorptive capacity of the local society and economy. Many LDCs lack a sufficient number of educated and trained people to manage and staff industries that are technologically complex. Yet a number of countries, such as India, Mexico, and South Korea, have succeeded in training a great many of their people for such activities. One element limiting the amount of new technology that host countries can gain from MNEs is the reluctance of such firms to part with proprietary information.

To calculate the actual net economic impact of foreign direct investment upon host countries calls for balancing a number of factors. On the plus side are MNE payments for local labor, capital, and land, the taxes paid to local governments, and the gains by domestic firms that benefit from a quickening local economy. On the minus side are the opportunity costs to domestic factors of production—labor, land, and capital—that might have been used otherwise, and the loss of funds sent out of the country as profits, dividends, interest, royalties, and fees. Most such calculations have shown gains for the host countries. The exceptions are usually those cases where host governments have made too many tax concessions to attract MNEs in the first place.

That disagreements should occasionally arise between MNEs and their hosts seems inevitable, considering that governments tend to look for unrealistically quick returns on foreign investments and that MNEs and their hosts usually have different perspectives on costs and benefits. Such disagreements may grow with the passing of time following the beginning of operations, as the initial inflow of investment funds tapers off and the firm commences repatriating profits to the parent concern. At this point the host government may make new demands, bolstered by its increased bargaining power now that the company has committed its resources and cannot afford to shut down operations. The government and the MNE may then do a great deal of jockeying to arrive at a mutually satisfactory agreement on how to divide the benefits from the investment. In the end, agreement on economic matters is usually reached, for both parties would lose if the investment were terminated.

The political issues that arise between a multinational and its host government are often more difficult to resolve because of the effects of nationalistic feelings, especially in less-developed countries. Public debate of such matters often involves not only officials and politicians but also labor leaders, local business interests, the press, and those in academia. Underlying such discussions is the invariable question of whether the economic benefits of foreign investment are sufficient to outweigh the perceived threat to national sovereignty. The usual presumptions are that a multinational exercises a certain power over the local economy, that it is directed in this from a control center in some alien land, and that the government of the home country exerts a possibly sinister influence over the company.

Although this picture may be overdrawn, company interests and host-country interests are not likely to coincide exactly. The multinational seeks to maximize returns to its entire MNE system, whereas the host government looks to its national welfare—eco-

nomic, social, and military. Local officials resent the ability of an MNE to make decisions that affect the country's welfare independently of their control. They suspect MNEs of avoiding taxes and manipulating prices to the benefit of company interests.

The most contentious issue dividing MNEs and host governments is the perceived threat to national sovereignty because of home-government meddling in company decisions. Giving some substance to this fear, the U.S. government has openly imposed its will upon the overseas affiliates of its MNEs. It has, for example, prohibited Canadian subsidiaries of American companies from trading with Cuba, and it has tried to prevent European affiliates from selling gas-pipeline equipment to the former USSR. In addition to the friction caused by these efforts to assert political control over MNE foreign operations, controversy arose in the 1990s as a result of attempts to apply U.S. antibias laws outside the country. American courts were being asked to decide cases involving alleged discrimination by foreign subsidiaries against employees on the basis of race, national origin, religion, or sex.

The "extraterritoriality" issue has severely strained American relations with other governments. Several countries have warned the United States that international law recognizes the rights of nations to regulate conduct within their own borders. These conflicts have created perplexing dilemmas for U.S. multinationals operating in countries whose laws are based upon very different cultural practices.

Political considerations may lead host governments to place various restrictions upon foreign ownership. Indeed, most countries exclude certain industries from foreign ownership entirely, particularly defense industries. Many governments prohibit foreign ownership of banks, public utilities, communications, and, increasingly, minerals. In the American Midwest, several states even restrict foreign ownership of farmland. Some countries—notably France, Japan, and Mexico—prohibit foreign acquisition of local firms, and several countries maintain

strict review procedures for all proposed foreign takeovers.

Today, more and more governments are requiring foreign investors to acquire local partners when setting up new affiliates. Such joint ventures are especially popular among LDCs, which perceive them as a way of gaining access to new technology, limiting the outflow of repatriated profits, and minimizing the influence of foreigners over the local economy. Arrangements of this kind have become fairly standard throughout Latin America and Southeast Asia. Mexico, for instance, requires 51 percent local ownership of all but a few, explicitly designated, industries.

Another policy tool favored by host governments is to impose performance requirements upon foreign-owned enterprises. For instance, as a way of creating jobs, the MNE may be required to use a specified proportion of local personnel. Some countries provide companies with timetables for employing local persons as managers and technicians. Governments may require that firms set up training programs or establish local laboratories to perform R&D. Or they may force MNEs to increase the local content of the products they assemble in the host country, especially automobiles. Some newly industrializing countries with large foreign debts—for example, Mexico and Brazil—have required MNEs to export specified percentages of their output. These and other trade-related investment measures (TRIMs) were among the topics addressed in the Uruguay Round of GATT talks (previously mentioned). GATT negotiators sought to establish some discipline over the use of performance requirements by host countries, which had grown increasingly chaotic.

The most extreme measure of all is government seizure of foreign-owned companies. In recent years a rash of such expropriations has occurred in some Third World countries where the political processes have fallen into the hands of economic nationalists, many of whom oppose foreign ownership in any form. International law actually

(*Continued on next page*)

recognizes the right of governments to expropriate foreign enterprises, considering this merely an exercise of national sovereignty, but this law also specifies that the previous owners of such properties receive prompt, adequate, and effective compensation for the loss. Compensation is a key issue today, for many LDCs are failing in this. When compensation is not forthcoming, home governments may retaliate against offending countries. The United States, for instance, has in some cases cut off foreign aid and credits to delinquent nations.

The opposite side of these questions has to do with the relationships between MNEs and their home governments. The United States has no overall policy toward American-based multinationals, but the government has asserted its authority regarding certain specific issues. Prior to World War II the United States not only placed no restrictions on foreign operations by its MNEs, but it also stood ready to ensure that other governments did not discriminate against them. In several instances it actually intervened militarily in their behalf.

After the war the government encouraged foreign direct investment by U.S. multinationals as a form of foreign aid, but focused this upon LDCs especially after Europe had fully recovered. The United States entered into treaties with other countries guaranteeing fair treatment of its MNEs. When balance-of-payments problems began to arise in the 1960s, the U.S. government set quotas on foreign direct investment, forcing its multinationals to do their borrowing abroad.

As foreign investment by U.S. firms expanded, domestic criticism of them grew louder. Labor unions claimed that American firms were exporting jobs with their "runaway plants"—factories set up in East Asia, along the Mexican border, and in other low-labor-cost places—to produce goods formerly made at home. Some domestic critics objected to what they saw as the loss of American production through the transfer of technology abroad. Others decried the "unfair" advantages gained by U.S. multinationals in the favorable treatment accorded them under U.S. tariffs and in their ability to avoid restrictive U.S. laws to take advantage of concessions from foreign governments. Empirical studies tend to discount these claims, finding that MNEs as a whole have enjoyed faster growth in output than domestic firms, have higher rates of export growth, and generally have favorable balances in their own trade with the world.

Tax policy is another area of controversy between MNEs and their home governments. How do you prevent these elusive firms from escaping taxation but at the same time avoid taxing them doubly? In the United States the problem is compounded by the desire of state governments to tax MNEs operating within their jurisdictions. Some states favor taxing all production that takes place within their borders but exempts their foreign production. Other states insist upon taxing all production of their MNEs throughout the world. The United States is unique among nations in its antitrust laws, which are designed to prevent companies from cooperating with each other in ways that reduce competition. The United States also prohibits American firms from making "questionable" payments abroad. Other countries make no such efforts to prevent bribery, which is an accepted part of doing business in many Third World nations and some industrialized ones as well.

The evidence indicates that under ideal conditions everyone gains from foreign direct investment. Most of the problems that arise between multinationals and governments can be attributed to the lack of a uniform international policy for such enterprises and the absence of a mechanism for regulating their activities worldwide. Agreement among nations is much needed to ensure that multinationals are good corporate citizens of the countries where they operate and to make certain that the world receives full economic benefit from this efficient form of business organization with its potential for allocating the world's resources in the most effective manner.

---

the colonial operations of British, Dutch, and French firms exploiting the resources of their governments' overseas possessions, a tradition continued into this present century by the overseas activities of giant oil, mineral, and fruit companies. Manufacturing firms, however, were slower to develop foreign operations, partly because of the lack of good transport and communications and, especially in the case of U.S. companies, a preoccupation with growing home markets. Nevertheless, a few pioneering industrial firms, such as Singer, Westinghouse, Kodak, and Western Electric, went abroad with their new products and manufacturing technologies during the late 1800s, and their number gradually increased until the Great Depression.

Following World War II, multinational enterprises truly burst upon the world commercial scene. The greatest surge came in the 1960s, when U.S. multinationals moved abroad in numbers, aided by new developments in transport, communication, and industrial technology and by new forms of corporate organization. At the same time, international trade was expanding rapidly, aided by the tariff reductions effected by GATT. As we have previously noted, investment follows trade, and American MNEs were quick to take advantage of the enlarged market afforded by the newly created EC and by opportunities elsewhere in the world to develop new sources of oil, minerals, and other commodities to replace dwindling supplies at home.

In the past decade the pace of U.S. direct investment in Western Europe and Canada has dwindled with the slackening of economic growth in those areas and as more attractive alternatives have appeared in the western Pacific. Meanwhile, American firms have begun to lose their competitive advantage as multinationals based in Europe, Japan, and other countries gained in size and strength. Not only are the latter seizing a larger share of opportunities in foreign areas but they have also precipitated a surge of foreign investment within the United States itself. Even as the global pattern of MNE activity has grown more complex, the character of the multinational concern has itself undergone fundamental changes.

The Nature and Role of the Multinational Enterprise

As multinational enterprises have increased their involvement in the world economy, they have developed a characteristic organizational form. Usually the parent company is headquartered in the country of principal ownership, although several exceptions to this exist. Royal Dutch Shell, for instance, is 60 percent Dutch owned and 40 percent British, and it maintains headquarters both in The Hague and in London. The stock in most MNEs is publicly held and is available to individual investors of any nationality, although a number of prominent multinationals are still privately held companies. During an MNE's early years its headquarters management and staff are typically natives of the home country, but in time the company brings into its home office individuals of talent from its overseas affiliates. The headquarters company is the control center for the firm's worldwide operations, and the decisions made here take on a global perspective. The management group in the home office is responsible for systemwide strategic planning and must decide what goods are to be manufactured, where in the world to make these, where to procure raw materials, and what global markets to target.

The company's foreign affiliates include both producing units and sales outlets. Today many companies have formed their overseas affiliates into an integrated system, within which the individual branches exchange products, materials, and capital. For example, European affiliates of Ford and General Motors exchange parts, subassemblies, and finished vehicles from one country to another in an elaborate intracompany network. In addition to their wholly or partially owned affiliates abroad, multinationals customarily maintain connections with other foreign enterprises not under corporate control, through such arrangements as joint ventures, distributorships, and licensing agreements.

The most significant feature of the MNE, from both a practical and a theoretical standpoint, is its role as an efficient agent for transferring capital, managerial skills, technology, and commodities among countries. Matching the scarcities of one country with the

surpluses of another, it helps to achieve a global equalization of factors; and by transferring innovations among nations, it is a major agent of technological change.

The transfer of managerial skills to other lands is a distinctive function of the MNE. Relying upon the firm's superior information-gathering ability, the headquarters company discovers and exploits opportunities in foreign areas that lie beyond the capabilities of domestic concerns in those lands. The MNE is also better able than local companies to bear the risk of such ventures because of its great size and financial strength and its experience in similar circumstances elsewhere.

Having decided to invest in a new foreign undertaking, the firm then performs its second key function, the transfer of capital. This can be in the form of real capital (machinery and equipment) or financial capital or a combination of the two. Depending upon political and economic circumstances, the company can fund the project with capital generated within its own system—obtained either directly from the parent concern or from the earnings of overseas affiliates—or it can rely upon borrowed funds, either in the host country or elsewhere.

The third major function of the MNE is to create technology and transfer it throughout its system. A newly established affiliate generally receives an infusion of technology from the headquarters company. Indeed, at one time all research and development took place in the parent concern, but today many MNEs share this function among their various constituent companies.

Finally, the MNE is a principal generator of international trade, notably the transfers of raw materials, components, and finished products that take place among the company's many branches. The current trend is for an MNE to integrate production and marketing among the parent and its overseas affiliates. Such coordination permits the firm to maximize the gains from international specialization: Each product is manufactured in that combination of locations having the lowest costs and in sufficient quantity to enjoy economies of scale. The company's ultimate aim in integrating its international operations is to serve every national market with a full line of its products and to do so at the lowest unit costs.

The international integration of an MNE can be either vertical or horizontal. In the case of vertical integration, a branch in one country sends partially manufactured subassemblies or intermediate products to another affiliate elsewhere for further processing or for final assembly. Finished products then go to all affiliates for sale in their own national markets. If integration is horizontal, each branch makes a particular line of finished products, the choice depending upon its comparative advantage, and shares these with all other units of the enterprise. In either case, every branch is able to offer its customers a complete set of company products.

Theories of the Multinational Enterprise

The multinational enterprise has attained prominence so recently that a cohesive theory on the subject has yet to emerge. Because most writers have approached the MNE from the perspectives of their individual specialties, the resulting works lack the generality essential to a true theory. We shall therefore attempt merely to draw together the common threads of this accumulating body of literature. Our concern will be to find answers to two sets of questions: (1) What causes a firm to go abroad and how is it able to succeed in a foreign environment against competition from both domestic firms and other multinationals, and (2) what happens to the fundamental character of the firm itself during the course of this internationalization process?

An Outline of Leading Theories.   What are the distinguishing characteristics of firms that enter into multinational production? One common trait cited by theorists is the expectation by MNEs of greater profits from their foreign ventures than those received by local competitors in those same areas. Indeed, it is essential that MNEs receive a higher return because they must overcome problems not borne by domestic firms. Local producers know the language and customs, can expect a greater measure of customer good will and government favor, have a closer awareness of local market conditions, and avoid the extra time and expense that the MNE has to bear because of operating from a distance. The MNE is able to obtain a larger return because it has certain advantages that no other firm possesses. Chief among these "monopolistic" advantages are (1) superior knowledge and (2) large size and scope of operations.

Leadership in innovation is the usual form of superior knowledge monopolized by MNEs. Innovativeness is a key element in technology-intensive industries such as pharmaceuticals and electronics. As a group, MNEs expend more on research and development than do other firms, and they are able to transfer this technology abroad with little additional cost. Local firms, on the other hand, would have to invest heavily to develop a competing technology themselves. Another kind of knowledge monopoly is found in those industries that rely upon high levels of marketing skill—for example, convenience foods and bever-

ages (McDonald's or Coca-Cola) or cosmetics (Estée Lauder). To acquire its superior knowledge, the MNE needs a home environment that offers high levels of technical and managerial skills and has a well-developed, affluent market. This is one reason why only a few countries serve as home bases for multinationals.

A second monopolistic advantage common to MNEs is superior size and scope of operation. In most industries foreign direct investment is dominated by only a few large concerns; in other words, these activities are oligopolistic in nature. These companies continually jostle with each other for larger shares of the world market. Because of their size and their ability to produce in many countries, they can achieve the most economical scale of operations. If the local market is too small to absorb all of the output, the affiliate can send its surplus to the company's branches in other countries. Domestic producers do not usually have this option. MNEs may also integrate their operations vertically to gain assured sources of supply. In this way they can avoid dependence upon others and, at the same time, are able to deny such supplies to their competitors.

Large size therefore permits the firm to assume a greater range of functions itself. By thus "internalizing" its various international operations, it can avoid buying and selling to other companies in foreign areas (or licensing its technology to them). The MNE thereby protects the secrecy of its technology and minimizes the effects of governmental restrictions. It is mainly for this reason that most international transfers of technology and managerial skills take place among units of the same firm, and that MNEs sell a high proportion of their exports to their own affiliates.

Because of the oligopolistic character of international business, MNEs intently watch their competitors' actions. If one company sets up operations in a new area or if it markets a new product, its competitors immediately take action to prevent any loss of their market shares. Each firm is concerned to maintain its rate of growth relative to its rivals as a way of preserving market share, and it seeks to erect barriers to the entry of any new firms into its markets.

MNEs are thus highly interdependent in their decision making. If one firm enters a foreign market, its rivals usually follow it there to minimize the risk to their market shares. These defensive actions therefore create a bandwagon effect in foreign direct investment. This kind of action also helps to explain so-called reverse investment, in which MNEs of different national origins compete in each others' home markets. For instance, the American tire company, Goodyear, operates in France, while the French firm, Michelin, makes tires in the United States. Although they turn out competing goods, these firms are careful to differentiate their products by means of brand names and advertising. Even this kind of product differentiation constitutes a knowledge asset of the firm.

To compete successfully in an alien environment, the multinational enterprise must choose carefully which countries to enter. Such decisions rely upon the theories of location and trade as well as foreign investment theory. A number of country characteristics enter into this decision: location, resource endowments, size and nature of market, political environment. Although the relative influence of these elements changes from one time to another, the strongest attraction for U.S. firms has been proximity—as suggested by the high proportion of investments made in nearby Canada and Mexico. U.S. multinationals have also preferred to invest in countries with familiar cultures—notably English-speaking Canada, Britain, and Australia—and with large markets offering economies of scale. To protect their investments, MNEs favor countries that have stable governments and a minimum of legal restrictions.

Not only do these country traits influence the decision to do business in a country, but they also determine the way in which MNEs will enter that market. For operating in those countries with stable governments and large, prosperous markets, multinationals generally prefer foreign direct investment. In dealing with those poorer underdeveloped countries having a high level of political risk, MNEs rely mainly upon exporting, together with some licensing of local production, but with only a minimum of direct investing.

Internationalization of the Firm.   The other aspect of MNE theory is concerned with the questions of how, when, and why a firm becomes multinational and what happens to its organizational arrangements during this process. The internationalization of a company typically occurs in three stages. In the first stage a firm that had previously served only its domestic market begins to export some of its output. Often this transition from domestic to foreign sales is unplanned, taking place in response to unsolicited orders received directly from potential customers overseas or indirectly by way of local buying agents for foreign purchasers. At this point the company has neither the specialized facilities to prepare shipments for export nor personnel skilled in export procedures. It therefore hires outside specialists to perform these functions. If orders from abroad continue to arrive, the firm will find it cheaper and more expedient to establish its own export department or foreign division, consisting of an experienced manager and a few clerks.

As this new foreign business commences to yield increased economies of scale and enhanced profit margins for the company, it begins to pursue export sales more actively. The firm appoints distributors in key market areas abroad, and in time it develops a network of such distributorships. Meanwhile, the firm may license its technology to local manufacturing firms in some host countries. When foreign operations become sufficiently extensive to warrant it, the company sends traveling representatives to service the network. At this point the firm may undertake a reorganization of its basic structure. It may form a separate corporate entity in the home country for the purpose of minimizing taxes and providing more efficient service, and it may establish foreign marketing subsidiaries in key countries. Up to this point the company has served its overseas customers solely with exports from its own production in the home country.

The second phase of internationalization arrives when the company decides to commence manufacturing in other countries. The decision to produce abroad usually follows the discovery that exports to a given national market have reached a level sufficient to justify building a factory there (the demonstration effect). Such a venture is especially attractive if production is market oriented, that is, it costs less to make at a location close to final consumption. A further incentive may be the sudden imposition of governmental barriers to imports in a key market. In some instances tax concessions or other special inducements by the foreign government may reinforce the decision. Having determined to set up production in the overseas market, the firm must then decide whether to build a wholly new factory or to acquire an existing firm in the foreign area. After production is under way in several overseas locations, the firm may integrate its foreign subsidiaries, either vertically or horizontally, to gain economies of specialization.

Foreign operations may eventually generate so large a proportion of the company's total revenue that the headquarters management comes to think of the firm's business primarily in global terms. Accompanying this change in perspective is the gradual internationalization of the headquarters staff, through worldwide recruitment of executives. Decision-makers no longer identify with the firm's home country but with the company as a global entity. Although the head office still makes strategic decisions affecting the system as a whole, it allows greater autonomy of larger overseas branches. In this final phase the firm has become fully internationalized.

Foreign Investment Trends

Despite the ever-growing importance of multinational enterprises in world production and trade, data for these activities on a world scale remain scarce and lack comparability. MNEs have gained prominence so recently that few countries other than the United States gather systematic information on them. In this review of global patterns and trends, therefore, the main emphasis will be on U.S.-based multinationals: the intensifying competition they are encountering from MNEs based in other countries, the shifting nature of foreign direct investment, and the rising level of FDI within the United States.

Rising World Competition Among Multinationals. American-based firms still hold first place in total value of foreign direct investment, but the size of this lead is steadily eroding in the face of heightened competition from other countries (Figure 13.4). In 1960 U.S. multinationals accounted for nearly half the world total and nearly triple the holdings of British firms, which ranked second. Dutch and Swiss companies made up most of the remaining one-third. In the expanding global market of recent decades, however, non-U.S. multinationals have proliferated, shrinking the dollar share of U.S. multinationals to only a third of the world total. British concerns still cling to second place, but Japanese and German MNEs are close behind in third and fourth positions. Multinationals are also springing up in other lands, including several newly industrializing nations.

Half of the world's 50 largest manufacturing companies and two-thirds of the leading petroleum concerns are based in the United States. Among the top firms nearly one-fifth are Japanese, one-seventh are German, and several are British. Certain small European countries are headquarters for some of the larg-

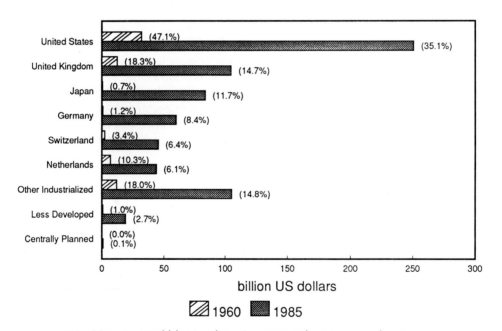

FIGURE 13.4 World foreign direct investment, by country and region, in billion U.S. dollars and percent of total. The expanding role of multinational corporations of all nations is seen in the growth of total foreign direct investment, which rose from $68 billion to $714 billion between 1960 and 1985. Though U.S. firms led this drive during the early years, MNEs based in other countries have more recently increased their foreign activities at an accelerating rate. Beginning at a low level in the 1960s, Japanese and German firms have since captured third and fourth places among the world's overseas investors. The number of countries serving as home bases to MNEs has also grown. These new entries are not confined to the older manufacturing regions but include several nations that have only recently become industrialized, especially those on the Pacific Rim. [*Source:* United Nations Center on Transnational Corporations, *Transnational Corporations in World Development: Trends and Prospects* (New York: United Nations, 1988).]

est firms, among them such giants as Nestlé (Swiss), Philips (Dutch), Unilever and Royal Dutch Shell (Dutch-British), ENI (Italy), and Volvo (Sweden).

Foreign production by U.S.–based MNEs has contributed a very high, and rising, proportion of the country's total sales. Indeed, by the end of the 1980s overseas output by affiliates of U.S. companies was more than three and one-half times as great as national exports. In the past decade, multinationals from Japan, Germany, Britain, France, Switzerland and a number of other countries have shifted much of their production overseas.

Many of the world's leading MNEs receive half or more of total company sales from foreign affiliates (Figure 13.5). Prominent among these are companies based in small West European countries. Leading the list is the Swiss food combine, Nestlé, which receives 98 percent of its earnings from foreign operations and has 95 percent of its assets outside of Switzerland. SKF has 96 percent of its sales outside its native Sweden, and Philips, the Dutch electronics firm, obtains 94 percent of total revenues from overseas affiliates. Of special interest is the Canadian communications giant, Northern Telecom, which earns 67 percent of reve-

nues abroad but produces more than 70 percent of its total output outside its home base. Foreign sales also constitute a major part of total earnings of the leading petroleum multinationals.

The Changing Character of U.S. FDI.   During the postwar era U.S. multinationals have substantially shifted their global focus (Figure 13.6). In the 1950s and 1960s Canada accounted for almost two-thirds of foreign investment by U.S. firms—nearly twice the amount going to Europe. Half of the U.S. total was in less-developed countries, mostly Latin America. Very little direct investment took place in Japan, which then, as now, interposed stubborn barriers to foreign investors.

In succeeding decades the pace of foreign investment by U.S. firms accelerated greatly. The main target area during that time was Western Europe, which had accumulated 47 percent of the total by 1988. The most rapid increases in U.S. investment during the 1980s, however, occurred in the Pacific Rim countries—Japan, Australia and New Zealand, and the Four Tigers, among others (Figure 13.6). Yet, by 1988 Japan still accounted for only 5 percent of U.S. foreign

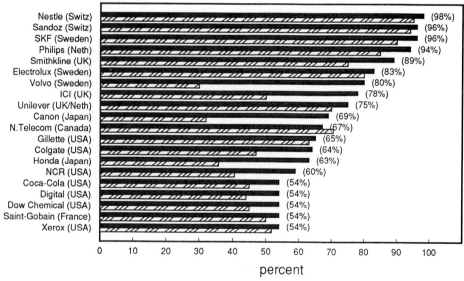

FIGURE 13.5 Global companies: percent of total sales and assets outside home countries. As they become more deeply involved in the international economy, multinational enterprises acquire ever-larger proportions of total company sales from markets outside their home countries. This growing dependence upon foreign sales in turn leads to increased investment in productive and sales facilities abroad, in order to enlarge market shares and to secure these against intensifying competition and the growing threat of protectionism. Among the firms shown here, seven of the first nine are based in small European countries with limited domestic markets. [*Source:* Company reports.]

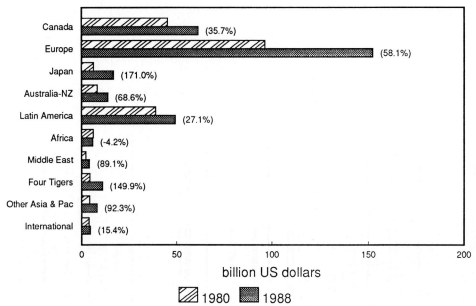

FIGURE 13.6 Foreign direct investment position of U.S. companies, by area, and percent change, 1980–1988. U.S.-based multinationals increased their total investments abroad by 52 percent between 1980 and 1988, but their attention shifted away from those areas favored in the past to new regions with greater growth potential. Western Hemisphere countries received a relatively smaller share of new investment, especially Latin American nations. The proportion going to Europe remained essentially unchanged. The greatest relative gains in overseas investment during the 1980s took place in Pacific Rim countries, which were targets for nearly one-quarter of all new FDI by American companies. The 1990s may see a reversal of this trend, however, if planned developments in economic integration succeed in Western Europe and the Americas. [*Source:* U.S. Bureau of the Census, *Statistical Abstract of the United States, 1990* (110th ed.) (Washington, D.C., 1990).]

direct investment in 1988, even though the Japanese economy has become the world's second largest. FDI by U.S. companies in debt-ridden Latin America stagnated during the decade, and it actually shrank in South Africa. U.S. investments also grew more slowly in Canada than in the rest of the world during the 1980s, but the pace promised to pick up in the wake of the 1989 Free Trade Agreement.

In addition to its regional shift, U.S. direct investment abroad has changed in sectoral composition. Manufacturing and mining companies had represented nearly three-fourths of total FDI value in the mid-1970s, but this proportion had slipped to little more than one-half by the end of the 1980s. Meanwhile, U.S. FDI in service activities had grown from less than one-fourth of all foreign investments to more than one-third. The rising importance of the services to the U.S. foreign investment position underscores the government's drive to reduce barriers to internationally traded services in recent GATT negotiations.

The Rise of Japanese Multinationals. Though U.S. firms led the world in FDI following World War II, their overseas activities have grown less rapidly in recent years than have those of multinationals based in Western Europe and Japan, especially the latter. As recently as 1975, the total value of foreign investments by American MNEs was eight times as large as that of Japanese companies; by the end of the 1980s, U.S. foreign holdings were only three times as large as Japan's. The total value of Japanese foreign operations is not an accurate measure of their importance, however, because many of these undertakings are joint ventures with local firms. Furthermore, Japanese multinationals have a very different functional and organizational makeup, which involves intercompany linkages that are not reflected in official data (See Box 13.7 for a discussion of the distinctive nature of Japanese and other non-Western MNEs.)

Foreign direct investment is a comparatively recent development for Japan. Because of an official ceiling on capital outflows imposed to save scarce foreign exchange during the early postwar period, Japanese firms were slow to go abroad. Until the Ministry of Finance lifted the ban in the late 1960s, therefore, Japan was mainly an exporter of domestically produced manufactured goods. During that period, most Japanese foreign involvement was undertaken by large trading companies for the purpose of providing assured supplies of raw materials for Japan's domestic industries.

Since 1969 the Japanese government has encouraged direct investment abroad. In addition to a mounting balance-of-payments surplus, a key incentive for this shift in official policy has been a planned restructuring of industry in favor of knowledge-intensive activities. The new policy has called for transferring abroad Japan's older labor-intensive industries, which polluted the environment and consumed great quantities of imported fuel and raw materials. The government has backed this policy with a variety of investment guarantees and other financial incentives to Japanese multinationals.

The latest thrust of Japanese investment is toward North America and Western Europe in response to growing import restrictions and accompanying pressures upon Japanese firms to manufacture locally in their foreign markets. Most Japanese investments in the West are in high-technology industries and involve state-of-the-art production methods. These ventures are very different from those undertaken by Japanese firms elsewhere. In Asia and Latin America, Japanese multinationals operate labor-intensive industries using standardized techniques, and in Australia, the Middle East, and Brazil they invest in extractive industries—petroleum, coal, and mineral raw materials. Hence, Japanese firms have gone abroad either to capitalize upon complementary resource endowments or to defend their goods from trade barriers in important market areas.

Foreign Direct Investment in the United States.
Direct investment in the United States by foreign companies has been expanding at a quickening pace, and this has had a major impact upon the U.S. economy. It has affected U.S. trade, industrial location, and employment conditions, and it has reinforced the shift in patterns of regional growth taking place within the country.

The influx of foreign FDI into the country began to swell during the 1970s; at the close of the decade MNEs from eight countries controlled nearly 2500 U.S. manufacturing operations. Thereafter the flow became a torrent: By the end of the 1980s more than a thousand new foreign enterprises were being added

every year, and the number of source countries for investment in the United States had multiplied severalfold. Also, during this period, foreign investors increasingly looked beyond manufacturing to other economic sectors.

These developments have brought a marked change in the U.S. foreign direct investment position (Figure 13.7). As recently as 1982, American FDI abroad still outweighed direct investment by foreigners in the U.S. by a substantial margin. This positive balance steadily eroded during the decade, however, as foreign FDI poured into the country faster than the rate of U.S. investment in other areas. By 1988 the traditionally positive U.S. FDI balance had slipped into deficit.

To some extent, the swift rise of FDI in the United States has stemmed from basic forces at work within the U.S. economy. During the 1980s the United States changed from being a net creditor nation to being a debtor nation (Figure 13.8). The spiraling national deficit has provided foreigners with huge accumulations of dollars for investment in the United States. Any European or Asian multinational pursuing a global strategy could not avoid entry into this, the world's largest market. Moreover, a rising U.S. protectionist sentiment in the wake of swollen trade deficits has obliged foreign MNEs to safeguard their shares in this crucial market by establishing production inside U.S. borders. Though the federal government places few restrictions on foreign investors, state and local governments compete vigorously for investments by offering all manner of tax and financial incentives to foreign firms. In many instances, the principal motivation for investment in the United States has been the desire to gain quick access to American technology.

A shift in source countries has accompanied this surge of direct investment into the United States. At the beginning of the 1970s, 88 percent of all FDI in the United States came from the United Kingdom, Canada, The Netherlands, Switzerland, and West Germany, in that order. By 1988 Japan had become the second-largest supplier, having climbed from a minuscule 2 percent of the total in 1970 to more than 16 percent (Figure 13.9). The United Kingdom remained an aggressive investor in U.S. enterprises, joined by several other European countries and a growing number of Pacific Rim and oil-rich Middle Eastern nations.

During the 1980s foreign multinationals substantially increased their share of U.S. manufacturing. By the end of the decade more than one-eighth of U.S. manufacturing assets were under foreign control. Prime targets for manufacturing investment were high-technology industries such as nonelectrical machin-

BOX 13.7 The Non-Western Multinational

As the twentieth century nears an end, many of the most dynamic multinational enterprises edging toward the center of the global economic stage come from East Asia. Though some of these non-Western concerns match the leading MNEs of Europe and America in size and power, they exhibit certain traits that do not seem to fit the general prescriptions of the theoretical literature.

The prime source country for MNEs in this group is Japan, whose successful postwar strategy for achieving economic superpower status has set the pattern for all aspiring nations. The other Pacific rim countries, having emerged from an impoverished colonial condition since the war, are now at the point of becoming newly industrialized countries. Principal among these NICs are the Four Tigers—South Korea, Taiwan, Hong Kong, and Singapore. Other East Asian countries striving for such status include Thailand, Malaysia, and Indonesia.

Though differing national circumstances and policies somewhat hamper direct comparisons between Japan and the Tigers, it is possible to point to several shared attributes that have helped to shape the new breed of multinational emerging on the Pacific rim. To a large extent, these traits arise from the blend of religions and ethical systems, especially Buddhism and Confucianism, that prevail in most East Asian cultures. Centuries ago these beliefs diffused from China to Korea and Japan, where they have intermingled with indigenous religions, notably the Japanese Shinto. In more recent times Chinese émigrés have transmitted these belief patterns to Hong Kong, Taiwan, and Singapore, as well as to other lands where Chinese entrepreneurs dominate local economies.

A fundamental source of motivation and discipline among East Asians is Confucianism, an ancient Chinese ethical system that places a high value on education and assigns a special virtue to hard work, obedience, and the obligations of the individual in a structured society. In Japan, Zen Buddhism has been influential, with its requirement of rigorous individual discipline and self-control, as well as its emphasis

upon simplicity and taste. East Asian societies are group-centered; the interests of the individual are subordinate to those of the whole, whether in the family, the village, or the place of work.

Japanese Multinationals. Though certain trading companies (*sogo shosha*) could lay claim to being among the earliest multinationals, the great surge of Japanese FDI overseas is a new phenomenon. Despite the recency of their appearance, some of these firms have already seized a major share of world markets. This swift success stems from a number of conditions relating to the organizational makeup of these companies, to the cultural system upon which they draw, and the unique economic and political environment from which they spring.

Japanese multinationals are not directly comparable with those of North America and Europe because they are organized differently. Japanese companies are divided into three functional classes: manufacturing, marketing, and financial. Firms of the three types often join together to form enterprise groups, called *keiretsu*, which are linked by mutual ownership, interlocking directorships, and operational ties based upon mutual understandings. Some of these enterprise groups are descended from family-controlled combines, *zaibatsu*, dating to the earliest period of Japanese industrialization. Commonly a trading company (*sogo shosha*) and a large bank form the core of such a group, together with a number of manufacturing concerns. Functionally, the member companies are closely integrated, but their relationship is so informal that they are not usually viewed in the same light as an IBM or a General Electric. Yet several *keiretsu* greatly exceed the leading European and American MNEs in total sales. Towering over other Japanese *keiretsu* is mighty Mitsubishi, with total global sales of $175 billion (see table of Japan's top six *keiretsu* and their principal member companies). In the past two decades some of the larger Japanese manufacturing firms, such as Sony, have internationalized their production independently of any enterprise group. This action has had a

bandwagon effect, drawing other Japanese competitors, as well as hordes of their suppliers, into overseas operations.

Japan's six leading *keiretsu*

	Core Companies in Group
Mitsubishi	28
• Mitsubishi Corporation	
• Mitsubishi Bank	
• Mitsubishi Heavy Industries	
Dai-ichi Kangin	47
• Seibu Department Stores	
• Shimizu	
• Yokohama Rubber	
Fuyo	29
• Marubeni	
• Nissan Motor	
• Canon	
Mitsui Group	24
• Toyota Motor	
• Toshiba	
• Toray Industries	
Sanwa	44
• Teijin	
• Ohbayashi	
• Kobe Steel	
Sumitomo	20
• NEC	
• Sumitomo Chemical	
• Sumitomo Metal Industries	

Source: *Business Week*, Sept. 24, 1990, 100.

The intragroup cooperation that takes place among member companies is consistent with the Japanese cultural heritage, which places group values over those of the individual. Pervading the entire corporate system, this outlook is expressed in a sense of togetherness within a family-type environment, a *ringi seido* (consensus) system of decision making, assignment of tasks to groups, with little differentiation among individual job definitions, and continuous on-the-job training. It is a system that relies upon close face-to-face contacts and the shared understandings of a homogeneous culture. Consequently, non-Japanese managers of overseas affiliates are often at a disadvantage in the decision-making process. This problem is all the greater because Japanese foreign operations tend to be tightly controlled from the home base.

Many factors have contributed to the growing success of Japanese foreign operations, some stemming from Japanese management techniques and others relating to conditions in the home country. Japanese multinationals benefit from a smoothly functioning production technology and a well-developed organizational technology that includes effective methods of quality control and minimizing inventory costs. Most Japanese overseas operations are located close to their local markets, as seen in the case of Japanese auto manufacture in the United States.

Among the many home-base advantages enjoyed by Japanese multinationals is the country's remarkable ability to create not only an abundance of money capital but also to upgrade human capital by means of an effective system of public education supplemented by corporate on-the-job training. MNEs have gained by high public investment in research and development. An informed public reacts instantly to perceived national crises, as in the concerted national effort to conserve energy. The Japanese consuming public, the world's second largest, also contributes through its insistence upon utter perfection in the products it buys. This creates an intensely competitive home market, which thoroughly prepares Japanese MNEs for competing in the world market with goods they have been forced to refine before taking them abroad.

Korea's Multinationals. Among the growing number of LDC-based multinational corporations listed annually among the *Fortune* 500 are many based in newly industrialized countries on the Pacific Rim. Unlike those Third World MNEs originating in resource-rich countries (for example, the oil-exporting lands of the Middle East), or those coming from countries with large markets (Brazil, Mexico, India), multinationals spawned by the East Asian NICs draw upon a labor-rich home environment as the foundation for their ventures abroad. Cheap labor may be more abundant in other newly developing countries, but East Asia's workers constitute a resource of unusual quality.

South Korea is typical of the East Asian NICs in its devotion to making the best of the human resources it has in order to compensate for the physical resources it lacks. As workers, Koreans are disciplined, hardworking, and well educated. The population is linguistically and racially homogeneous; and, in the aftermath of a bitter civil war, it is remarkably free of class divisions. Moreover, Korea has made an unusually strong commitment to upgrade this valuable resource by means of a highly developed secondary, university, and technical educational system, supplemented by advanced training abroad for many individuals.

Not only do Koreans look to Japan as a model for their development strategy, they also regard Japan as a competitor to be beaten. Korean companies have been quick to seize opportunities for invading Japanese product lines as structural changes in Japan make some forms of manufacture less economical. In standardized types of mass production, Korean firms are highly competitive on the basis of cost. However, Korea's population of 43 million offers a home market only one-third as large as Japan's, and consumer tastes are not as sophisticated. On the whole, Korea lags several years behind Japan in its level of advancement.

As their economy matured and as domestic wages rose, Korean firms began to enter into foreign ventures. Although the initial moves took place in the late 1960s, it was not until the early 1980s that outward FDI exceeded inward FDI. The first companies to go abroad were construction firms, which had gained their experience as contractors in the construction of U.S. military bases in Korea at the end of the Korean War and later in Vietnam. Korean construction companies were subsequently very active in the Persian Gulf oil states. Other industries that pioneered in foreign undertakings were plywood and textile manufacturers. Once started on this course, Korean firms have been remarkably quick to manufacture in other countries, in lines as diverse as consumer electronics, automobiles, and videotapes.

Very large industry groups, known as *chaebol,* dominate the Korean economy. Many of these giant firms grew out of the large general trading companies that predate them. Unlike Japan's *keiretsu,* which are loosely joined by informal links and interlocking directorships, the *chaebol* are closely held corporations run by strong, aggressive chief executives who usually were the company founders. The *chaebol* enjoy much government favor and support. The leading *chaebol* are Hyundai, Daewoo, Samsung, and Luck-Goldstar, all multibillion-dollar companies. These firms invest heavily in research and development and compete fiercely both at home and overseas.

MNEs Based in Taiwan. The other Tigers—Taiwan, Singapore, and Hong Kong—have produced similarly aggressive multinational enterprises. Unlike Korea, these three small nations are populated mainly by ethnic Chinese, the majority of whom escaped from their native land during the 1949 Communist takeover. The largest of the three, Taiwan, had been a Japanese colony prior to World War II. An island lying only a few miles off the coast of China, it became a sanctuary for the defeated Kuomintang (Nationalist) Chinese forces following the revolution. The native Taiwanese were overwhelmed by the flood of refugees, who took political control and shortly created a vibrant export-driven economy.

By several measures, Taiwan is the most successful of the Tigers. Now the world's twelfth-largest exporter, it has accumulated a cash surplus greater even than Japan's and has achieved the second-highest per capita GNP in East Asia—distributed among its 20 million people in an unusually equitable manner. Virtually all Taiwanese complete elementary school, and a remarkable 45 percent get at least some higher education.

(Continued on next page)

One of the world's most densely populated countries, Taiwan gained its manufacturing success by reason of an abundance of cheap labor and a robust entrepreneurial spirit. Its industries were largely of a low-technology, copycat type, involving only minimal research and development, and conducted in hundreds of small establishments. Government-imposed exchange controls, aided by a strong currency, kept the country's burgeoning supply of money at home. By the mid-1980s, however, pressures had begun to mount: Wages rose rapidly, inflation grew dangerously, and Taiwan's traditional manufactures could no longer compete with nearby Malaysia, Thailand, and Indonesia. Industrial output and exports slumped.

The country's response was two-fold. One solution was to shift from cheap assembly to higher levels of technology. Several new semiconductor factories sprang up, and Taiwanese computer companies aggressively doubled their share of the world market. The second reaction was to "go global." In 1986 the government ended the tight exchange controls that had restricted overseas investments, and a huge capital exodus ensued.

For Taiwan's countless small companies this meant transferring, unaltered, their low-wage, low-tech operations—shoes, garments, handbags, tennis rackets, plastics—to Thailand, Malaysia, the Philippines, Indonesia, and China. They poured billions of dollars into the nearby Chinese coastal province of Fujian, which, with its 29 million population, became essentially a Taiwanese industrial zone. In time, larger companies followed, bringing to Fujian more sophisticated products, such as chemicals, video recorders, and computers.

On the whole, however, the favored target for the larger investors was the United States. Taiwan's premier computer maker, Acer Inc., led the way in 1987 with its purchase of a U.S. firm, Counterpoint Computers. Following this came Taiwanese acquisition of the venerable American Bridge Company, eight Texas savings and loan associations, Princeton Publishing Labs, and Wyse Technology—one of Silicon Valley's leading manufacturers of terminals and personal computers—and Wyndham Foods (Girl Scout cookies), among others.

The City-States as Springboards for FDI.

The city-states of Hong Kong (population, 5.8 million) and Singapore (2.7 million), share similar histories of British colonial control. Singapore gained independence in 1965, but Hong Kong is to remain a crown colony until its scheduled return to Chinese control in 1997. Both are island countries with unusual locational advantages for trade and foreign investment: Hong Kong is the main point of entry into Kuangtung Province, China's leading industrial region, and Singapore is situated on the main sea and air routes linking East Asia with Europe and the Middle East. As a legacy of longtime British control, both have English-speaking populations, a positive attraction to foreign investors. Though each has enjoyed rapid growth and rising standards of living, Hong Kong has practiced freewheeling capitalism under a relaxed government policy of nonintervention in economic matters, whereas Singapore has achieved similarly successful results under a government program that closely managed all aspects of the economy after the Japanese model.

The same locational characteristics that, under British rule, had made Singapore the principal entrepôt of Southeast Asia, served to attract particular types of foreign investment in the post-independence era: shipbuilding and repair; refining; port and terminal services; airlines; printing; regional corporate headquarters for U.S., Japanese, and European MNEs; and a growing array of financial and business services benefiting from the presence of an English-speaking population.

Despite its small size, Singapore was also successful in developing into a manufacturing center for multinationals requiring a low-cost, literate work force within a setting that, in addition, offers excellent roads, air service, port facilities, and telecommunications. When, in time, the labor-cost advantage was lost to neighboring Asian lands, Singapore's steadfast policy of upgrading the quality of its work force and infrastructure enabled the country to restructure its economy to capital- and skill-intensive, high-value-added activities such as electronics and scientific equipment.

Playing an essential part in this economic restructuring was a rising group of Singapore-based multinationals. As rising wages deprived local industries of their competitive advantage in labor-intensive forms of production, they shifted their manufacturing activities to neighboring countries with abundant supplies of cheap labor. In this undertaking, these firms were able to build upon their accumulated production experience and to avail themselves of the well-developed Singapore banking community for the capital needed for these foreign ventures.

The Fourth Tiger, Hong Kong, was truly the pioneer in this type of outward FDI, and it has led the other NICs in the number of such investments throughout Southeast Asia. Indeed, Hong Kong interests established a stake in Communist Chinese enterprises even greater than that of their Taiwanese counterparts. As China's longtime window to the outside world, Hong Kong was uniquely situated for such undertakings. Reinforcing this locational edge were the many family ties and other personal links that Hong Kong entrepreneurs enjoyed within the Canton and Kuangtung areas. Hong Kong's highly developed international finance sector furnished crucial support for these and other foreign undertakings of locally based MNEs. Indeed, some of the financial institutions have themselves "gone global," a notable example being the Bank of Hong Kong and Shanghai, which entered the U.S. market through its acquisition of New York-based Marine Midland Bank.

Hong Kong's international role, however, has been severely threatened by the imminent resumption of Chinese political control upon expiration of Britain's 99-year lease in 1997. Distrusting China's assurances that it will not alter the existing economic framework, Hong Kong's ethnic-Chinese entrepreneurial class began an exodus from the colony during the second half of the 1980s, taking their very substantial supply of capital with them. Hong Kong's economic future is therefore clouded.

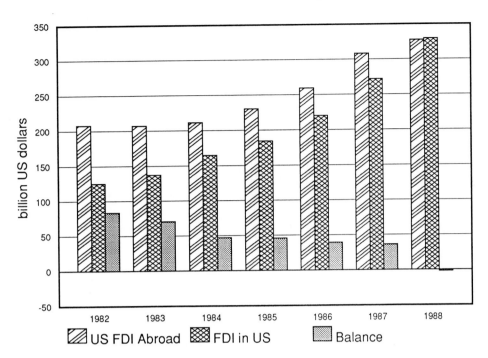

US FDI Abroad   FDI in US   Balance

FIGURE 13.7 U.S. foreign direct investment position, 1982–1988. For many years total direct investment abroad by U.S. multinationals greatly outweighed direct investment by foreign concerns in the United States. Although U.S. FDI has continued to grow, foreign investment in the United States rose at an even faster rate during the 1970s and 1980s. FDI in the country climbed from a mere $13 billion in 1970 to $125 billion in 1982, then soared to $329 billion by 1988. Within a period of only 6 years, therefore, the net FDI position of the United States slipped from a surplus of $83 billion to a deficit of $200 million in 1988, and the accelerating trend continued thereafter. [*Source:* U.S. Bureau of the Census, *Statistical Abstract of the United States, 1990* (Washington, D.C.: U.S. Government Printing Office, 1990).]

ery, chemicals and pharmaceuticals, electric machinery and electronics, and professional and scientific instruments. The percentage of foreign ownership was highest in chemicals and allied products; stone, clay and glass products; and primary metals. More than a quarter of the U.S. chemical industry was in foreign hands by 1990.

To the general public, however, the foreign presence was most visible in certain key consumer-goods industries. In the early 1990s the Big Three U.S. automakers became the Big Four: General Motors, Ford, Toyota, and Chrysler, in that order. Of all the major tire manufacturers in the country, only Goodyear remained under U.S. control. By 1991, major Japanese-owned industries in the United States included 66 steel works, 20 rubber and tire factories, 8 automobile assembly plants (plus three in Canada), and some 270 auto parts suppliers. As this suggests, Japanese auto manufacturing operations in North America were becoming highly integrated, including some research and development.

Public attention has increasingly focused upon foreign acquisitions in the nonmanufacturing sectors of the American economy, especially such highly publicized events as the purchase of Rockefeller Center, Columbia Records, Federated Department Stores, and a number of Hollywood filmmaking companies by foreign interests. Less noticed but equally important has been the rise of foreign ownership in finance, real estate, and business services. Altogether, between 1970 and 1988 the tertiary sector increased its share of total foreign assets in the U.S. from 31 percent to 53 percent, whereas manufacturing slipped from 46 percent to 37.

In their locational choices, most foreign companies had in the past favored the traditional manufacturing belt of the Northeast and Great Lakes, although firms of different national origins had tended to show

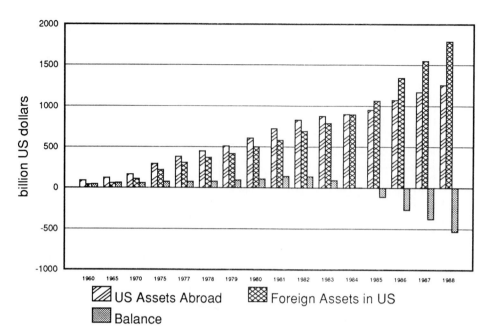

FIGURE 13.8 U.S. international investment position: U.S. assets abroad versus foreign assets in the United States. An important reason for the surge of foreign direct investment in the United States (see Figure 13.7) is the swelling hoard of dollars that foreigners have accumulated as a result of the mounting U.S. indebtedness to the rest of the world. This is shown here by a comparison of total U.S. overseas assets, both governmental and private, with total assets held in the United States by foreign interests. [*Source:* U.S. Bureau of the Census, *Statistical Abstract of the United States, 1990* (Washington, D.C.: U.S. Government Printing Office, 1990).]

preferences for particular parts of the country. Thus British and Continental firms had located mainly in the Northeast, following a long-established pattern of trade and investment in areas nearest to Europe; Japanese industrial firms had gravitated toward the two coasts, especially with their large investments in high-technology enterprises in those western areas closest to Japan. Canadian concerns, benefiting from long acquaintance with the nearby U.S. business environment, had tended to be more dispersed than the others; nevertheless, they had exhibited an inclination toward U.S.–Canadian border areas of the Middle West and Northeast, as well as the South Atlantic. Some of the new investment entering the country during the 1970s, however, followed the general migration of U.S. economic activity into the Sunbelt states of the Southeast and the Gulf and Pacific coasts.

As the volume of FDI entering the United States swelled during the 1980s, subtle shifts began to emerge in the spatial pattern of foreign ownership (Figure 13.10). The Pacific region assumed the lead in overseas FDI, with California replacing Texas as the state having the largest total. The highest rate of FDI growth occurred in the Middle Atlantic and southern New England areas. A major element is this surge of foreign

investment into New York, Massachusetts, and Connecticut, in particular, was the takeover of large retail chains, financial institutions, and other service organizations by foreign interests.

Most meaningful of all, perhaps, was the sudden emergence during the 1980s of a major Japanese automotive complex in the traditional Rust Belt states of Illinois, Michigan, Indiana, and Ohio—with extensions southward into Kentucky and Tennessee and westward to Missouri. Settling mainly in rural areas with weak or nonexistent unions, the Japanese "transplants" chose locations central to the national market at points affording maximum access to the interstate transport network. This unfolding situation helps to explain the high FDI growth rates experienced by some of these states during the decade (see Figure 13.10).

TOWARD A DYNAMIC NEW THEORY OF INTERNATIONAL COMMERCE

In this second of three chapters on the geographical dimensions of world commerce we have added a further set of modifications to conventional trade theory.

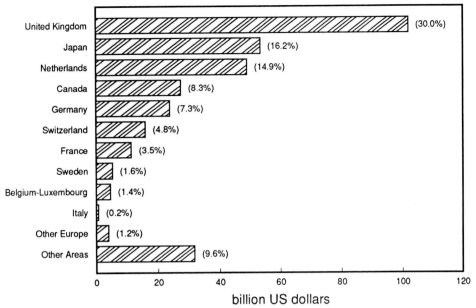

FIGURE 13.9   Foreign direct investment in the United States, by area, 1988 (book value at year end). As defined by the U.S. Department of Commerce, this includes all American firms in which foreign interest or ownership is 10 percent or more. Although Europeans and Canadians were the principal investors in U.S. enterprises in the past, FDI has come from a growing variety of other countries during the 1980s. The most important development has been the recent flood of Japanese investment, which has propelled Japan into second place behind Britain in U.S. holdings. Back in 1970, the Japanese had had only 2 percent of the total. In 1988 Europeans still owned nearly two-thirds of all FDI in the United States, but the Canadian share, almost a quarter of the total in 1970, had dropped to only 8 percent. The "other areas" category has proliferated: Among the new entrants are the Four Tigers, Australia, Brazil, several Middle Eastern oil exporters, and a great many others from Asia and Latin America. [*Source:* U.S. Bureau of the Census, *Statistical Abstract of the United States, 1990* (Washington, D.C.: U.S. Government Printing Office, 1990).]

In Chapter 12 we saw that the factor-endowments explanation fails to take into account the effects of demand, the barriers of distance and governmental intervention, and the impact of trade upon factor endowments. The present chapter has been concerned with the altering effects of change. We have noted the variable role of trade in the growth of national economies and the trade effects of technology, giving special attention to the question of whether or not the United States is losing its lead in technology-intensive trade.

Another major issue addressed here is the special trade problems of less-developed countries, which, some observers believe, cast doubt on the applicability of trade theory to the circumstances of LDCs. Seeming to belie this argument, certain developing countries have devised successful new trade strategies that have enabled them to become important actors in world commerce. Still another strategy—viewed by theorists as a form of selective discrimination—is regional economic integration. Cooperative ventures of this type have been undertaken by groups of industrialized nations, Third World countries, and members of the Communist bloc.

A final modifying element has been the multinational enterprise, a company with its headquarters in one country and sales and production branches in other countries. Within a surprisingly short time the MNE has become a prime agent for international transfers of capital, services, entrepreneurship, and technology—as well as a vital force in international trade. These MNEs have demonstrated a remarkable capacity for fundamentally altering the quality and quantity of factor endowments in those countries where they operate. This they have accomplished by efficiently moving human and physical resources from one part of the world to another.

The astounding growth of foreign direct investment, and the evolution of more powerful and versatile

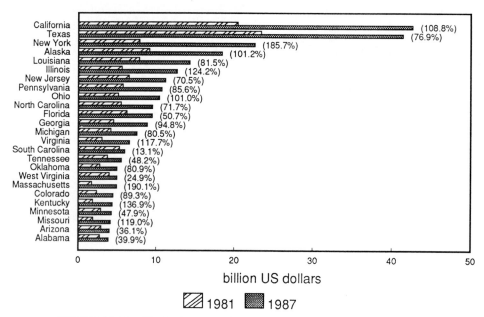

FIGURE 13.10   FDI in the United States, 25 leading states, and percent change, 1981–1987. As foreign investors became better acquainted with the business environment of the country, FDI began to reach into new areas. Nevertheless, in 1987 three states accounted for nearly one-third of all FDI in the U.S., and the 25 states shown here garnered 80 percent of the total. In the country as a whole, FDI grew by 84 percent between 1981 and 1987, but the states did not share equally in this increase. Rapid growth rates occurred particularly in certain states of the Middle Atlantic and southern New England areas, along the Pacific Coast, in the industrial Middle West, and in the national capital district. New FDI lagged somewhat in Texas, Florida, and various other high-growth states of the previous decade. [*Source:* U.S. Bureau of the Census, *Statistical Abstract of the United States, 1990* (Washington, D.C.: U.S. Government Printing Office, 1990).]

corporate forms for channeling this activity, has many implications for trade theory. As their global operations become increasingly integrated, MNEs generate more and more intrafirm trade. Thus, fully one-third of U.S. exports of manufactured goods represent shipments by American multinationals to their foreign affiliates. Although exchanges of merchandise among different branches of the same firm often take place for conventional reasons, such as the complementarity of resource endowments among countries, many of these transfers are in response to special company needs. Similarly, the investment behavior of an MNE may reflect the particular circumstances of the firm—for example, the necessity for responding to the actions of a competitor. As prime transfer agents, multinationals hasten the process of factor equalization among nations, thereby altering comparative advantages. Because they sell to the world, MNEs are not limited by the size of local markets in achieving optimal economies of scale in their production. Hence, an adequate

explanation of world trade and investment patterns must now take into account the behavioral characteristics and capabilities of multinational enterprises.

Although companies are thus the prime contenders in the arena of world commerce, we cannot forget that their competitive success relies to an important degree upon the characteristics of the countries that serve as their home bases. As Michael Porter has demonstrated, the home country is the ultimate source of a firm's competitive advantage. The national environment from which it springs importantly influences a company's ability to develop new production techniques and create new products and it affects the direction that such innovation takes. "Competitive advantage ultimately results from an effective combination of national circumstances and company strategy" (Porter 1990, p. 578).

It has, therefore, become increasingly apparent that trade theory and multinational enterprise theory are complementary: Trade theory is concerned with the factor endowments of countries, whereas MNE theory concentrates upon the knowledge assets of firms. The international location of production depends upon the spatial pattern of resource endowments, but control and ownership of this production and the flows that result from it relate to the special qualities of companies. A complete understanding of international economic interaction thus requires a new

body of theory that incorporates both aspects. It must also be a dynamic theory, one that takes into account the constantly evolving competitive advantages of countries and companies. All elements of this prospective new theory come into play in the analysis of evolving patterns of world commerce, which is the topic of the next chapter.

TOPICS FOR DISCUSSION

1. What are the two fundamental ways in which economic growth occurs? As economies grow and develop, how does their level of trade participation change and what shifts take place in the composition of that trade? Why do policymakers in some contemporary less-developed countries (LDCs) question the applicability of conventional trade theory to their own conditions? What special problems do LDCs have in their trading relations with industrialized countries? How may multinational enterprises affect the factor endowments of LDCs?

2. Explain why high-technology trade is so essential to the United States, indicate those high-tech commodities in which the U.S. trade balance has deteriorated, and propose a set of remedies for the country's declining technological lead.

3. Examine the alternative trade strategies available to developing countries and explain the differing results that have followed the pursuit of such policies in Latin America and East Asia.

4. How does the theory of regional economic integration relate to conventional trade theory? What organizational types of economic integration have been identified and to what extent are these ideal types represented among the integrated groups now in existence? What are the theoretically ideal characteristics that a group of countries needs to possess if successful integration is to occur?

5. Assess the effects that Western Europe's postwar integration experiments have had on intrabloc trade and on trade with the world at large. In what ways has integration influenced the location of production in Western

Europe? What changes in European trade and location might we anticipate if the European Community succeeds in its plans for closer integration in 1992? How might the collapse of Communism in Eastern Europe alter those plans?

6. Explore the incentives for creating a North American Free Trade Area and weigh the obstacles that appear to hamper this effort.

7. Why is the multinational enterprise (MNE) considered a prime agency for the international transfer of goods and factors of production? As viewed by the theoretician, what does the MNE contribute to the world economy? How do the theories of international trade and the multinational enterprise complement each other?

8. What causes a firm to go abroad and what makes it succeed in an alien environment against competition from local firms and from other MNEs? How, when, and why does a firm go multinational, and what happens to the organizational arrangements within the firm as this process continues? How do these events change the company's perspectives?

9. Discuss the international legal status of multinational enterprises and show how this poses problems both for the MNEs and for national governments. What are the economic and political impacts of MNEs upon host countries and upon their home countries?

10. Account for the changing U.S. balance of foreign direct investment. How is investment by foreign multinationals contributing to locational change within the United States?

FURTHER READINGS

BALASSA, BELA. *The Theory of Economic Integration.* Homewood, Ill.: Richard D. Irwin, 1961.

Introduces a system for classifying the organizational forms used by various groups of countries in their experiments with economic integration, and develops a comprehensive theory of integration within the general framework of modern international trade theory.

DUNNING, JOHN H. *International Production and the Multinational Enterprise.* London: George Allen and Unwin, 1981.

Develops an eclectic theory of international production that draws upon industrial organization theory, location theory, and the theory of the firm. Bringing together elements common to a variety of specialized works on the

MNE, the eclectic theory holds that the propensity for foreign direct investment depends upon the possession by a company of assets that its competitors lack, the willingness of the company to internalize these assets, and its ability to profit from exploiting them in foreign countries.

DUNNING, JOHN H. (Ed.). *Multinational Enterprises, Economic Structure and International Competitiveness.* New York: John Wiley, 1985.

Considers the extent to which multinational enterprises contribute to the process of restructuring now taking place in the world economy. Twelve authors pursue this question with respect to four different categories of home and host countries. They find that the impact of multinationals varies substantially from country to country and depends to a large extent upon the character of particular national economies and the public policies pursued in each.

HANSON, ROGER D. *Central America: Regional Integration and Economic Development.* Washington, D.C.: National Planning Association Studies in Development Progress, No. 1, 1967.

A theoretical and empirical analysis of the experiments in economic integration conducted by five Central American countries.

HYMER, STEPHEN H. *The International Operations of National Firms.* Cambridge, Mass.: MIT Press, 1976.

Emphasizing the owner-specific element in international commerce, this seminal work established industrial organization theory as a basis for the analysis of foreign direct investment.

KNICKERBOCKER, FREDERICK T. *Oligopolistic Reaction and Multinational Enterprise.* Boston: Harvard University Graduate School of Business Administration, 1973.

Shows the importance of examining the particular characteristics of industries in order to gain an understanding of why companies go abroad.

LINDER, STAFFAN BURENSTAM. *Trade and Trade Policy for Development.* New York: Praeger, 1967.

Analyzes the special trade problems of less-developed countries, explores the linkages between the theories of international trade and economic development, discusses the changes that take place in a country's trade as it grows and develops, and considers the options available to policymakers in addressing the problems of LDCs.

McCONNELL, JAMES E. "The International Location of Manufacturing Investments: Recent Behaviour of Foreign-owned Corporations in the United States." In *Spatial Analy-*

sis, Industry and the Industrial Environment. Vol. 3, Regional Economies and Industrial Systems (F. E. I. Hamilton and G. J. R. Linge, Eds.). London: John Wiley, 1983.

Examines within a theoretical framework the recent flows of foreign direct investment into the United States, giving special attention to the differing investment patterns of European, Canadian, and Japanese subsidiaries at national, regional, and subregional scales.

PORTER, MICHAEL E. *The Competitive Advantage of Nations.* New York: The Free Press, 1990.

Building upon some of the ideas advanced in his earlier best-selling works, *Competitive Strategy* (1980) and *Competitive Advantage* (1985), Porter identifies the fundamental determinants of national competitive advantage in an industry and the manner in which these function as a system. He emphasizes the influence that a company's home-country environment exerts over its competitive success in the world arena.

RONEN, SIMCHA. *Comparative and Multinational Management.* New York: John Wiley, 1986.

A psychologist's guide for managers who must contend with the complexities of operating in unfamiliar cultural environments. This work provides a basis for understanding cultural differences and the effects these may have on managerial policies and practices. Offers a valuable review of the literature on comparative management.

ROOT, FRANKLIN R. *International Trade and Investment,* 6th ed. Cincinnati: South-Western Publishing Co., 1990.

An integrated treatment of theory, governmental policy, and multinational enterprise relating to international trade and foreign investment.

STOPFORD, J. M., and L. T. WELLS, JR. *Managing the Multinational Enterprise.* New York: Basic Books, 1972.

Provides a helpful guide to the changes that take place in the organizational structure of a company as it evolves into multinational status. The authors identify three phases: autonomy consolidation, creation of a specialized international division, and integration into the mainstream.

VINER, JACOB. *The Customs Union Issue.* New York: Carnegie Endowment for International Peace, 1950.

A classic work on the theory of economic integration.

WILKINS, MIRA. *The Emergence of Multinational Enterprise.* Cambridge, Mass.: Harvard University Press, 1970.

Reviews in some detail the history of the foreign operations of U.S. business concerns prior to World War I.

14

Patterns of World Commerce

OVERVIEW

Previous chapters have established a theoretical framework for viewing the forces that foster international commerce, as well as those influences serving to divert, inhibit, or otherwise modify it. In this concluding chapter we examine the actual flows, using international data, in a search for meaningful spatial patterns, which we interpret conceptually.

Empirical evidence reveals the effects of recent economic and political events on the spatial patterns of world commerce. The changes now materializing in the economic linkages among major trading countries and regions follow a very long era of relative stability, a time of incremental development tied to structural advances in industry and the shifting fortunes of nations.

This placid period was terminated during the 1970s, however, by a series of global crises that upset the established system. Reinforcing the spatial changes in the global economy during the past two decades, world industry underwent a fundamental restructuring accompanied by an internationalization of production and services. In consequence of these de-velopments, the essential nature of resource endowments was basically altered, with important implications for spatial economic theory.

In the course of the 1980s the center of gravity of world commerce continued to shift from the North Atlantic, its traditional focus, toward the Pacific Basin. Building upon an impressive supply of human resources, a dynamic group of East Asian countries amassed a large store of the new kinds of factor endowments required to profit from a restructured international economy.

Even as world trade and investment increasingly focused upon this emerging Pacific realm, however, a renewal of economic cooperation was taking place in Europe, where the collapse of communism in the Eastern Bloc opened new vistas. A similar movement toward the economic integration of North America suggests the prospect of three competing regional centers of economic power in the twenty-first century, with globalized multinational enterprises operating simultaneously in all three.

OBJECTIVES

- to assess the theoretical implications of contemporary developments in the economic relations among countries
- to distinguish trends in the growth and composition of international commodity flows
- to evaluate the impact of recent global crises and political events on world trade and foreign investment
- to examine the shifting currents of world commerce; the effects these have had on international flows of goods, services, and factors of production; and the new economic regions that are evolving

THE GLOBAL ECONOMY IN TRANSITION

The dynamic elements of world commerce addressed in Chapter 13 are assuming an ever-greater role in the international exchange of goods, services, and factors of production. Trade and foreign investment are gaining prominence in national development strategies as newly industrializing countries adopt a greater openness to the world, and new technology is being created and transferred internationally at an accelerating pace. Central to all these developments is the multinational enterprise, which is itself undergoing a transformation in organizational form, scope of outlook, and economic functions. Change has thus become the new reality. Patterns of world commerce—dependably stable over very long periods in the past—are now in transition, the result of recent major world economic crises.

In this chapter, therefore, we turn attention to the changing composition and direction of economic flows among countries, the nature of the regional patterns produced by this type of spatial interaction, the shifting fortunes of countries and regions in an increasingly competitive world environment, and the potential shape of the world economic map in the coming century. Before undertaking this survey of international trends and emerging patterns, let us examine a few empirical studies to see what they tell us about the influences that have shaped economic flows in the recent past. This will provide a starting point for looking at the fundamental changes now taking place in the competitive positions of countries and the effects on the geography of world commerce.

The Changing Character of World Commerce

Investigating the Bases of Trade. In the postwar era a number of analysts examined the two-way trade between country pairs using interaction (gravity) models, which are based upon the premise that the intensity of intercountry trade flows is directly proportional to their trading capacities and inversely proportional to the physical distance (and other barriers) separating them. One such study was that of Dutch economist Hans Linnemann (1966), who identified three groups of influences affecting the size of trade flows: potential total supply of the exporting country, potential total demand of the importing country, and the "resistance" impeding the flow of goods between them.

Potential supply and demand, noted Linnemann, are a function of the differences between domestic output and demand, which in turn derive from the comparative advantages of the countries. The larger the

national economy, the more industries it can support at optimal economies of scale; however, the larger the population, the greater the proportion of output needed to accommodate domestic demand. Linnemann further reasoned that the trade flow between country pairs is likely to be greater if the commodity structure of one country's exports conforms closely to the structure of the importing country's demand. Linnemann acknowledged two types of barriers: distance and governmental intervention.

Based upon these premises, Linnemann's model incorporated the following variables for each country: (1) gross national product, (2) population size, (3) physical distance, (4) preferential trading relations, and (5) commodity composition of flows. The data consisted of 6300 commodity movements among 80 countries or colonies for the year 1959 (actually a 3-year average for 1958, 1959, and 1960).

All the variables proved to be important determinants of trade. The most influential were gross national product (a measure of total demand) and distance. Preferential trading relations contributed substantially to the explanation, especially in the flows between mother countries and their associated colonies, past or present. This was particularly strong in the case of France and other members of the French community, which also showed the greatest complementarity in the commodities exchanged among them. The study thus exposed the unrealistic nature of the assumptions underlying conventional trade theory, especially with respect to the barriers to trade.

Contemporary Determinants of Competitive Advantage. Though Linnemann's analysis—and other trade-flow studies of the 1960s—found that resource endowments continued to have a significant influence on commodity flows, subsequent work has shown that the nature of resources has undergone fundamental changes. A major restructuring of industry, a revolution in global communications, and a growing place for multinational enterprises—all have produced a new global economic environment that Adam Smith and Ricardo would have found hard to recognize. As Leamer (1984) discovered, this process was already under way in the 1960s and 1970s. His study of trade flows disclosed major changes in the factors of production, particularly in the rising importance of high-quality labor and the diminished effect of physical-resource endowments.

Later, Porter (1990) noted that the differences in factor costs among nations had continued to shrink with the rise of knowledge-intensive industries. Because of greater economies of scale and an increased differentiation of products—along with other basic changes—today's industries bear little resemblance to those of an earlier age. In addition, the distinction between high-technology and low-technology industry has been narrowed through such innovations as the now-routine use of microelectronics in the most commonplace items, from washing machines to motor cars.

The international transfer of advanced technologies has deprived the older industrial powers of their competitive edge over the newly industrialized states. Consequently, countries have grown more alike in their endowments. Reinforcing this trend, the globalization of multinational corporations has freed firms from dependence upon the factor endowments of individual countries.

At the same time, many countries have learned that a cost advantage in labor or physical resources can quickly evaporate as new lower-cost countries come into production or as technology creates substitute materials. Porter noted that many less-developed countries have allowed themselves to become trapped into dependence upon exports that require low-cost labor and materials and compete only on the basis of price. Usually they have no plans to move beyond such exports when the cost advantage disappears.

Because of these basic changes in the global environment, it is necessary to reexamine the conventional explanations for international commerce. A useful framework for looking at this subject has been offered by Porter, whose determinants of national advantage will serve as an aid in our interpretation of the new world patterns now taking shape. Chapter 1 described Porter's determinants in some detail. Box 14.1 should refresh your memory.

Trade Growth and Structural Change

The volume of world commerce has fluctuated widely in modern times, showing how sensitive trade is to the vagaries of war and peace and of prosperity and hard times. World War I produced the first major disruption of trade in this century. Upon the arrival of peace, world exports soared until, by 1929, they had doubled their level of a decade earlier. When the Great Depression struck, the total value of trade dropped precipitously, falling by more than 60 percent within a very brief time. Indeed, trade contracted even more than did global production, for most industrial countries reacted to worsening economic conditions by imposing tariffs, quotas, and other trade restrictions to protect their domestic industries from foreign competition. Not until 1939 did world trade recover to its 1929 level, and it continued to lag behind the growth of output because of persisting governmental interference.

World War II again seriously interrupted commerce, and trade patterns remained distorted for some years afterward because of wartime destruction of European and Japanese production facilities. World trade gradually returned to normal by the 1950s, and it gathered strength as the GATT agreements reduced governmental restrictions remaining from the prewar era. Trade continued to accelerate thereafter, rising more than fourfold between 1948 and 1968.

The commodity composition, or structure, of trade likewise changed during the first two-thirds of the twentieth century. The value of manufactured exports increased fourfold, whereas trade in primary commodities rose by a mere 50 percent. This relatively poor performance by primary exports occurred despite a rising demand for industrial raw materials and petroleum. One explanation for this is the increasingly elaborate processing that rising technology had brought about; another is the rising proportion of finished goods that entered trade. Indeed, a fairly reliable measure of a country's level of development is the proportion that finished goods comprise of its total manufactured exports. The growing trade in manufactured goods offered further evidence of the ever-increasing interdependence among industrial countries.

The composition of manufactured exports also

BOX 14.1   *Porter's Determinants of National Advantage**

- *Factor conditions.* A country's relative endowment of skilled labor, capital, and other requirements

* After Michael E. Porter, *The Competitive Advantage of Nations* (New York, The Free Press, 1990), pp. 71–130.

for competing internationally in particular industries
- *Demand conditions.* The characteristics of the country's domestic market for the goods of such industries
- *Related and supporting industries.* The availability of internationally

competitive supporting activities within the nation
- *Firm strategy, structure, and rivalry.* The national environment affecting the creation, organization, and management of companies, together with competitive conditions within the country

changed during this era. Shipments of textiles and clothing—leading items of international commerce in an earlier time—declined steadily. Meanwhile, exports of metals and miscellaneous manufactured goods remained fairly static. The most rapid growth of all was in machinery, transport equipment, and chemicals.

This comparatively placid era of steady growth and evolution came to an end with the 1970s, when a series of crises rocked the world economy. The economic and political forces underlying these events had been building for some time, but their effects were as unexpected as they were severe. One major occurrence was the collapse of the old Bretton Woods agreement, which had sustained world monetary stability for most of the post-war years. Based upon gold and the U.S. dollar, the system had shown signs of deteriorating during the 1960s as emergence of the EEC, and later Japan, had eroded the preeminent position of the United States in world economic affairs. The complex system of floating exchange rates that replaced Bretton Woods after March of 1973 has led to much uncertainty in world business.

The early 1970s also saw a sudden rise in the prices of industrial raw materials. This brought an end to the remarkably long period of commodity price stability that had contributed so much to industrial growth in the 1950s and 1960s. The inflation in commodity prices resulted from an abnormally high demand from the industrial countries, which were enjoying an unusual period of simultaneous prosperity, and it was reinforced by a rise in nationalism among the less-developed countries (LDCs) supplying these commodities.

Then, in September 1973, the first OPEC oil crisis erupted, followed by a second in 1979. The ensuing tenfold rise in oil prices added further to the worldwide inflationary spiral already under way, and the enormous transfer of wealth to the oil-exporting nations reduced incomes in the industrialized countries and halted development in the poorer LDCs. Global recessions followed both the 1973 and 1979 oil crises, accompanied by rising unemployment, uncontrolled inflation, mounting public debt, and soaring balance-of-payments deficits in oil-importing countries. (See Box 14.2.)

World trade growth was a major casualty of this crisis-ridden period, because the affected nations reacted to worsening trade deficits with a return to protectionism. Thus ended a remarkable era of international economic cooperation that had fostered structural change and raised living standards. The 1973 crisis slowed the rate of trade growth for a time; but in the depressed period following the second crisis,

world trade actually shrank 9 percent in value. In the mid-1980s, however, trade growth began a resurgence, despite continued protectionist pressures, and by 1990 combined trade in goods and services had mounted to $4 trillion. This represented a 13-fold rise in real (inflation-adjusted) terms since 1950.

This same era brought fundamental changes to the international economy. Beginning with the period of European colonization, the world had formed an international division of labor based upon comparative advantage and trade. Under this system, less-developed countries had traded their raw materials and agricultural goods to the industrialized lands in exchange for manufactured products. In the postwar age, however, the spread of foreign direct investment contributed to an internationalization of manufacturing. Relying upon advances in transportation, communications, and materials-handling technology, multinational enterprises were primary agents of this change. Many LDCs acquired their own industries, aided by multinationals attracted by the presence of literate, hardworking, low-cost labor and, in some instances, locally available raw materials. Guided by forward-looking national policies, several of these newly industrialized countries (NICs) have improved upon preexisting factor endowments and created new ones—educating and training workers, encouraging capital accumulation through savings, and investing in research and development (see Chapter 13).

Cheaply produced goods of growing sophistication have since poured into world markets from these NICs. Unable to counter this new competition, many long-established industries of Western Europe and North America retrenched or folded. The older industrial economies found themselves handicapped by aging plants and equipment, complacent and top-heavy management, and government policies incapable of adapting to changing world conditions. Moreover, some European nations had failed to keep up with innovations in the newer technology-intensive industries.

As deindustrialization continued in North America and Western Europe, manufacturing employment declined, offset in part by rising employment in the services. These older industrial nations have vied with each other in the development of new technology and have contended for leadership in supplying capital, entrepreneurship, and internationally traded services.

The progressive liberalization of international trade and the entry of new manufacturing nations into world markets have caused countries to become far more interdependent than in earlier times. Today, a quarter of the supplies of finished manufactured goods available in the domestic markets of Europe and North

America are made up of imports, five times the proportion four decades ago. This increased interdependence did not, however, result in greater interindustry specialization among nations, as conventional theory might lead us to expect. Instead, the trade structures of industrial countries, including the NICs, have tended to converge; that is, the goods exchanged among them have actually become more similar, often differing from each other only in such things as source, brand name, and reputation (for instance, Volkswagens, Fiats, Toyotas, Fords).

The kinds of merchandise entering international trade have therefore undergone significant changes during the postwar era (Figure 14.1). The value of world industrial exports continued to increase at the expense of other categories, rising from 61 percent of the total in 1965 to nearly 76 percent in 1988. In between, however, export shares fluctuated considerably as a result of gyrating oil prices.

As Figure 14.2 shows, the crises affected the various classes of manufactures differently. Least touched were exports of machinery and transport equipment, which mounted steadily, pausing only briefly during the global recession of 1981–83. This category includes many of the high-technology items for which world demand appears insatiable. After 1984 all three classes of manufactures climbed at unprecedented rates.

Fuel exports were the most dynamic category in the 1970s, doubling their value share from less than one-tenth to more than one-fifth before weakening demand and oversupply of oil forced a retreat in the 1980s (Figures 14.1, 14.2). This dramatic expansion was measurable only in value terms, however, being wholly a function of exploding OPEC prices; the total tonnage of world oil exports actually shrank as costs rose.

The export value share of other primary commodities—food, beverages, and crude materials—has steadily declined in recent years, continuing the long-term trend cited earlier. Indeed, the rate of decrease actually accelerated following the oil crisis: From a share of 29 percent in 1965, these commodities had slipped to only 15 percent by 1988 (Figure 14.1). Much of this change represents worsening terms of trade for primary goods as prices of manufactures and energy

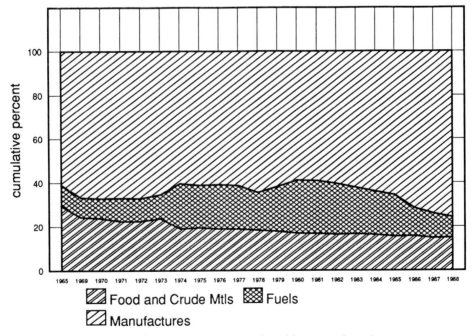

FIGURE 14.1 Changing composition of world exports (by value), 1965–1988. The explosion in petroleum prices during the 1970s temporarily halted the long-term rise in the relative share of manufactured exports. As oil prices declined in the early 1980s the share of fuel exports shrank to precrisis levels. The portion accounted for by other primary commodities has steadily declined throughout the present century, except for a short-lived expansion at the beginning of the 1970s. [*Source:* United Nations, *Yearbook of International Trade Statistics* (New York: United Nations, various years).]

BOX 14.2   World Trade and the Energy Crises

"It is now obvious that this decision was one of the pivotal events in the history of this century." So said former U.S. Secretary of State Henry Kissinger of the spectacular increase in oil prices posted by the Organization of Petroleum Exporting Countries (OPEC) in December 1973. The 10-fold increase in world oil prices during the 1970s profoundly altered the pattern and structure of world trade. This episode truly ranks as one of the four major global economic crises of an eventful decade. All the world's nations were affected but in very different ways, depending upon their resource endowments, where they were in the development process, and their roles in the international economy.

How did the world get into this vulnerable situation? In Chapter 5 we traced the evolution of energy demand and the reasons for the growing interdependence of nations in this most widely traded form of energy. The very cheapness of oil, less than $3.00 per barrel in 1973, encouraged its lavish use. Accounting for only 30 percent of total global energy in 1957, it had mounted to 43 percent of the total on the eve of the OPEC crisis and was still rising. With world consumption surging and production concentrated in only a few places, the world oil trade expanded nearly fourfold during this brief period, reaching one-tenth of all commodity trade.

Much of the new demand for oil resulted from the rapid postwar economic growth of Western Europe and Japan. Importing nine-tenths of its petroleum, Western Europe absorbed half of all oil shipments in 1972. Japan, with virtually no oil of its own, was importing one-sixth of the total. Meanwhile, the United States had shifted from being a net exporter of oil to being a net importer. Altogether, these industrialized countries took 80 percent of all internationally traded oil. This was also a period of substantial economic progress in much of the Third World, which was basing its industrialization upon cheap imported oil.

While the global demand for oil was climbing, the main sources of supply were shifting eastward. In the 1950s Venezuela had provided 35 percent of the world's petroleum exports, but by 1973 its share had slipped to only 8 percent. Much of the rest came

from the Middle East and North Africa, where more than two-thirds of global reserves are concentrated. Although founded in 1960, OPEC had spent its first years in fruitless efforts to extract better terms from the oil multinationals. By 1973, however, the cartel was supplying 85 percent of the world's oil, clearly enough to assure a global monopoly if only its 13 quarrelsome members could agree on common action.

The opportunity to test this notion came late in 1973 when the Arab members of OPEC declared an embargo on oil shipments to the United States and other Western nations giving aid to Israel in the brief "Yom Kippur War" with neighboring Islamic states. Surprised and delighted by this demonstration of its power, OPEC quickly seized control of world petroleum pricing, abruptly shifting world power relations. Two main periods of steep price increases followed. At the end of 1973 OPEC raised prices fourfold and placed a ceiling on the volume of oil the cartel would produce and sell. The takeover of Iran by Muslim fundamentalists in 1979, and the Iran-Iraq war that followed, panicked world oil markets, causing the base price to jump from $12.70 to $41 per barrel. Though oil prices have since slipped, owing to world recession, conservation, and increased output by non-OPEC sources, the world economy remains deeply affected by OPEC's eight-year lock on world petroleum pricing.

International trade absorbed much of the impact of OPEC's actions. One effect was to alter global terms of trade—the average price a country receives for its exports in relation to the average price it pays for imports. The major industrialized countries and non-oil-exporting LDCs alike were forced to allocate a major part of their foreign exchange earnings to purchase the suddenly more costly OPEC oil. For much of the Third World it was near disaster. As the OPEC-induced world recession forced down their own export prices, many LDCs went deeply into debt to avert a complete halt in their development.

The spatial pattern of trade flows shifted, too. Although higher prices drastically increased the dollar value of petroleum exports and imports, the total volume of these shipments actually

declined, idling much of the world's large tanker fleet. And needing more and more foreign exchange to pay for oil, most countries cut back their foreign purchases of other goods, especially the LDCs. The newly rich oil exporters, however, quickly increased their imports of manufactures—capital goods to speed their industrialization and consumer products to satisfy the rising demand from their prospering citizens. Hence, the emergence of this large new import market benefited the industrialized countries supplying such products, but it did little for LDC exporters of primary commodities. In time, the high price of oil brought new petroleum exporters into world markets—Mexico, the United Kingdom, Norway, and the former USSR—thereby diversifying the spatial pattern of energy flows. Note, however, that these new source areas are closer to the markets for their oil, many of which are connected directly by pipeline, further diminishing the need for ocean-going tankers.

Clearly the OPEC crises altered the composition of world trade, reducing the total volume of petroleum shipped and forcing LDCs to substitute oil purchases for capital goods. Although the imports of OPEC countries increased in amount and variety, their exports became even more specialized, partly because of the high valuation placed upon their petroleum shipments but also because their nonoil commodity exports—such as olives, dates, coffee, and cacao—declined because of neglect and inflated currencies.

The vast size of the global import bill for petroleum is a measure of the monetary impact of the OPEC crises. Ballooning prices meant the wholesale transfer of billions of dollars to the oil exporters from the rest of the world. The combined oil revenues of OPEC, which were only $7 billion in 1970, quickly rose to $72 billion in 1974 and to $300 billion by 1980. As a consequence, virtually all of the non-OPEC world found itself thrown into a balance-of-payments deficit. The problem was less severe for the industrialized countries than for the oil-importing LDCs, however, because the former were able to sell manufactured goods and services to OPEC at sharply rising prices (thereby exporting their inflation). The LDCs did not have this cushion, because their conventional exports fell sharply in quantity and price. Meanwhile, for a time OPEC was drawing in money faster than it could be spent, threatening a world financial crisis.

The effects of these events upon individual OPEC countries varied greatly. The organization is by no means monolithic; its members differ in history, religion, culture, systems of government, ideology, population, stage of development, size of oil reserves, and productive capacity. In general, they fall into two main divisions. One subset consists of countries that have populations relatively larger than their oil output and therefore have a crucial need to maximize their incomes (Iran, Algeria, Indonesia, Venezuela, Nigeria, Ecuador, and Gabon). Members of the second group, on the other hand, have small populations relative to output and have no immediately pressing need for large revenues (Saudi Arabia, the United Arab Emirates, Kuwait, Qatar, Libya, and Iraq). With more than 90 percent of OPECs total population, countries in the first group have little flexibility and are continually pressing for higher prices. The latter group can afford to wait, viewing oil left in the ground as a potentially valuable resource for the future.

The enormous global transfer of wealth from oil importers to oil exporters—at least $100 billion per annum—presented OPEC's Group 2 countries with unprecedented money-management problems (Group 1 had no such dilemma—its members can easily absorb any amount of revenue). The problems were of two kinds: how to manage vast financial resources, and how to plan national development in such a way as to use this one-time infusion of funds efficiently and with lasting benefit. In the short run they placed their surplus funds in short-term investments, mostly in the United States and selected other industrial countries. In the longer run they gradually increased their expenditures on development projects at home: roads, housing, ports, airfields, and new industries. Saudi Arabia, for instance, had emphasized energy-intensive industries that multiply the returns from its abundant supplies of very cheap oil and natural gas—such activities as petroleum refineries, petrochemical works, and cement plants.

Just as the benefits of their new riches varied among OPEC members, so did the effects of suddenly costly energy differ among oil-importing countries. For the older industrialized countries the initial impact was recession, high inflation, and declining incomes. Subsequently, however, those developed countries favored for OPEC investment and trade—the United States, Japan, and certain Western European nations—benefited from the recycling of OPEC wealth and the refocusing of their foreign sales upon the newly oil-rich lands. However, those industrialized countries passed by in the recycling process, such as Italy, had no such compensating benefits to relieve the impact of soaring energy bills. And, as we have seen, the effect of the energy crises was truly devastating for the oil-importing LDCs.

As it must to all cartels, the end of OPEC's complete command of world oil prices came in the early 1980s. The price-elasticity of demand for oil is low in the short run but is high in the long run: The immediate defense of consumers against soaring oil prices is limited because it takes time to develop more energy-efficient transportation, insulate buildings, and so forth. In time, however, the reaction to expensive petroleum was to give a high priority to energy efficiency, to develop new oil fields, and to find alternative forms of energy. The widespread recession and inflation following the initial shock of high prices had reduced global economic growth and thus the demand for OPEC oil. High prices also made feasible the development of high-cost petroleum sources, such as the North Sea and the North Slope of Alaska, and induced industries and consumers to prune their use of oil.

The net result of these events was to reduce sharply the demand for OPEC oil. Whereas the group had a combined output of 31 million barrels per day in the 1970s, this total had fallen to only 18 million barrels by 1983. This put downward pressure on the price of oil, causing it to drop from a high of $41 to only $29 within this same period. As a result, OPEC's combined surplus income, more than $109 billion in 1980, turned into an $18 billion deficit by 1982. Some of the more hard-pressed members of OPEC, such

as Nigeria and Iran, began to cheat on their agreed-upon production quotas, thus further weakening prices, which by mid-1986 had fallen below $10 per barrel on the world spot market. Several OPEC countries went into budgetary deficits and were no longer able to sustain their high expenditures for development. Some of those with large populations resorted to heavy borrowing abroad.

With OPEC discipline in disarray, prices falling, and economies recovering from recession, global oil consumption resumed its upward march through the remainder of the 1980s. From a postcrisis low of 58 million barrels a day in 1983, world consumption had risen to 65 million barrels by 1989, a rise of 11 percent. Thirty percent of this new demand came from the United States and Canada.

By the end of the decade world prices had returned to $20 and OPEC's daily output had again reached 23 million barrels. The group was unsuccessful in reasserting complete control over world pricing, however, because of dissension and cheating among its members and rising competition by non-OPEC producers, from the North Sea to the Eastern Pacific, Africa, and South America.

Consuming nations were shaken from their complacency, however, in August 1990, when Iraq seized Kuwait and threatened Saudi Arabia's main producing areas. Possession of all three oil producers would have given Iraq's rulers dominion over 45 percent of the world's oil reserves and a tight lock on global supplies and pricing. Spot prices on world markets quickly spiraled beyond $30 and would have gone higher had not other producing nations increased output to fill the gap. The ensuing Gulf War ended the Iraqi monopoly threat and restored prices to previous levels. World consumption resumed its expansion.

Oil analysts predict that the apparent emancipation from OPEC domination is only temporary. Non-OPEC supplies are expected to peak after 1995, and OPEC nations continue to hold more than three-fourths of global reserves. Thus, until the world can curb its appetite for energy or find viable alternatives to petroleum, every Persian Gulf flare-up will create panic in oil markets and imperil political and economic stability.

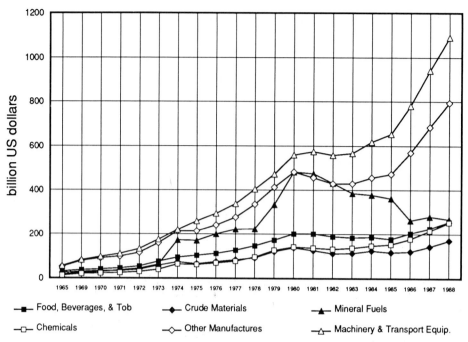

FIGURE 14.2 World growth of major export classes (by value), 1965–1988. Despite a 10-fold increase in oil prices between 1973 and 1979, which was responsible for the steepening curve of fuel exports, manufactured exports continued to rise throughout most of the period. Note, however, the effects of the two global recessions in the mid-1970s and early 1980s. Since that time, exports of all three manufactured categories have climbed steeply. [*Source:* United Nations, *Yearbook of International Trade Statistics* (New York: United Nations, various years).]

rose in world markets. Raw material exports showed the least growth of any major category, more than erasing their price gains of the early 1970s. Note from Figure 14.2 that nearly every major export category suffered a setback during the world economic recessions of 1972–1975 and 1981–1983.

Recent trends and events have affected some types of countries differently than others (Figure 14.3). Most striking was the meteoric climb in the value of OPEC exports following the 1973 Mideast crisis and again after the sharp jump in oil prices in 1979. Equally abrupt was the decline of OPEC's foreign earnings in the 1980s—a result of falling prices, energy conservation, and growing competition from non-OPEC producers. Just as significant for the longer-term, perhaps, was the steady rise in exports by the "Other LDCs," due mainly to the growing export strength of the newly industrialized countries. NIC exports hardly paused in their steady climb during the troubled 1970s and early 1980s. Foreign sales of the developed economies, however, were adversely affected by the recession of 1981–1983, though export growth of this group resumed by the mid-1980s. Exports of the 22 least-

developed countries, on the other hand, remained depressed throughout.

These diverging rates of export growth have altered the market shares of the various country groups (Figure 14.4). After many years of steady progress, the advanced countries commanded 71 percent of world exports at the beginning of the 1970s. This share fell below 63 percent during the crisis years but had rebounded to its old level by the end of the 1980s. OPEC's share expanded nearly threefold during the 1970s but fell to only 4 percent during the next decade. The other LDCs, led by a number of vibrant NICs, lost only a minor portion of their world market share to OPEC during the 1970s and eventually captured nearly one-sixth of world exports in the 1980s. The least-developed countries saw their meager share dwindle from 0.5 to a mere 0.3 percent during the period. After years of clinging to a one-tenth share of world exports, the centrally planned economies were losing ground at the end of the 1980s, foreshadowing the general collapse of communism in the 1990s.

Many of the fluctuations in export market share have been related to changing commodity prices, espe-

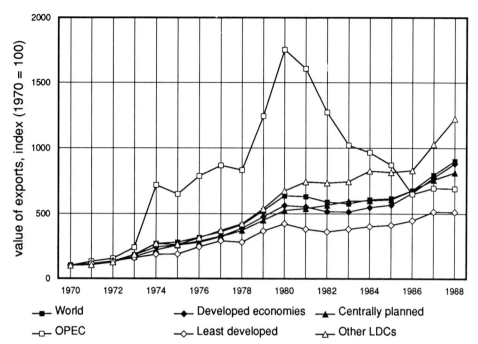

FIGURE 14.3 Growth of exports by major country categories (by value), 1970–1988. The most striking feature in the development of recent trade patterns was OPEC's spectacular rise in the 1970s and even more precipitous drop in the 1980s. In the period as a whole, the greatest gain was made by ''other LDCs,'' owing mainly to the robust trade performance of an aggressive group of newly industrializing countries. The exports of these NICs were little touched by the oil price rises and subsequent world recessions that so adversely affected other oil-importing regions. The least-developed countries—the world's 22 poorest—continued to lag behind all the rest. [*Source:* United Nations, *Yearbook of International Trade Statistics* (New York: United Nations, various years).]

cially oil. Another perspective on world export growth emerges, therefore, when this is expressed in quantum terms, as in Figure 14.5, which shows the rates at which the physical volume of exports have changed during the past two decades. Here we see the rapid drop in LDC export tonnage following the sharp run-up in oil prices in 1979, which caused the demand for oil to contract. This episode was also largely responsible for the ensuing global recession and its trade-depressing effects. The rising volume of LDC exports since the mid-1980s conceals divergent regional trends within that broad category of countries. For instance, the quantum figure for Middle Eastern exports in 1987 still remained at only 63 percent of its 1980 level, whereas the quantity of exports by the LDCs of East and Southeast Asia had exactly doubled within that same brief period.

In recent years important shifts have occurred in the spatial patterns of trade linkages, marking a trend toward greater diversity of trading partners. Throughout the 1950s and 1960s a major portion of total trade

had taken place among industrialized countries, whose factor endowments and structures of demand were fairly similar. Thus, by 1970 industrialized nations sold more than three-fourths of their exports to other advanced countries. Only 18 percent of these went to LDCs, which, on the other hand, relied upon advanced countries for the greater part of their exports and imports and traded comparatively little with each other.

The subsequent eventful period altered this pattern somewhat. The proportion of exports and imports exchanged by industrialized countries fell, and their trade with LDCs rose accordingly, especially imports. As might be expected, most of this change had resulted from the increased cost of imported OPEC oil and the sudden blossoming of OPEC as a market for their industrial goods. By 1988 the declining fortunes of OPEC had spelled a return to the old trade pattern of interdependence among advanced countries, and the pre-1973 allocations of exports and imports were largely restored.

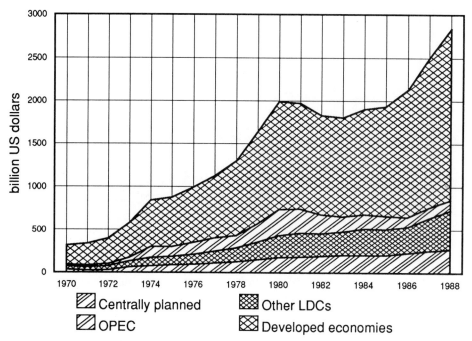

FIGURE 14.4 Changing shares of world exports, major country types (by value). In the early 1970s the developed economies were supplying 72 percent of world exports. This share decreased somewhat during the troubled 1970s but had recovered fully by 1988. After capturing more than 15 percent of the total during the crisis years, OPEC was earning a smaller proportion at the end of the 1980s than it had before 1973. The "other LDCs," however, increased their share from under 11 percent to 16 percent during the period, thanks to the remarkable achievements of the newly industrialized countries. The 22 least-developed countries saw their share shrink from 0.5 percent to a mere 0.3 percent, too small to show in this diagram. Note the sizable dip in combined world exports during the recession era of the early 1980s, the first such contraction since World War II. [*Source:* United Nations, *Yearbook of International Trade Statistics,* Table A (New York: United Nations, various years).]

A more durable legacy of the period was the growth of trade among LDCs. OPEC's activities contributed in some measure to this development, but possibly the most dynamic element was the expanded role of the newly industrializing countries. From a low of under 20 percent in 1970s, the share of LDC exports going to other LDCs had risen to one-fourth in 1980 and had exceeded 27 percent by 1988. Imports followed a similar path.

In 1990 another dynamic situation unexpectedly materialized in the Eastern Bloc countries, where the sudden collapse of communism introduced a new volatile element into world commerce. Throughout the postwar era the centrally planned economies traded predominantly with each other, but this interdependence had diminished over the years. In the 1950s this group relied upon each other for 70 percent of their exports and more than three-fourths of their imports; by the end of the 1980s intrabloc trade had shrunk to

little more than half of their total exports and imports. The new opening of these countries to the West holds the potential to transform the economic map of the continent.

THE SHIFTING FOCUS OF INTERNATIONAL ECONOMIC ACTIVITY

This dramatic turn of affairs in Eastern Europe and the former Soviet Union is only the latest in a series of important developments affecting the course of world commerce in recent times. Chief among these have been the spectacular rise in Japan's share of world exports, the growing prominence of the East Asia's NICs, slowing trade creation in Western Europe, and an expanding market for imported manufactured goods in the United States. In combination, these de-

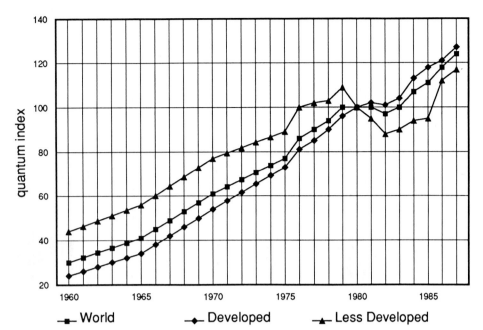

FIGURE 14.5 Export growth by market economies, quantum indices (1980 = 100), 1960–1987. A different picture of export growth emerges when this is measured in terms of its physical quantity rather than its monetary value, thereby eliminating the distorting effects of price inflation. Note the steep decline in quantities exported by LDCs after 1979. This is a result of the price hikes by OPEC, which for a time reduced oil shipments and depressed world markets for other commodities. The quantity of world exports as a whole shrank during the early 1980s because of widespread recession. All three country groups saw quantum gains for their exports following economic recovery, but the use of such broad categories obscures marked regional differences in export performance. [*Source:* United Nations, *Yearbook of International Trade Statistics,* Special Table F (New York: United Nations, various years).]

velopments are producing a major shift in the center of gravity of global economic activity.

Although the volume and composition of international flows had fluctuated from time to time, the basic spatial pattern of economic linkages among the world's nations had remained remarkably stable over a very long period. The North Atlantic basin had dominated international trade at least since the age of colonization, when the economic ties between Western Europe and North America were forged and this region become the focus for suppliers of primary commodities elsewhere in the world (Figure 14.6). So enduring was this arrangement that when Bruce Russett (1967) compared patterns of trade linkages prior to World War II with those of the 1960s, he could point to the erection of the Iron Curtain separating the communist Eastern Bloc from Western Europe as the only significant disturbance affecting the basic map of international trade in modern times. He concluded, therefore, that fundamental trade patterns change with glacial slowness.

No longer is this true. Today, the North Atlantic basin accounts for a shrinking proportion of world trade and investment as the pace of economic activity in Western Europe has slackened. Indeed, Western Europe's 44 percent share of world exports shown in Figure 14.7 is misleading: A full 70 percent of that amount consists of trade among Western European countries—a consequence of Europe's extreme political and economic fragmentation. If, as the European Community's founders had intended, the region had become a United States of Western Europe, their interregional commodity flows would be classified as domestic trade. Their remaining exports to the rest of the world represented only 13 percent of global trade in 1988—well below the 15.3 percent contribution of the United States and Canada (Figure 14.7).

Today, international economic activity increasingly focuses upon the Pacific Basin. The main participants in this development are 12 countries on the western rim of the Pacific, extending from Japan and Korea southward to Australia and New Zealand, together

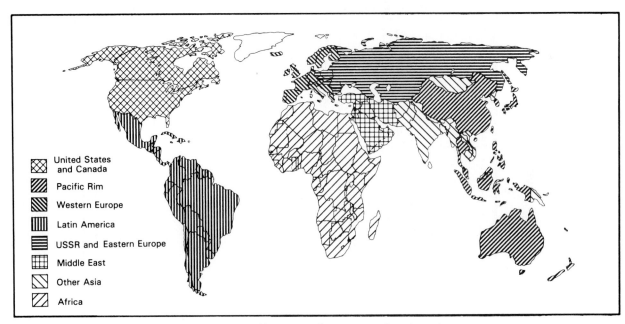

FIGURE 14.6   Major world regions of international trade and investment.

with the United States and Canada, both of which are turning westward with their trade and investment. Although trends of the past several years had foreshadowed this shift, the world crises of the 1970s undoubtedly hastened it, for the Pacific Rim countries have been much quicker to respond to changing conditions than has the rest of the world.

The Pacific Basin has evolved into a functionally integrated region whose 14 nations hold half of the population of the world and turn out half of its total output of goods and services. The United States and Canada are the prime targets for the rapidly expanding manufactured exports of the dynamic Pacific Rim countries, and the two are also leading suppliers of industrial materials and agricultural commodities, as well as investment capital and technology, to the region. Being active participants in the economic affairs of both the Atlantic and Pacific basins, therefore, Canada and the United States act as a fulcrum between the two realms. In the following pages we shall be looking more closely at the pivotal role of North America in the changing affairs of these and other major economic regions of the world.

North America

The United States remains a central focus of world trade and investment even though its trade has not grown as fast as world trade as a whole. During the early postwar period the United States accounted for a quarter of all world trade; today, its share has shrunk to only 11 percent of the total. Yet it is still the largest

trading nation, even though it has a much smaller ratio of trade to gross national product than most countries. This ability to sustain a high level of trade with so small a proportion of its output is a function of size: a $4.8 trillion economy (1988) and a varied resource base within a territory of more than 9 million square kilometers. The level of U.S. trade participation is rising steadily, however (Figure 14.8). Prior to the 1970s the United States sold no more than 4 percent of its goods abroad, but by 1988 it was exporting 6.6 percent of its GNP. The ratio of imports to GNP has risen even more rapidly, reaching 9 percent in both 1980 and 1988.

This enhanced level of trade participation is evidence of the extent to which the U.S. economy has become internationalized in response to the far-reaching changes taking place in the world at large, as well as within the country itself. These external pressures on the United States first surfaced during the 1970s, when the spiraling cost of oil pushed the country into a merchandise trade deficit after an extended period of positive trade balances (Figure 14.9). The deficit was $41 billion by the end of the decade, and it continued to widen even after the OPEC crises had ended, soaring to an alarming $170 billion by 1986.

The deepening of this predicament during the 1980s took place as a consequence of consumption and debt boom that helped depress the country's savings rate to unprecedented lows. This combination led to a soaring U.S. dollar, which made imported goods cheap for American consumers but priced U.S. exports out of world markets. The huge American market became a prime target for the world's exporters

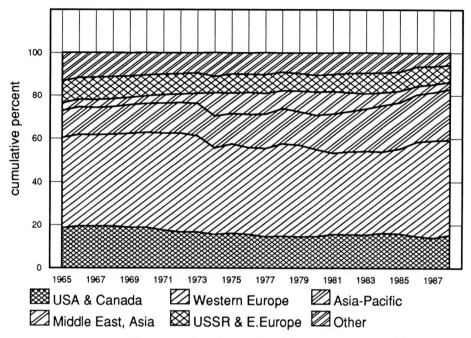

FIGURE 14.7 Changing value shares of world exports, major world regions, 1965–1988. Except for a brief slump during the recession years of the early 1980s, Western Europe's portion of global exports has remained fairly close to its 1988 figure of 44 percent, though a growing part of this has been diverted to intra-European trade. During this period, the United States and Canada have seen their combined exports slip from 19 percent of the world to only 15 percent. The largest overall gains were garnered by the Asia-Pacific region, which climbed from only 13 percent in 1965 to 24 percent in 1988. The 12 dynamic Pacific Rim countries were responsible for 23 percent of this; the other nations of South and Southeast Asia contributed a mere 1 percent of the Asia-Pacific total, despite their immense populations. The Asian Middle East briefly controlled as much as 11 percent of world exports during the oil crisis years, but its portion had dwindled to less than 4 percent by 1988. Exports from the former USSR and Eastern Europe also slipped in the late Eighties. [*Source:* United Nations, *Yearbook of International Trade Statistics,* Special Table A (New York: United Nations, various years).]

and a magnet for foreign investors seeking to widen their shares of that market. Domestic manufacturers were ill-prepared for this onslaught of competition at home and abroad, having failed to upgrade their products and industrial techniques during a period of innovative change by foreign producers.

Almost unnoticed, the deficit problem began to ease in the late 1980s. An international agreement to reduce the exchange rate of the dollar suddenly reopened world markets to U.S. companies. The ensuing revival of exporting, however, owed much of its strength to the restructuring that firms had been forced to undertake in order to survive in their period of trial. When the opportunity came, they were able to seize it. World conditions had meanwhile turned more favorable for them: The cost of capital in the United States was no longer higher than in competing lands, U.S. government negotiators had worked to break down protectionist barriers overseas, and new foreign markets had opened as a result of preparations in anticipation of the European Community's plans for full economic union in 1992.

Further easing the international deficit problem for the United States has been the recent vigorous growth in its "invisible" exports. An expanding surplus in internationally traded services—transportation, finance, tourism, entertainment, and so forth—has compensated for an important part of the merchandise deficit. As both components of foreign commerce move in a positive direction, the combined U.S. trade in goods and services promises to achieve a surplus in the early Nineties. Indeed, some analysts

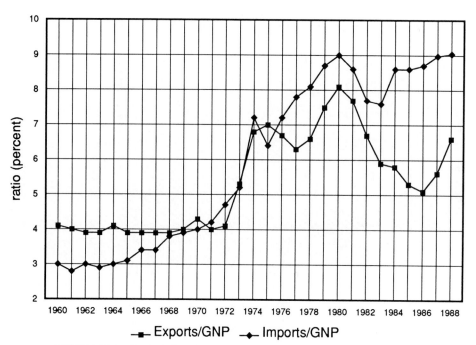

FIGURE 14.8   Ratios of U.S. exports and imports to gross national product, 1960–1988. Because of its very large economy, the United States is able to remain a major trading nation (see Figure 14.7), even though exports and imports do not constitute a large part of national output by comparison with most industrial nations. Through most of the 1960s, the size and diversity of domestic resources made it unnecessary to maintain imports at a level much above 3 percent of GNP, whereas exports continued steadily at about 4 percent. The tumultuous 1970s and 1980s changed this, forcing the U.S. into greater international involvement. Both export/GNP and import/GNP ratios rose, but imports climbed faster, reaching 9 percent in 1980 and again in the 1988. The Export/GNP ratio peaked at 8 percent in 1980 but slumped badly in the mid-1980s. At the end of the 1980s, U.S. export activity quickened substantially. [*Source:* U.S. Bureau of the Census, *Statistical Abstract of the United States* (Washington, D.C.: U.S. Government Printing Office, various years).]

insist that if the activities of U.S.-owned multinationals abroad and foreign-owned firms in the United States were weighed into the scale, then the country's foreign accounts would already be in surplus.

The United States sells an unusually broad range of goods on world markets, reflecting a national resource endowment of great diversity. Unlike most industrial countries, the United States is able to draw upon a very large and productive farm sector for a multitude of agricultural commodities grown under many different physical conditions. Complementing these are the country's exports of industrial goods, which rely upon a comparative advantage in high-technology production. As the competitive edge of American innovation diminishes, however, the manufacturing nations of Western Europe and the Pacific Rim are cutting into this lead in technology-intensive goods (see Chapter 13).

The structure of U.S. imports is also changing. With its enormous appetite for a growing variety of raw materials, American industry can no longer satisfy its needs from domestic sources and must therefore buy more and more of these abroad. Furthermore, now that U.S. oil production has peaked, the country must rely upon foreign suppliers for a growing portion of its energy. Meanwhile, Americans are acquiring a taste for foreign-made automobiles, appliances, electronic goods, and innumerable other consumer products. Figure 14.10 shows some of the effects of these developments upon the U.S. balance of trade in particular commodity classes. Comparing the composition of U.S. trade in the 1960s with that of the late 1980s, we see that the comfortable surplus in machinery and transport equipment has vanished, replaced by a $43 billion deficit. This reflects not only very large imports of motor vehicles but also a growing quantity of high-

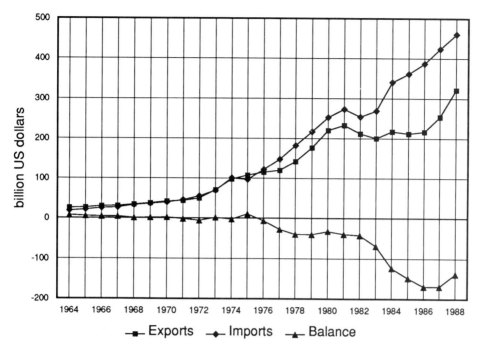

FIGURE 14.9 U.S. merchandise exports, imports, and trade balance, 1964–1988. Throughout the postwar era, the United States had usually exported more goods each year than it imported. The soaring price of oil in the 1970s pushed the U.S. merchandise trade balance into a deficit, which plunged still more deeply in the 1980s. Massive public debt and a consumption boom depressed the U.S. savings rate, and the dollar climbed to record heights. This made imported goods cheaper for Americans and U.S. exports prohibitively costly for foreigners, further widening the trade gap. A reversal began in the late 1980s, however, when an international agreement lowered the value of the dollar, prompting a revival of U.S. exports. Meanwhile, U.S. manufacturers had been forced into a painful restructuring, at the end of which their companies had been transformed into some of the lowest-cost, most-efficient competitors in the world. Export growth continued to accelerate until, by the early 1990s, the merchandise trade gap showed promise of narrowing considerably. [*Source:* United Nations, *Yearbook of International Trade Statistics* (New York: United Nations, various years).]

technology goods covered by this category. Between 1964 and 1988 the deficit in other manufactures (mainly nontechnology goods) had swelled to nearly $88 billion. The bill for imported fuels also yielded a large deficit, but this represented a substantial improvement since the oil crisis period. As in the past, surpluses in chemicals, farm products, and industrial materials helped cushion the burden. Despite this seemingly bleak picture, however, a recovery in U.S. industrial exports was already under way in 1988 and continued to accelerate thereafter.

The eventful 1970s and 1980s also produced major changes in the spatial pattern of U.S. trade linkages, as the two parts of Figure 14.11 reveal. Between 1970 and 1988 much of the country's trade had shifted away from Western Europe and toward the Asian-Pa-

cific arena. Imports from Japan and Other Asia (mainly East Asian NICs) had grown especially large by 1988, contributing four-fifths of the merchandise trade deficit in that year. During this period, the proportion of U.S. trade with Latin America had contracted somewhat.

Despite these overall shifts in U.S. trade links, certain ties have remained fairly constant. Among the most enduring relationships are the close ties of trade and investment with the country's North American neighbors. Canada is the largest trading partner of the United States, with 20 percent of total U.S. trade (exports plus imports), and Mexico ranks third (behind Japan). Canada and Mexico are even more economically dependent upon the United States, which accounts for two-thirds or more of their total trade in

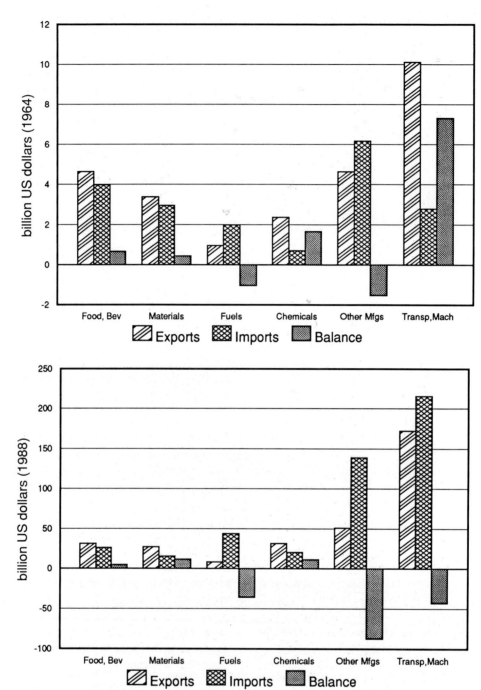

FIGURE 14.10   Changing commodity structure of U.S. exports and imports, 1964 and 1988. In the mid-1960s the United States was still enjoying a positive overall trade balance, which benefited from a very large surplus in machinery and transport equipment, as well as positive balances in chemicals, agricultural goods, and industrial materials. By that time U.S. petroleum output had peaked, leading to a trade deficit in fuels, and imports of mass-produced low-technology goods were beginning to exceed exports. A contrasting picture emerges in 1988. The overall merchandise trade deficit in that year had reached a worrisome $138 billion, and imports of manufactured goods in both low-technology and high-technology categories exceeded exports by large amounts. Subsequent information suggests that the U.S. trade balances in manufactured goods had substantially improved by the early 1990s. [*Source:* United Nations, *Yearbook of International Trade Statistics* (New York: United Nations, various years).]

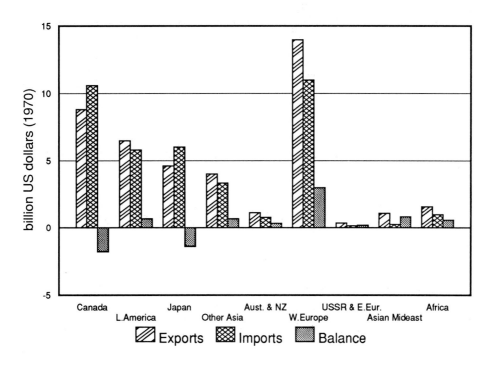

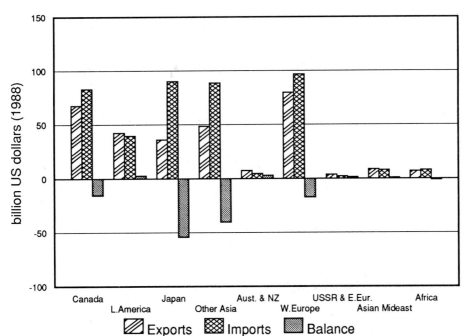

FIGURE 14.11   Changing U.S. merchandise exports, imports, and trade balances with major world regions, 1970 and 1988. In 1970, U.S. trade was in overall balance with the world at large. The only sizable deficits were with its leading trading partner, Canada, and Japan. By 1988, the deficit with Japan had swollen to $54 billion and a $40 billion deficit with Other Asia (mainly East Asian NICs) had developed. Newer information indicates that the trade balance with Western Europe has since turned positive. Note that in the late 1980s Canada was still the principal partner of the United States in trade but that the Asia Pacific region had risen in prominence. The positive balance with the Asian Middle East reflects U.S. success in marketing to that area, together with a pattern of U.S. oil procurement that entails importation from a variety of other sources. [*Source:* United Nations, *Yearbook of International Trade Statistics,* Special Table B (New York: United Nations, various years).]

most years and is their major source of foreign investment. One obvious reason for American dominance of
its neighbors is its huge economic size: The U.S. economy is 10 times as large as Canada's and 18 times as
large as Mexico's. Perhaps of equal importance, the
United States has a 6700-kilometer common border
with Canada and a 3200-kilometer border with Mexico. Because of this contiguity, transport costs are
minimized and commercial concerns are intimately familiar with conditions in these neighboring lands.
Long-standing business ties develop under these circumstances.

Another reason for the close economic interaction among the three countries is the complementarity
of their resources, reflecting differences in physical
conditions and in the availability of technology, capital, labor, and entrepreneurial skills. The United States
obtains certain land-intensive commodities from its
well-endowed neighbors—tropical agricultural products from Mexico and petroleum and mineral ores
from both countries—and relies upon Mexico for labor-intensive manufactured goods. Balmy climates,
attractive scenery, and exotic cultures also lure American tourist dollars, a vital source of foreign exchange
for Mexico (nearly $2 billion in 1982). In return, the
United States supplies temperate grains for food-short
Mexico and subtropical fruits and winter vegetables to
Canada, and it provides both countries with a range
of capital-intensive, high-technology manufactured
goods.

If current negotiations for a North American
Free Trade Agreement succeed, the flow of goods and
services among the three neighbors could expand substantially. In 1990 Mexico had the fastest-growing
economy in the region—a result of new outward-look-
ing government policies. The influx of foreign capital
following a trade agreement would further accelerate
Mexican growth, enhancing the buying power of a
population expected to number 109 million by the year
2000. Pooling the human and natural resources of three
prosperous North American nations could produce a
truly powerful economic bloc.

Canada relies upon foreign commerce to a far
greater degree than does the United States; in most
years the country exports more than one-fifth of its
output. This high trade dependence results from a special combination of factor endowments. With a total
land area second in size only to Russia, Canada has an
enormous store of mineral wealth and biotic resources, as well as a large expanse of land suitable for
temperate grains. Yet the population, which is about
the same as that of California, is too small to absorb
this great output of land-intensive commodities, leaving a huge surplus for sale abroad. At the same time,

Canada must import tropical and subtropical foods and
beverages for which its agricultural lands are climati-
cally unsuited. Moreover, Canada must import a wide
range of manufactured goods its own industries are
unable to supply because their production requires
economies of scale impossible to achieve with so small
a domestic market.

Although primary commodities figure importantly in Canada's foreign sales, industrial exports are
an unusually large part of the total. Some of these
result from the initial processing of mineral ores and
forest products, but many are finished goods. On the
whole, the country's manufactured exports neatly express the character of the land. Thus, Canada has been
especially successful in marketing heavy-duty hydroelectric generators and hydraulic turbines, benefiting
from the long experience gained by Canadian firms
involved in developing the country's great water-
power potential. Canadian companies have gained an
important competitive edge in the sale of high-technology communications equipment (including fiber optics) and small commercial aircraft—products that
have been developed to overcome the problems of living in a vast territory. Increasingly, Canadians have
concentrated upon exporting products, such as these,
in which they are able to compete successfully in
global markets. At the same time, they have dropped
many consumer goods that had been expensively produced for the limited domestic market under an umbrella of protective tariffs. This tariff shelter had been
rendered ineffective in recent years by a series of
GATT agreements.

Although the United States has long been the
principal market for Canada's abundant resource-
based commodities—such as oil, gas, hydroelectricity, minerals, and wood products—U.S. purchases of
vehicles and parts under the Canada—U.S. Auto
Agreement helped to shift the balance in favor of industrial goods. Today, motor vehicles and parts represent the single largest class of exports to the United
States, nearly half the total in 1988 (Figure 14.12). Altogether, three-fourths of the goods shipped to the
United States are of industrial origin, and nine-tenths
of U.S. sales to Canada fit into this category. Though
overwhelmed by the surging two-way trade in manufactures, Canada's exports of fuels and industrial materials to the United States continue to be important to
both countries and will likely increase under provisions of the new Canada–U.S. Free Trade Agreement.
Offsetting the large U.S. merchandise trade deficit
with Canada are substantial amounts of U.S.-provided
services and sizable capital flows representing repatriated profits on American investments in Canada.

The second-largest regional partner for Canadian

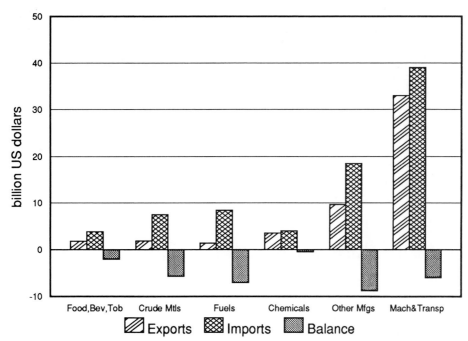

FIGURE 14.12 Composition of U.S. trade with Canada, 1988. The United States ran a trade surplus with Canada as long as that country was mainly a supplier of resource-based commodities. In recent decades, however, the bilateral balance turned negative as the manufacturing content of Canada's exports increased. The Canada–U.S. Auto Agreement contributed importantly to this shift. Note that the trade between the two is now heavily weighted toward industrial goods—90 percent of U.S. shipments to Canada and a surprising 76 percent of Canadian exports to the United States—with motor vehicles and parts dominating movements in both directions. Whether the Canada–U.S. Free Trade Agreement will tilt this proportion still further is uncertain because the pact calls for lifting Canadian export limits on certain basic commodities. [*Source:* United Nations, *Yearbook of International Trade Statistics, 1988,* Special Table B (New York, United Nations, 1990).]

trade is Western Europe, although its share of the total has slipped somewhat in recent years (Figure 14.13). This is the only region with which Canada sustains a persistent trade deficit. Among Canada's individual trading partners, Japan ranks second only to the United States. Japan has also invested heavily in Canada. Initially, Japanese investors concentrated upon resource industries in the western provinces, but increasingly they have set up manufacturing plants in Canada's industrial heartland of Ontario and Québec, in response to North American integration. For similar reasons, other Pacific Rim countries are also developing trade and investment ties with Canada.

The Pacific Rim

Since the 1960s a collection of vibrant nations along the western margins of the Pacific has developed into the world's most rapidly expanding economic region.

Between 1970 and 1988 the Asia-Pacific area boosted its share of global exports from only 12 percent to more than 23 percent (refer to Figure 14.7), and in the 1990s a select group of Pacific Rim nations has come to occupy a prominent position in international investment and finance.

Five sets of Pacific Rim countries have participated in this unfolding drama. Japan has been the leading figure, establishing a pattern of trade-led growth with its astounding economic performance since the early 1950s. Japanese enterprise has since played a central part in integrating the Pacific economies. Following later in Japan's path, the "Four Tigers" of Asia—South Korea, Taiwan, Hong Kong, and Singapore—are successfully competing in world markets with an increasingly sophisticated line of manufactured products. More recently, five other Asian countries have adopted similar export-led strategies: Thailand, Malaysia, Indonesia, the Philippines, and the

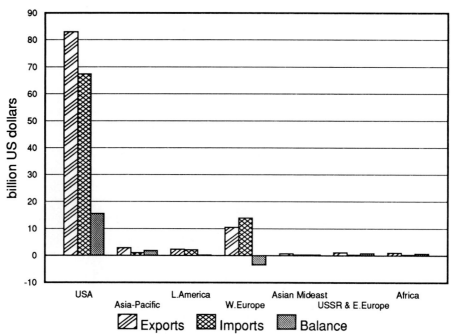

FIGURE 14.13 Canadian exports, imports, and trade balance with major world regions, 1988. Foreign trade is important to the Canadian economy, and an overwhelming share of that trade is with the United States: In 1988 the United States took 73 percent of Canada's exports and supplied 69 percent of its imports. The second area of importance for Canadian trade is Western Europe. Among individual trading partners, Japan has assumed a growing place. Canada's merchandise trade balance is positive with all the regions shown here except Western Europe, where it runs a substantial deficit. [*Source:* United Nations, *Yearbook of International Trade Statistics, 1988* (New York: United Nations, 1990).]

People's Republic of China. During this same period, Australia and New Zealand, having been cut adrift by the problem-ridden United Kingdom, have formed new economic ties in the Pacific realm. Here they have discovered new markets for their abundant physical riches in the newly industrializing Pacific lands nearby. Six of the Pacific Rim countries (Indonesia, Singapore, Malaysia, Thailand, Brunei, and the Philippines) have joined together in a loosely structured experiment in economic integration called the Association of Southeast Asian Nations (ASEAN).

This upsurge of economic activity along the Pacific Rim occurred during a period when the rest of the world was reeling from the major shocks of the 1970s—the inflation in commodity prices, the breakdown of monetary stability, two sharp oil-price rises, and two global recessions. The East Asian countries have demonstrated a remarkable ability to weather such crises. Drawing upon deeply imbedded cultural values that emphasize hard work and allegience to the group, laborers and managers work together for the success of their joint enterprises, and business leaders collaborate with government ministries to further na-

tional goals. Together they closely follow international economic developments and respond quickly to changing conditions of demand and supply. The general public is made aware of the country's circumstances and can be mobilized to the common good during times of crisis.

Unlike the older industrial countries, with their stable populations and sluggish economies, the Pacific Rim is an area of growth. Between 1965 and 1988 the combined GDP of this group increased 19-fold, adding mightily to the buying power and productive capacity of a region that holds a third of humanity. Moreover, unlike most of the underdeveloped world, the newly developing members of this bloc are successfully bringing population growth under control, thereby permitting a steady rise in per capita buying power. At the same time, literacy rates are rising, labor and management skills are multiplying, and support services are evolving.

This combination of growing productive capacity and rising consumer demand has brought a flood of investment to the western Pacific. During the 1970s foreign investment in the region as a whole quadrupled and investment in the Four Tigers actually grew six-fold. Meanwhile, investment in Western Europe has peaked and some investors are beginning to withdraw. Multinational enterprises are the prime agents for this transfer of capital and technology. United States MNEs have led, but Japanese and British companies have been close behind; German, Canadian, and Australian firms are also well represented.

The extent to which merchandise flows have shifted from the Atlantic Basin to the Pacific is to be seen in Figure 14.14. Prior to the 1970s, total trade (exports plus imports) between Anglo-America and the Pacific Rim had been consistently less than that with Western Europe; by the end of that decade the situation had reversed. During the interval, trans-Pacific flows had increased twice as fast as those crossing the North Atlantic.

At the same time, a marked change was taking place in the kinds of goods moving between North America and the Pacific Rim. Very quickly, the developing countries of the western Pacific advanced from being exporters mainly of primary commodities to becoming sellers of industrial products. More recently,

aided by the influx of multinationals, the Pacific Rim countries have further upgraded their output, moving quickly from the production of standardized labor-intensive goods, such as textiles and clothing, to the manufacture of ever-more sophisticated products, including machinery, electronics, and communications equipment. This development has spread sequentially through the region in a fashion that has now become typical of the Pacific Rim, beginning first in Japan and then moving to the Four Tigers and finally to the five newly emerging countries.

Perhaps the most remarkable development in the western Pacific is the appearance of new centers of corporate control and finance. Although Japanese firms had been actively investing abroad for some time previously, multinational corporations are now establishing headquarters in Hong Kong, Singapore, Taiwan, South Korea, and Australia. As they set up branch operations in neighboring lands, these Pacific-based multinationals serve to integrate the region ever more tightly.

Lately, as enormous trade surpluses accumulate, several East Asian capitals have become centers of

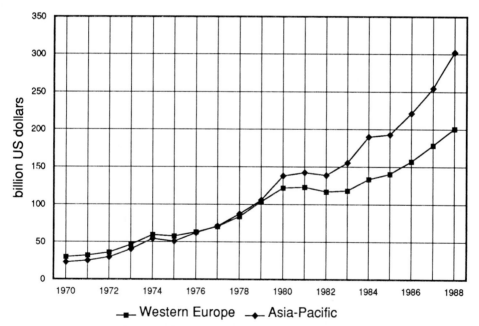

FIGURE 14.14   U.S. and Canadian trade (exports plus imports) with Western Europe and the Asia-Pacific, 1970–1988. The Pacific eclipsed the Atlantic as the leading avenue for North American commerce late in the 1970s, ending a centuries-old dominance of world trade by the Atlantic Basin. The Asia-Pacific realm as defined here includes all of East, Southeast, and South Asia, but 12 vigorous nations on the Pacific Rim contribute all but 1 percent of the trade generated in the entire region. These 12 have been lead actors in a rapidly changing international scene. [*Source:* United Nations, *Yearbook of International Trade Statistics,* Special Table B (New York: United Nations, various years).]

international finance. Japan is now the leading exporter of capital, and banks and brokerage firms headquartered in Tokyo operate branches throughout the world. Both Singapore and Hong Kong have lively money markets, and these are taking a prominent part in the current move toward the internationalization of financial trading on a 24-hour basis.

It is clear that Japan has done more than any other country to forge the Pacific Basin into a functionally integrated whole—an economic region whose complementary resources are linked together by trade and investment. In creating an export-led, innovation-driven economy based almost entirely upon human resources, Japan has shown the way for those Asian lands, notably the Four Tigers, that lack sufficient natural endowments of their own. Japanese multina-

tionals have also led in developing the resources of those Pacific countries, such as Australia, Indonesia, and Malaysia, that have surplus industrial raw materials and fuels.

With 123 million industrious people enjoying incomes comparable to Europe's, Japan has the world's most rapidly growing advanced economy and is the third largest trader. The Japanese have continually restructured their industries in adjusting to changing world demand and their country's advancing technical capabilities. This is apparent from the changing character of the country's trade (Figure 14.15). Japan's exports of textiles and yarns—mature, labor-intensive products that once dominated the country's foreign sales—now contribute only a minor share of the total. The big increases are in machinery and transport

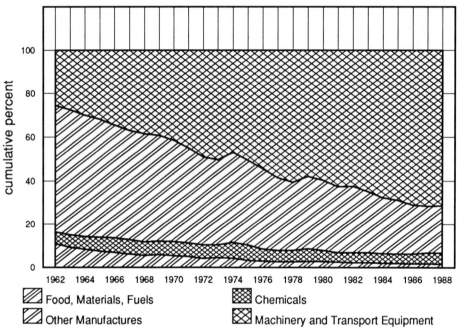

FIGURE 14.15 Evolution of Japan's export structure, 1962–1988. The composition of its exports faithfully mirrors Japan's longtime role as a workshop nation that sells manufactured products abroad to pay for the primary commodities its resource-poor home environment lacks. Even so, the nature of the country's exports has undergone a fundamental change corresponding to the restructuring that has taken place within the national economy. Thus, in 1962 nearly three-fifths of Japanese exports consisted of mass-produced, standardized goods classified by the UN as other manufactures (SITC 6 and 8). Only one-quarter of the total fell under machinery and transport equipment (SITC 7), a higher-technology heading. Steadily over the next three decades the contributions of the two classes came to be almost exactly reversed as the level of Japanese technology rose generally. During the period industrial exports of all kinds increased from 89 percent of the total to more than 98 percent, whereas food, materials, and fuels shrank from 11 percent to a mere 1.6 percent. Japan's import structure is essentially a mirror image of this. [*Source:* United Nations, *Yearbook of International Trade Statistics* (New York: United Nations, various years).]

equipment, now nearly three-fourths of all exports despite a decline in shipbuilding (captured by South Korea). Other rapidly expanding exports include electronics and communications equipment, which are representative of the knowledge-intensive industries now stressed by Japanese government policy. A diminishing share of exports comes from Japan's older energy-intensive, polluting metallurgical industries, which required massive imports of raw materials and fuels.

More than two-thirds of Japan's trade, both exports and imports, takes place within the Pacific Basin (Figure 14.16). Furthermore, one-third of its exports go to other Asia-Pacific countries, which in turn supply two-fifths of its imports. In a sense, therefore, the Japanese have succeeded by peaceful means in gaining economic dominance over a part of the world they had once sought to conquer militarily. Japan has also substantially enlarged its share of the European market, which now accounts for one-fifth of all foreign sales. The only major region with which Japan has a negative trade balance is the Middle East. Dependence upon

that politically explosive region has diminished substantially since the height of the oil crises—from 34 percent of total imports in 1980 to 10 percent in 1988—owing partly to Japan's policy of diversifying its oil purchases to safer sources and partly to a national campaign for increased energy efficiency. During that time, energy imports as a whole dropped from a high of 51 percent of all imports in 1981 to 21 percent in 1988.

In recent decades Japanese exports have grown much faster than imports, creating an embarrassingly high trade surplus with the country's principal trading partners and with the world at large. In 1988 Japan's exports to the United States were two and one-half times as large as imports, yielding a bilateral surplus of $54 billion. That same year it had trade surpluses of nearly $32 billion with Western Europe and $20 billion with the Asia-Pacific region.

Although this lopsided trade balance has added fuel to worldwide protectionist fires, it has also furnished Japan with an enormous hoard of capital with which to invest in foreign ventures. Prior to the 1970s,

FIGURE 14.16 Value share of Japanese exports (top) and imports (bottom) with major world regions, 1988. The Pacific Basin supplies more than two-thirds of Japan's imports and takes a like amount of its exports. Northern America and Western Europe are both more important to Japan as customers than as suppliers, and sales to these areas have climbed steeply in recent decades. The reverse is true of the Asia-Pacific region, which is more significant as a source for Japanese imports and has further enlarged this role as Japanese companies farm out more and more of their labor-intensive manufactures to other Asian countries. The Middle East actually supplies a smaller percentage of Japanese imports today than it did prior to the OPEC crises, evidence of Japan's canny program of diversifying its sources of oil. [*Source:* United Nations, *Yearbook of International Trade Statistics* (New York: United Nations, various years).]

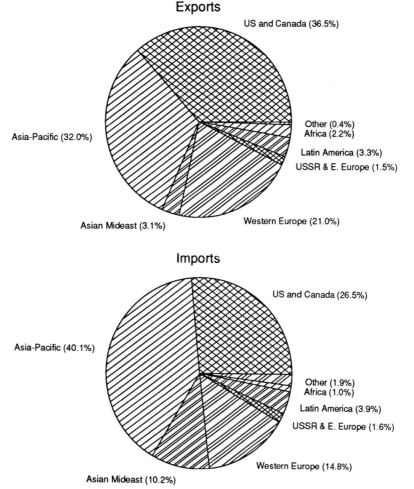

Japanese multinationals largely concentrated their overseas activities in the extractive enterprises, with the purpose of assuring long-term supplies of industrial materials for the resource-poor homeland. Since 1969, when governmental restrictions on exports of capital were removed, Japanese firms have greatly expanded their investments in foreign manufacturing and service ventures. Today, more than half of Japan's overseas investment is in the Pacific region.

The rise of the Pacific Rim as a powerful economic force is having a great impact on the rest of the world generally and on the United States in particular (Figure 14.17). Aside from its dangerously mounting trade deficit with the western Pacific countries (Figure 14.18), the United States finds itself in a paradoxical

position with respect to that region. The types of merchandise the country exchanges with East Asia place the United States rather in the role of a less-developed country dealing with more advanced ones: A high proportion of U.S. exports to the Pacific consists of primary commodities, whereas imports are mostly industrial goods. Indeed, one-third of all U.S. agricultural exports now goes to the Pacific Rim. This region still relies, however, upon certain high-technology items from the United States, especially aircraft, pharmaceuticals, and the more advanced types of capital goods.

So pervasive is the Pacific region's influence that it is lending added force to the westward movement of people, industries, and commercial activities within

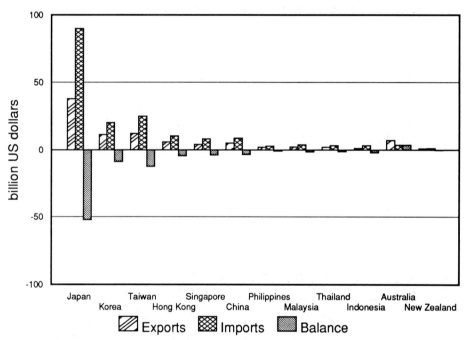

FIGURE 14.17 U.S. merchandise exports, imports, and trade balance with the Pacific Rim countries, 1988. As a group, the Pacific Rim nations were responsible for more than 35 percent of all U.S. trade (exports plus imports) in 1988. Amid all the attention paid to Japan's strained trading relations with the United States, it has gone little noticed that the other 11 Pacific Rim countries in combination actually generate a higher proportion of U.S. trade than does Japan. Furthermore, they are better customers; in 1988 they bought 40 percent more American goods than Japan. High-technology goods constitute a major element in the two-way exchange between the United States and the East Asian NICs. All four of the Little Tigers maintain close economic ties with the United States. In 1988 Taiwan led the four in trading with the U.S., followed closely by South Korea. Of all the Pacific Rim countries, only one, Australia, buys more from the United States than it sells. As a group, therefore, this region imposes a heavy drain on the U.S. trade balance (see Figure 14.18). [*Source:* U.S. Bureau of the Census, *Statistical Abstract of the United States, 1990* (Washington: U.S. Government Printing Office, 1990).]

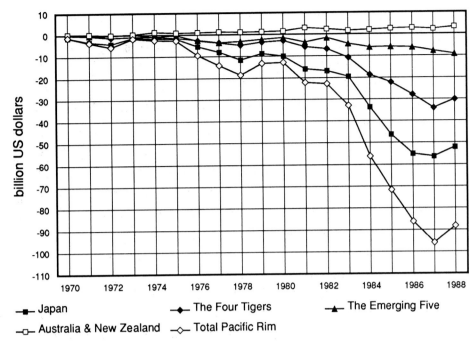

FIGURE 14.18 Deepening U.S. trade deficit with the Pacific Rim, 1970–1988. Although some slight easing took place in 1988, the combined U.S. trade deficit with the Pacific Rim was still $88 billion in that year. This represented 73 percent of the entire U.S. trade shortfall with the world. Of the 12 countries, only Australia buys more from the U.S. than it sells. Some of the group averages shown here mask significant intragroup differences, especially among the Emerging Five. The only member of that group with an improving balance is Indonesia; U.S. deficits with the other four continue to deteriorate rapidly. The worst problem is posed by China, which shipped $15 billion of merchandise to the United States in 1990 but took only $5 billion of U.S. goods in exchange. *Source:* U.S. Bureau of the Census, *Statistical Abstract of the United States* (Washington: U.S. Government Printing Office, various years).]

the United States. West Coast ports carry more than four-fifths of U.S. trade with the Pacific and are enjoying a boom in port industries and service activities associated with this rising tide of commerce. In addition, the western states are beneficiaries of more than a third of all investment by Pacific countries in the United States.

Latin America

The developing countries of Latin America offer a number of contrasts to those of East Asia, not only culturally but also in the fundamental character of their resource endowments, the makeup of their exports and imports, and the public policies that have shaped their commercial relations with the rest of the world.

Latin America's traditional role in the world economy, dating to the beginning of European coloni-

zation, called for exporting primary commodities—agricultural products and minerals—to the industrialized countries of the Northern Hemisphere. Although this exchange drew upon many natural complementarities between the two areas, Latin Americans had long been dissatisfied with the subordinate position in which this relationship placed them, and they worked persistently to change it through their development planning and trade policies.

Despite the shared colonial past and the economic and political problems with which it left them, the Latin American nations are surprisingly diverse. They range in size and level of development from Brazil, a giant of a country that aspires to superpower status by the end of the century, to the small, desperately poor island nation of Haiti. Among them are countries rich in valuable minerals, Mexico and Venezuela; or in agricultural lands, such as Argentina; or in both, such as Brazil. Others have neither of these.

Also highly variable from one country to the next are work-force skills, literacy levels, and quality of infrastructure.

Most Latin American countries export a large proportion of their national output. The median export/GDP ratio is more than 15 percent, as compared with less than 7 percent for the United States and 9 percent for Japan. The highest ratios are those of small Central American countries such as Costa Rica (27 percent) and mineral exporters such as Chile (32 percent). Certain large countries with lower ratios, however, are enjoying rapid export growth—Brazil and Mexico in particular.

Though primary commodities still command a prominent place in Latin American exports, industrial products are showing important gains. This is a recent development. As recently as 1970, 84 percent of the region's exports to its principal customer, the United States, had consisted of foods, materials, and fuels. This was a usual pattern for Third World countries. Imports, on the other hand, were not at all typical: Unlike most LDCs, the Latin American countries have for years imported only small quantities of manufactured consumer goods and a high proportion of capital goods. Thus, in 1970, manufactured products made up 79 percent of Latin American imports from the United States, but only 18 percent consisted of consumer products. The reason for this was the longstanding Latin American policy of import-substituting industrialization, as a result of which they had become largely self-sufficient in such products. Import substitution is much more difficult to achieve with higher-technology items.

By 1988, the structure of Latin American trade had changed markedly. Persuaded by the success of export-led industrialization policies in East Asia, Latin American countries are dropping old trade restrictions and opening to the world. Primary exports are now little more than half of total exports to the United States, much of the rest made up of a growing variety of manufactures. At the end of the 1980s—a decade of massive public indebtedness in the wake of the oil crises—Latin America entered upon an economic recovery. With North America's fastest-growing economy, a newly buoyant Mexico led the way.

The traditional markets and sources of supply for Latin American countries have been North America and Western Europe. Throughout the nearly two centuries since independence, Mexico, most of Central America, and much of South America have been tied to the United States. The southernmost countries—Argentina, Uruguay, and Chile—have had strong links to Europe; and the Caribbean islands, most of which have gained independence only recently, still maintain commercial connections with their former mother countries. Patterns of foreign investment have reinforced these trade linkages, and the resulting condition of economic dependence has made Latin America vulnerable to the vagaries of business cycles, politics, and wars in the North.

In the past two decades these long-established trade patterns have weakened. Since 1970, Latin America's trade with the older industrialized countries has shrunk from three-fourths of the total to two-thirds. Western Europe has suffered the major part of this decline; trade with the United States actually strengthened significantly, aided in part by growing U.S.–Mexico ties. Japan's share also grew. Less-developed countries have been the chief beneficiaries of the shift, however. Initially the oil-exporting lands absorbed a major part, but the East Asian NICs have since captured much of it. Although intra-Latin American trade increased for a time, it has recently fallen below 1970 levels. Today, Latin American exporters especially the semi-industrialized countries of Brazil, Mexico, and Argentina, are aggressively selling their new manufactures throughout the developing world (see Chapter 13). Latin American trade with the former planned economies remains relatively minor, much of it accounted for by Cuba's remaining links.

Western Europe

The international crises of the 1970s had an exaggerated effect upon the countries of Western Europe, mainly because they are so dependent upon trade. The large European countries generally export about a quarter of their GNP, but some of the smaller ones export half or more of their output. In part, their dependence is a function of political fragmentation—more than 20 sovereign entities occupying an area no more than a third that of the United States—and the substantial intra-European trade this produces. Many of these small countries are contiguous, distances are very short, transport networks are dense and superior in quality, and economic integration has greatly reduced the artificial barriers of earlier years. The high level of commercial activity also stems from the size and density of their populations—a third of a billion people in all—and their high per capita incomes. Standards of living throughout the region are today comparable to those of North America, and two European countries exceed the United States in per capita GNP.

With so much of Western Europe's output going into world commerce, it is not surprising that this region accounts for more than two-fifths of total world trade (refer back to Figure 14.7). As we noted earlier, however, the size of this contribution is deceptive because a very high proportion of it consists of trade among a score of small countries occupying a territory only two-fifths the size of the United States. Moreover, this intraregional proportion has increased in recent decades (Figure 14.19), from 55 percent of all West European exports in 1956 to 70 percent in 1988, with short interruptions during oil crises. The increase in intra-European imports has been even greater, from 49 percent to 71 percent, explaining why the region's trade gap with the rest of the world has closed. This offers a clear example of trade diversion.

This shift to intraregional trading partners closely parallels the growth in the European Community's size and cohesion, from its founding in 1958 to the present. During that period the EC has doubled its membership from 6 to 12 and has increased its share of the region's total exports from 53 percent to 84 and its imports from 59 percent to 86. The trend has accelerated since the mid-1980s, with the quickening pace of European integration.

Western Europe's trade is also keenly sensitive to events outside the area. The region's contribution to world commerce rose substantially during the 1960s as a result not only of European integration but also the general liberalization of international trade induced by the GATT agreements. Western Europe's prosperity peaked in 1973 on the eve of the first OPEC oil crisis; in the following year, trade slumped badly, especially its exports, with the onset of worldwide recession. In 1979, just as trade was beginning to recover, the second oil crisis struck. Imports continued to rise, because of the mounting cost of imported oil, but exports plummeted. Both exports and imports remained weak throughout the ensuing recession, and they recovered only slowly in the mid-1980s, a time of lagging European technological innovation and competitiveness. In the late 1980s, however, European trade growth resumed with the collapse of Communism and the preparations for full economic union in 1992.

These events likewise altered Western Europe's trade linkages with the rest of the world (Figure 14.19). The oil crises greatly increased, in value terms, the region's imports from the Middle East, offset only partially by higher export sales to that suddenly wealthy region and despite growing amounts of petroleum obtained from the North Sea and other sources. This shift came at the expense of trade with some of Europe's traditional trading partners; some of the losses have not been restored since, affecting long-standing relationships with present and former colonies. Thus, once-important trade with Africa has been reduced to a quarter of its former size, and exports to Australia and New Zealand have fallen well below 1 percent of

the European total. West European imports from Northern America have dropped from 17 percent in 1957, the year that the EC came in to being, to only 7 percent in 1988.

Within this same period, Japan and the East Asian NICs have enlarged their place in Western Europe, doubling their combined share of that market in the past decade. Note from Figure 14.20 that Western Europe had large trade imbalances with those countries in 1988. With most other parts of the world, the balance was positive in that year.

Being relatively well endowed with mineral resources and productive agricultural lands, Western Europe does not have to import as much food and industrial raw materials as might be expected from its high population density. In 1988, imports of primary commodities represented only 23.5 percent of the import bill. During the period of high oil prices, however, oil imports alone rose to 24.4 percent of the total, with a severely damaging impact on European economies. In normal times, however, industrial goods constitute more than three-fourths of West European imports and exports.

Western Europe's largest trader has been West Germany, which has experienced an economic resurgence in the postwar era remarkably similar to that of Japan. In 1988 Germany was responsible for 26 percent of the entire region's exports. It was also the world's leading exporter in that year, passing the United States by a small margin (the United States remained the leader in total trade, however, because of the enormous size of its imports). Following its historic reunification with East Germany in October 1990, the efficient German trading machine stood ready to exploit its economic strength and central location to effect a future integration of Western Europe with the newly liberated East.

The Former USSR and Eastern Europe

Even before the 1989 breakdown of the Communist systems in the Soviet Union and Eastern Europe, the Eastern Bloc countries were contributing less than 8 percent of the world's exports, down from an annual average of about 10 percent prior to the 1970s. Considering the human and natural resources at their disposal, the Eastern Bloc countries undoubtedly lagged far behind their trade potentials. This we would expect from systems that subordinated economic matters to political considerations, and held a lingering attachment to the Stalinist belief in *autarky,* or self-sufficiency. Politics limited trade between neighboring countries with seemingly complementary resource endowments, provoked hostility with the West, and led

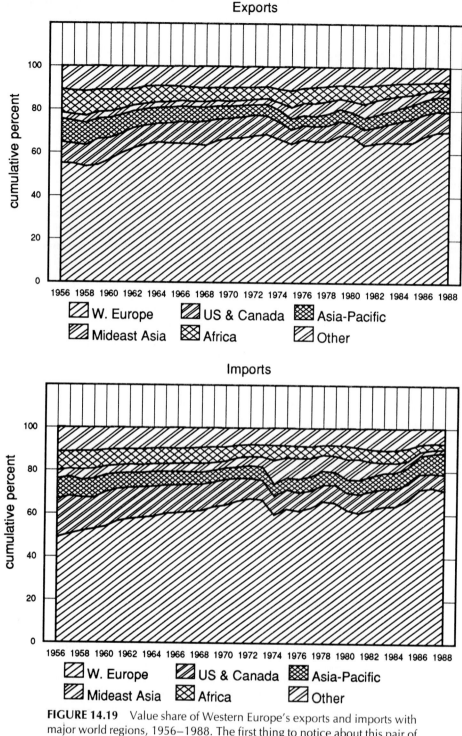

FIGURE 14.19   Value share of Western Europe's exports and imports with major world regions, 1956–1988. The first thing to notice about this pair of diagrams is the uncommonly high proportion of Western Europe's intraregional trade. This percentage has increased at irregular intervals over the years, in response to a number of significant influences. Most persistent of these has been the formation in 1958 of the European Community and its growth in membership and cohesion. Also apparent here are the various setbacks experienced by the west Europeans as a result of oil crises and recessions. Evidence of trade diversion and the effects of foreign direct investment in the EC are to be seen in the declining imports from the United States and Canada. Note the recent expansion in European imports from the Asia-Pacific region (mainly Japan and the NICs). [*Source:* United Nations, *Yearbook of International Trade Statistics,* Special Table B (New York: United Nations, various years).]

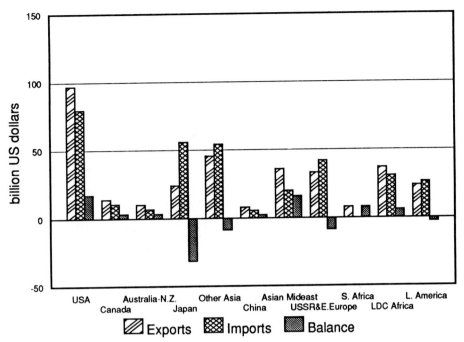

FIGURE 14.20 Western Europe's merchandise exports and imports and trade balances with other world regions, 1988. The United States is still the largest single trading partner of the West Europeans, but Japan and the East Asian NICs have risen quickly in importance during the past decade. Falling oil prices have reduced the Middle East's contribution. The past three decades have also seen the relative decline of several trading partners of historic importance to the Europeans. Western Europe's overall trade balance was positive in 1988, but mounting deficits with Japan and other Pacific Rim countries were provoking protectionist responses. According to late information, Europe's trade balance with the U.S. had also turned negative by 1990. [*Source:* United Nations, *Yearbook of International Trade Statistics,* Special Table B (New York, United Nations, various years).]

to ideological disputes within the Communist bloc itself.

On objective economic grounds, the opportunities for increased international involvement by the Eastern Bloc indeed appear great. Together, these countries occupy an immense territory, nearly 16 percent of the world's land area, which holds a combined population of nearly 390 million people. The group thus possesses a great storehouse of physical resources and would seem to offer a promising market for Western goods. Important complementarities exist between East and West. Indeed, in the pre-Communist era a lively trade took place between the two parts of Europe, based upon an exchange of the East's land resources for the West's manufactured goods. In recent times, the oil, gas, and metallic minerals of the former USSR have found a demand in the West, and the Eastern Bloc countries have sought Western capital goods and technology. In addition, the Communist

lands have had to import massive quantities of grain to make up for shortfalls in the output of their own badly managed farm lands.

Aside from the daunting problems of transforming state-run systems into market economies with convertible currencies and the infrastructure needed to support free exchanges of goods with the West, it may be asked just how great indeed is this potential for East-West trade. In addition to the mutual needs and wants of the countries on each side, several factors seem to argue for a truly important addition to world commerce from this source in the long run. One of these is the increased demand to be generated from the accelerated GNP growth resulting from the release of Eastern Bloc economies from their suffocating centralized bureaucracies.

A second consideration that favors expanded East-West trade is the likelihood that some of the present trade flowing among East Bloc nations will be transferred to other countries. The agreement by Bloc members to dismantle Comecon in June 1991 indicates a will to remove the controls that have favored intra-Bloc trade. The distorting effect this has had is seen in the fact that intragroup trade in 1988 constituted 57 percent of their total exports to the world and 64 percent of their total imports. This highly managed system was even more of a constraint for Eastern Europe than it was for the former Soviet Union, which had long been a supplier of resource-based commodities to world markets.

Another question concerns the kinds of goods likely to be exchanged with the West. With regard to exports from the former USSR, the answer is suggested by the eager reception that the Soviets found in the West for their oil, gas, and other mineral output (the USSR led the world in oil exports in recent years). For the Eastern Europeans, the solution is less clear. Until now their exports to other Bloc members have consisted predominantly of machinery and transport equipment but their shipments to non-Bloc countries have been very largely limited to simple basic manufactures. They have been unsuccessful in finding non-Bloc markets for their more advanced manufactures because their quality does not meet Western standards. Now that they face competition in their home markets from superior Western products in these sophisticated lines, East Bloc firms will have to concentrate on making simpler industrial goods until they can upgrade their equipment and their labor and managerial skills.

With regard to imports, one of the most obvious needs of the Eastern Bloc is for foodstuffs, at least in the short run, until this one-time breadbasket of Europe can regain its agricultural productivity. Another need is for a great variety of high-technology goods, especially those whose export to the former Soviet Bloc had previously been prohibited for national security reasons. In time, it can also be anticipated that rising incomes in Eastern Bloc countries will create a market for the wide variety of consumer goods to which Western populations have long been accustomed.

Finally, we may ask which Western countries are likely to participate most actively in developing East Bloc markets. Undoubtedly the country best positioned to benefit from an opening to the East is Germany. With its central European location, directly on the former border separating East from West, and its well-organized, experienced, and export-minded business community, Germany has already built up strong commercial relationships in the East and currently leads the world in sales to the area. Its reunification

with the former East Germany in 1990 also provided the country with an important early advantage.

Multinationals from a variety of countries are investing in Eastern Bloc ventures. Among these are German and U.S. automobile companies, machinery manufacturers, and consumer-electronics makers. In the former Soviet Union, U.S. oil companies have entered into joint ventures to modernize that country's flagging petroleum output. Western investors, however, face intimidating political and economic uncertainties in such undertakings. The opportunities offered by early entry into Eastern Bloc ventures may warrant the risks for well-financed industrial giants such as Occidental Petroleum or Volkswagen, but for most smaller concerns the uncertainties are as yet too great.

The Middle East

Living at a historic crossroads of world commerce, the people of the Middle East have been traders from earliest times. Although great-power interests have long focused upon this area because of its strategic location, the discovery of vast pools of petroleum beneath the region has attracted world attention as never before. The knowledge that they control two-thirds of all known oil reserves made it possible for the Arab members of OPEC to precipitate the crisis of 1973. Only half of the Middle Eastern countries are surplus oil exporters; most of the rest are resource-poor agricultural nations that do not share in the oil bonanza (except for such aid as OPEC may grant them). Indeed, farming is the leading occupation throughout the Middle East, even in those countries producing oil. Yet the population is growing so fast that the region as a whole has become a net importer of food.

During the 1970s the Middle East enjoyed a huge increase in its share of world exports, which jumped from only 3 percent to nearly 11 percent within a span of six years. This resulted solely from a 10-fold rise in oil prices; the volume of shipments actually shrank. For a time, oil revenues were pouring in so fast that imports could not keep up, and the oil-exporting countries acquired enormous balance-of-payments surpluses. In 1980, for instance, the Middle East as a whole had a positive balance of $114 billion on total foreign earnings of $211 billion. After that, oil revenues shrank as oil prices sagged in a weakening market. By 1988, the Middle East's share of global exports was again back to 3 percent, and the earlier trade surplus had turned into a deficit of $3 billion.

Prior to the oil boom the Middle East's traditional exports were agricultural commodities—such as cotton, figs, and dates—and various mineral ores. In fact, goods of this type still brought in 11 percent of the region's foreign earnings in the early 1970s. Exports of these commodities have continued to grow since, but they have been overwhelmed in the trade figures by the steep rise in oil receipts.

As industrialization reaches the Middle East, new classes of exports are beginning to appear. Egypt has now attained the status of a semi-industrialized country and is exporting cotton yarn, textiles, and other consumer manufactures. A sharp increase in Middle Eastern shipments of industrial products is taking place as Saudi Arabia's huge new petroleum refineries and petrochemical plants go on stream. Made from exceedingly cheap feedstocks of Saudi oil and natural gas, these commodities are very competitive on world markets. Many other energy-intensive manufacturing industries are rising throughout the region as oil-exporting nations prepare for a world after the oil is used up. Some Middle Eastern countries are earning substantial amounts of foreign exchange through invisible exports, especially Egypt and Israel with their prospering tourist industries. As a transit country, Egypt gains additional revenues from Suez Canal tolls.

The Middle East's imports, which have grown steadily since 1973, are very diverse. Being highly specialized producers of oil and other primary commodities, these countries nevertheless have varied needs, which can be satisfied only with imports. During the bountiful years, rising incomes caused the range of consumer demand to expand, and development needs called for a wide variety of capital goods and industrial raw materials.

Even before the crises of the 1970s, the Middle Eastern oil exporters had had unusually diverse trade ties throughout the world. Their largest regional market had always been—and still is—Western Europe, which was taking 44 percent of all Middle Eastern exports at the time of the first oil price rise. Since then, Western Europe's share has slipped, dropping to only 23 percent. Japan, the second largest customer, continued in 1988 to take a little less than one-fifth, and North America bought another tenth. Conscious of the political instability of the Middle East, however, the region's First World customers have been diversifying their oil sources, causing the Middle East's share of world oil sales to dip. The Persian Gulf crisis of 1990–1991 further reinforced this trend. At the same time, rising import shares have gone to several LDCs and newly industrializing nations in Africa, Latin America, and Asia. With the former USSR no longer supplying Eastern Europe with oil at concessional prices, Middle Eastern exporters are capturing some of that market as well. During the past decade the Middle East has seen a noticeable rise in intraregional trade.

Western Europe continued in 1988 to be the Middle East's chief source of imports, preserving its usual two-fifths share of the total market. The United States and Japan remain important suppliers, but with diminishing portions. Much of the difference has been made up by East Asian NICs and a variety of LDCs, including Brazil and other purveyors of war matériel.

The odd man in this virtually solid bloc of Islamic countries is the Jewish state of Israel. About the size of New Jersey, this tiny nation of 3 million people resembles its Arab neighbors physically but is very different culturally, economically, and politically. Having a highly skilled labor force and many experienced managers, Israel has joined the ranks of industrial nations and has forged formal economic ties with both the United States and the European Economic Community. Its industrial exports include cut diamonds (one quarter of foreign earnings), machinery, chemicals (based upon salts from the Dead Sea and phosphates from the Negev Desert), aircraft, and armaments. Relying upon its excellent transport connections and its climatic complementarity with Western Europe, Israel ships subtropical fruits, winter vegetables, and cut flowers to European capitals daily by air.

Despite its success as a diversified exporter of agricultural commodities and industrial goods, Israel runs a dangerously high trade deficit. Exports cover only a little more than half the cost of imports, which are kept high by the demands of a large defense establishment and heavy government subsidization of the economy.

THE GLOBAL ECONOMY IN THE NEW CENTURY

The world is a far more prosperous place today than it was at the close of World War II—at least for those living in modern industrialized societies—and the consensus among students of the subject is that major credit for these advances goes to the spectacular surge of international commerce in recent decades and to the liberalization process that made this possible. The resulting internationalization of national economies has materially contributed to the unfolding of a different kind of world scene, one marked by an accelerating rise and decline of national economies and a continual restructuring of industries.

Among the lead actors in this drama are the business concerns whose competition for advantage in the world market place inspires the innovations that prompt these advances. As Porter has shown, however, the competitive success of such firms depends importantly upon the economic and cultural environments of the countries that serve as their home bases. The other prime actors in the unfolding international economic drama, therefore, are the nations themselves. Their relative success in the competitive struggle, like that of the firms operating within their borders, is subject to the wider trends and events transpiring in the world at large: broad sweeps of political change, such as the liberation of Eastern Europe, pivotal episodes, such as the Persian Gulf crisis or German reunification, grand schemes for reconstituting world regions, such as Europe 1992 or a North American free-trade area, and evolutionary changes, such as the restructuring of world industry.

A main concern in this chapter has been to discern the new spatial patterns of world commerce now evolving and to examine the changing character of economic flows among countries. At this point, we need to see what lessons can be drawn from these developments and to learn what they suggest concerning the basic determinants of international competitive advantage. From this perspective, we can then attempt a look at the kind of global space economy the twenty-first century may bring.

Three Decades of Spatial Economic Change.
The global space economy looks very different in the 1990s than it did 30 years earlier. A prime feature of the world economy in that earlier period was the deep divisions that separated it into three distinct parts: a First World of non-Communist developed nations was responsible for more than 65 percent of all trade, an isolated Second World of Communist states accounted for another 12 percent, and a Third World of less-developed countries provided the other 20 percent.

The United States dominated international commerce, supplying more than one-seventh of all exports and a major share of foreign investment. Already, only 15 years after the close of World War II, the two defeated Axis partners, West Germany and Japan, had risen to distant second and third places behind the United States. As it had for more than three centuries previously, world commerce centered upon the North Atlantic Basin, including most of that of the Third World.

As the last decade of the century opened, the divisions of 30 years earlier were disintegrating. The Iron Curtain that had separated Eastern and Western Europe was gone, the Eastern Bloc's share of world trade had shrunk by a quarter, and the former Communist lands were seeking new economic ties with the West. By the start of the 1990s, U.S. dominance of international trade had eroded, and in some years Germany was the world's leading exporter.

The focus of world trade and investment had shifted westward to the Pacific Basin, where a resurgent Japan had doubled its share of world exports. The Pacific Basin's new central place in the world economy also derived from the meteoric rise of an aggressive set of newly industrializing countries in East Asia. The other anchor of Pacific commercial activity, the United States, had just formed a free-trade area with Canada and was negotiating with Mexico for a further agreement that would join the three in a North American Free-Trade Area.

At the beginning of the 1990s, Western Europe still retained its two-fifths share of world exports and imports, but the greater part of this was intra-European trade, after 30 years of economic integration. A newly reunited Germany dominated West European economic affairs and became a main force in the opening to Eastern Europe.

The ranks of the less-developed countries had been reduced by the shift of a sizable group that had risen to the status of Newly Industrialized Countries. Intragroup trade had increased among LDCs, but the 22 poorest LDCs had seen their share of global trade shrink to the lowest point yet. By the start of the 1990s, the global export share of oil-exporting LDCs had retreated to the same 3 percent level it had occupied 20 years earlier, following an extended interval during which they had captured more than 15 percent of all exports.

Given the magnitude of the differences between the global space economies of 1960 and 1990, fundamental forces for change have surely been at work. Of all the interrelated factors that contributed to this progression, perhaps none has been more basic and essential than the process of trade liberalization pursued in the postwar era through the GATT mechanism. In a sense, everything else has flowed from this. The unprecedented international cooperation of that period caused trade to expand enormously, and it led to the integration of the world economy.

At the same time that the processes of trade liberalization and economic integration were being initiated globally, similar processes were under way at the regional scale. It was during this early period that regional economic integration was seized upon by the Europeans as a way of stimulating their postwar recovery and solving persistent intraregional trade problems. Though this mechanism has the disadvantage of discriminating against nonmember countries, the gains that the European Community has enjoyed have caused the EC to become a model for similar regional organizations from Latin America to Southeast Asia, Africa, and North America. Regional integration, therefore, has been one of the forces for rearranging world patterns of trade and investment.

The liberalization of world trade was a prerequisite for the impressive rise of the Pacific Rim countries. Increased trade flows and the opening of world markets made it possible first for Japan and then for the East Asian NICs to introduce industrial technologies requiring economies of scale. Access to the global economy thus allowed them to manufacture product lines that their home markets were not large enough to support. The small countries of Western Europe benefited in this same way. Indeed, the quantitative evidence confirms that, in the postwar period of liberalization, small countries—which rely upon international trade to a greater extent than large ones—enjoyed the highest economic growth rates.

In an integrated world economy, trade exerts powerful pressures for change by unleashing the forces of competition. Nations and firms must adjust or perish. This competitive discipline has been a major impetus for the burst of product and process innovation of recent years. The growth of world trade and foreign investment has affected large countries and firms as much as small ones because it has made them all vulnerable to foreign competition both at home and abroad. This is the lesson American industrialists painfully learned in the early 1980s, and it was the force that goaded them into the restructuring that restored their international competitiveness in the early 1990s.

The liberalization process has been especially beneficial in the development of new high-technology goods. In the early postwar years such products were subject to unusually low tariffs, because at that time they represented only a minor element in world commerce; since then, tariffs on these items were further reduced in subsequent GATT rounds. This gave companies a powerful incentive to increase their competitive positions through product innovation.

Throughout this dynamic era the multinational enterprise has been a major agent of change, even as it was itself undergoing a transformation in organizational form and function. Manufacturing firms and international providers of services alike have internationalized their operations, competing worldwide and pursuing global strategies in procuring raw materials, assembling products, and selling these in a variety of countries. As Porter has observed, the globalization of an industry decouples a firm from the factor endowments of a single nation and enables it to secure its needs from the lowest-cost sources, wherever those

may be. Moreover, it permits a multinational to enter readily into new markets, taking with it the know-how it has accumulated elsewhere, and quickly establish a viable presence.

The modern-day shifts in the international focus of economic activity thus stem from changes in the competitiveness of nations and firms, made possible by the liberalization of world commerce. The nations of the Pacific Rim have prospered by increasing the productivity of their resources, which has enabled them to improve their competitive positions in existing industries and to develop competitiveness in new industries. A hierarchy of nations has emerged in the region as first Japan and then the Four Tigers have systematically moved into new, more-sophisticated export lines, shifting their old lower-technology industries to the next tier of nations below them.

Conversely, some of the older industrial nations of Europe and North America have failed to maintain their competitiveness in some types of high-technology production and have found their competitiveness in world markets impaired. Compounding this problem by means of various protectionist devices, they have persisted in clinging to low-technology industries—such as mass-produced textiles and clothing—in which their international competitiveness has long ago dissipated. Hence, the international market shares of these countries have suffered, their economic growth has lagged, and their unemployment rates have risen.

The transformation of the global economy in recent decades prompts a reexamination of the determinants of conventional international trade theory. If Linnemann were to use his interaction model to analyze today's world trade linkages, it seems possible that the gross national products of trading partners would remain a significant variable but that size of population and area would be much reduced in importance. Some of the world's most active trading nations in East Asia and Western Europe are small in size, but their trade-led prosperity creates relatively large GNPs.

Distance would likely remain a significant variable as well, in view of the exceedingly large trade flows among the tightly knit nations of Europe, among the three North American neighbors, and within the rising East Asian bloc. At the regional level, however, distance may have lost some of its force as a result of industrial restructuring. Because of this, a larger proportion of trade between countries consists of advanced manufactures, which command high prices in relation to shipping costs and thus move readily over long distances.

The determinants of conventional trade theory are still with us, but they require much modification, as Leamer and Porter have both noted. What Porter terms "basic factors," such as land resources, figure less importantly in global trade because of improvements in product design and in transportation and communications. Porter's "advanced factors"—educated personnel, research and development capabilities, and advanced communications—assume a greatly enhanced role in world commerce.

The Future Global Space Economy. Taking note of the economic and political trends of the early 1990s, as well as the structural changes in world industry, how might we expect the map of global economic activity to look upon the arrival of the new century?

Two conspicuous features of the global economic and political landscape loom at this time: (1) the opening to the West by the newly liberated lands of Eastern Europe and the now-independent republics that constituted the former USSR, and (2) the trade frictions clouding commercial relations between the nations of Europe, North America, and the Pacific Rim. The possibility exists that these two trends might converge, especially if the former Communist Bloc were to be absorbed into the West European sphere.

At the world scale, the postwar liberalization of trade is in danger of being reversed, at least in part, by contemporary tendencies toward the formation of three competing trade blocs. These would consist of (1) an augmented European Union growing out of the EC's Maastricht Accord of December 1991, (2) a Western Hemisphere bloc based upon the proposed North American Free Trade Area, and (3) a Japan-dominated Asian bloc.

The prospect that the 12-nation European Community would become a full economic union led several non-EC European countries to seek EC membership even before the Maastricht agreement set Western Europe upon a course leading to unexpectedly stronger economic and political union. In the aftermath of the accord, a much-enlarged European Union seemed virtually inevitable. Most of the EFTA nations either applied for EC membership or were seriously considering it, and much of Eastern Europe appeared likely to be drawn into its orbit. Earlier the former East Germany had been incorporated into the EC as a result of German reunification; Poland, Hungary, and Czechoslovakia had been admitted to associate membership on the eve of the Maastricht meeting. If in time the former Soviet republics should succeed in making the transition to market economies, some of these might likewise seek close ties with, if not active membership in, the EC or its successor.

The campaign to create a North American Free Trade Area joining the United States with both Canada and Mexico produced echoes throughout the Americas. A politically and economically resurgent Latin America saw in this movement the nucleus of a greater Western Hemispheric free trade area, and several Latin American nations began positioning themselves to take advantage of any such opportunity. One of the appeals of an enlarged North American Free Trade Area has been the greater economic strength that such a coalition could draw upon in the threatening competitive struggle with an enlarged European Union and a flourishing East Asian bloc.

The third group, in East Asia, does not currently have formal existence. However, the large and ever-strengthening ties of trade and investment among Pacific Rim nations essentially amount to a *de facto* trade bloc. To some extent the linkages among these countries constitute a defensive reaction to the barriers encountered by this group in their commercial dealings with North America and, especially, with Western Europe.

The picture of Global 2000 now emerging is of three economic entities jealously competing for advantage in global commerce and defensively limiting imports from each other. The potential for such barriers has led to a struggle for competitive advantage in the EC that pits Europe's own multinationals against each other and against MNEs from the United States and Japan. Because few of Europe's MNEs are as yet large or powerful enough to compete successfully in a Europe-wide market, they have been busily merging and buying each other out to gain sufficient strength. Europeans do not object seriously to closer links with U.S. multinationals, but they are most fearful of potential Japanese dominance of their economies.

This tripartite division of world commerce among industrial nations would appear a setback for efforts to complete the still-unfinished business of integrating the world's economies. The possibility of three suspicious and mutually hostile economic groups revives memories of the Smoot-Hawley era of the 1930s. In an earlier age this situation could have meant a collapse of world trade; in the 1990s, however, matters seem unlikely to proceed that far.

The difference this time is that powerful multinational corporations have become the ultimate creators of world trade. Even prior to Europe 1992, multinationals had evolved a "three-legged" corporate strategy under which each firm expected to maintain a substantial corporate presence within each of the three regions as a way of securing its global market share against loss to its competitors. Now the three-legged strategy has the added function of guarding against possible exclusion from any one of these vital markets by the forces of protectionism.

Though the offensive and defensive strategies of multinationals may help prevent a return to the dangerously fragmented world economy of the Depression years, any reversal of past progress toward trade liber-alization would cost the world some of its postwar gains in living standards. The continued growth of large and small economies today relies upon ensuring continued movement toward more trade liberalization, not less.

TOPICS FOR DISCUSSION

1. Weigh the theoretical implications of the variables used by Linnemann in his interaction model of trade flows, and consider how their relative importance for explaining trade flows may have changed since Linnemann's work was published. What does this type of analysis suggest concerning the potential for a North American Free Trade Area linking Canada, the United States, and Mexico?

2. In what ways have the trends and events of recent decades affected the basic character of national resource endowments? Show how some countries have capitalized upon these developments to increase their competitive strengths in world commerce.

3. How were world patterns of trade and investment altered by the major political and economic upheavals of the 1970s and 1980s? Why did some regions and countries respond to these events differently than others?

4. Why did OPEC succeed as a cartel when other primary producers have failed in similar efforts? Discuss the divisions among OPEC members and show how these differences have affected their abilities to absorb oil revenues and the positions they take in the setting of OPEC production quotas and prices. How have the effects of OPEC actions differed among oil-importing countries? How did the Persian Gulf crisis of 1990–1991 differ from previous Middle Eastern crises in its political and economic impacts?

5. Discuss the competitive positions of the leading exporters of technology-intensive goods and show how these relate to their changing comparative advantages for such products.

6. How has the Pacific Basin evolved into a functionally integrated economic region, and what impact has this had upon U.S. trade? What effects has the rise of the Pacific Rim had upon regional growth and the location of economic activities within the United States?

7. Describe the economic and cultural conditions that have contributed to the remarkable success of the Pacific Rim countries, interpret the trade strategies they have followed, and discuss the new roles these countries have assumed in world production, investment, finance, and trade.

8. Explain why the countries of Western Europe have such high export/GNP ratios, and interpret theoretically the spatial pattern and composition of that region's trade. How would you expect the EC's plans for Europe 1992 to modify the region's trade and investment patterns? How might these be affected by the new opening to Eastern Europe with the fall of communism?

9. Develop two alternative scenarios for the shape of future commercial relationships among Eastern Bloc countries, one based on successful liberalization of their economies and the other based on its failure.

FURTHER READINGS

KRAUSE, LAWRENCE B., and SUEO SEKIGUCHI, eds. *Economic Interaction in the Pacific Basin.* Washington, D.C.: The Brookings Institution, 1980.

Investigates the transmission of economic impulses among six representative countries within the Pacific basin, noting particularly the effects upon those countries of the economic upheavals of the 1970s and their responses to these.

LEAMER, EDWARD E. *Sources of International Comparative Advantage: Theory and Evidence.* Cambridge, Mass.: MIT Press, 1984.

This ambitious study rigorously tests the empirical validity of the Heckscher-Ohlin theorem and, based upon the results, describes the changing patterns of international trade and resource endowments. Provides an excellent carefully developed review of trade theory and a thorough critical review of previous empirical tests of the Heckscher-Ohlin theorem.

LINDER, STAFFAN BURENSTAM. *The Pacific Century: Economic and Political Consequences of Asian-Pacific Dynamism.* Stanford, Calif.: Stanford University Press, 1986.

Traces the rapid transformation taking place on the Pacific Rim and explores the economic implications this holds for the Asian–Pacific countries themselves, for other developing countries, for the established industrial countries of Europe and North America, and for the centrally planned economies.

LINNEMANN, HANS. *An Econometric Study of International Trade Flows*. Amsterdam: North-Holland Publishing, 1966.

A pioneering work in the development of interaction models for use in the search for generalized explanations for the existence of trade between countries. Tests a series of models of increasing refinement, using 6300 bilateral trade flows.

PORTER, MICHAEL E. *The Competitive Advantage of Nations*. New York: The Free Press, 1990.

Porter's theoretical interpretation of the fundamental determinants of national competitive advantage offers a productive new framework for analyzing the changing patterns of world commerce in the final decade of the twentieth century.

RUSSETT, BRUCE M. *International Regions and the International System: A Study in Political Ecology*. Skokie, Ill.: Rand McNally, 1967.

Uses factor analysis to group countries according to the strength of their relationships to each other in each of several forms of international interaction. Finds that the world's nations fall into nine regional groups on the basis of their trade linkages.

Index